THE ROOTS
OF AMERICAN
COMMUNISM

A VOLUME IN THE SERIES
COMMUNISM IN AMERICAN LIFE
CLINTON ROSSITER, *General Editor*

OTHER VOLUMES IN THE SERIES:

The Communists and the Schools BY ROBERT W. IVERSEN
The Decline of American Communism BY DAVID A. SHANNON
American Communism and Soviet Russia BY THEODORE DRAPER
Communism and the Churches BY RALPH LORD ROY
Marxism: The View from America BY CLINTON ROSSITER
The Social Basis of American Communism BY NATHAN GLAZER
The Moulding of Communists BY FRANK S. MEYER
Writers on the Left BY DANIEL AARON

THEODORE DRAPER

THE ROOTS

OF AMERICAN

COMMUNISM

THE VIKING PRESS

NEW YORK

COPYRIGHT © 1957 BY THEODORE DRAPER
ALL RIGHTS RESERVED

COMPASS BOOKS EDITION
ISSUED IN 1963 BY THE VIKING PRESS, INC.
625 MADISON AVENUE, NEW YORK 22, N.Y.

DISTRIBUTED IN CANADA BY
THE MACMILLAN COMPANY OF CANADA LIMITED

PRINTED IN THE U.S.A. BY THE MURRAY PRINTING COMPANY

To My Mother

Note

This book is one of a series of studies of Communist influence in American life. The entire survey has been made possible through the foresight and generous support of the Fund for the Republic. All of us who have taken part in it are grateful for this exceptional opportunity to study the most confused and controversial problem of the age and to publish the results exactly as we find them.

CLINTON ROSSITER

Contents

Introduction		3
1.	The Historic Left	11
2.	The Age of Unrest	36
3.	The New Left Wing	50
4.	Influences and Influencers	65
5.	The Left at War	80
6.	The Reflected Glory	97
7.	Roads to Moscow	114
8.	The Revolutionary Age	131
9.	The Real Split	148
10.	The Great Schism	164
11.	The Sibling Rivalry	176
12.	The Underground	197
13.	The Second Split	210
14.	Spies, Victims, and Couriers	226
15.	The Crisis of Communism	246
16.	To the Masses!	267

CONTENTS

17.	The Revolution Devours Its Children	282
18.	New Forces	303
19.	The Legal Party	327
20.	The Manipulated Revolution	345
21.	The Two-Way Split	353
22.	The Raid	363
23.	The Transformation	376

Notes 399

Acknowledgments 459

Index 463

THE ROOTS
OF AMERICAN
COMMUNISM

Introduction

IT IS possible to say many true things about the American Communist movement and yet not the whole truth. It is possible to be right about a part and yet wrong about the whole. The most contradictory things can be true—at different times and in different places.

After almost forty years, the Communist movement is like a museum of radical politics. In its various stages, it has virtually been all things to all men. All kinds of men and women have been able to find in it almost anything they have wanted to find.

In political terms, it has been "Left" and "Right," "sectarian" and "opportunist," "extremist" and "moderate." It has been a small sect and a rather large organization. It has been almost totally isolated from American life, and it has enjoyed broad influence out of all proportion to its numbers. It has operated under illegal, underground conditions, and it has flourished legally and openly. It has been shunned by other parties and groups, and its support has been welcomed by the most powerful and respectable institutions. The outward appearance and behavior of individual Communists, the discipline and type of activity expected of them in the party, the very language or expressions in vogue from time to time, have changed sharply with the changing political "line."

There are many ways of trying to understand such a movement, but the first task is historical. In some respects, there is no other way to understand it, or at least to avoid seriously misunderstanding it. Every other approach tends to be static, one-sided, or unbalanced. Anyone without a basic grasp of the historical development of the movement is likely to grope in the dark. He will find it hard to fit in the pieces and to discriminate between one bit of evidence and another.

The historical problem is not merely to establish what position the American Communists have held at any particular time but to seek out the dynamic forces that drove them from one position to another—and back again. The Communists have held so many different and conflicting positions that at first glance the total effect may be one of incredible inconsistency and confusion. They have been so inconsistent that they have even hopelessly confused themselves. But when the reasons for the changes are looked into, when the conditions that made them necessary are analyzed, a number of basic problems and forces appear—a pattern emerges.

This pattern began to emerge at a very early stage. Once the Communist movement matured, it became the prisoner of its own development. It gradually created precedents, traditions, rituals. But there was a time when everything was new, fresh, and spontaneous. Every crisis was the first crisis. Every move was unrehearsed.

As soon as we ask the question "Why?" about the fundamental aspects of the Communist movement, we are invariably driven back to the beginnings. The deepest, the most important secrets are hidden in the formative period. Once something happened, it was easy to repeat it. But the first time was never easy. It was not even entirely clear in its implications to the participants. It was like a game for which the rules had not yet been invented. Communists of a later period took for granted much that Communists in the first years had never expected.

Who were the first American Communists? Who were the first American ex-Communists?

Why did a revolution in Russia in 1917 mean so much to them?

Why did it shake up the existing American radical movement and

INTRODUCTION

bring about an altogether different line-up such as we still have with us today?

Why did the relations between the Russian Communists and the American Communists become so unequal?

What was the effect of official repression on the first generation of Communists?

Why did so many early Communists prefer the "underground" to an open, legal party?

When did the Communists become inhibited in dealing with subjects like force and violence?

Why was there so much Communist resistance to the "united front" when it was first proposed in Moscow?

Why and when did the first Comintern representative with plenipotentiary powers come to the United States?

What was the first Communist change of line and what can it tell us about all later ones?

To enable us to answer these questions and many others, the Communists themselves have provided the richest store of material. The Communists have written so much about themselves that no congressional committee is necessary to force them to testify about the really significant political and social aspects of their movement.

Communist source material, of course, contains innumerable traps for the uninitiated and the unwary. All of it is partisan and much of it is propaganda. In this respect, it resembles the familiar types of partisan and propaganda material throughout history that must be sifted in order to get at the truth about all movements. People and movements reveal themselves in their partisanship and propaganda, often in ways they do not intend.

It is difficult, if not impossible, for the Communist leadership at any given time to foresee how the Communist line is going to change at some future date. What seems desirable to say or to reveal today may be most indiscreet or compromising tomorrow, but then it is already too late. Thus, as one goes through old papers and records, a great deal of interesting and important information may be gleaned from them because their authors could not anticipate what might give them away ten, twenty, or thirty years later. Only by destroying their own papers and records can the Communists hide the truth about themselves. They have, indeed, done so on a large scale wherever they have taken power. In the United States, they have not been able to do more than withdraw works from sale or circulation as soon as they have become embarrassing or inconvenient. None of this would be necessary if Communist source material were not so self-revealing, consciously or unconsciously.

Major changes of line have almost always been accompanied by fierce factional struggles ending in changes of leadership. In every factional struggle—and there have been quite a few in the American party—both sides have poured out the most detailed and intimate information about the inner workings of the movement. Every time the leadership has changed, the new one has "exposed" the old one and thereby exposed to view what went on under the old one.

There are different levels of Communist source material. The mass propaganda intended for nonparty consumption does not speak the same language as inner-party documents or discussions. A daily newspaper may be revealing of one thing, an official theoretical organ of another thing, and an organizational bulletin of something else again. What the American Communist movement said about itself at one time or place may be revised by what it said at another time or place. In order to use Communist source material most fruitfully and with a maximum of safeguards, it is necessary to carry on documentary research on the largest possible scale. A little research on the Communist movement can be a dangerous thing.

The Communists themselves cannot write their own history. One reason may be found in the official *History of the Communist Party of the United States,* signed by William Z. Foster. This book is so extreme in its omissions and distortions that it is practically worthless except as an example of what the party leadership would like the public to believe. Since it was published in 1952, even this has changed. A surprisingly large number of factual errors shows that

INTRODUCTION

the book was done carelessly. But the main inability of Communists to face their own past truthfully has a deeper cause.

For almost twenty years, two men, Jay Lovestone and Earl Browder, were dominant figures on the American Communist scene one after the other, the former until 1929, the latter until 1945. But since it is Communist etiquette in such matters to pretend that "renegades" never amounted to anything, they are mentioned in Foster's book as infrequently as possible and then only for purposes of abuse. Almost all the other ex-leaders are completely wiped out of the record. The man who did more than anyone else to make possible the formation of the American Communist movement in 1919, is, as we shall see, not even mentioned. In a Communist state, these men would have been liquidated physically. In a non-Communist state, their liquidation takes a literary form. Apart from all other considerations, Communists cannot write their own history because they cannot reconcile so many changes of line and leadership with the aura of infallibility. When they admit "mistakes," the admission is almost always symptomatic of a struggle for power, not of a sudden reverence for historical truth. New leaderships habitually admit the sins of their predecessors to entrench themselves in power.

While it is necessary to dig more deeply into Communist source materials, Communist documents can be peculiarly frustrating and treacherous.

For one thing, Communist documents can be understood only in their historical context. They are invariably couched in sweeping generalizations expressed in the most absolute terms. At the same time, they are conceived for special purposes on particular occasions. Thus Communist dogmatism may be deceptive. When they are pursuing a sectarian policy, the Communists are dogmatic, and when they are pursuing an opportunist policy, they are equally dogmatic. A document which appears to be most rigid and fundamental in form may not be anything of the kind in practice.

A second limitation of Communist documentary sources is even more important. What we want to know about the most basic and far-reaching decisions can rarely, if ever, be found in published documents or records. What appears in the open is the result, not the background, of those decisions. But when was the real decision made? Where? By whom? Why?

Not many people in the Communist movement can answer such questions. As a general rule, the more important the decision, the fewer the leaders who took part in making it. In later years it is almost always necessary to know what went on in the Political Bureau, which at times consisted of as few as five members and never of more than a dozen. At certain periods, policies originated in the still smaller Secretariat of only three members and came to the Political Bureau ready made. The Central Committee has usually been considered too large to serve as anything but a rubber stamp or a sounding board.

When we get to the really major decisions, we have to leave the area of the American movement altogether. These were inextricably bound up with problems and forces of international proportions, and international decisions originated in Moscow, not in New York. It is necessary to know what went on in the Communist International and sometimes, in the final analysis, in the leadership of the Russian Communist party which determined the decisions of the Communist International. Obviously this presents the historian with a most difficult and tantalizing task—to peer behind the surface of the documentary material into the inner recesses of the movement where the power really resides.

In the formative period of the Communist movement, however, there was a minimum of mystery and reticence. The organization had not yet hardened into shape, and much was permitted that later became taboo. Oppositions functioned more or less freely. Communists were more contemptuous of outside opinion in the conduct of their own discussions. They were so confident of the future that they felt little need for mental reservations. In fact, they believed that the more frankly they made known their views, the sooner would they win over the masses of workers.

INTRODUCTION

As a result, some things came out into the open in the first years that were carefully concealed from view later on. The early records of the American Communist movement have never been properly collected and are hard to find. The papers of the underground period were published in small, ephemeral editions circulated within a narrow circle of trusted adherents and sympathizers. But they vastly repay the effort of tracking them down and studying them closely. They exhibit an innocent candor which went out of the Communist movement at a relatively early date.

Historians also have some reason to give thanks that so many early American Communist leaders were expelled from the party. A few of them * have been consulted personally in the preparation of this work. They were former leaders of the first rank, and they understood that there could be no strings attached to any material obtained from them. In the case of others who had already written at length, I have used published material.

At crucial points, the Communist documentary material could be filled out by one or more of these personal sources of information. The problem of what to believe, or how much to believe, again had to be faced. It was complicated by the passage of years, the fallibility of memory, and the human desire for self-justification. Without minimizing the risks, however, it need not be imagined that the historian is entirely at the mercy of anything told him. In order for answers to be convincing, they must be consistent with everything else that we know about the subject. It is not easy to concoct a tale that must be compatible with a large body of acknowledged facts and documentary evidence. In any case, the danger of misrepresentation is considerably lessened by scrupulously playing fair with the reader, by revealing all sources and enabling others to judge for themselves the nature of the evidence.

Some problems and personalities of the American Communist movement have been discussed in this volume at greater length than others. Sometimes the choice was made on the basis of the available material. Sometimes a problem emerged more sharply at

* See Acknowledgments, page 459.

a later period and could be analyzed with greater clarity in a subsequent volume. Some of the early leaders began and ended their Communist careers in the formative period; their stories had to be told completely in this book. Others went on for many years and have been reserved for fuller treatment in a sequel which I plan to write. Some careers were more symbolic than others and lent themselves to the personification of larger forces.

This volume has been conceived as an independent, self-contained study of the origins of American Communism. Though the essential character of the movement was shaped at the beginning, least interest has been shown in the historical forces which led to it and the first years of development which determined its nature. The formative period has remained a largely untold and even unknown story, despite the light it casts on the fully matured movement.

The American Communist movement is worth understanding more than for itself alone and its place in American history. The supreme paradox of the Communist movement is: though a child of the West, it has grown up most spectacularly in the East. Today, as a result, the threat to the West from the East appears at the same time as a Communist threat. But if the center of gravity of the Communist movement has continued to shift from West to East, the reason must be that communism had to seek easier channels of expansion in the East.

Because they were able to achieve power, the Russian and Chinese Communist movements have virtually monopolized scholarly attention. But strength is not necessarily the same as significance. There is no reason why the strongest sections of the Communist movement should represent it any more authentically than the weakest. A good many misconceptions might have been avoided in the past if most thinking about communism in general had not been based on the most successful Communist party. Even in the days of Lenin—the period dealt with in this book—communism was not merely what happened in Russia; it was just as much what was happening in the United States.

1

The Historic Left

THE older native American Communists were born, with few exceptions, in the decade 1881–91. They were still relatively close to the birth of the modern American labor movement; to the infancy of socialism, trade unionism, anarchism, and syndicalism; to the heyday of radical and reform movements now only dimly remembered.

The first Marxian Socialists in the United States were German immigrants who came over after the ill-fated German revolution of 1848. These German immigrants brought with them a degree of trade-union and political consciousness then unknown in the United States. No sooner had they arrived than they set about duplicating their old-world allegiances in their new homeland. But they did not get very far until after the Civil War. The International Workingmen's Association, the so-called First International, founded in London with the help of Karl Marx in 1864, obtained its first American section five years later.

The next and larger wave of German immigrants in the seventies and eighties, however, owed their socialism less to the exiled Marx than to the romantic founder of German social democracy, Ferdinand Lassalle. Lassalle taught that state aid through political action was the only road to the future revolution. He believed in the "iron law of wages"—that it was impossible in an economic system based on free competition for workers to receive more than the bare minimum for existence. Hence he left no room for trade unionism or at least for its primary function, the struggle for higher wages. His immigrant American followers formed "Social Democratic" and "Labor" parties but opposed trade unionism. On the other hand, the early American Marxists did not consider the time ripe for political activity. They believed in trade unionism as the best immediate medium for their political ideas. For the Marxists, the line between political and economic activity was not so sharply drawn, since Marx saw political implications in every economic struggle.

It was a fateful clash, transferred almost bodily from Europe to America. Modern American socialism had its origin in the rivalry between the Marxists and the Lassalleans. The reluctance of the orthodox Marxists to engage in general political activity was one of the main causes of a split in the American branch of the International in 1872. The Lassalleans formed a Social Democratic party of North America in 1874. It suffered from the same disruptive controversy of trade unionism versus politics. The Working Men's party of the United States came in 1876 under joint Lassallean-Marxist auspices. When the Lassalleans gained control, they changed the name to the Socialist Labor party of North America in December 1877. This party for the first time gave organizational continuity to American socialism.[1]

In those seminal years, the issues were posed in such a way that the opposing sides tended to go to extremes. In that small, immature Socialist world, it seemed necessary to choose between Socialist politics and trade-union economics. Though the Socialists suffered cruelly from their own fratricidal wars, they succeeded in stirring up a remarkably creative ferment in the labor movement. But this ferment produced an unexpected result. Out of it came ex-Socialists and former Socialist sympathizers who moved from trade-union socialism to trade unionism without socialism. Two cigar makers, Adolph Strasser and Samuel Gompers, traveled this road from socialism to "pure and simple" trade unionism. The American Federation of Labor, which they were largely instrumental in forming in 1886, in part grew out of the reaction against political socialism.

Also transferred across the Atlantic was the bitter feud between Karl Marx and Michael Bakunin, the son of a Russian nobleman and the father of modern revolutionary anarchism. Bakunin's ideas and methods became the stock in trade of the nineteenth century's revolutionary underground—the conspiratorial form of organization, the cult of violence, the loathing of all authority, the quixotic vision of liberty and equality through destruction and chaos. A Revolutionary Socialist party was organized in Chicago in 1881 by an extremist faction which split away from the Socialist Labor party. The arrival in New York the following year of a German Bakuninist, Johann Most, gave the anarchists a mordant spokesman. Most spread the gospel of the "propaganda of the deed," "expropriation" of the rich, and the beauty of a well-placed stick of dynamite. The "Revolutionary Socialists" and the anarchists united at a convention in Pittsburgh in 1883 and drew up a platform proclaiming that "there is only one remedy left—force." By 1885, this organization claimed about 7000 members, over twice as many as the politically minded Socialist Labor party.[2]

In a well-ordered society, this sort of agitation might have been dismissed as the ravings of madmen. But the United States of this time was not a particularly well-ordered society. Thousands of immigrants poured into the country from Europe each year—almost 9,000,000 from 1881 to 1900. The relations between labor and capital were largely undefined and uncontrollable except by sheer force on both sides. Employers fought labor organizations by every possible means. Strikes were ruthlessly crushed by armed guards, police, sheriffs, militia, and federal troops. Court injunctions tied the hands of unions on the mere threat of a strike. Working conditions often ranged from the primitive to the abominable. Bad times followed good times with monotonous regularity.

In this inflammable social climate, socialism, trade unionism, and anarchism were not the only panaceas. When the A.F. of L. was formed, the Knights of Labor boasted three times the membership of the trade unions. The Knights, founded in 1869, came out of a period when labor organizations were compelled to work in secrecy to overcome the lockouts, blacklists, and forcible resistance of employers. Originally conceived to promote education, mutual aid, and cooperation, it came to spend most of its energy on strikes and boycotts. In one respect, its struggles differed from those of the trade unions: the Knights organized the unskilled and semi-skilled, the trade unions the skilled workers. The decline of the Knights in the period 1886–1900 signified the ascendancy of the skilled craft labor of the trade unions, but the tradition of industrial unionism, which finally prevailed, goes back to the Knights of Labor.

The status quo was challenged from other directions. Henry George attacked land speculation as the source of all social evil and sought to stamp it out by taxing all profits from land equal to the full rental value—the "single tax." In the great American utopian tradition, Edward Bellamy's tremendously popular novel, *Looking Backward,* appeared in 1887. Bellamy's hero awoke in the year 2000 A.D. to find a world of perfect virtue and virtuous perfection because the state had peacefully expropriated all private industrial enterprise and taken charge of the entire economy on a basis of equality and cooperation. Bellamy's genteel and ethical vision of socialism appealed to many more native Americans than did Marx's analysis of the class struggle, but some of those who started with Bellamy ended with Marx. The Christian Socialist movement arose in the late 1880s. Some Protestant thinkers and ministers fought sin in the guise of capitalism and sought salvation in the form of socialism. The essential ideals of socialism were scattered far and wide, and incorporated into many different systems of thought.

The official Socialist movement, however, was little more than a small, moribund, foreign-language sect until the Socialist Labor party was taken over by that imperious, eccentric, and magnetic personality, Daniel De Leon, in 1890. A lecturer on international law at Columbia University, De Leon had supported Henry George's candidacy for mayor of New York in 1886 and had passed through both the Knights of Labor and the Bellamy movement. De Leon could not make the S.L.P. into a mass movement but he could give it an unprecedented theoretical vitality. The convert to Marxist doctrine quickly became its outstanding American interpreter and even went on to do his own thinking in order to fill the gigantic vacuum left by Marx on the nature of the future socialist state. De Leon was a doctrinaire, but a creative one, a combination rarely encountered in Marxian dogmatists. When the future Communist leaders were growing up, De Leon was already a force to be reckoned with, and he initiated some of them into the mysteries of Marxism before that other creative doctrinaire, Lenin, came along to replace him in their affections.

Industrial unionism and Bellamyite utopianism served Eugene Victor Debs as stepping stones to socialism. A former railway fireman born in Terre Haute, Indiana, Debs organized the American Railway Union on industrial-union lines in 1893. After a turbulent strike against the Pullman car company the following year, a sweeping court injunction, the intervention of government troops, and a debacle for the union, six months in jail for defying the injunction gave Debs the enforced leisure to start studying socialist literature. After this strike setback, Debs devoted himself to a scheme for the cooperative colonization of a sparsely settled Western state. Disappointed again, he announced his conversion to socialism in 1897. Instead of joining forces with De Leon in the Socialist Labor party, however, Debs formed a rival organization, the Social Democratic party, in 1898.

At about the same time, a rebellion began to erupt in the Socialist Labor party. The rebels, led by Morris Hillquit of New York, opposed De Leon's domineering personal rule and his anti-A.F. of L. trade-union policy. After much negotiation and maneuvering, the forces behind Debs and Hillquit combined to form the Socialist party of America in 1901. It brought together Christian Socialists and orthodox Marxists, immigrant workers and native intellectuals, trade-union officials and millionaire social reformers. Only a few of the delegates at the first Socialist party convention "had more than the haziest intellectual acquaintance with theoretical Marxism," writes David A. Shannon. "Certainly the anticapitalism of many of the delegates derived more from Edward Bellamy's *Looking Backward* than from *Das Kapital*." [3]

Those who were looking for a militant, extremist movement, however, were no longer likely to find it in socialism. The most exciting new phenomenon in the labor movement in the first decade of the twentieth century—the most impressionable early years of the future Communists—was syndicalism. It arose in the Western states where the craft unionism of the A.F. of L. could not or would not penetrate. The original impulse came from the Western Federation of Miners, formed in 1893. William D. (Big Bill) Haywood became its secretary-treasurer in 1901. The mine federation, an industrial union, had stormed out of the A.F. of L., charging lack of support, and had retaliated by setting up independent Western Labor centers, first the Western Labor Union, then the American Labor Union. Finally, a conglomeration of anti-A.F. of L. elements, including those in the American Labor Union, the Socialist Labor party, and the Socialist party, met together to form the Industrial Workers of the World (I.W.W.) at Chicago in 1905. At the outset, it was big enough to hold Debs, De Leon, and Haywood—but not for long.

Though most of the organizers of the I.W.W., including Haywood, were avowed socialists, they did not agree on the road to socialism. The fundamental dispute hinged on the old problem of political versus economic action. Should political parties or trade unions or both make the revolution? The orthodox Marxists put their faith primarily in revolutionary parties; the syndicalists, in revolutionary trade unions. The original preamble of the I.W.W.'s constitution referred to a struggle "on the political as well as on the industrial field." This phrase did not go far enough for those who believed in revolutionary political activity and went too far for those who believed solely in revolutionary trade unionism. Debs left the I.W.W. in 1906 because he felt that it underestimated the importance of political activity. De Leon was ousted in 1908 in a coup executed by an I.W.W. group more sympathetic to anarchism than to socialism. In that same year, the preamble was changed to eliminate the reference to political activity altogether. The I.W.W. developed into an American variety of anarcho-syndicalism whose battle cries were "direct action," "sabotage," and the "general strike."

The Left Wing of the American labor movement before World War I had its deepest roots in two movements—socialism and syndicalism. Therefore it did not have a single home. It was in the main divided in its loyalties among three organizations—the Socialist Labor party, the Socialist party, and the I.W.W. But that elusive and yet indispensable term—the Left Wing—cannot be fully understood organizationally. There are usually a number of rival groups within the Left Wing, each claiming to be the only true Left. The Left Wing of one period differs from the Left Wing of other periods. This instability is characteristic of a term which does not stand for a party or a program but rather for a relative position, and often only for a vague state of mind.

Nevertheless, there has been something like a historic Left in the American labor movement. As one Left Wing has followed another, a number of basic issues have recurred again and again. Since the Left Wing was less an organization than a fluctuating body of attitudes and ideas, these issues, more than anything else, gave it an enduring character.

Politics versus economics

One of the earliest and most persistent of these issues, as we have seen, was that of political versus economic action.

It split the socialist movement at its inception in the struggle between the Lassalleans and the Marxists. In the context of the time, the pure and simple trade unionists represented the Right Wing; they were regarded with disdain by the political socialists because they worked for the immediate and partial betterment of the working class. Since the political socialists scorned such palliatives and held out for a fundamental change in the social order, they considered themselves to be the Left Wing of the period.

The Lassallean-Marxist dispute still hovered over the socialist movement when De Leon appeared on the scene. He attempted to bring about a theoretical reconciliation. De Leon expected the Socialist party to come into power peacefully by elections, then dissolve itself and turn over the administration of the state to the industrial unions. In this way, he had one foot in parliamentary socialism and the other in syndicalism.

The Socialist party approached the problem somewhat differently. It was primarily a political organization that functioned most effectively at election time. But it recognized the vital role of the trade unions in improving the conditions of the workers. The dominant Socialist outlook, however, implied a division of labor. The socialists owed support to the trade unions in the economic field, and the trade unions owed support to the socialists in the political field. The Socialist party never tried to form revolutionary industrial unions, as the Socialist Labor party under De Leon tried to do. In effect, the Socialist party could officially live at peace with the A.F. of L., even if some individual Socialists could not.

The I.W.W. brought back the old feud with renewed force. The change in the preamble and the expulsion of De Leon bolted the door of the organization against all varieties of political-actionists. Haywood himself was less one-sided. As long as he remained a member of the Socialist party, he did not rule out the political weapon. He thought of political action, however, from the viewpoint of a trade unionist who was being shot at by police and troops. Political action was a possible means of neutralizing these foes. Though the general public identified the I.W.W. with Haywood, the organizing staff of the I.W.W. looked to the General Secretary-Treasurer, Vincent St. John, for leadership, and St. John came much closer to orthodox syndicalism.

The weight of the Left Wing tradition leaned over in the direction of the I.W.W. Trade-union struggles were exhilarating and electoral activity was anemic. In their first stage, the future Communists showed the effects of this conditioning.

Unionism—"pure" and "dual"

The Left Wing did not approve of any kind of economic action by any kind of trade-union movement. The tradition of De Leon, Debs, and Haywood declared war on the A.F. of L. and sought to replace it with industrial unionism.

De Leon agreed with the old Lassalleans that seeking higher wages and shorter hours through "reformist" unions was useless. Instead of rejecting trade unions altogether, however, he prescribed the remedy of revolutionary unions, industrial in form and closely linked to the Socialist Labor party. First he tried to take over the declining Knights of Labor for this end, and when this maneuver failed, he pushed through the organization of a new federation, the Socialist Trade and Labor Alliance, in 1895.

The A.F. of L.'s leader, Gompers, fought back by raising an anguished cry against "dual unionism." From that time on, any attempt to form rival unions has met with the same stigma.

De Leon's Socialist Trade and Labor Alliance never caught on and he merged it with the I.W.W. in 1905. After De Leon was expelled from the I.W.W. three years later, he retaliated by setting up a rival organization in Detroit, using the same name. For years there was a "Detroit I.W.W." and a "Chicago I.W.W." Only the latter ever represented a serious threat to the A.F. of L. De Leon, Haywood, and Debs had a standard answer to Gompers' charge of dual unionism. They simply refused to concede that the A.F. of L. was a bona fide trade union. For De Leon it was a band of "labor fakers." Haywood opened the first I.W.W. convention with the words: "It has been said that this convention was to form an organization rival to the A.F. of L. This is a mistake. We are here for the purpose of forming a labor organization." [4] Debs wrote: "To talk about reforming these rotten graft-infested [A.F. of L.] unions, which are dominated absolutely by the labor boss, is as vain and wasteful of time as to spray a cesspool with attar of roses." [5]

Dual unionism was never a very accurate epithet. It implied

that the A.F. of L. had organized the American working class, and that any other union would merely duplicate it. This was never remotely the case, least of all in Gompers' prime. At the turn of the century, when Gompers was storming about dual unionism, the A.F. of L. had organized about 3 per cent of the total number of gainfully employed workers in non-farm occupations. The A.F. of L.'s share in 1910 was only about 5 per cent.[6] In that era, the A. F. of L. was largely made up of craft unions with a membership of native skilled workers, mostly located in the East. It kept out the vast majority of unskilled and semiskilled immigrant workers in the East and lacked the aggressiveness to invade the unorganized territory in the West. The Western Federation of Miners had no competition from the A.F. of L. The immigrant men's garment workers flocked into the independent Amalgamated Clothing Workers because the older A.F. of L. union in the field could not organize them. The railroad brotherhoods antedated the A.F. of L. and never belonged to it. Dual unions came in various shapes and sizes for many different reasons, ideological and opportunistic.

Yet if there had been nothing to the charge of dual unionism, it would not have become for many decades a fighting issue. There was something to it, but not what Gompers implied. As long as the A.F. of L. fell short by so wide a margin of organizing the American worker, it could scarcely make good its claim to be the mainstream of the American labor movement. By failing to organize the unorganized, it held out a standing invitation to others to do the job. Dualism exposed the limitations of the A.F. of L., challenged Gompers' right to speak for the American worker, and held out the threat of future invasion of A.F. of L. territory.

In Left Wing dualism, two words were invariably linked—"revolutionary" and "industrial." This tradition enabled the A.F. of L. to fight industrial unionism as if it were a revolutionary plot. It enabled the Left Wing to use the popular appeal of industrial unionism to advance its revolutionary aims. But when industrial unionism finally came to the American labor movement in the 1930s, it required no revolution, and eventually the A.F. of L. made peace with it.

Violence—imported and domestic

The anarchists did not introduce violence into the American labor movement. Irish immigrants were blamed for riots in the middle of the 1830s. The Molly Maguires, as a secret society of Irish miners was popularly called, punished their enemies with death and destruction of property in the anthracite regions of Pennsylvania in the 1860s and 1870s. The great railroad strikes of 1877 were suppressed by federal troops waging small-scale battles with rioting crowds. But these outbreaks were spontaneous and localized, without a philosophy of violence.

The anarchists philosophized about violence; others benefited from it. The early anarchist movement never recovered from the tragic effects of the bomb that was thrown into the eight-hour-day demonstration in Haymarket Square, Chicago, in 1886, though its responsibility could not be proved. Several hundred Pinkerton detectives fought armed battles against steel workers to enforce a reduction in wages in Homestead, Pennsylvania, in 1892. Federal troops smashed Debs's strike against the Pullman company in 1894. A series of violent mine strikes broke out—at Coeur d'Alene in Idaho in 1892 and 1899, and in Colorado at Cripple Creek in 1894, at Leadville in 1896, and in the Telluride district in 1901. This protracted warfare culminated in the arrest in 1906 of two mine-union officials, Charles H. Moyer and William D. Haywood, and a former union official, George Pettibone, for complicity in the murder by bombing of Governor Steunenberg of Idaho. They were finally released, but the entire labor movement had to come to their defense, since the overshadowing issue of the case was the responsibility of the labor movement for the violence which had characterized the great American strikes for two decades.

The real source of violence was desperation. In the West, where the I.W.W. started, it was mostly successful in the lumber, agriculture, and construction trades, which used unskilled migratory workers who shifted from job to job and industry to industry. When it came East, it concentrated on the unorganized immigrant workers in the textile trades. Neither of these classes of workers voted. It was hopeless for them to think of winning reforms by political means. The employers in the fields invaded by the I.W.W. ruthlessly opposed any trade-union organization. Even A.F. of L. organizers, especially in the West, knew that buckshot won or lost many a strike and organizing campaign.

The I.W.W. accepted violence as a natural and inevitable part of the organizing job. It owed much less to the tradition handed down by the old Bakuninist immigrant intellectuals than to the gun-toting morality generally prevalent in the Western states. Some European theories happened to fit into the I.W.W.'s practice, but the practice would have existed without the theories. "Direct action" was the I.W.W.'s free translation for the facts of life in the neofeudal company towns. The I.W.W. reflected the facts of life at a particular time and place; it failed to survive because there was no longer a need for it when the facts changed.

Haywood and the I.W.W. were distinguished from the rest of the Left Wing by their admission of violent means of struggle to the economic arsenal. The violent, revolutionary, industrial unionism of syndicalism was a much more potent brew than anything Debs or De Leon could stomach. If they represented two of the Left Wings before World War I, Haywood represented the extreme Left Wing.

The immediate and the impossible

With the upsurge of trade unionism, socialism, and anarchism in the 1880s, the lines were sharply drawn for one of the great doctrinal controversies in the labor movement.

Adolph Strasser gave "pure and simple" trade unionism its classic formulation in 1883: "We have no ultimate ends. We are going on from day to day. We are fighting only for immediate objects—objects

THE HISTORIC LEFT

that can be realized in a few years." [7] The more extreme socialists and anarchists scorned such short-term, practical aims. They refused to countenance anything less than the ultimate goal—the overthrow of capitalism. With De Leon, this attitude hardened into a rigid dogma. "A political party that sets up 'immediate demands' by so much blurs its 'constant demand' or goal," he insisted. "The presence of 'immediate demands' in a Socialist platform reveals pure and simple politicianism—corruption, or the invitation to corruption." [8]

The newly formed Socialist party could never, as a whole, make up its mind. At its first convention in 1901, there were some who believed in socialism on the installment plan and some who held out for all or nothing. The former wanted a series of reform planks in the platform. The latter wanted nothing but a statement of socialist fundamentals. The final outcome was a compromise. Seven reform demands, such as more state aid to education, were put in, but capitalist-sponsored reforms were denounced on the ground that they helped to make exploitation safer for the capitalists. At the next convention, in 1904, immediate demands were again included, but to avoid giving them undue prominence, they were not placed in a special section. At the 1908 convention the immediate demands were promoted to a separate section, but each faction was free to stress publicly what it wanted.[9]

To the Left Wing, the proponents of immediate demands were "bourgeois reformers." The latter preferred to call themselves "constructive Socialists." To the Right Wing, the opponents of immediate demands were "impossibilists." The latter preferred to call themselves "scientific Socialists." Yet each wing was equally sure that it was both constructive and scientific. The Right Wing was able, in perfectly good faith, to equate the immediate objective of reforms with the ultimate goal of socialism because it was persuaded that every reform within the body of capitalism represented a degree of full-fledged socialism, as if socialism consisted of the sum-total of reforms.

To the Left Wing, this was dangerous nonsense. It took the position that socialism could begin to develop only after the overthrow of capitalism. Reforms were, as Debs put it, "the mask of fraud," staving off the overthrow of capitalism rather than advancing the cause of socialism.[10] Some Left-Wingers were opposed to reforms in principle; others were willing to tolerate them in "bourgeois" parties but saw no reason for socialists to sponsor them. This conflict of tendencies made it possible for a Center group, largely guided by Hillquit, to dominate Socialist policy for many years.

The I.W.W. had trouble with the problem in a somewhat different way. The workers involved in its strikes were just as much interested in getting higher wages and better working conditions as were the workers involved in the A.F. of L.'s strikes. But I.W.W. strikes were like revolutions in miniature. Organizers moved in on spontaneous outbursts of mass rebellion, gave them leadership to the extent of fiery and thrilling oratory, spurned negotiations and compromises, and personally led wild, bloody clashes with the police. I.W.W. strikes, like A.F. of L. strikes, were made possible by concrete grievances; they took on a different character because the I.W.W. specialized in lost causes. With rare exceptions, I.W.W. strikes failed to win any immediate demands but succeeded in arousing a great deal of revolutionary feeling.

The connection between immediate demands and the ultimate goal was historically an almost insoluble problem for the Left Wing. The favorite solution seemed to require a complete dichotomy, as the De Leonites argued in theory and the I.W.W. demonstrated in practice. In this respect, the Left Wing of the Socialist party had no position of its own; it agreed fundamentally with the Socialist Labor party and the I.W.W.

Orthodoxy and revisionism

The struggle between immediate demands and the ultimate goal was closely related to another struggle—between "revisionism" and "orthodox Marxism."

As long as Karl Marx or his co-worker, Frederick Engels, lived, there was a relatively simple way to determine what orthodox Marxism was: it was whatever Marx or Engels said it was. Marx's letters contain passing remarks which reveal his awareness of American conditions. In the early fifties, he expressed the opinion that "bourgeois society in the United States has not yet developed far enough to make the class struggle obvious and comprehensible." In the late sixties, he wrote an address to the National Labor Union, ending with the thought that its "glorious task" was to see to it that "at last the working class shall enter upon the scene of history, no longer as a servile following, but as an independent power." In the early seventies, he laid down for one of the German Socialist immigrants the important principle that economic struggles for a shorter work day or strikes were useful in building the organizational basis of a political movement of the working class.[11]

Marx paid relatively little attention to the American movement, but it was otherwise with Engels. After Marx's death, a steady stream of advice, encouragement, and criticism came from his pen in letters to American correspondents. Engels himself made a short trip to the United States and Canada in 1888. Unlike Marx, he was able to make a quite extensive and detailed analysis of the special problems of the American movement, and one that can still be studied with profit more than a half-century later. Engels' attitude toward the American problem was at least partly due to his disappointing experiences in England. Despite the fact that both Marx and he had been living there for over thirty years, the British labor movement had persisted in going its own way, ignoring their wishes and often their very presence. By the time Engels turned his attention to the Americans, he had learned to be more tolerant and forbearing. If the British workers refused to heed him, he could hardly expect more from the Americans.

Engels' image of the American working class of his time may be outdated but it is not altogether irrelevant. From his point of view, there were pluses and minuses. He was tremendously impressed with American "energy and vitality." The Americans did not have to contend with a feudal past as well as a bourgeois present. They were pre-eminently "practical," and judged everything on the basis of concrete results. On the other hand, they were lamentably backward in "theory"—so backward that he considered the *Communist Manifesto,* published in 1848, "far too difficult for America" in 1887. Engels' letters on America are studded with phrases like "untheoretical, matter-of-fact Americans," "quite crude, tremendously backward theoretically," "contemptuous of reason and science," "so conceited about its 'practice' and so frightfully dense theoretically," "ahead of everyone else in practice and still in swaddling clothes in theory." These peculiar conditions, Engels tried to teach the German Socialist immigrants, would lead to a peculiar type of American development. It would have to be based on practical experience rather than theoretical indoctrination. The best way to handle the Americans was to let them learn from their own mistakes. Meanwhile, the important thing was the mass movement, such as the unprecedented strike wave of 1886. He advised working inside the Knights of Labor, despite all of its political confusion, because it was a mass movement. He thought that the next step forward would be a Labor party and warned that a million or two workingmen's votes "for a *bona fide* workingmen's party is worth infinitely more at present than a hundred thousand votes for a doctrinally perfect platform." Though always the optimist, he expected the American movement to advance by "ups and downs" and by colossal "zigzags." [12]

Oddly enough, then, it would be hard to establish a dogmatic Marxist orthodoxy as applied to American conditions on anything that Engels himself wrote. The founders of Marxism were complex enough to plant in their own work the seeds for most of the schisms that have taken place in their name. It is not without significance that some of Engels' least doctrinaire sentiments were evoked by the American problem. One was: "Our theory is a theory of evolution, not a dogma to be learnt by heart and to be repeated mechanically." Another reads: "For the masses are to be set in motion only along the road that fits each country and the prevailing circumstances, which is usually a roundabout road." [13]

Despite Engels' advice, however, the American Socialist movement continued to suffer from dogmatism. The German immigrant doctrinaires were replaced, or rather supplemented, by the despotic De Leon, who was like Marx in one respect—he was fiercely jealous of his prerogative to decide what socialism stood for.

The rebellion against De Leon and the organization of the Socialist party at the turn of the century coincided with a doctrinal crisis in the international Socialist movement. In Germany, the largest and most influential section of the movement, a great theoretical struggle flared up between the "revisionist" critic, Eduard Bernstein, and the foremost guardian of "orthodox" Marxism, Karl Kautsky. Bernstein was no ordinary party member; he was Engels' literary executor. His book, originally published in 1899, and later translated into English as *Evolutionary Socialism,* shocked the Socialist world out of theoretical complacency. Bernstein tried to cut away what he considered to be the out-moded philosophical and economic preconceptions of the Marxian system. In the process, he developed a view that was remarkably similar to the practice of the Right Wing Socialists in the United States. In fact, Bernstein merely put into words what Socialist parties were doing almost everywhere. When he came out for a "party of reform," he was describing as much as he was advocating. When he boldly proclaimed that, for him, "the goal of Socialism is nothing, the movement everything," he expressed what many others were feeling. In this respect, Bernstein created nothing new; he gave an existing tendency a theoretical justification and the prestige of his name. It is noteworthy that Bernstein was also strongly influenced in his views by his experiences in England. In the United States, Bernstein's position was quickly adopted by Victor L. Berger of Wisconsin, the most successful leader of the Right Wing and the first Socialist member of Congress, though on occasion he could use revolutionary rhetoric with the best of orthodox Marxists. Berger liked to be called the "American Bernstein." [14]

The Left Wing in the Socialist party was identified with orthodox Marxism, the class struggle, the revolution, the supremacy of the proletariat. It rejected immediate demands, reforms, middle-class adulteration. Sometimes the same words could be used by both the

Left and Right Wing to mean different things. To the Right Wing, a "revolution" was merely a fundamental, deep-rooted change in the social system. It was not incompatible with the theory of piecemeal reforms, which could be interpreted to mean such a change eventually. For the Left Wing, "revolution" signified the road to power as well as the objective result; the enemy was personalized; his violent resistance to any fundamental change was taken for granted; and the "final conflict" was envisioned literally in more or less violent terms. The Right Wing referred to the "class struggle," if at all, as merely a way of describing the existence of classes with different interests. How these different interests might be best expressed, whether through the ballot box or physical violence, was another matter. The Right Wing was uncomfortable with many of socialism's fundamental formulas, used them rarely, or took the fight out of them. The Left Wing doted on revolutionary phrases and liked to serve them piping hot.

Since there was more than one Left Wing, the mutations and permutations could be most complicated. Both wings of the Socialist party had some things in common against the syndicalism of the I.W.W., especially on the score of political action. On the other hand, the I.W.W. was also dedicated to the class struggle in its most primitive form, and many an orthodox Marxist could not help but feel closer in spirit, if not in theory, to it than to the Right Wing.

Chosen people

One article of faith was shared by all Left-Wingers—the revolutionary nature of the proletariat and the counter-revolutionary nature of the middle class. The proletariat was the revolutionary hero, the middle class the reformist villain. The proletariat was the guarantee of the ultimate goal, the middle class the corrupting influence of immediate demands. The proletariat was dedicated to the class struggle, the middle class to class collaboration.

The reality was so much at variance with the theory that the theory had to be patched up. Marx and Engels themselves gave currency to both the crude theory and the more realistic refinement. Sometimes they wrote as if the proletariat as a whole constituted a necessarily revolutionary class. Sometimes they recognized the revolutionary nature of only a portion of the proletariat in some countries but not in others. Engels was constantly complaining that the higher standard of living of the British working class, which he attributed to British exploitation of other nations, was producing a "bourgeois proletariat."[15] This implied that there were revolutionary and nonrevolutionary sections of the proletariat, depending on the standard of living. There was nothing revolutionary about the better-paid "aristocracy of labor," though by definition it was part of the proletariat. On the contrary, this aristocracy was relegated to outer darkness as carriers of the bourgeois virus within the working class. The crude theory could not give a social explanation for what was wrong with the A.F. of L. but the refinement did. De Leon was fond of quoting Mark Hanna, who had said that the A.F. of L. was led by "labor lieutenants of capital." For De Leon they represented the "aristocracy of labor."

Yet the distance between Gompers and the Socialists was not as great as both of them imagined. The whole Socialist theory was based on the material interests of the proletariat. This type of thinking was also second nature to Gompers since his fledgling days as a Socialist fellow traveler. What separated Gompers from the Socialists was the difference in their interpretations of material interest, not the basic proposition itself. To Gompers, higher wages were material; shorter hours were material; better working conditions were material. Only the concrete and immediate were material. Whatever success Gompers had, and the Socialists did not have, was scarcely a repudiation of the Marxist emphasis on material interests. It might have indicated the need for American Marxists to take their materialism a little more materialistically.

In any case, the relation of the working class to the other classes of society was a problem which long plagued the Left Wing. For orthodox Marxists, the middle class was a dangerous enemy, not a potential ally. Everything wrong with the Socialist and labor movements was ascribed to middle-class or petty-bourgeois influences. Lawyers, ministers, dentists, doctors, and teachers were the traditional butts of Left Wing oratory—even if the orator himself was a lawyer, minister, dentist, doctor, or teacher. It was another case of doctrine triumphing over reality. Victor L. Berger, the "American Bernstein," was a former schoolteacher; the orthodox Marxist, Louis B. Boudin, was a lawyer. Haywood became a miner at nine years of age, but De Leon was a college teacher. As we shall see, the dentists, teachers, journalists, accountants, and lawyers who helped to form the Communist party were furiously contemptuous of the dentists, teachers, journalists, accountants, and lawyers who remained in the Socialist party. In truth, there were Left Wing and Right Wing teachers, lawyers, and proletarians. Relatively few proletarians were admitted into the leadership of either wing—and even these speedily became ex-proletarians.

The relation of the proletariat and the middle class was far more than a theoretical question. In terms of practical politics it prevented American socialism from working with predominantly middle-class liberal or progressive movements. Immediate demands and partial reforms were what liberal and progressive movements thrived on. The Socialists could complain that these middle-class movements pilfered their immediate demands from the Socialist platform; but the Socialists could not claim credit for taking part in the popular movements which translated their own demands into practical legislation. Thus, in the older tradition of American radicalism, the Left Wing doomed itself to political isolation. It could not make alliances; it reserved its hottest fire for its only potential allies. Despite Engels' advice, the Socialist party uncompromisingly opposed a Labor party until the early 1920s.

Long before there was a Communist movement, then, the Left Wing identified the revolution with the unskilled, the unorganized, and the poorest portion of the proletariat. The capitalists were the open enemies. The middle class represented rotten compromise and insidious seduction. The skilled, organized, and better-paid workers belonged outside the proletarian pale, henchmen of the A.F. of L. and of the Right Wing.

Immigrants and natives

The proletariat was not the only chosen people. From the very outset, the American Socialist movement was peculiarly indebted to the immigrants for both its progress and its problems. The first convention of the Socialist Labor party in 1877 was composed of representatives of seventeen German sections, seven English, three Bohemian, one French, and a general women's section.[16] Immigrants naturally assumed the role of teachers and organizers, but they were mainly concerned with teaching and organizing themselves.

The immigrants found themselves in a new world where the social conditions did not provide the fertile ground for socialist ideas that they had been accustomed to take for granted in the old world. There were no centuries-old rigid class distinctions and barriers to overcome. There was still the lure of free land. There were vast inequalities, and equally vast opportunities. It was a world by no means impervious to socialist ideas, but it did not fit the mold in which those ideas had been cast in their European birthplace. This native recalcitrance baffled the socialist-minded immigrants. They could not fathom the irrepressible American propensity for seeking salvation in monetary schemes. They were nonplussed by the get-rich-quick mentality rampant in all segments of American society.

The adaptation of socialist ideas to American conditions was the great challenge before these German Socialist pioneers. Some bravely grappled with it. The majority proved unequal to the task. Instead, they took refuge in a form of escapism typical of the Socialist movement. They made a sanctuary out of socialist theory. For it was in the theoretical realm that the Socialist immigrants felt themselves most comfortable and superior. The traditional phrases and formulas of "scientific socialism" were their impregnable strongholds. When they had to reinterpret these phrases and formulas in American terms and apply them to American conditions, their comfort and superiority faded.

Engels clearly and acutely sized up this unhealthy situation as early as the 1880s. He was appalled by the false pride of the German immigrants, which prevented them from taking part in the confused native movements, and even from learning the English language. Aware of his low opinion of them, the Germans paid him back by boycotting his books. "The Germans have not understood how to use their theory as a lever which could set the American masses in motion," he complained bitterly. "They do not understand the theory themselves for the most part and treat it in a doctrinaire and dogmatic way as something that has to be learned by heart, which then will satisfy all requirements forthwith. To them it is a credo and not a guide to action." Again and again he tried to save them from themselves. "They will have to doff every remnant of their foreign garb," he thundered at the German-American Socialist Labor party. "They will have to become out-and-out American. They cannot expect the Americans to come to them; they, the minority and the immigrants, must go to the Americans, who are the vast majority and the natives. And to do that, they must above all things learn English." [17]

The Socialist Labor party was never more than an American head on an immigrant body. The I.W.W. rested on native-born workers in the West and immigrant workers in the East. The Socialist party was not set up to appeal to the foreign-born and they in turn did not feel at home in it. As a result, foreign-born Socialists who did not speak English or preferred their native tongue resorted to more or less independent organizations. The Finnish Socialists were first to do so in 1904. By 1915, there were fourteen foreign-language federations affiliated with the Socialist party. In 1917, out of a total party membership of 80,126, no less than 32,894, or 40 per cent, belonged to the foreign-language federations. They were virtually autonomous, much closer in spirit to the Socialist parties of the countries of their national origin than to the American Socialist party.

The immigrants played a dual role in the development of American socialism. They were largely responsible for its birth. They were also largely responsible for stunting its growth. They could transplant the theory of socialism but they could not naturalize it. In the formative years, therefore, an unequal and uneasy relationship existed between foreign-born and native Socialists. The former enjoyed the prestige of intellectual superiority but could not effectively spread the gospel. The latter suffered from a sense of theoretical inferiority but were indispensable in presenting the face of the party to the general public. It was not unusual for the top leadership of local Socialist groups to be native-born while a majority of the rank and file were foreign-born. The Communist movement inherited much of this situation from the Socialist movement. The arrogance of the German immigrants in the early Socialist movement resembled that of the Russian immigrants in the early Communist movement.

The immigrants, however, cut across Left-Right lines. This can be seen from the local centers of strength of both wings in the Socialist party.

The Right Wing was particularly strong in Wisconsin, Pennsylvania, and to a lesser extent in New York. Yet the immigrants were most numerous in precisely these states. The Left Wing was dominant in such states as Ohio, Indiana, and Michigan. Shannon writes: "West of the Mississippi River, in Missouri, Kansas, Arkansas, Texas and especially Oklahoma, was a kind of emotional and radical Socialism that caused Berger, Hillquit and most moderate Eastern Social Democrats to shudder." [18] Berger was an Austrian immigrant and Hillquit a Russian immigrant. On the other hand, in some states, as in Massachusetts, the immigrants were among the extremists. The tendency of the Socialist movement in the home country accounted in large part for the difference. The German Socialist immigrants in Wisconsin reflected the moderate policy of the German Social Democracy. The Lettish Socialist immigrants in Massachusetts reflected the fact that the Lettish movement in Europe belonged to the extreme Left Wing led by the Russian Bolsheviks. Yet the extremism of the immigrant Left Wing manifested itself mainly in theory and propaganda. It had little of the "direct action" so dear to the native-born.

Oklahoma farmers who considered themselves Socialists were capable in 1917 of plotting a modern Shays' Rebellion—a march on Washington to seize the government and stop the war—despite official Socialist disapproval. This potential of violence within the Socialist movement had little or nothing to do with anything that the immigrants contributed, and they were often the ones most violently displeased. American society of the late nineteenth and early twentieth century, into which the Socialist movement injected itself, was sufficiently violent in some of its aspects without help from abroad. As the I.W.W. showed, the more violent native radicals could not be contained within the Socialist movement and were not content until they had a more indigenously militant expression of their temperament. Haywood could begin his autobiography with these words: "My father was of an old American family, so American that if traced back it would probably run to the Puritan bigots or the cavalier pirates." [19] Not a few American Communist leaders of a later generation could and did make a similar boast. Such people came to socialism, syndicalism, or communism because of a need within themselves, and not because they were converted to a foreign ideology alien to their background and upbringing.

In one sense, the immigrant character of the Left Wing was anything but "un-American." America was a land of immigrants and the American working class was largely immigrant in character. The disproportion of newly arrived immigrants in the Left Wing resulted as much from the rejection of these immigrants by the dominant political institutions as from the rejection by the immigrants of the dominant political institutions. The major political parties neglected them or permitted them to become pawns of corrupt political machines. For many immigrants the dream of American equality came true in the Left Wing where they were received without prejudice and given a means of political expression. Moreover, a large proportion of Socialists were immigrants, but a small proportion of immigrants were Socialists.

Yet the fact remains that the Socialist movement never succeeded in naturalizing itself in the United States as it did in a large part of Europe. The deeper reasons went far beyond the influence of the immigrants. At bottom, socialism was "foreign" to American life because of a shortcoming inherent in itself. The Socialist analysis and appeal had been conceived for a much more rigid and retrogressive society. If all the Socialist predictions of American capitalist decay and doom had stood the test of experience, the Socialist movement would have Americanized itself, with or without the immigrants. Socialism gained a precarious foothold in American life because it partially fulfilled a need. It did not go further because the need was not greater.

2

The Age of Unrest

THE generation to which the first American Communists belonged was tormented by intense doubt and anxiety about the state of American capitalism. The troubled conscience of this generation was fed far more by Populism and Progressivism than by socialism and syndicalism. All of them combined to create a general mood of discontent in the middle class as well as in the working class. The formative years of three typical native Communist leaders—William Z. Foster (born in 1881), Charles E. Ruthenberg (born in 1882), and Earl Browder (born in 1891)—were spent in an America deeply dissatisfied with the status quo.

For over a century and a half, every popular American movement has been openly antagonistic to or keenly critical of the course of American capitalist development. In Jefferson's time, the enemy was the fattening mercantile class. In Jackson's time, it was the monopolistic national bank and the privileged moneyed powers. After the Civil War, the trade unions, the Knights of Labor, the Greenback movement, the Single-Taxers, and many other local parties sprang up to protest in one way or another the headlong onslaught of industrialism. The chief political expression of Western economic unrest in the 1890s was Populism. James B. Weaver, the Populist presidential candidate in 1892, polled more than a million votes on a platform calling among other things for government ownership of the railroads.

In the next presidential election the Populist thunder was stolen by William Jennings Bryan, and Bryan frightened America's "organized wealth" as Marx never did.

But there was anticapitalism and anticapitalism. The Populist variety revealed the fears, expressed the hopes, and spoke the language of the Middle-western farmer. He was second to none in his hatred of "Wall Street," Eastern bankers, international financiers, "robber barons." What sent him into battle, however, was the war cry of "free silver," not desire for the socialization of production. The discontented American farmer wanted more of what the capitalist had. He wanted it without the annoyance of revolution or the encumbrance of ideology—just by coining more precious metal and putting more into circulation. There was in this yearning a peculiar disproportion between the end and the means. The end which inspired all the native protest movements from Jefferson to Bryan was a utopia of nostalgia. It was a dream of recapturing an imaginary idyllic past of independent freeholders capable of supporting themselves on their own land without debts or depressions. The road to this promised land was to be paved with "cheap money." It was the prototype of those "Share the Wealth" plans which have always appealed to the masses of discontented Americans. Never have they been able to make up their minds whether they dislike big capitalism or only the big capitalists.

The agrarian revolt never threatened the foundations of private property. Its shock troops were property-conscious farmers threatened with debt and bankruptcy. They fought against exorbitant railroad rates and extortionate credit terms in order to save private property—their own. It was for them, however, an unequal battle. So strongly entrenched were the railroads and banks that the farmers had to seek help from the government to redress the balance. But they demanded government ownership and control to disarm their enemies, not themselves—the desperate expedient of little capitalists besieged by big capitalists. Paradoxically, the demand for government ownership and control that came out of the Populist tradition was not a step toward collectivism, socialism, or communism. It was a peculiar American device to defend the capitalism of the many against the capitalism of the few.

The Socialist variety of anticapitalism, on the other hand, came over from Europe. It sought to reveal the fears, express the hopes, and speak the language of the proletariat. It wholeheartedly accepted industrialism. It looked to the future, not the past. Its favorite breeding ground was the city, not the countryside. The ideal of native anticapitalism was precapitalistic; the ideal of imported anticapitalism was postcapitalistic.

But there was—or seemed to be—a meeting ground for all varieties of anticapitalism. The everyday propaganda of populism and socialism could be virtually indistinguishable to the naked eye. When the Populist program of 1892 said, "The fruits of the toil of millions are boldly stolen to build up colossal fortunes for a few, unprecedented in the history of mankind," it was speaking the common language of all radicalism. This synthesis of Populism and socialism was the secret of success of the *Appeal to Reason*, which made its debut in 1895, the only Socialist paper ever to achieve a mass circulation of more than half a million copies a week.

Officially, Populism and socialism spurned each other. A Populist organ attacked socialism as the substitution of one slavery for another. The Socialists assailed the Populist money program as the ignorant illusion of a doomed class—the small farmers. But socialism could begin where Populism ended. The Populists could not restore the small farmer to political supremacy or dictate financial policy to the whole nation. But they stirred up social discontent which sometimes found an outlet elsewhere. One of these outlets was socialism. Debs was a typical example. He was a Democrat, and then a Populist, before he became a Socialist. His biographer comments: "If Bryan had been elected President in 1896, Eugene Debs might never have become a socialist."[1] In 1909, former Populists accounted for 15 per cent of the membership of the Socialist party.[2] In some parts of the country, and in many subtle ways, the Populist tradition intermingled with the Socialist tradition. A number of popular Socialist songs out West were Populist in origin.[3]

THE AGE OF UNREST   39

The older generation of American Communists still had some roots in the Populist tradition. Foster significantly named his autobiography *From Bryan to Stalin*. In Philadelphia Ella Reeve Bloor began her political career during Bryan's "free silver" campaign of 1896. At one political debate a young New York Socialist delivered a Marxist criticism of the free coinage of silver. He so impressed her that she promptly asked for a Socialist Labor party button. In Denver at the turn of the century, Israel Amter found his way to a Socialist club that had been formed by disappointed Populists. Kansas was one of the chief Populist strongholds when Earl Browder was a boy in Wichita. His father was a Populist sympathizer and filled the home with its evangel. The official history of the American Communist party criticizes the old Socialist and labor movements for their failure to support the Populists, implying that the Communists would have done otherwise. A Communist booklet on Populism treats the subject with a maximum of sympathy and a minimum of criticism.[4] Fifty years later, there was still something in the Populist tradition that the Communists considered useful for their own purposes.

The Progressive variety of disenchantment after the turn of the century was not the same as the Populist. Progressivism made its greatest appeal to the middle class. It was especially congenial to intellectuals. In addition, the steam of the old Populist rebellion had not yet completely evaporated, and what was left of it, together with the Bryanite agitation, helped to push forward the Progressive movement on a nationwide scale. For once, discontented farmers joined forces with discontented shopkeepers and professionals. It was the line-up that Franklin D. Roosevelt re-created a quarter of a century later, with organized labor added for good measure.

Intellectually and spiritually, the Progressive era represented an unusual kind of stocktaking. That generation had witnessed tremendous changes in the size, structure, and style of living of the nation. It was moved by a nagging need to open its eyes to the reality of American life. Industry had made colossal strides. But some of it was becoming trustified and monopolistic. Urban population had shot forward. But the new arrivals from the countryside and abroad were huddled in overcrowded, unsanitary, vice-breeding centers where ostentatious wealth rubbed against conspicuous misery. The cities were infested with corrupt political machines. Politicians up to the highest, financiers at the very top, the pillars of society provided the Progressive conscience with material for disillusionment.

The "muckraking" of Progressive journalism, the "realism" of Progressive literature, the "economic interpretation" of Progressive historians, and the "trust-busting" of Progressive politics were all of one piece. Their favorite genre was the exposé. Lincoln Steffens exposed municipal corruption in *The Shame of the Cities*. Frank Norris's novel *The Octopus* was an exposé of railroad expansion. *An Economic Interpretation of the Constitution of the United States* by Charles A. Beard was a retroactive exposé of the Founding Fathers. The best part of Progressivism was a literary exercise in disillusionment. This was both its strength and its weakness. It could criticize the way American capitalism had grown to maturity and deplore the price that had been paid, but it could not stop or even hinder the process. In the end, it proved to be more a symptom of growing pains than a signal of social crisis.

The Progressive intellectuals made one of the most sustained and broad-fronted critical assaults in our cultural history on the shortcomings of American capitalism. The Progressives exposed the evils of the existing order more effectively than the Socialists were able to do. They reached many more people in magazines of mass circulation through writers of nationwide celebrity. Few young men or women in that era with any interest in social problems could escape being caught up in the wave of indignation against greed, hypocrisy, and corruption in industry and politics. Like the Populists, however, the Progressives stimulated an appetite which they could not always satisfy.

Lincoln Steffens, the muckraker, gently steered admiring disciples to communism and followed them himself a decade later. Charles Edward Russell was a muckraking journalist turned Socialist. Sometimes one generation went as far as the Populists or Progressives and the next generation continued on to the Socialists or Communists. John Reed's father was caught up in the Bull Moose movement of Progressives and insurgent Republicans. Henry Demarest Lloyd wrote the first muckraking classic, *Wealth Against Commonwealth,* and tried to mediate between Populism and Socialism. His son, William Bross Lloyd, became a prominent Socialist and then one of the founders of the Communist movement. His sister, Caro Lloyd, joined the Communist party in 1935 at the age of seventy-six.[5]

The literary renaissance of the Progressive period was full of Socialist and Left Wing overtones. Sherwood Anderson wrote a long book called *Why I Am A Socialist* but destroyed it.[6] The greatest of all muckraking novels, *The Jungle,* Upton Sinclair's exposé of the Chicago stockyards, originally appeared in the *Appeal to Reason.* After the book's appearance in 1906, Sinclair founded a colony at Englewood, New Jersey, on utopian Socialist lines. The furnace was tended by a Yale student named Sinclair Lewis.[7] Carl Sandburg started out as a Socialist journalist and poet. Some of Jack London's most famous works, read by hundreds of thousands of Americans, amount to thinly disguised Socialist propaganda.

The Communist intellectuals of the next decade liked to think of themselves as the heirs of the social rebellion of the Progressive era.[8] The Progressives were not the product of a revolutionary ferment, but they stirred up a ferment which could produce some revolutionaries.

High tides

The high tide of Progressivism was also the high tide of Socialism. In the presidential election of 1912, the "New Freedom" of Woodrow Wilson received more than 6,000,000 votes, the diluted "Progressivism" of Theodore Roosevelt more than 4,000,000, and the diluted "conservatism" of William Howard Taft a poor 3,500,000. The Socialist vote of Eugene Victor Debs soared to 897,011, representing 5.9 per cent of the total vote—the highest percentage ever reached by the Socialist party. Almost four out of every five votes were cast for candidates who competed with one another in criticizing the status quo and promising various degrees of change.

When the Socialist vote for 1912 is more closely examined, the party's strength outside New York may come as a surprise. In terms of the percentage of Socialist votes out of the total vote cast, the most Socialist-minded states in the country were Oklahoma with 16.6 per cent and Nevada with 16.5; then came Montana, Arizona, Washington, California, and Idaho, all over 10 per cent; but New York was thirty-first with only 4 per cent of the total vote. Even in absolute figures, Ohio, Pennsylvania, Illinois, and California surpassed New York.[9]

A Socialist of 1912 who dared to foresee the ruin of the party in seven short years would have been accused of morbid hallucinations. The vote had increased ninefold in twelve years, had doubled in only four years. The party membership had grown sevenfold in nine years. The first Socialist congressman, Victor Berger, was sent to Washington from Wisconsin in 1910. By the beginning of 1912, the number of Socialist officeholders had reached 1039, including 56 mayors, 305 aldermen and councilmen, 22 police officials, and some state legislators. Cities and towns of the size of Milwaukee, Berkeley, Butte, Schenectady, and Flint were run by Socialists.[10] The perennial president of the A.F. of L., Sam Gompers, was opposed at the 1912 convention by a Socialist candidate, Max Hayes, who rolled up almost one-third of the votes. The Socialist party was able in 1912 to take credit for 5 English and 8 foreign-language daily newspapers, 262 English and 36 foreign-language weeklies, and 10 English and 2 foreign-language monthlies. The English dailies were published in Chicago, Milwaukee, New York, Belleville, Illinois, and Lead, South Dakota.[11] The weekly *Appeal to Reason* went out in great bundles from Girard, Kansas, at twenty-five cents a year. The Intercollegiate Socialist Society attracted many of the best minds of the time.[12]

The I.W.W. also saw its best days in 1912. Though it had fought hard in the West, where it originated, the migratory and unskilled workers whom it largely represented never permitted it to settle down and establish itself on a firm basis. The East offered the I.W.W. a more fertile field with a different type of worker—immigrant, semi-skilled, and largely unorganized. The I.W.W.'s chance in the East came when it was called in to lead a strike of textile workers at Lawrence, Massachusetts. After two months of virtual warfare, the strike of about 25,000 workers of twenty-eight different nationalities ended in a substantial victory. When the I.W.W. tried to follow up with a silk workers' strike at Paterson, New Jersey, it went down to defeat. As a labor organization, the I.W.W. staggered downhill after Lawrence.

For a while, however the Lawrence strike made an overwhelming impression on the Left Wing. It became the era's supreme symbol of militant struggle against industrial oppression. Like the Sacco-Vanzetti case in the next decade, the strike particularly aroused the social conscience of many intellectuals. For the Left Wing, the lessons of Lawrence seemed to be that immigrants could be organized, that their strikes could be won, and that what was hopeless for the A.F. of L. was not hopeless for the I.W.W. It further confirmed and strengthened the bias of the Left Wing in favor of pro-I.W.W. "dual unionism." It brought to life the "class struggle." It encouraged an idealized image of the revolutionary, unskilled or semiskilled, poorly paid, unorganized immigrant worker.

Future Communists participated in the I.W.W. strikes of 1912–13. The leading I.W.W. woman organizer, Elizabeth Gurley Flynn, played an outstanding role in all of them.[13] The special correspondent of the Socialist Labor party's paper at the Lawrence strike was an eighteen-year-old protégé of Daniel De Leon named Louis C. Fraina. He was so deeply moved by the strike that he joined the I.W.W. for about six months.[14] John Reed missed the excitement of Lawrence but made up for it at Paterson in 1913.

One night, in the midst of the Paterson strike, Reed met Big Bill Haywood, the I.W.W. leader of both strikes, at the lower Fifth Avenue salon of Mabel Dodge, a rich American woman who collected famous or unusual characters. Haywood told about the Paterson strike then raging. Reed was enthralled. It was the beginning of his long love affair with the I.W.W. He went from the salon to the front line of the class struggle in Paterson. He was arrested and thrown into jail for four days. Unable to remain an onlooker, he conceived the idea of a giant pageant in Madison Square Garden to dramatize the cause of the Paterson strikers. It was the forerunner of the successful Communist spectacles in the Garden two decades later.[15]

One historian has tried to prove that "it was while the Left Wing was most active in the party, from 1909 through 1912, that the Socialist movement achieved its greatest strength and influence." At the same time, however, he admitted that few local victories were won on the issue of capitalism versus socialism and "hundreds of thousands of moderately liberal citizens came to look upon a vote for the Socialist party as a vote for a specific reform or against corrupt machine politics." [16] This contradiction in his argument is related to the fatal flaw in the Left Wing of 1912 and anticipated the equally contradictory propaganda and practice of the American Communists in later years. The Left Wing was mainly a factor in the inner life of the party; as soon as the Left Wing went outside the party to ask for broad popular support, it became almost indistinguishable from the Right Wing. Charles E. Ruthenberg, who was then the Ohio Left Wing leader, acknowledged in 1912: "It was upon municipal reform issues that most of the Ohio victories were won." [17] In effect, there was not too much difference between an Ohio Socialist campaign and a Wisconsin Socialist campaign. Theoretical orthodoxy was one thing, popular influence another.

The stranger in the house

This dualism of American radical politics haunted the Socialist movement as soon as it tasted conventional success. From the outside, its future never looked brighter. Inside, a crisis festered. The sharply divergent tendencies in the party were always a latent source of trouble. As long as the party was relatively small and weak, however, the factions tolerated each other, since there did not seem to be much at stake. The showdown approached when the dominant Right Wing began to feel that it had to eliminate the extreme Left Wing to protect its gains.

The test came in California. Late in 1910, the Los Angeles *Times* building was dynamited and twenty-one persons were killed in the midst of bitter labor strife. A few months later, two labor leaders, the brothers J. B. and J. J. McNamara, were arrested and charged with the crime. They were induced to plead guilty in order to obtain a more favorable settlement of the case.[18] Debs, Haywood, and other Left Wing leaders threw themselves into the campaign to defend the McNamaras. Meanwhile, however, the municipal election of 1911 was coming to a head in Los Angeles. The Socialist candidate, Job Harriman, a Right Wing leader, was considered to have an excellent chance of winning. After the McNamaras made their arranged "confessions," the resultant scandal was so great that Harriman suffered defeat. The McNamara case thoroughly frightened the Socialist leadership. It made "force and violence" an issue which had to be resolved in order not to endanger the party's progress. Long a matter of dispute as a theoretical issue, it now had to be settled as a matter of practical politics.

The opportunity soon came. Haywood was nominated to the National Executive Committee of the Socialist party toward the end of 1911. Hillquit charged that Haywood was guilty of advocating illegal, anarchistic practices. The Haywood-Hillquit war of words, the McNamara affair, and the California debacle combined to split the party wide open. The party's outer life in 1912 seemed devoted to the presidential election. Its inner life was preoccupied with an intense and turbulent debate on questions of fundamental principle: political action or direct action, industrial socialism or political socialism, legality or illegality, opportunism or "impossibilism," anarchism or social democracy, economic class struggle or parliamentarism. The election of the new executive committee early in 1912 brought the showdown nearer. Of the seven members on the committee, the two Right Wing leaders, Berger and Harriman, led in the voting. But Haywood came in third, ahead of his chief adversary, Hillquit.

Neither Haywood nor the Right Wing would let the issue rest. In a characteristic speech at Cooper Union in New York, Haywood made a ringing declaration of faith: "We should say that it is our purpose to overthrow the capitalist system by forcible means if necessary." [19] He was answered at the next Socialist convention in the spring of 1912. Article II, Section 6, of the party's constitution was changed to expel anyone "who opposes political action or advocates crime, sabotage, or other methods of violence as a weapon of the working class." The Left Wing fought back vainly; a motion to delete was defeated 191 to 90; and the section was subsequently upheld by a referendum vote of 13,000 to 4000. Haywood continued to speak his mind, heedless of the consequences. Toward the end of 1912, at a rally held in connection with the successful conclusion of court cases arising out of the Lawrence strike, he made some favorable allusions to sabotage and direct action.[20] Two days later the first steps were taken to expel Haywood from the Socialist party's National Executive Committee. Early in 1913, a referendum to that effect was approved by a vote of more than two to one. The pro-Haywood states were Montana, Nevada, Oregon, Tennessee, Texas, Utah, Washington, and West Virginia. The heaviest anti-Haywood majorities were registered in New York, Massachusetts, Pennsylvania, and Wisconsin.[21]

Haywood's recall did not eliminate the Left Wing in the Socialist party. Haywood represented only one tendency in the Left Wing, the extreme syndicalist tendency whose true home was the I.W.W. Haywood stopped paying dues, and about 15 per cent of the membership dropped out from 1912 to 1913,[22] but the Socialist party was still the largest and broadest single center of social unrest.

Yet Haywood's ouster opened a wound in the party that could never be healed. To the syndicalist-minded, it proved that there was no future in the Socialist party. The Right Wing was too strong and also too headstrong. From 1912 on, the specter of a split hovered

THE AGE OF UNREST   47

over the Socialist movement. The precedent had been established. From then on, the Left Wing had to reckon with the almost certain knowledge that the dominant Right Wing would not tolerate any faction that advocated a policy of force and violence, or that interpreted the class struggle in terms of civil war. An unbridgeable gap opened between those who believed in the historical inevitability of violent revolution and those who believed that, as the standard Right Wing answer to Haywood put it, "nothing could prove more disastrous to the democratic cause than to have the present class conflict break into a civil war." [23]

A portion of those who left in disgust or stayed without enthusiasm were future Communists. A young Kansas City member of the Socialist party, Earl Browder, dropped out in 1913 in protest against Haywood's treatment.[24] One of the few Socialist women organizers, Ella Reeve Bloor, was sent into Ohio, West Virginia, and southern Illinois to try to restore unity because such "very bitter feeling" against Haywood's recall prevailed there.[25] A young New York clerk, Benjamin Gitlow, faced a typical dilemma. He sympathized with Haywood's position on violence but decided to vote against him in the referendum because he reasoned that advocating it publicly would open the party to *agents provocateurs* and government persecution. He stayed in the Socialist party but was drawn into I.W.W. activities.[26] In Ohio, the Left Wing tried to steer a middle course. Its leader, Charles E. Ruthenberg, took the position that "there was room within the movement for men and women of various shades of opinion as to tactics to fight for the goal at which Socialism is aiming." The Ohio executive committee apparently tried to keep out Right Wing speakers while disassociating itself from the direct-actionists.[27] A young philosopher-poet, Max Eastman, joined the party early in 1912. One of his first acts was to send off a letter to the party organ advocating "sabotage and violence as having been, and as likely to be in the future, excellent tactics in the fight of an oppressed class against its oppressors." [28] Among the Socialist intellectuals who signed a resolution protesting Haywood's recall were James P. Warbasse, Osmond K. Fraenkel, Max Eastman, William

English Walling, Rose Pastor Stokes, Louis B. Boudin, and Walter Lippmann.[29]

The Left Wing became a stranger in the Socialist house. Although many of the remaining Left-Wingers differed with Haywood intellectually, almost all sympathized with him emotionally. Those who chose to stay in the party did so under the threat of the treatment handed out to Haywood. They were forced to swallow their pride and dream of revenge.

The literary Left

The estrangement of the Left Wing revealed itself in the Socialist press. The Left Wing expressed itself in publications outside official party control. This had been true even before the Haywood crisis in the case of the monthly *International Socialist Review*. It was published by Charles H. Kerr and Co. of Chicago, the pioneer source of Socialist classics in English. Kerr himself became a sympathizer of the I.W.W. and made the magazine the unofficial organ of the Left Wing. It welcomed contributions with either a syndicalist or an orthodox Marxist slant, or with the hybrid that sometimes passed for either or both. Haywood was an editor, and Debs used the magazine for some of his more controversial pronouncements. The Right Wing was not amused but could do nothing, because the magazine was privately owned.

The *Masses* had started publication in January 1911 as a Right Wing magazine, which its founder, Piet Vlag, intended to speak for the cooperative side of the Socialist movement. When the fight over Haywood's direct-actionism flared up the following year, it joined in the attack on Haywood's position.[30] Though the new magazine boasted some well-known muckraking and Socialist writers, it attracted few readers and had to suspend publication after struggling for over a year. Then Max Eastman was brought in to resuscitate it—with the help of a tiny fraction of the Vanderbilt fortune—and a new era began in December 1912.[31] The revival of the *Masses* coincided with the climax of Haywood's recall. Eastman did not turn against the I.W.W. or leave the Socialist party. He converted the *Masses* into "a meeting ground for revolutionary labor and the radical intelligentsia," as he later put it. This meeting ground was broad enough for syndicalism, socialism, atheism, bohemianism, and the new sexual freedom. The big yellow pages of the *Masses* still communicate a quality of creative excitement and inspired horseplay which the literary Left Wing has tried vainly to recapture. It was exuberant, shocking, and stirring. Conventionality was an even greater enemy than capitalism. Serious verse, essays, propaganda, drawings, satire, and slapstick were jumbled together. A list of the *Masses* contributors reads like a Who's Who of artistic and literary America for the next two or more decades.[32]

At about the same time, in January 1913, a group of heavier thinkers began to put out *The New Review*. Though the contributors ranged from ardent syndicalists to moderate Socialists, the Left Wing had much the better of it. In its pages, sabotage could be commended, Section 6 passionately denounced, and Haywood apotheosized.[33] At the end of its first year, the Right Wing was so enraged that the New York local of the Socialist party officially forbade the sale or distribution of *The New Review* at public meetings.[34] Louis C. Fraina, who became a regular contributor in 1913 and a member of the editorial board the following year, made it a vehicle for his development from a disciple of De Leon to a disciple of Lenin. The political development of the other members of the same board would embrace a large part of the intellectual history of the American twentieth century. Among them were W. E. B. DuBois, Max Eastman, Arthur Livingston, William English Walling, Floyd Dell, Walter Lippmann, and Robert H. Lowie.[35]

The first generation of American Communists grew to maturity in a world hospitable to every variety of radicalism. A later generation, which has grown to maturity in a world hospitable to every variety of conservatism, may find it difficult to enter into the spirit of this age of unrest.

3

The New Left Wing

THUS FAR, we have been tracing the development of the historic Left Wing. We are now on the eve of the development of the specific Left Wing that led directly to the organization of the American Communist movement.

The transition started with the shot at Sarajevo on June 28, 1914. The Bosnian student who fired the bullet into the neck of the Archduke Franz Ferdinand also fired into the heart of the international Socialist movement.

In the face of the war the Marxist tradition proved inadequate. That tradition was far from clear cut. Until almost the end of their lives, Marx and Engels had taken the position that wars were engines of social progress and that the most "progressive" side deserved to win. Far from opposing or discouraging war, they had preached and pleaded for several kinds of war, especially one against Czarist Russia, in their view the principal bastion of European reaction. In 1848 they demanded war on Russia to free Poland and save the German revolution; in the Crimean War of 1853 they supported Turkey against Russia and berated England and France for taking so long to get into it; in 1859 they wanted Austria to defeat France; in 1866 they preferred to see Prussia defeated by Austria; in 1870 they favored Germany in the war against France and then changed sides after the German armies occupied Paris; in 1877–78, they were again pro-Turkish in the war against Russia. This tradition prevailed

THE NEW LEFT WING

as late as the Russo-Japanese war of 1905, when most of the Socialist movement cheered for a Japanese victory on the ground that Japan represented the more "progressive" force.

But Marx and Engels drew back as soon as they began to see—soon after the Congress of Berlin in 1878—the outlines of a different type of war "of an extension and violence hitherto undreamed of." They were "prowar" in the era of national wars; they became antiwar as the era of world wars approached. Marx foresaw in the event of a general European war "a useless exhaustion of forces for a longer or shorter period," and hoped that it could be avoided. "I would consider a European war a misfortune; this time a terrible misfortune," Engels wrote. "It would inflame chauvinism everywhere for years, as every country would have to fight for its existence." Beginning in 1879, they began to reverse themselves; they adopted the attitude that socialism would triumph by peace, not war. Yet the longer-lived Engels never left any clear prescription for the ultimate crisis. In 1890, five years before his death, he served notice that the German Socialists would and should defend Germany against a Franco-Russian coalition. When the French Socialists protested, he gave them his blessings to defend their own country against a German aggression.[1]

The Marxist tradition, then, cannot be summed up as prowar or antiwar. It began militantly prowar; then it became antiwar; but in the actual event of war, it made the guilt of aggression, the danger to national independence, and the relative "progressiveness" of the opposing sides the decisive factors in determining a concrete policy. It was not hard to gather from Engels' own final position that the German Socialists could find good reasons to defend Germany and the French Socialists to defend France.

The Second International, formed by the various Socialist parties in 1889, suffered from the same ambiguity. It voted fervent resolutions against war, but they were passed in such a way as to hold out little hope of effective action if war broke out. The stumbling block was always the question of concrete action. At the first few congresses, the extremists presented their panacea, a general strike, and invariably lost out by a wide margin. In 1907, at the Stuttgart congress, the German leader, August Bebel, offered a resolution which merely exhorted the workers to end a war rapidly. The extremist spokesman, Gustave Hervé, called for a general strike, desertions from the army, and insurrections. A compromise was arranged by Rosa Luxemburg, Lenin, and Martov. They introduced amendments to Bebel's resolution which included a passage about the duty "to utilize the economic and political crisis created by the war to rouse the masses and thereby to hasten the downfall of capitalist class rule." It was a successful diplomatic operation; the amended resolution was passed unanimously to cover up the disunity revealed in the debates. Again at the Basle congress in 1912, the emphasis was placed on preventing war but a passage warned that "the monstrosity of a world war would inevitably call forth the indignation and the revolt of the working class." The last meeting of the International Socialist Bureau on July 29–30, 1914, soon after the Archduke's assassination, proved to be a helplessly desultory affair.[2]

When the war feared by Marx and Engels broke out in 1914, their followers reacted in confusion. The prowar and antiwar Socialists refused to fall neatly into Right Wing and Left Wing categories. Hervé in France went from violent extremism to frenzied chauvinism. The orthodox French Marxist, Jules Guesde, accepted a post in the French cabinet. The pioneer Marxist popularizer in England, H. M. Hyndman, came out in favor of the war, and the non-Marxist pacifist, Ramsay MacDonald, came out against it. The majority of German Socialists accepted the war as their own. A minority, led by Rosa Luxemburg and Karl Liebknecht, denounced the majority for betraying socialism. The orthodox Kautsky and the revisionist Bernstein joined forces in trying to steer a middle course. The foremost Russian Marxist, George Plekhanov, supported the Allies. The two Serbian Social Democratic deputies voted against war credits and then reversed themselves after their country was deeply invaded.

Of the antiwar Marxists, a majority were satisfied to demand the end of the war at the earliest possible moment without making a Socialist revolution a condition of the peace. A few refused to give up the class struggle, even in wartime. Rosa Luxemburg's biographer notes that she made the simple slogan of peace the "center of her political agitation" and that she "spoke only of the class struggle, and not of revolution and civil war."[3] Trotsky held out for a proletarian revolution as the goal in war as well as peace. But a comparatively obscure Russian émigré in Switzerland, the Bolshevik leader, Vladimir Ilyich Ulianov, better known as Lenin, did not fit into any existing category.

Lenin's antiwar position was so extreme that most of his own followers could not swallow it. He demanded an active policy of "revolutionary defeatism" always and everywhere, to "turn the imperialist war into a civil war." Working indiscriminately for the defeat of one's own country irrespective of time, place, and circumstance had never been accepted in the Marxist tradition. It constituted a departure from the last phase of Marx's and Engels' thinking on the subject which still confined the Socialist position to the areas of peace or national defense. This departure was so drastic that Lenin could justify it only by cutting the ground from under the relevance of much of Marxism. He based his case on the premise that capitalism was capable of progressive wars in Marx's time but doomed to reactionary wars in the "final" stage of imperialism—as if Marx and Engels had not spent their lives trying to demonstrate that capitalism had exhausted its usefulness, as if Engels had not lived long enough to witness the heyday of British and French imperialism, and as if Lenin would live long enough to know what the final stage of capitalism would be.

Lenin's policy was also a departure from the Second International's tradition, which had never gone beyond merely predicting the revolt of the working class. Instead, the war fever which gripped the working class in the belligerent countries swept along Socialist leaders unwilling to be isolated from their own followers. For Lenin, working for the defeat of one's own country was equivalent to working for the revolution; even the majority of Bolsheviks could not see how it was possible, in practice, to work for a Russian defeat without working for the enemy's victory. As a recent study of Lenin's "revolutionary defeatism" has shown, he failed to define the concept with any clarity or consistency.[4] He never succeeded in breathing life into the slogan; it remained an empty revolutionary abstraction without exact definition or practical application in his own party. Defeat, not defeatism, made possible the later Bolshevik revolution. Nevertheless, the defeatist slogan separated Lenin from all but a few personal disciples, of whom the most important in the war years was Gregory Zinoviev.

Despite the important variations in the antiwar camp, a fundamental breach opened between the prowar and antiwar Socialists. With the war, antimilitarism, anti-imperialism, internationalism, working-class solidarity, became the exclusive possession of the new antiwar Left Wing. Prowar Socialists far outnumbered antiwar Socialists, who constituted a small and hard-pressed minority in all the major countries. But it was a minority with a new sense of destiny. It assailed prowar Socialism as a contradiction in terms. To be prowar was nothing less than sheer treason to Socialism. The more extreme antiwar Socialists dared to read the prowar Socialists out of the movement. A large part of the prowar majority was guilt-ridden with the betrayal of all the old speeches and resolutions. War weariness, misery, mountains of casualties, the fall of dynasties, the inevitable letdown of the peace negotiations, were bound to work for the Left. The differences over the war went much deeper than the old controversies over strategy and tactics. The war lent itself to an enormous simplification of the whole factional struggle.

Nevertheless, the differences within the Left Wing emerged as soon as it tried to organize. Thirty-nine delegates from eleven countries came together in September 1915 at Zimmerwald, a mountain village in Switzerland, to draw up a common program. Among them were Lenin and Zinoviev, Leon Trotsky and Julius Martov for other Russian groups, Karl Radek for the Polish Left, Mme. Henriette Roland-Holst for the Dutch, J. A. Berzin for the Letts, and others representing groups or tendencies in Italy, Rumania, Bulgaria, Norway, Sweden, France, and Germany. While all these delegates were more or less antiwar, they were not agreed on the immediate consequences or the next steps. All could see the profound split that had opened up in the international Socialist movement. But some wanted to revive the old International in a purified form, and others wanted nothing less than a new—a Third—International, immediately. Lenin gave the most extreme expression to the split and the new International. Because in theory he assumed that the war was supposed to produce a revolutionary situation, he was capable of seeing a revolutionary situation—as early as 1915.[5] When the majority refused to accept Lenin's full program, he formed his own "Zimmerwald Left." A second conference was held at Kienthal in April 1916, at which Lenin and his supporters again failed to win a majority for a new International—the demand which most sharply differentiated the extreme Left Wing from the main body.

The war also brought into being a new American Left Wing, but it responded to the same forces in a somewhat different way.

The house divided

There was no immediate war crisis in the American Socialist movement as there was in the European. The American crisis was rather a latent one, ticking away like a delayed-action bomb. For this, circumstances were largely responsible.

The European Socialists in the belligerent countries had to make up their minds without delay whether to support the war or oppose their own governments and suffer persecution. The American Socialists faced no such emergency. They could oppose the war without opposing their own government as long as the United States stayed out of the war. At first, they made up their minds about someone else's war.

On the surface, the Socialist party officially took a clear-cut antiwar position. It issued statements that unequivocally denounced the war and blamed capitalism for it. The Socialist slogan in the congressional elections of November 1914 was: "Every Socialist ballot is a protest against war."[6]

The official position of the American party seemed to put it on the side of the Left Wing in Europe. The American Left Wing was thereby deprived of the *raison d'être* of its European counterpart. It did not have the same provocation for raising a hue and cry about betrayal by the Right Wing.

Beneath the surface of the official statements, however, the American party was a house divided. Its most prominent public figures made no attempt to hide the fact that they were intensely partisan. Allen L. Benson was outspokenly anti-German. The electrical wizard, Charles Steinmetz, desired a German victory to destroy Russian autocracy. John Spargo wanted a "decisive victory" for Russia. Max Eastman's heart was with "invaded France." Robert H. Lowie, the anthropologist, admitted to a "pro-German view." George D. Herron confessed that he was pro-Russian. Jack London was violently pro-Allied. Victor Berger had a hard time restraining his pro-German sympathies. William English Walling and Charles Edward Russell did not try to restrain their pro-Allied sympathies.[7]

The most revealing line of reasoning was perhaps that of Morris Hillquit. More than any one else, he reflected the mixed feelings of the European Socialists. His natural sympathies went out strongly to the majority German Social Democrats with whom he was closely linked personally and politically. When they supported their own government in the war, he adopted a benevolently understanding attitude toward them. But he was equally broad-minded about the support which the French and British Socialists gave their own governments. He condoned them all on the ground that "the Socialists of each country have yielded to the inexorable necessities of the situation." Nevertheless, he went on to condemn the war as a whole and to oppose it in American politics. To top it all, he favored "a cessation of hostilities from sheer exhaustion without determining anything."[8]

Debs took a simpler view. He attacked the war and advocated complete neutrality, but there was little practical leadership in his earnest exhortations.[9]

The American prowar and antiwar groups did not fit into the old Left Wing and Right Wing grooves any more than the European ones did. For example, Eastman and Walling had been representative of the prewar American Left. The war drove Walling, but not Eastman, to the extreme Right.

Boudin's war

In the first years of the war, the new American Left Wing was still an amorphous tendency. It is best to think of it as a haphazard collection of individuals rather than as anything resembling an organized group. These individuals had, of course, some things in common. They were militantly antiwar. They refused to sympathize, emotionally or politically, with any of the belligerents. They condemned the French Socialists as much as the German Socialists. They fought against the spirit of nationalism which the war had intensified. They interpreted the conflict in Marxist terms as a capitalist struggle for markets. And yet, at this stage, more can be learned from looking at individuals than at the group. Such were the differences that there were almost as many Left Wings as there were individuals.

Of special interest at this time was an acknowledged Left Wing authority, Louis B. Boudin. He was one of the fathers of the Left Wing, but he was not one of the fathers of the Communist party which grew out of the Left Wing. Why he could be the one and why he did not become the other were equally significant.

Boudin was born in Russia and came to the United States at the age of fifteen. Only ten years later, he became a lawyer. He also became an ardent Socialist and a devoted student of Marxism. In his early thirties he wrote a series of articles for the *International Socialist Review* defending Marxian economics against its critics. When they were published as a book, *The Theoretical System of Karl Marx,* in 1907, Boudin's fame spread throughout the Socialist world. The work was quickly translated into many languages, including German and Russian, and impressed European Socialists even more than it did the Americans, who were less captivated by abstruse Marxist economic analysis. Boudin knew or corresponded with the most famous Socialist leaders of Europe as few Americans were privileged to do. The foremost German theoretical Socialist magazine, *Die Neue Zeit,* edited by Kautsky, invited Boudin to write on American affairs. Jessie Wallace Hughan made a survey of the American Socialist movement in 1911 in which she recognized Boudin as one of the two "chief Marxian apologists in America." Lenin compiled a bibliography of Marxism in 1914 which included mention of Boudin's book. A contemporary American Marxist economist has ventured the opinion that Boudin's book is the only prewar Socialist work "which, aside from historical interest, is worth reading today." [10]

In the American party, however, Boudin never played the role to which he thought he was entitled by his theoretical superiority. He developed an intense aversion for Hillquit who, he was convinced, was inwardly pro-German. The rivalry of the two Socialist lawyers from New York became one of the highlights of party life. Since the Left Wing regarded Hillquit as its most dangerous enemy, Boudin's feud with Hillquit served a much larger political purpose.

In the spring of 1915, Boudin became one of the most important contributors to the *New Review*. Every issue began to carry his extended comments on "Current Affairs." As far as the Socialists were concerned, the most controversial of current affairs at this time was the question of "Preparedness."

As long as the Socialists debated the war in Europe, they could disagree without reaching the breaking point. But the Wilson administration began to press for increased army and navy appropriations to prepare for a possible emergency. This presented the Socialists with a war crisis closer home. Again, the party reacted one way officially and another way in the statements of some of its most prominent figures. A resolution to expel any Socialist officeholder who voted for "military or naval purposes, or war" was adopted by referendum in May 1915 by the overwhelming vote of 11,041 to 782.[11] It was sufficiently uncompromising to please the most absolute pacifist or revolutionary. But Victor Berger and the Milwaukee Socialists had already declared for a larger army on the ground that it was needed to defend the United States against an Asiatic threat.

Hillquit took the position that the United States was justified in strengthening its naval and military defenses if there was any danger of becoming involved in the war. But he denied that there was such a danger. When the British liner *Lusitania* was torpedoed without warning in May of 1915 and over a hundred American lives were lost, the clamor for an immediate American declaration of war against Germany increased, and the Socialists were not immune to it. Even Debs was flushed with anti-German feeling, though he restrained himself from demanding war. The first well-known Socialist to make a public demand for war against Germany was Charles Edward Russell, toward the end of 1915. Russell's indiscretion was mitigated by the fact that he had dared to say publicly what other Socialist leaders were thinking privately. Abraham Cahan, editor of the widely read Jewish *Forward,* came out in support of Russell. The *New York Call* argued editorially that the referendum against voting for military expenditures was virtually meaningless. Debs himself pleaded that Russell should not be denounced or asked to leave the party. Socialist Congressman Meyer London of New York tried to belittle Russell's fear of Germany but called for "a great deal of latitude on such questions as preparedness, in view of the state of affairs in the world." When two defense bills came to a vote in Congress, London conveniently absented himself.[12]

Boudin set himself the task of developing a Left Wing position on war and preparedness. At the end of 1914, he delivered six lectures—published in 1916 as *Socialism and War*—which gave the Left Wing the closest thing it had to an authoritative analysis and policy. Without any help from Lenin, he traced the cause of the war to imperialism. He recognized the class struggle as the only basis for a Socialist policy. "Active, unrelenting opposition to war, irrespective of the demands of so-called 'national interests,' is therefore the 'natural state' of the Socialist who accepts the Class Struggle theory," he insisted. But any policy of working for the defeat of one's country at the risk of its national independence never occurred to him. "The working class of any nation or country is therefore vitally interested in *preserving the freedom from alien domination* of that nation or country," he wrote. "And the Socialist is ready to go to war in order to defend that freedom. His readiness to go to war in defense of his country is however strictly limited by his desire to preserve this national freedom." [13]

Boudin's antiwar position still came out of the orthodox Marxist tradition. The new Leninist position was presented in America at about the same time—but not by Americans. A visiting Russian lecturer, Mme. Alexandra Kollontay, wrote a letter and an article for the *New Review* in which, without mentioning Lenin's name, she put forward the view that "the only way to fight this war, as any imperialist war, is to turn the war into a 'civil war.'" [14] This hint was never followed up by Boudin or Fraina. A Dutch Left-Winger, S. J. Rutgers, wrote a favorable review of Boudin's book for the *International Socialist Review*, in which, however, he objected that it left the door open to support of certain types of defensive wars.[15] As we shall see, both Mme. Kollontay and Rutgers reflected Lenin's thinking, though the Americans were not yet aware of it.

Boudin could not unite the American Left Wing around himself, despite his great gifts and important contribution. Highly opinionated, he inspired respect but not emulation. For the task of transforming the Left Wing from an amorphous tendency into an organized movement, a different type of propagandist was necessary.

Fraina's road

If there was one man who led the way to a pro-Communist Left Wing, that man was Louis C. Fraina. Yet in 1952 the current leader of the American Communist party, William Z. Foster, in a 600-page book entitled *History of the Communist Party of the United States*, did not find room for a single mention of Fraina's name. By an almost unbelievable combination of circumstances, this name was wiped out of the consciousness of a generation. It is doubtful whether one per cent of all the thousands of people who have passed through the American Communist movement could identify Fraina or tell what he did.

Fraina's road to communism started in an Italian village.

In 1894 in the village of Galdo, in the province of Salerno, some sixty miles south of Naples, a boy was born to a poor Italian republican, Antonio Fraina, and christened Luigi Carlo. Two years later, like hundreds of thousands of his compatriots, Antonio decided to leave the poverty and antirepublicanism of southern Italy in search of freedom and fortune in the new world. He came to New York alone at first, and brought over his wife and children the following year when Luigi was three years old. The Fraina family exchanged the dirt of Galdo for the filth of the East Side. Luigi was brought up on the Bowery, Mulberry Street, and Christie Street, in the heart of the old slums.

Americanization started with names. Luigi Carlo became Louis C. Antonio learned to speak English, but his wife lived to be eighty without learning any English at all. Antonio worked as a waiter or at odd jobs, making barely enough to feed his family. At the age of six Louis sold newspapers on the Bowery near Chatham Square. After school, he worked in a tobacco factory as his mother's helper and picked up extra money shining shoes.

Years later, when he was, under another name, a professor of political economy, he delivered an address to the faculty and student body. In it, he made a rare reference to his past: "I remember that my mother refused charity, even when bread was scarce. There was something in her that resented charity. But there was no complete escape. My mother's pride gave in once. She sent a younger brother and myself to a parochial school of a different religious denomination because it gave the pupils free hot lunches. I was happy to eat the meals. But one day an attendant slapped my brother without, in my opinion, just cause. I arose (I was all of eight years old and my brother six) and walked out of the lunchroom. Then Christmas came. At the parochial school they gave Christmas gifts—shoes, sweaters, skates—and when I came home without any gifts I had to tell mother the whole story. She began to scold me terribly, but I started to cry; she cried too, and kissed me as she had never kissed me before."

When his mother discovered that he had stayed away from the parochial school for six months, she permitted him to transfer to a public school. He was a small, physically weak child, always a loser in sports and games. His favorite refuge was reading. Four months before his fourteenth birthday, in 1908, he graduated from elementary school. When his father died five weeks later, he quit school forever to go to work as a clerk for the Edison Company.

He began with the literature of revolt—Zola, Frank Norris, Shaw, Upton Sinclair, Jack London, Theodore Dreiser. Then came the politics of revolt. The first symptom of radicalism took the form of a rebellion against the Catholic faith. In his spare time, he began to write for an agnostic publication, *The Truth Seeker*. The well-known Hearst columnist Arthur Brisbane read one of his articles and got him a job as a cub reporter on the New York *Journal*.[16]

He was ready for radical politics. He joined the Socialist party, but stalked out six months later because it was not radical enough for him. He went over to the more extreme and doctrinaire Socialist Labor party in 1909. At the age of fifteen, he was speaking on street corners two or three times a week; he was elected secretary of the general committee of the New York section; he served with De Leon himself on a committee of three to draw up an important resolution; he wrote long theoretical articles, one on the relations of the proletariat and the intellectuals, another on the work of the Spanish educational reformer, Francisco Ferrer; and he acted as doorman at a party festival.[17] Soon he became an S.L.P. organizer and then a staff member of its organ, *The Daily People*. When his sympathies went out to the I.W.W. during the Lawrence strike of 1912, he joined it too, if only for half a year. He was a full-fledged revolutionary while other boys his age were struggling through high school.

Fraina quarreled with De Leon in 1914 and broke away from the S.L.P. When De Leon died that year, Fraina wrote an article on his former chief and teacher that was full of admiration but which may also reveal what had estranged him. De Leon, he charged, was "sometimes dishonest in his methods of attack. He was temperamentally a Jesuit, consistently acting on the principle that the end justified the means. And he attacked opponents with all the impersonal implacability of the Jesuit."[18] It was not the last time that Fraina had trouble with revolutionary Jesuits.

In effect, Fraina was that common phenomenon in radical movements, the self-taught intellectual. The Marxist movements have been especially favorable breeding grounds for this revolutionary type because they are so topheavy theoretically. Beginning with Marx himself, the "theoretician" has enjoyed exceptional prestige and authority. It would be difficult, if not impossible, to attain a position of leadership in Marxist movements without the ability to make an economic or political "analysis," or at least to demonstrate a command of the terminology. The very effort required to read the works of Marx and Engels—and later of Lenin and Stalin—can become a tremendous incentive to further study or self-improvement. The movements have learned from bitter experience that intellectuals formed from an early age within their own ranks are much more reliable and loyal than ready-made intellectuals from the outside. For many impressionable, ambitious, and idealistic young men, therefore, the radical movement has been a university as well as a faith.

By the age of twenty, Fraina had already gone through three movements, the Socialist party, the I.W.W., and the Socialist Labor party. He was then prepared to meet the outstanding radical intellectuals on equal terms. He made his appearance on the board of editors of the *New Review* in May 1914. Soon he also became a member of the board of directors, secretary of the publishing company, business manager, and chief contributor.[19] Increasingly, the policy and tone of the magazine took on his personal coloration.

The twenty or so articles that Fraina wrote for the *New Review* afford by far the best insight into the mind of the Left Wing before and after the outbreak of the war. Before the war, he wrote about the Catholic Church, new trends in the concentration of capital, and "futuristic" art.[20] After the war, he devoted himself chiefly to attacking American imperialism, militarism, Socialists, and liberals. He was not content to dispute with Hillquit as Boudin did; he flatly accused Hillquit of lying and distorting facts.[21] Most of all, Fraina concerned himself with the crisis of socialism. He was not the first contributor to an American Left Wing organ to bury the Second International and raise a cry for the Third; a Dutch Left Wing intellectual, Anton Pannekoek, did that. But he was the first American to make this demand his own and campaign for it.

Yet it is interesting to note how far from communism and the Russian Revolution Fraina still was. He expected "a new era of capitalist development," not collapse, to follow the war. He was particularly optimistic about the postwar progress of capitalism in Russia. As late as 1916, Fraina betrayed the distinctive syndicalist mark of the American Left Wing extremist. He was still a protagonist of the "revolutionary union," not the revolutionary party. He defined socialism as "industrial self-government." His antiwar program consisted of a confused mixture of traditional syndicalism and incipient Bolshevism. "The proletariat, as a revolutionary class, must project its own governmental expression, its own concept of the relations between nations—industrial government and the world state," he wrote. *"The embryo of this expression is industrial unionism and international proletarian organization.* This means a relentless struggle against the nation and its interests, and parliamentary government and its social manifestations." [22]

In the first two years of the war, then, the range of the pre-Communist Left Wing may be gathered from the different personalities of Boudin and Fraina. One was twenty years older than the other. Boudin prided himself on being the foremost orthodox Marxist in the Socialist party. Fraina stood much closer to the tradition of the Socialist Labor party and the I.W.W. He had much more of the fervor and extremism of the true revolutionary. Though both were immigrants, Boudin had made a professional as well as a political career for himself; Fraina had made a profession of his politics.

Boudin and Fraina worked together as long as the one crucial issue was the war. But the war gave the Left Wing a starting point, not an enduring reason for existence. Boudin went to the edge of communism and recoiled; Fraina went on.

4

Influences and Influencers

IN VIEW of the preponderant Russian influence in the American Left Wing and Communist movements after 1917, it may come as a surprise to learn that there was very little Russian influence before 1917. It may come as an even greater surprise that a much stronger European influence was Dutch.

The Dutch Left Wing had formed its own organization, the Social Democratic party, as far back as 1909. It contained only a few hundred members, as compared with the thousands in the Dutch Social Democratic Labor party, but three of them were outstanding intellectuals with international prestige.[1] Anton Pannekoek was a famous astronomer. Herman Gorter was a celebrated poet. Mme. Henriette Roland-Holst, a writer, was one of the founders of the international women's Socialist movement. Politically Pannekoek and Gorter were linked with the Left Wing in the German Social Democratic party. Pannekoek worked so closely with the German Left that he was often considered part of it.[2] Gorter was regarded as the "ablest theorist" of the group which was sometimes identified by his name.[3]

The popularity of anarcho-syndicalist ideas in Holland, as in the United States in that period, may have been the reason that the Dutch Left Wing was so congenial to the American Left Wing.[4] In any case, there was a simple, direct reason why Pannekoek and Gorter were familiar names to many American Socialists when Lenin

66   THE ROOTS OF AMERICAN COMMUNISM

and Trotsky were virtually unknown. The Dutch writers, especially Pannekoek, were among the most frequent contributors to the two Left Wing organs, the *International Socialist Review* and the *New Review*. The quality, not merely the quantity, of their articles counted. On the most crucial international problems of the day, both magazines featured leading articles by the astronomer and the poet.

Pannekoek was first to condemn the war as imperialist and attack the majority German Social Democrats, in the *International Socialist Review*.[5] He was first to signal the "downfall" of the Second International and raise a demand for the Third—which Fraina proceeded to echo—in the *New Review*.[6] Gorter and Pannekoek, as we shall see, were responsible for the slogan that was taken up by the incipient American Communists as the quintessence of revolution—"mass action."

Another and more tangible reason for this curious Dutch influence was the physical presence in the United States of a comrade in arms of Pannekoek and Gorter. He was S. J. Rutgers, a big, broad-shouldered, handsome man with a little beard and an aristocratic manner. By profession, Rutgers was a civil engineer. He had spent several years working in the Dutch East Indies where he came to know at first hand the worst aspects of pre-World-War-I colonialism. He appeared on the American Socialist scene in 1915 and immediately plunged into the thick of the struggle to win the Socialist party for the Left Wing. A prolific writer, he became a steady contributor to the *International Socialist Review* and the *New Review*, taking over the main burden of propaganda from Pannekoek and Gorter.

The Socialist Propaganda League

From Europe came many other influences to help form the American Communist movement. These influences worked through the foreign language federations of the Socialist party. By 1915, fourteen of these federations accounted for about one-third of the total Socialist membership.[7] A large part of the history of the American Socialist movement has remained shrouded in comparative obscurity because the language barrier has hindered an adequate study of these relatively autonomous organizations. Because no two were exactly alike, it would be necessary to study them separately in order to give them the attention they deserve.

For our purposes, however, one of these foreign-language federations—the Lettish *—stands out in importance. The organizational looseness of the American Socialist movement enabled it to live a life of its own irrespective of the main trend among the native-born, English-speaking Socialists.

The Lettish Socialist federation was peculiar in that it had long been controlled by the Left Wing. But it was a Lettish Left Wing with traditions and ideas that derived from the parent organization in Europe. The Lettish Socialists were first organized at the turn of the century as an American branch of the Lettish Social-Democratic Workers party, to which the branch paid dues and looked for leadership. In 1908, it affiliated with the American Socialist party without breaking its old ties to the European party. In Europe, the Lettish party was divided, as usual, into a Left Wing and a Right Wing, with the difference that the Left Wing was the dominant one, strongly influenced by and in closest contact with the Russian Left Wing led by Lenin. In the later Russian Revolution, the Letts supplied some of Lenin's most ardent and reliable supporters.

The counterpart of Lenin in the Lettish Left Wing was a man of exactly the same age and almost similar background, Fricis Rozins, or as he used to sign his name in English, Fr. Rosin.[8] His life was that of the typical East European revolutionary—conversion to Socialism as a university student, emigration to London and later to Berne where he edited the Lettish Social-Democratic paper, the writing of a pioneer Marxist history of Latvian agriculture, return to

* The term "Lettish," rather than "Latvian," was used before 1918 when Latvia was a Russian province generally known as Lettland from the German version of the name.

Latvia and arrest, exile to and escape from Siberia.[9] Rosin came to the United States in 1913 and settled in Boston, then the center of the Lettish federation. By 1915 he was editing its organ, *Strahdneeks (The Worker)*.[10] In that year, the Lettish federation boasted 1600 members.[11] There were two groups of Letts, the older and larger Lettish Workers Society of Boston, controlled by the Left Wing, and the Roxbury branch of the federation, controlled by the Right Wing. So affluent were the Boston Letts that they provided the Massachusetts Socialist party with a $50,000 building. Apparently the Left-Wing Letts and their allies controlled the state organization in 1913–14.[12] Then, in 1915, James Oneal of Indiana was brought in as secretary of the Massachusetts party, with the result that the Right Wing regained control.[13] From then on, Massachusetts was one of the main battlegrounds between the Left and the Right.

The fight came to a head at the Massachusetts Socialist convention in July 1915. Out of a total of 276 delegates only 16 represented the Lettish Workers Society of Boston, but they came well prepared for a showdown.[14] The Letts introduced four resolutions, the nature of which tells us what a man like Rosin had in mind at this time. The first forbade any Socialist from ever joining the army or navy "or any other military organization of the capitalists." The second called for the collaboration of European and American revolutionary Socialists to form a Third International. The third sent greetings to Karl Liebknecht for his struggle against the war. The fourth denounced American preparations for war against Mexico.[15] All four were rejected, though the Letts claimed the support of about one-third of the delegates. Since the total membership of the Massachusetts party in 1915 was 4450, the Left Wing could possibly count on the backing of about 1500 members in the state.[16] The great majority of Finnish, Jewish, and English-speaking members supported the Right Wing.[17]

The fight at the Massachusetts convention did not mean much in the rest of the country. It was not mentioned in Left Wing organs like the *International Socialist Review* and the *New Review* or in widely read official organs like the *New York Call*. The Massachusetts conflict was merely a local manifestation of a general condition in the party. Yet, as far as the future Communist party was concerned, the repercussions of this convention were historic. The soil was prepared for the first seed.

This seed was the Socialist Propaganda League. It was formed as a direct result of the defeat inflicted on the Left Wing at the Massachusetts convention of 1915. In revenge, the Left Wing decided to set up an independent organization, virtually a party within the party. The League made its debut with a manifesto, dated October 9, 1915, and signed by eighteen names, including that of its secretary, C. W. Fitzgerald. This manifesto went somewhat beyond the four Lettish resolutions rejected by the convention. It contained six points: revolutionary socialism instead of opportunism, true democracy within the party, industrial unionism, organic unity between the Socialist party and Socialist Labor party, immediate steps to organize a new International, and resistance against strengthening of or enlistment in the army.[18]

At this stage, there was still no thought of breaking away from the Socialist party. The League was organized to gain control of the party and prepare for the struggle for power at the next convention. The nominal leadership of the League was entrusted to native-born Americans with the names of Fitzgerald, Williams, Bennett, Moran, Smyth, and Edwards. But behind them were the Letts, who provided the bulk of the mass support and ideological ammunition—the traditional combination in the American radical movement of native spokesmen and immigrant backers.

At the next convention of the Massachusetts party in June 1916 the Socialist Propaganda League was hotly denounced for sowing dissension in the ranks. The League's delegates agitated in favor of the Zimmerwald conference of the European Left Wing which had taken place the preceding September. They also protested against sending an American delegate, Algernon Lee, to a conference of the Socialist parties of the neutral countries affiliated with the old International at The Hague the following month. Again their attacks were repulsed. The Letts claimed that the Socialist Propaganda League had about 50 members at the convention as against 70 to 80 for the

Right Wing majority.[19] If so, the proportional strength of the Left Wing was much higher in Massachusetts than anywhere else in the East.

The presidential election in November 1916 proved to be a windfall for the Left. The Socialist ticket was headed by Allan L. Benson, a journalist, relatively colorless compared with the evangelistic Debs. The result shook up the party and destroyed whatever complacency may have existed. For the first time in its history, the Socialist party lost votes in a presidential election. Debs's vote of almost 900,000 in 1912 was cut about one-third to less than 600,000 for Benson in 1916. The percentage of the total vote fell from 6 to 3. The Socialist vote dropped in twenty-four states and rose in only one, Oklahoma.[20] The causes of the debacle were cumulative. The defection of Haywood's sympathizers was partly responsible. But undoubtedly more important was the competition of Woodrow Wilson, who was promising to keep America out of the war with a popular appeal that the Socialists could not match. William English Walling, hitherto one of the sharpest thorns in the intellectual side of the Right Wing, expressed the Socialist dilemma by wishing that he, along with 99 per cent of Socialist voters, could cast a "protest vote" for Benson and an "effective vote" for Wilson.[21]

This electoral setback was bad news for the Socialist party but good news for the Left Wing. The party was losing ground under Right Wing leadership, as the Left Wing had long been trying to prove. In Massachusetts, the election made the inner-party struggle more acute than ever. State Secretary Oneal charged that the Boston party, controlled by the Left Wing, had refused to arrange a meeting for presidential candidate Benson.[22] After the election, he had even more to complain about.

The Socialist Propaganda League held a post-election meeting on November 26, 1916. It took place, significantly, in the headquarters of the Lettish Workers Society of Boston. The business transacted at this meeting was destined to occupy a peculiarly historic place in the development of the American Communist movement. A letter was read from Comrade S. J. Rutgers of New York offering a loan of

$100 to help defray the expenses of the forthcoming organ of the League, *The Internationalist*. The secretary of the Lettish Workers Society announced that the League was free to use its rooms for conferences, lectures, or committee meetings, without charge. A new manifesto was adopted and 10,000 copies ordered printed. The secretary of the Lettish Socialist Federation, who was scheduled to go on tour to Chicago for the Federation, was commissioned to organize simultaneously for the League.[23] But for Rutgers, the activity at this meeting might not have attracted any more national attention than anything else the League had done in the past year. The Dutch émigré, however, saw the potentialities of the League as the embryo of a new revolutionary Socialist organization and decided to spread the news.

He did so by means of an article, "The Left Wing," in the *International Socialist Review* of December 1916. Many years later, some students of the American Communist movement came upon this article and mistakenly made it the foundation stone of everything that followed.[24] Actually, as we have seen, the League had been functioning for over a year and had sent forth a manifesto in 1915 as well as in 1916. Nevertheless, Rutgers announced with considerable fanfare that the Socialist Propaganda League was the "actual beginning in trying to organize the Left Wing forces in the Socialist Party of America." He served notice that the organization had issued a revolutionary manifesto and was going to publish a weekly organ.[25] Two months later, the *International Socialist Review* reprinted the text of the manifesto and again called national attention to the League.

While Rutgers went a bit too far in calling this activity the "beginning," the steps taken by the Socialist Propaganda League at the end of 1916 were undoubtedly unprecedented in importance as a stage in the development of the pro-Communist Left Wing. The manifesto of 1916 was a much more comprehensive document than the one of 1915, and showed much more of the Dutch influence. Like most such documents, it began with a rather long, abstract analysis of capitalism. The capitalist economy was leading to war and militarism. A new era had dawned in which the class conflict was approaching a climax. The manifesto ended with a call for action—reorganization of the old Socialist party on the basis of industrial unionism; "parliamentary action" instead of pure and simple electioneering for votes and bourgeois parliamentary reform; "undivided mass action" on both industrial and political fields; and opposition to militarism and imperialism.[26] Such phrases as "dictatorship of the proletariat" or "Soviets" did not appear; these came into circulation only after the Russian Revolution the following year.

Of equal organizational significance was the new paper, *The Internationalist*, the first issue of which was dated January 6, 1917.[27] The Left Wing had been welcomed in the pages of the *International Socialist Review*, the *New Review*, and the *Masses*, but these magazines were by no means limited to any single Left Wing point of view to the exclusion of all others. The new development was a Left Wing organ of an exclusive, homogeneous type. Rutgers set the tone of the first issue with an article, "What We Are After."[28] Another article on the Third International was contributed by Pannekoek.[29] The Left Wings in Boston and New York were so little connected that Fraina did not know of the existence of the Socialist Propaganda League until he saw a copy of *The Internationalist*.[30]

The Socialist Propaganda League has generally been considered the first Left Wing organization in the direct line of ancestry of the American Communist movement. As such, it occupies a unique place in the formative years of the movement.

The Russian influence

Not until the Russian Revolution of 1917 did a specifically Russian influence make itself felt in the American Left Wing. Lenin was a mere name which had appeared so infrequently in the American Socialist press that scarcely a handful of non-Russians would have been able to identify him.

Lenin's name seems to have been mentioned for the first time in America in an article on "The Evolution of Socialism in Russia" by William English Walling in the *International Socialist Review* of

INFLUENCES AND INFLUENCERS 73

July 1907. On this occasion, Walling interpreted Lenin—not without cause—as believing that socialism in Russia could be achieved only after a Socialist revolution had broken out all over Europe. The following year, Walling published a book, *Russia's Message,* based on personal observations in Russia. He talked to both Lenin and Trotsky, and referred to Lenin as "the man who is perhaps the most popular leader in Russia." [31] But Walling was far ahead of his time, and Lenin dropped completely out of sight for several more years. The next time, in the *New Review* toward the end of 1915, Lenin was listed as one of the signatories of the Zimmerwald Manifesto.[32] Some excerpts from the pamphlet *Socialism and War,* by Lenin and Zinoviev, were published in the *International Socialist Review* of January 1916, with favorable comment. It seems likely that this was the first American publication of anything written by Lenin. Finally, in March 1916, the *New Review* promised to publish regular articles by European Left Wing Socialists and mentioned six names, in the following order: Lenin, the French trade-union leader Bourderon, Anton Pannekoek, Rosa Luxemburg, the German Socialist, Franz Mehring, and the Italian Socialist Lazzari. Even Fraina had never heard of Lenin before 1916.[33] Eastman became aware of Lenin's existence for the first time in 1917.[34]

If the American Socialists knew very little about Lenin, he knew almost as little about them. He was indirectly connected with the Americans through the Dutch. Both Pannekoek and Gorter earned high praise from him as "unflinching, sincere, ardent, convinced internationalists." [35] The article by Pannekoek on "The Downfall of the International," which the *New Review* published in November 1914, was circulated by Lenin. Never one to praise someone else's work wholeheartedly, Lenin paid tribute to Pannekoek as "the only one who spoke the truth to the workers, even if in half tones and occasionally not quite aptly." [36] But the Dutch were in no sense Lenin's mouthpieces, and he merely recognized them at that stage as kindred spirits.

Lenin probably had indirect relations with the Boston Letts also. The Lettish Social-Democratic Labor party was one of the national groups belonging to the Russian Social-Democratic Labor party. This circumstance would easily account for the fact that the first manifesto issued by the Socialist Propaganda League, in October 1915, was received by Lenin in Switzerland the following month. He hastened to send back "an *enormous* English letter" and some other material in German "in the hope that there is a comrade in your League who knows German." This suggests that the manifesto had found its way to him through party channels and not through personal contact with the Letts.[37] In his letter, only part of which has been preserved, he commented favorably on the League's manifesto and urged it to keep in touch with him.[38] A story, which has all the marks of being apocryphal, has come down to the effect that Lenin was so little known that no one bothered to answer his letter and it was thrown into the wastebasket.[39] It is hardly likely that the Letts were so ignorant of his name, and the real reason may be what Lenin himself suspected —that the letter was confiscated by French authorities and never reached Boston.[40]

Finally, toward the end of 1915, Lenin made direct contact with the United States. His personal informant was Mme. Alexandra Mikhailovna Kollontay. She came to America from Stockholm on a lecture tour that took her from coast to coast for over three months. Mme. Kollontay was a strikingly feminine figure in the gallery of almost all-male Russian revolutionaries. She had started out in life as the daughter of a Czarist general. Married to an engineer at an early age, she bore him a son, and left both them and Russia for a more exciting life abroad.[41] A slim, striking woman, then in her early forties, with finely chiseled features and perfectly groomed appearance, she generated a spark of romantic excitement in the grimly intellectual Slavic revolutionary milieu. For years, she had devoted herself, as a prolific writer and lecturer, to social and sexual questions from a Socialist and feminist point of view. Formerly a Menshevik, she went over to the Bolsheviks after the war broke out and became one of Lenin's chief collaborators. She visited the United States on the invitation of the German Socialist Federation and gave her lectures under its auspices—a rather roundabout way for Lenin to get a personal representative on the American scene.[42]

Mme. Kollontay's trip to America loomed large in Lenin's plans at the end of 1915. "We have been building not a few hopes on this journey," he wrote her. He wanted her to get the pamphlet *Socialism and War* published in English, to get in touch with Left Wing circles, and, above all, to raise money ("No money. There is no money! That is the *main* trouble!") He knew enough about the American movement to advise her to "link up" with the Socialist Propaganda League, the Socialist publishing house of Charles H. Kerr and Co. in Chicago, and the *Appeal to Reason* in Kansas, which he gave a reasonably high mark as *"not at all bad."* Evidently Mme. Kollontay had to report failure, for he followed up in the spring of 1916 with this startled outcry: "Do you mean to say there were no sympathizers in America and it was impossible to get the International leaflet published in English??? It is incredible." Of the most famous American Socialist of the time, Lenin wrote: "And who is Eugene Debs? He writes sometimes in a revolutionary manner. Is he only spineless like Kautsky?" Three months later, Lenin knew all about Debs, so she must have been responsible for enlightening him. In a speech at Berne, he read a quotation from an antiwar article by Debs, whom he now called "the American Bebel, the beloved leader of the American workers," to prove that the working class was rallying all over the world.[43]

Mme. Kollontay did not altogether disappoint Lenin's hopes in her. Her lectures were primarily propaganda meetings in behalf of the Zimmerwald movement. She succeeded in getting three of her own articles into the most important American Socialist publications. She agitated for a Third International, defended it against the charge of splitting the old movement, and gave American readers the first reasonably clear report of what the differences in the Russian movement were.[44] But she never once mentioned Lenin's name, though he was busily sending her instructions. She could not get the Kerr publishing house to put out a full English translation of *Social-*

ism and War, but the long excerpt in the *International Socialist Review,* published by Kerr, came out soon thereafter. It seems, however, that money was just as scarce in Lenin's vicinity after her trip as before.

The man responsible for inviting Mme. Kollontay to come over was Ludwig Lore.[45] Stocky, quick-witted, with black curling mustache and an overgrown mass of unruly dark hair, he was typically the partially-Americanized European. Lore was born in Germany and came to the United States at the age of twenty-eight, leaving behind him a Socialist career of some prominence in Germany.[46] At the time, he was executive secretary of the German Socialist federation and assistant editor of its organ, the *New Yorker Volkszeitung,* generally considered the best Socialist paper in any language in the country. Lore was basically an orthodox Marxist, closer in theory to Boudin than to Fraina within the broad confines of the emergent Left Wing. The German organ was far more militantly antiwar and international-minded than the Socialist papers in English. When Charles Edward Russell came out in favor of preparedness, the *Volkszeitung* demanded his resignation from the party.[47] For many of the most famous European émigrés driven here by the war, Lore served as the link between the old and the new. German was often their second language. His own background was similar to theirs. His leading position in the German movement enabled him to publish their articles or send them on lecture tours. He was secretary of a fund for the relief of European Socialists suffering from the war—to which, he bitterly complained, the American contributions were "astonishingly meager." [48]

Mme. Kollontay's second American trip was made at the end of 1916. At about the same time, in November, there arrived in New York a slight, sensitive-looking young man in his late twenties—Nikolai Bukharin.

He was already a revolutionary veteran with a decade of dangerous activity behind him. After his third arrest and release in Russia in 1911, he fled abroad, moving from one country to another as the police or his party demanded. Accused of antimilitarist activity in

Sweden, he was again expelled, arrested in England, and finally managed to get to the United States. In New York, he became editorial secretary of the *Novy Mir,* the organ of the Russian Socialist federation, and rapidly helped to make it an important source of Left Wing propaganda.[49]

Shortly thereafter, in the first days of 1917, an even more exciting Russian celebrity, Leon Trotsky, arrived. An American Socialist paper described him as "tall, well-built, and rather handsome."[50] Trotsky, known as the outstanding leader of the Russian revolution of 1905, was already famous enough for newspapermen to interview him at the pier. The *New York Times* credulously reported that he represented Jewish newspapers in Petrograd and Kiev, a slightly fictitious description which probably made it easier to pass himself off as a harmless Jewish refugee rather than as a notorious international revolutionary.[51] The Socialist papers played up his arrival as a major event. Grotesquely enough, however, the New York *Call* quoted him as saying at the pier, "I am not a revolutionist."[52] Trotsky also went to work for the *Novy Mir,* at a desk "in a dingy hole at the rear of the cellar" at 77 St. Mark's Place.[53] With his wife and two young children, he lived in a three-room apartment on Vyse Avenue in the Bronx. His main source of income came through Lore, who enabled him to write editorials and deliver lectures for the *New Yorker Volkszeitung.*[54] The paper arranged no fewer than thirty-five lectures for him at ten dollars a lecture.[55] Sometimes Trotsky, Bukharin, and Lore would speak at the same meeting, the first two in Russian, the last in German.[56] Lore became Trotsky's most intimate American friend, a circumstance that was to have fateful consequences for Lore's subsequent Communist career.

Russia was not the only country that sent important exiles to the United States, first into the Socialist movement and then into the Communist movement.

To the older generation of Socialists, Sen Katayama was already a legend in his own lifetime. He came to the United States from Japan for the first time in 1884, at the age of twenty-six, to complete his education. After graduating from Grinnell College, he spent two more years at Andover and one year at Yale. For twelve years, he supported himself mainly by working as a cook. Then he returned to Japan in 1896 and played a leading role in the young Japanese labor and Socialist movements until, in 1906, he was sentenced to nine months of hard labor for antiwar activity. After his release, he returned to the United States and lived in San Francisco for almost a decade, again earning his living as a cook and publishing a little monthly magazine, *Heimin,* written in Japanese and English. Toward the end of 1916, then almost sixty, he came to New York to see his old friend, S. J. Rutgers.[57] When the *International Socialist Review* published an article the following year telling the story of Katayama's life, Rutgers wrote it.[58]

The Finnish émigré, Santeri Nuorteva, became an appreciable power in the American Socialist party. He was originally a teacher of history and languages in Finland, where he joined the Socialist movement at the turn of the century. He edited Socialist papers and was elected a Socialist representative in the first Finnish Parliament, which the Russian rulers were forced to grant after the general strike of 1905. This activity incurred the wrath of the Czarist authorities and he found it healthier to move to the United States about six years later. He quickly acclimated himself to his new environment and was made editor of *Raivaaja,* organ of the Finnish Socialist federation, by far the largest of all the foreign-language organizations. Before long, he was also elected to the National Executive Committee of the Socialist party. Since the Finnish paper was published in Fitchburg, Massachusetts, Nuorteva found himself in the middle of the struggle between the Socialist Propaganda League and the Right Wing state leadership. At first he opposed the Left Wing, but after the Russian Revolution he became one of its most zealous and influential propagandists, able to lecture in Finnish, German, Swedish, Russian, and English. His decision to back the pro-Communist Left represented no small gain.[59]

The Irish were represented by James Joseph Larkin, Jack Carney, and Eadmonn MacAlpine. "Big Jim," one of the most appealing figures of the Irish Nationalist movement, came to the United States in 1914 and stayed nine years.[60] A man of many occupations—once listed as "dairy worker, butcher, sailor, sea-going fireman, French polisher, mechanical engineer, painter and paperhanger, soldier, in U.S. Navy, stowaway, docker, while in jail worked at baking, textile trade, shoemaking, tinsmithing, and bookbinding; professional football player; social worker; temperance advocate" [61]—he had founded the famous Irish Transport and General Workers Union. When Larkin put out his paper, *The Irish Worker,* in Chicago, Carney served as his associate editor. Carney and MacAlpine figured prominently in the publication of the first American Communist papers.

The Left Wing Americans and émigrés made up a closely knit little international community in those days. At one New York mass meeting in 1917, for example, Trotsky spoke in Russian, Lore in German, Nuorteva in Finnish, Boudin in English, and others in Lettish, Jewish, and Lithuanian.[62]

5

The Left at War

ONE EVENING in the winter of 1917—on January 14, to be exact—about twenty Left Wing Socialists came together at the home of Ludwig Lore in Brooklyn. Of those present, eleven can be definitely identified. There were five Russian exiles, Trotsky, Bukharin, Mme. Kollontay, V. Volodarsky, and Grigorii Isakovich Chudnovsky. There were two more émigrés—Sen Katayama from Japan, and S. J. Rutgers from Holland. The four known Americans present were Boudin, Lore, Fraina, and John D. Williams, the last representing the Socialist Propaganda League of Boston. Fortunately we have first-hand accounts of the meeting by two of the participants, Lore and Katayama, which they wrote in 1918 and 1919 respectively, while memories still were fresh. That they should have done so indicates how large the meeting loomed in their recollection of the development of the Left Wing.

The separate paths which brought this unique collection of real and would-be revolutionists to Brooklyn show how complex and far flung were the social and political forces moving in the direction of the American Communist movement. The presence of Trotsky, for example, was totally unforeseen. The meeting had been called a few days earlier without him. But when he happened to get off the boat from Barcelona on the thirteenth of January—Lore tells us that he arrived the day before the meeting, which is why it is possible to de-

THE LEFT AT WAR

termine the exact date—he was quickly invited to bring the others up to date on the latest developments in Europe.

The meeting was called to discuss "a program of action for Socialists of the Left, for the purpose of organizing the radical forces in the American Socialist movement," Lore related.[1] The Americans were very pessimistic. The Left Wing was still so weak and chaotic that the task of organizing for effective action seemed hopeless. But the Russians were not put off so easily. They plunged into a long, intense theoretical discussion lasting far into the night. Out of it, two schools of thought emerged. They were represented by the great Russian antagonists, Trotsky and Bukharin. For a brief moment, they held the fate of the American Left Wing in their hands.

Bukharin belonged to the Bolshevik wing of the Russian movement. But he was independent-minded and frequently brought down on himself the wrath of its leader, Lenin, on various theoretical grounds. Trotsky was politically a lone wolf and occupied an exposed personal position in the no man's land between the Russian factions. Then thirty-eight, he was immensely self-confident, eloquent, and combative. One of the main complaints of the Bolsheviks against Trotsky attacked his delay and hesitation in making a clean break with the Russian Right Wing. Twenty-four hours after Trotsky's arrival, he and Bukharin were able to carry on their European feud in terms of an American movement almost wholly foreign to both of them. In fact, their American dispute was virtually a continuation of their European disagreement.

Bukharin wanted the American Left Wing to split away from the Socialist party and form a separate organization. Trotsky held out for staying in the party, but proposed an independent organ to represent the position of the Left Wing. Both agreed on the need for a new publication. A vote was taken and Trotsky won. A subcommittee was elected to bring in a definite proposal at the next meeting of the group. The committee, which included Trotsky, came back with the proposal of a bimonthly periodical.

From Lore's account, it is clear that the Russians dominated the meeting. If it had not been for them, nothing of importance would have come of it. By the time Lore and Katayama wrote down their memories of this meeting, Trotsky had become a world-famous organizer and leader of the Red Army, second only to Lenin as an outstanding figure of the Bolshevik revolution. It may be necessary, therefore, to discount somewhat their reverential references to Trotsky's personal triumph at the Brooklyn meeting.

Lore and Katayama agree that Trotsky talked himself into the momentary command of the American Left Wing. "Had Trotsky remained a year in the United States, our movement would have found in him a good and splendid leader," wrote Lore, whose heart was wholly captured by Trotsky. But Katayama, a less prejudiced eye-witness, also recalled, "We intended to organize the Left Wing under the direction of Comrade Trotsky, and Madame Kollontay, who was going to Europe, was to establish the link between the European and American Left Wing movements." [2]

As for Mme. Kollontay, she was busy tattling on Trotsky and Bukharin to Lenin in Zurich. The *Novy Mir* was not big enough to hold both Trotsky and Bukharin. Before Trotsky's arrival, Bukharin wrote the chief articles in the paper. Trotsky soon forged ahead in the frequency and importance of his contributions. Judging from Lenin's letters to Mme. Kollontay, she kept him posted on the struggle between a group headed by Bukharin and another headed by Trotsky for control of the *Novy Mir*. One of her letters, about Trotsky's "bloc" against Bukharin, brought the rejoinder from Lenin: "What a swine that Trotsky is!" [3] Years later, in his struggle against Bukharin and Stalin, Trotsky could not shake off this phrase, though he went to the trouble of denying that Mme. Kollontay's reports to Lenin had any foundation in fact.[4] From Mme. Kollontay's gossip, Lenin also seems to have made the hasty deduction that Bukharin was somehow involved in the Socialist Labor party's antipathy for a "minimum program." [5] Obviously De Leonism was still a closed book to Lenin.

Trotsky apparently had a falling out with Bukharin over a conference, held in New York City on February 17, 1917, which called itself, somewhat overoptimistically, "The International Conference of

Socialist Organizations and Groups." The conference's main achievement was a decision to adhere to the Zimmerwald movement as "the embryo of the Third International." The following organizations and groups were represented: *Novy Mir,* Russian branch of the Socialist party, Lettish branch No. 1, Ukrainian branch, Manhattan Lithuanian branch, Brooklyn Lithuanian branch, Bolshevik section of the Russian Social Democratic Workers' party, Socialist Propaganda League of America, and Group of Social Revolutionaries.[6] Of the nine organizations and groups, eight were East European, almost half were Russian, and only one, the Socialist Propaganda League, contained any Americans at all. Since the organizations and groups in the list were obviously overlapping, the conference was even smaller and narrower than it claimed to be.

Trotsky evidently poked fun at this attempt to organize an American branch of the Zimmerwald movement. At the end of 1926, during the crucial debate in the Russian Communist party and the Communist International, Bukharin went all the way back to their vendetta in the United States for one of his accusations. In a long catalogue of Trotsky's alleged crimes and misdemeanors he said, "On many occasions he asked me ironically: have you got a Zimmerwald Left Wing in the North Pole (although as is known America is not the North Pole)."[7] If it is true that Trotsky twitted Bukharin in this way, it would indicate that Bukharin's group was chiefly responsible for the New York conference in February 1917, even though Trotsky had written the manifesto of the original Zimmerwald conference.

A month later, in 1917, Trotsky did lend his name to a different kind of public demonstration by the increasingly aggressive Left Wing. As all signs pointed to the imminent entrance of the United States into the war, a meeting of the New York local was called on March 4 to determine what the Socialist attitude should be. The Left Wing seized the opportunity to make its first important effort to capture the leadership of the New York local on the eve of the declaration of war. A majority and a minority report were submitted to the Manhattan membership. Both were antiwar, but the latter was more daring in its practical measures. In line with the Left Wing point of view, it demanded resistance to recruiting and conscription, and support of all strikes. This minority report was signed by Trotsky and Fraina. Since Trotsky could not speak English, Fraina made the main speech in behalf of their joint resolution, though he had only recently rejoined the Socialist party. The fact that Trotsky's name was used indicates that his prestige was considered a valuable asset. The Trotsky-Fraina report was defeated by a vote of 101 to 79, though the losers contended that the result was inconclusive because only a fraction of the total membership had turned out for the meeting. The report ended with the words: "No 'civil peace'! No truce with the ruling class! War does not change the issue, but emphasizes it. War against capitalism. On with the class struggle!" [8]

The conduct of the meeting was described by one of the participants, the future Right Wing lawyer, Louis Waldman: "This was the stormiest meeting I ever witnessed in a long career of stormy meetings. Two chairmen had to surrender their posts because they found it impossible to maintain order. Fist fights kept breaking out in the hall as partisans of opposing factions split into little sub-meetings, without benefit of parliamentary procedure to abate their passions. Trotsky was the leader of the faction which opposed the government's policy even if it led to civil war, while Hillquit directed the tactics of the moderates." [9]

Odd as it may seem in retrospect, the Russian exiles were planning to play leading roles in the American Left Wing because they thought that they were going to stay in the United States for quite a while. The imminence of the Czarist collapse was not anticipated by either Lenin or Trotsky. Lenin, who was much nearer to Russia than the exiles in New York were, delivered a lecture in Zürich at approximately the same time as the Brooklyn meeting, in which he sadly estimated that he might not live to see the coming Russian revolution—less than a month away.[10] When Trotsky had departed for the United States, he wrote in a letter: "This is the last time that I cast a glance on that old *canaille* Europe." [11] Trotsky did not behave as if he were going to stay in New York for only about two months. Though extremely modest about how much he managed to learn about the city in that period, he tells how he "plunged into the affairs of American Socialism too quickly and I was straightway up to my neck in work for it." [12]

Apart from his work on the *Novy Mir* and lecturing in both German and Russian, he spent most of his spare time at the New York Public Library studying the American economy. In retrospect, he never considered his American stay very important, except as a short interlude between his long exile in Europe and his return to Russia. His biographers have followed his example, with the result that no satisfactory account of his short but significant American visit exists.[13]

Unfortunately for the plan reported by Katayama and Lore to make Trotsky a leader of the coming American revolution, a faraway incident intervened. On February 15, 1917, Nicholas II, Czar of All the Russias, hastily abdicated. Six days later, he and his family were seized and imprisoned. The three-hundred-year rule of the Romanovs evaporated in a matter of hours. A provisional government of ten Liberals and one Socialist took over. In Zürich, Lenin immediately wrote to Mme. Kollontay, then in Stockholm, that this was only "the first stage of the first revolution." [14] He began to seek ways and means of making the long journey to speed up the second revolution. In New York, Trotsky, Bukharin, and the other Russian exiles also made immediate preparations to depart. An impassioned farewell meeting at the Harlem Casino was called by the German federation, at which Lore presided, Boudin spoke for the American party, and Trotsky delivered an address on "The Revolution." [15] Despite the fact that they were going home to fight together, the Russian exiles did not travel together. Trotsky's party left at the end of March, Bukharin's the following month. The Left-Wingers whom they left behind went with them in spirit, and many of them as soon as possible in body also.

Trotsky went back to become the first Commissar for Foreign

Affairs and then Commissar of War. Bukharin was put in charge of *Pravda*, the central organ of the Bolshevik party. Mme. Kollontay was made the first Commissar for Social Welfare. Chudnovsky was one of the three men responsible for the plan to capture the Winter Palace in Leningrad and then became its commandant.[16] Volodarsky, one of the great orators of the revolution, was assassinated in 1918 and became one of the earliest Bolshevik martyrs.[17]

The first organs

It is revealing that Trotsky should have sensed at the Brooklyn meeting, twenty-four hours after his arrival, that what the Left Wing needed most was a publication, an "organ."

The *New Review* was no more. As it went further and further to the Left in 1916, its editorial board became smaller and smaller, until only Boudin, Fraina, and four others remained. A last-minute effort was made to save the magazine by making it the "English edition" of the European organ of the Left Wing, *Vorbote*, edited by Pannekoek and Mme. Roland-Holst.[18] The plan was never carried out. The *New Review* expired in the summer of 1916 and handed over its small legacy to the *Masses*. Its departure showed that the Left Wing was still too weak to support a single publication of its own.

One of those at the Brooklyn meeting in January 1917, John D. Williams of Boston, had come as the emissary of the Socialist Propaganda League to raise money for its new paper, *The Internationalist*.[19] Instead, a New Yorker at the meeting, Fraina, took over the Boston paper, which also needed an experienced editor. Fraina, available for the job since the demise of the *New Review*, accepted on condition that the name of the paper should be changed to *The New International* and that he should have a fairly free hand in editorial policy. The editorial and business office was moved to New York, where Fraina remained for the time being. Rutgers became its financial "angel" as well as one of the main contributors. Fraina brought out ten issues of a four-page newspaper, the first dated

April 22, 1917. Since no more than a thousand copies of each issue were printed, its influence was limited. Nevertheless, *The New International* played a historic role as the first propaganda organ of the Left Wing.[20]

Soon afterward, the bimonthly magazine proposed at the Brooklyn meetings became a reality. Since the Russians were gone, the Americans carried out the project by themselves. The first issue of *The Class Struggle,* dated May–June 1917, appeared with three editors, Boudin, Lore, and Fraina.

By the spring of 1917, the Left Wing had a propaganda newspaper and a theoretical magazine. More than anything else, they gave the young movement meaning and identity. This was traditional. To no other movements have publications, no matter how small or obscure, meant so much as to radical movements. It is sometimes hard to determine whether a radical movement exists for the sake of its organ or vice versa. Trotsky's proposal of an independent organ was virtually a conditioned reflex. The only thing of special interest this time was the timidity of the proposal for a bimonthly, an indication of how limited the committee's backing still was. Especially in their first stages, there is very little radical movements can do but make propaganda; and no group, committee, league, society, club, council, or party would consider itself worthy of the name if it could not put out at least a typewritten propaganda organ. This is the reason why so many radical leaders have at one time or another engaged in some form of journalism. It is not that so many journalists become radicals as that so many radicals become journalists, at least to the extent of writing for or editing a political magazine or newspaper. A first-rate radical leader must be a political Jack-of-all-trades, beginning in most cases with some form of journalistic propaganda.

The first great American example was Fraina. In 1917, at the age of twenty-three, he dominated both *The New International* and *The Class Struggle.* As long as the Left Wing was primarily a propaganda movement, its development was practically coincident with his personal history.

Mass action

Of the two Left Wing organs, *The New International*, edited by Fraina alone, was more extreme than *The Class Struggle*, in which he had to contend with two other editors who did not always agree with him.

Yet even *The New International* advocated something quite different from the doctrine of communism, despite the fact that Fraina was closer to communism than almost anyone else. The first numbers were virtually syndicalist in ideology. Only "revolutionary unionism," exclaimed an editorial, was the historic instrument of the proletariat, "not alone for every-day struggles but for the *final* struggle against Capitalism." [21] Fraina's position was typical of the period. Max Eastman greeted the first Russian revolution of March 1917 with an article in the *Masses* entitled "Syndicalist-Socialist Russia." He announced joyfully: "One by one the facts fall out exactly as they were predicted by Marx and Engels and the philosophers of Syndicalism." It mattered little in New York that the first Russian revolution was neither syndicalist nor socialist, or that the founders of modern socialism and the philosophers of syndicalism were so far apart that no revolution could fall out exactly to satisfy them all. Eastman also translated "Soviets" into American terms: "A parliament of proletarian deputies, entirely unofficial politically—a body like an American Federation of Labor convention with a majority of IWW's—is in essential control of Russian affairs." [22] The American Left Wing was the offspring of syndicalism and socialism, and, at first glance, it saw in the upheaval in Russia what it had been preaching at home.

Theoretically, the gap between syndicalism and socialism was bridged by an oracular phrase that beguiled the American Left Wing for years—"mass action." The term itself was Dutch-German rather than Russian in origin. It seems to have arisen in the period 1910–12 during a great practical and theoretical controversy in the German Social Democratic movement. Early in 1910, vast masses of workers staged violent demonstrations in Prussia to force the government to adopt a democratic electoral system. The movement grew so strong that the Left Wing, led by Rosa Luxemburg, began to agitate for a political strike. In order to differentiate themselves from the syndicalists, however, these Socialists preferred to speak of a "mass strike" rather than a "general strike." Such revolutionary tactics were most distasteful to the dominant wing of the German party, and Kautsky took up the cudgels against Rosa Luxemburg.[23] One of those who rallied to her side in the great debate was Pannekoek, who carried on an extended war of words against Kautsky in 1912-13. In this controversy, Pannekoek made use of the phrase "mass action" in such a way that he transformed a common expression into an all-embracing slogan and article of faith. He defined it as "an extra-parliamentary political act of the organized working class, by which it operates directly and not through the medium of political delegates."[24] As early as 1912, the phrase turned up in a resolution presented to the national convention of the American Socialist party by Secretary C. Karklin of the Lettish federation. It was used in the sense of "meetings, demonstrations, petitions and similar means." What inspired Karklin to use the term does not appear.[25] An English-born lawyer, Austin Lewis, who had traveled the well-worn American road from socialism to syndicalism, seems to have been the first definite American victim of Pannekoek's literary spell. He shared his discovery of the Kautsky-Pannekoek controversy with the readers of the *New Review* in 1913 and introduced its readers to the nature of mass action. Lewis seized on the term because its antipolitical bias fitted in with a syndicalist ideology. "Real mass action is outside the sphere of parliamentary action," he explained.[26] After this, there was not much reference to the peculiar powers of mass action until Rutgers arrived. He was so successful in his propaganda that the *International Socialist Review* accepted it as editorial policy at the end of 1916.[27] The Socialist Propaganda League made it a key phrase in its manifesto of November 1916. But Rutgers' most important convert was the indefatigable Fraina.

Between them, Rutgers and Fraina made "mass action" into a Left

Wing shibboleth. The special quality of this term has been lost to later generations because the great bugaboo of pre-World-War-I socialism has virtually disappeared from the political scene. In that era, nothing enraged the Left Wing so much as the spectacle of Socialist leaders entering bourgeois governments and quickly betraying the movement which had nurtured them. "Ministerialism," the supreme sin, was the enemy which mass action primarily sought to destroy.[28] As authoritatively interpreted by Rutgers, mass action was antiparliamentary, not antipolitical. It forbade Socialists to take jobs in non-Socialist governing bodies; it did not bar voting on a pure Socialist basis. Parliamentarism implied that the ruling class could be voted out of power—an unforgivable heresy to the Left Wing. Mass action implied that every means, economic and political, should aim at the revolutionary seizure of power. In the narrowest sense, the term embraced the more physical methods of struggle. "Mass action means meetings, street demonstrations, political strikes," Rutgers taught. For the American Left Wing, the concept was especially important because it seemed to offer a way out of the old impasse created by the tug of war between "industrial" and "political" socialism. "As soon as conditions will be ripe for it," Rutgers promised, "industrial action and the political action will both emerge into the unit of one fighting organization on democratic mass action lines, in accordance both with the ideals of social democrats and industrialists." [29]

When Americans like Fraina were converted to the theory of mass action in 1917, they gave it a twist that made it more compatible with the peculiarly syndicalist tradition of the American Left Wing. *The New International* acclaimed the first Russian revolution as a demonstration of "the meaning and power of Mass Action" because the Czar had been overthrown without the benefit of an election. But the paper was not entirely satisfied with the European version of mass action and thought that it had to be adapted to "our particular needs and revolutionary practice." In Europe, it complained, mass action was used primarily "to fight the conservatism of the Socialist movement." It merely meant more aggressive action. In the United

States, something more was needed. The added ingredient was industrial unionism. "May our European comrades fuse *their* Mass Action with the theory and practice of Industrial Unionism," it admonished.[30]

In his book, *Revolutionary Socialism,* published in 1918 and the first attempt to develop a full theoretical basis for the pro-Communist Left Wing, Fraina virtually wrote political prose poems trying to explain mass action:

> Mass action is not a *form* of action as much as it is a *process and synthesis* of action. It is the unity of all forms of proletarian action, a means of throwing the proletariat, organized and unorganized, in a general struggle against Capitalism and the capitalist state. It is the sharp, definite, expression of the revolt of the workers under the impact of the antagonisms and repressions of Capitalism, of the recurring crises and revolutionary situations produced by the violent era of Imperialism. Mass action is the instinctive action of the proletariat, gradually developing more conscious and organized forms and definite purposes. It is extra-parliamentary in method, although political in purpose and result, may develop into and be itself developed by parliamentary struggle.

After more of this came the climax:

> Mass action is dynamic, pliable, creative; the proletariat through mass action adapts itself to the means and tactics necessary in a prevailing situation. The forms of activity of the proletariat are not limited and stultified by mass action, they are broadened, deepened and co-ordinated. Mass action is equally a process of revolution and the Revolution itself in operation.[31]

This conglomeration of ideas satisfied a deep need in the American Left Wing. Until the Russian influence completely eliminated the Dutch, no Left Wing manifesto or resolution was complete without the invocation of mass action, preferably as many times as possible. The great virtue of the phrase was its vagueness and all-inclusiveness. It was broad enough to admit the most variegated collection of radicals into the revolutionary fraternity. It was also perhaps a literary compensation for the real condition of the Left Wing. Only on paper was the Left Wing capable of committing any mass action.

The St. Louis resolution

The long-awaited opportunity for the Left Wing to force a showdown on the crucial issue of the war came at the emergency convention of the Socialist party held at St. Louis beginning April 7, 1917, the day after war was declared. An effort was made by L. E. Katterfeld of Washington, supported by Charles E. Ruthenberg of Ohio, to compel each candidate for the all-important Committee on War and Militarism to give a yes or no answer to the question: "Are you opposed to all militarism and to all war, either offensive or defensive, except the war of the working class against the capitalist class?" Morris Hillquit, the official strategist, and Adolph Germer, the executive secretary, succeeded in beating down the motion 96 to 66. Despite this initial setback, the Left Wing vote was threateningly impressive.

Katterfeld was a good example of the old-time Socialist Left-Winger who became a Communist. At the time of the St. Louis convention in 1917, he had been a member of the Socialist party for twelve of his thirty-six years. He was responsible for organizing the Lyceum Bureau of the Socialist party in 1911, a nationwide system of lecture courses which helped to recruit thousands of members into the party. His sympathy for Haywood led to his ouster from the bureau in 1913. He served as secretary of the Washington State Socialist party, then controlled by the Left Wing, in 1914–16. Unlike Ruthenberg, whose career had been restricted to Cleveland, Katterfeld had worked in the national office of the Socialist party and had lectured all over the country.[32]

Hillquit outdid himself at St. Louis. Hillquit, Ruthenberg, and Boudin were elected to the fifteen-member committee. A sub-committee of three—Hillquit, Ruthenberg, and Algernon Lee—was appointed to compose a draft of the resolution on the war. Hillquit succeeded in getting Ruthenberg to go along with Lee and himself in presenting the final version of the resolution. As a result, Hillquit was able to present a majority report signed by eleven members of the committee, including Ruthenberg and himself. This united front between Hillquit and Ruthenberg forced Boudin to present a minority report signed by only three members. There was more difference between the two in spirit than in content. For Boudin, the all-important consideration was to avoid lining up with Hillquit, whose sincerity he questioned. Boudin vainly complained that the majority report said one thing and meant another. Indeed, there was little else in it that the Left Wing could complain about, for it denounced the war in the most uncompromising terms: "We brand the declaration of war by our government as a crime against the people of the United States and against the nations of the world." By joining forces with Hillquit, however, Ruthenberg made it impossible for the Left Wing to emerge at the convention as a fully developed, independent political force. In effect, Hillquit succeeded in splitting the Left Wing. The old master had outmaneuvered it again.[33]

A third report, presented by a minority of one, John Spargo, represented the prowar position. The Hillquit-Ruthenberg majority report received 140 votes, to 31 for Boudin's and 5 for Spargo's, and was subsequently ratified in a referendum of the membership by 21,000 to 350.

In the end, however, the St. Louis resolution satisfied no one.

It caused the prowar group to desert the Socialist party. The loss was much greater qualitatively than quantitatively. Among the bolters were some of the best-known Socialist propagandists: John Spargo, William English Walling, A. M. Simons, Charles Edward Russell, William J. Ghent, George D. Herron, Gustavus Myers, Winfield R. Gaylord, Robert Hunter, J. Stitt Wilson, Allan L. Benson, Upton Sinclair, and others. Most important Socialist trade-union leaders were equally prowar, though they departed more discreetly. At one blow, the war deprived the party of the services of those who had enabled it to make the greatest inroads among the middle class and the organized working class. "In fact, except for Hillquit, Berger, and Debs, not one major 'name' remained in the ranks of American socialism after the war," Daniel Bell sums up.[34] The balance in the Socialist party was upset in 1917; the disruption was finished by the Communists two years later.

The St. Louis antiwar resolution also gave the government its chief legal weapon to prosecute Socialist leaders and suppress the Socialist press. After the Espionage Act was passed in June 1917, national and local authorities demonstrated little discrimination. The Socialist national office in Chicago was raided in September. Adolph Germer, the executive secretary, Victor Berger, the Wisconsin leader, J. Louis Engdahl, editor of the official national organ, William F. Kruse, head of the Young People's Socialist League, and Irwin St. John Tucker, former head of the literature department, were charged with obstructing the draft. This assortment of victims, from the prowar Berger to the antiwar Engdahl, had one effect the government did not intend. It deprived the Left Wing of a monopoly of antiwar martyrs. Among the approximately two thousand persons tried under the Espionage Act were martyrs enough for all.

A head-on collision with the government was not at all what the Hillquit-Berger team had intended. The resolution did call for antiwar demonstrations, "unyielding opposition" to conscription, and other militant measures. But some of those who voted for the resolution were more interested in inner-party maneuvering than in obstructing the war effort. Berger himself testified that he supported the St. Louis resolution in order to prevent the adoption of an even more radical program.[35] Even before the emergency convention was held, another backer of the resolution, former Congressman Meyer London, had come out for "national unity" if war was declared.[36] In the New York Board of Aldermen in the spring of 1918, six of the seven Socialist aldermen, including Algernon Lee, voted in favor of the third Liberty Loan.[37] Hillquit was far from consistent until his illness in 1918 temporarily took him out of action.[38] He was willing to denounce the war in general terms, at a safe distance from the kind of revolutionary opposition demanded by the Left Wing. "Whatever the reasons," writes Nathan Fine, "the fact remained that by the middle of 1918 important sections of the party were no longer seriously, if at all, opposed to the war."[39] The Right Wing was hammered on one side by the government for being too antiwar and on the other by the Left Wing for not being antiwar enough.

For the Left Wing, however, the lines were not drawn sharply enough. An organized Left Wing did emerge at the St. Louis convention, put forward its own resolutions and amendments, and maneuvered behind its own leaders. But the acceptance of a common resolution prevented it from coming out with a distinctive antiwar program. All it could and did demand afterward was that the official party leadership should live up to its own program. Officially there was nothing to attack. The Left Wing had to fire away at small moving targets instead of a single stationary one. Boudin went after Hillquit for not favoring withdrawal from the war.[40] *The New International* wanted to know why Berger and London were not expelled along with the openly prowar Charles Edward Russell.[41] *The Class Struggle* complained bitterly against the endorsement of the third Liberty Loan by the Socialist aldermen in New York.[42]

If the government had not flung its legal dragnet so wide, the Left Wing might have stood out more clearly as the only one to live up to the letter and spirit of the St. Louis resolution. In Cleveland, Socialist candidate for mayor Ruthenberg, state secretary Alfred Wagenknecht, and state organizer Charles Baker were arrested for making anticonscription speeches.[43] In Kansas City, Earl R. Browder, his two brothers William E. and Ralph W., and four others, were seized for opposing the war.[44] Louis C. Fraina and Ralph Cheyney, the poet, were arrested for addressing a meeting of conscientious objectors in New York City.[45] Rose Pastor Stokes was tried for writing a letter to a newspaper charging that "the government is for the profiteers."[46] Against the better judgment of the Department of Justice, Eugene V. Debs was prosecuted for a speech at Canton, Ohio.[47] Juries were easily persuaded to bring in heavy sentences, as much as ten years in the cases of Debs and Mrs. Stokes, though none served the longer terms of imprisonment in full. But "mass action" was most conspicuous by its absence. The only important Left-Wing-led mass protest during the war took place in Boston where the Socialist Propaganda League was most active. "Hundreds of Socialists were beaten and forced to kiss the flag on their knees," a Socialist paper reported.[48] Such mass protest was not soon repeated.

The chief victim of the government's drive was neither the Left Wing nor the Right Wing of the Socialist movement, but the I.W.W. The raids on Socialist headquarters and private homes were relatively few and mild compared to those launched against the I.W.W. There were no Socialist trials like the mass trials of 101 I.W.W. members in Chicago, 46 in Sacramento, and 38 in Wichita (tried in Kansas City). In the Chicago trial, the heaviest sentence was twenty years imprisonment and $10,000 fine for Haywood and fourteen others. The Communist movement a little later inherited a number of these I.W.W. prisoners, among them George Andreychine, Harrison George, Charles Ashleigh, and George Hardy.

Thus the American pattern in the war was not the same as the European. The prowar wing fled from the American Socialist movement, the antiwar wing from the European. The entire American movement was officially antiwar, superficially lining it up with the European Left Wing. But, on closer examination, there was the same fundamental cleavage in the American party despite the break away of the open prowar group. There still remained a militant antiwar and a covert prowar group. There was the same process of differentiation as in Europe, but it was not so sharp or clear.

The extremist antiwar position constituted the first political capital possessed by the Left Wing. Even though it came to have a virtual monopoly of this commodity, something more was needed to lead the way from the wilderness of Left Wingism to the promised land of communism. The antiwar position had a wide appeal. It could hold together pacifists and revolutionists in a loose, ambiguous alliance. But it could not become the basis of a centralized, single-minded, revolutionary party. For this, something else was needed, something much more rigid and selective.

6

The Reflected Glory

THE EARLY Communists never doubted what it was that made them Communists.

"It was the Russian Revolution—the Bolshevik Revolution of November 7, 1917—which created the American Communist movement," the American Communist leader, Charles E. Ruthenberg, proclaimed. "The Communist Party came into existence in the United States, as elsewhere, in response to the ferment caused in the Socialist parties by the Russian Revolution," he wrote on another occasion. And still later, he reiterated, "The movement which crystallized in the Communist Party had its origin and gained its inspiration from the proletarian revolution in Russia." [1]

American Communism proudly represented the Bolshevik revolution in the United States. It owed its reason for existence to something that happened five thousand miles away.

Before 1917, the revolutionary outlook in Russia was so gloomy and obscure that it offered little for other countries to imitate. Since it was generally assumed that Russia had to catch up with the West before the material and political conditions would be ripe for a socialist revolution, Russia had much more to learn from the West than the West had to learn from Russia. By common consent, the next stage for Russia was supposed to be a "bourgeois-democratic," not a socialist revolution. Marx had thrown out some hints that Russia might not have to go through the traditional stages of capitalism in order to get to socialism. Both he and Engels had considered the possibility that the Russian revolution might sound "the signal for the proletarian revolution in the West, so that each complements the other."[2] But these were isolated speculations. Within the Marxist movement, as distinct from some of the things which Marx himself wrote, the idea that Russia might lead the way was not taken seriously.

Lenin's thinking on this point was not materially different. "It is the task of the proletariat to complete the bourgeois-democratic revolution in Russia in order to kindle a Socialist revolution in Europe," he wrote in 1915.[3] On the eve of his return to Russia in the spring of 1917, he included the "American Socialist proletariat" with the European in the "decisive battles" which would be necessary for a socialist revolution in Europe and Russia. Lenin did not conceive of a socialist revolution limited to Russia.[4] When he first suggested that the Provisional Government should be overthrown and the Soviets should seize power, his own followers, including Stalin, were flabbergasted. He won them over, but their initial shock betrayed the strength of the tradition.[5]

The Russian Right Wing acted on the belief that Russia was simply not ripe for a socialist revolution. The Russian Left Wing, under Lenin, acted on the belief that the Russian Revolution was the first stage of a European revolution. No one believed in a revolution beginning and ending in Russia.

Repercussions in America

If Lenin's Russian followers had trouble making up their minds about what was going to happen in Russia, the Americans were understandably even more confused.

The official Socialist *New York Call* asked Alexander L. Trachtenberg to explain what was happening in Russia. A native of Russia who had taken part in the revolution of 1905 as a young man of twenty, he was a logical choice. Emigrating to the United States the following year, he soon began to play an active role in the Socialist student movement, first at Trinity College and then at Yale University. He came to New York in 1915 to head the Research Department of the Rand School of Social Science.[6] Two years later, when he was given the opportunity to interpret the first Russian revolution, Trachtenberg was another immigrant intellectual who had Americanized himself with remarkable speed without giving up his peculiarly European prestige.

When the Romanov regime gave way to the government of Prince Lvov in February 1917, Trachtenberg applauded the change. For him, the revolution was symbolized by two men—the Social-Revolutionary, Alexander Kerensky, and the Menshevik, Nicholas S. Cheidze. According to Trachtenberg, the goal of the revolution was a "democratic republic."[7] In another article, he listed the chief Russian Socialist leaders and included Trotsky but not Lenin.[8] For a while, the average American Socialist was just as hopelessly puzzled as most people about what Lenin stood for. The *New York Call* reprinted an article from the Jewish *Daily Forward* identifying Lenin as a "pro-German Socialist."[9]

But Lenin was not the only one impatient with a bourgeois-democratic revolution. Across the Atlantic, without any means of communication, Fraina also called for a second revolution, the real revolution. When Trotsky's party was held up at Halifax by the British authorities, Fraina protested: "Why does Great Britain fear Trotsky and his party of revolutionary Socialists? The answer is simple. The revolutionary forces of Russia are clarifying their aims and organizing their power. They are a majority. The provisional government is pro-war, the Working Class is *against the war*." And he added, "The hope of Russia lies precisely in the programme of men of the character of Trotsky. Their programme declares for a real revolution and a Social Republic."[10] An editorial in *The New International* said confidently: "A dictatorship of the Working Class in Russia today would serve the ends of progress."[11] Fraina saw the second Russian revolution in Trotsky's image, not Lenin's, for the obvious reason that the former was much better known to Americans.

Lenin's direct influence was somewhat delayed. The first post-Czarist statement by him in any American publication (in English) appeared in *The New International* of June 30, 1917. It consisted of a lecture on "The Russian Revolution" which he had delivered in Zurich shortly before his departure for Russia. Gradually he, not Trotsky, emerged as the dominant revolutionary figure in Russia. Not until the issue of October 1 was the extreme Left Wing in Russia identified by Rutgers as the "group Lenin." Only two more short messages by Lenin were published before the Bolshevik revolution.[12] The most important theoretical articles were still contributed by the Dutch. Besides the frequent comments and reports by Rutgers, basic analyses were furnished by Pannekoek.[13]

The difference between *The New International*, edited by Fraina alone, and *The Class Struggle*, edited by the triumvirate, Boudin, Lore, and Fraina, became evident with the Bolshevik revolution in November 1917.[14] *The New International* welcomed it unhesitatingly and unconditionally. A front-page announcement was headed: "Great News from Russia!"[15] *The Class Struggle* soon revealed a split personality. Boudin reacted to the Bolshevik seizure of power with dismay. In a bitter article, "The Tragedy of the Russian Revolution," he called the Bolshevik uprising "a counter-revolution which will rob the Russian people of the best fruits of the Revolution."[16] Orthodox Marxism did not make room for a socialist revolution in Russia in 1917, and Boudin refused to accept the accomplished fact. Fraina, on the other hand, rushed to the defense of the Bolshevik revolution in a long fiery polemic against Boudin.[17]

The distance between them became so great that Fraina demanded Boudin's ouster from the editorial board. Lore found himself in the middle. In this instance, he agreed with Fraina, but he did not wish to force a break with Boudin.[18] Finally Boudin had to go.[19] There was no room for a critic of the Bolshevik revolution in *The Class Struggle*. The split was a microcosm of the rupture that was rending the Socialist world.

The power and the glory

The impact of the Bolshevik revolution on the American Left Wing was stunning. It was as if some Left Wing Socialists had gone to sleep and had awakened as Communists. The Bolshevik revolution had a dazzling, dreamlike quality, all the more glamorous because it was far away, undefiled by any contact with the more recalcitrant American reality.

For this metamorphosis to be possible, it had to satisfy some deep, long-maturing need outside as well as inside Russia.

All over the world the Socialist movement had been suffering from a case of acute frustration. After decades of hard work and enormous sacrifice, the Socialists could not boast of power in a single country. And without power socialism was only a beautiful theory. Reformist Socialists were not too disturbed by this lack of fulfillment, because they were content to work for a far-off ideal, or because power frightened them. The plight of the so-called revolutionary Socialists was more painful. They denied the possibility of a peaceful, piecemeal growing-into the Socialist society. They believed in the seizure of power as the indispensable condition of fundamental social change.

The great lure of the Bolshevik revolution was that it took a problem that had baffled the whole Socialist movement for decades and, in a matter of a few months, seemed to present a ready-made solution that was irresistibly quick and simple. One thing could not be argued away: the success of the Russian Bolsheviks. In May 1917, there were only 11,000 members of the Bolshevik party in all Russia.[20] Yet five months later the Bolsheviks seized power. Somehow they had found a short-cut. They made it possible to believe that it was not necessary to build a party at a creeping pace to win over the majority of the population, or at least the great majority of the working class. It was possible for a handful of determined revolutionists to achieve power. If this was possible in Russia, the last country in Europe where a proletarian revolution had been expected, it now seemed even more feasible in the advanced capitalist countries where the classical conditions for socialism were far more developed.

This aspect of the Bolshevik revolution was almost hypnotic in effect. If great numbers were not necessary, the revolution in every country with relatively few revolutionists was much closer than anyone had dared to hope. What, then, was the secret of Bolshevik success? No one—certainly, no one in the United States—really knew. What Lenin or the other Bolshevik leaders had actually done or written for a decade and a half previously was still buried in obscure Russian émigré papers. Only the Russian exiles and immigrants had more than a dim notion of Russian conditions and history, let alone of the intricate background of the factional struggles in the Russian Socialist movement. What counted most was a vague, general impression that a revolutionary spirit and doctrine had triumphed in Russia. The Bolsheviks had won because they were more revolutionary than anyone else. They had made the revolution because they really wanted it, unlike the more moderate Socialists who talked about a revolution which they really did not want.

The supreme lesson seemed to be that a small party could seize power if only it had enough revolutionary zeal and purity of doctrine. No revolutionary group could guarantee numbers, but zeal and doctrine could be had for the asking. Such was the infinitely optimistic horizon that the Bolshevik revolution appeared to open up. Small wonder that its first impact on politically starved and spiritually depressed revolutionary Socialists everywhere was so overpowering.

The personal histories of Lenin and Trotsky—in those days their names were inseparable—were equally inspiring to the Left Wing everywhere. Lenin was a relatively obscure Russian Left Wing Socialist of whom not one American Socialist in a hundred had ever heard before 1917. He had labored in exile for over a decade at the head of a tiny group, had gone home in the midst of the chaos brought on by war and defeat. Before the year was out, his name symbolized the revolutionary conquest of one-sixth of the earth's surface. The element of personal contact made Trotsky's story even more impressive. Only a few months earlier, American Left-Wingers had known him as an émigré journalist—perhaps more brilliant than most but nevertheless only a journalist, without even a party—who had lived in an ordinary New York tenement house, hard-pressed to pay the rent. While these memories of him were still fresh, he became the first Foreign Commissar of the Soviet Russian government—itself a term mysteriously exciting in its novelty—and then the organizer and leader of the Red Army, the Communist Carnot. Every Left Wing journalist could dream of duplicating Trotsky's feat at home. After the Russian experience, one could not help wondering: who would be the American Lenin, who the American Trotsky? The message of Lenin and Trotsky seemed to be that revolutionaries had to hold themselves in readiness for the right moment. Then, despite all previous setbacks and lack of mass following, superior revolutionary principles and determination would carry them through to victory. In the first flush of the Russian Revolution, few American Left-Wingers were in a position to make a more profound analysis of the causes for Lenin's and Trotsky's spectacular success. Whatever the reasons, their example was bound to be blissfully contagious.

To this extent, the relationship between the Russian Bolsheviks and their Western disciples was totally one-sided. The Russians gave everything and received nothing. But there was more to the story as it was understood then. If the Westerners had a stake in the Russian Revolution, the Russians had just as much a stake in the Western revolution.

In the first period of the Russian Revolution, the Bolsheviks devoutly believed that their victory was only the prelude to revolution in Europe and the West. They went further and accepted as a basic tenet that the Russian Revolution could not survive without a victorious European revolution. Lenin was just as firm and fixed on this point as was any of the others. The Russian Revolution was the common property of the whole Left Wing movement in the sense that it would be saved and overtaken by the coming European or even world revolution. In the view of both Russians and Westerners the dependence of the Western revolution on the Russian example was only temporary.

In the spring of 1918, after six months of power, Lenin could say that it was an "absolute truth" that they were "doomed" without a German revolution.[21] In the spring of 1919, after eighteen months in power, he could still refer to the Russian Revolution as merely "the dress rehearsal, or one of the rehearsals" for the world proletarian revolution.[22] The scene of the real, the official revolutionary performance was looked for in Europe and especially in Germany. The Bolsheviks merely hoped to hold on long enough for the European revolution to rescue them from what still seemed like an impossible predicament. They had taken advantage of certain uniquely Russian conditions to set off an all-European revolution which, in turn, would be their "salvation."[23] They expected Russia to be outdistanced quickly in the second phase. Lenin spoke modestly even in relation to Poland. He related how he had remarked to a Polish Communist, "You will do it in a different way." The latter replied, "No, we will do the same thing, but better than you." And Lenin added, "To such an argument I had absolutely nothing to object."[24] Such was the attitude and outlook for at least two years after the Russian Revolution.

The contrast between the collapse of the Social Democracy in Germany and the triumph of Bolshevism in Russia was so overwhelming that the choice did not even seem debatable to many Left-Wingers. They jumped to the conclusion that the Russian path was right and the German path was wrong, not that there was one path for Russia and another path for Germany—and perhaps a third one for the United States. The Russian Bolsheviks did not need to organize a great international propaganda campaign to rub in this revelation. It went around the world before they were able to make any propaganda abroad. Any Left-Winger anywhere could take a proprietary interest in the Russian Revolution because it was somehow "his" own revolution, as if one were entitled to part of the credit by belonging to the same international movement.

"The call to action of the proletarian revolution in Russia will soon—*now, perhaps*—marshal the iron battalions of the international proletariat," wrote Fraina in his introduction to the first American collection of Lenin's and Trotsky's writings.[25] The Fraina of 1915 had seen capitalism emerging from the war stronger than ever, especially in Russia. The Fraina of 1918 saw the iron battalions of the international proletariat marshaled everywhere. The only question was when—"soon" or *"now, perhaps."*

Yet what had happened on the American radical scene in these three years to give him this confidence? In 1915 the I.W.W. was still a fighting organization. The Socialist party was still imbued with the optimism generated by its last and greatest presidential vote. By 1918, the I.W.W. was fighting for its existence. The Socialist Labor party was more than ever a ghostly reminder of past eminence. After a poor electoral showing in 1916, and a good one in the municipal elections of 1917, the Socialist party suffered a sharp setback in the congressional elections of 1918. The Socialist press was devastated by the government's hounding restrictions. The Left Wing was divorced from the solidly prowar trade-union movement. By all normal standards, the syndicalists and Socialists of the Left Wing should have been shrouded in gloom at the end of the war. Yet the reverse was true. The Left Wing was filled with boundless hopes and intoxicating dreams. The revolution was never closer, never more inevitable. For all this, the Bolshevik revolution was responsible. It hit the American Left Wing at a peculiarly vulnerable moment. At a time when there seemed nothing more to believe in at home, when all native radical movements seemed to have exhausted themselves, a triumphant peal of revolutionary thunder was heard from afar, and from the most unexpected quarter.

Some students have expressed the opinion that the American Communist movement was totally unrelated to the Socialist Left Wing of 1912.[26] This view seems to minimize historical continuity. The Bolshevik revolution transformed the Left Wing, but it did not create a new one out of nothing. On the contrary, the leading roles were played by men and women who were prepared for them by past inclinations and experience. The Bolshevik revolution came to fulfill, not to destroy. The peculiar development of American Communism can be understood only in terms of the way in which the new Bolshevik influence impinged on American radical traditions. The interaction of the two was a long, painful, complex process. Nevertheless, there can be no doubt that something new was born with the Bolshevik revolution. It was born precisely because the old Left Wing was famished for something new, different, more successful. But as with all newborn things, the flesh out of which it came was not new.

Red Guards

The Russian period of the American Left Wing effectively dates from 1917.

The New International, as usual, led the way. A new note of admiration and imitation of what was happening in Russia made its appearance midway between the March and November revolutions. Almost five months before the Bolshevik revolution, one writer ventured in the new direction: "However, we cherish one belief, and that is this: that the days are not far off when we shall have a Council of Workmen and Soldiers on the same pattern as the one in operation in Russia." [27] After the Bolsheviks came out on top, the paper unmistakably expressed the line of reasoning which enabled it to claim some of the glory for itself: "The Bolsheviki, representing the revolutionary Socialism of the Left Wing, are proving and emphasizing the bankruptcy of moderate Socialism. They are not simply a product of the temporary situation in Russia, but Socialists who have always been revolutionary, the same Left Wing Socialism that, organized in small or large minority groups, operates throughout the world." [28]

While waiting for the revolution to reach America, there was also a compulsion to do something more than watch the Bolshevik revolution from afar. This political and psychological need was so great that it soon became difficult to tell whether the American Left Wing existed to further the Russian Revolution or the Russian Revolution was made to further the American Left Wing.

The first American pro-Soviet organization, Friends of the Russian Revolution, or, as it was also called, Friends of New Russia, was formed in December 1917 to support the Soviets' peace proposals promulgated the previous month. Though Left-Wingers were prominent at its meetings, the initiating committee was not limited to them. The Soviets' demand for an immediate peace without annexations or indemnities was capable of soliciting broad support and led the way to President Wilson's Fourteen Points the following month.[29]

The Left Wing soon came out with its own pro-Soviet organization. Delegates from five Russian groups and the Socialist Propaganda League came together to form the American Bolshevik Bureau of Information early in 1918. The executive committee included Nicholas Hourwich of the Russian Socialist Federation, Ludwig C. A. K. Martens of the "New York Section of the Russian Bolsheviki," and Rutgers of the Socialist Propaganda League. Fraina was named director of the Bureau. Significantly, however, its inspiration was wholly American; the Soviet authorities were not yet able to set up such an organization. The ubiquitous Fraina combined in his own person the functions of chief propagandist for both the Left Wing and the Bolshevik regime.[30]

Fraina also brought out in 1918 the first American collection of post-revolutionary writings by Lenin and Trotsky. This book, *The Proletarian Revolution in Russia,* gave the American Left Wing its first extensive view of the Bolshevik program. Much of this program could appeal to the most idealistic of American radicals.

In the articles and speeches which Fraina presented, Lenin gave expression to some of the utopian elements in Marxism, derived in part from the short experience of the Paris Commune of 1871. The Soviet regime, he promised, "would not introduce, does not intend to introduce, and should not introduce any reorganization which is not absolutely ripe not only in the economic activity but in the consciousness of the majority of the people." The poor peasants "should be made to see the advantage of the machine-process, Socialist agriculture, by the force of example alone." All nationalities must be granted "full freedom of secession, the broadest local autonomy, full guarantees for the rights of minorities." The new type of Bolshevik government represented a revolt "against the re-establishment of the police, against an immovable and privileged bureaucracy, against an army which is separate from the nation." The Bolsheviks aimed "to attract *every* member of the *poorer* classes to practical participation in management." They desired to put into effect, perhaps within a year, "a policy of reducing high salaries to the standard of wages of the average worker." Not only would officials be elected but they should be subject to recall.[31]

In the light of the Soviet system's development, these precepts by Lenin constitute one of the cruelest deceptions and self-deceptions in history. A system which has wiped out millions of poor peasants in forced collectivization, which has expunged whole nationalities from the map, which has terrorized its people with secret police, and which has fostered the most extreme inequality of income, started out by promising the peasantry to use no force but that of example, by unconditionally guaranteeing the rights of all nationalities, by ruling out the re-establishment of the police, and by advocating absolute social equality based on the wages of the average worker. There is no more scathing critique of the Soviet reality than the Bolshevik promises, but in 1918 the promises seemed to be the reality.

Fighting for the Russian Bolsheviks in America soon did not seem enough for the American Left Wing. The logic of its involvement in the Russian Revolution drove it to take another step—fighting for the Bolsheviks in Russia itself. In New York, the Socialist Propaganda League started a campaign in February to recruit an "American Red Guard" for armed service in Russia. At one mass meeting, it was proudly announced that five hundred "Guards for the Revolution" had enlisted and were waiting permission from the War Department in Washington to sail for Russia.[32] In the name of the American Bolshevist Bureau of Information, Fraina, who also presided at the recruiting meetings, sent a telegram to the Council of People's Commissars, Smolny Institute, Russia: "Have taken steps to organize Red Guards." Another cable, signed by Fraina, Rutgers, and Mrs. Rovitch, read: "Socialist Propaganda League has unqualified faith in you. Have started recruiting Red Guard for service in Russia. Great enthusiasm among American workers. Your cause is ours. Cable instructions. Can League help any other way?"[33] Many other similar messages were sent. There was only one hitch in the plan. Telegrams were sent to get the approval of President Wilson. A reply from Acting Assistant Chief of Staff Brigadier General Henry Jarney discouraged the idea.[34] That was the quick inglorious end of the American Red Guard. Perhaps this incident as much as any other summed up the heroic and the pathetic in the Left Wing's infatuation with the Russian Revolution. Among the Red Guard's frustrated recruits was a struggling young writer and ex-anarchist, Michael Gold.[35]

After the fiasco of the Red Guards, Fraina was confronted with a rival as propagandist-in-chief for the Bolshevik regime. When the short-lived "People's Republic" of Finland seized power early in 1918, Santeri Nuorteva, editor of the Finnish Socialist organ, received a cablegram appointing him its American representative. The message was signed by Yrjo Sirola, the revolutionary Finnish Foreign Minister, who had once lectured and written for the Finnish Socialist federation in the United States.[36] He did not play as important a role in American Socialist politics as Nuorteva did, but he subsequently rose much higher in Moscow as a leading official of the Communist International. When the revolutionary Finnish regime was overthrown in the spring of 1918, Nuorteva continued his propaganda activities in behalf of the Russian Soviets. He participated in still another of the early pro-Soviet organizations, the Russian Soviet Recognition League, with Trachtenberg as its provisional chairman.[37] The press considered Nuorteva the foremost pro-Bolshevik propagandist in the United States until the official Russian agency was established in 1919.[38] Fraina made enemies in his meteoric rise—and Nuorteva was one that would cost him most dearly.

The Bolshevik bandwagon

It should not be imagined that the Left Wing had a monopoly on the enthusiasm for the Bolshevik revolution. In fact, the Left Wing had a hard time establishing its exclusive claim to the American rights. For a time, the Bolshevik revolution was a bandwagon on which many others tried to climb.

The Socialist party's top leadership went on record with unstinted approbation. "They come with a message of proletarian revolution," a proclamation on Russia of the National Executive Committee said early in 1918. "We glory in their achievement and inevitable triumph." [39] Later that year, a conference of state secretaries and party officials issued another proclamation on Russia, which began, "Since the French Revolution established a new high mark of political liberty in the world, there has been no other advance in democratic progress and social justice comparable to the Russian Revolution." [40] When Abraham Cahan, editor of the Jewish *Daily Forward,* heard that the Bolshevik government was erecting a statue of Karl Marx in Moscow, he wrote: "We have criticized them; some of their utterances often irritate us; but who can help rejoicing in their triumph? Who can help going into ecstacy over the Socialist spirit which they have enthroned in the country, which they now rule?" [41] Morris Hillquit also rejoiced: "With all the outcry of our reactionary press and our narrow-minded statesmen against the present [Bolshevik] regime in Russia, we know that the great country, which has heretofore been the strongest resort of the darkest reaction, is today the vanguard of democracy and social progress. It is from top to bottom in the hands of the people, the working class, the peasants." [42] Louis Waldman granted that the Bolshevik upheaval was an "awakening to freedom and to self-government." [43] James Oneal was full of scorn for critics who "say there has been violence in Russia. Some violence in a revolution! Just imagine! Do they think a revolution is a pink tea party?" [44] And Debs outdid them all with the declaration: "From the crown of my head to the soles of my feet I am Bolshevik, and proud of it." [45]

In the I.W.W., the Bolshevik revolution also struck a responsive chord. In the Cook County jail in Chicago awaiting sentence after the mass trial, Harrison George wrote the first pro-Bolshevik pamphlet by an American—*The Red Dawn,* based on information furnished by Russian cellmates.[46] John Reed brought the message of Russia to Haywood in person, and his *Ten Days That Shook The World* was circulated among the I.W.W. prisoners in Leavenworth Penitentiary.[47] In Kansas City, James P. Cannon left the I.W.W. and joined the Socialist party in 1918.[48] Harold Lord Varney, for a time acting secretary of the I.W.W. and author of one of the earliest "proletarian" novels, *Revolt,* greeted the Bolshevik revolution as his own because "Bolshevism was but the Russian name for I.W.W." [49] Emma Goldman and Alexander Berkman sailed off for Russia in 1919 with glowing expectations of the new world.

The Socialist Labor party was the unsuspecting victim of supersalesmanship on the part of John Reed and others. From Lenin's correspondence, it is quite clear that he had only vague notions about the party before 1917.[50] After the revolution, Lenin read a comparison of his own theories and De Leon's in an English Socialist paper. He borrowed some of De Leon's pamphlets from a former S.L.P. member, Boris Reinstein, then in Russia, and read them for the first time. De Leon's emphasis on industrial, rather than geographical, representation in the future Socialist legislative body impressed him as an anticipation of the Soviet system.[51] When John Reed came back from Russia in 1918, he tried to win over the S.L.P. by telling it that Lenin was practically a disciple of De Leon.[52] This was heartwarming news to the lonely De Leonites, who had little progress to show at home. As late as 1919, National Secretary Arnold Petersen expressed satisfaction over "the harvest so far reaped" by the S.L.P. —in Russia.[53] When the inevitable day of disillusionment came, only a few members of the Socialist Labor party became Communists.

The Bolshevik regime also had a special charm for some pacifists. Lenin's contempt for pacifists was boundless; he realized that they had to oppose his slogan of "civil war" as much as they opposed the "imperialist war." His definition of pacifism was one of the "means employed to fool the working class." [54] But the Bolsheviks proved themselves to be adepts at making popular yearnings and emotions which they privately detested serve their immediate, practical ends. The classic demonstration of this Bolshevik art came in 1917. After the overthrow of the Czar, the Kerensky regime refused to recognize the fact that Russia was no longer capable of carrying on the war. By ordering the war-weary Russian soldiers back to the front, it gave the Bolsheviks the priceless gift of an irresistible slogan of peace. The most withering critics of pacifism then rode to power on a wave of popular pacifism. As their first act, the victorious Bolsheviks sent out an appeal for immediate and universal peace. American pacifists who had opposed the United States's entry into the war received the news of Russia's departure from the war with joy. The People's Council of America, a movement launched by Socialists and pacifists for "Democracy and Peace," prominently featured the Bolsheviks' example in its propaganda. Yet this Council, its very name a translation of "soviet," was one of the Left Wing's favorite targets of abuse on the ground that it lacked revolutionary militancy.

There were some Socialist critics, but at first they found themselves hard-pressed. At the end of 1917, the Socialist *Call* in New York published an interview with Dr. Anna Ingerman, a New York Socialist who had just returned from Russia, sharply attacking the excesses of the Bolsheviks.[55] She was soon assailed by Fraina in a three-column letter.[56] Editorially the paper refused to commit itself. It rather pathetically admitted that "the Russian Revolution has got clean away from us; that we can make nothing of it at present, nor predicate anything for its future from present reports."[57] After the pro-Bolsheviks had had all the best of it for about a year, Bela Low, a Socialist engineer, in the fall of 1918, took issue with the prevailing trend.[58] Joseph Shaplen, a recent United Press correspondent in Russia, even attacked the *Call* at the end of 1918 for favoring the Soviets.[59] The Jewish *Forward,* afterward the bulwark of anti-Communism in the entire Socialist movement, did not print anti-Bolshevik articles until 1922.[60]

A confused situation was basically responsible for this confusion of voices.

Many months after it happened, the Bolshevik revolution was still a very hazy and contradictory phenomenon. It was not simple and clear even to the participants. In its first stage, the Bolshevik regime consisted of a coalition between the Bolsheviks, the Left Socialist Revolutionaries, and minor groups. Long-time Marxists and anarchists pulled together against the common enemy. The last semblance of a legal opposition in Russia was not destroyed until 1921. Onlookers from afar could not be expected to capture the essence of a revolution which was in flux. Another thing encouraged deception. For the first time, in 1917, the world became acutely conscious of the existence of Soviets, or Councils of Workers and Peasants. As far as anyone knew, the Soviets constituted the ruling administrative-legislative bodies of revolutionary Russia. Only with the evolution of the Bolshevik regime into a one-party state and gradual clarification of the principles and practices of the Bolshevik party were the impotence and dummy-existence of the Soviets revealed.

Thus it was possible for the American Left Wing to see the Bolshevik revolution in its own image. It could make itself believe that the Soviets were merely Russian equivalents of "industrial socialism" or "industrial unionism." When Harrison George joyfully embraced Bolshevism, he did so under the misapprehension that "the lesson of the Bolsheviki and the road to power of the I.W.W." were virtually one and the same, but the discovery of his error did not prevent him from becoming a Communist.[61] The same misunderstanding caused Arnold Petersen's premature adoption of the Bolshevik revolution. Unlike George, however, he drew back after the truth dawned on him.[62]

7

Roads to Moscow

To A growing number of American Left-Wingers events in Russia seemed closer than anything happening at home. Yet Russia was almost impossibly far away. The war and then the blockade made travel difficult and dangerous. Communications were cut down to a trickle. Anyone who could get to Russia and back in the first months of the Bolshevik revolution was assured of a sympathetic audience hungry for news from Russia—tales of suffering and heroism, glimpses of the new social order, an interview with Lenin himself.

The trek to Russia began very early in the course of the Russian Revolution, but it was mainly made by those who never expected to come back. In the middle of 1917, the State Secretary of the Socialist party of Massachusetts called attention to a novel problem. He complained about the loss of at least 500 members by the summer of that year. The reason he gave was unprecedented: they were returning to Russia.[1] In a hundred years, close to three and a half million Russian immigrants had poured into the United States, sometimes as many as a quarter of a million in a single year. Comparatively few chose to go back after 1917, but even a few thousand such cases signified a new Russian force in the world.

The Russian magnet also attracted a small group of Americans who had a professional reason for making the trip. They were forerunners of a new type in American journalism—foreign correspondents turned political missionaries. About half the pro-Soviet pamphlets available in the United States in 1918–19 were written by British or American journalists, M. Philips Price of the *Manchester Guardian*, Arthur Ransome of the London *Daily News*, and Albert Rhys Williams of *The Outlook*.[2] John Reed's book undoubtedly made more Soviet sympathizers than did all other Left Wing propaganda combined. Williams and Reed came back in 1918 and lectured up and down the country with an authority on Russian affairs that no other American could match.[3]

Four of the first Americans to see the Russian Revolution for themselves were foreign correspondents or writers. None of them was ever the same afterward. Yet each of them reacted to Russia in different ways. Their stories tell what Russia could do to some Americans.

Steffens

When the Progressive era came to a close, an old muckraker like Lincoln Steffens had a void to fill. Like many others, he filled it in Russia. He made his first trip to Russia in 1917 before the outbreak of the Bolshevik revolution and returned in 1919 with the Bullitt Mission sent officially to investigate post-revolutionary political and economic conditions. These trips made Steffens an intellectual convert to communism. He was disillusioned with the middle class. He was disillusioned with "honest government." He became a heroworshipper of the proletariat and of scientific revolutionaries.

A whole generation of American Communist intellectuals was weaned on an offhand remark by Steffens. After his return to the United States in 1919, Steffens happened to look in on the sculptor, Jo Davidson, while Bernard M. Baruch, the wartime economic administrator, sat for a portrait bust. "So you've been over in Russia?" said Baruch. "I have been over into the future, and it works," replied Steffens.[4] This casual comment traveled from mouth to mouth. It soon became one of the most seductive of Communist slogans in a streamlined version: "I have seen the Future, and it works."

Two things influenced Steffens. One was his own aching sense of emptiness and frustration with his liberal, muckraking past. The other was the contagious fervor and optimism of revolutionary Russia. Having lost confidence in himself, he was swept away by the confidence of the Bolsheviks in themselves. He considered himself too far gone and worn-out to become a Communist all the way. As he put it, he was content to stay in hell—then Paris—even though he knew where heaven was—Moscow.[5] He was by temperament an observer, satisfied to sit on the sidelines and send younger protégés and admirers into the battlefield. It was enough for him to lend a hand to the Communist cause by persuading himself and others that communism was inevitable, that it was the long-awaited scientific organization of society. In a letter of 1920, after his return from Russia, he admitted that he did not know what his own philosophy was; despite this slight void, he added that he was sure the future was in Russia.[6] Still later, Steffens saw the future in fascist Italy also. He admired Mussolini as well as Lenin because he thought both of them were "historically due."[7]

Yet Steffens became the great symbol of a liberal's conversion to communism in the Popular Front period in the 1930s. He served as American Communism's most valuable living link to the liberal age of the most recent past. By then, however, most Communists had forgotten—if they ever knew—that there had been two Communist images of Steffens: the sinner of the twenties and the saint of the thirties. Before Steffens became the model Communist liberal, he was the Communist model of a liberal laughing stock. As late as 1931, Michael Gold taunted him for going from war to war and movement to movement "with the exuberance of a drunk questing from speakeasy to speakeasy after new cocktails and new faces."[8] The first generation of American Communists gave Steffens no thanks for his services because, for most of his life, he cheered from the sidelines. Nevertheless, he was one of those whose personal influence over others makes them an extension of himself and enables him to give something through them which he cannot give himself.

Reed

If Steffens did not immediately go all the way to active participation in the Communist movement, the rest of the journey was traveled by his protégé, John Reed.

Twenty-one years separated Steffens and Reed in age, and the younger man could start where the older one had left off. Steffens had been a friend of Reed's father, a prosperous Portland, Oregon, businessman. When Reed in his early twenties was making his way as a young journalist in New York, Steffens still enjoyed the full success of his muckraking fame. Yet Reed shot ahead so fast that, in a few short years, they were like contemporaries, going through the same experiences together. In 1911 Steffens enabled Reed, then twenty-four, to get his first journalistic job. Two years later, both of them were reporting Pancho Villa's uprising across the Mexican border, with Reed gaining most of the journalistic glory.

If John Reed had deliberately arranged his life to contradict all the future clichés about Communists, he could not have done a more thorough job. He was not an immigrant; his grandfather had been one of the pioneer builders of Portland. He was not an Easterner; he came from the Far Northwest. He was not a poor boy; he was born into wealth and privilege. He was not self-educated; he attended private schools and Harvard. He was not a revolutionary turned journalist; he was a journalist turned revolutionary. Not a little of the attraction Reed had for the majority of the poor, immigrant Communists may be attributed to what he was, as well as to what he did. Communism was more than a movement of social outcasts if it could attract someone like Reed.

At Harvard, he showed little interest in politics and only occasionally attended meetings of the Socialist Club, then headed by Walter Lippmann. He preferred to be the football team's star cheerleader, urging the future Republican congressman, Hamilton Fish, Jr., on to greater glory as the team's star player. Steffens introduced the young poet and playboy to the world of radicals and nonconformists in New York. But Steffens was then no Socialist himself and did not exert the kind of influence that would lead to a political commitment. Reed was drawn into the radical movement by going beyond Steffens and associating with the more unconventional New York intellectuals who were closer to him in age and temperament.

Max Eastman gave Reed his first literary and political home in the *Masses* early in 1913. By the end of that year, they were putting out the magazine together, with Reed as managing editor, though he soon went off to make his reputation as war correspondent in Mexico and Europe for more commercial publications. For the next four years of the *Masses'* existence, however, the man and the magazine can hardly be separated. The *Masses* did not give Reed a political dogma because it did not have one itself. It provided him, as well as others, with a political climate, loose and disorderly enough for his still romantic and bohemian rebelliousness. It was also in 1913, as we have seen, that Reed was initiated into the class struggle by way of Mabel Dodge's salon, Bill Haywood, and the Paterson textile strike. The next important political experience in Reed's life was the Mexican revolution some months later. In it he found a strong man to admire, the swashbuckling Pancho Villa. Until the outbreak of the first World War, however, Reed's political education was spasmodic, emotional, and superficial. A strapping, fun-loving American boy in appearance, he was still playboy, poet, gilded youth, bohemian, and successful reporter.

The war, which he saw at close range on the eastern front for a few months in 1915, gave Reed his first profound, personal political cause. He was deeply, irreconcilably opposed to it, convinced that it represented merely a struggle between rival capitalist interests. Since the American press was almost totally prowar, he had to cut himself off from the important, lucrative assignments to which he had become accustomed. That he supported Wilson for the presidency in 1916 shows how far he still was from committing himself to any Left Wing political party or movement. But he was no ardent Wilsonian. He felt that he had to choose between "the lesser of two evils" because the Socialist party lacked "any real soul or vision." [9] More and more, as the war dragged on and his journalistic career suffered, he drew closer to the antiwar anarchists and Socialists. The third year of the war was perhaps the emptiest and dreariest which he had ever endured. He was dissatisfied with his work, disillusioned with many of his past associates, and discontented with the world in general. He was ripe for revolutionary Russia.

Soon after Lincoln Steffens came back from his first trip to Russia, Reed decided he belonged there. His imagination, his sympathies, his personal depression, and his interrupted career all impelled him toward the vast, turbulent upheaval which had overthrown a centuries-old tyranny and now struggled to extricate itself from the war. The decision to go to Russia was both escape and fulfillment.

Eastman scraped together the money, and he reached Petrograd in September 1917. Thus he had two months before the Bolsheviks seized power. These were the days that shook John Reed. He went to Russia purely as a journalist, but he was not a pure journalist. He could not resist identifying himself with underdogs, especially if they followed strong, ruthless leaders. Reed was first and foremost a great reporter, but he was at his best reporting a cause he could make his own. For the *Masses,* this was not only possible but necessary, and he did his finest work for it. It took him only a single week to become a partisan of the Bolsheviks, hardly enough time to entitle him to hold strong views about a country whose history he knew only sketchily and whose language he knew not at all.[10] Yet Reed was nobody's fool and his quick choice was as much inherent in the situation as in himself. Tourists and journalists have to make up their minds in a hurry or not at all. As Reed ran from meeting to meeting, interviewed one leading politician after another, the boldness, the zeal, the unbounded promises of the Bolsheviks overwhelmed him. That Lenin and his followers were able to impress an American radical like John Reed so quickly is perhaps one indication of what enabled them to impress so many people all over the world.

Reed stayed in Russia six months. For the first time in his life he made a real political commitment. He went to work in the Bureau of International Revolutionary Propaganda. He made speeches as an American revolutionary sympathizer. Just how far he was willing to go in adherence to the new regime was shown before his departure. Trotsky proposed Reed as Bolshevik Consul General in New York, and he was actually appointed. But evidently Reed, whose imagination sometimes ran riot with half-formed, grandiose projects of all sorts, from making money to making revolutions, conceived of some scheme for putting American money to work for the Bolsheviks.[11] Reed's plan was prematurely divulged to Lenin, who was alarmed by its capitalistic implications, and the consular appointment was abruptly cancelled. The incident ended unhappily on both sides; it was Reed's first disappointment with his new political affiliation. But the reason for the cancellation was less significant than the reason for the appointment. That an American should go home as the consul general of a foreign power appeared to both the Bolsheviks and Reed as a triumph of revolutionary internationalism. The line between what was Russian and what was revolutionary was still so indistinct that Reed was more upset by the cancellation than astonished by the appointment.

Instead, Reed went home in the spring of 1918 with something more important—his notes and his memories of the Bolshevik revolution. As his biographer puts it, Reed's next steps were "natural stages in the transition from the task of giving information about Bolshevism in Russia to the task of organizing Bolshevism in America."[12] Indeed, there was almost no transition, because organizing Bolshevism in America consisted mainly of propagandizing about Bolshevism in Russia. This was why a newcomer like Reed—he did not join the Socialist party until the summer of 1918—could forge ahead so rapidly and immediately play such a leading role in the Left Wing. He had one inestimable advantage over old-timers like Fraina, Lore, and Boudin: he had been there. He had seen it with his own eyes. He had talked on terms of intimacy with Lenin and Trotsky. As a public speaker, Reed was more in demand than any other Left Wing figure, and with his native-born, educated accent and slouching, pants-hitching, boyish charm, he could reach people none of the others could. The newspapers and general public treated him as if he were the No. 1 American Bolshevik, a reputation which he had hardly earned, but which fed his growing political ambition.

Of all the first Communists, Reed was the hardest to classify. That he was capable of becoming a Communist leader of the first rank despite his family background, his education and upbringing, his anarchistic and pleasure-loving temperament, can serve as a warning against all easy generalizations about how Communists are made, where they come from, how they should behave, and why they should be converted. A movement capable of converting Reed had potentialities which cannot be too simply dismissed with a formula. Yet a movement which had to convert him in Russia in conditions so foreign to anything he had known at home had in store some unpleasant surprises.

Minor

Another American, Robert Minor, came to Russia in 1918 but, unlike Reed, was not carried away and converted on the spot.

On his father's side, General John Minor had served as Thomas Jefferson's campaign manager for the presidency. On his mother's side he was related to General Sam Houston, first president of the Texas Republic. But Robert Minor was not born into any American aristocracy. He was brought into the world of the hard-up, run-down middle class in an "unpainted frontier cottage" in San Antonio. His strong-minded mother was a physician's daughter, his "dreamy, improvident" father a lawyer by profession. He left school at the age of fourteen and home two years later, working at farming, railroading, carpentering, riding freight trains and living on handouts. It was the half-hobo, half-migratory-worker experience of the I.W.W. rank and file in the Southwest. A self-trained genius for drawing enabled him, at twenty, to escape from this harsh, uncertain proletarian existence. From a small San Antonio paper he made the jump to the

St. Louis *Post-Dispatch*. Seven years later, in 1911, his official biographer says, he was the highest paid cartoonist in the country. The family's fortunes also rose. An election the year before had transformed his father from an unsuccessful lawyer to an influential district judge.[13]

Minor came to communism by way of socialism and anarchism. His interest in radicalism arose after his material circumstances had improved. When he was still a carpenter, two members of the union tried to talk to him about socialism without making any impression. But after his cartooning career started in St. Louis, he consulted a doctor about his increasing deafness. The doctor gave him Socialist propaganda along with medical treatments. Whenever Minor tried to explain why he joined the Socialist party in 1907, he made this coincidence paramount. His Socialist activity made a place for him on the City Central Committee. Five years later, however, socialism gave way to anarchism. His anarchist period began about 1912 when he sympathized with Haywood in the inner-party struggle and became fully formed the following year when he went to Paris to study art. He quickly rebelled against the academic instruction but easily absorbed the anarcho-syndicalist philosophy that flourished in the studios and garrets of Montparnasse and Montmartre. When he came back to New York to work for the *Evening World,* he was a full-fledged, outspoken anarchist. Bill Haywood was his hero and Alexander Berkman his bosom friend and teacher. The European war broke out that year and Minor was able to draw his brawny, massive cartoons sprawled over a quarter of the editorial page without compromising his political conscience. Fortunately for him, the Pulitzers' editorial policy was antiwar. Unfortunately for him, it did not remain so.

At this point, Minor and Reed faced the same problem. The war came athwart their professional careers. When Minor was asked to draw prowar cartoons for the *Evening World* in 1915, he had to choose between his job and his convictions—and he chose his convictions. He immediately shifted to the Socialist *Call,* which was glad to get a famous cartoonist even if he was an anarchist and ex-

Socialist. But Minor was no longer content to express himself with pictures only. Minor the cartoonist became Minor the war correspondent. After his return from Europe, he was ready to take his first step as a political organizer. The opportunity came in 1916 when he was suddenly called on to lead a campaign to save the lives of people of whom, as he later admitted, he had never heard before.[14] The California labor leaders, Tom Mooney and Warren K. Billings, and three other defendants were accused of dynamiting a "Preparedness" parade in San Francisco. Minor organized the first Mooney defense committee, wrote the first pro-Mooney pamphlet, and did more than any other single man to save the defendants. The Mooney-Billings case was much more than a landmark in the development of one future Communist. It was a crisis of conscience for Minor's generation of radicals. Not a few young men traced their active participation in the radical movement to righteous indignation at the plight of Mooney and Billings.

Minor went to Russia for nine months in 1918. He was then thirty-four, a huge man with extraordinarily bushy eyebrows, intensely staring eyes, and a booming voice. He looked at the Bolshevik reality through the eyes of a convinced anarchist, and it repelled him. Though Lenin himself tried to win him over, he remained unmoved. When he left Russia, he published a famous interview with Lenin in the New York *World,* which he later claimed had been tampered with but which he did not deny reflected his basic attitude. It commented on Lenin's remark that the Soviet system was first formulated by Daniel De Leon in the form of industrial unionism: "There is no more industrial unionism in Lenin's highly centralized institutions than in the United States Post Office. What he calls industrial unionism is nothing but nationalized industry in the highest degree of centralization." It compared the old and new economic administrators with bitter disillusionment: "There is a difference now. The business types ride in fine automobiles as before, live in fine mansions, and are again managing the old industries, with more authority than ever before. Now they are 'People's Commissaries'—servants of the proletariat—and the iron discipline of the army under red flags has been developed in order to protect them against all annoyance. A rose smells as sweetly to them under any other name." [15]

This disenchantment with an all-powerful state was to be expected of an orthodox militant anarchist like Minor. Berkman and Emma Goldman went through it the following year.

Completely unexpected was the sequel. A year and a half later, Minor changed his mind. He tried to explain why he did so in an article which is intellectually incredible and psychologically fascinating.[16] Since Minor had no political finesse, he put down his thoughts with unashamed and disarming naïveté.

Minor told how, after leaving Soviet Russia "far from clear" about the Russian Revolution, he was "bothered with the elusive impression that a great natural law was at work which I did not understand." No one ever tried to explain this "natural law" as primitively as Minor did: "It was plain that the Russian Revolution had set this current in motion, and that its form was predetermined somewhere in the origin of the race." He also asked: "What strange power has Lenin? Why does every adversary, one by one, fall before him?" He explained: "The answer is that Lenin is a scientist in an unscientific world." In a previous age, Minor might have venerated Lenin as a prophet or even as a wizard. In the twentieth century, he worshipped Lenin the Scientist.

In an age of science, the great masses of men, even educated men, marvel at the revelations of science without understanding them. The least scientific of men, like Steffens, Minor, Floyd Dell, and Max Eastman, artists by nature, made a cult of communism by identifying it with the cult of science. "There will be something almost supernatural in the hold upon historic forces that Marxian science and the philosophy of change will give into the hands of this man," wrote Eastman of Lenin.[17] To Dell, Lenin represented a "scientifically daring, mathematically confident social-engineering genius." [18] They sought something in the "science" of communism which they did not have in themselves. What really captivated them was the mysticism, not the science, or perhaps the mysticism of science. When they permitted themselves to tell what it was that really fascinated them about communism, as Minor honestly and painfully tried to do on this occasion, the mystical element could not be concealed. It was no less mystical because it substituted for older mysteries the mysteries of science.

The identification of communism and science was also another way of paying tribute to the Russian Revolution as a practical success. In 1918, when the fate of the revolution was still very much in doubt, Minor was not particularly impressed, though he was there in immediate contact with the revolutionary reality. But by 1920, when its survival seemed assured, all those who considered themselves revolutionaries were confronted with the choice of associating themselves with the one successful revolution or remaining with frustrating little movements that had nothing but practical failures to their credit. What made the Russian Revolution seem so scientific was primarily its success, since by any other standard, such as the predictability of its development, it was more nearly a work of improvisation. The confusion was between something which "worked" because it was scientific and something which was scientific because it "worked," as if only science can make something "work."

In this respect, Minor's development was just the opposite of Reed's, though their ideas were not so far apart at the start. Reed was immediately won over by the physical presence of the revolution and went further away from it as time passed. Minor was not immediately won over but came closer to it as time passed.

Yet Minor had to reconcile his anarchist ideals of liberty and antistatism with his new Russian passion. He did it in such a way that he managed to change more than his ideas did. As an anarchist, he had rejected the dictatorship of the proletariat because it was based on a centralized, all-powerful, tyrannical form of state rule. Ironically, the ex-anarchist was still of the same opinion. "The dictatorship of the Proletariat is not liberty, nor an instrument of liberty," he declared. "It is tyranny. It is a State." He repeated: "A State has but one way of functioning—by curtailing liberty." He thought that the problem was solved by reading in the Marxist classics that the proletarian state was destined to "wither away." Short of that remote faith, however, Minor's views on the tyranny of the Soviet dictatorship did not change; only his own relationship to that tyranny changed.

Minor is a study in extremes. A truly gifted and powerful cartoonist, he renounced art for politics. He made this gesture of total subservience to politics after years as an anarchist despising and denouncing politics. But he could not transfer his genius from art to politics. The stirring drawings were replaced by boring and banal speeches. Since he had none of the gifts of the natural politician, his stock in trade was limited to platitudes and slogans. The wild man, tamed, became a political hack. If as an anarchist he had believed that politics was a filthy business, as a Communist he still seemed to believe it was—only now it was his business.

Eastman

Steffens went to Russia and converted others. Reed went to Russia and immediately converted himself. Minor went to Russia, refused to be converted there, but changed his mind at home. Eastman went to Russia already converted and came back unconverted.

Max Eastman also came from good, old American stock. He could trace his genealogy back to the Puritans. Daniel Webster's name appeared on one of the outlying branches of the family tree. His background, like Reed's, was a most unlikely one for a future devotee of Lenin. Both his father and his mother were Congregationalist ministers.

In his twenties, Eastman came to New York, taught philosophy at Columbia University, wrote poetry, made speeches for woman suffrage and ended up a Socialist, a very revolutionary Socialist. His political career started in earnest when the *Masses* was reorganized at the end of 1912 with himself as the new editor. For the next ten years, he lived and worked at the center of the half-artistic, half-political Left Wing. He held together the most remarkable collection of rebels and revolutionists in many decades. The younger revolutionary intellectuals idolized him. One of the most sensitive, Joseph Freeman, then twenty, attended a meeting in 1917 at which Eastman, then thirty-four, spoke. "He looked Beauty and spoke Justice," Freeman recalled many years later.[19] "The intellectual development of Max Eastman is the story of all healthy, idealistic minds," wrote young Mike Gold in 1918.[20] As late as 1926, Gold volunteered that Eastman and Floyd Dell, the associate editor of the *Masses* and its successor, *The Liberator,* were "the best teachers youth could have found during those years." [21]

Eastman had taught that Lenin was a "statesman of the new order," the living embodiment of Plato's philosopher-king.[22] When Romain Rolland issued a "Declaration of Intellectual Independence" calling on all intellectuals to recognize no master other than "the Mind," Eastman had taught that intellectuals had to place themselves on the side of the class-conscious proletariat.[23] When Henri Barbusse took the initiative to form an independent organization of revolutionary intellectuals, Eastman had taught that "the [Communist] party is the only *organization,* the only corporate source of intellectual guidance." [24]

But Eastman and Dell had one foot in an older order. They could never give themselves over wholly to politics. Eastman was capable of writing on "Bolshevik Problems" and "China's Paintings" within four pages of each other.[25] During the *Masses* trial, Dell used to ask himself, "Why am I not at home writing a story?" [26] Nor could they give themselves over wholly to a party. In his very answer to Barbusse in favor of the Communist party's exclusive intellectual guidance, Eastman remarked that he could not submit to "the official control of a party." [27] He always kept sufficient distance from the party to enable him to criticize it as a kind of disinterested sympathizer. Rolland and Barbusse went on to become faithful servitors of communism in the spirit of Eastman's replies to them; Eastman did not take his own advice. For Dell, the break with communism took the form of a rebellion against the tyranny of politics. "As a citizen, I would always be passionately interested in the political destinies of mankind," he wrote later, "and as an artist, I would always find in my political hopes a stimulus to creative effort. But, as an artist, I felt the wish to detach myself from the immediate and daily anxieties of the political situation, and to renew my contacts with the ageless and timeless aspects of nature, which afford a deep refreshment to the restless mind." [28]

The teachers did not take their own teachings as seriously as some of their students did. Some of the early Communists wore their politics like a hairshirt. If it was necessary to choose between politics and his art, Minor gave up art. If it was necessary to choose between politics and music, Israel Amter sacrificed his career as a pianist. "Let us fling all we are into the cauldron of the Revolution," cried Gold.[29] But Eastman published a volume of nonpolitical poetry a year after the Bolshevik revolution.[30] Dell gave up communism for marriage, fatherhood, and personal expression in literature.

In the spring of 1920, the readers of *The Liberator* were delighted to find a pro-Soviet article by Bertrand Russell. The distinguished British philosopher came out strongly for the victory of International Socialism, even if it could not be achieved by peaceful means. "When I speak of Socialism," Russell added, "I do not mean a milk-and-water system, but a thorough-going, root-and-branch transformation, such as Lenin has attempted." [31] But Russell soon made a trip to the Soviet Union. He came back thoroughly disillusioned. He wrote in *The Nation* about his dislike for what he found,—among other things, the concentration of power in a few men, the symptoms of future Soviet imperialism, the danger of a "Bonapartist military autocracy." His indictment of the Soviet system strikingly anticipated the vast literature of future Communist disillusionment.[32]

Eastman and Dell counterattacked in favor of the Soviets. They answered Russell the way many other disillusioned Communist sympathizers were to be answered. Eastman accused Russell of "a degree of the fantastic, of sheer professorial gullibility, in his manner of swallowing down the whole established Menshevik propaganda—lies, truths, and true lies, and lying truths, all together—which makes it quite certain that he found his place among the Mensheviks *before* this intellectual process began." Dell dismissed Russell as "a familiar Russian phenomenon. The political woods in Russia are full of people like that. Under the label of Menshevik, Right Social Revolutionist,

Left Social Revolutionist, and Anarchist, they have been cluttering up the progress of Russian history for the past three years." [33]

Two years later, Eastman himself went to Russia "to find out whether what I have been saying is true." He was received as a trusted and devoted friend. Trotsky agreed to cooperate with him on a book about his youth. At just about this time, however, the campaign against Trotsky was launched by Stalin, Zinoviev, and others in the Russian Communist party. Eastman was able to watch it develop at peculiarly close range. Trotsky encouraged him to leave the country with documents designed to expose the internal Russian struggle for power. When Eastman's book, *Since Lenin Died,* came out in 1925, the official Communist movement forgot all about his great contribution in the preceding decade and turned on him with the venom reserved for former comrades in arms. At this time, Eastman defended Trotsky in the name of true Leninism. It would take him another fourteen years to shake off the allegiance to Lenin's basic objectives. But Eastman was one of the very first to realize the implications of Trotsky's downfall. No other American Communist or sympathizer saw so clearly that the attack on Trotsky signified "a dictatorship of the officialdom within the Communist Party," and no one else did so much so soon to make it known.[34]

Trotsky continued to haunt the Communist intellectuals. Even after Eastman's book appeared, Gold could not resist extolling Trotsky as "almost as universal as Leonardo da Vinci." [35] As late as 1930, Gold wrote, among some tritely derogatory remarks, that "Trotsky is now an immortal part of the great Russian Revolution. He is surely one of the permanent legends of humanity, like Savonarola or Danton." [36] Even later, in 1936, what Freeman wrote about Trotsky enraged the Stalinist regime. Self-pride and aloofness were the worst sins that Freeman could bring himself to hold against Trotsky in his autobiography, *An American Testament,* one of the few Communist human documents worth preserving. But other passages—such as this one: "You could not question his [Trotsky's] great intellectual powers, his character, his integrity, his devotion to the cause, nor his brilliant services to it—" [37] were regarded more seriously in Russia. Literally on orders from Moscow, Freeman was excommunicated.

The teacher did not permit the party to become "the only corporate source of intellectual guidance." Eastman supported an individual and a principle against the main body of the party. But, meanwhile, the doctrine of party "guidance" had become so deeply ingrained in some of his younger disciples that they could not follow his example. What Russell had divined almost at the outset came to Eastman a few years later and to Freeman still later. It did not help Eastman that Russell had told him so, or Freeman that Eastman had told him so. Each generation has gone through the process of Communist infatuation and disillusionment in its own way, and yet the same way.

8

The Revolutionary Age

MEANWHILE, in the first months of the Revolution, few native Americans could make the trip to Russia. The rest of the Left Wing had to find its inspiration at home.

As long as *The New International* carried the main burden of propaganda for the Left Wing, no great progress was possible. The Socialist Propaganda League was too small and poor to be able to put its paper out regularly, though it claimed to have twenty branches in twelve states by the summer of 1917.[1] At first the paper appeared every two weeks, but lack of funds forced a suspension of publication between July 21 and October 1, 1917, the very period the Bolsheviks in Russia were rapidly moving toward the seizure of power. The paper reappeared as a monthly for two months, then it took three more months to get out a number on February 1, 1918, and two more months for the last number of April, 1918.

The Boston Left Wing was able to lead the way for another year by capturing control of the official Socialist city organization. As a result, in the spring of 1918, the Boston City Committee decided to call Fraina to take charge of its educational work.[2] When he moved from New York to Boston, the propaganda center of the Left Wing moved with him. By the end of the year, he was able to put out a successor to *The New International*. As the official organ of the Boston local of the Socialist party, *The Revolutionary Age* came out in November 1918.[3] It was scheduled to appear three times a week, but it was never able to do better than twice a week, and it soon became a weekly. Compared to its predecessor, however, it was a solid institution. The Letts were still "the core of the Left Wing," as even the Russian *Novy Mir* had to admit,[4] though their leader, Rosin, had returned to Europe. In his native Latvia, he served as the first head of the short-lived revolutionary government.[5] Subsequently, he rose to one of the highest posts in the new Russian regime, the Central Executive Committee of the Soviets.[6] His death in 1919 cut short a promising revolutionary career.

The staff of *The Revolutionary Age* indicated some of the changes that had been taking place in the Left Wing. Fraina remained as editor, but Eadmonn MacAlpine came in as associate editor. The contributing editors were Scott Nearing, John Reed, Nicholas I. Hourwich, Ludwig Lore, Sen Katayama, and Gregory Weinstein. Nearing was a young Socialist economics teacher whose dismissal from the Wharton School of Economics of the University of Pennsylvania and from the University of Toledo had been *causes célèbres* of academic freedom during the war. Of the eight, he and Reed were the only native Americans. Lore was about to become editor of the German Socialist organ following the death of Hermann Schlüter, the long-time patriarch of German Socialist journalism in the United States.[7] Katayama's name added some international luster to the list, though the old man was hardly able to contribute much practical assistance. Of greatest interest, however, were the two new Russian names, Weinstein and Hourwich, the editor and associate editor of the *Novy Mir* respectively. They were fast emerging as the strong men of the Left Wing as a result of the swing of the great majority of Russian Socialist immigrants to the Bolshevik side.

Nothing was more revealing of the spirit that motivated *The Revolutionary Age* than its subtitle: "A Chronicle and Interpretation of Events in Europe." The first four issues lived up to this promise. They did not contain a word about anything happening in the United States. The imminent upheaval in Germany claimed first attention. All the news from Central Europe seemed an echo from the east. Germany was teetering on the brink of revolution, just as the Bolsheviks had

THE REVOLUTIONARY AGE 133

been predicting. And after Germany, there appeared to be plenty of other candidates for the next eruption. "Europe is seething, Europe is a-fire," exulted a front-page summary of "The Trend of Socialism in Europe" at the end of 1918. Bolshevism in Austria was sweeping onward almost as rapidly as in Germany. Strikes, riots and demonstrations had broken out in Switzerland, Holland, Sweden, Denmark, and Spain. The Socialist movement was being driven to the extreme Left in Italy, France, England, Ireland, and Norway.[8] Closer home, Mexico was seething with its own peculiar brand of revolution. Some American Left-Wingers took refuge in Mexico to escape from the war, and the Mexican Revolution seemed to them like an extension of the Russian Revolution.

Fraina's head was then almost completely in Europe. In 1918, he had lost himself in the Russian Revolution. In 1919, he flung himself into the German revolution. From his pen came a series of long articles on Germany which became the basis of another book, his third in three years.[9] His front-page manifestoes thundered exultantly. The first one began as follows: "In these most glorious of all glorious days in history, when thrones and Capitalism are crumbling and the workers determining to become the masters of the world, the glory of it all is the despair and the gloom of the tyrants of capital and industry everywhere, who feel their supremacy tottering to its end."[10]

Before the year was out, *The Revolutionary Age* had published "A Letter to American Workingmen" by Lenin. Despite the pressure of the German army and the civil war raging in Russia, Lenin went to the trouble of sending a special appeal to the United States, and it was far from perfunctory. He used it as a vehicle for discussing some of the most pressing questions of the moment as well as his more fundamental program. Incidentally, he revealed fewer illusions about the American future than most of his American disciples had. "We know it may take a long time before help can come from you, comrades, American Workingmen," he wrote, "for the development of the revolution in the different countries proceeds along various paths, with varying rapidity (how could it be otherwise!)." But when his American readers came to the end and read, "We are invincible, for invincible is the Proletarian Revolution," they could be stirred to their depths by the monumental confidence of a revolutionary victor addressing himself to his future peers.[11]

All this was real enough to Lenin then, and yet it was only a substitute for reality to Americans. American Communism was born in the storm and stress of a revolutionary period. The time was authentically revolutionary. Revolution was authentic in Russia, in Germany, in Hungary. In America it was vicarious. As long as the would-be American Bolsheviks kept their eyes fastened on Europe, there was more than enough to sustain them in all their hopes and dreams and fantasies of the world revolution that was not going to leave them out once it had started on its ponderous way. This preoccupation with the revolutionary wave in Europe was the source as much of their strength as of their weakness. It gave them the strength of profound faith and optimism. It gave them the weakness of future disorientation and debasement.

Reed's premonition

An important part of the story of American Communism might be described as a struggle between a glittering Communist dream and a stubborn American reality. This struggle was personified at different times by different people. One of the first to give it expression, even if as little more than a premonition, was John Reed.

Although he was devoting most of his time to writing and speaking about the Russian Revolution, Reed's lecture trips at the end of 1918 and beginning of 1919 provided him with some unusual food for thought about his own country. His sense of reality as a reporter never deserted him, or perhaps he was still new enough to the movement to be able to look around him with a fresh eye. In any case, he made one of the earliest efforts to cope with the blasphemous idea that somehow American conditions and American workers were disturbingly different.

He tackled it in a somewhat sardonic way six months after his return from Russia. Ironically entitled, "Bolshevism in America," he began with tongue-in-cheek gusto: "In response to anxious queries from our capitalist acquaintances as to the danger of a Bolshevik Revolution in the United States within the next two weeks, we wish to settle the question once for all." He tried to settle it in this vein: "The American working class is politically and economically the most uneducated working class in the world. It believes what it reads in the capitalist press. It believes that the wage-system is ordained by God. It believes that Charley Schwab is a great man, because he can make money. It believes that Samuel Gompers and the American Federation of Labor will protect it as much as it can be protected. It believes that under our system of Government the Millennium is possible. When the Democrats are in power, it believes the promises of the Republicans, and vice versa. It believes that Labor laws mean what they say. It is prejudiced against Socialism." [12]

No one else wrote like this in the Left Wing press at the end of 1918. That Reed was not entirely joking was shown by another article written in deadly earnest. He asked why the American worker was more attracted to the A.F. of L. or the I.W.W. than to the American Socialist party which, he said contemptuously, was composed of American clerks, shopkeepers, administrative officers of small business, a few farmers, some journalists, foreign-born workers, and intellectuals. Out of his efforts to cope with this problem, one major and not entirely original thought emerged—the American worker respected and heeded "practical" programs and organizations only. The A.F. of L., the I.W.W., and the newly formed Labor party movement could win the support of men who worked with their hands because they held out practical rewards and achievements. The Socialist party failed to win over the American worker for two reasons. "In the first place, he probably doesn't like Socialism, which means to him only a system worked out in foreign countries, not born of his own particular needs and opposed to 'democracy' and 'fair play,' which is the way he has been taught to characterize the institutions of this country. In the second place, if he has become conscious of his *class* interests, voting for the Socialist party seems to him *impractical*. 'They won't win,' he says, 'it will just be "throwing away my vote." ' "

Reed's direct impressions of the American scene were his own; his solution of the problem was the orthodox one of the entire Left Wing. He had no patience with the "Menshevik appeal" that American socialism was really "Jeffersonian democracy" interested only in reasonable reforms, labor legislation, and the full dinnerpail. He scornfully attributed a third of the Socialist vote to middle-class persons "who think that Karl Marx wrote a good Anti-Trust Law." With this kind of propaganda he had no quarrel, except that he did not think that it made Socialists. What would? "My idea is to make Socialists," he answered, "and there is only one way of doing that—by teaching Socialism, straight Socialism, revolutionary Socialism, international Socialism. This is what the Russian Bolsheviki did; this is what the German Spartacus group did." In the last analysis, then, Reed also fell back on the European experience, after he had labored so hard to demonstrate that there was something different and peculiar about the American worker. It seemed as if he were willing to leave all the practical tasks to the A.F. of L., the I.W.W., and the Labor party, and save the ultimatist, millennial role for the revolutionary Socialists. Yet, before he was through, he caught himself and tried to reconcile the two:

Revolutionary Socialism, above all other kinds, must be *practical*—it must *work*—it must make *Socialists* out of workers, and make them quick.

Comrades who call themselves "members of the Left Wing" have an immediate job to do. They must find out from the *American workers* what they want most, and they must explain this in terms of the whole Labor Movement, and they must make the workers want more—make them want the whole Revolution.

They must do this in words which can be understood immediately by the workers, in terms of their own lives.[13]

It can hardly be said that Reed solved or settled anything. His instincts were taking him in a strange, new direction and when he went too far, he recoiled from the most troublesome implications.

He never really grappled with the problem of how the Left Wing could be "revolutionary" and "practical" at the same time in American terms. Unlike almost all the others at this time, however, he felt and stated it. He was not intellectually equipped then and he did not live long enough to push the frontiers of this age-old revolutionary problem much farther. He went as far as he did because he had an uninhibited, stubborn streak in him.

Spreading out

By the end of 1918, the slow, hard spadework of the Left Wing began to pay off.

It had taken a while for the full significance of the Russian Revolution to sink in. The odds against the Bolsheviks' holding on to power had seemed even greater than those against their seizing it. But when a year went by and they managed to survive, the wavering sympathizers were more willing to commit themselves in action. This was especially true among the Russian immigrants, who had a most practical reason for demonstrating their good will to the new Russian regime. If they had any intention of returning home, the first step on the long journey was a token of support for the revolution in their homeland.

The clearest and most direct way to subscribe to the Russian Revolution in the United States, was, first, to join the Socialist party, and, second, to join the Left Wing within the Socialist party. From 80,379 in 1917, the membership of the party increased to 104,822 in 1919, the second highest point in its history. But this marked increase was accompanied by a curious and most revealing disproportion, which betrayed the fact that something outside the Socialist party and the United States was largely responsible for the influx of new members.

The trouble was most clearly visible in the growing ratio of the foreign-language federations to the total Socialist membership. From about 40 per cent in 1917, the federations rose to 53 per cent in the middle of 1919.[14] The most spectacular gain was registered by the

Russian federation. It had not been formed until 1915, an indication that the Russian immigrants before the revolution were far from the most Socialist-minded group. Yet its average membership shot up from only 792 for the year ending March 1918 to 3,985 for the year ending March 1919.[15] When Gregory Weinstein, editor of the Russian organ, *Novy Mir,* was nominated for the Socialist New York state committee early in 1919, he was disqualified because he had not been a party member for as much as two years.[16] Nevertheless, the Russian federation in general, and Weinstein in particular, became the most arrogant and vociferous force within the Left Wing as it moved to win control of the Socialist party.

In Chicago, where the Slavic influence was particularly strong, the Left Wing organized itself in November 1918, on the first anniversary of the Bolshevik revolution, as the Communist Propaganda League, with Isaac E. Ferguson as secretary.[17] The use of the word "Communist" showed how far the Left Wing had traveled since the formative days of the Socialist Propaganda League in Boston three years before.

The most interesting American figure in the Communist Propaganda League was William Bross Lloyd, son of the Populist intellectual, Henry Demarest Lloyd. Through his mother, William Bross Lloyd inherited a sixteenth-share of the Chicago *Tribune,* which her father, William Bross, a former lieutenant governor of Illinois, had helped to found.[18] William Bross Lloyd took a step beyond his father into the Socialist party and ran for senator on the Socialist ticket in Illinois in 1918. When he went over to the Left Wing, the embryonic American Communist movement acquired its first millionnaire, but could not keep him for long. He became a rabidly anti-Roosevelt Republican in the nineteen-thirties.

Isaac E. Ferguson came from a totally different social milieu. The son of a Jewish butcher in Winnipeg, Canada, he graduated from the University of Chicago Law School and once ran for office in Wyoming on the Republican ticket. He found himself in the Socialist party early in 1918 because William Bross Lloyd hired him as "literary secretary" to assist in the senatorial campaign.[19] Before the

THE REVOLUTIONARY AGE 139

year was out, Ferguson had progressed as far as the Communist Propaganda League.

The postwar atmosphere in the labor movement as a whole also helped the Left Wing. A series of big, unusually turbulent strikes erupted all over the country. Three of them were raging simultaneously in February 1919. In Seattle, Washington, the first American general strike closed down the entire city. In Lawrence, Massachusetts, over 30,000 textile workers shut down every mill in the city for sixteen weeks. In Butte, Montana, for the third time in three years, the miners walked out in rebellion against a wage cut. In some places, the terminology of the Russian Revolution was noticeable. In Butte, the strike was controlled by "The Soldiers', Sailors' and Workers' Council" to which every union except that of the engineers was affiliated.[20] In Portland, Oregon, John Reed's birthplace, a "Council of Workers, Soldiers, and Sailors" was formed "to strike the final blow against the capitalist class."[21] The Portland "Soviet" inspired the *Soviet World* of Philadelphia to predict the birth within the next two years of the Socialist Soviet Republic of the United States of America.[22] Both "Soviets" expired with the strikes. Only the Lawrence strike succeeded in winning any concessions for the workers, but for a while the whole labor movement seemed to be rocking with a spirit of revolt.

The younger generation

In the struggle that developed to take over New York, a new Left Wing group came to the fore.

The situation in New York was almost a battle of the boroughs. The Brooklyn local had for years been a stronghold of the Left Wing. Among its members were Boudin, Lore, Rutgers, and Edward I. Lindgren, all of them long-time, highly respected spokesmen of the old Left Wing. The Queens local, with Fred Briehl, and the Bronx local, with Benjamin Gitlow and others, also could be swung over to the Left. But the New York local (Manhattan) was, as one of the earliest Communist papers complained, "the citadel of Right Wing resistance." [23] It was the center of Morris Hillquit's personal influence. Its executive secretary, Julius Gerber, fought the Left Wing by every means in his power. As long as the Right Wing held on to the New York county organization, it more than counterbalanced Left Wing strength in the outlying boroughs.

Boudin and Lore were typical of the older Left Wing which antedated the Bolshevik revolution. They were now in their mid-forties, too independent and experienced to succumb easily to a sudden vogue, even one as potent as the Russian Revolution. The Socialist movement had suffered so much from splits that Lore shrank from inviting another one. Boudin was totally disqualified by his fundamental reservations about the historical justification for the Bolshevik revolution. Such men could not keep pace with the Left Wing that the revolution brought into existence.

The new Left Wing was typified by younger men with fewer inhibitions. Outstanding among them for the next few years were Benjamin Gitlow, Bertram D. Wolfe, William W. Weinstone, and Jay Lovestone.

Gitlow, the senior in both years and political experience, was only twenty-eight years old in 1919. The son of poor Russian-Jewish immigrants, he spent his childhood in the grimmest poverty. The boy grew up in a home filled with stories of the Russian Socialist movement—its heroes, their experiences in prison and Siberian exile, their dreams of a future paradise on earth. He was a full-fledged Socialist at eighteen and, shortly after, head of the Retail Clerks Union of New York. Soon the gust of Big Bill Haywood's syndicalist heresy swept through the Socialist party and young Gitlow was drawn into I.W.W. activity, though he did not go all the way with Haywood on the subject of violence. Not content to remain a clerk, he spent a couple of years studying law.[24] This varied experience led to his nomination for assemblyman on the Socialist ticket in the Bronx in 1917 and he was one of the ten New York Socialists elected that year. Gitlow had put in almost a decade of Socialist activity and enjoyed the prestige of an elective office when the Russian Revolution hit him with full force and caused him, in the spring of 1918, to throw in his lot with the revolutionary Left Wing.

Wolfe was American-born of a German immigrant father and an American-born mother also of German family background. At the College of the City of New York in the early war years, his first political interest took the form of pacifism rather than socialism. But his pacifist activity led him to take an active part in Morris Hillquit's campaign for mayor in 1917, and he became one of the outstanding young speakers in the Brooklyn local of the Socialist party. After a year teaching high school and a year at law school, he went to work as publicity director of the Rand School for Social Science, the intellectual center of socialism in New York, at the time the pro-Communist Left Wing was taking shape. Soon he was caught up in the enthusiasm that flowed out of the Russian Revolution and completed the cycle from pacifism to communism. Yet, at this stage, he thought that the secret of the revolution was to be found in the works of De Leon, not Lenin.[25]

Weinstone and Lovestone—twenty-two and twenty-one respectively in 1919—came from Russia as children and embraced socialism in their teens. Lovestone was also a former De Leonite. Unlike virtually all the other early Communist leaders, their radical apprenticeship was served in the student movement. They were leaders together of the Intercollegiate Socialist Society's chapter at the College of the City of New York.[26] It was not literally true, as was sometimes said disparagingly, that they went from City College into the leadership of the American Communist movement, but the statement was close enough to hurt at a time when the student movement did not rank high as a preparatory school for Communist leadership. In the three years between Lovestone's graduation from City College in 1918 and his first full-time job in the Communist movement, he studied accountancy and law, and held various short-term jobs such as statistician and social worker.

Most of the others in the up-and-coming New York group were more or less of similar background. They included Dr. Maximilian Cohen, a dentist; Joseph Brodsky, a lawyer, and his brother Carl;

Rose Wortis, a dressmaker; and Harry M. Winitsky. They had a number of things strikingly in common: almost all were in their twenties, some in their very early twenties; they were mostly Jewish; they came over from Russia as children or were first-generation Americans of Russian-Jewish parents; they became active in the Socialist movement in their late teens and were generally about twenty or a little older at the time of the Russian Revolution. The Right Wing in New York was not very different in social background, but it had many more older people with a much longer record in the party. The indignity suffered by the older Right Wing Socialists who had devoted the best part of their lives to the party and now found themselves being told in no uncertain terms what real socialism stood for, by young extremists, some of them in the party for no more than a year or two, embittered the party struggle.

The uncomfortable Center

An influential little group held on to a very precarious position in between the major factions in New York.

As a young veteran of the Russian revolution of 1905, Alexander Trachtenberg was far from immune to the lure of the Russian revolutions of 1917. Though he made the mistake, from the later Communist point of view, of applauding the first, bourgeois-democratic revolution, he slowly came around to applaud the second, Bolshevik revolution, too. But his hesitation cost him heavily in prestige with the first echelon of unconditional American Bolsheviks. At a debate with Algernon Lee in New York in the spring of 1919. Fraina flung out the contemptuous charge: "It wasn't more than one year and a half ago that certain individuals in the party, now praising the Bolsheviki, were calling Lenin and Trotsky 'anarchists,'" and he named Trachtenberg as one of the guilty individuals.[27] By this time, ironically, Trachtenberg himself was defending the Bolshevik revolution in a debate with a Right-Winger, but it was hard to forgive and forget.[28] When it came to the inner-party fight in the Socialist party, Trachtenberg again hung back. He scandalized the Left Wing by asserting in the heat of the struggle that the official policy of the Socialist party during the war years had made it deserve the unhesitating endorsement of the Russian Bolsheviks.[29] In the hectic months of 1919, Trachtenberg found himself uncomfortably in the middle, an object of suspicion from both sides of the New York barricades.

Another sorely troubled soul was an outstanding Russian-Jewish intellectual, Moissaye J. Olgin. He had emigrated from Russia in 1915, but his book written in English, *The Soul of the Russian Revolution,* came out only two years later, and Professor V. G. Simkhovitch hailed it as "the most scientific that has so far appeared in the English language." In this work, Olgin committed the monumental indiscretion—for a future Communist—of taking the Menshevik side in the struggle between the Russian factions. "The Mensheviki were more realistic, the Bolsheviki more dogmatic," was his first view.[30] Early in 1918, Olgin also brought out in English translation the first representative collection of Trotsky's writings. Though he disassociated himself from many of Trotsky's ideas and policies, he wrote about Trotsky with what amounted to personal adoration.[31] Olgin had to pay for each of these imprudences. By disassociating himself from Trotsky's ideas, he temporarily cut himself off from the pro-Bolshevik Left Wing.[32] Almost two decades later, Olgin wrote an official anti-Trotskyist pamphlet, purging himself retroactively of the transgression of having admired Trotsky personally in 1918.[33]

Of the old-timers, Lore found himself in the least enviable position. Emotionally, he could not tear himself away from the new, post-Bolshevik Left Wing, which he had done so much to create, even though he could not stifle misgivings about splitting the old party. He told himself that he agreed with the Left Wing in principle and differed only in tactics. In the spring of 1919, his confusion became too much for him. First, he lined up with a "Centrist" group which tried to mediate between the extremes.[34] No sooner had he taken this position than his Left Wing conscience began to plague him and he pledged his allegiance to the organized Left Wing.[35]

Doubt from still another quarter beset Scott Nearing, who also signed the appeal of the Centrist group. He lectured in behalf of the Russian Bolsheviks so enthusiastically that he even ventured to predict, in the spring of 1919, that Russia, Germany, and parts of Central Europe would form a league of their own within six months.[36] Then his pacifist conscience got the best of him. He came out with a pamphlet entitled *Violence or Solidarity? or Will Guns Settle It?* which pleaded that the use of violence had never benefited the labor movement. The reply of the Left Wing was: "There is no place for pacifists in the Social Revolution."[37]

The range of reactions from Trachtenberg to Nearing showed how hard and tortuous the development of some future Communists was destined to be. The Russian Revolution was the turning point for all, but some rounded it more quickly and easily than others.

New York catches up

By the end of 1918, there was an organized Left Wing in Boston and Chicago, but none in New York. In Boston, the situation looked so bright that the Central Committee passed a resolution in November 1918 demanding an immediate emergency convention of the Socialist party to prepare for the "final struggle" between socialism and capitalism.[38] First, however, the Left Wing had to prepare for a slightly less ambitious "final struggle"—within the party itself. As long as the New Yorkers remained unorganized, much preparation remained.

The Socialist aldermen in New York gave the Left Wing the opportunity to launch a frontal attack. In the spring of 1918, they had voted in favor of the third Liberty Loan. That fall, they also voted for a temporary Victory Arch at Fifth Avenue and Madison Square, though they later regretted this.[39] In any case, it was the last straw. Bursting with righteous indignation, the Left Wing raged against the aldermen and demanded retribution. A joint meeting of the central committees of all the locals of Greater New York was called, early in January 1919, to pass judgment on the aldermen's actions.

Julius Gerber ran the meeting. First he asked the chairman of the aldermanic delegation to read a long report, which studiously avoided the very questions the Left-Wingers were seething over. Then he asked for questions from the floor which the aldermen proceeded to answer leisurely. He seemed, to the panting Left-Wingers, to have no visible intention of permitting them to make revolutionary speeches and offer resolutions in the long-awaited discussion period. At eleven-thirty that night, the Left-Wingers could stand no more. Some Queens delegates tried to get the floor and Gerber declared them out of order. In protest, the Queens group rose and stormed out of the room. The Brooklyn group followed suit. Some Manhattan and Bronx delegates also left. The bolters crowded together angrily in the corridor and demanded a meeting room of their own, which was granted after a bitter argument. A City Committee of Fourteen, with Dr. Maximilian Cohen as executive secretary, was elected to draft a manifesto and wage a compaign to win over the rank and file.[40]

With this City Committee, which met for the first time on February 2, the New York Left Wing caught up with Boston and Chicago. The committee organized itself as a party within a party. It elected an "International Bureau," a speakers' committee, and county organizers. It decided to print regular membership cards and charge ten cents monthly dues.[41] A suitably long manifesto was drafted by Reed and Wolfe. Meetings were called in Brooklyn, Manhattan, and the Bronx to endorse it. After these preparatory steps, an all-day convention was held in Odd Fellows Hall, St. Mark's Place, on February 15.[42] The Left Wing Section of the Greater New York Locals of the Socialist Party, as it was formally called, came into existence. The "Manifesto and Program" as revised by Fraina, was adopted, and the City Committee was enlarged to fifteen members, with an executive committee of nine.[43]

The New York group soon became the organizing center for the still far-flung and loose Left Wing throughout the country. Requests for information or messages of support began to come in from every part of the country. Gitlow was sent out to tour New York State. The New Yorkers were so impressed with their own importance that they demanded the transfer of *The Revolutionary Age* from Boston to New York. When the Boston group refused to give up the paper without a national convention of the Left Wing, the New Yorkers decided to put out one of their own.[44] The first number of the *New York Communist,* with John Reed as editor and Eadmonn MacAlpine as associate editor, was dated April 19, 1919. It was the first Left Wing organ with "Communist" in the title. By this time, about twenty-five New York branches had affiliated with the Left Wing, including all the Russian, Lettish, Ukrainian, and Hungarian branches.[45] When the headquarters were raided by the Lusk committee in June, approximately 2000 signed membership cards were found.[46]

The two versions of the Manifesto and Program offer another opportunity to understand the state of mind of the American Left Wing more than fifteen months after the Bolshevik revolution. The original draft contained an assurance that it did not "contemplate splitting the party," but this was left out of the final version. Evidently there had been some objection to a forthright commitment, though the anti-secessionists continued to hold the upper hand a few months more. On the theoretical side, the original draft was almost naïvely syndicalist in inspiration. To do away with political parties without exception was the only reason for political action, it said, and only a *"Revolutionary Economic Organization"* could take over and keep permanent control of the means of production and distribution. This was toned down in the second version, but plenty of syndicalist ideology remained. That version still maintained that the goal was not government ownership or state control of industry but rather workers' control exercised by the industrial organizations, defined as "industrial unions or Soviets" as if they were the same thing.

Another thing was still taken for granted—the old, infallible way to distinguish between false and real socialism. The belief that social reforms should be demanded from the capitalist state was expressed in the first draft. The removal of all such planks from the platform was urged in the second. To demand factory laws, old-age pensions, unemployment insurance, sick benefits, and "the whole litter of bourgeois reforms" was equivalent to "playing into the hands of the American imperialists." Real revolutionary Socialism scorned the consumer's point of view, the cost of living, taxation. It recognized only one revolutionary principle: "The party must teach, propagate and agitate exclusively for the overthrow of Capitalism, and the establishment of Socialism through a Proletarian Dictatorship." [47]

The state of mind of the new Left Wing, then, was not so different from the state of mind of the historic Left Wing. There was still a great deal of syndicalism in this conception of socialism. Immediate demands and social reforms were still anathema. The historic Left Wing had been interested chiefly in the final goal—socialism. The new Left Wing took more interest in the so-called transition period—proletarian dictatorship. But, at first and for some time to come, much more of the old than the new prevailed. The new battle cry—dictatorship of the proletariat—out of Marx, but long neglected until Lenin popularized it, was tacked on almost as an afterthought. The Americans still welcomed the Russian Revolution because they imagined that it vindicated the ideas most native to them. The Russian influence was still far away. Except for a handful of returning travelers, and a few articles and pamphlets, mainly by Lenin and Trotsky, communications between Russia and the United States remained extremely difficult and spasmodic. The Americans still had to think almost entirely for themselves.

9

The Real Split

A TABLE and chairs stood in one corner of the vast room. Only a single electric lamp cast some light on the table, leaving the rest of the room in darkness. The four men at the table could see a painting on the wall—a young girl reclining at the mouth of a cave reading a book resting on a skull. A precious screen separated the table, the chairs and the men from the remainder of the room. Behind the screen was an opulently emblazoned canopied bed.

It was in this room—the royal bedchamber of Nicholas II, last of the Czars—that Lenin took the decisive step in January 1919 to form the long-awaited Third International. The three others were the Commissar for Foreign Affairs, Georgi Vassilievich Chicherin, the Finnish Communist, Y. Sirola, and the Russian-British Communist, J. Fineberg. Lenin showed them the draft of a manifesto inviting thirty-nine Left Wing parties, groups, and tendencies all over the world to send delegates to a Congress in Moscow. After a brief discussion, his proposal was adopted.[1] Chicherin sent out the message by radio on January 24.

Among the signatories of this manifesto were the Lettish exile, Rosin, in the name of the Russian bureau of the new Latvian Communist party, and Boris Reinstein, in the name of the Socialist Labor party. The way Reinstein came to play this role reveals a great deal about the problems of launching the Third International.

Reinstein was born in the town of Rostov, on the river Don, received an above-average education, was apprenticed to a druggist and soon thereafter found his way into the revolutionary movement. The Czarist police chased him out of the country in his early twenties and then succeeded in getting him arrested and jailed as a conspirator in Paris. When he was released from prison, he emigrated to the United States in 1901 at the age of thirty-three. He opened a drug store in Belleville, New York, a suburb of Buffalo, joined the Socialist Labor party under the influence of Daniel De Leon, and soon became a prominent figure in its dwindling ranks. He added English to his fluent Russian, Polish, and German, a useful asset in his party activity.[2]

Reinstein had been sent to Europe in 1917 by the S.L.P. to take part in a Socialist conference in Stockholm. Lenin would have nothing to do with this conference because he feared that it would serve to revive the Second International. Refused a passport, Reinstein sailed illegally, thus jeopardizing his safe return. In Stockholm, he was won over by a group of Bolshevik sympathizers and persuaded to go on to Russia.[3] He made himself so useful that for years he acted as one of the chief mentors and guides of virtually every American Communist who came to Moscow. The British journalist, Arthur Ransome, described him in appearance as "a little old grandfather" who was "a prodigy of knowledge about the revolution" and tireless in helping Americans.[4]

Reinstein quickly won the confidence of the Bolshevik leaders, who put him to work in the Commissariat for Foreign Affairs under Chicherin. He organized a Department of International Propaganda in the Commissariat, and this became a rudimentary model of the future Communist International. Among other things, this department was responsible for propaganda aimed at British and American soldiers then stationed in Russia. John Reed and Albert Rhys Williams helped to put out a German paper for it. In the early days, Soviet diplomatic and revolutionary activities were so closely related that they were carried on in the same commissariat. Indeed, only five weeks after the Bolshevik revolution, a decree dated December 13, 1917, put 2,000,000 rubles at the disposal of the foreign representatives of the Commissariat for Foreign Affairs "for the needs of the revolutionary internationalist movement." [5] Like Reed's appointment as Soviet consul in New York, this decree exemplified the early interchangeability of the diplomatic and the revolutionary. It did not seem to matter much then, since the world revolution was considered so imminent. Only as the world revolution receded and the Communist International developed did a division of labor become necessary.

Of the thirty-nine different groups to which the manifesto for the new International was specifically addressed, four were American:

33. The S.L.P. (U.S.A.)
34. The elements of the Left Wing of the American Socialist Party (tendency represented by E. V. Debs and the Socialist Propaganda League)
35. I.W.W. (Industrial Workers of the World), America
36. The Workers International Industrial Union (U.S.A.).[6]

Not a single one of these groups was able or willing to send representatives to the congress. Why they were chosen and why they failed to act can be understood only in terms of the lack of contact between Moscow and the United States and the illusions which distance bred.

The Socialist Labor party qualified, of course, as Reinstein's organization, even though it had nothing to do with his presence in Moscow. The "tendency represented by E. V. Debs" was somewhat of a misnomer, because, strictly speaking, Debs did not represent an organized or even a definable tendency. The reference to the Socialist Propaganda League, which was about to go out of existence,[7] showed how far behind American developments the organizers of the Third International in Moscow were. The greatest hopes were held out for the I.W.W., which was actually divided in sentiment toward the Communists. The Workers International Industrial Union was the De Leonite offshoot from the original I.W.W., which, like the S.L.P., remained small and undefiled by power.

The two organizations that would have been glad to send delegates to the congress in Moscow, if they had received notice in time and if they could have overcome the blockade, were the Left Wing Section of New York and the Communist Propaganda League of Chicago.

They were not mentioned in the manifesto because no one in Moscow had then heard of their existence.

The Comintern

But there was Reinstein. And there was Rutgers, who had made his way to Moscow in 1918. These two came nearest to representing the American Left Wing movement at the First Congress of the Third International.

Unsatisfactory contact with the rest of Europe forced a postponement of the opening of the Congress from February 15 to March 2, 1919. Of the fifty-one persons who attended, the only delegates from abroad were Hugo Eberlein of the Spartacus League of Germany, Rutgers from Holland, and several Finns.[8] All the others were Russians or emigrants living in Russia.

Reinstein took part as an official delegate of the Socialist Labor party with voting rights.[9] Admittedly he did so without authorization.[10] So desperate were the organizers for some non-Russians that a native Russian who had an official post in the Soviet Government and had readopted Russia as his homeland pretended to represent an American party that had sent him two years earlier to a different congress in a different country. The British delegate, Fineberg, was equally resourceful. He attended the First Congress in the name of the British Socialist Party without authorization.[11] The Socialist Propaganda League was represented by Rutgers, who was there primarily on behalf of the Social Democratic party of Holland. For both of these he was given an "advisory voice" only. Despite Reinstein's valiant efforts, the Socialist Labor party never joined the Third International.

The Congress itself was symbolic of the contradiction in which the Bolsheviks found themselves. In theory, they believed that the European revolution was imminent, not merely inevitable. Practically, they had to operate from day to day on a totally different basis.

Virtually the only connection the Russians had with the European and American revolutionary movements was through émigrés in Moscow cut off from their own countries. Make-believe representatives were pressed into service because real ones were lacking. Significantly, no German could be found to sign the manifesto for the new International, though the German revolution and the German Communist movement were considered second only to the Russian in immediate importance, and much more significant in the long run. Lenin was ready to launch the new International on Russian initiative alone for the same reason that he had been ready to set off the Bolshevik revolution itself—that a European revolution was imminent and inevitable. The greatest irony in modern history resulted. His assumption proved wrong, but he had his revolution and his International.

To Lenin's dismay, Eberlein reported that Rosa Luxemburg and her closest associates unanimously opposed the Russian position. She had stated her opinion to Eberlein only three days before her brutal murder. Rosa Luxemburg believed that Communist parties had to arise in almost all countries of Europe before a Communist International should be formed. Meanwhile, she favored the establishment of a preparatory commission and the postponement of the inaugural congress until the end of the year. Eberlein was sent to Moscow with instructions to hold fast to this position, which was supported by all the available Spartacus leaders.[12] Thus, two different points of view were clearly represented by Lenin and Luxemburg—the one that the International should be formed at once; the other that the parties should come first. Thinly veiled in this difference of opinion was a deeper question—whether the Russians should control the new International or whether the other parties should be strong enough to hold their own. The fateful decision was made at the very outset.

According to Eberlein, Lenin had his way as a result of something of a fluke. At first, Eberlein's opposition seemed an insuperable obstacle to the execution of the original plan. Even the Russians were not willing to take the responsibility against the expressed resistance of the Germans. But an Austrian delegate, J. Gruber (Steinhart), suddenly arrived in Moscow on the third day. He came with a tempestuously exciting story—seventeen days of crossing borders illegally, the revolutionary upheaval in Austria, the break-up of the entire Hapsburg empire. Gruber's fervor was infectious. The delegates felt that they had to rise to the occasion. After all, the Bolsheviks seemed right—Europe was teetering on the edge of revolution. Even Eberlein was overwhelmed. When he agreed to abstain from the vote, the Third, the Communist, International was voted into existence on March 4, 1919.[13]

Reinstein's only contribution to the congress was a rather pathetic statement that he could not offer any fresh information about America because he had been in Russia for almost two years. This fact did not prevent him from promising that the American revolutionary movement would not lag behind in the hour of need.[14]

The president of the new International, Zinoviev, and virtually its entire staff were Russians. Much of what was done in those hectic days was undoubtedly considered provisional. The provisional became permanent when the basic assumption—the all-European revolution—refused to materialize.

Out of the first syllables in the name arose the shorter and more familiar form—the "Comintern." This is the form generally used in this book, though the initials "C.I." were also frequently employed by the Communists themselves.

War in New York

Meanwhile the American Left Wing had to fight its own battles without benefit of the newborn Comintern.

The crucial battle was fought in New York where there was a strong Right Wing as well as a strong Left Wing. The Left Wing started out at a decided disadvantage because the Right Wing controlled the party machinery in Greater New York and in New York State. The chief party organ in New York, the *Call,* was owned by an independent association dominated by the old party leadership. On the other hand, the Left Wing could count on the three outlying boroughs, Brooklyn, Bronx, and Queens, with an aggressive group in Manhattan. The East-European language branches in the city were Left Wing strongholds.

The documents that issued from the First Congress of the Comintern were eagerly scanned for their American aspects and implications. The Russian authors, however, did not write them with the American situation uppermost in their minds and their message for the American Left Wing was somewhat blurred. Nevertheless, some phrases struck home.

The call for the Congress demanded a "merciless fight" against the Right Wing "social-patriots" who had supported the war. It urged "criticizing pitilessly" the leaders of the "Center" and systematically separating them from their followers.[15] The manifesto of the Congress repeated uncompromisingly: "War against the Socialist Center is a necessary condition of successful war against imperialism."[16]

The injunction against the Right Wing was easy to apply in American terms. But where and what was the American "Center"?

At first, the term was applied to a small group which included David P. Berenberg, Benjamin Glassberg, Louis P. Lochner, Scott Nearing, and, for a short time, Ludwig Lore. They had injected themselves into the argument between the two major antagonists by offering a "basis for discussion" in an effort to head off the approaching hostilities. Like the more extreme Left Wing, they came out for the abolition of all social reform planks; for teaching, propagating and agitating exclusively for the overthrow of capitalism; and for an international congress attended by the revolutionary Socialist parties of all countries. But they substituted the establishment of an "industrial democracy" for the proletarian dictatorship, and refused to mention the Russian Bolsheviks by name as the chief revolutionary party which had already called an international congress. One shaft was aimed at the Left Wing's most vulnerable spot—a protest against "organized separatism and division."[17] *The Revolutionary Age* responded pitilessly, as it had been told to do: "The center must be smashed as a necessary means of conquering the party for the party, for revolutionary Socialism."[18]

The so-called Center did not remain in the center very long. On one issue—organizational unity and loyalty—it fundamentally opposed the Left Wing. To be sure, the Left Wing did not admit that

THE REAL SPLIT

it was threatening the party's unity. All factions were still vowing undying loyalty to the party. But the Left Wing made abundantly clear that it intended to keep the party "united" on its own terms or not at all. The violence of its language, if nothing else, signified a policy of rule or ruin. By charging the Right Wing with the "betrayal" of socialism, it left no room in the same party for itself and the Right Wing. If the Center had to be "smashed," too, there was no possibility of sharing the party organization with it. The Left Wing slogan of "No compromise, no hesitation" could only mean all or nothing. Above all, the steps taken by the Left Wing to set up a completely parallel organization with membership cards, dues, county organizers, and a city committee left nothing to the imagination. It was the kind of dual authority which the Left itself, in the same circumstances, would never have tolerated. In fact, in its own ranks the Left Wing already demanded absolute and unconditional allegiance and discipline. When Boudin applied for membership with reservations, he was told to come in without reservations or to stay out. Eastman was informed that he had to shape the policy of *The Liberator* to conform to the Left Wing Manifesto and Program and pledge himself to be subject to the discipline of the organization.[19] No one could doubt that the Left Wing intended to remake the party in its own image.

To the Right Wing the organizational issue proved a godsend. It simplified the struggle into a matter of who would expel whom first. The Right Wing was not sure of winning a majority of the membership ideologically, but thanks to its control of the top committees it could not lose organizationally. The treatment of Bill Haywood earlier in the decade had already set a precedent. Many Right-Wingers saw very little difference between the syndicalism of 1912 and the communism of 1919. In 1912, however, it had been necessary to make an example of only one man. In 1919, it was necessary to get rid of thousands. The Right Wing did not flinch from such a course because it did not have much use for most of the new members anyway. The old-timers saw no cause for rejoicing in the growth of the foreign-language federations or in the new type of young, aggressive, pro-Bolshevik extremists. The sudden growth in membership looked good on paper, but the Right Wing harbored deep misgivings as to whether it was healthy for the party as a whole.

The first open move toward the inevitable split was made by one of the so-called Centrists, David P. Berenberg. He introduced a resolution at a meeting of the New York State Committee in Albany on April 13 to revoke the charter of any local that affiliated with the Left Wing. It was carried by a vote of 24 to 17, with 2 abstentions.[20] Since the Left Wing already boasted the affiliation of about twenty branches, this move threatened about 4000 members.[21] If it was intended to scare the Left Wing, it failed. *The New York Communist* gleefully reported the vote under the heading: "We're Gonna Be Expelled! Help!!"[22] When the Right Wing had to stage a walkout in the Bronx on April 18, Julius Gerber swung into action.[23] He hastened to call a meeting of the City General Committee on April 21, at which a decision was made to "reorganize" a Left Wing branch.[24] The war in New York was on.

Preventive war

In the spring of 1919, the outlook for a clean sweep of the American Socialist party by the Left Wing seemed excellent. Local after local, branch after branch, went on record endorsing the Left Wing program—Boston, Cleveland, Toledo, Akron, Buffalo, San Francisco, Oakland, Portland, Philadelphia, Detroit, Seattle, Queens, Bronx, Brooklyn, and many others. Seven of the foreign federations endorsed it—the Russian, Lithuanian, Ukrainian, Polish, Hungarian, South Slavic, and Lettish. The demand of the Left Wing to quit the Second International and affiliate with the Third carried in a referendum by a vote of more than 10 to 1. Even more conclusively, the Left Wing walked off with the referendum to elect a new National Executive Committee. It won twelve of the fifteen seats. The best-known figures of the old moderate leadership went down to smashing defeat. According to the official figures, Fraina was the most popular man in the party, closely followed by Ruthenberg. Victor Berger, a Right Wing stalwart, received little more than a third as many votes. In the referendum for international delegates, the first four elected were all backed by the Left Wing—Reed, Fraina, Kate Richards O'Hare, and Ruthenberg—with Hillquit a poor fifth.[25] By April, the prospect seemed so bright that a call was issued for a national conference of the Left Wing to be held in New York City on June 21. It was signed by Louis C. Fraina, who had become the secretary of the Boston local, Charles E. Ruthenberg, the secretary of the Cleveland local, and Maximilian Cohen, the secretary of the Left Wing Section of New York.

But the Right Wing had no intention of stepping aside merely because it had been outvoted in the elections. After giving the figures close scrutiny, the Right Wing decided to cry "fraud." Its case was built around the fact that only about one-fifth of the total membership had bothered to vote in the election and referendum. The organized Left Wing and some of the language federations were charged with voting as a bloc on an agreed-upon slate. It was not hard to deduce that the Left Wing candidates owed their overwhelming victory to the federations. The moral case of the Right Wing would have been somewhat stronger if the old National Executive Committee had not been elected by a somewhat similar minority of the total membership and if the undesirable preponderance of the foreign-language federations had been discovered before the votes were counted.

The signal for a purge was given by Morris Hillquit, who was then recuperating from tuberculosis in upstate New York. He returned to party activity long enough to send an article to the *New York Call* which constituted a bill of divorcement. Both factions had been piously pretending that they were tearing the party apart in the interests of unity. Hillquit coldly cut through the hollow pretense. After a characteristically circuitous analysis of national and international problems, he abruptly came to the point: "Better a hundred times to have two numerically small Socialist organizations, each homogeneous and harmonious within itself, than to have one big party torn by dissensions and squabbles, an impotent colossus on feet of clay. The time for action is near. Let us clear the decks."[26] To which the pro-Communist organ in New York replied that "when the time comes for clearing the decks we will handle the mop."[27]

Hillquit's "time for action" was the meeting of the National Executive Committee on May 24, three days after the appearance of his article. This meeting demonstrated that the Right Wing still handled the mop. Of the ten members present, only two represented the Left Wing—Alfred Wagenknecht of Ohio and Ludwig E. Katterfeld, then of Kansas.

On the first day, the entire Socialist party of Michigan was expelled. Its charter was revoked on the grounds that a recent convention of the Michigan party had amended its constitution to repudiate legislative reforms. This action cleared the Socialist decks of about 6000 members. On the fourth day, the seven Left Wing foreign-language federations were cast out. They were suspended for sending in a letter in which they protested against the suspension of several New York branches and endorsed the Left Wing program. This cleared the decks of over 20,000 more members.[28] With this mopping up as a start, the committee proceeded to hold up the tabulation of the vote for new officers and to agree on a national emergency convention to meet in Chicago on August 30.[29] The Left Wing had been vainly clamoring for months for an emergency convention. Now one was going to be held—without the Left Wing.

In the next few weeks, the state organizations of Massachusetts and Ohio, the Chicago organization, and numerous locals elsewhere were ruthlessly suspended or expelled. In six months, about two-thirds of the Socialist party was expelled or suspended. The second highest point in the Socialist membership was reached in January 1919 with a total of 109,589. In July of that year, the total fell to 39,750.[30]

Thus the real split took place in the middle of 1919. In effect, the Right Wing had declared preventive war on the Left Wing. The result was the relatively small Socialist organizations that Hillquit had foreseen, but they were still far from homogeneous and harmonious.

The Communist potential

From the end of May 1919, then, the Left Wing could claim almost 70,000 members or sympathizers. They constituted the potential backing of the Communist movement that was to come into existence only three months later. No new American radical movement had ever jumped off to a more promising start. The Socialist party had required almost ten years to reach this figure. In order to understand what happened to these 70,000 homeless Socialists, it is necessary to analyze them a little more carefully.

The single largest body of potential Communists came from the seven suspended language federations—Russian, Lettish, Lithuanian, Ukrainian, Hungarian, South Slavic, and Polish. By 1919, however, a marked change had taken place in the relative strength and influence of these federations. The Lettish leadership was now a thing of the past. The new phase was characterized by Russian leadership. The Russian federation would have enjoyed a great deal of influence in any case because of the influx of new members and therefore of money into the organization. But the material consideration was not the main thing. Everything Russian had taken on an irresistible glamor as a result of the successful Russian Revolution. The Russian federation's leaders began to develop unmistakable signs of delusions of grandeur—as if the genius of Lenin or Trotsky had rubbed off on all Russians. Their special claim to supreme authority was based on a unique sense of national affinity with the one country where communism had won power. Ironically, the great majority of the Russian federation had been pro-Menshevik. What had rubbed off on them was the success of the Bolshevik revolution.

The second important Communist reservoir was native born or at least English-speaking. It was most actively represented by the Left Wing Section in New York. Similar groups sprang up in about fifteen states. The Massachusetts, Illinois, Ohio, Minnesota, and Kansas City Socialist organizations were controlled by Left Wing forces; and the last three were far more "Americanized" than the

New York group. Six of these groups were issuing their own organs —*The Revolutionary Age* (Boston), *The Ohio Socialist* (Cleveland), *Truth* (Duluth), *The Bolshevik* (Minneapolis), *The Communist* (Chicago), and *The Workers' World* (Kansas City). There were more potential Communists as far west as California, as far north as Montana, and as far south as Kentucky. It was often impossible, however, to draw a clear line between English-speaking and foreign-language groups. In some places, notably New York, Chicago, and Boston, the English-speaking leaders were like captains at the head of foreign-language companies—which easily made hostages of them.

Besides the true adherents of the Left Wing, others sympathized with it for less compelling reasons. The mass expulsions and suspensions without hearings shocked many middle-of-the-road Socialists. This group was least likely to survive a real crisis in the Communist movement.

The Michigan group belonged in a class by itself. Its main leaders were Dennis E. Batt, a former machinist, and John Keracher, a shoe-store owner. They differed with the rest of the Left Wing on a number of vital points. They took the unpopular position that American capitalism had emerged from the war stronger than ever, and that it was destined to survive for an indefinite period. They believed that the most effective means of bringing the revolutionary message to the American people were political and educational. They rated trade unions very low in the revolutionary scale. The Michigan theory of educating for the revolution had the effect of conveniently bypassing the discouraging present in favor of the great day when the vast majority would be intellectually prepared to vote the Socialist revolution into existence.[31]

Most of these ideas were British in origin. They came from the small, extremist Socialist Party of Great Britain to the Socialist Party of Canada which, in turn, passed them on to a number of Left Wing centers in the United States, particularly Detroit and Seattle. According to this doctrine, the struggle for wages and hours was merely the struggle to sell a commodity and therefore an aspect of capitalist competition. Since trade unions were engaged in a commodity struggle, they could not contribute to the emancipation of the working class from capitalism. This point of view was scoffed at by all the other American Left Wing groups, which tended to go to the other extreme by overrating the revolutionary importance of trade unions.

The Michigan group was forced out of the Socialist party and temporarily moved in the same direction as the Communists for only one reason—the deep-seated Michigan prejudice against partial reforms or immediate demands. Otherwise, the Michigan group was closer to the Socialist than to the Communist position. It was classically reformist in its means and abstractly revolutionary in its end, a contradiction which earned it the abuse of both reformists and revolutionists. Yet there was something to the Michigan claim that it was closer to American experience and American conditions than the rest of the Left Wing was. It was more nearly right about the survival of American capitalism, the preference for political activity by the American people, and the long-term resistance against the revolutionary movement by the trade unions. On the other hand, ignoring the unions and ruling out all partial reforms as the objective of political activity were not policies likely to influence the mass of American workers.

These three principal groupings—the foreign-language federations, the scattered elements of the native or English-speaking Left Wing, and the Michigan organization—emerged from the Socialist purge in the summer of 1919. They were sufficiently different to make their unification a difficult problem.

Martens' bureau

To complicate the problem, a Russian center of power outside the Russian federation made its appearance in 1919. A courier arrived in New York from Moscow in January with instructions for Ludwig C. A. K. Martens to set up an official American agency of the Soviet regime. Martens, a mechanical engineer by profession, born in Russia of German parents, had joined the Russian revolutionary movement as a student and, after the usual experiences—arrest, jail, deportation

—had settled in Germany and then in London. He came to New York in 1916 as the representative of a large Russian steel firm, and proceeded to make equally good contacts with both American capitalists and the *Novy Mir*.[32] Martens took over Nuorteva's old bureau and in April opened the Russian Soviet Government Information Bureau, with Nuorteva as its secretary. Martens' staff of thirty-five contained some unusually interesting personalities, past and future. The office manager was Gregory Weinstein, former editor of the *Novy Mir*. The commercial department was headed by Abram A. Heller, a successful businessman and old-time Socialist. Nuorteva's assistant secretary was Kenneth Durant, later to be head of the American branch of the official Soviet news agency (TASS). The disillusioned former research director for the Socialist aldermen, Evans Clark, served as director of information and publicity. The strangest name on the list—yet one which explains a great deal about this period—was that of Morris Hillquit, who consented to lend his prestige as head of the legal department, though too ill for active service.

There were no precedents for Martens' bureau. It was set up as a diplomatic mission, without diplomatic recognition. It was made up mostly of Americans, and the others, like Martens himself, had been cut off for many years from direct contact with Russia. Couriers constituted the only method of communication, but they were so slow and uncertain that it took two months for Martens to get in touch with the Soviet government.[33]

Meanwhile, the greatest confusion reigned over what his mission was or even where he was supposed to get his orders. Martens himself preferred to emphasize commercial and trade relations with American capitalism and to stay out of the stormy battle for control of the Socialist party and the Left Wing. The leaders of the Russian federation, however, had other ideas. They did not hesitate to extend their jurisdiction over the official Soviet agency as well as the Left Wing. They felt that commercial and trade relations were foolish objectives. Only the spread of the proletarian revolution mattered. If the revolution conquered outside Russia, then commercial and trade relations would come of themselves. If the world revolution failed, commercial and trade relations could not help the Russian Revolution to survive. In effect, the American Russians had taken literally what the Russian leaders themselves were saying about the necessity for a world revolution to save the Russian Revolution, and in doing so, they became more doctrinaire than their teachers.

Nicholas I. Hourwich of the *Novy Mir,* the son of one of the most highly respected members of Martens' staff, Isaac A. Hourwich, a veteran of the American Socialist and trade-union movements, went so far as to "sound a warning to the American workers—and to Comrade Martens himself—against exaggerating the importance of purely diplomatic and commercial activity here." Hourwich instructed Martens that "the center of his attention, the compass directing his activity here into proper channels, should serve the interests of the revolutionary Socialist movement of the American proletariat, the interests of the advance guard of the movement—*the left or Bolshevik wing of the American Socialist Party.*" [34] Soon after this warning, Martens took steps to avow "his allegiance and support to the Left Wing movement." [35] Nevertheless, Martens and Nuorteva refused to confine themselves to the Left Wing and rebelled against taking orders from the leaders of the Russian federation. The feud raged behind the scenes for many months and contributed to the bitter feeling building up among the would-be American Bolshevik leaders.

In later years, both Soviet representatives and American Communists learned to draw a line between Soviet diplomacy and American revolutionary activity. Such a line proved necessary for purely tactical reasons. The early Communists were less worried about tactical expediency, because the revolution was right around the corner. They were not yet accustomed to double bookkeeping in their thoughts and actions. As a result, they followed their impulses more freely and naïvely looked at official Soviet and their own revolutionary activity as different sectors of the same battlefront. Later, even when the tactics changed, the basic, simple impulse remained the same. Working for the Soviet regime and working for a Communist revolution in the United States might be separated publicly, but inwardly they could never be severed.

10

The Great Schism

ANOTHER Russian specter came to haunt the American Communist movement as it struggled to be born.

To their American disciples, hurriedly catching up with decades of Russian revolutionary history, the Bolsheviks seemed to have prepared for power by spending most of their time fighting among themselves or against other factions in the Russian Socialist movement. The Bolshevik-Menshevik split of 1903 had been followed by innumerable other splits, always justified as the way to strengthen the revolutionary movement by removing foreign excrescences.

If this was the school of revolution in Russia, what self-styled disciple of Lenin dared say that it could be otherwise in the United States?

In order to take full advantage of its favorable position, the American Left Wing had to make up its mind that it wanted to fight for control of the Socialist party. Demanding a national emergency convention of the party was pointless if the Left Wing had no intention of going to it in order to win a majority and capture its machinery. Denouncing the expulsions and suspensions was meaningless if the Left Wing had no intention of staying in the party.

When the call was issued in April 1919 for the National Conference of the Left Wing to meet in New York two months later, the Left Wing clearly aimed to fight within the party for control of the party. The first notice of the call said distinctly: "The purpose of the Conference is to formulate a national declaration of Left Wing principles, form a national, unified expression of the Left Wing (a sort of General Council—not a separate organization) and concentrate our forces to conquer the Party for revolutionary Socialism." [1]

To the American leaders of the Left Wing, most of whom had matured politically within the Socialist party, it seemed only natural to start by taking over the party, especially when the chances for doing so seemed so good. The obvious strategy was to pin the responsibility of splitting the party on the Right Wing and to protest that the Left Wing was virtuously attempting to save it.

But where, then, was the American split? Two of the groups within the Left Wing—the foreign-language federations and the Michigan organization—had an answer to the question. The split was in the Socialist party—the sooner the better.

An emergency state convention, held in Michigan in June, issued a call for a national convention in Chicago on September 1 to organize a "socialist" party in the United States affiliated with the Third International.[2] The plain implication of the Michigan action, only a week before the scheduled opening of the National Conference of the Left Wing in New York, ran counter to the previously accepted strategy of the whole Left Wing. If it was going to Chicago to organize a new party, it could not very well go with clean hands to the official Socialist emergency convention.

The Michigan threat might have been beaten off as a minor irritation. But the Michigan leaders, Batt and Keracher, had found strong allies—none other than the seven suspended foreign-language federations.

Nicholas Hourwich of New York and Alexander Stoklitsky of Chicago, the most vociferous of the Russian spokesmen, had gone along with the original plan to fight for control of the Socialist party.[3] After the first documents of the Comintern became available, however, they began to have a change of heart. More and more it seemed to them that the Left Wing strategy contravened the Bolshevik tradition. After all, the American Socialist party had been for many years an integral part of the most dangerous enemy, the Second International. It was a hodge-podge of all tendencies and groups. Would Russian Bolsheviks have tried to curry favor with the heterogeneous membership of an organization with such a compromising past? Or would they have done their best to make a clean break? Had not Lenin always chosen principle above numbers? To the Russian generalissimos in America, the Left Wing itself was permeated with "centrism," exemplified by the policy of fighting for control of the Socialist party.

From different directions, then, the Michigan organization and the foreign-language federations joined paths. Both found themselves ousted from the Socialist party with no desire to go back. That their community of interest was purely negative mattered little for the time being. As the terms were used then, the Michigan group actually stood to the right and the foreign-language federations to the left of the Left Wing Program. In the long run, they were bound to clash. At the moment, however, they needed each other. By teaming up with the foreign-language federations, the Michigan group obtained mass backing on a national scale for its ambitious plan to set up a new party. By teaming up with the Michigan group, the foreign-language federations temporarily overcame their chief political weakness—lack of English-speaking spokesmen in an English-speaking country.

On the eve of the long-awaited national conference to unite the Left Wing, the Left Wing was disunited on a crucial issue—whether to form a Communist party immediately or to wait and try to capture the Socialist convention, ten weeks off. In either case, the Left Wing was determined to form a Communist party. The only question was how and when.

The National Left Wing Conference

From twenty states, as far apart as New York and California, 94 delegates came together at the Manhattan Lyceum in New York City on June 21, 1919, for the conference. It was the first nationwide gathering of most of the future leaders of the American Communist movement—Charles E. Ruthenberg and Alfred Wagenknecht from Ohio; James P. Cannon from Kansas City; William Bross Lloyd and

Isaac E. Ferguson from Chicago; Alexander Stoklitsky and Nicholas I. Hourwich of the Russian federation; and the largest group of all from New York, including John Reed, Benjamin Gitlow, James Larkin, Carl Brodsky, and Bertram D. Wolfe.[4] In recognition of his outstanding services, Fraina was assigned the opening address as temporary chairman. William Bross Lloyd was rewarded with the role of permanent chairman.

A loose coalition of the foreign-language delegates led by the Russians, the Michigan delegates, and a few others, soon showed their determination to force through a decision to organize a Communist party immediately. Batt of Michigan, supported by Hourwich, fought against postponement. The old policy of waiting was vigorously defended by most of the English-speaking leaders in New York—Reed, Gitlow, and Wolfe—as well as Fraina of Boston. To their support came other English-speaking delegates from the west—which, to many New Yorkers, meant almost anything west of the Hudson River. This was the first personal contact between the New Yorkers and midcountry delegates like Ruthenberg and Cannon. The leaders from outside New York were even less prepared to leave the Socialist party hastily. The three-day debate showed that, on the whole, the great majority of English-speaking delegates were lined up against the great majority of foreign-language delegates and the Michigan group.

A proposal to turn the Left Wing conference into a full-fledged Communist organization was defeated by a vote of 55 to 38. A majority of 43 to 14, with 14 abstentions, decided that the objective was still "the capturing of the Socialist party for revolutionary Socialism." As a last resort, Hourwich proposed that the federations should be given one member each on the proposed national council, a maneuver designed to give the federations control despite their defeat on policy. When this proposal was decisively rejected, the federation delegates, the Michigan group, and a few others staged a walk-out. They had come to make sure of a split and they were going to have it—inside the Left Wing.[5]

The remaining two-thirds went ahead. A national council of nine was elected—Louis C. Fraina of Boston, Charles E. Ruthenberg of

Cleveland, I. E. Ferguson of Chicago, John J. Ballam of Boston, and James Larkin, Eadmonn MacAlpine, Benjamin Gitlow, Maximilian Cohen, and Bertram D. Wolfe of New York. Ferguson was named national secretary. *The Revolutionary Age,* with Fraina remaining as editor, was adopted as the official organ. No conference could be complete without a manifesto, and the one for this occasion was exceptionally long and ambitious. As usual, it was composed by Fraina.[6]

In general, the June manifesto expanded on the themes already stated in the February manifesto. Capitalism was collapsing; the proletarian revolution was sweeping onward; the Second International had surrendered to imperialism; the Russian Revolution had demonstrated the validity and power of revolutionary socialism. But some of its points struck closer home. To take the sting out of criticisms that the Left Wing had no American basis, the manifesto found it necessary to say: "The upsurge of revolutionary Socialism in the American Socialist Party, expressed in the Left Wing, is not a product simply of European conditions. It is, in a fundamental sense, the product of the experience of the American movement—the Left Wing tendency in the Party, having been invigorated by the experience of the proletarian revolutions in Europe." This represented a slightly different emphasis. And indeed portions of the document betrayed the telltale signs of the American rather than the European revolutionary tradition. Mixed with the new ideology of Bolshevism was much from the old arsenal of syndicalism and De Leonism. A labor party was just as dangerous as "petty bourgeois socialism"; the A.F. of L. had to be exposed and broken; parliamentarism was useful only to the degree that it made possible "mass strikes"; the initial form of mass action was the "mass strike of the unorganized proletariat"; the revolutionary state of the proletariat "must reorganize society on the basis of union control and management of industry." Only an aspiring American Bolshevik who had gone through the schools of the I.W.W. and the Socialist Labor party would have used some of these expressions.[7]

The National Conference of the Left Wing tried to adopt a flexible strategy. If the old Socialist party executive went through with the scheduled emergency convention on August 30, the Left Wing would try to win control and transform it into a Communist party. If the Socialist convention was not held or if the Left Wing could not win control, it would hold its own convention in Chicago on September 1 to form a Communist party. And just to cover all possible contingencies, the conference decided to issue a call for a convention in Chicago on September 1 of "all revolutionary elements" to unite with either a revolutionized Socialist party or with a new Communist party.[8]

One way or the other, there was going to be a Communist party in the United States by September 1, 1919. The only question was who would be able to claim credit for it—the National Council of the Left Wing or the foreign-language federations–Michigan alliance.

Orthodoxy and opportunism

Despite the excitement generated at the time, it is hard to take too seriously this quarrel over whether a Communist party should be formed in June or in September. It is easy to laugh at the protagonists for taking themselves too solemnly and to dismiss this factional split as one of the innumerable tempests in a teapot brewed in the revolutionary movement.

Yet few things left a deeper and more lasting mark on the American Communist movement than this seemingly unnecessary split. For this was the precursor and prototype of all the splits and factionalism for years to come. It was the embryonic form of the great schism in the Communist movement.

In the broadest terms, the schism has its origins in this dilemma: to hew to an orthodox political line or to win the broadest mass influence? Theoretically such a choice should not be necessary. If Communist theory is valid, as the Communists claim, the orthodox line should be the short cut to mass influence. But in practice this has been rarely if ever the case. Orthodoxy is determined by a theory, a doctrine, a dogma. It seeks to impose itself on the complexity of life and society, to make them conform to its principles and preconceptions. It operates with abstract formulas, historic parallels, and quotations from sacred writings. This type of Communist orthodoxy has invariably been sectarian. It has isolated the party from the masses which it seeks to attract. Opportunism has time and again paid off in large-scale, widespread influence. Opportunism tells the masses what they want to hear, rather than what Communist doctrine says they should want to hear. It gets the masses closer to the Communists by getting the Communists closer to the masses. It enables the Communists to increase their mass following without increasing the masses' understanding of communism or even by deluding them about the true nature of communism.

This contradiction has baffled and plagued every Communist movement in the West. It began to baffle and plague the American Communist movement in June 1919. At the National Left Wing Conference, the self-appointed guardians of the orthodox political line were the representatives of the Russian federation and their close followers in the other foreign-language federations. They were the ones who virtuously proclaimed that devotion to principle was the only thing that mattered. They attacked the majority for seeking to woo and win a few more thousand vacillating members of the Socialist party. They proudly called themselves the "Communist" minority. When they could not sway the conference, they stormed out self-righteously and set up their own organization. They confidently waited, as sectarians always do, for the tide to turn in their favor. Psychologically, they enjoyed a superior feeling of integrity and purity. Organizationally, they seemed more daring and independent.

The victorious majority at the June conference vainly protested that no question of principle was at stake. All were agreed on the necessity of forming an American Communist party affiliated with the Third International. All were agreed on the Left Wing political program. The only thing separating them was the matter of timing. The majority merely wanted to wait only ten weeks more in order to start the Communist party on a larger mass basis. In fact, they charged, the Russian federation was guilty of compromising with principle by getting together in a marriage of convenience with a Michigan group that really differed on fundamental points of doctrine. On both sides, then, what was practical politics to one was unprincipled opportunism to the other. Back and forth went the recriminations: "centrism," "a small clique of deserters," "opportunistic vacillation," "lust for power."

But the Russians in America had one great advantage—they could cite the example of the Russian Bolsheviks. Had the Bolsheviks tried to capture the Second International before going ahead with a handful of non-Russian delegates to form the Third? Were the Bolsheviks ever squeamish about a split? Did the Bolsheviks ever hesitate because they wanted the masses to catch up with them? Like all recent converts, the Russian federation leaders were anxious to show how well they had learned their lessons by reciting them in the most dogmatic form. Their newly discovered ideal was the prerevolutionary Russian Bolshevik party under Lenin as they conceived it—deliberately and rigidly small, disciplined and politically pure (which it had never been, except in the legend that grew up after 1917). They were not interested in winning a large majority of the Socialist membership even if they could. They were interested in keeping out anyone not a 100-per-cent Bolshevik. Much more was involved, therefore, than the issue of whether to form the Communist party in June or in September. The reason for waiting until September was intolerable to the Russians. The desire to maneuver a few months more for the sake of a few thousand members smacked of opportunism, conciliationism, vacillation—the earmarks of centrism.

To the argument that the best way to expose the injustice and bureaucracy of the Socialist National Executive Committee was to fight for admission to the Socialist convention, the head of the Russian federation, Alexander Stoklitsky, replied scornfully:

> Must we stoop so low as to beg admission in order that we may capture the masses? Bolsheviki never run after the masses: Communists are not satisfied to be in the tail. They are ever in the lead. To be the tail is the characteristic peculiarity of the Centrists.

For good measure, he added:

> The builders of the Communist Party dare not run after masses whose hearts must be softened by the injustice of the N.E.C. We do not care for a Communist Party minus communist principles.[9]

To which Fraina flung back:

> There is danger ahead, comrades, and particularly comrades of the Russian Federation. The vanity and the lust for power of leaders must be crushed. We must have revolutionary discipline. We must have a mass movement. There is only one Left Wing, organized in the National Council. All power to the Left Wing! [10]

As Fraina intimated, there was more to this quarrel than a difference over principles or tactics. Personal animosities were beginning to come to the surface. The Russian leaders were behaving more and more dictatorially. The number of candidates who wanted to play the role of the American Lenin had increased. The struggle for power had made its appearance.

By a strange combination of circumstances, even before any direct influence could be exerted from Russia itself, the "Americans" were pitted against the "Russians"—or, more broadly, the English-speaking elements were pitted against the foreign-language forces led by the Russians. The Americans began to entertain thoughts about the need for an American leadership and the dangers of estrangement from American life. They were not willing to act merely as a native front for the foreign-language federations. They were playing for time in order to invite into the Communist party the maximum number of English-speaking members who were for any reason still in the Socialist party. The postponement of the Communist party's organization was, therefore, a weapon in the struggle for control against the foreign-language federations. The Russians were convinced that they were "more advanced" politically and alone deserved to be entrusted with the responsibility of giving leadership to the Communist party. To them, the Americans were novices in need of a long apprenticeship and a strong hand. The foreign-language federations were much more homogeneous and more tightly organized than anything the

Americans had immediately available. Above all, the Russian federation leaders felt a direct kinship with the Russian Bolsheviks and with a European revolutionary tradition from which the Americans were by definition debarred. The sooner the Communist party was organized, the more likely the foreign-language federations would be to be able to control it from the start.[11]

In this forerunner of all Communist factional struggles, the Americans found themselves in favor of the broadest mass influence, the Russians in favor of the orthodox political line. The debate between them was actually conducted in these terms, especially by the foreign-language federations; for them, more mass influence meant more American influence, and they were frankly contemptuous of the Americans. The more extreme proponents of foreign-language control actually conceived of the American Communist party as primarily a foreign-language party that had to be protected from "American" contamination. For the Americans, more was at stake than a fight for control. They had to prove that they were fit to occupy a place of leadership in the revolutionary movement in their own country.

The first Russian victory

In the first test of strength, mass influence won out. But, as was so often to prove the case, it was only a temporary victory.

The Russian-Michigan alliance went ahead as threatened. A new call for a national convention in Chicago on September 1, 1919, "for the purpose of organizing the Communist Party of America" was issued early in July by a "National Organization Committee" of seven members, including Batt as secretary, Stoklitsky as organizer, and J. V. Stilson, head of the Lithuanian federation, as treasurer.[12] This committee began to publish an official organ, *The Communist*, with Batt as editor.[13] Headquarters were set up at the Chicago office of the Russian federation, 1221 Blue Island Avenue. Besides the seven suspended federations, a portion of the Jewish federation, a Left Wing conference in Minnesota, the Michigan organization, and about a dozen city locals made up the immediate backing of the National Organization Committee.

The National Council elected by the majority of the June conference went its own way. It made a gesture to show that the strategy of taking over the Socialist party still held good. Though the official Socialist National Executive Committee had set aside the referendum to elect a new N.E.C., the Left Wing went through the motions of holding a session of the new "committee" in Chicago on July 26-27. Eight Left Wing candidates who claimed election, including Reed, Fraina, and Ruthenberg, came together, solemnly tabulated the votes, and imperiously demanded the appearance of the executive secretary of the Socialist party, Adolph Germer, to turn the party's national headquarters over to them. L. E. Katterfeld was named temporary party chairman and Alfred Wagenknecht temporary executive secretary. The "committee" also voted to reinstate the suspended and expelled organizations, to adopt *The Revolutionary Age* as the official party organ, and to affiliate with the Communist International.[14]

While this elaborate tomfoolery was going on in Chicago, a much more important meeting was taking place in New York on July 27. The suspended foreign-language federations gave two representatives of the National Left Wing Council, Ferguson and Gitlow, a chance to make a final plea for staying a few weeks more in the Socialist party. As Gitlow has described the scene, it was more like a court-martial than a conference. The would-be revolutionary inquisitors sat solemnly around a long oblong table, making no effort to hide their boredom as he argued against them. When he finished, they talked among themselves in Russian without bothering to give the two worried Americans a translation. The tribunal was adamant—no participation in the Socialist convention on any terms. Ferguson and Gitlow were dismissed "like two schoolboys who had just received a spanking." Ferguson was shaken. He was ready to concede to the superior wisdom of the Russians. Gitlow was stubborn. The Russians' arrogance succeeded only in making him more irascible.[15]

THE GREAT SCHISM

The cave-in of the National Council came the next day, July 28. By a vote of 5 to 2, the majority reversed itself and decided to go to Chicago to form a Communist party instead of making a last effort to win over the Socialist party. The five were Ruthenberg, Ferguson, Ballam, Wolfe and Cohen. The hold-outs were Gitlow and Larkin. Two members did not vote because they worked on the party organ. Fraina sided with the majority, MacAlpine with the minority.[16]

The Russians had worked themselves into a position to dictate. They had two English-speaking groups to do their bidding, the Michigan organization and the majority of the National Council. In the end, the Russians kept both on leash.[17] After considerable negotiation, a Joint Call was issued by I. E. Ferguson, of the National Left Wing Council, and Dennis E. Batt, of the National Organization Committee, for a constituent assembly in Chicago on September 1, 1919, to organize the Communist party of America.[18]

Meanwhile, the National Council's minority, Gitlow, Larkin, and MacAlpine, refused to become a party to the deal. They were backed by Reed and Wagenknecht—and any movement backed by Reed, a popular idol, could not be easily dismissed. To Reed and Gitlow, the capitulation of the National Council was a craven betrayal. Their aversion for the Russians was now matched by their contempt for their English-speaking former associates. By August 15, the new minority had an official organ, *The Voice of Labor,* with Reed as editor and Gitlow as business manager. They were still going to attend the Socialist convention in Chicago on August 30. After that, they were still going to form a Communist party—of their own. What had started out for them as a war on one front—against the Socialist Right Wing—had broadened out into a fight on all fronts at once—against the foreign-language federations, the Michigan organization, and the rest of the English-speaking Left Wing.

11

The Sibling Rivalry

As the summer of 1919 waned, all the wings of the mangled Socialist movement converged on Chicago for the battle of the conventions.

The Right Wing mobilized for the convention of the official Socialist party which opened at Machinists' Hall, 113 South Ashland Boulevard, on August 30.

The main body of the Left Wing moved into position for a separate convention to organize a pure, genuine Communist party at the headquarters of the Russian Federation, 1221 Blue Island Avenue, on September 1.

The Reed-Gitlow flying column was planning to stage a raid on the Socialist convention at Machinists' Hall before camping down to form a second Communist organization.

The first engagement was the battle for control of the Socialist convention.

The official Socialist party was preparing to dig in for a siege in the auditorium on the second floor of Machinists' Hall. Special precautions were taken against the threatened Left Wing invasion. It was not enough for delegates to appear with credentials from state organizations. Special white cards were issued to keep out enemy infiltrators. When Reed and Gitlow learned of the rigid security regulations, they hurriedly called a caucus of their cohorts, fifty-two in number, in the billiard and bar room on the ground floor of Machinists' Hall on Friday evening, August 29. A plan of operations was agreed on. Only a few Left-Wingers had been able to get the precious white cards. The others were to come early the next morning, ignore the cards, rush into the second-floor auditorium, grab seats, and demand recognition. If this strategy failed, they were to withdraw in a body and hold their own convention in the name of the Socialist party. A steering committee, including Reed, Gitlow, Katterfeld, and Ruthenberg, was appointed. Ruthenberg had previously gone over to the other Left Wing faction which believed in boycotting the Socialist convention, but he attended this caucus in the interests of Left Wing unity.

The plan of operations miscarried immediately. The janitor of the building doubled as the bartender. He was also a friend of Executive Secretary Adolph Germer, with whom he had once worked in the South Illinois mine fields. He found the minutes of the caucus on a table in the bar room and turned them over to Germer, who had them mimeographed and distributed to the Right Wing delegates. Unknown to the Left Wing plotters, everyone was forewarned and forearmed the next morning, including a detail of police. The police were there apparently as a result of another Left Wing *faux pas*. Wagenknecht had incautiously boasted to a reporter for the *Chicago Tribune* that his group was ready to "take over the convention by storm" if necessary. The reporter passed on the word to a detective who saw to it that police were present to calm the storm.

Early the next morning, August 30, the Left Wing appeared in a group according to plan. They rushed into the second floor auditorium and occupied seats. When Julius Gerber, the New York nemesis of the Left Wing, arrived a little later to check credentials, he found them waiting. Gerber ordered Reed out and, when the latter refused to budge, tried to remove him forcibly—without success. Adolph Germer was hurriedly called to the scene and again ordered Reed and his band to leave. According to Germer, Reed began to fan the air and shout, "Make the police clear the hall!" Germer gladly obliged; the Left-Wingers were thrown out of the auditorium and retreated to the billiard room on the floor below. They were elated with the results of this morning's work, because it enabled them to make indignant propaganda about the use of capitalist police. Another caucus was held at which the decision was reached to meet as the duly authorized Socialist convention the following day.[1]

This was not the last walk-out from the official Socialist convention. A sizable group of Left Wing delegates whose seats were contested remained for a decision in their cases. When the committee on the contested seats failed to report on the first day, Joseph M. Coldwell of Rhode Island rose to protest, was ruled out of order by the chairman, Judge Jacob Panken of New York, announced that he was withdrawing from the convention, and called on other Left-Wingers to follow him. Still another walk-out was led by James H. Dolsen of the California delegation the following day. In all, twenty-six more delegates seceded from the Socialist party.[2] This did not mean, however, that the party was now "homogeneous and harmonious," as Hillquit had expected it to be after the split. There was still another Left Wing group, which included J. Louis Engdahl and William F. Kruse of Illinois, and Alexander Trachtenberg, J. B. Salutsky, and Benjamin Glassberg of New York, which could not yet bring itself to break away.

The Communist Labor party

At 6 p.m. on Sunday, August 31, eighty-two delegates from twenty-one states, led by Reed and Gitlow, came together in the billiard room on the first floor of Machinists' Hall. They included the entire delegations from California, Colorado, Delaware, Florida, Kentucky, Nebraska, Oregon, Rhode Island, Texas, Utah, Washington, Virginia, and West Virginia, and partial delegations from Illinois, Indiana, Kansas, Missouri, New Jersey, and New York.[3] Alfred Wagenknecht of Ohio rapped the gavel as temporary chairman to start the proceedings. Immediately everyone rose and sang the "Internationale." Cheers rang out—three cheers for Eugene V. Debs, then in jail, and three cheers for the I.W.W. The spirit of this convention was jubilant and, until some serious political differences were uncovered, lighthearted. The name of the new party, the Communist Labor party of America, was not adopted until September 2, though the actual birth is often dated from the opening of the convention on August 31. The last half of the convention was moved to the I.W.W. hall at 119 Throop Street.[4]

In a sense, the Communist Labor party lost its reason for existence by coming into existence. The original split between the Left Wing factions had taken place over the advisability of making an attempt to capture the Socialist convention. The attempt had been made and had failed. If there had been no more to the split, it could have been healed at this point. But there was more. A move by Ruthenberg, who attended the first session of the Communist Labor party convention, made this clear. He proposed that the first order of business should be consideration of uniting with the other Communist convention scheduled for the following day. He was voted down 37 to 31, after an angry debate lasting all night. Jack Carney threatened to go back to Duluth and denounce all concerned if any concessions were made to the foreign-language federations. Reed said, in effect, that the federations could come crawling to this convention if they wanted a joint party. Basically, then, the reason for the split was a question of power as well as principle—who was to control the new party, the "Americans" or the "foreigners"? This question kept coming to the surface in various ways long after the quarrel about the Socialist convention had ended. Finally, a committee of five was appointed to negotiate with a similar committee from the other Communist convention.

Boudin, true to form, precipitated another minor crisis. He had been elected a delegate to the Socialist convention by the expelled Brooklyn local and had gone downstairs to the Left Wing convention in the billiard room after the Brooklyn delegates were refused seats. Boudin's big moment came during the debate on the platform. He wanted a simple statement appealing to the workers to support the new party in the political field. He objected to what he considered unorthodox terminology by John Reed in calling for "the conquest of political power." When Reed tried to defend his proposal by quoting from the *Communist Manifesto* of Marx and Engels, Boudin laughed scornfully. Reed, whose reputation as a theorist was notoriously weak, was no match for Boudin's irony and erudition. Control of the convention seemed to hinge on the right quotation. Reed slipped out of the building and returned with a copy of the famous Marxist classic. Triumphantly, he pointed out the exact words which Boudin had contemptuously rejected. All that Boudin could muster in reply was, "It's a very poor translation," forgetting that this was one English translation Engels himself had personally approved. Then Gitlow arose and castigated Boudin for attempting to dilute and destroy the scientific Marxist integrity of the platform. Boudin could suffer no more. Shaking with rage, he fled out of the hall crying, according to one version, "It's a lie, it's a damn lie!" According to another version, his parting shot was "I did not leave a party of crooks to join a party of lunatics!" [5]

Reed's formula carried by a vote of 46 to 22. The one-third minority was large enough to indicate that the Communist Labor convention was far from agreed on fundamentals. The basic leadership was made up of people like Reed, Gitlow, and Wagenknecht, who considered themselves full-fledged Communists and unconditionally pledged their loyalty to the Third International in Moscow. Others were there, however, to protest against the Socialist leadership's undemocratic methods and mass expulsions. The unifying element was negative—a common antipathy for both the Old Guard Socialists and the foreign-language federations in control of the other two conventions. It was much too weak a bond to make the Communist Labor party a healthy, homogeneous organization.

Lore was another casualty. He had the misfortune of being elected to the National Executive Committee of the new party. But such was his in-and-out record in the Left Wing that the leaders of the convention feared that he would embarrass them in their feud with the other Communist group. Reed, Gitlow, and others attacked him as unfit to participate in the leadership of a Communist party. They hastily called for another election and substituted Max Bedacht for

Lore.[6] This repudiation did not save Lore from violent attack by the other side. After the conventions, the editors of *The Class Struggle,* the original intellectual organ of the Left Wing, were split in their allegiances. Lore at first favored neutrality, then changed his mind in favor of the Communist Labor party, which was then able to take over the magazine by a vote of 16 to 13. This service earned Lore a blast from the other group as one of the enemy's "compromisers, Centrists, masters of the revolutionary phrase and poltroons in action."[7] Lore's genius for pleasing no one rarely deserted him.

On the organizational side, Alfred Wagenknecht was elected executive secretary; Reed and Wagenknecht as international delegates; Gitlow, Charles Baker of Ohio, R. E. Richardson of Utah, and Arne Swabeck of Washington to the Labor Committee; and Max Bedacht of California, Alexander Bilan of Ohio, Jack Carney of Minnesota, L. E. Katterfeld of Kansas,[8] and Edward I. Lindgren of New York to the National Executive Committee. Most of these became familiar names in the Communist movement, but few of the other sixty-odd delegates lasted much longer. A number of papers supported the Communist Labor party—*The Voice of Labor* and later *Communist Labor* in New York, *Truth* in Duluth, *The Workers' World* in Kansas City, and *The Toiler* in Cleveland. National headquarters were established at 3207 Clark Avenue, Cleveland.

The Communist party

At about noon on September 1, the convention of the Communist party of America opened with 128 delegates and 9 fraternal delegates at the headquarters of the Russian federation in Chicago. The delegates liked to call it "Smolny" after an educational institute for the daughters of the Russian nobility in Petrograd, which became the first headquarters of the Russian Soviets.

The hall of the American Smolny was decorated with red bunting and revolutionary placards. Two large floral designs were made up of roses on a red background shaped as a flag. Behind the speakers' rostrum hung pictures of Trotsky, Marx, and Lenin. Just before the convention was about to open, the Chicago police's Anarchist Squad broke into the hall. A platoon of detectives tore down the red bunting, the placards, and the floral decorations. Police photographs were taken of the entire assemblage. Then a ten-piece brass band struck up the "Internationale." The singing and cheering were long and loud. Just as Batt of the Michigan delegation was about to mount the platform to open the convention, he discovered that he was about to be arrested for having violated the Illinois anti-espionage law in a speech three days earlier. After Batt said a few words, greeting the delegates and denouncing the "political tricksters" of the rival Communist convention over at Machinists' Hall, a detective stepped forward and handed him a warrant of arrest. Rose Pastor Stokes cried, "They are arresting our comrade—three cheers for the revolution!" The detective roared back, "Shut up—it's always a woman that starts the trouble!" A local Communist lawyer who protested was badly beaten. Sitting quietly in the gallery was Jacob Spolansky, in charge of the Chicago office of the Bureau of Investigation,* taking notes of everything that went on for the next five days. After all this preliminary excitement, Louis C. Fraina made the opening keynote address, which ended with these wishful words: "We now end, once for all, all factional disputes. We are at an end with bickering. We are at an end with controversy. We are here to build a party of action." [9]

Fraina's optimism was premature. The convention was a tug of war between three tightly knit and highly disciplined blocs. The foreign-language federations, led by the Russians, were the strongest. The English-speaking majority of the former National Left Wing Council, with Fraina and Ruthenberg as its outstanding figures, was almost as large numerically. The Michigan organization was about half the size of the other two, with approximately twenty votes. The weakest of the three blocs held the balance of power. From the outset, the federations met in caucus and voted as a unit. When the so-called Council group realized its disadvantage, it also resorted to a caucus form of organization. Then both blocs formed a joint

* Forerunner of the Federal Bureau of Investigation.

THE SIBLING RIVALRY

caucus with nine members from each. The real decisions of the convention, therefore, were made behind the scenes.

The first dispute almost split the three blocs at the start. The Council group was still sorely troubled by the break with the other Communist convention and wanted to make overtures for a reconciliation. The federations and the Michigan group were opposed to even a gesture in this direction. A motion by Ferguson to appoint a committee of five to confer with the rival convention was defeated by a vote of 75 to 31. The English-speaking minority had to resort to a desperate measure to break the hold of the federations-Michigan alliance. On the morning of the second day, they staged a protest "strike." The minority members, including Fraina, Ruthenberg and Lovestone, announced their resignations from an important committee. The Russian chieftains were temporarily stunned. The federations' caucus met and saw fit to reverse itself. On the committee of five, however, the federations made sure they had a majority.

The negotiations came to nothing. The Communist party merely offered to accept as delegates to its convention any Communist Labor delegates who were acceptable to its credentials committee. The Communist Labor party countered by proposing that the two negotiating committees should meet as a joint credentials committee to agree upon recommendations to both conventions. The C.P. answered by reiterating its original condition. The C.L.P. made a second and more drastic proposal that the two conventions join in an informal meeting. The C.P. coldly replied that it had already invited its rival's delegates to attend as special guests.[10]

In effect, the Communist party was much the more self-confident and self-satisfied of the two. It refused to make any real concessions, except that it would admit some Communist Labor delegates who could pass its tests. Though the C.L.P. seemed to be much less demanding, it knew well that any proposal implying equality of the two conventions ran little risk of acceptance. The negotiations on both sides were entered into and carried on less with the intention of coming to an agreement than for the purpose of maneuvering for a favorable position in the party warfare sure to break out.

184   THE ROOTS OF AMERICAN COMMUNISM

The second important dispute reversed the convention's alliances. This time it was a question of basic policy, and the Michigan group found itself up against a solid coalition of the other two major blocs.

The break between the Michigan group and its erstwhile allies, the Russians, took place in the program committee. Fraina presented one draft of the proposed program, Batt another. Hourwich and Stoklitsky voted for a condensed version of Fraina's draft, which won by a vote of 7 to 2 with Batt and Wicks in the minority. When the same line-up put across Fraina's program at the convention, it was the turn of the Michigan group (the term was used to include a small number of similar-thinking delegates from other states) to go on strike. Twenty delegates announced solemnly that they were going to refuse to vote for or against the Manifesto and Program and, furthermore, refuse nomination for any future post in the party. This second strike went unheeded. It meant the virtual end of the role played in the Communist movement by the Michigan group.[11]

But the alliance between the foreign-language federations and the English-speaking Council group was obviously a temporary and uneasy one. A Socialist observer reported that not a single Russian hand went up when Ruthenberg, Ferguson, Fraina, or other English-speaking delegates were nominated for committees.[12] Yet the Russians themselves were not always united. Hourwich of the New York Russians and Stoklitsky of the Chicago Russians fell out over the location of the party's future headquarters. With the help of the non-Russian delegates, Chicago won by a big vote.[13]

The most important posts in the newly organized Communist party went to Ruthenberg and Fraina, the former becoming National Secretary, the latter International Secretary and editor of party publications. The Central Executive Committee of fifteen included Ruthenberg, Fraina, Charles Dirba of Minnesota, Harry M. Wicks of Oregon, John J. Ballam of Massachusetts, Alexander Bittelman of New York, and Jay Lovestone of New York.[14] The official party organ, *The Communist,* which replaced *The Revolutionary Age,* was entrusted to Fraina's editorship. National headquarters were established at 1219 Blue Island Avenue, Chicago.

The old and the new

What was old and what was new about the American Communist movement at its birth in 1919?

The two Communist parties showed clearly that they had their roots in the old tradition of socialism and syndicalism. In some respects, indeed, there was little above the roots.

Like the historic Left Wing, both Communist parties were still fighting the battle of immediate demands versus the ultimate goal. Both were true to the tradition of excluding all immediate demands or partial reforms. The Communist party's program specifically insisted that its parliamentary representatives "shall not introduce or support reform measures." Any Communist elected to office had to limit himself to analyzing "capitalist legislative proposals and reform palliatives as evasions of the issue and as of no fundamental significance to the working class." The Communist Labor party's program instructed its political candidates to emphasize that "the chances of winning even advanced reforms of the present capitalist system at the polls is extremely remote; and even if it were possible, these reforms would not weaken the capitalist system." It went on to recognize "only one demand: the establishment of the Dictatorship of the Proletariat."

For the Communist founders, then, there was no such thing as the "united front." They considered it just as reprehensible to cooperate in any way with reform groups or parties as for Communists themselves to preach reforms. The Communist party's program took the precaution to name the Socialist party, Labor party, Non-Partisan League, People's Council, Municipal Ownership Leagues, "etc.," as the type of groups and parties with which cooperation was forbidden. The Communist Labor party took the same prohibition for granted. This revolutionary isolationism was another link to the historic Left Wing.

Unlike the pure syndicalists, however, the Communists did not reject political action in principle. For them the class struggle was essentially political in nature, in the sense that Communists aimed at the conquest of political power. But, in practice, the difference was not so great. The early Communists' conception of practical political activity was strictly negative. It was limited severely to exposing "parliamentary democracy" and making "revolutionary propaganda."

The trade-union policy of the first Communists was also inherited from the historic Left Wing. "Dual unionism" was obligatory for both parties, the only question being what kind of dual unions. In this respect, the Communist Labor party was the most traditional. It merely endorsed the I.W.W. Its program lauded the "propaganda and example" of the I.W.W. without reservation. In the midst of their convention, Reed and Gitlow made a pilgrimage to pay their respects to Haywood, who was too busy with his court appeal to give much attention to the Communist conventions.[15] It was as if the Comintern were considered the official guide internationally and the I.W.W. the chosen instrument in the American labor movement —a close approximation of the way Reed, for one, felt about them. The Communist party also dismissed the A.F. of L. as a "bulwark of capitalism." But it came out for the formation of a "general industrial union organization, embracing the I.W.W., W.I.I.U. [Workers International Industrial Union], independent and secession unions, militant unions of the A.F. of L., and the unorganized workers, on the basis of the revolutionary class struggle." In its press, the Communist party subsequently adopted a more critical attitude toward the I.W.W. than did the Communist Labor party. The two parties did not differ so much about dual unionism in general as about the I.W.W. in particular.

Organizationally, the Socialist party was the basic model for the new Communist parties. They carried over the custom of electing an executive secretary, national executive committee, international secretary, and international delegates, though the latter two offices were dropped as soon as it was discovered that they had no counterparts in foreign Communist organizations. In the Communist party, the foreign-language federations were virtually maintained intact with the same functions and privileges. Even the Communist Labor party could not get along without federations. It tried to clip their wings by ruling out "autonomous federations" and defining them as "propaganda organizations" only. But the difference was more verbal than real. The Communist party continued to be plagued more than its rival by the foreign-language organizations, chiefly because it had more of them.

What was new? There was a new ring about the theoretical parts of the program, especially those dealing with war and imperialism, the nature of the state, and the dictatorship of the proletariat. A new vocabulary had come into vogue as the writings of Lenin, Trotsky, Bukharin, and other Russian leaders had become available. At the same time, however, some of the pre-Russian influence lingered on. The Communist party's program still devoted an entire section to "Mass Action," followed by one devoted to the "Dictatorship of the Proletariat." The Communist Labor party's program referred to "action of the masses," a slightly different formulation into which the other Communist group read an insidious attempt to water down the true faith. Long and bitter was the doctrinal warfare that broke out over the difference between the two phrases.

Above all, both parties pledged their total and unconditional allegiance to the Communist International. The internationalism of the Communist Labor party, however, was impugned because it made such a to-do about the need for an American movement not controlled by the foreign-language federations. "And this party protests its thorough internationalism!" scoffed the organ of the Communist party.[16] Soon it let loose a bigger and more deadly blast at what it considered the Communist Labor party's most vulnerable spot: "The Socialist Party and the Communist Labor Party agree on one thing—an 'American' movement, not a 'foreign' movement, is necessary. It is appropriate that the Communist Labor Party, which has not yet severed the umbilical cord binding it to the Socialist Party, should express this treacherous ideology of 'Americanism'."[17] To the Communist party, as its program put it, internationalism meant that "the problems of the American workers are identical with the problems of the workers of the world."[18]

This was the first appearance in the American Communist movement of the "treacherous ideology of 'Americanism'." The American heresy was discovered almost as soon as the American movement was born. It was to make many more appearances and take many other forms.

The founders

How many and what sort of people made up the Communist movement at its inception?

As might be expected, statistical information for this period is scarce. It was almost impossible even for the parties themselves to discover what they were like before the government drove them underground, as it was shortly to do. Yet a careful analysis of such information as is available can be enlightening. Since the statistical machinery was primitive and haphazard, the figures need not be considered as anything more than approximations. They do reveal tendencies, however, which can be confirmed by later and fuller figures.

Both parties, of course, claimed the maximum for themselves and the minimum for their rivals. The Communist party gave itself 58,000 members and gave the Communist Labor party only about 10,000.[19] The Communist Labor party gave itself 30,000 members and gave the Communist party only 27,000.[20] The total for the two was 68,000, according to the first, and 57,000, according to the second. The Communist party was much the stronger of the two in the foreign-language federations. It claimed the Hungarian, Lettish, Lithuanian, Polish, Russian, South Slavic, Esthonian, and Ukrainian.[21] The Communist Labor party was admittedly much stronger in the west. It was recognized as the dominant force in Washington, Missouri, Colorado, Oregon, Kansas, Nebraska, Utah, and Kentucky.[22]

But these figures, based on the representation claimed by the delegates to the conventions, were virtually equivalent to the number that broke away from the Socialist party. The circumstances leading to the conventions were so complex and confused, however, that there was no way of knowing which portion of the delegates or the members they claimed to represent really belonged to the Communist movement. At best, the figures tell us what the Communist movement *might* have been able to claim if it had succeeded in winning over and holding the great majority of ex-Socialists. What the delegates said they represented at the conventions and what they could bring into the organizations were two different things.

There is reason to believe that the maximum figure of those who signed up after the conventions was closer to 40,000. "More than 40,000 dues-paying members" for both the Communist and Communist Labor parties within two months of the conventions was claimed by one official Communist source.[23] For the Communist party alone, we have the actual dues payments for the three months following the convention:

October 1919	27,341
November 1919	20,261
December 1919	23,624
Average	23,744

An official estimate of the language composition of the Communist party at the end of 1919 arrives at a slightly larger figure:

English	1,900 *
Non-federation Language members	1,100
Esthonian	280
German	850
Hungarian	1,000
Jewish	1,000
Lettish	1,200
Lithuanian	4,400
Polish	1,750
Russian	7,000
South Slavic	2,200
Ukrainian	4,000
Total	26,680

* Including 800 of the Michigan organization which soon dropped out.

These figures tend to bear out the Communist Labor party's estimate of about 27,000 for the Communist party.[24] If we estimate the figure for the Communist Labor party itself at about 10,000, the total falls somewhat short of 40,000. Gitlow believes that the two Communist parties' membership totaled slightly less than 25,000.[25] It seems safe to assume that the American Communist movement started out with a minimum of 25,000 and a maximum of 40,000 enrolled members after the conventions. Whatever the figure was, the fact that only a small portion represented individual membership must be taken into account. Ruthenberg and Bedacht later admitted that 90 per cent of the total membership of both parties was contributed by the foreign-language federations which enrolled their members *en masse*. If we distinguish between those who were swept into the Communist movement for political reasons and those who were swept along for nationalistic reasons, the number of genuine Communists should be reduced even further.

The most startling and significant aspect of the American Communist movement in 1919 was its national composition. For the Communist party, the Russian members represented almost 25 per cent of the total, and the entire East-European membership accounted for over 75 per cent. The English-speaking members represented only 7 per cent with the Michigan group and 4 per cent without it. Though the percentage of English-speaking members was higher in the Communist Labor party, it could not have been very high if 90 per cent of both parties came from the foreign-language federations. Gitlow believes that about one-tenth of the Left Wing before the conventions was English-speaking and that after the split the percentage was reduced still further.[26] It seems fair to accept a figure of about 10 per cent as maximum for the native-born or English-speaking membership. How low the minimum might have been was indicated the following year by Ruthenberg when he professed that the Communist party did not have five speakers "who could present its cause in English and the same was true in regard to writers and editors"—an exaggeration made for factional purposes but not too wide of the mark.[27]

THE SIBLING RIVALRY 191

The parties' national composition most eloquently proved that the purely political or ideological impact of the Russian Revolution was not the only, or even the most important, force at work in the birth of the American Communist movement. The Slavic preponderance was so great that it can be ascribed only to a nationalistic identification with the mother country. In fact, even the English-speaking members tried to exploit their own identification with the Slavic delegates and the Russian tradition. "For one thing, the fact that the Federation delegates were largely Slavic emphasized the close union between the organization of the Communist Party here and the parent organization which came into being in Moscow in March of this year—the Communist International," Ferguson boasted in the official account of the Communist party's convention. "It was the Russian expression of Marxism which predominated this Convention, the Marxism of Lenin, and the party traditions of the Bolsheviki." [28] For the Americans, the Russians in the United States were like surrogates of the Russians in Russia, so closely identified had Russia and Russians become with the revolution, despite the fact that most of the American Russians were "November Bolsheviks," converted after the Bolshevik revolution.

Yet it is easy to exaggerate the long-run importance of the Russian preponderance in the early Communist movement. That it was overshadowing in both numbers and influence for the first two or three years cannot be doubted. But this predominance did not last, for one reason because so many of the Russian leaders went back to Russia. The Hourwiches and Stoklitskys vanished from the American scene, the Ruthenbergs and Lovestones remained. Small as it was in the beginning, the English-speaking group provided the core of long-run leaders, if not the majority of the rank and file. It is just to say that the American Communist movement started out as a predominantly Slavic movement, but it did not remain that way for very long. More and more, the Americans took over the leading positions, while other nationalities supplanted the Russians and other East Europeans among the rank and file.

Among the foreign-language federations, the two considered

strongholds of the Right Wing were the Jewish and the Finnish, with the German and Italian in the doubtful category.[29] A Left Wing was organized in the Jewish Socialist federation by five young men early in 1919.[30] They made such headway that they were able to put up a fight for control of the federation at its convention in Boston in June that year. Of the 136 delegates, 53 were counted in the Left Wing. When their demand to abolish all reform planks in the party's platform was defeated, 38 walked out and held a Left Wing convention on the floor below.[31] This Left Wing faction transformed itself into the Jewish Communist federation at a Philadelphia convention in October.[32] Its organ, *Der Kampf,* was edited by Alexander Bittelman. It was officially estimated that the Jewish Communist federation contributed less than 4 per cent of the total membership in the Communist party.[33] The increased importance of the Jewish element in the Communist movement came somewhat later.

The Negroes counted least of all in the early Communist movement. Not a single Negro delegate seems to have attended either convention. So little was the Negro problem in the Communist consciousness that the Communist Labor program had nothing at all to say about it. The Communist party's program connected the "problem of the Negro worker" with that of the unskilled worker. The basic analysis was inherited from the Socialist movement: "The Negro problem is a political and economic problem. The racial oppression of the Negro is simply the expression of his economic bondage and oppression, each intensifying the other." The American Communists did not depart from this traditional Marxist attitude until the next decade. In this area, as in so many others, the American Communists at first followed in the footsteps of the historic Left Wing.

In the beginning—and for a long time afterward—women played a subordinate role in the movement. A few stood out, though they never gave the men much competition in the policy-making leadership. The oldest active woman organizer was Ella Reeve Bloor, fifty-seven years old in 1919 and still going strong. She had served as a Socialist organizer in several states before she helped to set up a branch of the

Communist Labor party in Kansas City and later became the national organizer of its Eastern Division. The Communist Labor party in California enrolled Charlotte Anita Whitney, then fifty-two, a former social worker, a descendant on her father's side from *Mayflower* settlers, with an uncle who was a justice of the United States Supreme Court. The most colorful female figure in the Communist party was Rose Pastor Stokes, the beautiful Russian-Jewish cigar-sweat-shop worker who married an aristocratic American millionaire, J. G. Phelps Stokes. She wrote poems and plays, drew pictures, agitated for birth control, and mounted soapboxes for socialism. She belonged to the group that had left the Socialist party in support of the war, but she changed her mind after the Russian Revolution and went on to become an ardent Communist, though she could not persuade her husband to go along with her. The strongest female political personality and the only one ever considered a threat to the male monopoly in the top leadership was Juliet Stuart Poyntz. She came from a middle-class background in Nevada, was educated at Barnard, Columbia, Oxford, and the London School of Economics, taught history at Columbia, founded and directed the educational work of the International Ladies Garment Workers Union, and went over from socialism to communism with the rest of the pro-Bolshevik Left Wing. Rose Wortis, a slight-looking needle-trades worker, became the most effective woman trade-union leader developed in the Communist movement.[34]

Ruthenberg's leadership

The man who emerged from the conventions in 1919 as the outstanding American Communist was Charles Emil Ruthenberg, a tall, balding, thirty-eight-year-old veteran of the Socialist movement.

Nothing in his background particularly distinguished him from hundreds of thousands of other first-generation Americans. His father, an immigrant from Germany, had been a longshoreman. The son was born in Cleveland, Ohio, and attended a German-Lutheran elementary school for eight years and a business college for two. School came to an end for him at the age of sixteen when he went to work sandpapering moldings in a picture-frame factory. He spent eight years working for the Cleveland branch of a New York book company, as house-to-house salesman, stenographer, bookkeeper, and finally head of a department. For seven years more, until 1917, he worked in the sales department of a roofing company, estimated bids for a building company, and purchased supplies for a ladies' garment manufacturer. Until he was thirty-five, then, he worked at white-collar jobs which required an orderly, efficient administrative ability.[35]

He came to socialism, he once explained, as a substitute for the ministry. When he was still working for the book company, he began studying the Bible and theology in his spare time to prepare himself for the pulpit. Instead, he became interested in evolution, then sociology, and finally socialism.[36] When he joined the Socialist party of Cleveland in 1909 at the age of twenty-seven, he wasted little time in becoming an active organizer and perennial candidate. He ran for state treasurer of Ohio on the Socialist ticket in 1910, for mayor of Cleveland in 1911, for governor of Ohio in 1912, for United States senator in 1914, and for mayor again in 1915. Cleveland was a stronghold of the Left Wing, and Ruthenberg became its outstanding local spokesman. In the 1912 crisis, this meant that he wanted the party to emphasize its revolutionary goal instead of vote-catching "municipal reform tactics."[37] His career leaped ahead in 1917. In April, he stood out in the St. Louis convention of the Socialist party as the principal leader of the Left Wing. He was the Left Wing representative in the subcommittee of three that wrote the famous St. Louis antiwar resolution. In June, he left his job with the ladies' garment manufacturer to become a full-time organizer and secretary for the Cleveland local of the Socialist party. In July, he was sentenced to one year in the workhouse for making antiwar and anticonscription speeches. In November, he again ran for mayor of Cleveland and received 27,000 votes out of a total of 100,000. Though his political activity had been confined to Cleveland, he was now one of the few nationally known Left Wing leaders with a record of real achievement behind him. Nevertheless, he was still far from the Communist ideology he was soon to embrace. In 1917 he wrote a pamphlet which used the traditional vocabulary of "industrial democracy" and the "Cooperative Commonwealth" without a trace of the new Bolshevik literary style.[38]

The next big year for Ruthenberg was 1919. Cleveland was the scene of the American Socialist movement's "baptism of blood," as *The Liberator* put it.[39] A big May Day demonstration was violently attacked by police, and blood flowed as army trucks and tanks, police cars, ambulances, and patrol wagons drove into the crowds. Ruthenberg, the principal speaker, tried to make himself heard and was arrested.[40] When he came to New York the following month to attend the National Left Wing Conference, he stood out both as a successful organizer and as an eminent martyr. As long as the Left Wing had its center of gravity in Boston or New York, Ruthenberg was not able to play a major role in its development, but this conference launched him as a strong contender for the leadership. He was elected to the nine-man National Left Wing Council, seven of the remaining eight coming from New York or Boston. His greatest obstacle was the hostility of the foreign-language federations, caused by his lining up with the other English-speaking delegates against the premature split in the Socialist party. But Ruthenberg was one of those who capitulated on this issue and attended the convention of the Communist party, even though fourteen of the sixteen Ohio delegates went to the convention of the Communist Labor party. As we have seen, his conscience bothered him, and he made some attempt to prevent an irrevocable breach between the two Communist groups, a show of independence which also helped to estrange him from the foreign-language federations.

Nevertheless, Ruthenberg was the natural choice for National Secretary of the Communist party for two reasons—he was a native-born American, and he had demonstrated his ability to run an organization. Almost no one else qualified on both counts. Fraina had done more for the pro-Communist Left Wing in the lean years, but he was almost exclusively a propagandist. Once the party was born, an organizer was needed, and Fraina totally lacked the taste and talent for organization. Unfortunately for Fraina, when his dream came true, the organizer became more important than the propagandist, and he had to accept what was at best the number two position in the Communist party. In later years, a legend spread that Ruthenberg was the "outstanding founder and leader" of the American Communist movement.[41] Until 1919, this was far from true. If we look at the foundation of the Communist movement as a process which lasted much longer than a few months, Ruthenberg's "outstanding" role came at the very last stage. There is no need to detract from Ruthenberg's importance, but the legend arose to serve factional purposes and incidentally enabled the later Communist leadership to blot out Fraina's outstanding role.

For all of his proved ability, Ruthenberg was not the one to set the American movement on its own political path. He was not creative enough intellectually and his personality was not of the magnetic kind. His manner was cool, efficient, and reserved. Like many business executives, he liked to be called by his first two initials. C.E.'s strong point was inner-party administration, with just enough of a theoretical bent to get along from one practical situation to the next. His virtues were sorely needed by the young movement which had so few first-rate leaders to choose from. But if what was needed was an American Lenin, Ruthenberg was a pallid substitute.

12

The Underground

Four months after the American Communist movement was organized, it was driven underground. In so short a period, not much could be expected from the two young parties. But their failure was due to sterility of policy as well as to shortage of time, and of the two the former was far more costly in the long run.

The opportunities for every variety of radicalism on the American scene of late 1919 were immense.

The strike wave was one of the greatest in the history of American trade unionism. The Seattle general strike, the Lawrence textile strike, the Boston police strike, the national coal strike, and the great steel strike all occurred in 1919. The steel strike alone involved 365,000 workers, and it broke out the very month the Communist parties were formed. More workers were involved in labor disputes in 1919 alone than the total number for the next six years. More than fifteen years would pass before the trade-union movement again burst into so much militant activity.

The political expression of the forces that let loose the strike wave was the movement for a Labor party, which to some extent was also inspired from abroad. The postwar program of the British Labour party attracted much attention in liberal and labor circles in the United States. Local American Labor parties, modeled more or less after the British original, began to spring up. The most promising was the Cook County Labor party, whose candidate, John Fitzpatrick, head of the Chicago Federation of Labor, received 60,000 out of 580,000 votes in the Chicago mayoralty election in November 1919. Encouraged by this showing, Fitzpatrick summoned a national convention of all the local Labor party movements in Chicago on November 22 of that year. Thus the Communist movement and the national Labor party movement were born at approximately the same time and entered the race neck-and-neck for the favor of the same American worker.

The unprecedented strike wave and the new Labor party movement confronted the Communists with their first great challenge.

"In the Communist Party and the Communist Labor Party conventions of 1919," Ruthenberg subsequently stated, "it would have been difficult to gather together a half-dozen delegates who knew anything about the trade union movement." [1] The others talked and wrote about the trade unions with vast authority but had little contact with them. The membership of the American Federation of Labor in 1919 was 3,260,068, the largest number in its history up to then. The Communist contact with this organized body of workers was very slight among the rank and file and almost nonexistent among the leadership. What made the Communists imagine that they belonged to the labor movement and knew more about it than anyone else did were the formulas of a theory, not the facts of life.

According to the theory, partial economic or political demands were only a corrupting substitute for the revolution. Strikes for increased wages and better conditions were written off in advance as wasted effort, unless they developed into revolutionary manifestations. "These strikes, moreover, must always strive to cease being strikes and become *revolutionary mass action against Capitalism and the state*," *The Revolutionary Age* expounded early in 1919 as the strike wave began. "Every strike must be a small revolution, organizing, educating and disciplining the workers for the final revolutionary struggle." [2]

Even the great steel strike, led by William Z. Foster, failed to rouse any enthusiasm among the Communists. They criticized it sharply for demanding the check-off system of union dues collected by the employers. "But here, in the steel industry, the A.F. of L. is imposing this reactionary system upon the workers—assisted by the Syndicalist E. Z. Foster!" cried *The Communist* in horror.[3] Its instructions to the Communists themselves went: "Our task is to participate in this action, to make the strike general, to make it conscious of its larger purposes, to develop the general political strike that will break the power of Capitalism and initiate the dictatorship of the proletariat—all power to the workers!"[4] At its most extreme, the Communist view maintained "The revolution is the issue in the steel strike."[5]

Any union member who took the Communist press seriously had to leave the union or work against it. Commenting on the course of the steel strike, *The Communist* declared, "Trades unionism is the arch enemy of the militant proletariat." It added, "This is one of the tasks of the Communist Party—the destruction of the existing trades union organizations."[6] A resolution on the strike situation by the Central Executive Committee complained that a million workers had gone out on strike "without any fundamental action developing." It demanded independent strike councils to unify all the strikes and break the power of the old unions. What it meant by "fundamental action" was made clear in the final sentence: "The actual conflict will itself determine the moment when that mass movement shall merge all of its economic and political demands into the revolutionary demand: *All power to the Workers!—for the Communist reconstruction of society!*"[7]

As Ruthenberg later admitted, "the Communist Party of 1919 stood outside of the labor movement, endeavoring to draw the workers into its ranks through agitation and propaganda which pointed to the necessity of a revolutionary party fighting for the overthrow of capitalism."[8] To stand outside the labor movement in 1919 was to stand outside the greatest strike wave in a generation.

The Communists had no more use for the Labor party movement, whose mass base was located in the trade unions and whose political program was a watered-down version of reform socialism.

"A minor phase of proletarian unrest is the trade unions organizing a Labor Party, in an effort to conserve what they have secured as a privileged caste," said the Communist party program of 1919 loftily. "Laborism is as much a danger to the proletariat as moderate petty bourgeois Socialism—the two being expressions of an identical social tendency and policy. There can be no compromise either with Laborism or reactionary Socialism." The Communist program forebade any cooperation with the Labor party. The Communist Labor program merely ignored the subject.

Another political problem was more difficult to handle. Was it permissible to take any part in political elections? Was participation a form of recognition and acceptance of the capitalist state? Or was nonparticipation tantamount to a refusal to utilize the regime of political democracy against capitalism, a syndicalist error condemned by the manifesto of the Third International?

Strong influences in the American Communist movement made nonparticipation most congenial. The whole American revolutionary tradition, so closely bound up with the I.W.W., favored a boycott. The overwhelming majority in the foreign-language federations were neither citizens nor union members.[9] Most Communists did not want to vote and could not vote even if they wanted to do so.

But some Communists were already on the ballot in the New York municipal election of 1919. In the days of the Left Wing, they had contested the primaries with the Right Wing of the Socialist party, and a number of them had come out ahead. Now that they were Communists, they found themselves in the embarrassing position of running for office.

A compromise solved this awkward problem. It was decided that the Communist party could take part in the campaign but not in the election. A distinction was drawn between participation in the campaign to emphasize that the sole objective was the conquest of power, and nonparticipation in the election to emphasize that general political strikes were the only way to achieve power. Thus the chief Communist slogan in the 1919 elections was "Boycott the elections!" In practice, this meant that the Communist candidates were permitted to wage a campaign to persuade the workers not to vote—for them or for anyone else.[10] The inspiration for this ambidextrous policy was hinted at in the official Communist organ: "At the moment when it is necessary to strengthen this mass action tendency of the proletariat, as at this moment, it becomes necessary to boycott the elections, as the Bolsheviki boycotted the elections for the second Duma in 1906."[11]

The following year, an unprecedented protest vote against the two old parties was rolled up in some states. Two Socialists, from Wisconsin and New York, were sent to Congress; ten Socialists were elected to the Wisconsin Legislature and five Socialists to the New York Assembly. The Labor party movement broadened out to become the Farmer-Labor party movement. From this storm of economic and political unrest in 1920, the Communists held themselves scornfully aloof. It was not revolutionary enough.

There was method in this madness. The whole pattern of Communist behavior went back to the assumption that the period was revolutionary in the United States as well as in Eastern and Central Europe. Therefore, it was the duty of real revolutionists to be uncompromising and inflexible. It was no time for subterfuge and evasion. Half measures that postponed the cataclysm were worse than none at all.

For all the political and economic turbulence, the Communists in the United States lived in a world of unreality. The unreal seemed real because after the Russian Revolution nothing could be dismissed as unreal any more. There was nothing at the beginning of 1917 so absurdly unreal as a "proletarian revolution" in Russia, and there was nothing by the end of the year so excitingly real. To tell the American Communists of 1919 that their war against the trade unions, against the Labor party, and against the elections was unrealistic was like telling them that the Russian Revolution had never taken place.

The "reign of terror"

A jury in Indiana took two minutes to acquit a man for shooting and killing an alien because he had shouted, "To hell with the United States." The Vice-President of the United States cited as a dangerous manifestation of radicalism in the women's colleges the fact that the girl debaters of Radcliffe had upheld the affirmative in an intercollegiate debate on the subject: "Resolved, that the recognition of labor unions by employers is essential to successful collective bargaining." Properly elected members of the New York State Assembly were expelled because they had run on the Socialist party ticket. For such excesses, during and after World War I, Frederick Lewis Allen charged: "It was an era of lawless and disorderly defense of law and order, of unconstitutional defense of the Constitution, of suspicion and civil conflict—in a very literal sense, a reign of terror." [12]

Before the first World War, only two states, New York and Tennessee, had laws against "sedition," and no one had ever been prosecuted under them. After the war, thirty-five states passed legislation against "sedition," "criminal anarchy," "criminal syndicalism," and the like. An epidemic of prosecutions broke out. A mass deportation drive was launched against aliens suspected of subversive affiliations or beliefs. Thousands were rounded up in raids on homes and meetings. The hysteria communicated itself to school boards, college presidents, self-constituted "vigilante committees," and pulpits. Spies and secret agents infested the labor movement in behalf of the big corporations. Little distinction was made between anarchists, syndicalists, Communists, Socialists, and pacifists.

A committee of twelve distinguished lawyers and constitutional authorities issued a report in May 1920 denouncing the Department of Justice's excesses. Among the signatories were Dean Roscoe Pound, Zechariah Chafee, Jr., and Felix Frankfurter of the Harvard Law School, Acting Dean Tyrell Williams of the Washington University Law School, Alfred S. Niles of the Maryland Law School,

THE UNDERGROUND

and Frank P. Walsh of New York City. The Twelve Lawyers' Report, as it was called, said in part:

> Under the guise of a campaign for the suppression of radical activities, the office of the Attorney General, acting by its local agents throughout the country, and giving express instructions from Washington, has committed continual illegal acts. Wholesale arrests both of aliens and citizens have been made without warrant or any process of law; men and women have been jailed and held *incommunicado* without access of friends or counsel; homes have been entered without search warrant and property seized and removed; other property has been wantonly destroyed; working men and working women suspected of radical views have been shamefully abused and maltreated.[13]

Raids and arrests had been going on for over two years before the Communists began to feel the brunt of them. The first large-scale anti-Communist raids took place in New York City on November 8, 1919, about two months after the Communist parties were formed. They were made on behalf of the Lusk committee of the New York Senate, appointed to investigate "seditious activities."[14] Over 700 policemen and special agents swooped down on headquarters and meetings, carried away tons of papers and literature, and hauled off hundreds of people. About seventy-five were prosecuted, including such well-known Communists as Benjamin Gitlow and James J. Larkin (of the Communist Labor party) and Charles E. Ruthenberg, I. E. Ferguson, and Harry M. Winitsky (of the Communist party). The first four were indicted for publishing the Left Wing Manifesto in the defunct *Revolutionary Age* four months earlier, before the Communist parties were formed.[15] The New York Communists went underground immediately after these raids. The parties operated more or less openly in the rest of the country for about two months longer.

The high point of the anti-alien drive was the deportation of 249 Russians aboard the *Buford,* otherwise known as the "Soviet Ark," an army transport dating from the Spanish-American War. Its two most famous "passengers" were the anarchists Emma Goldman and Alexander Berkman.[16] The ship sailed for Finland—there being no regular relations with Russia—on December 21, 1919, arriving four weeks later after some harrowing experiences. Some of the deportees were admitted anarchists, some were happy to get a free trip to the workers' fatherland, and some were poor devils, separated from their wives and children, who happened to be caught in the raids. By hitting at Russian aliens, the *Buford* deportations struck indirectly at the Communist party which had so many Russian aliens in its ranks.

A warning signal that the entire Communist movement throughout the country faced the same fate as the New York organizations came from Chicago on January 1, 1920. From four p.m. until far into the night, raiding parties brought in prisoners, mostly Communists and I.W.W.'s—real or suspected. It turned out that the Chicago District Attorney, a Republican, had acted prematurely in order to steal some of the limelight from the Attorney General, A. Mitchell Palmer, a Democrat. On the night of January 2, the Palmer raids went off as scheduled in thirty-three cities from coast to coast. A second round-up was staged on January 5. Over 5000 arrests were made. For the next two years, so many Communists were indicted all over the country that everyone in the movement regarded himself as a potential political prisoner or fugitive from the law. Most of the prosecutions took place in Illinois, New York, and California. In Chicago, twenty Communists, including L. E. Katterfeld, Charles Krumbein, and Max Bedacht, drew sentences of from one to five years. In New York, Ruthenberg, Ferguson, Larkin, Winitsky, and Gitlow received sentences of five to ten years, and actually served about two years. In California, an estimated five hundred arrests resulted in 264 convictions in 1919–21.[17] Actually, in the end, many sentences were handed out and few served, except by the New York group and Katterfeld. Nevertheless, at the time, the fact that the bark of the inquisitors was much worse than their bite could not be known. The Communist leaders lived in a half-world of indictments, trials, defense committees, convictions, sentences, and appeals. John Reed once faced three indictments at the same time. To the day of his death, Ruthenberg was never free of his appeals from convictions, always living, so to speak, on borrowed time.

The subterranean stream

The answer to informers, raids, and arrests was the underground. After the January 1920 raids, both the Communist party and the Communist Labor party hastily converted themselves into conspiratorial organizations. Though they had spent much time and energy proving that they were different, the government treated them with magnanimous impartiality. When it came to throwing their members in jail, no distinctions were made.

The illegal Communist party organ published instructions on how to work illegally. Whereas the basic unit of the organization had formerly been the branch, with a minimum membership of seven, the new unit of the illegal party became the group, usually composed of ten members. Each group was headed by an organizer whose responsibility it was to collect dues, distribute leaflets, papers, and pamphlets, and in general keep in touch with the party organization as a whole. All membership cards and charters were ordered destroyed. Meeting places changed constantly. Only those willing to risk imprisonment or arrest were considered worthy of membership.[18]

The party papers continued to come out, but suddenly all the names mentioned in connection with party activities became unrecognizable. Ruthenberg became "David Damon"; Lovestone was known at different times as "Langley," "Wheat," and "Roger B. Nelson"; Gitlow as "Tom Paine" and "John Pierce"; Max Bedacht as "James A. Marshall"; Bittelman as "A. Raphael"; and so forth. For the historian, the pseudonyms make reading the underground papers an exercise in a kind of political cryptography.

One official Communist document listed ten rules for underground work:

1. DON'T betray party work and party workers under any circumstances.
2. DON'T carry or keep with you names and addresses, except in good code.
3. DON'T keep in your rooms openly any incriminating documents or literature.

4. DON'T take any unnecessary risks in party work.
5. DON'T shirk party work because of the risks connected with it.
6. DON'T boast of what you have to do or have done for the party.
7. DON'T divulge your membership in the party without necessity.
8. DON'T let any spies follow you to appointments or meetings.
9. DON'T lose your nerve in danger.
10. DON'T answer any questions if arrested either at preliminary hearings or in court.[19]

The membership of the underground can be analyzed with some accuracy. The information for the Communist party is quite full and precise.[20]

We have official figures of the dues-paying membership of the C.P. for the months immediately before and after the Palmer raids:

1919		1920	
October	27,341	January	1,714
November	20,261	February	2,296
December	23,624	March	4,517
Average:	23,744	April	8,223
		Average:	5,584

We also have a different set of figures for the same periods based on an estimate of the foreign-language federations' membership.

	Before raids	After raids
English	1900 *	700
Non-federation language members	1100	400
Esthonian	280	140
German	850	500
Hungarian	1000	
Jewish	1000	500
Lettish	1200	1000
Lithuanian	4400	2500
Polish	1750	1000
Russian	7000	3000
South Slavic	2200	1000
Ukrainian	4000	2000
Total	26,680	12,740

* Including 800 of the Michigan organization which dropped out in January 1920.

The dues-paying figures in the first table show that the first shock of the raids was almost disastrous. Then came a gradual recovery to a point about one quarter of the pre-raid average. The second set of figures, in terms of the language composition, shows a decline to about one-third of the pre-raid figure. The Russian members represented almost 25 per cent of the total before the raids and over 23 per cent after the raids. The East European membership accounted for over 75 per cent before and 82 per cent after. The English-speaking members (excluding Michigan) represented 4 per cent before and 5 per cent after. Thus the East-European preponderance became even greater as a result of the raids though, individually, the Russian and English-speaking proportions remained practically the same.

As for the Communist Labor party, Gitlow says that it retained only a "few members" after the raids.[21] Ruthenberg and Bedacht said that the January 1920 raids reduced the membership of both parties from between 50,000 and 60,000 to about 10,000, or a drop of at least four-fifths. In the next two years of underground existence, even the latter figure was cut in half.[22]

Ironically, the Palmer raids came as a blessing in disguise to the foreign-language federations. More than ever they were able to imagine themselves Russian Bolsheviks in America. Had not the Russian Revolution been forced to work illegally almost to the very eve of the seizure of power? Was there any fundamental difference between Palmer's prisons and the Czar's dungeons, the Bureau of Immigration's deportations and the Ochrana's exiledom in Siberia? If the Russian road to the revolution was right, then the postwar repression in the United States merely offered additional proof that the American revolution was really approaching. The underground character of the movement became the supreme test of its revolutionary integrity. A truly revolutionary organization by definition had to suffer repression, as in Czarist Russia. The Russia hypnosis made a necessity into a virtue.

At the same time, the isolation of the Communist movement from the vast majority of the American people, workers included, increased. The movement had been doing its best to isolate itself by means of its extreme sectarianism in trade union and Labor party policies. The government's repressive campaign completed the process from the outside.

Psychologically, it seems necessary for Communists to erect certain defenses to withstand the worst effects of isolation. One of the most extraordinary of these defenses is the belief that the revolution is coming nearer rather than going further away. The combination of estrangement and extremism is very common. The further away the American Communists have been from practical mass activity, the more eagerly have they taken refuge in the immediate goal of socialism.

If the Russian Bolshevik movement was able to survive Czarist illegality, it was not too great an achievement for the American Communist movement to survive American illegality. Revolutionary movements have survived so many different kinds of persecution in so many different places that it is a particularly ignorant illusion to imagine that that is the way to get rid of them.

An underground movement, therefore, should not be confused with a nonexistent movement. The Communist choice is never between having or not having a movement. The choice is between an open or a secret, a legal or an illegal, an aboveboard or an underground movement—or a combination of both.

The rank and file on which the Communist movement depends for its influence, and the leadership on which it depends for its very existence, react differently. As soon as party membership became dangerous, most of the rank and file was scared off. Those who accepted the risks of imprisonment or deportation were made of stronger stuff. The underground was the breeding ground for future leaders. It was an ordeal by fire. It provided the first real-life experience of conspiratorial methods. It created martyrs and heroes, real and imaginary. For those who stayed, it made communism more rather than less precious, because a movement which requires greater risks and sacrifices is capable of evoking greater devotion and fervor, since no one wishes to take risks and make sacrifices in vain.

As long as a hard core of Communists could survive the dangers

THE UNDERGROUND

and rigors of the underground, the movement itself was never at stake. The rank and file could come and go, as times changed. Only the "cadres"—the Communist equivalent of commissioned and noncommissioned officers—could not be improvised. Anyone who remains in an illegal party demonstrates qualities of loyalty, discipline, and leadership which may, in the end, result in reinforcements from the rank and file to the cadre. The first trustworthy cadre of the American Communist movement came out of the first underground.

13

The Second Split

IT WAS easier for the Communists to run away from the police than to run away from their own problems. Despite the trials of the underground, the unfinished business of the founding conventions could not be postponed. At no time did the two parties, or the factions within them, call a truce just because their leaders were being hounded and arrested, and their rank and file terrorized and deported.

The struggle for control between the American groups and the foreign-language federations in the Communist party erupted at the height of the government's anti-Communist campaign.

The founding convention of September 1919 had barely been able to hold together the three major factions—the foreign-language federations, the Michigan group, and the other English-speaking Left Wing Council group. The Michigan group remained in the party only by a technicality, since it refused to accept any official position or take responsibility for the program. The Council group stayed in by dint of concessions to and from the federations.

The first to go was the Michigan group. Its major stronghold was the so-called Proletarian University in Detroit, a school to spread the gospel of the Michigan faith. Since its teachings were considered heretical in the Communist party, the Central Executive Committee decided to take it by storm in January 1920. The committee ordered the "university" to become a party institution under its supervision.

The Michigan group refused to accept the decision and chose to leave the party for good.[1] It reorganized as the Proletarian party in 1920 and lingered on as a small, self-satisfied sect.

This left the two dominant factions to bicker and maneuver for control.

One of the first squabbles arose over a very touchy matter—who was to represent the party in Moscow? The natural choice was Fraina, the International Secretary. When the question was first broached three weeks after the convention, Ruthenberg objected on the ground that too few English-language writers and speakers were available for the editor of the party's publications to be spared. He was overruled by the Russian-led majority, which decided to send two delegates abroad, Fraina and Hourwich. Ruthenberg succeeded in preventing them from leaving immediately because no word had come of any definite meeting in Moscow. The decision to let Fraina go was finally made in November, but Hourwich was less fortunate. He fell afoul of Ruthenberg's wrath by allegedly scheming to get unauthorized funds for his unauthorized trip.[2]

Of deeper organizational significance was the struggle that developed over unity with the Communist Labor party. In the postconvention competition between the two parties, the Communist party had, in effect, taken the position that there was nothing to discuss except the suicide of its rival. As long as both parties worked openly, Ruthenberg's group did not try to upset this uncompromising decision. When the Communist Labor party proposed a meeting of the two executive committees to seek some basis for unity, the Communist party haughtily offered to swallow up any C.L.P. branches which accepted its program and constitution and, to rub it in, benevolently volunteered to appoint a special committee to arrange for the liquidation of the national organization of the C.L.P.[3] No progress was possible on this basis, and the two parties went on insulting and denouncing each other.

This stalemate was abruptly broken by the Palmer raids. Confronted by the same repression, the English-speaking groups in both parties quickly forgot the old grievances and sought each other's support. After four months of party life, the Ruthenberg group in the Communist party had been made painfully aware of the fact that it could be easily outvoted by the federation members in the top committees. Rather than resign itself to being a loyal "minority," it was tempted by the prospect of strengthening the English-speaking faction by uniting with the predominantly English-speaking Communist Labor party. The Palmer raids gave the Ruthenberg minority a more persuasive argument against the chief objection to the Communist Labor party—that it contained wavering, opportunistic, centrist elements. It was now possible to reply that the raids had scared off the "centrists" and the C.L.P. was stripped down to its hard core of true revolutionists. In January 1920, therefore, the Ruthenberg group launched a unity campaign in earnest. It scored a partial victory when the Communist party made a gesture of proposing a call for a joint convention on the basis of its own program and constitution.[4]

In return, the Communist Labor party went much further. It asked for immediate working unity, even before the convention, by merging the two top committees and conducting propaganda, organizational, and defense activities in common. The Communist party countered with a proposal for a joint convention in six months on condition that the Communist Labor party agreed in advance to preserve the privileged status of the foreign-language federations. This condition set off a howl of protest from the Communist Labor side, which hit back by demanding unity immediately and not in six months. When a vote was taken on the immediate unity proposals in the Central Executive Committee of the Communist party, Ruthenberg's pro-unity group lost out 9 to 4.[5]

In revenge, Ruthenberg's minority struck at the foreign-language federations directly. It criticized the Communist party itself for being a federation of federations instead of a unified organization. It accused the Hungarian federation of "desertion" after the January raids and the Jewish federation of withdrawing in order to remain "neutral" in the inner-party struggle. To bring about a more centralized organization and, incidentally, cut down the autonomy of the federations, it proposed that dues payments be made to the party's district organizations rather than to the nine federations. In this way, financially at least, the federations would be made dependent on the central office of the party instead of the other way round. This proposal was, of course, totally unacceptable to the majority and never had a chance.[6] Nevertheless, with every defeat for the minority, the split came nearer.

One of the most revealing battles was fought out on a question of principle—force and violence. The controversy was characteristic of what may be called the uninhibited period of communism. In later years, such a delicate question was never discussed in the same way.

A proposal was made in the Central Executive Committee in February 1920 to issue a leaflet to the railway strikers calling for armed insurrection. Again the Ruthenberg group showed its displeasure. No difference in principle separated the two factions. The Ruthenberg minority said that it was firmly convinced that:

The party must be ready to put into its program the definite statement that mass action culminates in open insurrection and armed conflict with the capitalist state. The party program and the party literature dealing with our program and policies should clearly express our position on this point. On this question there is no disagreement.[7]

The Ruthenberg group limited its protest to the tactical inadvisability of injecting the issue of force and violence in a leaflet to striking railwaymen. It maintained that such a leaflet could be used by the government as a pretext for using force and violence against the strikers, that it would put the party in a position of "acting as the agent provocateur of the capitalist state," and that it would play into the hands of the prosecution at a time when the government was imprisoning hundreds of Communists.

The same majority that opposed unity took up the cudgels for force and violence:

We maintain, that if the lessons of the history of all revolutions—and particularly, the proletarian revolutions—means something and teaches us anything (lessons which the 2nd International completely failed to learn), —we must propagate to the workers the USE OF FORCE as the ONLY

MEANS of conquering the power of the state and establishing the dictatorship of the proletariat. And that, instead of remaining silent on this question, we must constantly STRESS it, in order to show the workers the utter futility of hoping for any "peaceful revolution," accomplished either through the parliaments, as the opportunistic Socialists teach—or, by mere general strikes, as the syndicalists teach.

And to indicate the source of its inspiration, it added:

Those familiar with the discussion in the Russian Social-Democratic literature on the same subject (some years ago), will easily recognize that the "majority" takes the same position as the Bolsheviki took at that time; while our friends of the "minority" are innocently repeating the arguments of the Mensheviki . . .[8]

Ruthenberg did not push this fight to a showdown, but the two factions were drawing so far apart that almost any issue was good enough for a split.[9]

The blow-up was detonated by a local crisis in Chicago. The District Committee forced Ruthenberg's hand by threatening to call an insurgent convention to overthrow the foreign-language leadership. Ruthenberg was sent there to crack down on the rebels and, instead, prevailed on them to withdraw their threat of secession on the promise of immunity from reprisals. He made clear that he agreed to a large extent with the Chicago revolt but considered it unnecessarily disruptive organizationally.[10] This settlement did not please the majority of the smaller Executive Council, which proceeded to vote the removal of the Chicago district organizer. The line-up was 4 to 3 against Ruthenberg.

The split in the Communist party took place on April 20, 1920. With Ruthenberg went two other members of the Central Executive Committee, one of them Lovestone (Langley), while ten remained in the old party, including Hourwich (Andrew) and Bittelman (Raphael).* Ruthenberg carried off with him a majority of the English-speaking members and a minority of the foreign-language federations. Instead of adopting a new name for what was temporarily a third Communist party in the field, Ruthenberg's group

* All names in parentheses are pseudonyms of the underground period.

insisted on clinging to the old one in order to assert its claim to being the official Communist party. Two Communist parties proceeded to put out two official organs, each called *The Communist*. Ruthenberg went on signing papers with his old official title. To add injury to insult, he also tied up the original C.P.'s funds and made off with the records.[11]

The second split in the Communist movement followed the first one by less than seven months. If splitting was necessary to forge a real revolutionary movement, as not a few believed to be the lesson of the Russian Revolution, the American Communist movement was well on its way.

Ruthenberg's heresy

Ruthenberg's rebellion against the Russian federation's domination in 1920 was a direct continuation of the Communist Labor party's rebellion in 1919. As always, the conflict was a compound of personal rivalries, fortuitous circumstances, and clashes of principle. Yet the fact that Ruthenberg had refused to go along with John Reed in the first battle and then had found himself in essentially the same position signified that something deeper than personalities or circumstances was involved.

What made the second battle even more interesting than the first was the increased clarity and candor with which the fundamental causes were recognized. Both sides were fully aware that there was more to the split than the unity negotiations or the fate of the Chicago district organizer. They expressed it so clearly, even so naïvely, that it would be hard to find a clearer expression of the schism which has persisted throughout the entire history of the American Communist movement. The factional argument was also a fascinating political dialogue.

The Ruthenberg wing analyzed the schism as follows:

Since the beginning of the party there have been two viewpoints represented in the Central Executive Committee. The majority members of the committee considered themselves "great theorists." They constantly talked about the word "principle," but never about how to relate Communist principles to the working class movement of this country and to make these principles a living reality in action . . .

The Executive Secretary [Ruthenberg] and the minority group, on the other hand, stood for a policy which would make the Communist Party in reality the "party of action" which its Manifesto so proudly proclaims it. They endeavored to relate the party to the life struggle of the workers. They sought to inject the party viewpoint in every struggle of the masses. They believed that a Communist Party should be, not a party of closet philosophers, but a party which participates in the every day struggles of the workers and by such participation injects its principles into these struggles and gives them a wider meaning, thus developing the Communist movement.[12]

What could be objectionable about breaking through the party's isolation and establishing contact with the masses? The anti-Ruthenberg wing answered:

This cry of "contact with the masses" holds in itself the seeds of future compromise, vacillation, and betrayal. It is the cry of confusionists and sentimentalists who seem to think that a Communist Party must have "contact with the masses" at all stages of its development. They do not see, that if they attempt to run after the masses, at a time when the masses are not ready for them, they will, in their zeal, reduce Communism to a theory and practice that will meet with the approval of the politically immature masses. *They will compromise principles and tactics in order to get "contact with the masses."*

What if the masses came into the party without accepting the full program and before the situation was revolutionary? The anti-Ruthenberg group maintained:

And when the Communist Party is swamped with these politically immature masses, they will clog and hamper the revolutionary effectiveness of the Communist Party, holding it back when the time for real action arrives. These masses flocking to the party when it was silent on the necessity of the USE OF FORCE to overthrow the bourgeois state will refuse to accept that tactic when the revolution comes. It will mean that these masses, having not yet cut the Gordian knot which binds them to the Socialist ideology of a "peaceful" revolution, will come into the Communist Party and by sheer weight of numbers compel it to change its Communist course of propaganda and agitation,—compel it to revise its whole position until it will meet with their politically immature ideals,—compel it to recede until it will effect a juncture with the social-patriotic Socialist Party which is even now luring weak-minded Communists with the cry of "unity."

The Communist Party, if it is to learn anything from the bitter experiences of the past, cannot afford to attempt to get "contact with the masses" at the expense of sacrificing Communist principles and tactics. Essentially the Communist Party represents ideas and not numbers. We can afford to remain small in numbers for the present, if we shape our organization to hold Communist principles and policies unsullied and free from the base ingredients of compromise and opportunism and carry on our Communist propaganda to the workers with the full implication of all that it implies.[13]

Abstract ideas or mass influence, principles or power? The choice was obviously an impossible one. Both sides wanted and promised both. The Ruthenberg wing tried to solve the problem in terms of stages of development:

The party must and will remain a party of clear understanding of principles. But such a party is valueless unless it applies those principles to the life struggles of the workers and develops the progressive stages of mass action that culminate in the social revolution itself.[14]

The anti-Ruthenberg wing held out for the attraction of the masses at one climactic stroke as the reward of revolutionary integrity:

We must try to reach the workers with our propaganda—we don't expect to make much of an impression on them at present. Well and good. We shall continue our agitation, confident that the social forces, the economic disintegration of world capitalism since the war—and which can no longer succeed in rehabilitating itself—will compel the masses to listen to our message.[15]

If the Communist movement could hew to abstract principles and at the same time gain broad mass support, such debates would not be necessary. Because the American Communist movement has never been able to attract any significant mass support on the basis of a clear Communist program, the pendulum has swung from one extreme to the other—from sectarianism to opportunism and back again—in a vain effort to achieve an equilibrium.

In one respect, the anti-Ruthenberg wing worried unnecessarily. It feared that mass support on a nonrevolutionary basis would hold back the Communists in a revolutionary situation. This fear betrayed pathetic ignorance or misunderstanding of the Bolshevik revolution by those who claimed to know most about it. The Bolshevik revolution was made with alluring slogans like "Bread and Peace." The peasants who supported the Bolsheviks were lured by the promise of land which the Bolsheviks had every intention of taking away from them at the earliest opportunity. The Russian workers were rallied in the name of Soviets, which were turned into empty shells as soon as they had served their purpose. The early American Communists, however, saw in Russia what they wanted to see at home—a small band of isolated revolutionists armed with irresistible abstract principles.

Ruthenberg recognized the problem of abstract principles and practical activity very clearly, though he contributed little to a solution. An inveterate organizer, he was not enchanted by illegality. Uppermost in his own mind was the undeniable fact that the party had lost contact with the masses, that it was increasingly isolated from the life of the country. The organizer had less and less to organize. The organizational vacuum of the underground forced him to work his way back to the original position of the Communist Labor party on the need for an American approach to communism. "It may be said, in all candor, that up to this time our zeal has been more in the direction of faithful imitation of phrases than in Communist expression of the class struggle as it develops from day to day in the United States," the Ruthenberg group stated in the spring of 1920. "Our crying need is a more precise and more understandable expression of Communism as part of the everyday working class fight in the United States." [16] In other words, Ruthenberg had come to the conclusion that it was easier to "Americanize" the Communists than to "communize" the Americans.

The United Communist party

For about a month, from the end of April to the end of May, 1920, there was a three-way split in the Communist movement—two Communist parties (the original one dominated by the foreign-language

THE SECOND SPLIT 219

federations and the rump led by Ruthenberg) and the Communist Labor party. The latter suddenly found itself wooed by the rival Communist parties. It chose to accept the offer of the Ruthenberg organization, which had made unity one of its chief causes. The two new allies agreed to preserve some form of split by leaving the other Communist party out of the negotiations. They decided to call separate conventions and then come together in a Unity Conference to take the final step of amalgamation.[17]

It was a delicate operation, considering the man hunt for Communist leaders then raging in the country. For seven days at the end of May, a total of fifty-seven delegates, one fraternal delegate, and an unidentified "representative of the Executive Committee of the Communist International" without the authority of later representatives, secretly plotted to reorganize the better part of the Communist movement in a clearing in the woods near Bridgman, Michigan.[18] After the first day of separate conventions, they came together for the Unity Conference on the second day. Most of the delegates had pinned on their bosoms in large black letters the words, "AT LAST," torn from the caption of a circular.

The rejoicing was premature. Not until noon of the seventh day was unity assured. All the theoretical and personal feuds and factions which had plagued the Communist movement from the start came out again in full force.

Was capitalism going to collapse because it failed to "produce" the needs of life or because it failed to "provide" them? This dispute lasted two hours. "After considerable uncertainty," says the official account, the word "provide" won out.[19]

A much longer and fiercer fight raged over force and violence, a sore point with the Ruthenberg followers, who were being charged with pussyfooting by their former colleagues in the Communist party. At the first mention of the overthrow of the capitalist system in the discussion on the program, an amendment to add the word "forcible" was hastily proposed. At every opportunity, "one amendment was piled upon the other—a veritable 'force' panic," the official report relates. The opposition came from the Communist Labor delegates, who wanted to say the same thing in a different section of the program. Only a well-timed move to recommit this portion for overnight consideration prevented serious consequences. Everything went smoothly the next day, and enough force and violence was put in the program to satisfy everyone. It said in part:

The United Communist Party will systematically and persistently familiarize the working class with the inevitability of armed force in the proletarian revolution. The working class must be prepared for armed insurrection as the final form of mass action by which the workers shall conquer the state power and establish the Dictatorship of the Proletariat.

The worst and longest dispute involved industrial unionism. The question was how far to go in endorsing the I.W.W. or condemning the A.F. of L. The decision shows how faithful a large part of the Communist movement was to the American leftist tradition of pro-I.W.W. "dual unionism" as late as the spring of 1920. After many stormy sessions and dozens of amendments and substitutes, the following wording was adopted:

The Socialist Party policy of "boring from within" the A.F. of L. is vicious in that it is only an indirect and hypocritical method of supporting an inherently reactionary labor organization. A Communist who belongs to the A.F. of L. should seize every opportunity to voice his hostility to the organization, not to reform it but to destroy it. The struggle against the A.F. of L. must not be purely negative. The I.W.W. is the obvious medium for giving the advocacy of industrial unionism affirmative character. The I.W.W. must be upheld as against the A.F. of L. At the same time the work of Communist education must be carried on within the I.W.W.

The same traditional hostility to political action was also evident. The United Communist party did not go as far as the I.W.W. in condemning political action in principle, but the same purpose was achieved in a more roundabout way. The concrete issue at the convention was whether to nominate Communist candidates for political office. The extremist group opposed all nominations. A more moderate group, represented by Ruthenberg, tried to make a fundamental distinction between legislative and executive offices. The former included Congress, state legislatures, and city councils, the latter the presidency, governors, mayors and local officials. The distinction hinged on the permissibility of representing the people and the impermissibility of running the capitalist state. Executive offices were ruled out totally, but legislative offices were considered theoretically permissible—if Communist legislators refrained rigorously from introducing any reform measures and limited their legislative activity to the slogans: "Down with the parliamentary sham of capitalism! Hail to the soviets and real working class democracy!"

Ruthenberg's point of view prevailed by a narrow margin. But there was no need for the losers to fret, because the convention went on record against all nominations in the 1920 political campaign, in effect boycotting the elections for the second year in succession. The reasoning behind the boycott went: "When the revolutionary crisis shatters the mass illusions as to capitalist democracy, it becomes unnecessary for the Communists to direct their agitation to the destruction of these illusions." The revolutionary crisis in the America of 1920 was supposedly so far advanced that the Communists could afford to ignore the presidential election—won by that herald of normalcy, Warren Gamaliel Harding.

After these and other basic principles were agreed on, the last and greatest crisis arose. The Ruthenberg group had a slight advantage in numbers, with 32 delegates against 25. If both groups held firm, the former was always able to outvote the latter, a most poignant consideration in every question pertaining to factional control of the unified party.

The first test of strength came over the name of the new party. The Ruthenberg delegates were able to roll up a majority for their own name, Communist party. The Communist Labor delegates refused to accept it on the ground that it seemed symbolic of factional control. At the next session, another vote was taken whether to call it "United Communist Party" or "Communist Party" with "united" written underneath. The former came out ahead. Unity had been saved by a word in the right place.

It was saved just long enough, however, to get to the crucial business of electing the leadership. Again the caucuses went into action and the old party lines reappeared. By some adroit maneuvering, the outvoted Communist Labor delegates were able to put across a majority for five of the nine members of the Central Executive Committee. To the losers, this upset was unbearable. As they put it, how "could the C.P. delegates report back to their members that they had been outwitted in strategy in a way to give the minority control of the united party"? Ruthenberg and two others resigned from the committee. After a tug of war lasting into the middle of the night and right through to the last morning of the convention, a compromise was reached. The C.E.C. was increased to ten members, with five from each side. Unity had finally been saved for the last time. The Communist Labor party made its exit from the scene, and the United Communist party came into existence.

Alfred Wagenknecht (Meyer) was named Executive Secretary of the new party, with Ruthenberg editor of the official organ.[20] Foreign-language federations continued to be recognized, though nominally stripped of their "autonomy." To make the work of future historians more complicated, *The Communist* was chosen as the name of the official organ.[21] As a result, two underground papers with identical mastheads, both full of fictitious names, came out from the summer of 1920 to the summer of 1921. It was hard on the uninitiated and almost as hard on the devotees.

The darkest hour

"The year of 1920 must be considered the worst year in the history of our movement," one of the founders admitted a few years later.[22]

How many Communists were there in 1920? The maximum figure claimed by the Communists themselves was about 15,000. There is no need to take it too seriously, since it was put forward for factional purposes—and each faction invariably reduced the other's claims by about 50 per cent. If they were right about each other, the total figure was closer to 8000.[23]

These 8000 to 15,000 Communists were more than ever foreign-

THE SECOND SPLIT

language forces. The Communist party organ said brutally: "The membership of the Communist Party as well as the U.C.P. is overwhelmingly composed of foreign comrades who do not speak or understand English." [24] Even the United Communist party organ reported that a majority of the delegates to the Unity Conference were "foreigners." [25] It may be surmised that no more than 1000 to 2000 English-speaking Communists were left in both parties.

It was a year of lost opportunities on a spectacular scale. The greatest opportunities were lost in the nascent Labor party movement and in the vast strike wave, from both of which the Communists were excluded and excluded themselves. There were symptoms of self-criticism and recovery in the Ruthenberg tendency, but it was too timid and immature to strike out very far on its own and translate its incipient principles into practice. When Ruthenberg was taken off to jail in 1920, moreover, his personal influence was removed for about two years. Despite all the brave reasons which made him break away from the Communist party, there was little evidence of reform in the United Communist party.

How little reform was accomplished by the second split may be seen from typical manifestoes issued to workers on strike in the fall of 1920. The older Communist party addressed the trolley-car employees of the Brooklyn Rapid Transit Company in these terms:

> Get ready for armed revolution to overthrow the Capitalist Government and create a Workers Government—as your brothers did in Russia.
>
> Stop asking merely for a little more wages.
>
> Overthrow the dictatorship of the capitalist—the present Government of the United States—and through the Soviets and Proletarian Dictatorship take possession of the B.R.T. and of every mill, mine, factory, railroad, field and farm in the U.S.
>
> The Communist Party of America sounds the call for revolution—for the armed uprising of all the workers.[26]

Not to be outdone, the newer United Communist party issued a "Proclamation":

> YOU MUST DIRECT YOUR STRIKES AGAINST THE GOVERNMENT AND MUST OVERTHROW THE CAPITALIST GOV-

ERNMENT. WHEN THE FINAL STRUGGLE TO OVERTHROW THE GOVERNMENT COMES YOU MUST HAVE GUNS IN YOUR HANDS, EVEN AS THE WEST VIRGINIA MINERS HAVE NOW, AND BE PREPARED FOR AN ARMED INSURRECTION TO WIPE OUT THE GOVERNMENT OF THE CAPITALISTS AND ESTABLISH YOUR GOVERNMENT—THE GOVERNMENT OF THE WORKERS COUNCILS.[27]

Most of this violence was more verbal than real. These calls to revolt belonged to the realm of literary make-believe. No preparations accompanied them; no consequences followed them. The Communist factions were talking to themselves; they were not communicating with the outside world. Their Russian manifestoes and proclamations in translation hurt no one but their authors, whom they estranged from the very American workers they were intended to influence.

The two parties agreed on what to tell the strikers but not on what to do about the unions. The United Communist party wanted to support the I.W.W. against the A.F. of L. The Communist party spurned both. In fact, the latter wanted to remain untainted by any kind of practical union activity. In its program, adopted at the second convention in New York in July 1920, it stated:

Wherever the workers are, whether in the A.F. of L. or similar organizations, or in the I.W.W., there the Communist Party must constantly agitate, not for industrial unionism, but for Communism.

Another section of the same program added:

The Communist Party shall participate in strikes, not so much to achieve the immediate purpose of the strike as to develop the revolutionary implications.[28]

In practice, supporting the I.W.W. or not, propagating communism in the A.F. of L. or attempting to break it up, did not amount to a great deal of difference. These were the empty formulas of men whose contact with the trade unions was limited to their own pronouncements.

Both parties agreed that political campaigns should be waged for revolutionary propaganda and agitation only, that nominations for public office should be limited to legislative bodies, and that the elections of 1920 should be boycotted anyway.

The chief organizational quarrel was still over the foreign-language federations—whether they should be "autonomous," as the Communist party insisted, or not, as the United Communist party maintained. Actually, as long as the federations existed in both parties, the difference was largely verbal. They continued to lead lives of their own in both parties, but this did not in the least discourage the intolerant and interminable polemics on the subject.

Thus, a year after its birth, the American Communist movement seemed to be dying. A major portion of its energies was exhausted in defending itself, not attacking the enemy. But it was not primarily the flight from the police that made 1920 such a black year. It was rather the flight from reality. The worst sickness was within. Factionalism poisoned the inner life of the movement. There was something glamorous and heroic about hiding from the police and assuming false names. There was nothing but morbid demoralization in internecine warfare.

14

Spies, Victims, and Couriers

THE UNDERGROUND was riddled with spies, informers, and government agents.

The Twelve Lawyers' Report of May 1920, stated: "Agents of the Department of Justice have been introduced into radical organizations for the purpose of informing upon their members or inciting them to activities; these agents have even been instructed from Washington to arrange meetings upon certain dates for the express object of facilitating wholesale raids and arrests."[1] More light on these agents' activities was shed in the *New York Times:* "For months Department of Justice men, dropping all other work, had concentrated on the Reds. Agents quietly infiltrated into the radical ranks, slipped casually into centers of agitation, and went to work, sometimes as cooks in remote mining colonies, sometimes as miners, again as steel workers, and, where the opportunity presented itself, as 'agitators' of the wildest type. Although careful not to inspire, suggest or aid the advancement of overt acts or propaganda, several of the agents, 'under cover' men, managed to rise in the radical movement and become, in at least one instance, the recognized leader of a district."[2]

It seems to be a general rule in revolutionary movements that government agents behave like " 'agitators' of the wildest type." At least, this can be established about several known cases in the American movement, including one of the first and most spectacular of all operatives. Among his many exploits was a web of intrigue that meant the beginning of the end for the Communist career of Louis C. Fraina.

N-100 and FF-22

As International Secretary of the Communist party, Fraina was expected to represent the Communist party at any conferences or congresses abroad. One such conference of representatives of the Western Communist parties was soon announced to take place in Amsterdam, Holland. When Fraina left Chicago for New York after the founding convention, he immediately went underground because the Lusk Committee raids had forced the New York Communists to take cover. Meanwhile, he applied to the Russian Soviet Government Bureau headed by Martens for credentials to facilitate his ultimate mission as a representative to the Third International in Moscow.

The problem was how to get Fraina across the Atlantic. A party committee in New York was given the task of finding someone to help Fraina. The committee reported that a certain Russian by the name of Jacob Nosovitsky was the man for the job. He had been acting as a trans-Atlantic courier for Martens, and, therefore, knew just how to arrange such matters. But there was a hitch. Nosovitsky, a former member of the Russian federation, had once offered automatic pistols to the Russian leaders. He urged them to accept the guns with such eagerness that they suspected him of being a *provocateur.* There was no definite evidence against him, but the suspicion was enough to lead to his expulsion as an undesirable. Nosovitsky, a tall, slender, glib young man of thirty, produced documents to prove his innocence. The New York committee was sufficiently impressed to propose him as Fraina's guide across the Atlantic. In order to clear up the old charges against him, however, he was sent to Chicago to see Ruthenberg.

Nosovitsky appeared in Chicago wearing the regalia of an assistant surgeon of an ocean liner. He failed to talk Ruthenberg into taking him back into the party. But he was sufficiently convincing to get a note authorizing him to receive printed literature from abroad to deliver to the party and to make the technical arrangements for Fraina's trip to Europe.[3]

In New York, Fraina received a letter from Ruthenberg to the effect that arrangements had been made for him to go abroad and that he was to meet his helpmate, Nosovitsky, at a given time at a certain New York hotel. He was to recognize him by a flower in his lapel.[4]

Some years later, Nosovitsky wrote a series of articles in the *New York American* telling his side of the story.[5] He claimed that he had joined a revolutionary organization in Russia at the age of fifteen; received a bullet wound near his heart in a pitched battle with the Czarist police in 1907; spent three years in Siberia; served only three months of a five-year sentence in the northern part of Archangel; and escaped to Norway by walking through the marshes. Such were the tales he no doubt told in order to win the confidence of Martens and others. He turned spy and informer in 1919, so his story went, because his father and mother had starved to death and two brothers had been killed as a result of the Bolshevik revolution. To revenge himself, he went to the Department of Justice in New York and offered his services. He was employed as undercover agent "N-100."

Nosovitsky became one of the most indefatigable organizers of the Russian federation. He spoke at meetings almost daily, set up new branches, collected funds—and wrote reports for the Department of Justice. He was even brutally beaten up by the police for the cause. Such devotion brought him to the attention of Martens, who was looking for a secret courier to England.

According to Nosovitsky, the courier service in behalf of Soviet Russia was successfully arranged with the thoughtful assistance of Scotland Yard. A false document was obtained from a Detroit medical college making him a doctor. Next, he was appointed to the post of "assistant surgeon" by the Cunard line and assigned to the *Mauretania*. Martens sent for him, congratulated him on these excellent arrangements, and began to send him across. Nosovitsky speedily became the most reliable courier ever employed by the Russian Soviet Government Bureau. He never failed. When Nosovitsky was asked to arrange for Fraina's passage across the Atlantic, he knew just what to do. All he did, he related, was to go to Washington, confide his mission to the Department of Justice, and everything was cared for. A foreign passport was obtained in the name of "Ralph Snyder" for the benefit of Fraina.[6] Nosovitsky used the name "Dr. James Anderson." Reservations were made for them to sail on the steamer *Lapland*.

Just as they were about to depart, a second spy appeared on the scene.

Ferdinand Peterson had been manager of the Finnish Socialist paper formerly edited by Santeri Nuorteva, the Russian Soviet Government Bureau's secretary. After spending sixteen months in the United States Army, Peterson related, he was visited by a Colonel Willard who offered him a job as an agent of the Department of Justice to spy on the Finnish Socialists and others, particularly Nuorteva himself. Before accepting the offer, however, Peterson came to see Nuorteva, who admittedly did not try to dissuade him. Evidently Nuorteva thought it was better to be spied on by someone he knew than by a total stranger. In the summer of 1919, Peterson went on the payroll of the Department of Justice at $5 a day as Special Agent FF-22.

Early in September, the month the Communist movement was formed, Peterson came to Nuorteva with a sensational tale. He called Nuorteva's attention to an article in the Finnish Socialist paper calling Fraina an "agent provocateur." Since such charges were loosely flung about in the heat of the internecine war in the Socialist movement, Nuorteva first greeted it incredulously. Subsequently, however, he took the accusation more seriously and offered Peterson $1000 for documentary evidence incriminating Fraina.

To earn the money, the spy came back with more and more "proof" that Fraina was working for the Department of Justice. He began to see a man who looked like Fraina in the New York headquarters of the Department of Justice. One official told him that Fraina worked for the Department; another denied it. Finally, a girl in the file room supposedly showed him a check for $140, allegedly endorsed by

Louis Fraina. Later she showed him two other checks and a thick bunch of written reports in the same handwriting as the signature on the checks.

One day, as Peterson told the tale, the girl left him alone in the file room for a half hour. He made off with one check and one report to qualify for Nuorteva's reward. Instead of going straight to Nuorteva with the papers, however, he noticed that he was being followed and hurried home. About an hour and a half later, he tried to sneak out through the basement. The two men, Federal agents, walked over to him, searched him, and found the papers. After six nights in jail, he was released and fired, as was the file clerk. To add the final touch to his woe, Peterson complained that the Department of Justice owed him money and refused to give him references for another job.

On the basis of this incredible hodge-podge by a self-confessed spy spurred on by the lure of $1000, Fraina's revolutionary reputation was called into question and he had to fight for his political life. Nuorteva openly accused him of working for the Department of Justice. Because the charge came from such a powerful source, the Communist leaders in New York could not ignore it.

Two days before the *Lapland* was scheduled to sail, Fraina was ordered to appear at the office of the Russian Soviet Government Bureau in New York to stand trial. Around a big table in a large conference room sat Martens, Nuorteva, and Weinstein of the Bureau, and Bittelman, Lovestone, and several others of the Communist party. Fraina came with Nosovitsky. When he had mentioned his trouble to the courier, the latter had volunteered to come along and help him. Fraina thought nothing of it and took him along.

Almost as bizarre as the fact that the "trial" was held at all was the fact that the Communist party found it necessary to publish a stenographic record of the proceedings as a pamphlet.[7] It remains to this day one of the rarest and weirdest of all the rare and weird publications ushered into the world by the Communist movement. Peterson's story is taken from his own testimony in this pamphlet.

In the middle of the "trial," the informer himself was brought into the room to confront Fraina. At first Peterson could not recognize him. When the chairman asked him, "Do you think that there is in this room anyone whom you can identify as Louis Fraina?", Peterson replied, "No, I would not say so." But, after a while, as he was describing the alleged appearance of the spy, he happened to look in Fraina's direction, and said: "It was just like that gentleman's," pointing to Fraina's forehead. Then he added: "Will you please get up for a second?"

Only the stenographic report can do justice to the climax:

FRAINA (*rising*): Do you want me to take off my glasses? (*as he began taking them off*).
PETERSON: You are the man!
FRAINA: Thank you (*sits down*).
NOSOVITSKY: A political move!! [8]

Now there began a battle of wits between the two spies. Nosovitsky took over most of the cross-examination. He was by far the more cunning of the two. More than anyone else in the room, he forced Peterson to expose himself. Nosovitsky made Peterson confess that Department of Justice agents never signed names to any documents, only their secret numerical designations. This admission cut the ground from under Peterson's claim that he had seen Fraina's name on a report or a check. Realizing this, Peterson turned on Nosovitsky and complained that it was very strange that the latter knew so much about the Department of Justice's procedure. No one seemed to take the hint that Peterson, No. FF-22, might also have been exposing Nosovitsky, No. N-100. When Nosovitsky got through with him, Peterson's credibility had gone down sharply.

What completely shattered Peterson's case against Fraina was the dates he chose to allege that he had seen him in the New York headquarters of the Department of Justice. Fraina was able to prove conclusively that he could not have been there on any of the three occasions mentioned by Peterson. Lovestone and Bittelman confirmed that Fraina was in Chicago, not in New York, on at least two of the dates.

After the testimony, Fraina asked everyone present to state

232 THE ROOTS OF AMERICAN COMMUNISM

whether the matter had been sufficiently cleared up to permit him to leave on schedule. All those present, except the chairman and Nuorteva, answered affirmatively. The chairman wanted to recall Peterson to confront him with Fraina's final refutation. Weinstein reserved opinion and urged Fraina not to leave immediately. The leaders of the Russian Soviet Government Bureau were clearly leagued against Fraina for reasons of their own. In any case, the Communist leaders decided to exonerate Fraina and approve his departure for the Amsterdam conference the next day. Nosovitsky says that he sat up all night writing a full report for the benefit of the Department of Justice. Then he cabled Scotland Yard to expect his arrival with Fraina aboard the *Lapland*.[9]

Fraina thus slipped out of the clutches of Peterson, a small-fry operator, only to fall into the clutches of Nosovitsky, a much bigger one. Nosovitsky had been fighting Peterson in order to save Fraina as his own victim.

Amsterdam vs. Moscow

In all the history of the Comintern—the most neglected of all aspects of Communist history—only once were the Western Communists permitted to get together without the benefit of Russian chaperons to draw up a program of their own. An American, Fraina, played a prominent role on this unique and little-known occasion.

The Russian Bolsheviks had been sorely disappointed at the lack of foreign representation at the First Congress of the Comintern in March 1919. Since the blockade made it so difficult for foreign sympathizers to get to Moscow, emissaries were sent out to make contact with them abroad. One such emissary was S. J. Rutgers, one of the few Westerners at the First Congress. He came out of Russia in November 1919 with a threefold mandate from the Comintern: to set up a Communist propaganda center, to establish relations with the various Communist parties and groups of Western Europe and America, and to organize a Communist conference.[10] Amsterdam became his headquarters and the site of the proposed conference.

Fraina, accompanied by the indispensable Nosovitsky, left New York in December. As "Ralph Snyder" and "Dr. James Anderson," they arrived in London en route to the forthcoming conference in Amsterdam. According to Nosovitsky's tale, they lived in grand style at the expense of Scotland Yard. Nosovitsky would like us to believe that he concocted a plot to break down Fraina's puritanical revolutionary morale by giving him a taste of luxurious living. He persuaded the British Exchequer to finance the experiment, admittedly unsuccessful, at an alleged cost of $2800 in two weeks.[11]

At any rate, Fraina and Nosovitsky proceeded in the middle of January 1920 to attend Rutgers' conference in Amsterdam. Only sixteen official delegates were present—from Germany, England, Switzerland, Belgium, Holland, and the United States. A few others, from Hungary, China, and the Dutch East Indies, took part without voting privilege. Still others arrived from Germany, Austria, Rumania, and Spain after the main conference was forced to disperse.[12] The preponderance of delegates from England and the continental countries nearest Holland virtually made it a conference of Western Communists.

The conference itself took place early in February 1920.[13] It proved to be one of the most ludicrous secrets of the conspiratorial period. For one thing, there was Nosovitsky, faithfully sending reports to the Department of Justice and Scotland Yard. For another, so accustomed were the Dutch Left-Wingers to working in the open that they housed the foreign delegates at one of the best hotels. They ate at a well-known restaurant, where they sang radical songs.[14] On the fourth day, a startling discovery was made by another Russian emissary, Michael Borodin. He spotted a dictaphone machine operated by the Dutch police in the room next to the secret conference. The delegates quickly scattered, but not before the Dutch police had succeeded in arresting most of the foreigners. Borodin, Fraina, and a few others managed to hide out and continue the discussions at Rutgers' home, a few yards from an army barracks at Amersfoort.[15]

The decisions reached at the conference were "ultra-leftist." Rutgers himself was an ideological extremist, and some of the English delegates were only partially reformed syndicalists. The chief resolutions were hostile to political action and existing trade unionism. Fraina introduced the basic "Thesis on Unionism." In general, the Amsterdam Conference reflected the current state of mind of the Western Communists, particularly in England, Holland, and the United States, where extremism took the form of refusing to use parliamentary methods or to work inside the conservative trade unions.

The Amsterdam meeting was not the only effort to set up a Communist center outside Moscow. The German Communist party had previously decided to organize a "Secretariat for Western Europe," and a conference in Germany had been announced for the latter half of January 1920. After it became clear that the state of siege in Germany would prevent the German conference from taking place, the Amsterdam group went ahead with its conference, but a delicate problem of the relationship of the two efforts remained. It was decided provisionally to solve the problem by means of a division of labor—Central and Southwestern Europe for the German Secretariat, Western Europe and America for the Amsterdam organization.[16]

In the end, the Amsterdam Conference decided to create an "International Sub-Bureau" for England, Germany, France, Italy, Holland, and the United States. An Executive Committee composed of Henriette Roland-Holst, S. J. Rutgers, and D. I. Wynkoop set up headquarters in Holland. One of its functions was to issue a bulletin in German, English, and French. Two subsidiary bureaus were also created. Since the German Secretariat was not functioning, a Central European Bureau was formed for Germany, Austria, Poland, Rumania, Hungary, and Bulgaria. An American Bureau, to be provisionally set up by the Communist party of America, was commissioned to call a Pan-American conference to organize a permanent bureau to represent the Comintern in Latin America, Canada, and the United States.[17]

A Pan-American Provisional Bureau was actually set up in the United States, but it split into no less than three parts when Ruthenberg led his followers out of the Communist party into the United Communist party. The latter then proceeded to form a Pan-American Sub-Bureau in competition with the C.P.'s original Bureau.[18] No Pan-American conference was ever held and these offshoots of the Amsterdam Conference were largely paper organizations.

The Amsterdam Bureau itself lasted less than three months. By the time word of the antipolitical and anti-trade-union resolutions adopted at Amsterdam reached Moscow, a change of line was already in full swing. As a result, the Comintern's mandate to the Amsterdam Bureau was brusquely revoked in May. The Bureau's functions were handed over to the West-European Secretariat of the Comintern and the latter's big three, Zinoviev, Bukharin, and Radek, were appointed to draw up a memorandum and theses castigating the Amsterdam "ultra-leftists." [19]

Such was the short, somewhat inglorious career of the only opportunity ever given the Western Communists to form a subsidiary Communist center of their own. It was a half-hearted effort at best, snuffed out as soon as the Moscow leaders saw the possibility of independent thinking as well as independent organization. The hasty suffocation of the Amsterdam effort provided at the very start a flash of insight into the future mechanism of the Russian monopoly of wisdom and power in the Comintern. The alternative would have been a more decentralized international Communist movement with subsidiary regional organizations outside Moscow, which was represented by the Amsterdam meeting in embryo. But decentralization was the last thing the Russians wanted. Their ideal was a totally centralized international organization. At Amsterdam, this ideal was unintentionally threatened for the first and last time. Western Communism was never again permitted to have a life of its own.

Amsterdam was also the parting of the ways for Fraina and Nosovitsky. The Dutch police raid aroused Fraina's suspicions, and he decided to shake off Nosovitsky. They made arrangements to meet at a Dutch port to return to England and then to the United States. Instead, Fraina, with the help of his Dutch acquaintances, walked across the frontier into Germany and made his way to Berlin. His next destination was Moscow. Nosovitsky had to return alone and empty-handed.

But the indefatigable Nosovitsky went back to the United States and on to bigger, if not better, things. According to Nosovitsky, the financier, Henry W. Marsh, of the American Defense Society, a private radical-hunting organization of the twenties, gave him $25,000 to find evidence that Mexico was about to be taken over by the Red Army. With the help of the Department of Justice, Nosovitsky relates, he entered Mexico to get the evidence. It did not take him long to discover that the Mexican Communists were nothing to worry about and that the Red Army in Mexico was a figment of his employer's imagination. But Nosovitsky was not one to admit defeat on such a lucrative assignment. He says that he stayed in Mexico for almost two and a half years manufacturing documents to scare his clients about a nonexistent Red Army. These forged documents, which he boldly reproduced in his published memoirs, were faithfully transmitted to Secretary of State Charles Evans Hughes. Nosovitsky proudly boasted that they helped to stave off American recognition of Mexico for over two years.[20]

Borodin's mission

One of the Russian emissaries at the Amsterdam conference, Borodin, was also one of the Comintern's first couriers to the United States.

His real name was Michael Gruzenberg. He was born into a Jewish rabbinical family in the town of Yanovichi, near Vitebsk, in Byelorussia, and entered the revolutionary movement at the age of sixteen through the Jewish Bund. He gave up the Bund for the Bolsheviks three years later in 1903. Arrested on returning from a Socialist conference in Stockholm in 1906, he preferred exile and chose to come to the United States. There he shortened his name to Berg, studied at Valparaiso University in Indiana, married another Russian student, and with his wife set up a "progressive preparatory" school in Chicago. In 1917 the Russian Revolution called him back home.[21] "He is a man with shaggy black hair brushed back from his

SPIES, VICTIMS, AND COURIERS 237

forehead, a Napoleonic beard, deep-set eyes, and a face like a mask," wrote the English sculptress, Clare Sheridan.[22] He was also one of the most persuasive and fascinating Bolshevik propagandists ever sent out from Moscow to spread the revolution abroad.

One of Borodin's earliest missions involved getting propaganda and money into the United States. Unable to deliver them in person, he had to find an intermediary. By a strange combination of circumstances, his choice fell on the famous American poet and biographer, Carl Sandburg.

One day, toward the end of 1918, Sandburg was sitting on a bench on the broad boulevard outside the Grand Hotel in the city of Oslo, when Borodin walked over to him. Sandburg had recently arrived to report the short-lived Finnish revolution for the Newspaper Enterprise Association. Borodin smilingly explained that they had something in common—both came from Chicago. Though they had never met before, Borodin undoubtedly knew about Sandburg's old Socialist sympathies and had sought him out for that reason. He made himself useful to Sandburg as a source of information and they were drawn together for a few weeks.

When Sandburg decided to return to the United States, Borodin's opportunity came. First he asked Sandburg whether he would like to take back home some literature of the kind that they were getting out in Russia. Sandburg received an entire trunkful of printed documents and propaganda material which he intended to turn over to the University of Chicago. Just before his ship sailed, Borodin handed him a $10,000 check on a bank in New York to be delivered to Nuorteva, 400 Norwegian kroner for his own wife who was still in Chicago, and the English translation of a pamphlet by Lenin. At the last moment, Sandburg says, he told the United States Minister, whom he knew, about the check. When Sandburg arrived in New York, he was greeted by an official reception committee which made a thorough search of his baggage. The United States government thereby came into possession of a trunkful of Communist propaganda. Sandburg was not searched personally but he voluntarily handed over the $10,000 check. He did not hand over the 400 kroner, which he duly

238 THE ROOTS OF AMERICAN COMMUNISM

delivered to Borodin's wife, or the translation of Lenin's pamphlet, which he turned over to Nuorteva.

And thus *A Letter to American Workingmen* by Lenin, the pamphlet in question, was brought over by the future biographer of Abraham Lincoln. It soon appeared in *The Revolutionary Age* and *The Liberator,* and in many pamphlet editions.[23]

Borodin's next attempt to invade the United States was much more adventurous and expensive. We know about it from several sources, each of which has a different tale to tell.

Borodin himself told one story to the ex-Communist Indian leader, M. N. Roy, who retold it in his memoirs more than twenty years later. According to Roy, Borodin had two purposes. The Soviet Russian Trade Delegation in Washington was desperately short of funds as a result of the blockade which prevented contact with Russia. Not having any available foreign exchange, the Foreign Commissariat had to use crown jewels worth about a million rubles to finance the Delegation. Borodin was chosen to smuggle the jewels into the United States on the strength of his American experience. His instructions were to rescue the Trade Delegation from financial embarrassment and to use the remainder of the proceeds from the sale of the jewels to help set up a Communist movement in the United States. The jewels were hidden in two heavy leather valises.

In Vienna, Borodin picked up a young, aristocratic Austrian ex-officer who dreamed of leaving Europe to its doom and emigrating to South America in quest of a remote hacienda. Borodin decided that he would make an excellent companion. With the help of some of Rutgers' colleagues in Holland, the ex-Austrian officer in search of solitude and the ex-Chicago schoolteacher in search of revolution boarded a Dutch freighter bound for the West Indian island of Curaçao, where it was supposed to pick up a cargo of gin. The two heavy leather valises went aboard safely.

The ship was stopped and searched by American customs officials in Haiti. Borodin and his Austrian companion were taken off the boat as "undesirable aliens" and held in custody pending an investigation. Borodin dragged the two heavy leather valises ashore. He decided to break loose and escape without them. The Austrian agreed to take them over and, whenever he might be set free and allowed to travel, to deliver them to Borodin's wife in Chicago. A few days later, Borodin managed to reach Jamaica in a sailing boat. There he booked passage on a ship to New York.

But, as we know from the Bureau of Investigation agent, Jacob Spolansky, Borodin was already a marked man. By chance, Spolansky and Borodin were old Chicago acquaintances. Reports on Borodin had been coming in from abroad, and Spolansky knew all about the consignment of jewels but did not know that Borodin had abandoned them. When Spolansky searched Borodin's luggage at Ellis Island, the precious stones were missing. Borodin's next move was to pay a visit to D. H. Dubrowsky, an important member of the official Soviet bureau headed by Martens. According to Dubrowsky, Borodin told him to expect the delivery of a quarter of a million dollars worth of diamonds. Meanwhile, Borodin himself went off to see his wife in Chicago. Spolansky says that Borodin telephoned him for a conference in Chicago and tried to talk him into becoming a Soviet agent like himself! The reply of Spolansky's chief at the Bureau was, "Drop all further negotiations." Borodin calmly proceeded to Mexico.

In Mexico, Borodin converted the remarkable Roy, then an Indian Nationalist with Socialist leanings, to communism. In due time, a message arrived from Moscow instructing Borodin to return as quickly as possible for the forthcoming Second Congress of the Comintern. Roy was chosen to go along with him to represent Mexico. They made preparations to depart by different routes and meet secretly in Berlin.

The story has three, or possibly four, different endings.

According to Roy, Borodin's former Austrian companion decided to stay in Haiti. He found his peace and solitude by living like a hermit in a hut on the beach. Not expecting the two heavy leather valises to be of any use to a hermit, he had left them behind. When Borodin arrived in Moscow without the jewels, he was accused of misconduct. To get him exonerated, Roy had to testify on his behalf. Borodin's wife was also called to Moscow. She arrived with the two heavy leather suitcases. The Austrian had finally realized that there must have been something of value in them and had delivered them to her in Chicago as he had promised. When they were opened in Moscow, the contents were found intact.

According to Dubrowsky, who testified before a congressional committee almost twenty years later, a man had actually come to his office with a bag of diamonds two weeks after Borodin's departure. Dubrowsky handed it over to the Produce Exchange Corporation, a forerunner of the official Soviet Amtorg agency. When it was reported that the diamonds were sold for only $12,000, an explanation was demanded from Borodin in Moscow. Borodin met Dubrowsky in Red Square on May Day of 1920, and asked him to come to the Foreign Commissariat to vouch for the fact that a quarter of a million dollars' worth of diamonds had been delivered to him.

Louis Fraina also thought he knew what had happened to the diamonds. After Fraina arrived in Moscow in 1920, he became friendly with Borodin. Fraina recalled, years later, that Borodin told him he had dumped the diamonds in the ocean before landing in New York.[24]

Some jewels, possibly the same ones, can be traced from Russia to the United States to Ireland and back to Russia. Martens needed money so badly that he gave Russian jewels to the Irish Republican delegation in New York, then headed by the future Irish prime minister, Eamon De Valera, as security for a loan of $20,000. Martens was deported from the United States in 1921 and the jewels were deposited in an American bank by Harry Boland, one of De Valera's colleagues. Boland brought the jewels to Ireland at the end of 1921, and the following year, as he was dying, he instructed his mother and sister to hold them until the Irish Free State should become a republic. After the Irish Constitution was passed in 1938, Boland's sister handed over the jewels to De Valera as head of the government. On one occasion in Geneva, De Valera suggested to Maxim Litvinov, the Russian representative to the League of Nations, that the loan should be repaid and the jewels returned but received no response. In 1948 the whereabouts of the jewels became a hotly disputed issue in the Irish general election. The newly elected government proceeded to get in touch with a Russian representative in London; the Russians agreed to repay the original loan in dollars, without interest; and the jewels were finally repatriated after twenty-eight years as a strangely disturbing factor in men's consciences.[25]

There is no secret about Borodin's mission, even if there probably will always be a mystery about the diamonds. The substratum of truth and the aura of mystery were both characteristic of the underground's atmosphere.

Advice and instructions

The Comintern's first messages and couriers to the United States were plagued by extraordinarily bad luck.

At the very moment that the American Communist movement was being formed in Chicago, a "circular letter" dated September 1, 1919, was sent out from Moscow by the Comintern. It was not received in the United States until after the Palmer raids had driven the party underground. In the English version at least, it was published in the *New York Times* before it appeared in the official Communist organ.[26]

This letter tried to answer the question to what extent it was justifiable for Communists to utilize parliamentary institutions. The answer was twofold. It was wrong to think of parliamentarism as a desirable form of state organization. It was right to utilize parliamentarism in order to overthrow or destroy parliaments. The answer was boiled down in the following catechism:

Are we for the maintenance of the bourgeois "democratic" parliaments as the form of the administration of the state?
No, not in any case. We are for the Soviets.
But are we for the full utilization of these parliaments for our Communist work—as long as we are not yet strong enough to overthrow the Parliament?
Yes, we are for this—in consideration of a whole list of conditions.

This emphasis on utilizing parliamentary institutions, albeit for the purpose of destroying them, went counter to the historic tradition of the American Left Wing. In the underground period, the Comintern's directive did not seem to apply to American conditions. Indeed, the Comintern was still so far removed from the American scene that it referred in this document to the I.W.W. as the organization which was leading "the fight for the Soviets" in the United States. It failed to give the slightest indication that it was aware of the birth of the two Communist parties. Obviously no one in Moscow had received reliable information from the United States in months.

The first Comintern messages specifically addressed to the American Communists appeared in a well-known news magazine, *Current History*.*

Shortly before Christmas of 1919, a pro-Bolshevik conspiracy to overthrow the Latvian government was uncovered at Volmar, near Riga. Among a hundred persons arrested was a Russian sailor on whom was found a large sum of money and jewels of great value, and, in the soles of his boots, two letters. The letters were intended by the Comintern for American sympathizers. The sailor had spent considerable time in Latvia waiting for an opportunity to sail for the United States. Tired of lying in hiding in an old house, he had sent a woman messenger to Moscow for instructions. She was caught trying to pass the lines. His arrest followed.

The first letter began: "Dear Comrades, permit us to give you a full résumé of our advice and instructions regarding current work in America." It proceeded to give "advice and instructions" on how to organize an American Communist party, thereby indicating that the Comintern still had to catch up with American events. It expected the components of an American Communist party to come from four sources—the defunct Socialist Propaganda League, the extreme elements excluded from the Socialist party, a split in the Socialist Labor party, and the I.W.W. Significantly, it added: "The organization of this party should be effected in Moscow."

The political side of the letter also betrayed more about the illusions in Moscow than the reality in the United States. It solemnly advised the Americans to organize small Communist nuclei in the

* It has not been possible to confirm these messages from official Communist sources.

armed forces "to carry on energetic propaganda in organizing Soviets of soldiers and sailors, and in preaching fanatical hostility towards officers and Generals." More military advice went: "It is most necessary to develop propaganda to instill into the minds of the workers the paramount necessity for *arming*. Revolutionary soldiers who are demobilized should not give up their rifles." The enemy was also taken care of—in Russian style: "Use the utmost efforts to oppose the organization of White Guards. This should be done in most ruthless and violent manner." The Comintern cautioned that there was a special American danger that Workers' Soviets in the United States would degenerate into philanthropic or cultural organizations instead of *"militant* units of the fight for national control and proletarian dictatorship." It counseled: "The organization of strikes and of unemployed and the fomenting of insurrections—that is the task appointed." The fate of the A.F. of L. was settled in no uncertain terms: "This must be *smashed in pieces.*" A general platform for the American Soviets was suggested:

(a) Down with the Senate and Congress.
(b) Down with capitalists in the factories. Long live the management of the factories by the workers.
(c) Down with speculators. All organizations of food and supply to be in the workers' hands.

The second letter contained a reference to the desire of the Russian federation to control the official Soviet agency under Martens. It ruled that Martens' office was not to be controlled by, or subordinate to, any "local organizations." Thus a precedent was set for the formal separation of the local Communist movement and the official Soviet representation.[27]

A few weeks later, another courier from Russia was captured in Latvia. Two more documents for American consumption were taken from him. This time the New York *World* enabled the American Communists to get the benefit of the Comintern's guidance.*

The first one, typewritten closely in English on both sides of pieces

---

* These messages were confirmed by the official Communist press.

of cotton cloth of foolscap size, was addressed to the top committees of both the Communist and Communist Labor parties. It differed markedly from the previous efforts of the Comintern, which had mainly revealed the Comintern's ignorance of the American situation. This one finally showed considerable knowledge. Dated January 12, 1920, and signed by Zinoviev as head of the Comintern, it may be considered the first Comintern message of consequence to American Communists. It set the precedent for the hundreds of messages, letters, directives, and instructions, by courier, cable, and mail, major and minor, large and small, that streamed out of Moscow in the direction of America for many years.

The Comintern came down heavily in favor of unity between the two parties. It advocated limiting the autonomy of the foreign-language federations to propaganda work in their own languages and making them subordinate to the central party organization in political and economic matters, as well as depriving them of their right to collect party dues. It urged a combination of legal and illegal methods of work. Other proposals showed which way the wind was blowing in Moscow. The Comintern strongly favored "a *mass* organization and not a narrow, closed circle." It called for more active participation in strike struggles. On the other hand, it still referred to "the period of immediate revolutionary struggle for power" and approved of "the speedy split of the American Federation of Labor." In general, this communication indicated that the Comintern was entering the American field warily, feeling its way to a new line without breaking too sharply with the past.[28]

On a separate piece of cloth was written an agreement reached in Moscow by unidentified American delegates, calling for the unification of the Communist and Communist Labor parties. It ordered the American Communists to call a unity convention and adopt the United Communist party of America as the new name of a single party.[29] Since the agreement, at least in substance, appeared in the New York *World* at the end of March 1920 and the United Communist party came into existence at the end of May, this message from Moscow probably played a role in American developments. Nevertheless, it did not succeed in unifying the entire American Communist movement, and the foreign-language, anti-Ruthenberg wing of the original Communist party defied it with impunity.

The same courier also carried with him a letter from the Comintern to the I.W.W., written on small sheets of tissue paper. It tried to wean the I.W.W. away from its long-time opposition to any kind of state, even a workers' state, and political activity. The I.W.W. organ did not publish it in full for more than seven months, by which time it did little to win over the last die-hards of American syndicalism.[30]

15

The Crisis of Communism

On the surface, the underground period seems like the dark age of American Communism. Little attention has been paid to it, as if nothing important could happen while the Communists were so busy trying to stay out of jail.

But something of the utmost historical importance did happen—a crisis so profound and far-reaching that the entire future of world communism was at stake in it.

The crisis came because world communism could not live on the proceeds of the Russian Revolution indefinitely. The Russian Revolution was enough to start it off; it was not enough to insure survival. For the impulse that came from the Russian Revolution was based on an illusion—the illusion that the entire capitalist system was about to go down. As long as this illusion persisted, the Russian Revolution and the world revolution were parts of one whole. The problems of the world revolution seemed to have been solved in Russia. The belief that the Russians had at long last found the answers gave Russians and non-Russians alike a contagious sense of destiny and confidence. Faith in the Western revolution was a necessary ingredient of the Russian Revolution, and faith in the Russian Revolution was a necessary ingredient of the Western revolution.

But what if the Russian Revolution had not solved the problems of the world revolution? What if it were necessary to rethink all the old problems again in specifically Western terms?

Disillusionment of such magnitude was bound to cause a crisis. By chance, Lenin saw it coming just about the time the American Communists were driven underground. This coincidence did not mean that the Americans could postpone facing the issue until they were able to come up out of the underground. On the contrary, a solution was most urgent in the United States because the disadvantages of working underground reinforced and exaggerated the basic trouble. The underground made the American crisis the most acute of all, but there would have been a crisis without it.

Nevertheless, the American problem was peculiar in that it had to be faced under the most difficult and unfavorable conditions. The Americans had to conduct a great debate on the new tactics necessary in the new situation at the same time that they were forced to devote most of their energies to staying out or getting out of jail.

This debate was conducted largely in the underground papers, which came out more or less regularly. The underground Communist papers were far more preoccupied with the fight among the Communists themselves than with the fight against the police. So furious was the internal struggle that Max Eastman contemptuously referred to the Communist movement as "a lively underground debating society." [1] Out of this debating society, however, came the fully formed Communist movement that would function in the open for years to come. In the end, the internal crisis was infinitely more important than the external one.

Because the American crisis was part of a much larger one in the Communist world, it is impossible to understand it in exclusively American terms. One impinged on the other, as major Communist crises have always done. To understand fully what happened in New York and Chicago, it is first necessary to understand what was happening in Moscow.

The end of an illusion

The great illusion that the entire capitalist world was about to go down was as much Russian as American—in 1919. At the First

Congress of the Comintern, Lenin made the extraordinary statement: "The Soviet system has conquered not only in backward Russia but also in the most developed country of Europe—Germany, and in the oldest capitalist country—Great Britain." The proclamation issued by the Comintern for May Day of 1919 declared: "The great Communist International was born in the year 1919. The great International Soviet Republic will be born in the year 1920." In July 1919, Lenin made a speech which guaranteed "the victory of the International Soviet Republic, and this victory will be complete and irrevocable"—by July 1920.[2] One of Lenin's first questions to Emma Goldman was: "When could the Social Revolution be expected in America?" Zinoviev asked her "how soon the revolution could be expected in the United States."[3] Such questions were the common experience of American visitors to Moscow.

Day after day, week after week, then month after month, the victorious Russian Bolsheviks waited for the European revolution that never came. By 1920, Lenin became so convinced that the revolutionary wave had receded that he began to turn his attention primarily to the economic development of Russia itself. He continued to believe in the inevitability of the Western revolution, but no longer in its imminence. Once this was clear to him, a whole constellation of practical implications followed. Lenin's peculiar opportunism was based on a simple rule: new situations demand new tactics. Since the new situation in the West was nonrevolutionary, he reasoned that offensive tactics had to give way to defensive ones.

Instead of permitting the Western Communists to work out the new equation for themselves, Lenin did it for them. The result was his little book, *"Left-Wing" Communism: An Infantile Disorder,* written in the spring of 1920. It remains the most powerful and systematic textbook of Leninist tactics in the postwar period with special emphasis on Western rather than Russian conditions.

In this work Lenin declared war on the "ultra-Left." He hit out ruthlessly against what he considered the two main errors: the refusal to participate in "bourgeois parliaments" and the unwillingness to work in "reactionary trade unions." His most biting criticism was reserved for those Communists who did not see the need to "compromise" if necessary and to "maneuver" by every possible means. These new tactics of compromise and maneuver were not, as Lenin had to concede, very novel. These were the terms with which he himself had belabored his old enemies, the opportunists and reformists. He admitted that there was no hard-and-fast line between revolutionary and nonrevolutionary opportunism. He pointed out all the political compromises and deals that the Russian Bolsheviks had made in order to come to power. What he had to fall back on, in the end, was the familiar concept of revolutionary opportunism—revolutionaries were justified in making any kind of compromise or opportunistic maneuver as long as the circumstances warranted and the ultimate goal remained intact.[4]

Whatever the abstract merits of the case, this was not at all what Lenin's more recent Western converts had been led to believe. They had been lashing away at everyone else's opportunism on the basis of the most rigid, absolute, and intolerant standards. Now, so long as they were convinced of their own revolutionary virtue, no kind or amount of opportunism was forbidden to them.

A point of no return was passed in Communist history when Lenin decided to give up the illusion of the imminent world revolution. Compared with this decision, all other landmarks of the Communist movement become secondary.

Once the Bolsheviks realized that they had miscalculated—providentially in terms of their power but catastrophically from the viewpoint of doctrine—they were plunged into an intellectual vacuum. They could not turn back and there was nothing in their creed that told them how to go forward. They could not make a revolution according to their principles; henceforth they were doomed to make a revolution without principles.

There came a day when Lenin had to admit publicly that there was nothing in the "old books" to prepare the Russian Communists for such an important innovation as the New Economic Policy of partially restoring capitalism. Lenin complained, "It did not even occur to Marx to write a word about this subject; and he died without leaving a single precise quotation or irrefutable instruction on it. That is why we must get out of the difficulty entirely by our own efforts." [5] Lenin finally confessed that the Russian Communists had failed "to present our Russian experience to foreigners." He advised the Russians "to sit down and study things after five years of the Russian Revolution" and "to start learning from the beginning." [6] In effect he had led the Russian Communists into a Marxist *cul-de-sac*. The men who made the Russian Revolution could never escape from the paradox that they had won power not because of their principles but in spite of them. At the very moment that the Bolsheviks had to put their theories into practice, they discovered that their practical position made their theories utterly useless. There was only one thing for them to do—improvise. They have been improvising ever since.

We have been accustomed to think and talk of the "Communist revolution" in Russia. There was instead a revolution made by Communists. Men took power; no ideal was realized. They took power in conditions which made it impossible for them to realize the ideal. Before the Soviet regime became a political jungle in which some Communists could rule by force, intrigue, and improvisation, it had become an intellectual jungle in which all Communists had lost their way.

For the first time, every Communist in the world was called on to change his mind in accordance with a change of line. A faith which had seemed so simple, pure, and direct was transformed into something devious, tortuous, and complex. A Communist of the 1919 vintage suddenly became an anachronism. Unless he was prepared to defend what he had attacked and attack what he had defended, he was a heretic to the Communist of the next vintage. The propaganda of yesterday was repudiated or conveniently forgotten. Old comrades in arms denounced one another. The dogmas changed; dogmatism remained. In the beginning, the Communists had simplified capitalism so much that they could also simplify themselves. When they changed their perspective of capitalism, they changed themselves. So long as they believed that the world revolution was around the corner, they could afford to take a position of no reforms, no compromises, no maneuvers—only the revolution. When the imminence of revolution went out, compromise and maneuver came in.

Lenin did not mention the American Communists specifically in *"Left-Wing" Communism*. He did cite "a certain *section* of the Industrial Workers of the World and the anarcho-syndicalist trends in America." His chief targets were the German, British and Dutch "Leftists." But the Americans were most vulnerable on exactly the two points that Lenin considered most important—work in the old trade unions and political activity. Both were alien to the dual-union, antipolitical tradition of the American Left Wing. The first American translation of *"Left-Wing" Communism* did not appear until January 1921, and its full impact on the American Communists was therefore somewhat delayed.

Meanwhile, however, two Americans, Reed and Fraina, were vying with each other to get to Moscow first. Without knowing it, they were heading into Lenin's new position.

New York to Moscow

The race to Moscow started soon after Fraina was elected International Secretary of the Communist party and Reed the International Delegate of the Communist Labor party at the Chicago conventions in September 1919. Reed left late that same month. Fraina was held up for two more months disposing of the "spy" charges and beating off competitors in the Communist party who wanted to make the trip in his stead. He was then held up by the Amsterdam Conference for another two months. Both knew the stake in Moscow: that party would survive which succeeded in winning the recognition and support of the Comintern.

Reed easily won the race by starting first and going by a more direct route. A trip to the capital of the world revolution was then high adventure as well as a political mission. As "Jim Gormley," he worked his way across the Atlantic as a stoker on a Scandinavian ship. From Norway, he stowed away on a ship bound for Finland. He was supposed to be taken in hand by two workers on the dock, followed the wrong pair, trudged back to the dock to flirt with arrest a second time, and luckily found the right men—without possessing a passport or knowing the language. Eventually he was passed on from sympathizer to sympathizer through the Finnish lines into Russia early in 1920.[7] From Reed, the highest Soviet leaders, including Lenin and Trotsky, received a first-hand if not unprejudiced version of what had been happening to the American Communist movement. Lenin liked Reed and often called him to the Kremlin to discuss American conditions.[8]

It took Fraina from March to June to get through the blockade of 1920 on the way to the promised land.

When he reached Berlin from Amsterdam, the German capital was totally paralyzed by a general strike in answer to the Kapp Putsch. With a British Communist, John T. Murphy, he tried to make his way to Russia via the northern, Scandinavian route. First they walked across the German border into Schleswig-Holstein. At Flensburg, arrangements were made to get them to Copenhagen where a motor boat was to take them to Finland and from there to Russia. But they were given away, arrested, and thrown into prison for nine days. Deported back to Germany, they made a second attempt. With a police agent trailing them, they managed to get to Hamburg where they were smuggled aboard a ship bound for Reval (Tallin), carrying Russian prisoners of war. Murphy and Fraina, pretending to be prisoners, were hidden on the ship, put aboard a train with other prisoners at Reval, answered *"Da"* when the prisoners' names were called out at the frontier, and reached Petrograd five days later.[9]

In Moscow, Reed's headstart was the least of Fraina's troubles. The old New York charges had reached the Comintern ahead of him. In addition, he had to explain his relations with Nosovitsky and his freedom of movement after the raid on the Amsterdam Conference. The Comintern had already taken the precaution of appointing an investigating committee of three to look into the charges, and Fraina had to go through the ordeal of a second "trial." The committee was composed of an American, Alexander Bilan, a Frenchman, Alfred

Rosmer, and a Hungarian, A. Rudniansky. They studied the full stenographic record of the New York "trial," listened to more testimony by all the Americans present in Moscow, including Reed, questioned delegates from Holland on the Amsterdam incident, and examined Fraina himself. The Committee unanimously decided in favor of Fraina's complete innocence, and he was admitted to the sessions of the approaching Second Congress of the Communist International.

During the Congress, however, his chief accuser, Santeri Nuorteva, arrived in Moscow. In view of Nuorteva's presence, Fraina requested the Comintern to reopen the whole case. On a motion by Zinoviev, Nuorteva was given forty-eight hours to present any new evidence with the warning that, if he failed to sustain his accusations, the case would be closed and severe measures taken aganist him if he ever repeated the charges. After listening to Nuorteva at length, the investigating committee gave Fraina a clean bill of health for the third time.[10]

Lenin himself took a personal interest in Fraina's plight. It reminded him uncomfortably of the old charge that he was a German spy because the German government had made it possible for him to return to Russia in 1917. Fraina had two interesting conversations with Lenin. In the first, Lenin tried to convince him that the Communists in America, as well as in England, should support a Labor party. Fraina argued against it, and no definite instructions were given him.[11] In the second conversation, Lenin brought up the subject of the charges against Fraina, read the Comintern resolution exonerating him, and suggested that it did not go far enough. To satisfy Lenin, a supplementary resolution was adopted: "The Executive Committee of the Communist International insists that Nuorteva must retract publicly, in the press, all the accusations made by him against Comrade Fraina."[12] During the second interview, which took place while the Red Army was knocking on the gates of Warsaw, Lenin tried to impress Fraina with the need for philosophy in the revolutionary movement![13]

The Russians did more than make Nuorteva retract. They arrested him and held him in jail for about a year, apparently on the charge that he himself had been acting as a foreign spy. After his release, he was removed from Moscow and sent to the far north as the Commissar for Education of the Karelian Workers Commune.[14]

The Second Congress

The First Congress of the Comintern in March 1919 had been so poorly attended that the second one was really the first in terms of policy and organization. Whereas the first one lasted only five days, the second took three weeks, from July 17 to August 7, 1920. The number of delegates had grown to 169 from 37 countries, though the Russian delegation was still by far the largest with 64. In the eighteen months between the two congresses, Communist parties had sprung up all over Europe. Over 100,000 Communists were reported in Germany, about 50,000 each in Italy and Yugoslavia, and over 35,000 in Bulgaria. Louis C. Fraina and Alexander Stoklitsky represented the Communist party of America, John Reed and Alexander Bilan the Communist Labor party. In view of the Comintern's demand for unity, the two groups decided to work as one delegation at the congress.[15] Actually, the Communist Labor party no longer existed, having been merged into the United Communist party in May, but the news had not yet reached Moscow, and neither Reed nor Fraina knew of the reshuffle back home.

A Comintern congress was then the most important event in Russia, and no effort was made to hide the fact. The first session was held in Petrograd in the Tauride Palace to please the head of the Comintern, Zinoviev, who was also the President of the Petrograd Soviet. The pageantry and enthusiasm of the ceremonies overwhelmed the foreign delegates. John Reed wrote ecstatically of

the great demonstration at Petrograd, where the tremendous masses flowed like a clashing sea through the broad streets, almost overwhelming with their enthusiastic affection the delegates as they marched from the Tauride Palace to the Fields of Martyrs of the Revolution, protected on both sides by long lines of workers holding hands, forming a living chain: the vast throng on Yuritsky Square, in front of the Winter Palace, where seventy thousand people crowded, roaring, to greet the delegates; the pageant at night on the steps of the old Stock Exchange—now the Sailors' Club—where more than five thousand people in gorgeous costumes took part, depicting the history of the proletarian revolution, from the Paris Commune to the International Revolution, and the cruisers of the Red Fleet, decked with flags, saluted with cannon the opening of the Congress and the Red Army marched past in review.[16]

Special trains transported the delegates to Moscow—at a time when trains were rare and rarely ran. The other sessions of the Congress took place in the grand Vladimir Throne Room of the Imperial Palace in the Kremlin.

The great singer of Imperial Russia, Chaliapin, sang for the Communist delegates at a banquet.[17] They were housed, fed, and entertained gratis. While they were deliberating in the Kremlin, the Red Army was marching on Warsaw. A huge map was hung up to keep the Comintern delegates abreast of its day-by-day advance.[18]

This was the Comintern in its youthful heyday. Small wonder that American revolutionaries like Reed and Fraina, famished for power and glory at home, were swept away by the spectacle. It brought them into direct contact with the revolution of their dreams, with their heroes who made the revolution, with the masses who fought for it. It was the promissory note of their own even greater revolution. For years to come, a trip to Moscow, a mission to the Comintern, was capable of stirring the same vast hopes and vicarious pride.

Reed's revolt

But despite the intoxicating atmosphere, for Reed and to a lesser extent for Fraina, the discussions and decisions of the Second Congress were little short of an ordeal. Nothing had prepared them for Lenin's new line of working in "reactionary trade unions."

Reed was the more headstrong and disrespectful of authority. A fervent admirer of the I.W.W., he could never bring himself to accept the A.F. of L. even in the hope of capturing it. He had been saying for years that the A.F. of L. had to be smashed, and he had no intention of saying something else, even if Lenin and the Comintern demanded it. As soon as the business sessions of the Congress got under way in Moscow, he rose as the spokesman of twenty-nine other delegates to propose that the trade-union question should be placed near the head of the list on the order of business in order to give plenty of time for the fight which he was itching to make on this issue. He also proposed that English be made one of the official languages, at least while this question was under discussion. He was defeated by the Russian steam roller on both motions.[19] Even more provoking to him personally was the Anglo-American group's choice of Fraina and Jack Tanner, a representative of the Shop Stewards' movement in England, as their spokesmen on the trade-union question.[20] Reed was not one to take these rebuffs lightly.

The biggest Russian guns, Zinoviev and Radek, were brought out to put down the revolt against the new trade-union line. Zinoviev hit the Anglo-American united front with a salvo of irony:

On the one hand, the English and American comrades are very optimistic. The social revolution is coming from today to tomorrow; we have the victory of the social revolution in our pocket, and so forth. But now that we are dealing with the trade unions, we suddenly and immediately see an unheard-of pessimism with regard to the working class. Here is what they say: we will do away with the Morgans and the Rockefellers but we will never be able to do away with the bureaucracy in the trade unions.[21]

As a horrible example of the American malady, Zinoviev pointed to the program of the United Communist party, news of which had arrived in the midst of the Congress. He held up to ridicule its instructions not to reform the A.F. of L. "but to destroy it," though he ended by offering a reluctant concession. "If the Communists go into the A.F. of L. taking for granted that their objective is to destroy it, they will destroy their own work. If it turns out, nevertheless that the result of their struggle makes it necessary to destroy the A.F. of L., then they may do it." On one thing, however, the Russians were adamant: the place of the American Communists was now inside the A.F. of L.

Radek's treatment of Reed was virtually insulting. He went so far as to accuse Reed of "sabotage." When Reed protested against cutting off further discussion, Radek replied brutally that it was not necessary for the Congress to listen to Reed for two days. Radek took the position that a mixed policy was necessary. He advocated working within the A.F. of L., collaborating with the I.W.W., and forming new unions where necessary.[22] Fraina disassociated himself from Reed and adopted a position much closer to Radek's.[23] The vote went against Reed, 57 to 8.[24]

The British delegates found themselves in a similar predicament. Lenin had advised them to seek admission into the British Labour party, which was roughly the equivalent of telling the Americans to work in the A.F. of L. The future Communist M.P., William Gallacher, pleaded pathetically, "You cannot demand from us that we should work against and speak against that which we have spent years struggling for."[25] That was precisely what Lenin, in no uncertain terms, did demand. In the end, both the Americans and the British had to go back home and eat their words.

Reed held out to the end. To the official organ of the United Communist party he sent a report on the Congress, which showed that he, for one, was eating nothing. Instead of changing his mind, he predicted that the Executive Committee of the Communist International would have to change its attitude. "At the next Congress, these theses must be altered," he wrote unrepentantly.[26] To the day of his death, he refused to make peace with the new line or even to pay lip service to it. Yet Reed survived unscathed. He, not Fraina, was chosen to represent the American Communist movement on the Executive Committee of the Communist International.

It was possible to defy the highest leaders of the Comintern, to stand up openly and fearlessly for what one believed, to go down to defeat proclaiming victory for one's ideas the next time, and to be rewarded with the highest honor bestowed by the Comintern on its most faithful servants. John Reed proved that it was possible—in 1920.

Reed and Fraina were the first American Communists to bring their splits and squabbles to Moscow for arbitration and decision.

It was another of those fateful steps taken so easily and confidently in the early days. The Americans were incapable of resolving their differences by themselves, and they took them to the Comintern as to a higher authority, an ultimate tribunal. It was not merely that the Comintern insisted on dictating to them. Even if there had been a greater willingness in Moscow to pursue a hands-off policy, the Americans themselves would not have permitted it. For many years, whenever the American Communist movement found itself incapable of solving its own problems, it took them to the Comintern as the only alternative to a split.

The spectacle of two fiercely hostile Communist parties, both swearing absolute allegiance to the Comintern, clearly violated Communist doctrine. The factions were saved from themselves by Moscow and thereby lost themselves to Moscow. Nor were the Americans the only ones. As soon as it appeared that the European revolution was far from imminent and that all the newly born Communist parties outside Russia were rickety structures, the same thing happened in party after party. The Comintern was only too glad to intervene, and the parties were sick enough first to accept intervention and later to seek it.

Zinoviev's system

The Second Congress also indicated why no American would be able to stand up to the Russians much longer.

To some extent, the change was bound up with the personality of the head of the Comintern, Zinoviev. Of all the old Bolsheviks, he was considered closest to Lenin, whose authority towered above all the rest. Zinoviev was Lenin's chief co-worker during their years of exile in Switzerland, unlike Trotsky, who was then considered an opponent, or Stalin, still a minor cog in the Bolsheviks' conspiratorial

THE CRISIS OF COMMUNISM

machine. On the eve of the Bolshevik seizure of power, Zinoviev made the fatal mistake of opposing Lenin's demand for the insurrection, an error in judgment that, as the future proved, would haunt him to the end of his life. But Lenin was not one to bear grudges, and Zinoviev was quickly restored to his good graces after the success of the insurrection. The years of intimate collaboration earned Zinoviev two of the highest posts at the disposal of the Bolshevik regime, President of the Petrograd Soviet and Chairman of the Executive Committee of the Communist International. That he was chosen to head the Russian regime in Petrograd, the birthplace of the revolution, the party's proudest stronghold, showed how high his postrevolutionary prestige was. In the Comintern, he was given precedence over the other two Bolshevik representatives in the E.C.C.I., Radek and Bukharin.

The fact that Zinoviev held these two key posts simultaneously, the one so outstanding in purely Russian terms, the other so prominent internationally, again indicates the ambivalence of the Communist movement at its inception. Because the Russian leaders played such double roles, it was hard to tell where the Soviet regime ended and the Comintern began.

Though Zinoviev had spent years as Lenin's right-hand man, as human beings they had little in common. Despite the ruthlessness with which Lenin conducted his political relationships, his personal influence on many Western Communists might be described as a kind of fatherly despotism. He asked questions so voraciously and listened so intently that his visitors often left him with the glowing feeling that they had participated actively in the great man's development and decisions. He was capable of exercising such a spell that they felt converted after talking to him for an hour. This was one of his greatest advantages over Trotsky, who gave an impression of haughty aloofness. One of the British delegates to the Second Congress, J. T. Murphy, who demonstrated his independence of mind a dozen years later when he broke with the British Communist party, was typical of the many syndicalists whom Lenin converted almost single-handed. After a session with Lenin, he "felt so drawn to this man that had he told me that the best service I could then render to the cause of the Socialist Revolution was to go back to England via the North Pole I would have been prepared to attempt the journey." [27]

Zinoviev was given the opportunity to play Lenin's role on an international scale. He was primarily responsible for justifying the Communist faith in the world revolution. Success in the Comintern was his trump card in the struggle for power among Lenin's successors, and failure was equally sure to deal a fatal blow to his ambitions. For him personally, there was another reason why it was necessary to demonstrate that he was capable of making a revolution outside Russia. Ever since he had flinched on the eve of the Bolshevik revolution, he had to prove that he was made of stern stuff. As head of the Comintern, therefore, Zinoviev strained every nerve, drove through every opening, manipulated every available pawn to "make" a revolution elsewhere. Zinoviev's personal stake in a successful Western revolution, however, was scarcely consistent with Lenin's diagnosis that the revolutionary wave in the West had receded, and from this contradiction arose some of the Comintern's most serious early reverses.

At the time of the Second Congress in 1920, Zinoviev had spent nineteen of his thirty-seven years in the revolutionary movement. Though unprepossessing in appearance, he was one of the great revolutionary orators and magnetic figures on the rung of leadership just below Lenin and Trotsky. Without a strong hand to guide him, however, he was erratic, unstable, and superficial. Many foreign Communists feared and hated him even while they did his bidding. He surrounded himself with favorites, giving or taking away power according to the lip service paid him and his temporary policies. He thought nothing of making and unmaking top leaders in the Western Communist parties, sometimes more than once in a single year.

Zinoviev's system in the Comintern prepared the way for Stalin's system, which was in many ways a continuation and a development rather than a new departure. For this reason, many of the Communist leaders whose school was Zinoviev's Comintern graduated into Stalin's Comintern with little or no trouble.

Russia's International

A more subtle and tactful person than Zinoviev might have made a different system—but different only in degree, not in kind. Zinoviev was heavy-handed in the way he applied the principles on which the Comintern was founded. However, he did not invent those principles, and he would have been powerless to change them. All Bolsheviks were agreed on the basic principles of the organization. No one stepped forward to dispute Zinoviev when he expressed them for the first time with the utmost force and candor at the Second Congress in the name of the Executive Committee.

By chance, Zinoviev utilized the situation in the American Communist movement to make his point.

He reported to the Congress that the Executive Committee had called representatives of the two rival American Communist parties to Russia. It had studied the literature of both groups. It had devoted two special sessions to the American problem. A subcommission had drawn up a plan to unify the parties and had invited them to accept it. He went on to point out that the Comintern had also intervened in the parties of Germany, Finland, Ukraine, Austria, the Balkans, France, as well as those of United States. Comintern representatives had been sent to Germany, Austria, France, Italy, Sweden, Norway, Bulgaria, the United States, and other countries. The Comintern was glad to give funds to various parties, and certain activities of the Italian Communist party, for example, were possible only because the Comintern had supplied the money. No effort was made to hide the fact that the Comintern's money came from the Russian party, the only one in a position to provide it.

Zinoviev made no apologies for "interfering" in the internal affairs of member parties. On the contrary, he proclaimed that it was the Comintern's duty to "interfere." He put it this way:

In this epoch, the international proletariat must absolutely build a genuine General Staff to take into account all the peculiarities of the movement in the various countries, to combine all the peculiarities of the proletarian movement in the whole world, but at the same time to understand how to centralize the struggle of the proletariat of all countries.

In the name of the Executive Committee he summed up:

It considers it not only as permissible but as obligatory to "interfere" in the work of the parties which adhere to or wish to adhere to the Communist International.[28]

The Second Congress spelled out this principle in detail by adopting twenty-one points of admission to the Comintern. These conditions of membership were designed to keep out parties and individuals that might have threatened the monolithic character of the Comintern. The sixteenth condition, for example, stated:

All the resolutions of the congresses of the Communist International, as well as the resolutions of the Executive Committee, are binding upon all parties joining the Communist International.[29]

In later years, this candor became embarrassing. The control of the individual parties by Comintern representatives and the subsidizing of weak parties with Comintern money contributed by the Russian party were carried on with the greatest secrecy and even hotly denied. But in the early years, these activities were taken for granted and little attempt was made to hide them, as the official report of the Second Congress shows. When the Soviet Ambassador in Berlin, A. A. Joffe, was expelled from Germany in December 1918 for interfering in internal German affairs, *Izvestia,* the official organ of the Soviet government, calmly published his reply accounting in detail for all the marks and rubles that he had handed over to German sympathizers "in the interests of the German revolution."[30] No hard-and-fast line was drawn to separate the individual parties, the Comintern, and Soviet Russia as a state. A resolution was passed at the second convention of the Communist party of America in 1920 which combined all three, as follows:

The Communist Parties of the various countries are the direct representatives of the Communist International, and thus, indirectly of the aims and policies of Soviet Russia.[31]

It would be vulgar oversimplification to imagine that American or other Western Communists submitted to the direct control of the Comintern or the indirect control of the Soviet state because they were willing to be "foreign agents." They did not consider themselves mercenaries in a foreign army. On the contrary, they gave themselves freely to the Comintern because they agreed on a certain conception of *their* movement.

According to this conception, the Comintern was not merely the central organization of separate parties—it was *the party*, the world party. The various parties were only subdivisions of a single international unit with its headquarters in Moscow. They were "sections" of the Comintern. All Communists literally "belonged" to the Comintern as much as they belonged to their own individual parties. The application card of the Communist party in 1919 stated:

The undersigned, after having read the constitution and program of the Communist Party, declares his adherence to the principles and tactics of the party and the Communist International: agrees to submit to the discipline of the party as stated in its constitution and pledges to engage actively in its work.[32]

The application card in 1925 was especially interesting for the order of precedence:

The undersigned declares his adherence to the program and statutes of the Communist International and of the Workers (Communist) Party and agrees to submit to the discipline of the Party and to engage actively in its work.[33]

The statutes of the Comintern adopted at the Second Congress were unequivocal on the subject of instructions:

The Executive Committee makes the necessary appeals on behalf of the Communist International, and issues instructions obligatory to all the parties and organizations which form part of the Communist International.

The E.C.C.I. could also demand the expulsion of whole groups of members from affiliated parties. If deemed necessary, it could set up within the parties its own "technical and auxiliary bureaus, completely subordinated to the Executive Committee."[34]

Zinoviev's use of the term "General Staff" was no accident; it was the stock analogy in Communist literature for many years. The E.C.C.I. in Moscow was the General Staff of the World Revolution; the leadership of the various parties represented field commanders; and the Comintern representatives were like general staff officers assigned to field duty, as in the German Army.

It was a grandiose conception. The entire world was one battlefield; all Communists everywhere were soldiers in a single army; all battalions were controlled from a single center. The head of the Comintern was like a marshal; the head of a party, a general; the district organizer, a captain; the rank and file, privates. The orders of the marshal could be transmitted down through a recognized chain of command to the lowest private. Yet each private was imbued with a sense of his own superiority over everyone outside the organization.

It would be shortsighted to underestimate the persuasiveness and plausibility of this organizational plan. The enemy was everywhere, deeply entrenched and sometimes brilliantly led. The early Communists were devout internationalists, playing for the highest stakes on a worldwide scale. They had bitterly criticized the Second International as merely a congeries of individual parties which put their own interests above those of the whole. The founders of Communism were determined to go just as far in the opposite direction. In so doing, they betrayed their internationalism and, step by step, came to serve the interests of revolutionary Russian nationalism. There could be no true internationalism in the Comintern without a more equal distribution of power and authority. The Russian preponderance made one party and one country the supreme arbiter over all the others. By a complex and subtle process, the non-Russian Communists exchanged the nationalism of their own countries for the nationalism of another country—in the name of internationalism.

American and other Communists accepted the political authority of the Comintern because it became their only direct human and organizational link to the Russian Revolution, the reason for their very political existence. If it was not possible to be a soldier in the Red Army, at least it was possible to be a soldier of the Comintern.

American Communists did not consider themselves to be "foreign agents" because they did not consider Russia to be a "foreign" country. The political and psychological identification was so close that it was "their" country, too. In the early twenties, James P. Cannon put it this way: "For, after all, Soviet Russia is not a 'country.' Soviet Russia is a part of the world labor movement. Soviet Russia is a strike—the greatest strike in all history. When the working class of Europe and America join that strike it will be the end of capitalism." [35] In 1930, William Z. Foster was asked, "Now, if I understand you, the workers in this country look upon the Soviet Union as their country; is that right?" And Foster, reflecting the training of the older generation of Communist leaders, answered without hesitation, "The more advanced workers do." [36]

The Communist contradiction

The Russians and the Americans in the Comintern made a curious combination.

The Americans represented the most advanced capitalist country in the world. Both the American economy and the American working class were developed to a point that backward Russia could hope to reach only in decades. Economically the Bolsheviks made no secret of the fact that they intended to overtake the United States by imitation and example. That they entertained no false pride in such a matter was indeed one of their strong points.

Politically, however, the Americans came to them as novices. The authority which Lenin, Trotsky, and their fellow leaders enjoyed was based on genuine admiration and devotion. In the first flush of the Russian Revolution, their authority did not need to be propped up by organizational pressure or unscrupulous deals. The whole revolutionary world looked to the Bolsheviks as pupils to masters.

This was the paradox, the contradiction, which took root in the Comintern at the very start and became progressively more acute as time went on. From the Communist point of view, history had played a cruel joke on the development of the revolution: Russia had to learn from America technically, and America had to learn from Russia politically. The material basis of the Russian Revolution was in America; and the political fulfillment of the American economy was in Russia. This was not at all what anyone had expected, least of all the Marxists, who had taught for decades that politics and economics move together.

The Western Communists never extricated themselves from this contradiction. In order to capitalize on the Russian Communists' victory, they had to assume that it was possible to follow the Russian example. It was easy to take the next step—the best way to follow the Russian example was to follow the Russian leadership.

Yet if politics and economics moved together, this reasoning was as specious as it was seductive. Just the opposite results could be expected if Russian methods and leadership were carried over to Western Europe and America. The assumption of the imminent Western revolution which gave Lenin the courage to go ahead with the Russian Revolution, shows how important it was for the Bolsheviks to identify Russian conditions with Western conditions. By the time of the Second Congress, Lenin was thoroughly disillusioned. The Western revolution had failed to materialize. But Lenin and the Bolsheviks suffered no loss of authority or prestige thereby. On the contrary, as one abortive Western revolution after another disappointed them, as their most extravagant hopes proved baseless, their authority and prestige rose all the higher. The failure of the world revolution only served to increase the splendor of the Russian success.

16

To the Masses!

THE Comintern began to crack down on the American Communists at the Second Congress.

When the Congress opened in July 1920, the delegations of the Communist party and the Communist Labor party were allotted five votes each. What the Congress did not know was that the United Communist party had swallowed up the Communist Labor party two months earlier. In the middle of the proceedings, a representative of the United Communist party, Edward I. Lindgren (Flynn), arrived unexpectedly in Moscow. He immediately demanded the ousting of Fraina and Stoklitsky as delegates of the Communist party on the ground that the overwhelming majority of the Communist party had gone into the United Communist party. Lindgren claimed that the United Communist party had been formed by 30,000 members from the Communist party and 20,000 from the Communist Labor party. The figures were preposterously high, but, as Fraina had to admit, no one in Moscow was in a position to challenge them. The Comintern refused Lindgren's extreme demand against Fraina and Stoklitsky, but it was sufficiently impressed to allot six votes to the United Communist party and four votes to the Communist party.[1]

By this time, the Comintern leaders were determined to do something drastic to force unity on the American factions. The Second Congress decided to give the Communist and United Communist parties two months to get together. The deadline was set for October

10, 1920. If the parties failed to carry out this injunction, both were threatened with expulsion from the Comintern. Lindgren was sent back with an ultimatum signed by Zinoviev himself. It sternly advised both parties: "You will receive all material from the Second Congress. We demand now, ultimateively [sic] from you all, that an immediate full unity should be accomplished on the basis of the decisions adopted by the Congress. Further split cannot be tolerated and cannot be justified by anything. We wait from both sides an immediate formal reply." [2]

Communications were so poor that the news of the ultimatum with its October 10 deadline did not arrive in New York until October 13, and then accidentally. Someone happened to see it in a copy of *Izvestia* dated September 14, 1920, which had taken a month to reach the United States.[3] Meanwhile, however, another Communist party emissary, Nicholas Hourwich (Andrew), had arrived in Moscow. He requested a delay, and the whole question was reopened.

This time the Comintern was more specific. A six-point plan for American unity was drawn up. The chief point made representation at the future unity congress of the American factions depend on dues payments for the months July to October 1920. The deadline was extended to January 1, 1921. A supplementary decision even instructed the united party to call itself the Communist party of America.[4]

The Communist party and the United Communist party thereupon entered into the required negotiations. There was little difficulty in agreeing on the program, because the Comintern had stipulated that it must be based on the decisions of the Second Congress. But the proposed representation at the unity congress contained a big loophole in depending on dues payments. The Communist party claimed that it had over 9000 members to only 4000–5000 for the United Communists.[5] The latter charged that its rival had faked its membership figures. The C.P. insisted on a majority of the delegates, while the U.C.P. was willing to compromise on equal representation.[6] The issue was of course decisive for control of the "unity" congress.

When the deadline of January 1, 1921, came, there was still no semblance of agreement. "Unity" negotiations that failed always made matters worse, by providing additional opportunities for the negotiators to attack each other. In the foreign-speaking Communist party, feeling ran so high that anyone who openly supported unity was treated like an enemy. Two of the founders, Alexander Bittelman and Maximilian Cohen, were temporarily expelled. They formed their own Communist Unity Committee, which criticized both sides and hardly made matters clearer.[7]

One of those caught in the middle of this fierce factional struggle was Fraina. He had been won over to the idea of unity at all costs in Moscow. Out of touch with the Communist party back home, to which he still belonged, he had proposed equal representation at the coming unity congress. This position infuriated the party's bosses and Fraina found himself unceremoniously repudiated.[8] It was more of the hard luck that had dogged him politically for over a year.

In Moscow, new steps were taken to get results. An "American Agency" was set up in the Comintern. The United Communist party was represented by Carl Jansen or Johnson, the Lettish Communist from Roxbury, Massachusetts, who had adopted the Comintern name of Charles E. Scott.[9] The Communist party was nominally represented by Fraina. The third member, and the chairman, was Sen Katayama, the Japanese exile who was now working in the Comintern. Katayama's pseudonym for the occasion was "Yavki." These three were given the task of ending the deadlock.

The Comintern had an additional reason for impatience. Plans were being rushed to set up a new trade-union organization, the Red International of Labor Unions (R.I.L.U.) at a congress in Moscow originally called for May 1, 1921. At the end of March, Scott, Fraina, and Katayama received word that the Third Congress of the Comintern would be held in June and that the First Congress of the R.I.L.U. had been postponed to July. The Comintern did not want two wrangling American delegations at its own congress, and it wanted the strongest possible American delegation at the R.I.L.U. congress. A good American delegation was sought in order to enable the new trade-union organization to boast of its truly international character. Since the Comintern's support was top-heavy in Europe and almost nonexistent in the Far East and Latin America, it had to fall back on the United States as the best bet to broaden the base of its trade-union protégé.

As the time for these congresses approached and American unity seemed as far away as ever, the Comintern decided on a policy of unity or else. On April 2, it empowered the American Agency to unite the two American parties by June 1, "otherwise the whole movement will be reorganized without regard to the existing parties." Scott transmitted this ultimatum to the American parties with more detailed instructions for the summons of a unity convention.[10] If the two American parties did not make peace between themselves, the Comintern would make war on both.

Determined to leave nothing to chance, Scott, Fraina, and Katayama came to the United States in person. Through their efforts, a unity convention took place at Woodstock, New York, in May 1921.

The chief credit for this step clearly belonged to the Comintern. Without its extreme pressure the two parties would certainly have gone on fighting each other a good deal longer. The fratricidal war gave the Comintern the first opportunity for large-scale intervention in the American movement. No doubt it would have intervened anyway on some other occasion later on, but the peculiar circumstances of this first important and direct intrusion into the American situation made it easy to accept. The American Communists could not justify such suicidal disunity. The more level-headed American leaders were tired and ashamed of it. Yet they were incapable of achieving unity by themselves. The more helpless they were, the more readily they accepted the Comintern's dictation.

The Communist party of America

Like most shotgun marriages, the Communist party of America that came out of the Woodstock convention represented a union in name more than in fact. Since the Comintern was bent on getting one party, there would be one party—but two of everything else.

Even so, it was a close call. Sixty delegates, equally divided between the former Communist party and United Communist party, took two weeks to make up their minds and almost parted enemies. After full agreement had been reached on the program, the usual questions of control came up: how many members on the top committee and what to do about the controversial language federations.[11] The committee on constitution split 3 to 3. Then the convention split 30 to 30. At eleven o'clock at night, after a long, acrimonious day, the thick veneer of unity that had taken over a week to lay on almost came off. The official account relates the scene: "No constitution had been adopted. The Convention was hopelessly deadlocked. Neither side left their seats. No motions were made; no one took the floor. The chairman announced that he would entertain a motion to adjourn. This was answered by the humming of the 'Internationale.' The chairman waited and then declared the session adjourned, and left the chair." [12]

But no one dared to move, fearing that they would never get together again. An unidentified Comintern delegate saved the day. The chairman reopened the session and gave him an opportunity to propose that the delegates should separate into two caucuses which would negotiate through small committees. The caucusing continued all night; the committees met the following day. Only after a session that lasted forty-eight hours without interruption were compromises reached and a constitution adopted. What this meant to personal relationships that had been disrupted by political differences may be gathered from the phrase in the official report—"Comrades who after having been separated for years embraced each other."

But they embraced almost too soon. According to the new constitution, the Central Executive Committee was supposed to have nine members. The first eight were elected without difficulty. Two nominations were made for the "impartial" ninth member. Each received 30 votes. At the last minute, the convention was deadlocked over the one committeeman who could give control of the united party to one of the former factions. At every crisis, the caucuses went into action and the convention split up once more into rival camps. At last, a compromise was proposed and accepted. Since it appeared impossible to get a ninth man, both "impartial" candidates were unanimously elected to make a ten-man C.E.C.

For the first time—almost twenty months after the first Chicago conventions—the American Communist movement was represented by a single party. Because the party was formed mainly to please the Comintern and was not an organic growth, the old wounds were merely covered, not healed. The last split was by no means in sight. In fact, this one-party set-up represented only a short interlude. Six months later, the two-party problem was resurrected in a somewhat different form, and almost two years would pass before a permanent one-party set-up was established.

The state of the party

The organization of the Communist party of America gives us an opportunity to see what the American Communist movement was like in the middle of 1921, after a year and a half of underground existence.

The membership claims had gone down from a high of about 70,000 for the two 1919 parties to 10,000–12,000 for the C.P. of A.[13] For each party member, however, there were many more sympathizers, if the claimed circulation of the merged parties' publications may be taken as an indication. The former United Communist party submitted a report to the unity convention boasting of thirty-five publications with a total monthly circulation of 1,642,000. The former Communist party reported nineteen papers with a monthly circulation of 999,000.[14] Even if duplications and exaggerations are discounted, about ten sympathizers for each party member is a fair estimate. The overwhelming majority of both members and sympathizers, probably as high as 90 per cent, were foreign-speaking.

Financially, the Communist movement was still a relatively small business. The operating expenses of both former parties amounted to about $50,000 monthly, including everything from wages to literature. By the end of 1921, the newly formed C.P. of A. had run up a deficit of $25,000. It had nineteen paid organizers, most of them in the East. Some idea of the party's wage scale may be gathered from the proposal to reduce salaries to the level of $25 per week for those without dependents, $35 for those with a wife or parents to support, and $40 for married members with children.[15] The initiation fee was $1 and monthly dues 60 cents.

The most important organizational compromise at the unity convention involved the foreign-language federations. There was so much opposition to abandoning them that they were retained with some modifications. The central party leadership was given more control over them, and all dues payments had to go through regular party channels. No less than twenty-one language federations were affiliated to the Communist party of America, though only ten of them were credited with more than 250 members.[16]

The basic organizational unit was the "group" with five to ten members. About 1700 groups were reported at the end of 1921.[17] Up to ten groups in the same city or locality made up a "branch," about ten branches a "section," not more than ten sections a "subdistrict," and on top of the whole local structure came the "district," usually made up of one or more states, except for New York State where the membership was large enough for two districts. There were twelve territorial districts at the end of 1921.

The Communist party of America had no daily newspaper in English, but there were eight daily papers in other languages and over thirty weekly, semimonthly, and monthly publications, the great majority of them in foreign languages.

Not much had changed in the human material in two years.

Politically, the Communist party of America represented a much sharper break with the past. It would take time for practice to catch up with principles, but at least the principles were new and, indeed, unprecedented in terms of the American revolutionary background.

For the first time, the dual-union and anti-political tradition was formally surrendered. The new program said unequivocally: "The

Communist Party condemns the policy of the revolutionary elements leaving the existing unions." It instructed them to fight against being expelled. Splits were not to be tolerated or encouraged because of "some remote revolutionary aim." The I.W.W. policy of "artificially creating new industrial unions" was condemned. The program also promised to participate in municipal, state, and national elections, though it recognized that the underground party could not do so in its own name. However, the idea that elected Communist officeholders might think of "parliamentary" activity as a means of improving the condition of the masses was still too terrible to contemplate. Special emphasis was put on the duty of Communist representatives to propose "demonstrative measures, not for the purpose of having them passed by the bourgeois majority, but for the purpose of propaganda, agitation and organization."

To hammer home the futility of political activity, this apotheosis of force and violence was proclaimed: "The Communist Party will systematically and persistently propagate the idea of the inevitability of and necessity for violent revolution, and will prepare the workers for armed insurrection as the only means of overthrowing the capitalist state." And lest anyone have any illusions, the constitution also took the trouble to state: "The Communist Party of America is an underground, illegal organization." [18]

Though the unified party was a new departure in many ways, the time was not yet ripe for a really clean-cut break with the past. It was impossible to put the new line into effect in underground, illegal conditions. The summer of 1921 was a turning point for the American Communist movement, but only a partial one.

The Third Congress

No sooner had the Comintern forced formal unity upon the American Communists than it started a campaign for something else—a legal, open, mass party. The Americans were even less prepared for this step than they had been for unity.

The Comintern sprang its surprise on the American delegation to its Third Congress, June 22–July 12, 1921, less than two months after the American unity convention. The delegation was made up of Max Bedacht (Marshall), Robert Minor (Ballister), Nicholas Hourwich (Andrew) and Oscar Tywerousky (Baldwin).

In a sense, the Third Congress was more important than the first two. The first was predicated on a nonexistent European revolution; the second was transitional. But the third started off on the assumption that the European revolution had been indefinitely delayed. The last straw for the Russians was the disastrous uprising in Germany in March 1921. Despite the fact that Lenin had begun to see the recession of the revolutionary wave and had advised the Western parties of the need for a corresponding change in tactics the year before, the resistance to the new line was so great that the German Communists had a final fling at insurrection. When they suffered a one-sided defeat, the Comintern criticized them unmercifully and punished the leadership, even though the Germans accused the Comintern of having egged them on.[19] Most of the Third Congress was devoted to an autopsy of the German defeat.

The Russians were more than ever convinced that the revolutionary wave had degenerated into hopeless "putschism." They wanted no more revolutionary attempts because they wanted no more defeats. Trotsky said in his report on the international situation: "Now we see and we feel that we are not so near the goal of the conquest of power, of the world revolution. We formerly believed, in 1919, that it was only a question of months and now we say that it is perhaps a question of years." [20] As a result, the Third Congress was much closer than either of the previous two congresses to the reality of the next twenty years. The first two had been dominated by the victorious Russian Revolution. The third was held in the shadow of the victorious German counterrevolution. As far as postwar Europe was concerned, the German experience proved more typical than the Russian.

The great debate at the congress—there were still great debates then—was extraordinarily ironic.

On the basis of the German defeat and the partial economic

recovery of Western capitalism, the Russians demanded that the Western Communist parties give up their immediate revolutionary aspirations and settle down to a lengthy period of winning over the majority of industrial and rural workers. They lectured the Western Communists on the stupidity of always using aggressive revolutionary tactics and on the need for sometimes beating a strategic retreat. If this was a Right Wing position, Lenin and Trotsky were willing to associate themselves with the Right Wing.[21] It required all Lenin's vast authority and his most browbeating methods to force the congress to accept the Russian proposals. "He who fails to understand that in Europe—where nearly all the proletarians are organized—we must win over the majority of the working class is lost to the Communist movement," he insisted. He "declared war" on those who would not agree that the support of "large" masses was necessary. "We Russians are heartily sick of these Left phrases," he exclaimed in disgust.[22] The slogan of the Third Congress—To the Masses!—told what the Russian leaders wanted.

It was a topsy-turvy debate. If there was one thing that had overwhelmingly impressed the Western Communists, it was the fact that the large Social Democratic parties in the West had failed to win power and the small Bolshevik party had succeeded. When the Western Communists tried to point this out at the Third Congress, the Russians told them that conditions in the West were different, and that a Russian revolution was incomparably easier to make than a revolution in the West. Even if this were true, it is doubtful whether so many Left Wing Socialists would have taken the trouble to split the old parties and create new Communist parties had they been told it so unequivocally a little earlier. Now the tables were turned. The Russians wanted large parties. The Westerners protested that they were less interested in size than in revolutionary spirit and purity. The Russians told them to fall back temporarily on the defensive. To the Westerners, Bolshevism meant taking the offensive always and everywhere in preparation for the final triumphant offensive. The Russians, with Lenin and Trotsky leading the attack, chastized the Germans for engaging foolishly in an unsuccessful uprising. The Germans were rather proud of having had the courage to stage any kind of an uprising.

If the European revolution was written off at the Third Congress, the American revolution was simply dismissed with a few biting words.

The policy was set forth in the "Theses on Tactics," proposed by the Russian delegation consisting of Lenin, Radek, Bukharin, Trotsky, Zinoviev, and Kamenev. They did not content themselves with merely laying down the general line. They gave concrete instructions to all the other parties, including the Americans, on how to carry it out. The whole procedure was refreshingly open and straightforward. It was possible to accuse the Russians of telling everyone else what to do, but it was not possible to accuse them of pretending that they did not do so.

The Russians put the American Communists in their place by informing them that they "are still before the first and simplest task of creating a Communist nucleus and connecting it with the working masses."

This was the official end of the American Communists' dream. They had once imagined themselves on the verge of taking power. Now they were publicly informed by the highest authority that they had not yet taken the first, let alone the last, step toward victory.

The Russians also had a surprise in store for the Americans on how to go about discharging the first and simplest task before them. The Americans were told to "try by all ways and means to get out of their illegalized condition into the open among the wide masses." [23]

The main American spokesman, Robert Minor (Ballister), accepted the implied rebukes humbly. He began his speech as follows: "The delegation of the Communist Party of America declares its agreement with the proposed Theses on Tactics of the Bureau of the Russian delegation. We approve everything unconditionally with respect to the fundamental points and accept the principles under consideration without reservations."

But he took issue on some "small technical points." He remarked that the Russian theses mentioned the United Communist party as if the American split still existed. Since the U.C.P. and C.P., had merged into the Communist party of America, he ventured the opinion that the first step of creating a Communist nucleus had been achieved in the United States. But the Russian criticism of American illegality was the one thing he could not swallow easily. He tried to make it clear that the proposed legal organization would be merely an appendage and under the unqualified control of the illegal organization.[24]

Minor's statement showed that the Americans were not going to give up their illegal, underground existence readily. For the time being, they were willing to go only halfway by setting up some sort of legal organization in addition to the illegal one. Yet the difference in attitude of the American delegates at the Second and Third Congresses revealed a change that had come over them in a year. Reed and to a lesser extent Fraina, had stood up to the Russians at the Second Congress and had presented their views without diffidence. Minor adopted a manner that would become more traditional. The ritual of approving everything unconditionally in advance even when some things were obviously problematic and puzzling was something new.

The biggest contribution of the Americans to the Third Congress was a one-sided dispute among themselves. The change of line had many victims, and one of the most bewildered and bewildering was John Reed's old idol, Bill Haywood.

Earlier that year, Haywood had been persuaded to become a fugitive from the United States and take refuge in the Soviet Union in order to avoid a twenty-year prison sentence. He arrived in Moscow with the aura of a martyr, was welcomed a few days later by Lenin personally, and was generally treated with the honor and esteem befitting a world-famous revolutionary. In an effort to exploit his prestige among syndicalists, he was put on the Executive Committee of the Communist International. When Haywood agreed to go to Russia, he was under the impression that the Comintern favored the I.W.W., as some of its earlier statements had indicated. At the Third Congress, however, he found himself in a most embarrassing position, because the line had changed in favor of working in the A.F. of L.

Haywood refused to go along. He pleaded with the congress to support the I.W.W. All the other American delegates repudiated and ridiculed him.[25] Haywood, sick in body and at heart, a shell of the old warrior, lingered on doing odd jobs of propaganda for a cause never really his own, spurned by most of his former syndicalist comrades, who could not forgive him for escaping alone and leaving the other I.W.W. defendants in the lurch. When he died in Russia in 1928, the broken hulk of a mighty man, it was a pathetic ending to a lifetime of defiance.

Interviews with Lenin

Behind the scenes at the Third Congress, a struggle went on within the American delegation. Despite Minor's unconditional approval of the new line in the name of the entire delegation, the representatives of the foreign-language federations, Hourwich and Tywerousky, were far from happy.

Toward the end of the congress Lenin himself intervened in the American controversy. He called the American delegates to see him in his "dingy, little office" in the Kremlin at the usual time for Russian leaders—after midnight.[26]

The main thing Lenin sought to impress on the Americans was the necessity for building a mass Communist party in the United States. To do so, he emphasized, they needed a daily newspaper in the English language. Since those who did not believe in a mass party also believed that a daily paper was impossible, Lenin faced opposition on both counts. Tywerousky and Hourwich argued that the American workers were so backward politically that it would be harmful for the Communists to engage in mass activity, that the masses would corrupt the Communists more easily than the Communists could convert the masses.

Lenin dismissed the argument as "very foolish." It reminded him of an argument against the building of a bridge in Berne on the ground that it was a dangerous operation and sure to cause some loss of lives. It was necessary, he assured them, to build the bridge despite the cost of lives. Holding up an American edition of Bukharin's pamphlet, *The Communist Program,* he asked whether it had been printed illegally.[27] Told that it was put out by a regular printer and sold publicly, he exclaimed that there was no need for an illegal party if such a pamphlet could be printed and sold legally. Lenin also berated the American Communists for boycotting the elections and refusing to support the presidential candidacy of Debs on the Socialist ticket in 1920. He even raised the question whether a Labor party would not facilitate the task of the American Communists. This suggestion had been made by Lenin to Fraina the previous year without evoking any reaction. This time it was reported back by the delegates and taken more seriously.

Hourwich was apparently the chief victim of the meeting. He aroused Lenin's ire by interrupting him repeatedly and finally brought down on his head the rebuke that he was a Russian, not an American. Hourwich was never permitted to come back to the United States, which was one way of solving the problem.

A few months later, Lenin had another interview with American delegates, this time with Katterfeld and Minor. After many years, Katterfeld was still able to become enthusiastic about the unexpected turn taken by the conversation between them. "What impressed me was that I was there all primed to tell him all about the inner party situation here," he related. "You see the whole thing always was a struggle between the two groups to have recognition and so on, and thereby the stamp of approval which would help them here. But Lenin didn't seem much interested in that, and he asked me what was I doing when I started working for the party. And of course I told him I was farming out in western Kansas. So then he sat up, and wanted to know all about the farming process, and most of the time it was on questions like that." [28]

For the first time the American delegates learned that Lenin had once written a fairly long study on *Capitalism and Agriculture in the*

United States of America."[29] After the interview, the booklet was brought to Katterfeld's room, and a young woman translated it for him. Though Katterfeld was expelled from the American Communist movement at the end of the twenties, he never gave up the belief that Lenin was a "great man."[30] Fraina never forgot that Lenin had talked to him about philosophy in 1920; Bedacht never forgot that Lenin had urged the Americans to publish an English daily newspaper; and Katterfeld never forgot that Lenin spent an hour discussing American agriculture instead of American inner-party politics. Lenin's personal influence was one of Communism's most important assets in the early years, and much of that influence seems to have derived from his personality as well as his politics and power.

17

The Revolution Devours Its Children

AFTER 1920, two familiar names soon dropped out of the American Communist movement. John Reed died. Louis C. Fraina ceased to exist.

Important as their contributions were, something else makes these men stand out for special attention—the symbolism of their lives. They went through in the first months of the new movement what many other Communists were to go through in the years to come. Controversy and mystery clouded the end of their lives. An effort to clear up what happened to them has been long overdue.

Reed lived and died an undomesticated American radical. He did not fit into the established order before he became a Communist, and he did not fit into the order established by Communism. For some Communists, especially intellectuals, the act of joining a disciplined movement represents a sharp break in their lives. They may say and do things, in public at least, that they had previously scoffed at. This adaptation to the Communist movement was foreign to Reed's nature. Partly because he remained essentially himself and partly because the movement was still so young that personal patterns of behavior were not yet set, he fought his organizational superiors with a temerity that would have scandalized the John Reed clubs named after him if they had known the man instead of the myth.

Reed was not the same man after the Second Congress. He was resentful and heartsick at his treatment by Zinoviev and Radek. Radek was a licensed court jester in the Comintern, and his attacks were easier to laugh off. Zinoviev was the embodiment of the Comintern's top leadership and Lenin's inner circle of collaborators. His arrogance and rudeness enraged and depressed Reed. This oppressive authoritarianism was not at all what he had been seeking in Greenwich Village, Lawrence, Massachusetts, Mexico, or Moscow. The Bolsheviks' seizure of power in 1917 had carried him away emotionally as a victory for the underdogs against overwhelming odds. But the underdogs in power were not underdogs any longer. Reed had to discover for himself the great gulf between a movement striving for power and a movement enjoying power.

The immediate issue was the new trade-union line. For years Reed had been preaching the necessity of building the I.W.W. and destroying the A.F. of L. He had been taught this creed in the American revolutionary movement, which had clung to it tenaciously for two decades. His experiences with the I.W.W. gave him some of the richest moments of his life; they were responsible in no small measure for his revolutionary conversion. Now he was expected to say and believe that the place of revolutionists was in the A.F. of L., not in the I.W.W. Lenin demanded it on a lofty level of thought; Zinoviev rammed it down Reed's throat as if he were a delinquent child. Lenin's arguments did not convince him; Zinoviev's methods appalled him.

Like so many Communists after him, John Reed stood alone at a crossroads of political and personal integrity. Whether the I.W.W. should be sacrificed to the new line of capturing the A.F. of L. was only the husk of the problem. At the core was the choice between loyalty to an ideal and loyalty to an organization. To remain faithful to his convictions or to remain a Communist in good standing? Reed was a good enough Communist to know that the necessity of discipline was a fundamental Communist conviction. The choice was not merely between a conviction and a movement, but between two types of conviction—the political and the organizational.

After the Second Congress, Reed was caught between these two fires. He lived only ten weeks more.

The mystery is what happened to him in these ten weeks.

The mystery of John Reed

The best way to understand the mystery is to see all the different ways it has been "solved."

The Communist version was given in 1936 by Granville Hicks in the only full-scale biography of Reed.[1] Though Hicks himself ceased to be a Communist three years later, he has not changed his mind about the problem of Reed's disillusionment.[2]

Was Reed so thoroughly disillusioned that he resigned from the Executive Committee of the Communist International? On this, one of the most controversial points, Hicks wrote: "During one of the sessions of the executive committee, Reed peremptorily offered his resignation from the E.C.C.I. in protest against Zinoviev's decision on an organizational question. It was not, of course, a thing that a disciplined revolutionary would have done, and Reed was persuaded by his fellow-delegates to withdraw his resignation and offer his apologies to the committee."[3]

As Hicks saw it, Reed was assigned at the end of August 1920 to attend the Congress of Oriental Nations at Baku, the Comintern's first effort to gain a foothold in the East. He went, made speeches, and returned with enthusiastic stories about the Congress. At the end of September, he was struck down by illness, at first diagnosed as influenza, then as typhus. Despite the best medical attention possible in war-torn Russia, he failed to recover. His death came on October 17, 1920. His body lay in state, guarded by Red Army soldiers, for seven days. Thousands of workers braved the rain and sleet to attend his funeral. Six Comintern leaders, headed by Bukharin, delivered funeral orations. He was buried under the Kremlin wall.

This version of Reed's last days soon stirred furious controversy. The attack was spearheaded by Reed's friend and the former editor of the *Masses,* Max Eastman. Since he was not in Russia at the time, Eastman had to depend on information from Louise Bryant, Reed's wife, and from Angelica Balabanoff, the first secretary of the Comintern. Eastman's most extreme version was attributed to Louise Bryant, from whom he heard the story several years later, the last time in 1934.

According to Eastman, Reed's fight with Zinoviev and Radek reached its height at the Baku Congress. Reed was offended by Zinoviev's demagogy and Radek's cynicism. He was shocked by their luxurious living on the way to and from Baku. After their return, Reed had a final interview with Zinoviev and Radek at which he handed in his resignation. They threatened to "destroy" him if he went through with it. He refused to back down. Then came his illness. None of the Russian leaders came to see him and Louise Bryant had to appeal to Lenin to get the best physicians and care available in Moscow. Thus Reed's burial under the Kremlin wall was a mockery; he had given up Communism before his death.[4]

Another Louise Bryant story has been told by Benjamin Gitlow, who says that she confided in him when she visited him in Sing Sing in 1921. When Gitlow wrote his first book, *I Confess,* published in 1939, he did not hint at any such revelation or even mention Reed's disillusionment. But in his second book, *The Whole of Their Lives,* published in 1948, twenty-seven years later, Gitlow was able to give three full pages of direct quotation of what she had told him.

As Gitlow tells it, Reed did not want to go to Baku, protesting that his health had been undermined in Finland on his way to Russia. Zinoviev insisted; Reed obeyed. The trip infuriated him. He was sickened by the lavish meals and sexual orgies on the train. The Congress added to his growing disillusionment. He objected to the behavior of Zinoviev and Radek. After his return, however, he questioned his own political judgment rather than theirs. He blamed himself for not being cut out to be a politician and thought that perhaps the Russians were right. His self-questioning was so intense that he lost his will to survive. When he fell ill, "he died because he did not want to live." [5]

There is nothing in Gitlow's version of Louise Bryant's story about Reed's resignation, the climax of Eastman's version. In fact, in direct conflict with Eastman, Gitlow implies that Reed wavered in his opposition to Zinoviev and Radek, and that his own weakness led to his self-destruction.

Emma Goldman was responsible for not one but two Louise Bryant stories. Neither of them goes as far as Eastman's version or Gitlow's and in fact the first Goldman version is curiously different from the second Goldman version. In *My Further Disillusionment in Russia,* published in 1924, she wrote:

Ever since I had come to Russia I had begun to sense that all was not well with the Bolshevik regime, and I felt as if caught in a trap. "How uncanny!" Louise suddenly gripped my arm and stared at me with wild eyes. " 'Caught in a trap' were the very words Jack repeated in his delirium." I realized that poor Jack had also begun to see beneath the surface.[6]

Seven years later, in 1931, Emma Goldman published her autobiography, *Living My Life,* in which she re-enacted this very scene. Either she remembered it differently or she did not bother to consult what she had already written about it, for she made some startling changes in the dialogue:

"I could not understand what he meant," Louise replied, "but he kept on repeating all the time: 'Caught in a trap, caught in a trap.' Just that." "Did Jack really use that term?" I cried in amazement. "Why do you ask?" Louise demanded, gripping my hand. "Because that is exactly how I have been feeling since I looked beneath the surface. Caught in a trap. Exactly that."
Had Jack also come to see that all was not well with his idol, I wondered, or had it only been the approach of death that had for a moment illumined his mind?[7]

In the first version, Emma Goldman had surprised Louise Bryant by uttering the words, "caught in a trap." In the second version, Louise Bryant had surprised Emma Goldman with those very words. In the first version, Emma Goldman was sure of Reed's disillusionment. In the second version, she merely raised the question.

By the time she came to write both of these books, Emma Goldman had apparently forgotten that she had already taken a stand on the

THE REVOLUTION DEVOURS ITS CHILDREN 287

question of Reed's final attitude. In *My Disillusionment in Russia*, published in 1923, she had reported without qualification that Reed had died believing fervently in the Communist future.[8]

Still another Louise Bryant story is easily the most incredible. Granville Hicks was told by a prominent journalist, Will Irwin, that Louise Bryant had talked to him in the Republican party's headquarters on election night in 1932. She allegedly told Irwin that Reed had been a secret agent of the United States government.[9]

And, finally, Louise Bryant assured Hicks's assistant, John Stuart, who spent several weeks interviewing her in Paris in 1935, that Reed was a devout Communist to the end and that she had never said anything to the contrary.[10]

This small collection of Louise Bryant stories may reveal more about Louise Bryant than about John Reed. She was his wife and was with him after his return from Baku to the end. Nevertheless, she was an unstable woman and apparently never told the same story twice. In her own writings, she never made the slightest reference to Reed's disillusionment. It is entirely conceivable that she told different stories depending on her own state of mind and that of her questioner.

If Louise Bryant were the only source of information about Reed's final attitude toward the Communist movement, the mystery would be difficult enough to solve. There are other witnesses, however, whose stories also vary.

The first is Angelica Balabanoff. Reed liked her and confided in her. In large part, she confirms portions of the various Louise Bryant stories and gives them such force that, though they cannot be integrated to form a single, consistent account, they demand some explanation.

According to Mme. Balabanoff, Reed was "profoundly disillusioned and disgusted" by the methods of "certain Bolshevik leaders," personified by Zinoviev, Radek, and others. His experience at the Second Congress confirmed his worst fears and brought his "moral sufferings and indignation to a high point." In a terrible state of depression, he was determined to avoid the spectacle of another manipulated Congress and told her of his decision not to go to Baku. Yet, after going to see Zinoviev and Radek for a showdown, he changed his mind and went. "He did not want to give them an excuse to attack him," Mme. Balabanoff tries to explain. "He wanted to go back to America and to work there in the revolutionary labor movement as an independent honest revolutionary." Why did he come back with enthusiastic reports of the Baku meeting? Because, she answers, he could admire other things besides Zinoviev's and Radek's "vulgar intrigues." She is also of the opinion that his disillusionment "contributed to the causes of his death" and affirms that Louise Bryant spoke to her in the same vein.[11]

When Mme. Balabanoff was asked what she specifically remembered of Reed's resignation, she replied, "When he was nominated as a delegate to the Baku convention, he decided to decline the nomination even if he would have to renounce membership of the C.I. That was his decision when he asked Zinoviev for an appointment. I don't exactly remember what he told me about his talk with Zinoviev whose appeal to discipline and responsibility may have influenced Reed not to insist on his resignation notwithstanding his disillusionment; it was an effort he made which cost him very much self-abnegation. From Baku he returned as a totally broken man, even physically. What he saw and heard there was the last blow."[12]

This would place Reed's resignation before Baku rather than after, as Eastman's version claims. Unfortunately, Mme. Balabanoff does not recall a crucial detail—what happened between Reed and Zinoviev as a result of the resignation. That Reed decided to go to Baku after all suggests that his mind was far from made up, even if the rest of Mme. Balabanoff's recollections are given credence. It is only fair to add that Mme. Balabanoff considers Reed's resignation to have only a very secondary importance in comparison with the essential fact of his general disillusionment.

Another important witness is Fraina. He was willing to answer Hicks's questions during the preparation of the biography and provided some of the most authoritative information about Reed's last days. They were together at the Second Congress and, though their

THE REVOLUTION DEVOURS ITS CHILDREN 289

political relations were strained, a measure of last-minute reconciliation took place. Reed called Fraina to his death bed and asked him to edit his speeches at the Congress, which had been garbled in translation. Hicks referred obliquely to Fraina's material but gave so little of it that one of the main points remained somewhat mystifying.

Hicks wrote that Reed had offered his resignation from the E.C.C.I. on an "organizational question." What Fraina had written was this: "The E.C.C.I. had, after demanding that the two American parties must unite, made a decision in regard to the personnel of the new united party. Reed opposed the decision, with not a single member of the E.C.C.I. supporting him. After the E.C.C.I.'s refusal to change the decision, Reed resigned. He was bitterly denounced by Zinoviev, Radek, Bukharin and several other E.C.C.I. members for false reasoning, for reprehensible factional and personal politics, for acting as a petty-bourgeois journalist." [13]

This flare-up took place soon after the Second Congress. It had nothing to do with the Baku affair. What Fraina did not tell Hicks was the concrete content of the "decision in regard to the personnel" of the united American party. This missing link was supplied by Fraina years later: "John Reed tries to get me suspended from the Party, the E.C.C.I. refuses, he resigns, is denounced unanimously, and withdraws his resignation." [14] On another occasion, Fraina revealed in greater detail what Reed had suggested to the E.C.C.I. Reed had argued that, while no one believed the "spy" charges against Fraina, the charges had been made and circulated in the United States, with the result that it might be a good idea if Fraina became inactive in the party for several years upon his return.[15] So hostile was the reaction that Reed was goaded into the defiant act of resigning, bringing on more recriminations and ending in his withdrawal of the resignation.

To deepen the Reed mystery, however, Fraina made short shrift of all the stories about Reed's disillusionment. He wrote unequivocally: "As one of the two or three Americans who saw him shortly before his death, I can affirm that Jack Reed kept all his loyalty to the Soviet Union and communism." [16] Hicks found that this view was shared by others on the spot, such as the American anarchist, Owen W. Penney, who, like Fraina, had no reason to exaggerate Reed's loyalty to the Comintern at the time he sought their views in the middle thirties.[17]

In order to make the Eastman, Gitlow, Balabanoff, Fraina and other versions compatible with one another, it is necessary to assume at least two resignations. However, Fraina had first-hand knowledge of the inner struggle in the Comintern, and it is unlikely that he would not have known of a second resignation over the Baku Congress.

The latest Communist version of Reed's life simply passes over the period of the Second Congress and its unpleasant repercussions with embarrassed haste. It copes with the problem of Reed's final disillusionment by ignoring it.[18]

And, finally, what can we learn from John Reed himself? He wrote several articles after the Second Congress, one of which, on the Congress itself, is most revealing.[19] He refused to budge as far as the new trade-union line was concerned. He did not hesitate to write back to the American party organ that nobody in Russia or Europe seemed to understand industrial unionism. He promised a fight at the next Congress. The tone of the article is such that he seemed to be spoiling for a fight. If he did intend to continue the struggle against the new line, it is hardly likely that he decided to resign for good and give up the struggle within the Comintern. Moreover, the article ends on a high note of pride and enthusiasm for the mass demonstrations staged in honor of the Congress. The author of this article was unrepentant and headstrong rather than self-questioning to the point of physical self-destruction. On the other hand, it is easy to believe that Reed said much harder things in private against the new line and the Comintern leadership than he permitted himself to put down on paper for publication. The wonder is not that he was so reticent in print but that he was so belligerently uninhibited about exposing his differences publicly. If there is no suggestion of a break with the Comintern in Reed's last writings, there is more than enough basis for a break sooner or later if Reed had persisted in his militant resistance.

Reed's disillusionment

All the existing versions, from Hicks to Fraina, agree on some things. At the Second Congress Reed put up a last-ditch fight against the Comintern's line and leadership that was unique even in 1920. He never gave the slightest indication of repenting his own position and, indeed, went to the opposite extreme of publicizing his opposition. His personal relations with the Comintern leadership had degenerated into an ugly feud. He made no secret of his contempt and hatred for Zinoviev and Radek, whose authority in the Comintern was then pre-eminent. On at least one occasion—when and why may be debatable but the fact is not—his anger or embarrassment or both brought him to the edge of *lèse-majesté,* as that crime of extreme insubordination was understood in the Comintern—he proffered his resignation from its Executive Committee. As far as we know, however, he was induced to withdraw the resignation, and he died before he was driven into another, irrevocable decision to revolt.

Was Reed a "disillusioned" Communist? If disillusionment means a final accounting with the Communist movement and its ideology, there is room for differences of opinion, with the burden of proof on those who claim a definitive break. But if disillusionment is understood intellectually and emotionally rather than organizationally, Reed was probably as disillusioned as it was possible to be and still remain in the movement. His disillusionment was cumulative, and it was heading toward a break on both sides if he had persisted in his course. That he was capable of offering his resignation at least once showed what was incipiently in his mind. To confidantes like Angelica Balabanoff he expressed his disappointment, if not his total disillusionment, with too much agitation to leave any doubt that he was going through a terrible crisis. Nor should it be forgotten that the Comintern would have had something to say about his future role in the Communist movement. Because the organization was still so young, there was more leeway for someone of Reed's rebellious temperament, but the reins were tightening almost visibly month by month. If Reed had gone on fighting the new line and the old leadership, the Comintern would probably have saved him the trouble of resigning. More important leaders than Reed were soon drummed out for less.

A possibility that has not been sufficiently explored is suggested by something on which Granville Hicks and Mme. Balabanoff agree. For a host of reasons, Reed was utterly fed up in Moscow and looked forward eagerly to returning home to take part once more in the American Communist movement. In her moving letter to Eastman on Reed's last days, written only a month after his death, Louise Bryant stated: "He was consumed with a desire to go home." [20] He may have been disillusioned with the Comintern, but most probably he was not entirely disillusioned or finished with communism. Whether he would have survived another bout in the still sick and split American Communist movement is something else. Nevertheless, he was willing to try it, and this would most probably have been his next step if he had survived the attack of typhus. Disillusionment there was, deeply implanted, but like many Communists after him, John Reed had probably paid for his faith too dearly to give it up without another struggle.

Would he have been able to survive the fierce rivalries and intrigues in Moscow? Four years after his death, the work that was his greatest monument, *Ten Days That Shook the World*, became one of the storm centers in the struggle between Stalin and Trotsky. On one point in connection with the Bolshevik uprising of 1917, Trotsky had found confirmation in Reed's book. Stalin counterattacked by charging that Reed had been "remote" from the Bolshevik party, that he had picked up hostile gossip from enemies, and had spread one of their "absurd rumors." [21] It is hard to imagine Reed rallying to the defense of Stalin, who was virtually unknown to him in 1920 and who was moreover allied with Zinoviev in 1924

THE REVOLUTION DEVOURS ITS CHILDREN   293

against Trotsky, whom Reed knew intimately and had portrayed as one of the greatest heroes of the Russian Revolution.

Death took him prematurely, not only as a human being but as a political symbol. The mystery of John Reed is what he would have done in the last act of his own life's drama. No one really knows, and everyone has written it differently in his or her own image.

The secret of Louis Fraina

After the Second Congress in 1920, Fraina spent two more years in the Communist movement. Those two years have hitherto constituted the greatest enigma of the early Communist movement. After playing such a prominent role, Fraina literally vanished without a trace. His name was wiped out from all Communist records as if it had never existed. Whenever the case was raked up, it was done in such a way that the worst possible interpretation of Fraina's actions was planted in the reader's mind.[22] Half truths and malicious gossip hounded him for the rest of his days.

Until the Second Congress, as we have seen, no one had contributed more to the American Communist movement. The only shadows that had fallen across his path were the spy charge brought against him by Peterson, a self-confessed spy, and his fortuitous association with Nosovitsky, another spy. To all appearances, Fraina had successfully cleared himself of suspicion. He had submitted to no fewer than three "trials," one in New York and two in Moscow. The all-powerful Executive Committee of the Communist International had exonerated him. Its official decision was duly published in the American Communist press.[23] Lenin had personally intervened in his behalf to punish Nuorteva for spreading the false charges. The Attorney General of the United States testified before a Congressional committee that Fraina had never been an agent of the Department of Justice.[24]

Nevertheless, the spy charges started Fraina's downfall. He had won a pyrrhic victory in Moscow. In principle, Reed's proposal that he should not return to any leading position in the American party was turned down. In practice, Reed had his way. The same end was achieved by putting Fraina on the American Agency with Katayama and Scott. Fraina was given the mission of organizing in Mexico. According to Roy, this idea came from Borodin and himself.[25] It removed Fraina effectively from the American party scene except for a short visit en route to Mexico.

Fraina left Moscow in December 1920. To carry out his mission in Mexico, he received $50,000 or $55,000 (in dollars) from the Comintern. While in Berlin, he gave $20,000 or $25,000 to the British Communist, John T. Murphy. Another $20,000 went to Scott for use in the United States. Fraina himself kept $10,000, which he carried in $1000 bills because they could be most easily concealed.[26] From Germany he traveled to Canada in the guise of a motion-picture representative. To make his role more convincing, he actually bought one German film, *The Arabian Nights*. After reporting to the party in New York, he went on to Mexico with Katayama. Scott remained for a time in the United States.

In Mexico, Fraina floundered helplessly. He did not know the language, the people, or the problems. The two emissaries, the American and the Japanese, stuck out glaringly in the chaotic Mexican political scene. Fraina had to work with young Mexican revolutionists who were anarchists at heart. According to one account, he wanted them to take part in an election campaign. They were scandalized, since no self-respecting Mexican revolutionist believed in such fastidious tactics. Finally, to please him, they agreed. They duly reported on meetings, trips, candidates, and, of course, expenses. Everyone was satisfied—the two isolated Comintern representatives because they were getting the right reports, the Mexicans because the whole campaign was purely imaginary. In any case, Fraina's organizing mission in Mexico was thoroughly disheartening. He was cut off from the work and people he knew best just as the party of his dream was painfully taking shape. He began to feel disillusioned and betrayed. Some of his best friends had turned against him in his absence. Letters made him aware of the sickening factionalism in the American party. The nomadic existence of a Comintern representative did not appeal to his young wife, whom he had met and married in Moscow. Mexico was a kind of exile that would have been hard to bear in the best circumstances. After months of frustration, it became intolerable.

Fraina returned to Germany. At the age of twenty-eight, in 1922, he had to make a crucial decision. For almost three years, ever since the bizarre "trial" in New York brought on by the preposterous tales of a self-confessed informer, his career in the Communist movement had suffered blow after blow. The first thing that had met him in Moscow was a second ordeal of accusation, investigation, and exoneration. Then came the Second Congress of the Comintern and his realization that the Russians were hard taskmasters. Those who disagreed found themselves at a hopeless disadvantage. Ironically, Fraina had sided with the Comintern against the instructions of his own party; the party paid him back by repudiating him. Fraina was mentioned in an American Communist organ for the last time in February 1922. "Comrade Louis Fraina was sent as a delegate of the C.P. of A., and unfortunately took a position with respect to work in the trade unions and parliamentary work totally different from the attitude of our party on these questions as set forth in the C.P. of A.'s program adopted at its Second Convention," it reads. "Comrade Fraina, in discrediting himself, also brought discredit to the party he represented." [27] This report indicates how much backbiting there was against him at home by 1922. Now almost friendless in the movement he had done so much to create, he made his decision.

Many years later, he tried to explain why he had broken with the Communist movement in the fall of 1922. He mentioned the factionalism, the Russian domination, and the disappearing freedom of thought. Yet he did not try to oversimplify. He called it a "complicated thing" and a "sort of process." At the time of the break, he still considered himself an orthodox Marxist. He knew that he could no longer work in the Communist movement, but he was still a Communist at heart.[28]

Once the decision was made in Germany, the problem arose—

where to go? In the face of the hostility of both the government and the Communists in the United States, it seemed too dangerous to go back. A new start in Germany was equally unthinkable. For the time being, Fraina decided, the best refuge was Mexico again. The only money he had with him was the balance of the Comintern funds. Before leaving Germany, he sent a letter of resignation and a financial report to the Comintern. Copies were also sent to the American secretary, Charles E. Ruthenberg.

Almost thirty years later, he discussed the matter with two representatives of the Federal Bureau of Investigation. When he could not remember the exact amounts he had distributed, they produced the financial report that he had sent to the American party. The F.B.I. had obtained it in a long-forgotten raid on the office of the American Communist leader, Israel Amter! This old document confirmed that he had kept $4200 of the Comintern's money for the second trip to Mexico.[29]

This rather modest sum became the basis of a lifetime of insinuations and gossip that he had been expelled by the Comintern for "embezzlement." The sum involved in the stories varied between $50,000 and $500,000.[30] It was tragic that Fraina needed the money so desperately; it was ironic that he took so little. If he had taken as much as some of his enemies claimed, the next life of Louis Fraina would have been much easier.

Two or three years later, Fraina sent a letter to the American party offering to make arrangements to pay the money back in installments from the meager wages he was earning. When enquiries were made for this book in an attempt to check on this letter, confirmation was obtained from James P. Cannon, then a member of the top committee. Cannon recalled that such a letter was handed to him on a trip to New York. He took the matter up with the Political Committee in Chicago; the Committee decided that the matter was outside the jurisdiction of the American party since it concerned Comintern funds.[31] An "embezzler" of huge sums—as some of the stories have alleged—would hardly have acted as Fraina did in offering to repay the money.

Mexico was even worse the second time. Nothing seemed to go right. He rented a small apartment over a garage (transformed in one published legend to "the large and luxurious hacienda of a wealthy Mexican senorita" [32]). He tried to write without success. One job after another disappointed him. For so many years devoted passionately to politics, he was cut off from all political activity. Money began to give out. Meanwhile, a child was born. In Mexico, early in 1923, he sank deeper and deeper into despair. Not yet thirty, he seemed to have burned himself out.

The ordeal of Lewis Corey

Louis C. Fraina ceased to exist in 1923. "Joseph Charles Skala" took his place. This was the name on the Czechoslovak passport he was using when he came back home. He arrived alone in New York in May; there was not enough money to bring the whole family. "My life is not to be described," he wrote the following month to his wife. He lived on twenty cents a day. Before the end of the year, the family was reunited. They moved into an old tenement house on Broome Street in the East Side slums where Fraina had spent his boyhood. He went to work in a dry-goods store at $12 a week, doing menial jobs from early morning to late at night. His wife found a job in a perfume factory. For a while, they could not afford a baby carriage.

A few months later, Charles Skala began to work as a substitute proofreader at the *New York Times*. A steady job as a regular proofreader for Street and Smith, the magazine publishers, followed. The Skala family moved to Marble Hill. It was a period of hard-working, obscure recovery. While Charles Skala lost himself in the city's millions, Louis Fraina was believed to be in Mexico. Only once was the past raked up. That was when the indefatigable Nosovitsky boasted of his exploits in a long series of articles in the New York *American* in 1925, a number of them devoted to the strange case of Louis C. Fraina. Charles Skala read them and continued to correct proofs.

One day, in 1926, he came across a book by Professor Thomas Nixon Carver, *The Present Economic Revolution in the United States*. It tried to show that the ownership of stock in the great corporations was becoming so widespread that the workers would soon own and control American industry. This thesis stirred the old Marxist blood in him. In his spare time, he started collecting data to refute Carver. The result was an article entitled "How is Ownership Distributed?" The second magazine to which it was submitted, *The New Republic*, published it. With that issue of May 5, 1926, another life opened before him. The article was not signed Louis C. Fraina or Charles Skala. Afraid of disturbing his new-found peace, he used a new name—Lewis Corey. The article attempted to show that corporate ownership was not being democratized, despite the multiplication of stockholders. It was a remarkable anticipation of the type of analysis made famous six years later by Adolph A. Berle and Gardiner C. Means in *The Modern Corporation and Private Property*. Four more articles in the same magazine during the next three years continued to subject the American economy, then at the height of its prosperity, to skeptical scrutiny. A half-year before the stock market crash of 1929, he began one article with the words: "The stock-market situation is recognized as dangerous." [33]

Charles Skala read proofs during the day. Lewis Corey wrote at night. A name that no one had ever heard of suddenly began to live a life of its own. Corey won recognition as an economist almost immediately. His earliest work was appreciated by some well-known academic economists.[34]

By 1929 he was well on his way to another outstanding career. In that year came a one-year fellowship at the Institute of Economics of the Brookings Institution in Washington, D.C. Corey's first book, *The House of Morgan*, was published in 1930. While writing it, he still put in three days a week proofreading. His first full-time intellectual job came in 1931 with the *Encyclopedia of the Social Sciences* on which he served as an associate editor until its completion in 1934. He was now working feverishly, driving himself to make up for lost time. Out of the encyclopedia period came his most ambitious project,

The Decline of American Capitalism, published in 1934. It was a monumental attempt to analyze the American economy in terms of orthodox Marxism.

Two names of one man symbolized two historical periods. Louis Fraina came into his own with the Russian Revolution. Lewis Corey shot up out of nowhere in the Great Depression. The prosperous twenties were no time for either of them.

One piece of unfinished business remained in Corey's life—the American Communist movement. Corey and Communism came into prominence in American life at approximately the same time in the early thirties. Corey's first direct contact with the Communists took place in 1932 when he was invited to join a committee of professionals and intellectuals in support of the Communist presidential candidates, Foster and Ford. He accepted, and played an important role in its activity—so important that the Communists in the committee started a campaign to get rid of him. The clash over Corey was one of the principle reasons for the committee's dissolution. When *The Decline of American Capitalism* came out two years later, the Communist press at first treated it respectfully.[35] On second thought, however, the higher authorities in the party decided that Corey's emergence as the leading Marxist economist in the country endangered them. He confronted the party, which had no economist of equal achievement or stature, with the threat of an independent center of intellectual authority. In retaliation, two of the leading Communist pundits, Alexander Bittelman and V. J. Jerome, devoted a 64-page pamphlet to his intended intellectual annihilation.[36] Corey was so little annihilated, even within Communist ranks, that when his next book, *The Crisis of the Middle Class,* came out in 1935, it was given a friendly review in the *New Masses.*[37] One of the by-products of the Popular Front line was a shift in the attitude toward Corey; the Communists suddenly began to woo him. He was invited to edit a special "Middle Class" issue of the *New Masses* in 1936.[38] At about this time overtures were made to induce him to rejoin the party. Instead Corey drifted further and further away.

The Trotskyists once thought that Corey was coming close to them.

The American Trotskyist leader, James P. Cannon, discussed Corey's case with Trotsky himself in 1934. They wanted Corey to work with them but they were troubled by "the old cloud over Fraina." Trotsky finally made an extremely curious proposal. He advised Cannon to tell Corey to go back into the Communist party, "straighten out his financial entanglements and get an official clearance from them." Only then could the Trotskyists accept Corey into a new party which they were planning to launch. Cannon agreed, but nothing ever came of the plan.[39] Corey chose instead to work with another group of expelled Communists led by Jay Lovestone.*

In retrospect, Corey dated his revulsion from communism to the great Russian purges of 1936–37.[40] They forced him to go beyond his distaste for the official Communist movement; he had to question the fundamental principles of communism, a process which was not completed until the German-Soviet pact of 1939. The shock of the pact not only liberated him, as it did so many others, from a lifelong loyalty to the ideal of communism—but destroyed his belief in the very basis of Marxism itself. In three articles in *The Nation,* entitled "Marxism Reconsidered," early in 1940, he went all the way— Marxism was a failure, and the mission of the proletariat was a delusion. He strove toward a new social goal which he called "people's functional socialism," "the progressive transformation of capitalism toward democratic socialism," and a "system of pluralism in government."[41] These ideas were worked out systematically in his book, *The Unfinished Task,* two years later. It is impossible here to do justice to, or even to make note of, all the fresh beginnings and false starts which he inspired or participated in during the last fifteen years of his life. He never knew any real economic security or peace of mind until he went to Antioch College in 1942 as professor of political

---

* Cannon had been expelled from the American Communist party in 1928, and Lovestone in 1929. Cannon had formed a "Left" (Trotskyist) and Lovestone a "Right" Opposition. Cannon remained a Trotskyist, but Lovestone and most of his group, including Bertram D. Wolfe, went through a process of development which led them to become active enemies of communism and Marxism.

economy, one of the few professors in American academic history who never went to high school.

But for the Lewis Coreys of our time, there is no escape from the past. The Communist movement continued to haunt him. When the war broke out in 1939, Corey took a position of nonintervention. A year later, he changed his mind and helped to found the Union for Democratic Action which came out for American assistance to defeat fascism.[42] When he wrote an article in *The Nation* in 1941 urging war against Hitlerism, the *Daily Worker* excoriated him under the headline: "Lewis Corey—Ludicrous Salesman of 'Nice Imperialism.'"[43] Ten days later, Germany attacked Russia and the ludicrous war against Hitlerism became Communist policy. The following year, when he had been at Antioch only three weeks, he was called in by the president; the school was receiving anonymous letters about his Communist past. Throughout his stay at Antioch, it was like that. The Communists inside and outside of the student body tried to make life miserable for him by spreading the old tales about his "embezzlement." At the same time, organizations of the extreme Right circulated a leaflet throughout the state of Ohio accusing Antioch's trustees of having given Corey "unlimited opportunities to implant communist doctrine in the minds of the innocent students who are not informed that Corey is a leading communist."[44]

After ten years at Antioch, Corey's restlessness returned. Though he had deeply enjoyed the experience of teaching, he came to feel that it took him too far from the mainstream of political life. When he was offered a post in 1951 as educational director of the Amalgamated Meat Cutters and Butchers Workmen, A.F. of L., for which he had written an outstanding union history, *Meat and Man,* he could not resist. And then a blow fell from the most unexpected quarter. On Christmas Eve, 1952, the United States government served him with a writ of deportation. He was caught up in the campaign to deport alien Communists. A month later, the union dismissed him. The chief government witness against him at the hearing the following April was Benjamin Gitlow. Corey was shocked by the testimony of his old opponent. According to Corey's lawyer, who was present at the hearing, "Gitlow testified quite freely as to Corey's activities in the 1920s but claimed to be totally unaware that Corey later became actively anti-Communist." [45] Corey's whole world seemed to have fallen in again.

Six months later, Corey suffered a cerebral hemorrhage. He died the next day, September 16, 1953, at the age of fifty-nine. The government's decision to issue a visa enabling him to leave the country to become a citizen arrived two months after his death.

The man who began as Louis C. Fraina and ended as Lewis Corey provided the complete symbol of the American radical in the first half of the twentieth century—the poor, immigrant boy; the self-taught radical intellectual; the Left-Winger in search of the revolution in the Socialist Labor party, the I.W.W., and the Socialist party; the Communist born of the Russian Revolution; the disillusioned ex-Communist struggling for almost two decades to tear himself away from the magnetic field of communism; the victim of Communist vindictiveness who became a victim of anti-Communist vindictiveness.

18

New Forces

THE revolution devours its children. But there are always more children to devour.

By the middle of 1921 new life was stirring in the battered body of American communism. The two-year old invalid was beginning to show signs of recovery, some generated from the inside, some from the outside. Old names vanished; new names came into prominence.

Inside, the formal end of the split represented the biggest gain. Outside, a new climate of public opinion gradually wore down the government's anti-radical drive.

Unity in itself, however, was useless. A united movement could be just as isolated and impotent as a disunited one. The old line had doomed the American Communists to political paralysis with or without the government's unkind assistance. To contain the breath of life, the new line had to express itself in new ideas, attitudes, slogans, and day-by-day activities. It had to pay off in increased membership, dues payments, newspaper circulation, votes, and trade-union positions. The Comintern was not interested merely in a united party. It wanted a mass party with mass influence, particularly in the labor movement.

On the government's side, the presidential election of 1920 came providentially. The Republican party's sweeping victory retired A. Mitchell Palmer, the Democratic Attorney General who had driven the Communists underground at the beginning of that year. It fell to a conservative Republican administration to moderate and eventually to abandon the repressive campaign of the Democrats. But there was no sudden change of political atmosphere, and the Communists could not afford to take chances.

At this point, the Communists found themselves up against an old problem. One of the peculiarities of the American radical movement had long been the divorce between politics and trade-unionism. In this respect, the early Communists were even worse off than the old-time Socialists. They were almost exclusively politically minded, with little actual organizing experience. When the new line required working inside the A.F. of L. they did not have sufficient strength within the unions to do very much about carrying it out. What they needed desperately and without delay was new forces within the trade unions themselves.

Exactly this happened at exactly the right moment. In addition to the new line and the new political atmosphere, new forces made their appearance in the Communist ranks.

First, the party's leadership was shaken up. Ruthenberg and Gitlow were serving jail sentences. Others, like Wagenknecht and Katterfeld, had suffered a loss in prestige, because they were slow to adapt to the new line. Those who wholeheartedly supported the line of broadening out gained ground. A new driving force was provided by Lovestone, Weinstone, Bedacht, Bittelman, and Cannon. This new team assumed increasing responsibility until the underground was liquidated. None of them was a newcomer to the party, but the change of line enabled them to play new roles in the leadership.

Lovestone was elected to the Central Executive Committee at the unity convention in Woodstock in May 1921. He was appointed editor of the official organ, *The Communist,* the following month, his first full-time paid position in the party. At the end of October, he gave up that post to become assistant secretary and in January 1922 rose to be national secretary.[1] Weinstone was also elected to the top committee at the same convention, preceded Lovestone as national secretary for a short period, and then served as New York organizer.[2]

Bedacht and Bittelman represented a different type. Bedacht, a native of Germany, was then thirty-eight years old; Bittelman, a native of Russia, thirty-five. They had come to the United States in their mid-twenties, old enough to have participated in the European Socialist movement. Their political activity in the new world was a continuation of their political activity in the old. Bedacht, another self-educated worker, had left school at the age of thirteen to earn a living as a barber. He worked at that trade for seven years in Switzerland, France, and Austria and for two more years in New York before he went out to Detroit to edit a German paper. When the Communist Labor party was formed in 1919, he was editing a German paper in San Francisco. After Reed died in Moscow at the end of 1920, Bedacht was sent to take his place on behalf of the still existing Communist Labor party. He was one of the official American delegates to the Comintern's Third Congress in the summer of 1921 and returned one of the most ardent partisans of the new line.[3] Bittelman came up by way of the Jewish federation. Unlike the European immigrants who dominated the Russian federation, Bedacht and Bittelman tried to Americanize themselves by using the language of their new country and trying to assimilate its ways. As soon as possible, they left the foreign-language work and took part in the general political leadership. Bedacht was essentially an agitator, at his best stirring up a crowd. Bittelman was more studious and reserved, the model of a Communist "theoretician."

Cannon came from still other stock. Unlike the other four, he was American-born. The Midwest was his native environment. His parents were born in England of Irish parentage. They were steeped in the Irish nationalist tradition of Robert Emmett, the patriot who was hanged at the dawn of the nineteenth century for an unsuccessful uprising against British rule. After coming to the United States and settling in a suburb of Kansas City, the father identified himself with the old Knights of Labor, then with the Populists, then the Bryanites, and, at about the turn of the century, the Socialists. The *Appeal to Reason* arrived weekly at their home. At the age of twelve, the boy went to work for the Swift packing house, a sixty-hour-a-week job. At sixteen, in 1906, his first feeling of social consciousness was stirred by the Moyer-Haywood-Pettibone case. He decided to go to high school at the unusual age of seventeen—a desire for "culture" and a receptivity to radicalism came together to rescue him from the factory and the poolroom. After leaving school, he joined the I.W.W. as a traveling organizer, a member of what the Wobblies called the "soap-box union."[4] Then came the Russian Revolution in 1917. It shook Cannon out of the I.W.W. and steered him into the Socialist party with the rest of the pro-Bolshevik Left Wing the following year. While the Communist movement was struggling to be born in 1918–19, he earned a living as an office worker during the day, went to law school three nights a week, and devoted the rest of his time to the local Left Wing in the Socialist party.[5]

Cannon attended the National Conference of the Left Wing in New York in June 1919 and found himself in sympathy with the Reed-Gitlow tendency, which opposed the domination of the foreign-language federations. He did not attend any of the Communist founding conventions the following September because, he says, he was opposed to a premature split in the Socialist party. Afterward, however, the Kansas City local went over to the Communist Labor party and Cannon was appointed secretary for the Kansas-Missouri district.[6] When the United Communist party was formed in the spring of 1920 at the first Bridgman convention, he was elected to the Central Committee and assigned as organizer of the St. Louis–Southern Illinois district. Toward the end of 1920, he was moved to Cleveland to edit *The Toiler,* an organ of the U.C.P.[7] He was shifted to New York the following year and began to take part in the top leadership of the Communist party of America.[8]

When Cannon came to New York, he was something of a curiosity in that stifling underground atmosphere. The tall, rawboned Midwesterner with an Irish gift of gab seemed to personify the kind of "American" movement to which the Comintern had given its blessing at the Third Congress. More than any one else, he embodied the free-swinging Western tradition of the I.W.W. At the same time, his organizing experience in the field made him stand out as a "practical" worker in a leadership top-heavy with "theoreticians." Cannon came on the scene at a propitious moment. The change of line had minimized his shortcomings and magnified his strong points. He had a long way to go before he could catch up with the New Yorkers in Marxist or Leninist phraseology. They had a long way to go to catch up with his trade-union experience.

While Cannon was becoming a front-rank Communist leader, a fellow Kansas City radical was quietly trying to earn a living in New York.

Browder

Over a hundred years before the American Revolution and about two hundred and fifty years before the Russian Revolution, two Browder brothers set sail from the British Isles, probably from Wales, to the distant shores of Dinwiddie County in the colony of Virginia. Browders settled in Kentucky, and other Browders pushed on as far as Illinois. There the grandfather of the future Communist leader settled down as a circuit-riding preacher and carried on some farming on the side to support his brood of eighteen children.

William, the eighteenth, married Martha Hankins, age sixteen, whose family was Scotch. They mounted a horse with all they owned and rode away to the free land farther West. When the horse had carried them as far as Medicine Lodge, Kansas, William staked out a claim to a quarter section of virgin soil on the nearby prairie. It was early in the 1870s, a decade of hard times following the Civil War, and William Browder was one of the unlucky ones. Eventually, he gave up the grim struggle with the soil and moved the family to Wichita, where his eighth child, Earl Russell Browder, was born in 1891.

The boy had to leave school before reaching the age of ten because his father had become an invalid and could not support a large family. After the usual youthful jobs, such as messenger, he was hired by a wholesale drug firm as errand boy and ended up six years later as its accountant and credit manager. After Wichita came six years in Kansas City. Browder, in his twenties, first attempted to set up a small business of his own. When it failed after a few months, he went back to work for others, usually as an accountant, and completed a law school's correspondence course in 1914. It is interesting to note that the three most important Communist secretaries in the first twenty-five years of the movement, Ruthenberg, Lovestone, and Browder, were a bookkeeper, an accountant, and a statistician, respectively. The number of law students who never became lawyers—Lovestone, Gitlow, Browder, Wolfe, Cannon, Dunne—is also striking.

The Populist and Socialist traditions intermingled in the Browder family. The father was a Populist sympathizer in a state that was a stronghold of Populism and, like so many of his generation, absorbed Socialist propaganda from the strongly Populist-tinged *Appeal to Reason*. Of his ten children, seven grew to maturity, and four of them found their way into the Communist movement.

Before he became a Communist, Earl Browder had spent some time in almost all the radical and labor movements of his day.

He joined the Socialist party in Wichita in 1907 at the age of sixteen. As he later put it, he was a "promising young executive in a local corporation on working days" and an ardent Socialist the rest of the time. When he moved to Kansas City in 1912, the great Haywood crisis was convulsing the Socialist movement. Browder reacted to Haywood's defeat by leaving the party. He did not follow Haywood into the I.W.W., however, because he was influenced by an offshoot of the syndicalist movement which believed in working in the A.F. of L. It was a local Kansas City group, called the Workers' Educational League, which propagated the ideas of the Syndicalist League of North America headed by William Z. Foster. Though Browder never considered himself formally a member of the syndicalist organization, he was closely associated with it in practical work for about three years after 1912. Both Cannon and Browder helped to put out a little labor paper, *The Toiler,* which represented the Syndicalist League in Kansas City, but their paths diverged when it came out against the I.W.W. Cannon departed, and Browder went into the A.F. of L. union of his trade, a Bookkeepers, Stenographers and Accountants local, which made him its president late in 1914 and sent him as one of its delegates to the City Central council. A shift from trade unionism to the cooperative movement took place in 1916. He went to work managing the store of a farmers' cooperative near Kansas City. The Cooperative League of America put him on its technical advisory board, and he wrote occasionally for its journal.

Until the United States entered the war in 1917, Browder had never really found a political home for himself. Socialism, syndicalism, trade unionism, cooperativism—he had tried them all, but none had held him for long.

Browder took an extremist position on the war. He was arrested in 1917 on a charge of conspiring to defeat the operation of the draft law, to which a second charge of nonregistration was later added. At the trial in December of that year, he was sentenced to two years for conspiracy and one year for nonregistration. While the conspiracy case was being appealed, he went to jail to serve the nonregistration sentence. The revelation of the Russian Revolution came to him in prison with the same force with which it had overwhelmed the frustrated Left-Wingers outside. He rejoined the Socialist party as soon as he was released and, reunited with Cannon and others, moved in to take over the Kansas City party for the Left Wing.

In the spring of 1919, with Browder as first editor, this group put out *The Workers' World,* one of the first pro-Communist papers outside New York. When Browder—together with his brothers, William E. and Ralph W.—went to jail in June 1919 on a conspiracy charge, Cannon took over the editorship. The paper survived for about nine months until Cannon was arrested for agitating against a government injunction in the Kansas coal strike.[9]

Browder's second prison term, of which he served sixteen months, prevented him from taking part in the formative stage of the Communist movement. He was not released until November 1920, over a year after the first parties were formed in Chicago. Out of jail, he hastened to leave Kansas City for New York, where he obtained a job as head of the bookkeeping department of a wholesale firm. His first direct contact with the Communist movement came in New York in January 1921. The United Communist party admitted him with the honorary distinction of a "charter member" because he had been unavoidably detained in jail at the time of the founding conventions, and his pro-Communist sympathies had been well known. He was working quietly in what was still a strange, big city when Cannon, by then in New York, unexpectedly came to see him with an intriguing proposition.[10]

In the spring of 1921, the three members of the American Agency formed in Moscow after the Second Congress—Scott, Fraina, and Katayama—arrived in New York. One of their missions was to raise a large, impressive American delegation to the first Congress of the Red International of Labor Unions. They soon discovered that no Communist leader in New York had enough trade-union experience to organize such a delegation around the country. Cannon hit on the idea that Browder was the man for the job. He came to see Browder, told him what the situation was, and played up the magnificent opportunity for starting at the top by taking on the task of organizing the delegation. Browder was thinking of settling down to a few years of comfortable, private life but the lure of big-time revolutionary politics was too much for him to resist. Cannon proposed his name to the party leadership, recommending him as one who had worked in the A.F. of L. and knew Left Wing labor leaders out West personally. Browder came to a meeting, was interviewed by Katayama, who approved of him, and accepted the mission. Thus, his trade-union experience was his first big asset in the Communist movement and enabled him to start, if not at the top, in the second echelon of leaders.[11]

Browder set out across the country to round up suitable candidates for the trip to Moscow. The single most important center of radical trade-union activity was then Chicago. The single most important radical trade-unionist in Chicago was then William Z. Foster, who was waiting impatiently for something to turn up.

Browder owed his introduction into the Communist leadership to Cannon; Foster to Browder. Ironically, when it came to leaving the

Communist movement, Cannon went first; then Browder; Foster remained.

Foster

There was nothing remotely Slavic about William Z. Foster. His father was an Irish immigrant; his mother came from English-Scotch stock. Born in Taunton, Massachusetts, near Boston, he spent his childhood in the slums of Philadelphia. His father washed carriages and plotted against the English. His mother produced twenty-three children, most of whom died in infancy, and devoted herself fervently to Catholicism. After quitting school at the age of ten, young Bill could not settle down to a place or a trade. For the next twenty-six years, he worked all over the country in a half-dozen industries—as logger, dockworker, farm hand, trolley-car conductor, metal worker, seaman—rarely staying at one job or in one place for more than a few months. When nothing else turned up, he took to hoboing. He was a restless, self-educated, rebellious worker, a type that radicals dreamed about but rarely were.

Politics interested him early. At fifteen, he says, he was stirred by William Jennings Bryan's campaign for the presidency in 1896.[12] He came to the Socialist party in 1901. Eight years later, he was expelled as a member of a Left Wing faction in the state of Washington. By coincidence, it was the same year, 1909, that Ruthenberg first joined the Socialist movement. The different paths they took at about the same time brought them to communism from different directions. Ruthenberg was able to go directly from Left Wing Socialism to Communism. Foster had to make a long detour to get to the same place.

For an American radical so "native" as Foster, European influences were destined to play a curiously crucial role. Trips to Europe determined the two turning points in his career.

He was carried away the first time by what he heard and saw in France and Germany in 1910–11. In France, the anarcho-syndicalists controlled the official trade-union movement. In Germany, they were impotently aloof from the trade unions. To Foster, the lesson for the United States was clear: get into the official trade-union movement and "bore from within." This was his advice to the I.W.W., which he had joined after leaving the Socialists. He maintained that the I.W.W. was wrong to oppose the A.F. of L. with its own pure, revolutionary unions. It was better to go into the A.F. of L. and take it over. He returned home in the fall of 1911 to fight inside the I.W.W. for his great discovery. Though he failed to convince the great majority of syndicalists, he succeeded in winning over a small group of disciples.[13]

Disappointed by the I.W.W. as he had been disillusioned by the Socialist party, Foster went into the business of radicalism for himself. He formed the Syndicalist League of North America in 1912. It lasted about two years. Then he formed the International Trade Union Educational League in 1915. It lasted about a year. These were small organizations on the fringe of the I.W.W., with which they mainly quarreled over trade-union tactics.

While working as a car inspector in Chicago and as a member in good standing in the Railway Carmen's Union of the A.F. of L., Foster conceived of a more direct way to put his ideas into practice. He persuaded the A.F. of L. in 1917 to start an organizing campaign among the packing-house workers in the Chicago district. To his own surprise, he became secretary of the organizing committee, with John Fitzpatrick, president of the Chicago Federation of Labor, as chairman. Over 200,000 workers were soon enrolled.

In the postwar ferment in the labor movement, Foster suddenly found himself, as a result of the packing-house success, a key figure. In 1918, he conceived of an even more ambitious operation—to organize the great open-shop, mass-production industries, starting with steel. Again he was able to put the idea across; he became secretary of the National Steel Committee, with Fitzpatrick as organizer. In the fall of 1919 an exceptionally violent strike of 365,000 steel workers broke out under Foster's leadership. After three and a half months, it went down to total defeat in January of the following year. The first great effort to organize the mass-production industries had failed and Foster's dream of taking over the A.F. of L. was shattered.

Thus Foster was deeply engrossed in the steel organizing campaign just when the Communist movement was being founded. To the Communists of 1919, he was little short of a renegade and traitor. Anyone who worked in the A.F. of L. or who led a strike for any other reason than to overthrow the capitalist system would have displeased them. The Communist press jeered at him as "E.Z. Foster" for taking the easy way out.[14] What made Foster's crime particularly unforgivable, however, was his testimony before a Senate Committee in the midst of the steel strike. As an A.F. of L. official, he had learned to moderate his public statements, and he felt it necessary to make a prowar statement as well as a declaration of allegiance to Gompers' policy.[15] In return, Gompers and Fitzpatrick gave assurances of their confidence in him.[16] In later years, Foster tried to explain away this compromising testimony as not representing his true convictions and as intended to protect the steel strike from the anti-Red hysteria.[17] At the time, however, the Communists would not have had a higher opinion of him even if he could have convinced them that he was lying. The early conception of revolutionary conduct under fire required him to defy the enemy honestly rather than get off easily with falsehoods. For years, Foster's enemies in the Communist movement raked up the old indiscretion to embarrass him both in Moscow and at home.

The packing-house and steel strikes proved that Foster was a great organizer. They did not prove that he was or could be a great revolutionary organizer within the A.F. of L. In order to carry on his organizational work, he had adapted himself to the existing bureaucracy of the A.F. of L., which sought to use him as much as he sought to use it. He was able to rationalize this process of adaptation by watering down the traditional syndicalist distinction between revolutionary and reactionary trade unions. Foster took the position that all trade unions were revolutionary—in the long run. He made organizing the unorganized in itself a revolutionary act. In practice, he limited himself to militant organizational methods and left the revolutionary propaganda to others. While the Left Wing was busy agitating against the war, he merely wished to take advantage of the wartime situation to build up the unions.

In the light of Foster's subsequent powers of adaptation in the Communist movement, it does not appear entirely fortuitous that he was first capable of adapting himself to the A.F. of L.

Foster was thirty-nine years old in 1920. He was through with the Socialist party, through with the I.W.W., through with the A.F. of L. Isolated except for a small band of devoted followers, yet still full of tireless ambition, he went back to the consolation of a more or less personal organization. He formed the Trade Union Educational League (T.U.E.L.) with himself as the inevitable secretary-treasurer in November 1920. The Communists refused to have anything to do with it because it was prematurely pro-A.F. of L. No one on the extreme Left had Foster's personal prestige as a mass working-class leader, but he had no immediate way of making use of it because the anti-A.F. of L. prejudice of the Communists was shared by the Left Wing in general. No American radical seemed less fitted to spend the rest of his life in the Communist movement.

At this propitious moment, Browder turned up in Chicago bearing tidings of the new trade-union international planned in Moscow and the vast new field of operations which it could open up to Foster. They had met before in Kansas City, but had never developed an intimate relationship. Foster was ten years older than Browder, with a national reputation as a strike leader. Browder was virtually restarting his radical career. It was in Foster's power to help the younger man make good on his first important assignment as a Communist simply by consenting to go along on the delegation to Moscow.

Foster was tempted. Without the Communists, his Trade Union Educational League had nowhere to go. Now he was being offered a chance to tie up with them on his own terms. Nevertheless, Foster had some qualms. Except for his pro-A.F. of L. slant, he was still an anarcho-syndicalist with a strong aversion for the rule of the state —even a Communist state. Unable to resist Browder's bid and unable to accept it unconditionally, Foster compromised by agreeing to go to Moscow as an "observer."

The Profintern

The new trade-union international was part of the new line to gain greater mass influence in the labor movement.

The older International Federation of Trade Unions—the "Amsterdam International"—was led by Social Democrats. By themselves, the Communist trade-unionists outside Russia were too weak to constitute a real threat to the existing organization. The most likely Communist allies were the syndicalists, who were strongly organized in France, Italy, Spain, Germany, and elsewhere. The Comintern was especially hopeful about the cooperation of the American syndicalists. The General Executive Board of the I.W.W. had made favorable statements about Soviet Russia and the Third International in 1919 and 1920.[18]

A visit to Russia of British and Italian trade-union delegations gave the Comintern the opportunity to set up a provisional council for the new trade-union international. Zinoviev himself presided as chairman of the first conference on July 16, 1920. The only American organization which took part in the preliminary conferences was the I.W.W., and an I.W.W. representative named Yochichago took part in the work of the provisional council.[19]

But as the Communist-syndicalist negotiations progressed, it became clear that the alliance was not a happy one. The Russians wanted the new trade-union organization to put the dictatorship of the proletariat into its program and to be directly affiliated with the Comintern. The syndicalists resisted supporting any form of state in principle and preferred a wholly independent trade-union organization. These difficulties caused a year's delay before a congress could be convened. Nevertheless, the Russian unions always held the upper hand—for one reason because the provisional council was financed by them.[20]

As the time for the inaugural congress of the trade-union international approached, the relation of the I.W.W. to the whole enterprise became increasingly uneasy. By then the Comintern had decided to shift its orientation from the I.W.W. to the A.F. of L. Despite pleas, persuasion, and pressure, the I.W.W. stubbornly refused to commit suicide. A new General Executive Board of the I.W.W. elected toward the end of 1920 adopted a hostile attitude toward the Comintern.

The first congress of the Red International of Labor Unions (R.I.L.U.) opened in Moscow on July 3, 1921. It came to be known more familiarly as the "Profintern," a telescoping of the Russian form of the name.

The American Trade Union Delegation to this congress was made up of Pascal B. Cosgrove (Crosby) of the Shoe Workers Union of Haverhill, Massachusetts, Joseph Knight (Emmons) of the One Big Union of Canada, Hulet Wells of the Seattle Central Labor Council, Dennis E. Batt, representing the Detroit Central Labor Council, Ella Reeve Bloor of the Minneapolis Trades and Labor Council, George Williams of the I.W.W., and Earl Browder (Joseph Dixon), ostensibly representing the Kansas miners, as secretary of the delegation.[21] Foster, the "observer" was a more important catch than any of the delegates or indeed than all of them combined.

After the delegation had left, William F. Dunne tried to get to Moscow on his own. Dunne was born in Kansas City of an Irish immigrant father and a French-Canadian mother, raised in Minnesota, and entered the trade-union movement as an electrician in Vancouver, British Columbia. During the war he moved to Butte, Montana, where he served as chairman of the joint strike committee of the violent metal trades strike in 1917–18 and edited the Butte *Daily Bulletin,* official organ of the Montana Federation of Labor and Butte Central Labor Council. Dunne dominated the radical Butte labor movement as secretary of the local electricians' union, vice-president of the Montana Federation of Labor, and member from 1918 to 1920 of the Montana State Legislature, to which he was elected on the Democratic ticket, then temporarily invaded by the extreme Left Wing.[22] Six Dunne brothers were once active in the labor movement; four became Communists; and three—Vincent R., Grant, and Miles—later became Trotskyists.[23]

A Socialist since 1910, Bill Dunne brought the Socialist party branch of Butte into the Communist Labor party in 1919. Unlike most of the other former Socialists, Dunne was never completely housebroken in the Communist movement. It seems that he tried to get to Moscow in 1921 by working his way across on a boat bound for Stettin, Germany. There he went on a spree with some shipmates, invited the attention of the German police, and never reached his destination. He returned to New York to add one more radical trade-unionist to the new Communist leadership.

The first session of the Profintern's first congress took place simultaneously with the last sessions of the Comintern's Third Congress. For the Americans, the main issue was the same in both—the struggle over dual unionism. Haywood accepted his defeat at the Comintern congress; the official I.W.W. delegate, Williams, refused to do so at the Profintern congress.

The syndicalist bloc, including Williams, made a fight on three basic points. It objected to any affirmation of the dictatorship of the proletariat, demanded complete independence of the Profintern from the Comintern, and rejected the policy of boring from within the old unions. On the first two, the Communist bloc was willing to strike a semblance of compromise. The Profintern's program came out openly for socialism, the overthrow of capitalism, the revolutionary class struggle, and the dictatorship of the proletariat, but the phrase used most often in the basic documents was the less provocative one of "workers' control." Organizationally, the Profintern was set up as nominally independent, but provision was made for the "closest possible contact" with the Comintern by giving each organization three representatives on the other's executive committee.[24]

No compromise was made on the question of dual unionism. On this crucial point, the I.W.W. was decisively rebuffed. The decision for the United States said emphatically: "Therefore the question of creating revolutionary cells and groups inside the American Federation of Labor and the independent unions is of vital importance. There is no other way by which one could gain the working mass in America, than to lead a systematic struggle within the unions." [25]

The European syndicalists also had their troubles. The larger syndicalist organizations in France, Italy, and Spain wanted to stay and work in the Profintern as a syndicalist minority opposition. The smaller organizations in Germany, Sweden, Norway, and Holland wanted to get out altogether.[26] The immediate result was a syndicalist split, with the better part of the syndicalist bloc remaining in the Profintern—for about a year. By 1923 the syndicalists had enough and launched their own international in a final break with the Communists.[27]

Williams sided with the more extremist syndicalist group from the outset and proved to be a thorn in the side of the Communists in Moscow. His report of the congress gave the I.W.W.'s leadership one reason for voting against affiliation with the Profintern at the end of 1921. Nevertheless, since a minority went over to the Communists, the effort to woo the I.W.W. was not entirely wasted. Over one-third of the I.W.W.'s membership had voted pro-Communist in a referendum held in 1920. It has been estimated that the I.W.W. may have lost as many as 2000 members, or from 10 to 20 per cent of its total following, to the Communist party.[28]

Next to the ex-Socialists, the ex-syndicalists accounted most for the original base of the American Communist movement, with the ex-liberals a poor third. By the end of 1921, the lines were sharply drawn between syndicalism and communism, and no insults were spared in behalf of the true revolution.

Though the Profintern was a child of the Comintern, the very existence of two centers of international Communist activity, both in Moscow, proved a fertile ground for family intrigues and rivalries. Theoretically their functions were clear enough. The Profintern was supposed to carry out the general line of the Comintern in the trade-union field. But this division of labor was often deceptive. The Profintern developed its own staff, held its own congresses, sent abroad its own representatives, and disposed of separate funds. The line between general political activity and trade-union work was frequently hard to draw, especially in terms of personnel. Some Communist leaders stayed in the trade-union movement, others took assignments in the unions or the party interchangeably. The "trade-union Communists" and the "political Communists" often vied for party leadership. If the trade-unionists temporarily lost out, they could take refuge in the Profintern apparatus until they were ready to stage a comeback. The Profintern gave them an independent line of communication and information to the real source of power, the Russian Communist party. A number of future Communist leaders, including George Dimitroff of Bulgaria and Harry Pollitt of England, came up via the Profintern, not the Comintern. In the United States, Foster and Browder were for years closer to the Profintern and its leader, Lozovsky, than to the Comintern and its leaders, Zinoviev or Bukharin.

To some extent, Lozovsky's personality molded the Profintern. For some years before the Russian Revolution, he had been closer to Trotsky, with whom he had collaborated in putting out a Russian émigré paper in Paris, than to Lenin, whose high-handed methods had irritated him as they had many other future Soviet leaders.[29] Under his real name, Solomon Abramovich Dridzo, Lozovsky had headed a small trade union of Jewish hat-makers in Paris. A short, nervous man with a broad black beard, Lozovsky never played an independent role. He became an expert at guessing which way the wind was blowing in the Russian party and in changing his course accordingly before it was too late. He prided himself on his ability to shift position without notice. He was so successful that he outlived all the top leaders of the Comintern. They came and went; Lozovsky remained entrenched in the Profintern, assiduously building up his own machine, encouraging his agents and protégés to make bids for more power in their own parties. Such a man was peculiarly useful to Stalin in his struggles against Trotsky, Zinoviev, Bukharin, and their sympathizers in the international movement. Since the Comintern and Profintern networks were often in bitter competition, the latter provided an alternative source of leadership in party crises. Nowhere was this behind-the-scenes rivalry to be more virulent than in the American party.

From Moscow to Chicago

Foster stayed in Moscow for three and a half months. At the end, he was ready to go over to the Communists.

What induced a man like Foster to change his political faith in Moscow? Before Foster went to Russia, he admitted, he "was very much in doubt as to the outcome of the Russian revolution." He still held the old-fashioned view that "Socialism could only be brought about" in a highly industrialized country.[30] As correspondent for the Federated Press on this trip, he sent his impressions back home, and it is possible from them to see what made him change his mind.

He was delighted, of course, to find the Profintern espousing his old views on dual unionism. On this score, it was saying, in effect, that he had been right and the American Communists wrong. But what seems to have impressed him most was, ironically, the omnipotent and ubiquitous nature of the Russian Communist party in power. He had no illusions, for he wrote with more candor than he could ever afford after his conversion: "In practice, as well as in accepted theory, the dictatorship of the proletariat resolves itself into the dictatorship of the Communist Party."[31] The anarcho-syndicalist who had despised all political parties and centralized governments, who had ardently preached that the trade unions were going to make the revolution by themselves, was charmed by the very aspects of the Russian Communist movement and government that had previously repelled him.

Not for nothing had Foster been preaching a peculiar form of syndicalism. The essence of it had been that, if only the trade unions —even A.F. of L. unions—could become big and strong enough, the revolution would take care of itself. It was a theory of revolution by organization rather than by propaganda. And now, in Russia, he saw for the first time the full fruits of revolutionary organization. Wherever he turned, in the army, in the government, in the trade unions, he saw the same organization at work. At the head of this organization were men like himself, who had come up from the bottom after years of drudgery and disappointment. Translated in terms of a party instead of a union, it was the organization which he had dreamed about. The jump was not too big for a man who had never cared much for books or theory in his revolutionary schooling. The contempt of many old-time syndicalists for theory made Communist theory less objectionable to them if other aspects of the Communist movement happened to appeal to them.

The bargain was struck in Moscow. The Profintern adopted Foster's Trade Union Educational League as its American section. Both sides had much to gain. Lozovsky was anxious to get a foothold in the American trade-union movement. The T.U.E.L. provided him with a ready-made American branch office. Foster had nowhere else to go. He had already learned that, without Communist support, the T.U.E.L. was doomed to sterility. With the Profintern's political and financial backing, and the change of line by the American Communists, the T.U.E.L.'s prospects suddenly became exceedingly bright.

In order to make a place for Foster back home, a most unusual division of labor and authority was arranged. Responsibility for political activity was allotted to the party under the leadership of Ruthenberg; responsibility for trade-union activity was assigned to the T.U.E.L. under the leadership of Foster. The political headquarters stayed in New York; the trade-union headquarters in Chicago. Browder was assigned to work with Foster in Chicago. The physical separation of the two centers had the advantage of keeping them from getting too close to each other for comfort. It was so inconvenient organizationally, however, that Browder was appointed in 1922 to act as liaison between the New York political headquarters and the Chicago trade-union headquarters.[32]

This distribution of power immediately made Foster a Communist figure of top rank. It was his comeback from the limbo into which he had been cast after the collapse of the steel strike. Foster joined the Communist movement on his own terms as head of its trade-union activity. He came back home from Moscow still identified with the T.U.E.L. only, proclaiming his willingness to work with all Left Wing trade-unionists alike. No public announcement of his Communist affiliation was made until 1923, but actually his membership dated from his return from Moscow in 1921.[33]

For a long time, however, Foster was regarded as a Communist in name only by the politically minded Communists in New York, who had a two years' lead over him in membership. To them, the road from Left Wing socialism to communism was much more consistent and desirable than the road from anarcho-syndicalism to communism. Foster's quick conversion in Moscow on such advantageous terms left them skeptical. For years to come, he would have to suffer being called a "syndicalist" or at best a "trade-union Communist" by his party opponents. The division of labor was a dangerous expedient. By creating two centers of power in the party, it planted the seeds of a more permanent and malignant type of factionalism than anything the party had yet experienced.

For almost a decade the main struggle in the American Communist movement was primarily between those who formed it in 1919 and those who came to the fore in 1921. There were exceptions; the line-up took some time to become clear and it fluctuated from time to time; but the 1919 group of Ruthenberg, Lovestone, and Gitlow provided the hard core of one great faction and the 1921 group of Foster, Browder, and Cannon that of another. The 1919 group was predominantly Socialist in background; its strong point was political theory; its national roots were largely European. The 1921 group was predominantly syndicalist in background; its strong point was trade-union activity; its national roots were largely native American. In numbers, the first was larger; in mass influence the second was potentially more important. It is even misleading to compare the two groups numerically, because the second did not amount to much more than a few individuals.[34] But they were more willing and able to build a mass movement than were the earlier ex-Socialists, who were able but not willing to do so in 1919, and willing but not able to do so in 1921.

The new initiative

Why was the American Communist movement capable of getting such an infusion of new blood after two years of an almost uninterrupted slide downhill? What did this small but vitally important native American contingent see in the Communist movement?

The Russian Revolution was still the main magnetic force. Such a staunch syndicalist as Foster had to go to Russia to be converted. It was, in essence, the story of John Reed all over again. What had happened at home was not so important because the source of strength was elsewhere. All the blighted hopes and bitter realities in the American party could be compensated for by the comforting reflection that, after all, there was one place where communism worked, where it had started from nothing and achieved everything, where what was happening was really important historically, as if everything elsewhere was merely a shadow of reality.

Nevertheless, an American did not become a Russian by believing in the Russian Revolution. Browder did not shed two hundred and fifty years of American ancestry by losing his heart in Moscow. Foster's roots in the American labor movement were not pulled up in Russia. On the contrary, they both found in Russia what they had been looking for in the United States. Their generation had looked for it in the Socialist movement and in the I.W.W. before coming to communism. Their fathers' generation had looked for it in the Knights of Labor or in the Populist movement. Every generation had had its organized form of social and political radicalism. The name and the causes changed; the spirit of revolt remained. When the Communist movement appeared, the question was whether it would become the main expression of American radicalism. The Socialists and the I.W.W. had been going downhill for some years, but there was still much life in them and they were capable of putting up a good deal of resistance. The competition was not decided all at once. In its first two years, the Communist movement was so completely isolated from all aspects of American life that its position in the race was far from clear. The Socialists and the I.W.W. were holding on grimly; their chances of staging a comeback could not be entirely discounted.

With the change of line, however, the Communists recovered the initiative. The background and development of Foster, Browder, Cannon, Minor, Dunne, indicated that the Communists had scored some success in linking up with an older, more indigenous radical tradition. These men had gone from one radical movement to another; if they ended up as Communists, it signified that communism succeeded with them in taking over the radical tradition. They were not bookish, ideologically punctilious types. They adopted communism emotionally long before they mastered it intellectually. They were less interested in the party's abstract principles than in its day-by-day practice. The change of line enabled them to make the transition from old-time radicalism to newfangled communism with a minimum of shift in practical activity.

First, they made a change in the Communist movement. Then it made a change in them.

Though the Communists scored a success by acquiring Foster in 1921, they suffered a setback by failing to win over someone even more important—Eugene Victor Debs. Ruthenberg visited Debs in Atlanta Penitentiary in June 1920 to ask him to join the Communist party. Debs rejected the overture on the ground that he could not accept the necessity for a dictatorship of the proletariat. The Communists punished Debs by refusing to support his presidential candidacy on the Socialist ticket in 1920 and by showing little interest in the campaign for his amnesty. When he sent Lenin a telegram in July 1922 protesting against the trial of Russian Social Revolutionaries, the Communist press treated him roughly. In behalf of his brother, Theodore Debs wrote to J. Louis Engdahl, then editing the Communist organ: "Gene wishes me to say to you that personally he owes nothing to the Communists. When he was in that hell-hole at Atlanta the Communists with but few exceptions ignored him and the rest of the political prisoners, and their papers, including the one you now edit, were cold-bloodedly silent, not raising a voice nor lifting a finger to secure their release, and as far as they were concerned Gene would still be rotting, were he alive, in his dungeon in Atlanta." Despite these harsh words, the letter ended by declaring that Eugene V. Debs still considered himself "a loyal supporter of Lenin, Trotzky and the Soviet Government." At the end of 1922, in his first public speech after his release from jail, Debs was reported as saying that "Sovietism is the only good thing that came out of the war." The Communist organ commented peevishly: "If Debs is honest in his declaration then he means that the universal workers' republic will be established by the 'dictatorship of the proletariat' in the form of Soviet Rule. And this includes the United States. Otherwise his remarks have no meaning." [35]

Debs's reaction to Communism has been generally confused in both pro-Communist and anti-Communist writings. Pro-Communist writers have doted on his sentimentalized eulogies of the Bolshevik revolution or his friendly attitude toward the Trade Union Educational League. Anti-Communist writers have lingered on his telegram in behalf of the Social Revolutionaries or his rejection of the dictatorship of the proletariat.[36] In truth, Debs was much clearer and more consistent in his sympathies than he has been given credit for being. He tried, not always successfully, to distinguish between what might be good for Russia in terms of Russian development and what was good for the United States in terms of American radical traditions. In so doing, he accepted Russian Bolshevism and rejected American Communism. He did not apply the same rules to both.

In all the history of American radicalism, no one succeeded in reaching out and touching the hearts of more people than did Eugene Victor Debs. When his gaunt body sagged virtually to the floor and his long finger stretched out to make a point, his audiences gazed at him reverently as if they were privileged to be in the presence of a socialist saint. The Communists, to become a popular American movement, desperately needed someone like Debs. He came close enough to them to make him symbolic of both their success and their failure. He could not tear himself away from those who claimed the patronage of the Russian Revolution or offered a class-conscious trade-union substitute for the A.F. of L.; he would not accept all the new formulas and slogans that came from abroad or fail to protest against the suppression of civil liberties, whether it concerned the Social Revolutionaries in Russia or William Z. Foster in the United States. There was no room for a Debs in the American Communist movement, and that is perhaps as good an explanation of its shortcomings as any.

19

The Legal Party

Few words have created more hope and wreaked more havoc in the labor movement than the words "united front" have done.

The germinal idea of the united front was contained in a suggestion to the British Communists in Lenin's *"Left Wing" Communism*. He advised them to wage a campaign for an electoral agreement with the leadership of the British Labour party against the alliance of Lloyd George and the Conservatives. His reasoning was brutally candid. The British Communists were few and weak. It was hard for them to get the masses to listen to them. The Labour party was large and amorphous. If the Communists came out and called upon the workers to vote for the Labour party leaders, Arthur Henderson and Philip Snowden, they could be sure that the rank and file would at least listen to them.

But Lenin had to explain away one delicate matter. After all, the Communists considered the Hendersons and the Snowdens traitors to the working class. According to Lenin, the Communists could use the united front to destroy them politically on one condition—*"complete liberty"* for the Communists in the electoral bloc. If the Labourites accepted, "we will not only help the Labour Party establish its government more quickly, but also help the masses understand more quickly the Communist propaganda that we will carry on against the Hendersons without curtailment and without evasions." If they refused, "we will gain still more, because we will have at once shown the *masses"* that "the Hendersons prefer *their* closeness with the capitalists to the unity of all the workers."

It is impossible to sum up Lenin's thought more cold-bloodedly than he did himself—that "I want to support Henderson with my vote in the same way as a rope supports one who is hanged." [1]

The broader implications inherent in Lenin's acrobatic opportunism were not immediately explored. They were held in abeyance during the Comintern's Second Congress in the summer of 1920 because the invasion of Poland by the Red Army caused a temporary resurgence of faith in the imminent European revolution. The disastrous Ruhr uprising in Germany in 1921 shattered the dream. The Third Congress in the summer of 1921 finally and officially buried the corpse of the European revolution in the international Communist movement. The Third Congress's slogan "To the masses!" reflected the shift, but just how the Communist parties were supposed to win the confidence of the masses was not fully and clearly thought out.

If the masses were not going into the Communist movement, where were they going? Those who were going anywhere were going into a movement that the Communists had long ago pronounced "dead." Ever since Lenin had solemnly proclaimed it as a fact in 1914, every Communist had believed devoutly in the "collapse" of the Social Democratic movement.[2] Yet the comeback of the Social Democratic organizations was a most remarkable and significant political phenomenon. The disparity in numbers between the Communist and Socialist parties and their sympathetic trade unions became perceptible very early in the twenties and continued to be more and more marked toward the end of the decade.[3] Not only did the mass of workers remain in the old or revived organizations; they resented the splits engineered by the Communists. The theory and the reality were so far apart that no Communist dared to make a fundamental analysis of the cause. No Communist could admit that the mass of workers were quite capable of recognizing their own best interests.

The united front, however, was tacit admission of this state of affairs. It was a calculated effort to remove the onus of splitting from the Communists and bestow it upon their enemies in the labor movement. Lenin's advice to the British Communists in 1920 could be adapted by all Western Communists. All the parties outside Russia were relatively weak and isolated. Only three of them, the German, French, and Czechoslovak, could be considered "mass parties" by any standard, and even these were no match for the German, French, and Czechoslovak Social Democratic parties.

The slogan of the "united front" was first introduced in December 1921.[4] The details were worked out at the Comintern's Fourth Congress the following year.

A basic distinction was made between two types of united fronts—"from above" and "from below." A united front "from above" signified that it was made by Communist leaders with the leaders of other workers' parties. A united front "from below" signified that it was made under Communist leadership exclusively. Only in certain circumstances were negotiations and agreements with leaders of other organizations considered permissible. Wherever and whenever possible, the Communists were to go over the leaders' heads and establish direct contact with the rank and file under Communist leadership. Though the united front could take different forms in different countries, it was admittedly only a new "tactic" to an old end, a more roundabout way of convincing the workers of "the inevitability of revolution and the importance of Communism."[5]

Thus the united front was born under an unlucky star. For the Communists, it was a child of defeat and retreat. It was not something they desired or preferred. It was forced on them by unpropitious, uncontrollable circumstances. Soon after the slogan of the united front was adopted, Zinoviev admitted sadly that it would not have become necessary if the Red Army had succeeded in capturing Warsaw in 1920.[6] One of the most important Comintern officials once explained that the united front rose whenever the revolutionary wave declined and the united front declined whenever the revolutionary wave rose.[7] It was, as Zinoviev frankly put it, a "strategic maneuver," to enable the Communists to recuperate by building up new and broader ties with the existing mass organizations of the workers at the expense of their leaders.[8] In a united front from above, other leaders were expected to participate forewarned that the Communists intended to make it an engine of their destruction. In a united front from below, the same masses who refused to accept Communist leadership by its own name were expected to accept it under a different label.

In essence, the united front was no change in the product; it was a change in the advertising.

The Workers' Council

The Comintern was far ahead of the American Communists.

While the Comintern was moving toward the united front in 1921, the American Communists were still too deeply embroiled in the struggle over the legal versus the illegal organization to care about anything else. A party which could not make up its mind to come up from the underground was scarcely in a position to make a bid to respectable legal organizations to form a united front.

Nevertheless, the American Communists could not stand still. While the Comintern from one direction and the Foster group from another were putting pressure on them to broaden out, a third push came from a new Left Wing within the Socialist party.

The original split of 1919 had driven away three quarters of the membership of the old Socialist party. From a membership of 104,822 in 1919, its second highest point, the party sank to 26,766 in 1920. The leftovers, however, were by no means "homogeneous and harmonious," as Hillquit had hoped. The lure of the Russian Revolution was still too strong to ignore. In a matter of months after the exodus of the Communists, the Socialist party had to go through a second siege of internal dissension and disruption.

The Socialist Left Wing of 1920–21 was led by a group of well-known officials and propagandists—J. Louis Engdahl, editor of the Socialist party's official publications; William F. Kruse, head of the Young People's Socialist League; Alexander Trachtenberg, director of the Department of Labor Research at the Rand School of Social

Science in New York City; Moissaye J. Olgin, an outstanding Jewish writer; Benjamin Glassberg, a former New York City schoolteacher dismissed in 1919 for radical activity; J. B. Salutsky (Hardman), editor of the Left Wing Jewish weekly, *Naye Welt* (*New World*).

This group had stayed in the Socialist party after the Communist split of 1919 for several reasons. Some of its members took a little longer to make up their minds about the desirability or durability of the Russian Revolution. Certain features of the underground Communist movement repelled them. They were not ready to accept the full program and tactics of the Comintern. Or they still hoped to win over the official Socialist party, where they felt more at home. This hope was not entirely unfounded. At the Socialist convention of 1919, Engdahl and Kruse had submitted a minority resolution supporting the Third International without completely endorsing the "Moscow programs and methods." A referendum completed in January 1920 showed a majority of 3475 to 1444 in favor of this resolution. An official Socialist request for admission to the Third International was actually made two months later. But the Comintern was not yet in any mood to welcome such belated and qualified adherence. Two Communist parties were already warring in the United States, and a third party was not likely to improve the situation. In its most ferocious style the Comintern rejected the petition by "declaring war upon you traitors to the working class who, on the eve of the World Revolution, sold out to the enemy to save your skins." The Engdahl-Kruse minority was brushed off as being "permeated by cowardly compromise and petty bourgeois prejudices." [9]

This was not the last Socialist overture. At the next convention in May 1920, the majority, led by Morris Hillquit, voted in favor of affiliation with the Third International on condition that autonomy in internal party matters be recognized and that the principle of the dictatorship of the proletariat need not apply to the United States. Though these conditions had no chance of acceptance by the Comintern, they showed that even the official Socialist leadership could not simply wave aside the whole question of some link to the international Communist movement. This time, the Engdahl-Kruse minority came out for unconditional affiliation. In another referendum, the Hillquit position won out narrowly by 1339 to 1301. After the convention, the Left Wing minority formed a "Committee for the Third International" with Engdahl as secretary.

The position of the Engdahl committee was exposed on both flanks. While it devoted most of its energies to fighting the Right Wing of the Socialist party, it was at the same time attacked without mercy by the Communists. The Communists were so extremist in their attitude that they scarcely deigned to take an interest in the second split that was clearly approaching in the Socialist party. In December 1920, a convention of the Finnish Socialist Federation decided by a two-thirds vote to withdraw from the Socialist party. The last hope of ever winning over the Socialist party to the Third International was dashed at the Detroit convention the following June. A motion to affiliate unconditionally was defeated 35 to 4, and another, to affiliate with reservations, 26 to 13. A motion to remain without any international affiliation won 31 to 8. When a majority of the membership sustained the convention's decision, the second split became unavoidable. By a vote of almost 10 to 1, the Bohemian federation decided to leave the party at the end of August 1921.

The final blow to the Socialist movement was the defection of the Jewish federation at a convention in September 1921 by a vote of 41 to 33. The Olgin-Salutsky group was chiefly responsible for the delay in the federation's action. This group was Left Wing enough to please most of the members, but it had also held them back from making the break to the Communists two years earlier. Virtually the entire leadership, and probably a majority of the membership, went with Salutsky, Olgin, Paul Novick, Rubin Saltzman, and Melech Epstein. Since the total membership of the Jewish federation in June 1921 was slightly under 1000, no large numbers were involved in the shift.[10] In 1921, the total Socialist membership fell to its lowest point —11,019.

In April, the "Committee for the Third International" began to publish a new biweekly magazine, *The Workers' Council,* edited by Benjamin Glassberg. The committee officially severed its connections with the Socialist party in September when the Jewish federation broke away. The federation became the backbone of a new organization, which adopted the same name as the magazine. Considerable support was also claimed among Finnish, Czech, German, Italian, and English-speaking groups. Engdahl shifted over as secretary from the defunct committee to its successor, the Workers' Council.

For a few months in 1921, the Council group played an independent role between the Socialist and Communist parties. Its leaders were no longer Socialists, but neither were they in any organizational sense Communists. They swore allegiance to the Russian Revolution and the Communist International, but they professed to have nothing but contempt for the local, officially recognized Communists. Though late-comers, they believed that they knew what communism needed to make it successful in the United States. Like Foster, they wanted to come into the Communist movement on their own terms, which would have been condemned as the most arrant of heresies the year before.

The heresy was the simple but insidious idea that Russia was not America.

As the Workers' Council took stock of the situation in October 1921, the Russian Revolution had "carried us off our feet," but its powerful appeal had been "romantic." The American Communists had "thought and acted as if the Russian Revolution had been bodily transplanted upon American soil." Now the time had come to give up "romance" in favor of "brutal realities." The world revolution had not materialized. Instead, imperialism was temporarily "more powerful than ever." The idea that a small minority of determined revolutionists could overthrow capitalism and lead the proletariat into communism was only a "fantastic dream." Even in Russia, the Communist dictatorship might stretch out "over decades" because the Russian masses were unprepared for the revolution.

In the end, the Workers' Council came to the conclusion that the

American Communists were suffering most from the disease of illegality. They denied that the Palmer raids had forced the Communist party to become a secret organization. They charged that it "had been lurking in the minds of most Communist enthusiasts ever since the outbreak of the Russian Revolution" because "it was a part of the atmosphere of revolution and romanticism that the Russian upheaval had created." They insisted that a secret organization could prosper in Czarist Russia but not in the United States, and demanded an "open, aboveboard mass movement," instead of an underground conspiracy. What the Workers' Council wanted most was clearly expressed in the title of its manifesto: "The Open Communist Party—The Task of the Hour!" [11]

There was a striking disparity in this line of reasoning between the broad principles and the narrow conclusion. If the Russian Revolution could not be "bodily transplanted" onto American soil, there was still the problem of how much of it could be transplanted and how much of the American tradition should be preserved. The Workers' Council group made the switchover from illegality to legality the complete solution of the whole problem. As a result of this oversimplification, the group never contributed much to the deeper problem of the relation between the Russian and American revolutions. At the first sign of the willingness of the official Communists to come up for air, the Workers' Council lost its reason for existence. Nevertheless, the attack against the underground struck an exposed nerve. It hit hard enough for the official Communists to react abusively. Insults like "centrists," "compromisers," and "opportunists" were brought out to put the interlopers in their place.

Foster did not challenge the underground party's leadership; the Workers' Council did. Hence the official Communists could accept the Foster group more easily. As long as the Communist party cherished the underground and the Workers' Council considered the underground the source of all evil, one or the other had to give way.

The new factionalism

Despite this ferment and pressure, a major convulsion lasting over a year was needed to bring the American Communist movement up from the underground.

Ever since the first days, every important decision had been accompanied by a fierce factional struggle—in 1919 over the premature split in the Socialist party, in 1920 over the unification of the two Communist parties. In 1921 the factions fought over the underground.

In the factional struggle of 1921, three main groups confronted one another.

At one extreme was the Workers' Council, headed by Engdahl. It was totally opposed to the illegal party and totally committed to an exclusively legal party.

In the middle were seven of the ten members of the Central Executive Committee of the Communist party of America, including Lovestone, Bedacht, and Minor. They wanted both to maintain the illegal party intact and to launch a new Communist-controlled legal party. This C.E.C. majority was backed by the Comintern.

At the other extreme were the three minority members of the committee—John J. Ballam, Charles Dirba, and George Ashkenudzie. They wanted only the illegal party and rejected any fully formed legal party, even if it was Communist-controlled. This so-called Left Opposition was backed by about 4000 members, admittedly a majority of the rank and file.[12]

No one in the Communist party, therefore, was bold enough to come out flatly against the underground. Only the Workers' Council, which still stood outside the party, went that far. Inside the party, the underground was still regarded as the natural habitat of a revolutionary movement, illegality as the indispensable token of revolutionary integrity.

In fact, the question was not raised in the form of illegality versus legality. The C.E.C. majority wanted both, but it did not give both the same status. For it, too, the illegal party remained the real revolutionary party. It conceived the legal party as a pawn or decoy to enable the underground to make contact with the masses above. The legal party was not to have a life of its own on an equal basis with the underground party. In principle, at least, there was no disagreement about the preservation and predominance of the underground. The only question was whether some sort of camouflaged and controlled legal organization should be added.

The fight against the legal organization was the last stand of the extremists in the foreign-language federations. Though their influence had been waning for some time and they no longer controlled the top leadership, they still represented the majority of the membership and could not be ignored in carrying out a radically new policy. A legal superstructure on the illegal party threatened them with an influx of new members as well as an unwelcome change of line. They were afraid that the legal tail would soon wag the illegal dog. They harked back to the good old days in Czarist Russia when a revolutionary movement worthy of the name had to work underground or not at all.

The branch office

After the May 1921 convention, the first rather timid effort was made to set up some sort of legal organization.

Fifteen of the party's own language federations and closest auxiliary organizations, ten of which were officially represented, came together in New York City in July 1921 to form the American Labor Alliance. The A.L.A. was only a federation of already existing organizations, not a new political party with its own dues-paying membership. Caleb Harrison of the Industrial Socialist League was elected national secretary, with headquarters at 201 West 13th Street, New York City.[13] Not much effort was made to camouflage the nature of the A.L.A. Article 1 of its "Rules" promised to propagate "the idea of the abolition of the capitalist system through the establishment of a Workers' Soviet Republic."

THE LEGAL PARTY

The ten organizations officially represented at the A.L.A. convention made an interesting list of the chief Communist auxiliary organizations in this period: Friends of Soviet Russia, Irish American Labor League, National Defense Committee, Finnish Socialist Federation, Associated Toiler Clubs, American Freedom Foundation, Ukrainian Workers Club, Industrial Socialist League, Marxian Educational Society (German), and Hungarian Workers Federation. Half were foreign-language groups and half letterhead organizations with little or no membership.

The A.L.A. soon proved to be a false start. One of the delegates to the Third Congress of the Comintern, Max Bedacht, returned from Moscow with the bad news that the Comintern considered it inadequate.[14] Something more far-reaching was desired.

Meanwhile, the Workers' Council approached the underground Communist leadership to form an open Communist party.[15] The Communists advised the individual members of the Council to join the underground party and the Council and the Alliance to merge above ground. The Council was ready to agree on a joint legal party on condition that the illegal party liquidate itself.[16] On the basic issue of the continued existence of the underground, both sides refused to give way. The underground was fighting for its life, the Council for its main principle.

As a result, the Alliance took steps to organize a new, underground-controlled legal party. The Council made a similar move in behalf of an uncontrolled party. By the middle of October, plans were made for two separate national conventions sponsored by the Alliance and the Council.

As preparations for these legal conventions speeded up, the Left Opposition became more and more alarmed. It demanded a convention of the underground party to give the underground membership a chance to be heard. The majority of the top leadership, knowing its weakness among the rank and file, refused to accede, on the ground that they had a mandate from the Comintern to go ahead. The mandate from the Comintern, however, lent itself to more than one interpretation. The minority claimed that it empowered the underground convention to decide whether or not to go ahead with the legal party. The majority contended that it had decided in favor of the legal party and merely gave the underground convention the function of putting the final touches on the preparations.

By now, every step was referred to Moscow for approval. One of the American representatives to the Comintern in 1921, Minor, tried to prove that the committee's majority enjoyed the full confidence of the Comintern. He also succeeded in demonstrating the extent of the Comintern's role in determining not only what should be done but how as well.

The American leadership had already fallen into the habit of sending a steady stream of telegrams to the Comintern. These telegrams kept the Comintern up to date on the latest developments relating to the proposed legal party, such as the committee's plans, the different elements involved in the organization, and the proportion of influence. Minor called it "fairly complete information." The telegrams were read by most members of the Comintern's highest body, the Presidium, in the presence of the two American representatives, Minor and Bedacht, and all expressed approval. But the Americans called attention to the fact that the plan omitted the underground convention before the legal party's organization. They protested that this was "a very bad mistake" and asked the Comintern to send a telegram telling the American leadership to delay arrangements for the legal party for a few weeks in order to enable the preliminary underground convention to take place. The Presidium agreed that it would be incautious to leave out the underground convention but hesitated to authorize such a telegram on the ground that the time was too short to change the plan. When the two Americans insisted, the telegram was sent, though not without some misgivings about changing arrangements on such short notice. This telegram from Moscow did not arrive in time, and another telegram was later received from the Comintern "exonerating" the Central Executive Committee of failure to comply with the "command" to hold the preliminary underground convention.[17]

Minor's report reveals that the practical operations of the Comintern in relation to its American section had taken on a definite character by 1921. The Comintern dealt with its American section as if it were a branch office. The local leaders were permitted a good deal of leeway in making plans and carrying them out, but the Moscow leaders wanted to be kept informed even about relatively minor details and reserved the right to make the final decisions.

The struggle over the underground convention showed that the two sides had reached the breaking point. One was entrenched in the rank and file and could afford to demand a "democratic" procedure. The other was entrenched in the leadership and was determined to draw in a new and broader rank and file, even if a large portion of the old one would be sacrificed. A showdown had to take place before a legal party could be launched.

The three leaders of the Left Opposition, Ballam, Dirba, and Ashkenudzie, were suspended by the majority of the Central Executive Committee on November 2, 1921.[18] The three submitted a written appeal to the Comintern. In Moscow, both factions frantically pulled wires to get a decision favoring one against the other.

A telegram from Moscow of November 14, 1921, brought good news for the legal-party partisans. It is worth giving in full for the peculiar flavor of the code used in these communications:

Telegram received. Stop. Shipment arranged so accounts will balance in a few days. Stop. Further ten thousand bid M. S. Epstein Company provided can do business daily. Stop. See Jewish customers about this and answer quick because immediate payment offered. Stop. Also you must raise ten quick for E. Daley to secure fifty quotation. Stop. Riley Company shipment made. Stop. Car arrived good condition. President chamber commerce sent you letter approving immediate manufacture new goods for open market declaring delay not permissible now.

Block and Co.[19]

The business of international communism was best expressed in the language of international business. In this telegram, "Block and Co." was the code name of the American representatives in Moscow. Lovestone subsequently interpreted the last sentence as the Comintern's instructions to go ahead with the immediate formation of the legal party. The "president [of the] chamber [of] commerce" was of course Zinoviev, and "new goods for open market" was the legal party. The reference to the "ten thousand bid" apparently refers to $10,000 offered by the Comintern for the publication of an American Communist daily organ in the Jewish language. It also seems clear that the Comintern offered $50,000 for the publication of an English daily newspaper if the American Communists were able to raise $10,000.[20]

The Comintern handed down a written decision on December 8 on the suspensions of the three minority members. This document was sent to the United States through a special "messenger," Minor, with a caution not to publish it. The decision found the minority guilty of "a serious and intolerable breach of discipline" and fully approved of the suspensions. It left room for their reinstatement with full membership rights if the rebels agreed to obey the new line.[21] Instead, the Left Oppositionists dared to declare the decision unsatisfactory and moved toward the organization of a rival Communist party. Minor appeared before a national conference called by the Opposition and read the Comintern's decision—to no avail.

The "Right" opposition, represented by the Workers' Council, which was not a homogeneous group, proved easier to handle. At one extreme was Salutsky, who was just beginning his outstanding career as a labor editor in the Amalgamated Clothing Workers Union. He was most determined to prevent the underground Communist party from controlling any new party. At the other extreme was Olgin, who had gone over to a Moscow-controlled conception of the American movement. As negotiations dragged on, the Workers' Council group tended to divide into two divergent tendencies, with Salutsky in the minority.

After the suspension of the "Left," the underground Communist leadership was able, in November 1921, to reach an agreement with the "Right."[22] Although some concessions were made on both sides, on the fundamental point at issue—the complete liquidation of the underground party—the Workers' Council gave way.[23] In return, the Communists gave the Workers' Council a much larger representation in the top leadership of the new legal party than its numerical strength justified. An agreement was also reached to publish a Jewish daily newspaper to rival the powerful daily organ of the Right Wing Socialists, the *Forward*. The first issue of the *Freiheit* (Freedom) appeared on April 22, 1922, nearly two years before the American Communists were able to put out a daily organ in English.[24] The agreement provided for an editor from each of the two groups, the Workers' Council choice going to Olgin.

The Workers party

The long-awaited legal organization, the Workers party of America, was born at a convention in the Star Casino, New York City, December 23–26, 1921.

The convention was thoroughly controlled by the underground Communists from the outset. Of the 94 official delegates, the Communist-controlled American Labor Alliance accounted for 47, the Workers' Council for 13, and remaining organizations for 34.[25]

The keynote speech was made by James P. Cannon of the illegal party's Central Executive Committee. But the Communists in control were thoroughly chastened ones. Gone were the fantasies of 1919, the dreams of power, the illusions of grandeur. Cannon talked as if the Communists had at last awakened from a nightmare and wanted everyone to know that they were conscious of the bitter reality:

> We have a labor movement that is completely discouraged and demoralized. We have an organized labor movement that is unable on any front to put up an effective struggle against the drive of destruction, organized by the masters. We have a revolutionary movement which, until this inspirational call for a Workers Party Convention, was disheartened, discouraged and demoralized.

As for the call itself, he thought it necessary to explain why it was so short.

> In our Conference Call you will notice we are not very verbose. We did not put in very many revolutionary words or foreign phrases, because that period is past and the time has come for action.

The same could be said about the party's constitution. The reason for existence of the new party was defined in a single sentence:

> Its purpose shall be to educate and organize the working class for the abolition of capitalism through the establishment of the Workers' Republic.[26]

What the program and the constitution of the Workers party left unmentioned was just as significant. There was nothing about Soviets, the dictatorship of the proletariat, or armed insurrection.

The indispensable condition of Communist control was threatened once. At the end of the first day, Salutsky rebelled against the domination of what he called the "subway party." About one-third of the delegates sympathetic to the Workers' Council met that night at Olgin's home to discuss whether to stay or to bolt the convention. Salutsky demanded a walkout on the ground that the underground Communist leadership would not leave the Workers party alone. But the majority of the group had gone too far. The new Communist line made it easier to swallow Communist control. The decision was to stay, and Salutsky himself agreed to go along with the majority, though he did not last long in the new party.[27]

When the Central Executive Committee was elected on the last day of the convention, the Workers' Council was rewarded with five of the seventeen seats.[28] Caleb Harrison, one of the few recruits from the Socialist Labor party, was named secretary with national headquarters in New York.[29] Foster's trade-union policy was adopted wholeheartedly.[30]

By means of the Workers party, the American Communists doubled their organizátional influence. The two biggest acquisitions were the Finnish and Jewish federations, which had stayed out of previous Communist set-ups. The new party also enabled Ludwig Lore, who was connected with the Workers' Council group, to get back temporarily into the good graces of the official Communists. In general, it gave every Communist sympathizer a pretext for leaving the sidelines without venturing all the way into the illegal party.

The Workers party was formed the same month that the Comintern coined the slogan of the "united front." It was not even a reasonable facsimile of a united front, but it was the best the American Communists could do for over a year. Bittelman was more nearly right when he called the Workers party a "transmission apparatus between the revolutionary vanguard of the proletariat and its less conscious and as yet non-revolutionary masses." [31] It was a legal extension of the illegal party rather than a united front with other independent workers' organizations.

The youngest Communists

One by-product of the Workers party was the first real Communist youth organization.

The delayed development of a youth organization was one of the paradoxes of the American movement. The Communist party's leaders were relatively young men. In 1921, Foster was forty, Ruthenberg thirty-nine, Bedacht thirty-six, Bittelman thirty-one, Browder and Gitlow thirty, and Lovestone a mere twenty-three. Early Communism had its greatest appeal for the twenty-to-forty-year age group; it did not fare so well above or below.

The first efforts to organize a Communist youth organization were abortive. A Left Wing secretary, Oliver Carlson of Michigan, had been elected at a mid-1919 convention of the Young People's Socialist League. After the Communist-Socialist split in September of that year, the League's executive committee voted to expel him, but he succeeded in calling an emergency convention in December at which the tables were turned. The organization's name was changed to the Independent Young People's Socialist League "affiliated with the Third International" and dedicated to the "principles of International Communism." However, this victory was short-lived. The splits among the older Communists carried over into the new youth organization with disastrous results. During the Palmer raids in 1920, efforts were made to set up an underground Young Communist League without much success. Two more years passed before the youth movement could recover from disorganization and repression.

The Young Communist League was organized at an underground convention at Bethel, Connecticut, on April 20, 1922, and a Young Workers League was formed at a "legal convention" in New York on May 13–15, 1922. For about a year, the Communist youth duplicated the legal and illegal organizations of the party.[32]

The American Communist youth movement has always been peculiar. In Communist theory, it should be broader and larger than the party. In the United States, the Young Communist League came into existence three years after the party and has been smaller and weaker organizationally. Yet the small Young Communist League born in 1922 provided the main reinforcements to the party's top leadership for the next two decades.[33]

20

The Manipulated Revolution

IF THE American Communist movement was born in 1919, it was reborn in 1921. The Communist movement of 1919–20 existed in a world of its own, which later Communists would have had trouble recognizing. But from 1921 on the whole future development became clearly marked out, the road ahead visible, the signposts familiar.

The Communists of 1919 believed piously in the principles of force and violence, the dictatorship of the proletariat, and the world revolution. They put these principles into practice by propagating them on any and all occasions, and by propagating almost nothing else. If they had to pay the price of illegality for the privilege, they solved the problem by making illegality a principle. After two years of preaching what they believed, they found themselves in the position of a typical radical sect—small, ingrown, harmless. Those who realized the real plight of the party tried to undo the damage by partially revolting against one of the principles—total illegality. But this partial revolt could not be carried out partially. The implications and repercussions were so far-reaching and fundamental that a new type of Communist movement had to develop out of it. The old type had reflected a period considered imminently revolutionary. The new type would reflect a revolution indefinitely postponed.

As in every struggle within a sect, there were fundamentalists and reformers.

The fundamentalists were not troubled by the fact that they were so few in numbers or that so many of them were foreign-born. This merely confirmed them in the belief that true revolutionaries were rare, and that native Americans were rarely true revolutionaries. Nor were they discouraged by their apparent weakness and isolation. This was the normal condition of true revolutionaries until the time came for an irrepressible revolutionary wave to swell up and sweep them into power. Meanwhile, it was up to them to prove that they were the only true revolutionaries by jealousy guarding the purity of their revolutionary principles. They looked inward because this decisive prerevolutionary struggle was conducted within the sect itself. They welcomed splits as the way to cast off foreign excrescences. They were impervious to setbacks and defeats because the final victory was guaranteed by their devotion to abstract principles.

The reformers were good enough Communists to protest against the slightest suggestion that they wanted to tamper with Communist principles. They proceeded as if they were merely changing the practical application of the accepted principles. The reformers wanted a mass party instead of an isolated sect, a party of action instead of a party of propaganda, a legal organization in addition to the illegal one, and a predominantly American party instead of a collection of foreign-language federations with a few American mouthpieces. The reformers insisted, as reformers always do, that the new means were the best, quickest, and only means of achieving the old end. They were righteously indignant when they were accused of betraying the true revolutionary faith. They believed sincerely that they were saving communism in America from hopeless sterility. Since the American reformers were encouraged and supported by the highest authorities in Moscow, including Lenin himself, they could hardly think of themselves as traitors to the cause.

If we compare the new line of the American Communists with the old line of the historic Left, we can judge more clearly the distance traveled.

The historic Left believed that the ultimate goal alone was worthy of the attention of real revolutionaries. Immediate demands constituted the stock in trade of middle-class reformists. Now one of the rising young Communist leaders wrote:

> We must also remember that the broad laboring masses never fight for general, abstract ultimate ideals. They struggle for immediate, concrete, tangible needs.

From this he concluded:

> We might talk ourselves blue in the face about our holy cause, about the wonders of Communism, about the necessity for shouldering guns against capitalism and yet not enhance the revolution by an iota. But let us talk to the workers about their long hours, their disemployment, their hardships and the why and wherefore of these, and they will be ready listeners and doers.[1]

Right Wing Socialists like Victor Berger and trade-union leaders like Samuel Gompers had made this discovery long ago. But their immediate demands and the Communists' immediate demands differed fundamentally, because Gompers accepted capitalism and the Communists did not. For the traditional Right Wing, the tactical use of immediate demands grew out of a long-range view of social reform. For the newly converted Communists, immediate demands aided and abetted a revolutionary purpose. This became a peculiarly Communist combination—old reformist means adapted to new revolutionary ends.

A basic Communist assumption made the new line seem more revolutionary than it proved to be. Though the Comintern was willing to admit the postponement of the Western revolution, it could not bring itself to believe that it would be postponed for long. In both Europe and the United States, the economic situation was dark enough to make the gloomiest prognostications seem plausible. For this reason, the Third Comintern Congress in 1921 thought it safe to make the following prognosis:

> The chief revolutionary characteristic of the present period lies in the fact that the most modest demands of the working masses are incompatible with the existence of capitalist society. Therefore, the struggle, even for

these very modest demands, is bound to develop into a struggle for communism.[2]

If this were true, the Communists could ask for immediate demands and get ultimate revolution. This reasoning was the theoretical justification for taking a different path to the same goal. It was, of course, utterly false. There was much more life left in the existing system, especially in its American form, than the Comintern foresaw. For the working masses, immediate demands would lead to more and greater immediate demands, not to the Communist revolution. But if struggles for higher wages, shorter hours, or better conditions did not necessarily lead to communism, they could and frequently did lead to more influence for Communists. Thus, wrong as their prognosis was, the Communists were able to boast of positive results from the new line.

The change of line also raised anew the age-old problem of leaders and masses.

According to the credo of the historic Left, the working class was inherently revolutionary. If the workers did not always behave like revolutionaries, the corrupting influence of other classes was responsible. Straight revolutionary propaganda was the best cure for insidious bourgeois vices. The old Socialists were filled with a touching faith in the ability of the masses to liberate themselves, if only their fundamental interests were made clear to them and a fighting spirit instilled in them.

For the first two years, the Communists more or less remained true to this well-established tradition. When it did not pay off, however, they became disillusioned. Bittelman put it somewhat bitterly:

All along we have been working contentedly on the theory that by spreading general Communist propaganda and building up active nuclei in the labor movement, the desired end will be achieved. This is a very simple theory. What has been its result? Almost complete failure.[3]

The new theory was more devious and roundabout. Its basic proposition was the idea that the workers could be made to learn from the struggle for immediate demands what they had failed to

THE MANIPULATED REVOLUTION

learn from pure revolutionary propaganda. One Communist writer explained it this way:

> The necessity of the revolutionary struggles for power must develop out of the hard knocks of the daily struggles for immediate demands. We may never succeed in teaching the workers theoretically the political character of their struggles. But what our abstract reasoning will not accomplish, the steady interference of the police power of the state in their daily struggles will.

According to this theory, an all-important difference separated the immediate demands of the Socialists and those of the Communists. For the former, they were everything; for the latter, they were merely stepping stones.

> The working class must travel the road of these immediate struggles to reach the battlefields of the struggle for power.[4]

The final step was fateful. The historic Left had no problem of concealment or subterfuge. It sought to make the revolution by direct, open, unequivocal revolutionary propaganda. For the Communists, this approach had lost its charm. Instead of gearing the masses to them, they were going to gear themselves to the masses. They would give the masses only as much as they thought the masses capable of swallowing. Now some things could not be divulged. The Communists had to dole out the truth in stages or installments, especially if it involved a dangerous subject like force and violence.

Bittelman tackled the question bluntly:

> The whole truth does not mean telling the workers, at every turn of the game, that the seizure of power will have to be accomplished by force of arms. The injection of the idea of armed force, whether as a means of defense or offense, at the *wrong* psychological moment can only harm the revolutionary movement. There are stages in the class struggle that do not call for the introduction of the idea of armed force. *Telling the workers the whole truth about a given situation does not mean giving the workers the full Communist program.* A Communist program is not a Bible to be brought to the workers always in full, with all its implications. It is a guide to action for the advanced guard of the working class—The Communist Party. It is to be applied in practice according to the demands of every particular situation.[5]

This theory was worked out by Foster in the trade-union field with disarming candor. In the spring of 1922, he said publicly:

> The American militant is most inexperienced. He has never dealt with masses. He does not even know how to arrange a meeting properly. He believes that the workers can be won over with talk. If he did less talking, if he kept his seat, and his mouth shut more often, and would do more work, his task would be easier. He must participate in the unions, and through day-by-day detail work through close association with the masses, convince the masses that he is a good union man, interested in their welfare.
>
> The idea was to use their control to put across their radical philosophy, not to use their radical philosophy to get control.
>
> The American workers are ripe for radical ideas. If the militants get control of the unions they can put their radical philosophy across very easily.
>
> The American worker will accept it by some complex form of reasoning something like this: He will say: "Well, John has got nutty ideas, but John is a good union man. He went to jail in the last strike. He works hard in the union. And if his ideas are good enough for him, they are good enough for me."
>
> Let the militants offer a practical program, participate in labor's everyday struggles with concrete demands, let them learn how to handle masses and his task of radicalizing the unions will be accomplished soon.[6]

The key word in this little speech, dutifully reported in the Communist press, was, of course, "control." If the Communists could not win control of unions as Communists, they could do so as good trade-unionists. When they won control as good trade-unionists, they were to make use of it as Communists. Radical philosophy was not the path to power; it was the reward of power. Consciously or unconsciously, Foster harbored a deep-seated contempt for both the Communists and the masses—for the Communists because they talked too much about the masses without knowing how to work with them; for the masses because they could be lured into accepting the leadership of men with "nutty ideas" for reasons that had nothing to do with those ideas.

Both as a syndicalist and as a Communist, Foster betrayed the same peculiar duality. He was temperamentally an extremist in politics, most at home in extremist movements. Yet his hunger for power and position brought out a strong opportunist streak in him. As a result, he was capable of veering sharply from extreme opportunism to extreme sectarianism, depending on which temporarily best served his interest.

Basically, the outlook of Foster in this phase was remarkably similar to that of Gompers. They were identical in their emphasis on the day-to-day, the practical, the concrete. But Gompers stopped there. He developed a philosophy of the practical and the concrete. Mistaken or not, his activity and his philosophy were consistent. He did not try to sell the workers one thing and give them another. Foster agreed with the Communists about a radical philosophy and he agreed with Gompers about practical activity. He reconciled the two by using practical activity to get control and control to put over the radical philosophy.

Foster was listened to because he was saying in trade-union terms what the Communists themselves were saying in political terms. The idea that the workers could not be trusted with the whole truth about the full Communist program and the idea that a radical philosophy was no help to win control of a working-class organization were closely related.

The Left Opposition failed to see that the new American line was part of a much larger phenomenon. A crucial decision had to be made on whether Western communism should become a sect or a mass organization. Because of the Communist preoccupation with power, the decision inevitably went in favor of a mass organization. Because of the contradictory tendencies inherent in the movement, it was not the last of such decisions. Whether to be a sect or a mass organization was a life-and-death question which recurred again and again in innumerable ways. The same people did not always answer it the same way. The two tendencies struggled against each other not only in the party but also within each individual Communist.

Both tendencies stemmed from Lenin, who, at different times and in equally characteristic pronouncements, came forth as a rigid sectarian and as an inspired opportunist. For many years before the

Russian Revolution, he was the leader of a small, isolated, impotent sect. Yet he was also the author of the bible of Communist opportunism, *"Left-Wing" Communism*. He demonstrated his greatest versatility after the Russian Revolution, when he proved capable of working with contradictory dogmas, stressing the dictates of orthodoxy or the drive to the masses as the need arose. This was a feat few of his followers could duplicate, and it is one of the reasons why Lenin stands out so high above all the others.

But Lenin could not work without dogmas. He was a Leftist dogmatically and he was a Rightist dogmatically. He was a dogmatic sectarian and a dogmatic opportunist. At any one time or in any one work, he appears to be absolutely rigid, static, uncompromising. It is only when the entire span of his life and body of his work is considered as a whole that he reveals himself to be anything but dogmatic. Such leaders, however, leave a very difficult heritage. Their followers find it much easier to imitate the dogmatic expression than to reproduce the undogmatic thinking.

There would have been much clearer thinking about the nature of communism if less attention had been paid to the Russian Revolution of 1917 and more attention to the revised version for the West which came into vogue four years later. The Russian Revolution owed its success to the exhaustion of a sick social system. The Bolsheviks did not invent the sickness of the social system or fabricate the revolution at the head of which they managed to place themselves. In the West, however, the Russian preconditions were lacking. The Communists had to give up the objective of revolution or try to make it another way. For a revolution of mass exhaustion they substituted a revolution of mass manipulation.

21

The Two-Way Split

THE Workers party caused another split in the American Communist movement.

Just before the split, one Communist leader wrote: "It cannot be denied that the Communist Party of America practically does not exist as a factor in the class struggle."[1] Another added: "We have virtually disappeared from the public scene."[2] The total number of American Communists was estimated by the Communists themselves at about 10,000.[3] Weak as the party was, it was capable of making itself weaker.

The split came after only eight months of "unity." Most of these months were spent preparing for the split. The majority of the official party's leadership had moved toward a break by suspending the three Left Opposition leaders. The Left Opposition countered by organizing itself as a caucus on a national scale. When the Workers party was launched without a preliminary underground convention, the caucus was ready to hit back by transforming itself into an independent party.

The split was consummated at an "emergency convention" of the Left Opposition early in January 1922. The 38 delegates claimed to represent 5000, or half of the former membership. Over 80 per cent of the Opposition came from the foreign-language federations.

The new organization refused to give up the old name. Again there were two underground parties in the field; both called themselves the Communist party of America; and both published organs called *The Communist*.[4]

The split seemed to put the Communist movement back where it had started from. The foreign-language federations again confronted the "Americans." To the federations, the split was a continuation of the fight against the Socialist party, the Communist Labor party, and the United Communist party. "The so-called Workers Party is a menace to the proletariat of America," their party's manifesto thundered. "It is a party of dangerous compromisers, opportunists and centrists, masking themselves as Communists. The [new] Communist Party of America calls upon all workers and workers' organizations to refuse to support or to join this prototype of the decadent Socialist Party—this aggregation of Compromisers, opportunists and centrists—this party of American Mensheviki called the Workers Party of America."[5]

The most serious objection against the Workers party turned on the old question of force and violence. The extremists were old-fashioned enough to take programs seriously. If a program did not promise the violent overthrow of the bourgeois state and the establishment of the proletarian dictatorship in the form of Soviet power, it could not pass muster with them. Since the program of the Workers party deliberately ignored these extreme formulas, it proved most vulnerable to fundamentalist criticism.

The promoters of the Workers party protested that they did not have the slightest intention of abandoning the principles of violent revolution or the dictatorship of the proletariat. Their Communist Party adopted "theses" after the split containing these words: "The overthrow of the capitalist system can only come through the violent overthrow of the capitalist state."[6] The question, as Bedacht put it, was whether it was necessary "to shout it from the housetops here, there, everywhere; now, tomorrow, anytime." No one believed more than he did in the inevitability of the violent overthrow of capitalism, he protested, but "when the open existence of the Communist party is at stake, then the insistence on this phrase in the program is little short of lunacy."[7] Minor wrote: "It is not necessary to write our program in language best suited to prosecutors. The object must be to make clear to those who join our Party, that such will be the inevitable development of the struggle and that the working class must be prepared to engage in the struggle accordingly. To establish the historical-political principle in the minds of the workers is the task of the program on this point. We don't have to use bucket-of-blood rhetoric just to show how brave we are."[8]

The Communist philosophy of violence has not been a static one, at least for public consumption. This dispute in 1922 represented the transition from open espousal of the inevitability of violence to a more guarded, implicit understanding of the same principle. The transitional phase was purely tactical in its motivation.

Whose comrades?

The cards were stacked against the Left Opposition because it never dared to question the ultimate authority of the Comintern. It attacked the program of the Workers party as if it were a purely American aberration, but it could not attack the Comintern for having really inspired it.

The underground extremists knew that the Comintern had ordered the American Communists to set up a legal organization. They were not opposed to it in principle, they insisted; they merely opposed the timing, the method, and the threat it held out of supplanting the illegal party. To prove that they were just as faithful followers of the Comintern's line as their rivals, they were obliged to set up their own legal organization.

A "legal apparatus," therefore, was formed by the Left Opposition at a conference in New York City on February 18, 1922. It adopted the name of "The United Toilers of America" and proceeded to publish the *Workers' Challenge* as its official organ. Largely recruited from the foreign-language federations, it boasted John J. Ballam, H. M. Wicks, and P. P. Cosgrove among its English-speaking mouthpieces.[9]

Each illegal Communist party, then, had its puppet organization—one the Workers party, the other the United Toilers.

Such factional struggles were by now automatically taken to Moscow for adjudication. This particular case was tried in Moscow in March 1922. The defense was represented by Katterfeld and Bedacht of the old official party. The prosecution was represented by Ballam of the Left Opposition's new party. The Comintern appointed a "commission" consisting of Heinrich Brandler, a German; Mátyás Rákosi, a Hungarian; Ottomar V. Kuusinen, a Finn; Boris Souvarine, a Frenchman; and Boris Reinstein. Ballam never had a chance. Not a single representative of a foreign party in the Comintern supported him. Only Katayama, the Japanese, gave him any sympathy at all, and even he opposed Ballam's position on the legal party. To Ballam's consternation, the Comintern leaders were little impressed with his claim to represent a majority of the American Communists. He wrote home:

They care nothing for majorities. They will support a minority who will carry out their policies against a majority that is opposed to them. They consider the greatest crime against the International is splitting. They say, "You report 5,000 comrades in America, whose comrades are they? Dobin's, Moore's and Henry's?* or are they Lenin's, Trotsky's and Bucharin's? You must obey the discipline first."[10]

Whose comrades are they? It would be hard to find words filled with deeper meaning for the future of American communism. Ballam came to Moscow representing a majority of American Communists. He tried to play this majority as his trump card in the game of power. But the Comintern did not play the game according to the ordinary rules of majorities and minorities. Not that it crudely refused to recognize the existence of a majority; it refused to recognize the staying power of an anti-Comintern majority. It proceeded on the assumption that every Communist everywhere owed his primary loyalty to the ruling power in Moscow, not to his own party. It sought to instil in every Communist leader a nervous awareness of

---

* Pseudonyms of Dirba, Ballam, and Ashkenudzie.

the provisional character of his leadership. It could make and unmake majorities because no majority could hold out against its will. It could make and unmake leaders because no leader could survive against its displeasure. Majorities evaporated and leaders disappeared as soon as the Comintern made loyalty to itself the decisive issue.

The Comintern ruled against Ballam's "majority." It ordered them to go back into the old party and turn over all "records, addresses, connections and properties" within sixty days. The decision was one of the most peremptory in the early history of the American party: "All members that do not comply with the instructions within two months from the time that they are sent out by the C.E.C. of the C.P. of A. stand outside of the C.P. of A. and therefore also out of the Comintern." [11] This ultimatum was somewhat softened by a concession to the extremists. The official American party was scheduled to hold a convention that summer. It was "instructed" to reinstate the oppositionists with full membership rights and to give them the right to take part in the election of delegates to the convention, if they applied for reinstatement within the two months' time limit. Since the intervening period was so short, the official party was also instructed to postpone the convention if necessary in order to give the rebels a chance to comply with the offer.

Faced with the full force of the Comintern's authority, Ballam capitulated. Together with Katterfeld for the victorious faction and Rákosi for the Comintern, he signed a "declaration" promising "to do all" to carry out the decisions.[12]

"Block and Co." hastened to send the good news to the "home office" in New York. One of their delightful "business" cablegrams read:

Henry, Curtis Dow Company * instructed quit using our firm name and trademark. They must dissolve and rejoin our company immediately or lose their stock. John [Ballam] is wiring them to quit competing and attacking our business. You must accept them without prejudice and postpone shareholders conference so they can participate.

* Other pseudonyms for Ballam, Dirba, and Ashkenudzie.

The "shareholders' conference" was, of course, the forthcoming party convention. A follow-up cable served notice that two factional representatives were coming back with final instructions for the convention.

Both salesmen returning home with full instructions from Board [of] Directors. Postpone stockholders meeting until they arrive. Acknowledge receipt.[13]

Ballam proved his loyalty to the Comintern by touring the United States in favor of an agreement which he admittedly considered unjustified. His former colleagues refused to go along with his agreement on the ground that the Comintern had been misinformed and misled. They did not dare to challenge the final authority of the Comintern. They had to pretend that they were challenging the authority of the Comintern's informants.

Geese and Liquidators

The American Communist movement of 1922 was split in still another way.

Those who stayed in the old organization and identified themselves with the Workers party were far from agreed among themselves. In fact, they soon found themselves so far apart that a fully formed split developed inside as well as out.

In the code of the underground, the official Communist party was known as "No. 1"; the Workers party as "No. 2," or "L.P.P." (Legal Political Party); the Trade Union Educational League as "X." There were so many code names for different groups in and around the party that the papers and documents of this period cannot be understood without a key for deciphering them.[14]

The Workers party was organized with the most exemplary speed, simplicity, and efficiency. All members of the Communist party simply enrolled in the Workers party. For the most part, the leadership of the two parties was interchangeable. There was so much duplication that the underground instructions on organizing the Workers Party read: "Distr. Comm. of No. 1 will function as Distr. Comm. of No. 2, except where it is advisable or necessary to have others." For the benefit of the district organizers who had to play dual roles, the instructions went: "Where DO's of No. 1 and No. 2 are the same, DO No. 1 shall make arrangements to take care of No. 2. Special attention must be given to the matter of files, records, literature and connections, so as not to expose the connections between No. 1 and No. 2 in writing." Since the same people could not be in two different places nor pretend to be officials of two different parties at once, the following precaution was taken: "The meetings of No. 1 and No. 2 shall be held in accordance with previous instructions, alternately, each week." [15]

These convenient arrangements created an inconvenient problem. On paper, the difference between the two parties was clear. Decisions were made underground by the illegal Communist party. They were to be carried out in the open by the Workers party. In practice, however, this division of labor did not give the Communist party enough to do. Once the decisions were made, it was relegated to a shadowy existence.

The political climate in the United States had changed so much that the new organization had little to fear from government persecution. Virtually everything the Communist party did furtively on a small scale, the Workers party was able to do openly on a larger scale. It held public meetings with impunity. It published a newspaper. It was not barred from elections. Those Communists who did not play a leading role in the Workers party became jealous of those Communists who did. At the same time, the Communists in control of the Workers party chafed at the control of the underground leadership or saw no sense in the duplication of functions.

The factional struggle that arose out of this situation was like a parody of the situation which arose among the Russian revolutionaries after the ill-fated revolution of 1905. The American Communists even used the same term of abuse.

The problem of legal and illegal organizations in Czarist Russia had been one of the reasons for the increasing rift between the Right and Left wings—the Mensheviks and Bolsheviks—of the Russian Social Democratic party. To the former, the legal mass organizations that had sprung up during the revolution held out the best hope for the future. To exploit these organizations fully, the Mensheviks wanted to make them the basis of a single party of the entire working class, uniting all different groups and tendencies. The Bolsheviks, especially Lenin, were scandalized. Lenin recognized the usefulness of legal mass organizations but mainly as a "cover" for the operations of the underground movement. He hurled one of his choicest epithets, "liquidators," at the advocates of the broad labor party, on the ground that such a party implied an end to the independent existence of the Social Democratic party.[16]

These relics of the post-1905 Russian revolutionaries came to life in the American Communist movement after the formation of the Workers party. Lenin's old epithet, "liquidators," was resurrected to stigmatize those who saw no further necessity for the illegal party.

Ruthenberg and Bedacht emerged as the strongest spokesmen for the American Liquidators. Ruthenberg was released from prison in the spring of 1922 and replaced Harrison as secretary of the legal Workers party.[17] With Bedacht, he proceeded to draw up a statement that adopted the most extreme position for the "liquidation" of the underground Communist party. They proposed that the Workers party should be transformed into an open Communist party and the dual set-up eliminated. Though they ruled out an illegal party, they did not rule out illegal work. They provided for "an illegal apparatus for the conduct of such work as cannot be carried on openly." Since no legal party could advocate "armed insurrection," they fought to keep it out of the program.[18]

The opposition's peculiar name—the "Geese"—went even further back into history. It was bestowed on them by the sharp-tongued Lovestone, because they cackled so much about saving the party, like the legendary geese that had saved Rome.[19] The Goose position was stated in "theses" by Israel Amter (J. Ford) and Abraham Jakira (A. Dubner). Under certain circumstances, they conceded, the Workers party could be transformed into an open Communist party.

THE TWO-WAY SPLIT

They refused, however, to tolerate the idea of giving up the underground party. Even if an open Communist party became possible, they insisted on maintaining the underground party as the "directing and controlling body." They foresaw, in effect, two Communist parties, a legal one and an illegal one, with the latter making all the important decisions in advance.[20]

The winning formula was Minor's work. It came down heavily on all sides of the question. It agreed with the Liquidators that an open, legal Communist party was desirable and also agreed with the Geese that a legal party had to include the "violent overthrow of the capitalist state" in its program. It permitted the Communists to operate openly with a "restricted program" and insisted on preserving the underground intact indefinitely.

The last and most interesting section reads:

The underground machinery of the Communist Party is not merely a temporary device to be liquidated as soon as the Communist Party with its full program can be announced in the open. The underground machinery is for permanent use. It is not a machinery to be used only on emergency occasions. It is for constant use. It must continue to operate not only while a legal party operates with restricted program, but also at all times, before and after the Communist Party with a full Communist program shall exist in the open. There is never a time, previous to the final overthrow of the Capitalist State, when a truly revolutionary party does not have to perform a considerable amount of work free from police knowledge and interference. The Communist Party will never cease to maintain its underground machinery until after the establishment of the dictatorship of the proletariat in the form of the Workers Soviet Republic.[21]

On balance, the position officially adopted in the summer of 1922 represented a victory of the Geese over the Liquidators. At this time, the total membership of the Communist party amounted to about 5000 or 6000,[22] of which a majority probably supported the "Geese." [23] Both the Liquidators and the Geese met in separate caucuses as fully formed factions. The chief figures in the Goose caucus were Katterfeld, Wagenknecht, Minor, Jakira, Amter and Lindgren. They were joined by Gitlow, who was released from prison a few days after Ruthenberg and needed more time to readjust to the freer atmosphere outside. Ruthenberg, the Liquidators' tower of strength, was supported by Bedacht and Lovestone. The so-called trade union group, represented by Foster, Browder, and Dunne, sympathized with the Liquidators but were too new to the movement to carry much weight in the argument.

If the American Communist movement did nothing else in 1922, it succeeded in setting something of a record in splits. Four parties have to be disentangled—two calling themselves Communist, both underground, and their two satellites, the United Toilers and the Workers party, both above ground. One of the underground Communist parties contained two factions, the Geese and the Liquidators, virtually equivalent to parties within a party. If the reader has not been slightly confused by all this, he cannot be sure that he has fully recaptured the Communist atmosphere in this peculiar period.

22

The Raid

AGAIN the American Communist movement found itself in one of those demoralizing factional struggles from which it could not extricate itself alone.

The stage was set for the first plenipotentiary from Moscow. The mission of Fraina, Scott, and Katayama in 1921 had not been entrusted with the same full powers. These three had originally come from the United States and could not dictate to their old associates. The first fully accredited Comintern representative with no previous tie to the American party enjoyed a much more exalted status.

The decision to send such a representative came during the negotiations with Ballam and Katterfeld in Moscow. The news was broken to the Americans in a letter of March 30, 1922: "The Communist International sends its plenipotentiary representative to America, whose task will be to help you in overcoming the still existing difficulties. We already had to contend with even greater obstacles than yours in some countries, and have learned to overpower them." [1]

This plenipotentiary representative was Professor H. Valetski (or Walecki), a mathematician by profession, long active in the Polish revolutionary movement. As an adherent of Karl Radek against Rosa Luxemburg in the prewar split of the Polish movement, he was an old hand at factional warfare.[2] Gitlow describes him as "a rather aristocratic Polish intellectual, who, notwithstanding his origin, looked like the American cartoonist's idea of a Russian Bolshevik—hooked nose, disheveled mop of hair on his head, an unkempt and unruly beard, looking rather ludicrous in the ill-fitting white linen suit that accentuated the angularity of his frame. But you could not help liking and respecting him, once you saw his eyes, sparkling with intelligence, wisdom, wit, and sheer human charm."[3] Bedacht recalls him as "a well-educated, jolly person around the fifties."[4] Evidently he won the respect of all the American factions.

Valetski was accompanied by two others, Joseph Pogany, a Hungarian, and Boris Reinstein, the former Buffalo dentist. Pogany came along ostensibly to work in the Hungarian federation of the American party, and Reinstein nominally represented the Profintern, though Valetski was the only one vested with special authority from the Comintern. They arrived in July 1922, a month before the postponed convention, and plunged immediately into the thick of the factional struggle. Valetski adopted the *nom de guerre* of "Brooks," Pogany that of "Lang," and Reinstein that of "Davidson."

We have the minutes of the meetings of the Central Executive Committee of July 26–28, 1922, convened on the arrival of the three envoys from Moscow.[5] They enable us to watch at close range the way the first Comintern representative functioned.

The first thing on the order of business was a report by Valetski on the purpose of his mission. In a formal declaration the following day, he called upon the factions "immediately to take proper steps for the liquidation of the factional regime and to create real guarantees for party unity which is so extremely endangered." The response to this by the Americans ranged from the obeisant to the obsequious. The agenda for the coming convention, drawn up before Valetski's appearance, was set aside. Minor made the motion to have a new committee of three, including Valetski, revise the agenda. Minor and Lovestone tried to outdo each other in seconding Valetski's plans to bring back the opposition. Minor even invited Valetski to formulate the "motion on the Opposition" for the committee, a step that went too far for Valetski. Minor moved to accept a recommendation by

THE RAID 365

Valetski to appoint a new "commission" to write "theses" on the "relations between #1 and #2." Lovestone came back with an amendment to an amendment making a place for Valetski on the commission. And so it went for three days, whenever any question of special interest to Valetski arose.

The next three weeks were devoted to preparations for the underground convention. Valetski virtually took charge. One faction tried to use a cable from Moscow to get the convention postponed. The other faction cried out indignantly against the "maneuver." Valetski ruled against the postponement on the ground that it would merely make matters worse. He was determined to come to the convention itself with ready-made resolutions to which all factions would be committed in advance. An "Adjustment Commission," unofficially called the "Disarmament Commission," made up of five representatives from each tendency plus the three men from Moscow, was entrusted with this task. After a dozen meetings, Valetski succeeded in extracting ten "unanimous" resolutions from the commission.

He described his methods in his own report to the Comintern: "I did not assume the role of a pacifier or arbiter, but, on the contrary, openly combatted everything that in my opinion represented witch-hunting or a political judgment or standpoint, in the Theses published. On the one hand, I particularly attacked the 'optimistic' estimation of the possibilities of political development, as expressed by Marshall [Bedacht] and Damon [Ruthenberg], which ignored the growing sharpness of the class struggle in the country and thereby gave rise to illusions that led to charges of 'liquidation.' On the other hand, I pointed out the falsity of the 'illegalistic' conception of the role of the Party in the Theses of Ford [Amter] and Dubner [Jakira], which was in opposition to facts as they are and also contradicted our Congress Theses on this subject." [6]

On the eve of the convention, Valetski had reason to be satisfied. Both factions had promised to behave themselves and support the made-to-order resolutions of the "Disarmament Commission."

Special Agent K-97

Everyone was ready for the underground convention, including the Department of Justice's favorite secret agent.

Francis A. Morrow was a short, slight man of nondescript appearance. Not quite forty years old, he seemed prematurely middle-aged, chiefly because of his graying hair. He lived with his wife and two daughters in Camden, New Jersey. He worked at the local shipyard as a shipfitter, an undeniably proletarian occupation.

Some time in 1919, Morrow began to work in his spare time for a new employer, the Department of Justice, as Special Agent K-97. He was paid only $1 a day at first, then $2, and at the height of his success $5.

The Department of Justice assigned him to keep in touch with radical organizations. For about a month or two, he belonged to the Socialist party, then in the throes of the original split. After the Communist party was formed, he switched over to it early in 1920. For a time, he devoted two nights a week to his Communist activity, one to the meeting of an English-speaking group of 12 to 15 members in Philadelphia, the other to a study class. Like all the others, he adopted a party name; he was known as "Comrade Day."

After the Communist party of America was formed at the unity convention in May 1921, he formed his own group in Camden. It consisted of Comrade Day, his wife, his son-in-law, and two friends, both pledged to help the Department of Justice. Since this group of five was the only one in Camden, Comrade Day became a section organizer.

His ability and reliability soon earned him special recognition. The local party leadership learned to count on him. He was asked to do more and more important jobs and fill more and more important posts. When the district committee needed a new secretary, Comrade Day's merits were rewarded with one of the highest posts in the district.

Meanwhile, he was sending the Department of Justice a steady

THE RAID

stream of reports and documents. One of these reports brought him to the attention of the highest authorities in the Department. It revealed the secret code then used by the underground leadership with which to communicate with the district organizers, who were the only ones authorized to possess the key to the code.

The secretary of the Communist party's district committee made it his business to be on the closest and friendliest terms with the district organizer. One day, the latter had somewhat too much to drink and pulled a piece of paper out of his pocket. It was an application blank for a United States postal money order. It was also the key to the secret code. As K-97 peered over his shoulder, the tipsy organizer permitted him to help in deciphering a message.

The special agent's report to the General Intelligence Division of the Bureau of Investigation of the Department of Justice the following day carefully explained the relation between a United States postal money order and the secret code of the Communist underground. The messages were written in the form of a series of arithmetical fractions. In each fraction, the numerator represented a line of type in the printed matter on the back of the money-order blank, and the denominator represented a particular letter in that line. Anyone caught with the money order had nothing to fear.

By the summer of 1922, K-97 was the key link in the chain of government informers and spies in the Communist movement. As the time for the underground convention approached, he was ordered to get himself elected as a delegate. As usual, he succeeded in carrying out his order, though this time by a narrow margin. The Philadelphia-Camden district convention was entitled to two delegates. In the voting, Comrade Day came in third, which made him the first alternate. Fortunately for him, a last-minute change was made to send three delegates from the district instead of two and he slipped in as the third.

Only one flaw spoiled this latest success. The convention was planned with such painstaking secrecy that the delegates were not told in advance where it was going to take place. Instead, a complex route was worked out with several destinations at each of which they were to be told how to get to the next one. As a result, K-97 was unable to inform the Department of Justice where the convention was going to take place, and no advance preparations for raiding it were possible.

Comrade Day and the other two delegates were instructed to attend a district convention of the legal Workers party in Philadelphia on a Sunday, August 13, 1922. There, a trusted representative of the underground leadership told them to proceed to an address in Cleveland. Another representative in Cleveland directed them to take a boat to Detroit. The fourth destination was Grand Rapids. It was now three days later and the party had increased to fourteen.

In Grand Rapids, Comrade Day and the others were given train tickets to St. Joseph, Michigan. Before leaving Grand Rapids, he managed to send a letter home. He arrived at the final destination the night before the opening of the convention and thereafter was completely cut off from any communication with the outside world.

The information in K-97's letter was rapidly transmitted to William J. Burns, then head of the Bureau of Investigation. From Washington, a message marked "urgent" went out to the head of the Bureau's Chicago office, Jacob Spolansky: "Secret convention of Communist Party now in progress somewhere in vicinity of St. Joseph, Michigan. Proceed at once to locate same and keep under discreet surveillance."

The hunter and the hunted were curiously alike. Spolansky himself was a Russian immigrant. He had founded the first Russian newspaper in Chicago before World War I. As a former sympathizer of the Russian revolutionary movement, he was intimately acquainted with the Russian Left Wing, including such Chicago figures as Gruzenberg-Borodin. Spolansky changed sides politically after the Bolsheviks came to power. He refused to support them and the circulation of his paper began to drop sharply. The swing of the Russian Left Wing community to the Bolsheviks forced him to sell the paper at a heavy loss. He was recruited into the Intelligence Branch of the United States Army in 1918 and transferred to the Bureau of Investigation of the Department of Justice the following year. He specialized in hunting the American Communist movement from the moment it was born.

Now Spolansky sprang into action. With another special agent, Edward Shanahan, he made a dash for a train to St. Joseph. They still did not know the exact location of the Communist convention but they were hot on the trail.

The Bridgman convention

About fifteen miles from St. Joseph was a quiet little village named Bridgman, with a railway station and a few homes. Less than a mile from Bridgman in the hills near Lake Michigan was the sprawling farm of Karl Wulfskeel, called Forest House, with a large, old-fashioned main house and several cottages scattered in a nearby grove of trees. The lake, woods, and hills made it most picturesque. The Wulfskeels used to make ends meet by turning the farm into a summer resort.

This pleasant site was chosen for the last underground convention of the Communist party of America because the Communists had successfully held a secret convention in Bridgman two years earlier. The Wulfskeels thought that they were playing host to a "singing society" on a week-long outing. As groups of delegates began to appear in Bridgman and make their way to the Wulfskeel farm, the strange assortment of accents and faces mildly surprised the townspeople.

The Communists took the most extreme precautions to prevent discovery. Lookouts were placed on the surrounding hills. Others made periodic reconnaissances of the village. A strict and detailed set of rules was drawn up for the benefit of the delegates. They had to rise at six in the morning and retire at ten in the evening. They could not leave the grounds, talk to strangers, take notes, keep incriminating documents on their persons, mail letters, or bathe in Lake Michigan except at certain periods. A committee enforced these rules.

The meetings of the convention were held in a hollow in the midst of the woods with hills rising on all sides. Tables for officers and stenographers stood in the center of the clearing. A tent was filled with typewriters, mimeograph machines, and records. Delegates sat on benches made of wooden planks laid on cement blocks. During the night sessions, a lantern hung from a nearby tree provided a dim, flickering light. As crickets chirped, the delegates' voices rose higher and higher in factional arguments.

The first session was held on August 17. Spolansky and Shanahan arrived in St. Joseph two days later. When the local sheriff was asked where about eighty people might be congregated for a secret meeting, he immediately guessed that Bridgman was the likeliest place. There the local postmaster was equally helpful. He informed them that the train had brought in "a bunch of foreign-looking people" who had gone off in the direction of Lake Michigan.

The two sleuths wasted no time but went out to hunt for the meeting place that night. As they wandered around in the woods between the farm and the lake, a heavy rainstorm descended. They pushed the search until the small hours of the morning without finding the right road and then returned to their hotel in Bridgman soaked to the skin, slightly frustrated.

Early the next morning, they went out prowling again, this time disguised in overalls. Just as the delegates had finished eating breakfast and were standing around in discussion groups, Spolansky and Shanahan put in an appearance. They went up to the pump, asked Mrs. Wulfskeel for a drink of water, and chatted with her for a few minutes about renting a room. Spolansky looked around carefully for the best way to stage a raid and spied some familiar faces. One of them was that of William Z. Foster.

Unknown to Spolansky, however, Foster had also caught a glimpse of him. As the two agents walked back through the woods to the town, they saw Charles Krumbein trailing them. Two more government agents arrived in Bridgman as reinforcements. At the convention, an argument broke out whether to stay or flee. The Comintern representatives decided in favor of an orderly retreat.

The final preparations for the flight were made in the woods in the dead of night. Whispered orders for the departure were communicated to the delegates. The highest priority was given to the

THE RAID

Comintern representatives, then came those immediately threatened with jail sentences or former prisoners, after them the aliens, and finally a group of American citizens. The latter were given the responsibility of getting rid of the convention's records. Couriers were sent to Bridgman and St. Joseph to hire cars for the getaway.

Meanwhile, Spolansky was marshaling his forces for the raid. They consisted of the four government agents, the local sheriff, and about twenty hastily mobilized townspeople. They attacked on the morning of August 22. To their disappointment, most of the delegates had succeeded in getting away the previous night. Only seventeen, including Ruthenberg, who had lingered behind to burn and bury incriminating documents, were left. They surrendered without resistance and were locked up in the county jail in St. Joseph. Another hour and they would have escaped, too.

One of the prisoners was K-97. When arrested, he gave his name as "Francis Ashworth." While Spolansky was questioning prisoners, one of the special agents whispered to him that "Francis Ashworth" claimed to be the redoubtable K-97. The slight little man convinced Spolansky of his identity by drawing a rough map showing where the records of the convention had been buried. Two agents were dispatched to the spot and started digging. First they brushed away an eight-inch layer of leaves. Then they hit a layer of sand. Finally, they struck some heavy tar paper. Beneath the tar paper were two sugar barrels full of documents. The barrels contained a registration of all the delegates, checks, instructions from Moscow, texts of the speeches, and an assortment of similarly revealing papers.

What to do with K-97 presented Spolansky with something of a problem. Spolansky telephoned for instructions to Director Burns who told him to keep K-97 locked up. When the master spy was finally released, his fellow prisoners were still kept in ignorance of his role. One of the deputies who happened to be a doctor swathed him in bandages in order to enable him to pretend that he had been beaten and that he had gained his freedom by signing an agreement not to prosecute the agents for assault.

Spolansky was still determined to track down those delegates who had missed the Bridgman raid. He caught up with another group of sixteen, including William Z. Foster and Earl Browder, at a meeting in Chicago. Late in December 1922, the list of witnesses in Foster's trial was made public. It contained the name of Francis A. Morrow. For the first time the Communists realized that Comrade Day, Francis Ashworth, Francis A. Morrow, and K-97 were the same man. He was the star witness the following April in Foster's trial which resulted in a hung jury of 6 to 6. Foster later discovered that he owed his good fortune to a member of the Daughters of the American Revolution. Much to his surprise, she proved most sympathetic to the defense appeal for freedom of speech. Ruthenberg was sentenced to five years' imprisonment a month later, but he was freed on appeal and died before the case was closed. The rest of the Bridgman defendants were never tried, though the cases were not dropped until 1933.

At the trials, K-97 demonstrated a phenomenal memory. But a few names proved too much for him. Instead of Valetski, he incorrectly identified the mysterious plenipotentiary, "Brooks," as "Arnold Losovsky," thereby presenting the head of the Profintern with a new first name as well as an imaginary trip to Michigan. "Lang" (Joseph Pogany) and "Albright" (Bertram D. Wolfe) stumped him completely.

K-97's public testimony exhausted his usefulness as a spy in the Communist movement. That there was no shortage of informers, however, was demonstrated at Foster's trial. Ruthenberg was questioned about a complete report in possession of the government of a secret meeting of the Communist leadership in New York seven months after the Bridgman raid. He had to admit that the report was substantially correct. The incident seemed to confirm an insistent rumor in radical circles that the Department of Justice had a secret agent in the Central Executive Committee of the Communist party.[7]

Sauce for the Geese

For the most part, the Goose caucus came out ahead at the unfinished Bridgman convention.

The convention represented a party of only about 5000–6000 members. Of these, 500 at most were "American comrades," as Ruthenberg and Bedacht put it. A mere 5 per cent were actively engaged in trade-union work.[8]

Valetski dominated the proceedings. He made the first important address on the "World Situation and the Comintern." He delivered the report of the "Disarmament Commission." Only two other items on the agenda were reached before the raid—a report by Foster on trade-union work and the Executive Secretary's report by Lovestone. Otherwise, most of the time was spent in wrangling for organizational control. For the first time an American Communist convention considered it necessary to appoint a "Presidium," in imitation of the Comintern's set-up in Moscow. Since each faction was determined to control the Presidium or prevent the other one from controlling it, the convention came to a standstill. Valetski, as usual, was called upon to break the deadlock. He agreed to become the thirteenth member of the Presidium with the deciding vote. "Several days [were] lost through this sort of debates and endless caucus meetings, which, as a rule, paid no heed to reality—not only no attention to the big reality, but not even to the trifling immediate realities of the convention itself," he wearily reported to the Comintern.[9]

It was clear from the outset that the Goose caucus could count on a safe lead over the Liquidators. In the vote for temporary chairman, the Geese won by a margin of 22 to 18. A few unattached delegates, like Bertram D. Wolfe, threatened the Geese's control by merging with the Liquidators. Wolfe had spent the underground period in San Francisco, far from the main centers of American factionalism.[10] The gap between the two main factions became so small that the Geese once won by one vote—23 to 22.[11] Since Francis A. Morrow, alias Comrade Day, alias Francis Ashworth, alias

K-97, had with the unerring instinct of a secret agent attached himself to the more extreme Goose caucus, the real credit for the victory belonged to him.

Valetski himself tried valiantly to stay out of the clutches of all the factions and caucuses. He played the role of the impartial arbiter who appeased the Geese by criticizing the Liquidators and appeased the Liquidators by criticizing the Geese. One of his "unanimous" resolutions, a Solomonic judgment on the "underground and open work," tested his diplomatic agility to the utmost. It was made up of three parts, so deftly arranged that they faced in all directions at once. The first part was written to win over the Geese: "1. The Communist Party of America must continue to exist as an underground party." The second part was written to pay off the Liquidators: "2. Its main task consists in the open work, especially through the L.P.P. [legal political party] and the trade unions." The third part was written to leave the future open for any contingency: "3. Should conditions change and the possibility of an open Communist Party arise, then a convention of the Communist Party alone can decide." The Bridgman formula was "Strong underground organization, but the center of gravity in the open work." [12]

The convention ended abruptly with the election of a new Central Executive Committee. All other crises paled before this one. The Geese demanded a clear majority of six to three. The Liquidators threatened to stay off the committee altogether on this basis. Valetski threw his weight behind the Geese on the ground that a majority of only one or two would not sufficiently discourage the future struggle for control. He advocated a majority of three for the Geese, and compulsory participation of the Liquidators. In the end, a new executive committee of twelve was named, including two proposed by both caucuses, six by the Geese, three by the Liquidators, and one representing the Young Communist League. Lovestone, a Liquidator, was first replaced by Katterfeld, a Goose, who was in turn succeeded by Jakira, another Goose.

The Bridgman raid came at a most unfortunate moment for the advocates of an open Communist party. The Department of Justice seemed to have provided a decisive argument in favor of remaining underground.

Left to themselves, the American Communists would surely have decided that it was no time to give up the illegal party. Yet the opposite course was adopted almost immediately after the Bridgman convention. The Americans were not left to themselves.

23

The Transformation

THE united front gave the Comintern trouble on both sides of the Atlantic.

The European Communists greeted the new line with outraged innocence. They were appalled at the idea of denouncing their enemies in the labor movement as traitors one day and making overtures to them the next. The fact that it was only supposed to be a tactical maneuver did not reassure them. Many of them had become Communists in rebellion against just such tactical maneuvers. They were confronted with a dilemma that was to become peculiarly characteristic of the Communist movement: it had recruited them on the basis of one policy and then told them to carry out another.

The great majority of the French Communist party at first refused to have anything to do with the united front. In Germany, Italy, Norway, and elsewhere, a large portion of the movement also rebelled. The Comintern spent most of 1922 forcing these parties into line. The greatest pressure was put on the French party. French representatives came to Moscow to engage in long, acrimonious disputes with the Russian leaders of the Comintern. Two representatives from Moscow, one of whom was Dmitri Z. Manuilsky, a longtime power in the Comintern, were sent to Paris. The French leadership was cast out and a new one more amenable to Moscow's orders installed. Only one-third of the French party's original membership remained to carry out the new line.[1]

In essence the Comintern met the new problem in the old way.

When the Comintern was formed in 1919, the enemy stood on the Right and splits were the order of the day. In every country and party, irrespective of national traditions or local conditions, disunity prevailed. Two years later, the enemy had shifted to the Left and the united front was the order of the day. Again, in every country and party, irrespective of national traditions or local conditions, "unity" prevailed. The tactics changed; the method remained the same.

The Comintern had not been able to do much under the old line. The organization was too new, and communications too difficult. The change to the united front was, as Zinoviev put it, "really the first large-scale international campaign which the Executive [of the Comintern] tried to carry out." [2] In effect, the Comintern's vital precedents for the future were set in establishing the new line. Franz Borkenau has pointed out that "the period of the united-front policy, paradoxically, was a period of the growth of rigid centralization of the Comintern under the lead of Moscow." [3] The paradox for the Communists in each country consisted of a loosening up of the relationship to non-Communists and a tightening up of the relationship to the Comintern. The first was a short-term tactical maneuver. The second was a long-range organizational reality. Any change of line would have served the same organizational purpose.

Toward the Labor party

Initially, the American Communists reacted to the united front evasively.

Unlike many European Communists, the Americans did not go so far as to accuse the Comintern of betraying its own revolutionary principles. The Americans tried to hold back on more cautious grounds and chose to think of the united front as a European tactic inapplicable at home. "The basis for a United Political Front which will embrace the working masses has not yet been created in the United States," said the first theses of the Workers party on the new line.[4]

With their long antipolitical tradition, the American Communists found the political aspect of the united front the most troublesome.

In the guise of the "Workers' League" the Communists participated for the first time in an election in New York City in November 1921. It was an abortive, half-hearted effort. Gitlow, then serving his jail sentence, was put up for mayor and promptly ruled off the ballot by the Board of Elections.[5]

The Communists began to take elections more seriously the following year. The question of candidates was now complicated by the newly injected problem of the united front. Concretely, the Communists had the choice of running their own candidates in the name of the Workers party or making some gesture of uniting with the Socialists on whom they had lavished for the past three years their most insulting denunciations. The issue flared up in New York in anticipation of the gubernatorial election campaign of 1922.

At the first general membership meeting of the Workers party in April, for which the party organ claimed an attendance of over 500, two groups emerged. One came out for an "electoral United Front." The other wanted to limit the united front to economic struggles and opposed an electoral united front on the ground that it would mean "the destruction of the movement—the abdication of the party to the Socialists." The second group enjoyed the support of Weinstone, then executive secretary of the New York District.[6] With the blessings of the national leadership, the New York party proceeded to put up its own slate of candidates, headed by William F. Dunne for governor.[7]

After the Bridgman convention, however, the Communists had second thoughts about the election. The Socialist candidate for congressman in one of the East Side districts, Meyer London, presented them with a special problem. His district had been gerrymandered to ensure a Democratic victory. In addition, the Republican candidate had withdrawn in favor of the Democratic. The predominantly Jewish working-class voters in the district, accustomed to voting for London, resented the intrusion of a Communist candidate who could win votes only at London's expense. So great was the

THE TRANSFORMATION

pressure that the Workers party candidate for congressman in this district withdrew just before the election.[8]

The Communist electoral campaign in the 1922 election constituted a weak and hesitant start. The Workers party succeeded in putting up only four state tickets and local candidates in half a dozen other states.[9]

At the same time, the Communists began to take a more active interest in the growing Farmer-Labor party movement. This interest was stimulated more by what had happened in Moscow than by what had been happening in the United States. The Farmer-Labor movement had been struggling along for three years without the Communists and despite their best efforts to discourage and destroy it. But that was before the Comintern discovered the united front. An American Communist leader later admitted, "And only after the party became more intimately familiar with the United Front tactics of the Communist International, and particularly, with Lenin's advice to the British Communists, to fight for admission into the Labor Party, did the C.E.C. finally feel justified in adopting a complete thesis which committed the party to a labor-party policy." [10]

This thesis made its appearance in May 1922. An official Communist pronouncement said: "The problem of the United Political Front of Labor in the United States is the problem of the Labor Party." [11] By making the Labor party the specific American form of the united front, the American Communists embraced both the Labor party and the united front at the same time, though they were not yet ready to do anything about them. The united front theses of the Workers party the following month went a step further: "To make the labor party an instrument of the class struggle and the revolution the participation of the Communists is an imperative necessity." Nevertheless the same document also held that the United States lacked a basis for a united political front.[12] While there was still so much dispute in the Communist movement over its own illegal status, pronouncements in favor of the Farmer-Labor movement merely amounted to abstract literary exercises. How difficult it was for the American Communists to make up their minds about the Farmer-

Labor movement was revealed in the preparations for the Bridgman convention in August. The Comintern representative, Valetski, decided to withdraw a resolution on the Labor party in the so-called Disarmament Commission "since I was convinced that the moment was not opportune for arriving at a decision in the party." [13]

After the Bridgman convention, Valetski took a stronger stand in favor of the Labor party. His parting advice to the American Communists gave them little leeway: "We must take a stand on the question of a Labor Party; we cannot evade it any longer. And this can only be in favor of the formation of a Labor Party containing millions of workers." He pulled aside the curtain for a brief peek behind the scenes of the inner-party struggle: "There was opposition to our Party being the main bearer of the idea of a Labor Party. There was the justified feeling that this would lead to a fiasco and to confusion in our ranks." Then Valetski indicated what had helped him to make up his own mind: "The idea of a large independent class party, the idea of a Labor Party, is being propagated independently of us by hundreds of labor unions of various shades. A fight on this question is going on in the labor movement. Hence it would be a very serious mistake if we should hesitate for a minute to take a clear and definite position to it. We must participate in it. When the Labor Party is formed, we must be in it." [14]

In the middle of October, soon after Valetski's departure, the American Communists came out with an unequivocal declaration favoring the Labor party. It called on the new party to represent the working class only and not the "hopeless small-business clique." In the anti-middle-class spirit of the old historic Left, it insisted: "A Labor Party will grow provided it attempts not to be a party for and of everybody, but to be a class party—of the working class." It included "working farmers," by which it meant tenant farmers and small-farm owners, in the "class party." At this stage, however, the Communists allotted a secondary role to the farmers. The necessity for the trade unions to take the initiative in forming the party was emphasized. By a "class party," the Communists meant one that clearly set its goal from the very outset as "the abolition of wage slavery, the establishment of a workers' republic and a collectivist system of production." [15]

Important as this statement was for the immediate future of American Communism, it was not written by an American Communist. Credit for it went to one of the recent arrivals from Moscow, "John Pepper," * the post-Bridgman pseudonym of Joseph Pogany.[16]

The Fourth Congress

Every struggle in the American party went on in two places, continents removed. One part took place in the United States; the other in Moscow. Since no policy and no leadership could long survive against the Comintern's wishes, the second scene of the struggle was decisive. Nevertheless, it was not merely a simple matter of handing down decisions in Moscow.

For one thing, factional struggles in the Russian party were reflected by factional struggles in the Comintern. In principle the Communist movement disapproved of factionalism; in practice it was impossible to prevent the foreign parties from possessing factions as long as the Russians enjoyed the privilege. For another thing, the dominant Russian leaders of the Comintern had already burned their fingers so often in the West that they began to fight shy of overhasty, one-sided actions. They were increasingly willing to hear all sides of a controversial question before making up their own minds. For these reasons, the decision-making process in the Comintern became more protracted and complex. For the foreign parties, the problem was not always simply to obey the Comintern's decision; it was sometimes to get the Comintern to make a decision that could be obeyed.

This was the situation in Moscow when James P. Cannon, chairman of the Workers party, arrived on June 1, 1922. It was his first trip to the seat of Communist power. The regular American representative to the Comintern was then Katterfeld, a leader of the Goose

---

* The story of the extraordinary career of this mysterious figure belongs in another volume.

caucus. Cannon came there in behalf of the Liquidators. The old line favoring the Geese was still so strong that he received a chilly reception. "For a long time I was somewhat a pariah," he wrote, "because this campaign about 'liquidators' had reached ahead of us, and the Russians didn't want to have anything to do with liquidators." [17] The next American arrival in Moscow that summer was Alexander Bittelman, who came to get money for the newly started *Freiheit,* the Jewish organ of the American party, from the Jewish Bureau of the Russian Communist party and similar sources.[18] Cannon and Bittelman worked together to influence the Comintern leadership.

"I noted that all the leaders, as though by a prior decision on their part, remained noncommittal in all these discussions of American policy at that time," Cannon recalls. "They were extremely friendly and patient. They gave us freely of their time, which must indeed have been strictly limited, and asked numerous pointed questions which showed an intense interest in the question. None of them, however, expressed any opinion. The net result of the first round of conversations, which extended over a considerable period of time, was an informal decision to wait for the arrival of the delegates from the other faction, who would be coming to the World Congress and to defer any decision until that time." [19]

The Comintern's Fourth Congress opened in Moscow on November 5, 1922, and lasted a month. An American Commission was named, with Kuusinen as chairman; three top-ranking Russians, Bukharin, Lozovsky, and Radek; the recent Comintern representative, Valetski; and eight others. In his main report, Zinoviev paid little attention to the American party beyond remarking that the great American problem consisted of uniting legal and illegal work. The three main American factions were given an opportunity to present their cases to the congress.

Katterfeld (Carr) led off for the Geese with a speech that betrayed a lingering reluctance to apply the united-front tactic to the United States. He argued that the American situation was not the same as the European. He attacked the withdrawal of the Communist congressional candidate in favor of Meyer London. Bedacht (Marshall) spoke for the Liquidators. He defended the decision of the American Communist leadership to take over the Farmer-Labor movement. He protested that the American Communists were forced to withdraw their candidate against Meyer London in order to avoid being accused by the Socialists of having helped to defeat a candidate of the workers. The "United Toilers" faction was represented by an unidentified Lett from Boston whose pseudonym was "Sullivan." He assailed everyone else and even roared his defiance of the Comintern. He demanded the immediate expulsion of the "Right Wing Mensheviks"—by which he meant Communists like Bedacht—from the American party, and accused the Comintern's top leadership of having supported the "Right Wing." [20]

One superficial paragraph was devoted to the American Communists in the "theses" of the Fourth Congress. On the main problem at issue in the American party, it merely noted that all the "Left elements" of the American trade-union and political movements were beginning to unite. The American Communists were advised to put themselves at the head of this trend by exploiting the slogan of the united front.[21]

Actually, the Fourth Congress represented much more of a turning point for the American Communist movement—but the real work was done in private meetings with the Russian leaders and in the closed sessions of the American Commission. Fortunately, two of the leading Americans present, Bedacht and Cannon, enable us to reconstruct what happened.

Cannon says that an interview with Trotsky turned the tide in favor of the Liquidators. Though Bedacht considers it only one of several similar meetings, none of which he regards as decisive, Cannon's story is worth relating for what it reveals about the kind of early "lobbying" that went on in the Comintern.

According to Cannon, the interview was hurriedly arranged by Max Eastman. "Trotsky, the most businesslike of men, set the interview for a definite time. His fearsome insistence on punctuality, in contrast to the typical Russian nonchalance in matters of time, was a legend, and nobody dared to keep him waiting. Eastman had only had about one hour to arrange it, and came within an inch of failing to round us up. He got hold of us at the last minute, as we were blithely returning from a visit to the Russian steam baths—my first and only experience with this formidable institution—and hustled us to Trotsky's office by auto just in the nick of time to keep the appointment."

Trotsky gave the three Americans—Cannon, Bedacht, and Eastman—an hour. Cannon stated the case for the Liquidators, with some supplementary remarks by Bedacht. Trotsky asked a few questions and then: "Trotsky stated unambiguously that he would support us, and that he was sure Lenin and the other Russian leaders would do the same. He said that if Lenin didn't agree, he would try to arrange for us to see him directly. He said he would report the interview to the Russian Central Committee and that the American Commission would soon hear their opinion. At the end of the discussion he asked us to write our position concisely, on 'one sheet of paper— no more,' and send it to him for transmission to the Russian leadership." [22]

By chance, the only document preserved by Bedacht from this early period was the memorandum given to Trotsky and others on this occasion. It was signed by "Marshall, Cook, and Lansing" (Bedacht, Cannon, and Swabeck) for the "Minority of the Delegation to the Comintern," and endorsed by six others, two representing the American Young Communist League, three the Trade Union Educational League, and the sixth the American farm organizer. Written in German, it filled two pages, not one. It came out strongly for an open, legal American party and ended with these uncompromising words: "We demand a clear statement of principles on the above-mentioned problems from the Comintern and request that, in the event a split should materialize from the realistic execution of these principles in America, the Comintern should not again insist on a mechanical formal unity." [23]

During the congress, the American delegates occasionally talked privately in the corridors and anterooms with Zinoviev, Bukharin, and other Comintern leaders. Bedacht says that they clearly indicated "their affinity with the ideas of the Liquidators." [24] The showdown came in the American Commission.

Katterfeld and Cannon were given about an hour to state the positions of their respective factions. Other American delegates were called upon for supplementary remarks. Cannon describes the dénouement: "Then the big guns began to boom. First Zinoviev, then Radek, and then Bukharin. The noncommittal attitude they had previously shown in our personal conversations with them, which had caused us such apprehension, was cast aside. They showed a familiarity with the question which indicated that they had discussed it thoroughly among themselves. They all spoke emphatically and unconditionally in support of the position of the Liquidators."

The Russians lectured the Americans on the subject of revolutionary legality and illegality. They took the position that it was purely a practical question. They "castigated" the tendency to transplant Russian experiences under Czarism to American conditions in a mechanical way. Zinoviev contributed an amusing story about a Bolshevik underground worker who insisted on carrying her old false passport even after the Bolsheviks had seized power. The Russians spoke with vast confidence and absolute assurance, as if it had not taken them about three years to make up their own minds.

When the Russians had finished, the Goose caucus was annihilated. The American Commission gave its unanimous blessings to three things—full legalization of the American Communist movement, a Labor party based on the trade unions, and the return of the Left Opposition to the Communist ranks.[25]

From these decisions there could be no further appeal or retreat. The Comintern's next "instructions" to the American Communists were "categorical." They maintained that "a legal party in America is now possible." Only a partial concession was made to the partisans of the illegal party. The Comintern was willing to admit that it was still necessary to have "in reserve an illegal apparatus," as long as the latter was considered "an auxiliary organization to the broad legal mass movement." The Comintern hastened to add, however, that it might be possible "almost totally to abolish the apparatus of the illegal party" within a year. This left little doubt of the real objective—a fully legal party unencumbered by illegal habits. The Comintern summed up its position in five points:

1. The main efforts must be devoted to work on legal field. 2. All energy must be directed toward building up a Labor Party. 3. The greatest attention must be paid to the Left Wing in the Labor movement. 4. The illegal Party shall continue to exist only as an auxiliary organization. 5. The merging of the Central Committees of the illegal and the legal parties must be brought about as soon as possible.

An interesting paragraph in this letter of instructions dealt with the old, painful subject of immigrants and natives. It showed how much had changed since the domination of the Russian federation in the formative period.

The immigrants, including Communists, who have migrated to America from Europe, play an important part in the American Labor movement. But it must not be for the moment forgotten that the most important task is to arouse the American-born workers out of their lethargy. The Party must systematically and willingly assist American-born workers, whenever the opportunity offers, to play a leading part in the movement. The Communist immigrants have brought many virtues with them to America, self-sacrifice, revolutionary courage, etc. At the same time, however, their greatest weakness lies in the fact that they desire to apply the experience they have acquired in the various countries of Europe, mechanically to American conditions.

The Comintern ended on an unmistakably threatening note:

The tasks that now confront the American Party are so important that we frankly declare: He who refuses to adopt these tactics let him leave the Party! [26]

This decision did not go far enough for Max Eastman. He submitted a statement to Lenin and Trotsky which argued against the "specious unity" achieved at the Fourth Congress. He expected the Slavic federations to continue their efforts to control the American Communist movement and advised the Russian leaders that the only way to prevent another split was to separate them organizationally.

But Eastman had lost touch with the fast-changing American situation; the Slavic federations had been beheaded and never dared to assert themselves again. More splits loomed ahead, but not for the same reason.[27]

Otherwise, the Fourth Congress was notable for the first extended discussion in Moscow of the American Negro question. Two Negro speakers, Otto Huiswoud (Billings) and Claude McKay (Mackay), reported on the conditions and prospects of the American Negroes. Huiswoud, a West Indian by origin, defined the Negro question as "another part of the race and colonial question to which no attention has hitherto been paid." McKay, a young Negro poet, had traveled to Moscow on his own but attended the Congress as a "special delegate." He created something of a stir by accusing both the American Socialists and Communists of neglecting the Negroes because of their own prejudices. A Negro Commission produced "Theses on the Negro Question." This document represents the first real effort of the Comintern to formulate a position on the Negro question and deserves more attention than it has received.
of the Comintern to formulate a position on the Negro question and deserves more attention than it has received.

One of these theses placed the emphasis on the colonial exploitation of Africa. The second one stated the main theme: "The history of the Negro in America fits him for an important role in the liberation struggle of the entire African race." It added that industrial development and brutal persecution had placed "the American Negro, especially of the North, in the vanguard of the African struggle against oppression." In effect, the Comintern in this period conceived of the American Negroes as part of an international Negro question rather than as a special American problem. It also chose to place the Negro question within the context of the whole colonial question—an outlook which eventually led by a somewhat different process of reasoning to the theory of "self-determination." Concretely, the Fourth Congress decided to hold a Negro World Congress in Moscow. Evidently the forces for such a major effort were lacking, and this congress never materialized.[28]

End of the underground

Unity and legality came to the American Communist movement after three years of disunity and illegality.

The first phase of unification had been stage-managed by the Comintern representative, Valetski, before his return to Moscow. As his major contribution, he forced the underground-at-all-cost Left Opposition to capitulate. A convention of the Opposition took place at the end of September 1922. With Valetski in attendance, it debated the Comintern's conditions for going back into the official party. For a while, the outlook for re-unification seemed very dim. A majority insisted upon obviously inacceptable demands, such as the expulsion of the most prominent Liquidators, Cannon, Bedacht, Ruthenberg, and Lovestone, and no obligation to join the Workers party. Valetski solemnly warned the convention that he would consider the adoption of these demands "a complete rejection of the letter and spirit of the decisions of the Comintern on the question of unity." Faced with the choice of standing by their principles or standing by the Comintern, the majority found it harder to give up the Comintern. The vote went 19 to 4 in favor of Valetski and unity.[29]

The last stand of the bitter-end minority was made by "Sullivan," the old-fashioned Lett from Boston. Six years later, in 1929, the newly organized American Trotskyists heard about an underground group, with headquarters in Boston and a branch in Cleveland, that was somewhat sympathetic to Trotskyist ideas. On a visit to Boston, the Trotskyist leader, Cannon, held a conference with the group. Cannon tells the story:

> They were very conspiratorial and took us in the old underground manner to the meeting place. A formal committee met us. After exchanging greetings, the leader said: "Now, Comrade Cook, you tell us what your proposition is." Comrade "Cook" was the pseudonym he knew me in the underground. He was not going to trifle with my legal name in an under-

ground meeting. I explained why we had been expelled, our program, etc. They said they were willing to discuss the Trotskyist program as the basis for unity in a new party. But they wanted agreement first on one point: The party we were going to organize would have to be an underground organization. So I passed a few jokes with them and went back to New York. I suppose they are still underground.[30]

Cannon recognized the group's leader as the "Sullivan" of the old days.[31]

The American Communist movement was unified in principle by the end of September 1922, though it took a few more weeks to work out the organizational details. By the end of the year, the opposition to legality had also surrendered unconditionally. It was political suicide to confess to an underground mentality after the Fourth Congress of the Comintern, which ended on December 5. Instead of delaying the inevitable, the former adherents of the United Toilers and the Goose caucus decided to jump on the bandwagon of all-out, immediate legalization. As soon as everyone realized that the underground had become a political corpse, all the old factions vied with one another to get credit for burying it.

A quick and easy way to make the transition from illegality to legality offered itself—the retirement of the illegal Communist party of America in favor of the legal Workers party. This plan was adopted in time for the second convention of the Workers party which opened in New York on December 24, 1922.

This convention elected a Central Executive Committee of 24 and a smaller Executive Council of 11 representatives of the united movement.[32] It also adopted a new program closely enough patterned on the old Communist program to enable the Workers party to come forth as a real Communist party in fact if not in name. Whereas the original program of the Workers party the year before had asked for "the abolition of capitalism through the establishment of the Workers' Republic," the new program came out for "supplanting the existing capitalist government with a Soviet Government" which would be a "dictatorship of the workers." [33] The Workers party formally accepted the leadership of the Comintern; the Comintern merely accepted the Workers party as a "sympathizing party." [34]

Later that same month, December 1922, a Party Council was held by the still underground Communist party to take stock of the situation. It served notice of what was coming by calling attention to the fact that the Workers party "daily is functioning more and more completely as an open Communist party." Nevertheless, one observation by the party's executive secretary betrayed the difference between dissolving the underground party and discontinuing underground work: "At last we must seriously take up the self-protection of the Party. The present underground party is only an underground in name. We must organize various confidential and secret departments of the Party for ensuring its safety and carrying on the Party's underground work, in order to protect ourselves from future attacks." [35]

All that remained for the underground Communist party was to make the final gesture of going out of existence. A third national convention of the Communist party of America was held in New York on April 7, 1923. It went through the motions of signing its own death warrant. A formal communication was sent to the Workers party to the effect that the Communist party of America had decided to dissolve because the Workers party "has developed into a Communist Party." [36]

In this way, the name of the Communist party was temporarily relinquished in the United States. For the next two years, it was known as the Workers party of America. The name was changed to the Workers (Communist) party of America in 1925 and to the Communist Party, U.S.A., in 1929.

People, places, and occupations

At this turning point, when unification finally came to the American Communist movement, how many Communists were there, where did they live, in what occupations were they concentrated?

We have fairly full official Communist figures for most of 1922–23.

THE TRANSFORMATION

They are worth considering if we take the proper precautions in evaluating them.

The Workers party claimed an average membership of 12,058 for 1922 and 15,395 for 1923. The number jumped from a low of 8339 for the months of March–June 1922, before unification, to 16,421 for April 1923, the month the underground party dissolved itself.[37]

These may be regarded as maximum figures, since it was in the interest of the leadership to make as good a showing as possible. Even at their face value, they indicate the basic four-year trend— the American Communist movement of 1923 was able to hold on to only about one-third or less of the total represented at the founding Communist conventions in 1919. But there is reason to believe that the real number in 1923 was much smaller.

Membership figures for the first half of the twenties were based on the "dual stamp" system—a single dues stamp for husbands and wives. This system was especially prevalent in the foreign-language federations which contained the vast majority of members. When it was discontinued in October 1925, the membership figure was roughly cut in half. The Comintern pointed out that all previous statistics of the Workers party had been woefully "inaccurate." If this factor is taken into account, the membership figure for 1922 would be nearer 6000 to 8000 and for 1923, 8000 to 10,000.[38]

Geographically, the Communists were clustered in a few places. In April 1923, according to the official figures, almost one-quarter of the total membership was concentrated in the New York District. Chicago ranked second with 15 per cent. Four-fifths were huddled together in six centers: New York, Chicago, Boston, Minneapolis, Cleveland, and Detroit, in that order. The "dual stamp" system tended to inflate the figures outside New York; it would probably be closer to reality to estimate that well over 50 per cent was concentrated in the Northeast, about 30 per cent in the industrial Midwest, and about 5 per cent on the Pacific Coast.[39]

American Communism in 1923 was predominantly an urban, northeastern movement. There was virtually nothing south of Philadelphia and Kansas City, and virtually nothing between Kansas City and San Francisco. This geographical distribution remained roughly the same for the next decade.

The "national composition" continued to be the most striking single aspect of the American Communist movement. By April 1923, the old Lettish influence and the Russian preponderance had completely passed away. So many Letts and Russians had returned home that the two federations had become mere shadows of their old selves. The Russian federation was officially rated as "completely disorganized" and the Lettish as in "difficulties." [40] The American party even started a campaign against "mass emigration of the workers to Soviet Russia." [41] In April 1923 the Russians constituted only about 7 per cent and the Letts less than 4 per cent.

Fundamentally, however, nothing else had changed. The preponderance of foreign-language groups was still overwhelming. What had changed was the relative standing within the foreign-language groups. Numerically, the lead was now held by the Finnish federation, which accounted for almost 45 per cent of the total membership. The Finns were to the Workers party what the Russians had been to the old Communist party, except that the Finnish federation never tried to dominate the entire movement as the Russians had done. After the Finns came the South Slavs with 8 per cent, the Lithuanians with 6 per cent, and the Jews with about 5 per cent. The English-speaking percentage accounted for only about 5 per cent. In his report at the end of 1923, Ruthenberg tried to minimize the preponderance of the foreign-language federations by offering the opinion that at least 50 per cent of the total membership could speak English as a second language.[42] If so, it may be inferred that about 50 per cent of the membership could not speak English at all, about 45 per cent used a foreign language as primary tongue and English as a secondary one, and about 5 per cent used English exclusively. In Chicago, for example, the Workers party had 52 branches, of which 10 were Czechoslovak, 6 Lithuanian, 5 English, 5 Italian, 4 Scandinavian, 4 Ukrainian, 4 Polish, 3 Russian, 2 German,

2 Hungarian, 2 Jewish, 2 South Slavic, 1 Finnish, 1 Lettish, and 1 Roumanian.[43]

We have partial information, based on a registration of only one-third of the total membership, on the occupational status of the party membership at the end of 1923. Metal and machinery workers ranked first with 14 per cent. Then came building workers with about 12 per cent, miners with about 10 per cent, and clothing workers with about 8 per cent. Only 35 per cent belonged to unions. It appears from the imperfect official figures that possibly two-thirds to three-quarters of the party could be classified as "proletarian," a much larger percentage than it ever achieved in later years. In this early period the foreign-language federations gave a working-class character to the American Communist movement. The federations contained chiefly immigrant workers, many of them in the basic industries. The Communist bid against John L. Lewis for power in the mine union in the twenties was based on this foreign-language strength. When the organic tie with the foreign-language federations was broken in the reorganization of 1925, the "proletarian" character of the American party dropped sharply. In later years, until the upsurge in the late thirties, the party's industrial strength was mainly concentrated in the needle and building trades.[44]

The great seduction

On the whole, then, it was a small, weak, isolated party, a far cry from the promise held out in 1919. Yet the Communist weakness was not absolute. It must be considered in terms of the strength or weakness of its rivals in the radical movement. In this sense, the Communist strength was not to be despised. The Socialist decline from 1919 to 1923 was even more catastrophic—from almost 110,000 to 12,000. In only four states, New York, Wisconsin, Massachusetts, and Pennsylvania, did the Socialists have as many as 1000 members by 1922.[45] The Socialist Labor party was a much smaller, impotent sect. The I.W.W. was still going downhill precipitously.

The plight of the Communists in the twenties was part of a trend throughout the radical movement.

Scott Nearing made a trip through the Middle West just about the time the American Communists came out of the underground. He reported that the Socialist party was "almost extinct" in the Middle West. He added: "The Workers party has fallen heir to the present radical political situation in the United States." The one thing that seemed to hold Nearing himself from going over to the Communists at once was the fear of Moscow's "system of dictation." [46]

Nearing was answered by Cannon. It was an extraordinarily revealing reply by one of the "American" Communists who had fought most vigorously for an "American" party. Cannon defended the American Communists against Nearing's misgivings by citing the recent victory for his point of view. Yet he did not try to deny Nearing's charge of Moscow domination. Instead, he countered with this argument: "The fraternal union of native and foreign-born workers in our party; realistic tactics adopted to the concrete situation in America; leadership of the movement, as a rule, in the hands of the native workers—that is the sound point of view finally adopted in our party. And who said the final word in favor of it? The 'Moscow Dictators'!" He added triumphantly: "We who have fought for a realistic party have found our best friend in 'Moscow.'" [47]

Cannon and those like him in the American party had reason to be grateful to Moscow. Without Moscow's intervention they might have had their way eventually, but at much greater cost and with far more delay. They repaid Moscow with years of service and subservience, some more, some less. In the beginning, however, they were lured by what seemed a not entirely one-sided bargain. They were genuinely delighted with the fact that they appeared to be able to solve internal problems in Moscow that they could not solve at home. In addition to all the other boons which Moscow held out to them—the reflected glory of the Russian Revolution, the international glamor of the Comintern, the desperately needed subsidies and other technical assistance—this last discovery of Moscow's usefulness was the most seductive and the most ruinous.

THE TRANSFORMATION

For Moscow in 1923 was just entering on a period of fierce and ugly fratricidal struggle to determine the succession to Lenin's leadership in Russia. This struggle poisoned the life of the Comintern and seeped into the bloodstream of every Communist party in the world. What were "realistic tactics" for the Americans in 1923 at the behest of the Comintern could be transformed into suicidally unrealistic tactics in 1924, also at the behest of the Comintern. Moscow's line changed; Moscow's domination remained. Some "American" Communists learned this lesson—and rebelled. Some learned the lesson—and built their careers on it.

The first change of line was every other change of line in embryo. A rhythmic rotation from Communist sectarianism to Americanized opportunism was set in motion at the outset and has been going on ever since. The periodic rediscovery of "Americanization" by the American Communists has only superficially represented a more independent policy; it has been in reality merely another type of American response to a Russian stimulus. A Russian initiative has always effectively begun and ended it. For this reason, "Americanized" American communism has been sporadic, superficial, and short-lived. It has corresponded to the fluctuations of Russian policy; it has not obeyed a compelling need within the American Communists themselves. Despite the fact that the American Communists have increased in numbers and influence only in periods of "Americanization," they have again and again surrendered their gains in order to demonstrate their loyalty to Russian leadership.

This book has tried to reconstruct the birth and early childhood of the American Communist movement. It was a difficult birth and an unhappy childhood. Like most people with unpleasant memories, the older Communists would rather forget them; they prefer to give the impression that the real history of the movement started much later. But something crucially important did happen to this movement in its infancy. It was transformed from a new expression of American radicalism to the American appendage of a Russian revolutionary power. Nothing else so important ever happened to it again.

NOTES

ACKNOWLEDGMENTS

INDEX

Notes

Partial key to sources

The following list is not in any sense a bibliography or a selection based on relative importance, but simply a key to sources which recur at widely spaced intervals in the notes, supplied to enable the reader to find the complete information easily. The words "see Key" in parentheses following the first reference to a source in a new chapter indicate that the source appears in this list.

KEY	SOURCE
American Labor Who's Who	*The American Labor Who's Who*, edited by Solon De Leon (New York: Hanford Press, 1925).
Bell	Daniel Bell, "The Background and Development of Marxian Socialism in the United States," in *Socialism and American Life*, edited by Donald D. Egbert and Stow Persons (Princeton, N.J.: Princeton University Press, 1952), Vol. I.
Bittelman	Alexander Bittelman, "History of the Communist Movement in America," in *Investigation of Communist Propaganda:* Hearings before a Special Committee to Investigate Communist Activities in the United States, Part V, Vol. 4, pp. 435–48 (Washington, D.C.: Government Printing Office, 1930).

Borkenau	F. Borkenau, *World Communism* (New York: Norton, 1939).
The Communist	The various publications of this name are explained in note 21, Chapter 13, and note 4, Chapter 21.
Deutscher	Isaac Deutscher, *The Prophet Armed* (New York: Oxford, 1954).
Fine	Nathan Fine, *Labor and Farmer Parties in the United States 1829–1928* (New York: Rand School of Social Science, 1928).
Foster's *History*	William Z. Foster, *History of the Communist Party of the United States* (New York: International, 1952).
Hicks	Granville Hicks, with the assistance of John Stuart, *John Reed* (New York: Macmillan, 1936).
Lenin's *Letters*	*The Letters of Lenin,* translated and edited by Elizabeth Hill and Doris Mudie (New York: Harcourt Brace, 1937).
Murphy	John T. Murphy, *New Horizons* (London: John Lane, 1941).
People vs. Ruthenberg	*People vs. Ruthenberg.* Transcript of Record, Supreme Court of the United States, October Term, 1925. This is the transcript of the appeal containing a portion of the original record of the trial held in St. Joseph, Michigan, 1923.
Recognition of Russia	*Recognition of Russia:* Hearings Before a Subcommittee of the Committee on Foreign Relations, U.S. Senate, 68th Congress, 1st Session (Washington, D.C.: Government Printing Office, 1924).
Revolutionary Radicalism	*Revolutionary Radicalism:* Report of the Joint Legislative Committee Investigating Seditious Activities, filed April 24, 1920, in the Senate of the State of New York (Albany: J. B. Lyon Co., 1920), 4 vols.

Shannon   David A. Shannon, *The Socialist Party of America* (New York: Macmillan, 1955).

Notes

Chapter 1: The Historic Left

1. Howard H. Quint, *The Forging of American Socialism* (University of South Carolina Press, 1953); Hermann Schlüter, *Die Internationale in Amerika* (Chicago: Deutschen Sprachgruppe der Sozialistischen Partei der Vereinigten Staaten, 1918); John R. Commons and Associates, *History of Labour in the United States* (Macmillan, 1926), Vol. II, part VI. *Socialism and American Life* (Princeton University Press, 1952), Vol. II, provides a bibliography by T. D. Seymour Bassett, which covers almost all the subjects and names mentioned in this chapter.
2. Samuel Yellen, *American Labor Struggles* (Harcourt, Brace, 1936), p. 48; Henry David, *The History of the Haymarket Affair* (Farrar & Rinehart, 1936), pp. 82–105.
3. Shannon (see Key), p. 3.
4. *Proceedings of the First Annual Convention, Industrial Workers of the World* (Labor News Co., 1905), pp. 1–2.
5. Letter by Debs, *Chicago Socialist*, December 23, 1905.
6. The A.F. of L.'s membership was 548,321 in 1900 and 1,562,112 in 1910. The number of gainful workers in non-farm occupations was 18,161,235 in 1900 and 25,779,027 in 1910 (*Statistical Abstract of the United States*, Government Printing Office, 1953, p. 184).
7. *Report on Relations between Capital and Labor:* Hearings before the Senate Committee on Education and Labor (Government Printing Office, 1885), Vol. 1, p. 460.
8. Cited by Bell (see Key), p. 247.
9. Ira Kipnis, *The American Socialist Movement, 1897–1912* (Columbia University Press, 1952), pp. 152–53, 159, 207.
10. Ray Ginger, *The Bending Cross* (Rutgers University Press, 1949), p. 211.
11. Karl Marx and Frederick Engels, *Letters to Americans, 1848–1895* (International, 1953), pp. 44, 76, 93–94.
12. Ibid., pp. 141, 154, 157, 160, 167, 177, 185, 190, 196, 223, 238, 240, 287, 289.
13. Ibid., pp. 168, 192.
14. Kipnis, op. cit., p. 118.
15. Karl Marx and Frederick Engels, *On Britain* (Moscow: Foreign Languages Publishing House, 1953), pp. 491–92, 522.
16. Commons, op. cit., Vol. II, p. 277.

17. Marx and Engels, *Letters to Americans,* pp. 162–63, 290.
18. Shannon, p. 25.
19. *Bill Haywood's Book* (International, 1929), p. 7.

CHAPTER 2: THE AGE OF UNREST

1. Ginger, op. cit., p. 191.
2. Julius Falk, *The New International,* Fall 1955, p. 153.
3. Shannon (see Key), p. 26.
4. Ella Reeve Bloor, *We Are Many* (International, 1940), pp. 46–47; Sadie V. Amter (Sadie Van Veen), *Daily Worker,* November 17, 1955; Foster's *History* (see Key), pp. 85–86; Anna Rochester, *The Populist Movement in the United States* (International, 1943).
5. Grace Hutchins, *Daily Worker,* January 17, 1939, p. 7.
6. *Sherwood Anderson's Memoirs* (Harcourt, Brace, 1942), p. 186. But Anderson also wrote that the book was called *Why I Believe in Socialism* (*New Masses,* September 1932, p. 8).
7. Floyd Dell, *Upton Sinclair* (Doran, 1927), pp. 121–24.
8. Michael Gold, "Three Schools of U.S. Writing," *New Masses,* September 1928, p. 13.
9. *American Labor Year Book,* 1916, pp. 97–100.
10. Fine (see Key), pp. 214; Kipnis, op. cit., p. 346.
11. Fine, pp. 232–33.
12. Shannon (pp. 55–56) lists: Upton Sinclair (who originally conceived the I.S.S.), George Strobell, Oscar Lovell Triggs, Thomas Wentworth Higginson, Charlotte Perkins Gilman, Clarence Darrow, William English Walling, J. G. Phelps Stokes, B. O. Flower, Leonard D. Abbott, Jack London, Owen R. Lovejoy, George Willis Cooke, Morris Hillquit, Robert Hunter, Harry W. Laidler, Mrs. Darwin J. Meserole, Walter Agard, Roger Baldwin, Louis B. Boudin, Randolph Bourne, Paul Blanshard, Bruce Bliven, Paul Brissenden, Robert W. Bruère, Louis Budenz, Howard Brubaker, Stuart Chase, Albert De Silver, John Dewey, Paul H. Douglas, Morris Ernst, Zona Gale, Lewis Gannett, W. J. Ghent, Felix Grendon, Paxton Hibben, Jessie Wallace Hughan, Ellis O. Jones, Horace M. Kallen, Edmond Kelley, Florence Kelley, Freda Kirchwey, William Ellery Leonard, Lewis Lorwin, Robert Morss Lovett, Alexander Meiklejohn, Broadus Mitchell, A. J. Muste, Harry Overstreet, Ernest Poole, Selig Perlman, Jacob Potofsky, Anna Rochester, David Saposs, Vida Scudder, John Spargo, Charles P. Steinmetz, Ordway Tead, Norman Thomas, Alexander Trachtenberg, Walter Weyl, Bouck White, Edwin Witte, Helen Sumner Woodbury, and Charles Zeublin.
13. Elizabeth Gurley Flynn, *I Speak My Own Piece* (Masses and Mainstream, 1955), pp. 116–60. This autobiography ends with the Sacco-Vanzetti case in 1925–26.
14. See *Daily People,* February 16–25, 1912, for Fraina's signed reports

NOTES: CHAPTER 2

of the Lawrence strike. His membership in the I.W.W. is mentioned in the outline for the autobiographical "One Rebel's Years" by Lewis Corey (see note 16, Chapter 3).
15. Hicks (see Key), pp. 96–104.
16. Kipnis, op. cit., pp. 347–48 and 424.
17. *New York Call*, July 30, 1912, p. 4.
18. *The Autobiography of Lincoln Steffens* (Harcourt, Brace, 1931, 1-vol. ed.), pp. 658–89.
19. See *International Socialist Review*, February 1912, pp. 461–71, for the full text of the speech.
20. Kipnis, op. cit., pp. 413–15.
21. Shannon, pp. 77–78.
22. *American Labor Year Book, 1916*, p. 95, gives the figures as 113,371 in 1912 and 95,401 in 1913.
23. Robert Hunter, *Violence and the Labor Movement* (Macmillan, 1914), p. xi.
24. Earl Browder, "A Political Autobiography" (in manuscript), Part I, p. 47.
25. Ella Reeve Bloor, op. cit., p. 113.
26. Benjamin Gitlow, *I Confess* (Dutton, 1939), pp. 15–16.
27. Ruthenberg, *New York Call*, July 30, 1912, p. 4.
28. *New York Call*, May 29, 1912.
29. *International Socialist Review*, February 1913, p. 623.
30. See *Masses*, February and March 1912, especially the editorials.
31. Max Eastman, *The Enjoyment of Living* (Harper, 1948), pp. 403–404.
32. Max Eastman lists the following names from the *Masses* and its successor, *The Liberator:* Jo Davidson, Stuart Davis, Glenn O. Coleman, Cornelia Barns, James Hopper, George Bellows, Robert Carlton Brown, Gelett Burgess, Oliver Herford, Horace Traubel, Upton Sinclair, Witter Bynner, William Rose Benét, Carl Sandburg, Harry Kemp, Ernest Poole, Leroy Scott, Wilbur Daniel Steele, Susan Glaspell, Franklin P. Adams, Sherwood Anderson, James Oppenheim, Djuna Barnes, Helen R. Hull, Arthur Bullard, Mabel Dodge, Vachel Lindsay, Alice Duer Miller, Sara N. Cleghorn, Leslie Nelson Jennings, Phillips Russell, Amy Lowell, Norman Matson, William Carlos Williams, Konrad Bercovici, Randolph Bourne, Babette Deutsch, Elizabeth Coatsworth, Philip Littel, George Creel, Romain Rolland, Bertrand Russell, Maxim Gorky, Bernard Shaw, Maurice Sterne, Arthur B. Davies, Randall Davey, Morris Kantor, Mahonri Young, John Barber, Eugene Higgins, Abraham Walkowitz, Robert Minor, Boardman Robinson, André Ruellan, J. J. Lankes, William Gropper, Elmer Rice, John Dos Passos, Clive Weed, S. N. Behrman, Claude McKay, James Weldon Johnson, Evelyn Scott, Ruth Suckow, Frances Winwar, Genevieve Taggard, William Ellery Leonard, Edmund Wilson, Stuart Chase, Joseph Freeman, David Morton, Carlton Beals,

Marya Zaturenska, William Troy, Helen Keller, Alexander Berkman, Maxwell Bodenheim, Siegfried Sassoon, Olive Tilford Dargan, Freda Kirchwey, Lewis Gannett, Arthur Ransome, Roger Baldwin, Francis Biddle, Art Young, John Sloan, Maurice Becker, Ellis O. Jones, Charles Winter, Alice Beach Winter, Eugene Wood, Horatio Winslow, Mary Heaton Vorse, Inez Haynes Gillmore, Finley Peter Dunne, Robert Henri, Arturo Giovannitti, John Reed, Howard Brubaker, Floyd Dell, Frank Bohn, William English Walling, K. R. Chamberlain, Louis Untermeyer, H. G. Glintenkamp, Michael Gold (*The Enjoyment of Living*).

33. *New Review*, "Direct Action and Sabotage" by Moses Oppenheimer, January 25, 1913, pp. 113–15; "Let Us Recall the Recall," April 12, 1913, pp. 450–52; "Haywood" by André Tridon, May 1913, pp. 502–506.

34. *New Review*, November 1913, pp. 927–28.

35. The first issue of the *New Review* is dated January 4, 1913. The publishing company was headed by Alexander Fraser, president; Moses Oppenheimer, treasurer; and Joseph Michael, secretary. The magazine changed from a weekly to a monthly with the issue of April 12, 1913. A new board of editors was announced in May 1914: Frank Bohn, W. E. B. DuBois, Max Eastman, Arturo Giovannitti, Isaac A. Hourwich, Arthur Livingston, Herman Simpson, William English Walling, William Bohn, Floyd Dell, Louis C. Fraina, Felix Grendon, Paul Kenneday, Walter Lippmann, Robert H. Lowie, Helen Marot, Albert Sonnichsen.

Chapter 3: The New Left Wing

1. I am indebted to Bertram D. Wolfe who generously enabled me to benefit from a portion of the manuscript of a work dealing in part with this subject. The writings of Marx and Engels on war were collated by Karl Kautsky, *Sozialisten und Krieg* (Prague: Orbis Verlag, 1937). A number of the most relevant references may be found in Wolfe, *Three Who Made A Revolution* (Dial, 1948), pp. 569–637; Boris Nicolaievsky and Otto Maenchen-Helfen, *Karl Marx: Man and Fighter* (Lippincott, 1936), pp. 169, 249, 302–14, 373–74; and Gustav Mayer, *Friedrich Engels* (Knopf, 1936), pp. 98, 107–108, 115, 145, 152, 154, 193, 210, 213, 288–92, 307–19).

2. See Milorad Drachkovitch, *Les socialismes français et allemand et le problème de la guerre, 1870–1914* (Geneva: Imprimerie H. Studer, 1953), for the most recent and most conscientious review of the source material on the pre-1914 position on war of the French and German Socialist movements. This book also includes valuable sections on the changing attitudes of Marx and Engels, and the policy of the Second International. G. D. H. Cole, *The Second International*

NOTES: CHAPTER 3

(Macmillan, 1956), Part I, Chapter 2, also deals with the position of the Second International on the war question.
3. Paul Fröhlich, *Rosa Luxemburg* (London: Gollancz, 1940), p. 240.
4. Hal Draper, "The Myth of Lenin's 'Revolutionary Defeatism,'" *The New International,* September–October 1953, pp. 255–83; November–December 1953, pp. 313–51; January–February 1954, pp. 39–59. These articles also discuss the Socialist reaction to the Russo-Japanese war of 1905 and the war policies of Rosa Luxemburg and Leon Trotsky.
5. V. I. Lenin, *The Imperialist War,* (*Collected Works,* Vol. XVIII, International, 1930), p. 353.
6. Fine (see Key), pp. 305–306.
7. Benson (*New York Call,* August 6, 1914, p. 6); Steinmetz (*New Review,* December 1914, pp. 702–703); Spargo (ibid., July 1, 1915, pp. 109–110); Eastman (*Masses,* October 1914); Lowie (*New Review,* November 1914, pp. 642–44); Herron (ibid., December 1914, pp. 733–34); *Jack London, American Rebel,* edited by Philip S. Foner (New York: Citadel Press, 1947, p. 126); Walling (*New Review,* September 1914, pp. 512–18); Russell (*New York Call,* September 14, 1914).
8. *The Metropolitan,* December 1914 and January–May 1915; *American Socialist,* January 9, 1915.
9. Ginger, op. cit., pp. 328–29.
10. Jessie Wallace Hughan, *The Present Status of Socialism in America* (New York: John Lane Co., 1911), p. 55; Lenin, *The Imperialist War,* p. 54; Paul M. Sweezy, in *Socialism and American Life,* Vol. I, p. 462. The correspondence of Boudin for the years before 1914 has been deposited in the Columbia University Library. I am indebted to Vera Boudin for personal information about her father, who died in 1952.
11. *The American Socialists and the War,* edited by Alexander Trachtenberg (Rand School of Social Science, 1917), p. 21.
12. See *New Review,* February 1915, pp. 107–108, for the quotation from the *Milwaukee Leader;* May 1, 1915, p. 3, for quotations from Hillquit; June 1, 1915, p. 38, for Debs; *New York Call,* November 29, 1915, p. 3, for Russell; magazine section, December 19 and 26, 1915, for Cahan; editorial, November 22, 1915; Fine, p. 305, for Debs; *New Review,* December 15, 1915, p 368, and March 1916, p. 55, for London.
13. Louis B. Boudin, *Socialism and War* (New Review Publishing Co., 1916), pp. 72, 245, 259 (italics in original).
14. Alexandra Kollontay, *New Review,* January 1, 1916, p. 21, and March 1916, p. 60.
15. S. J. Rutgers, *International Socialist Review,* February 1916, pp. 496–99.

406   THE ROOTS OF AMERICAN COMMUNISM

16. For the material on Fraina's early years, I am indebted to Mrs. Esther Corey for personal information, and to the following: An outline for an autobiography by Lewis Corey entitled "One Rebel's Years: A Contribution to the Autobiography of a Generation" (a 12-page typewritten manuscript submitted to Doubleday & Co.). The typewritten manuscript of a speech by Lewis Corey on "A Rediscovery of Liberal Democracy" at Antioch College, 1945.
17. By the time he made his outline for the unwritten "One Rebel's Years," Lewis Corey had forgotten how early his activity in the Socialist Labor party had begun. In this outline, he wrote that he had joined the Socialist party when he was not quite seventeen years old, resigned after six months, and joined the Socialist Labor party in 1912. However, the activity mentioned in this paragraph was reported in the *Daily People,* July 3 (first street-corner meeting), August 31, September 3, October 3 and 19, November 23, 1909—three years before the date mentioned in the outline.
18. *New Review,* July 1914, p. 397.
19. The others were Frank Bohn, W. E. B. DuBois, Max Eastman, Arturo Giovannitti, Isaac A. Hourwich, Arthur Livingston, Herman Simpson, William English Walling, William Bohn, Floyd Dell, Felix Grendon, Paul Kenneday, Walter Lippmann, Robert H. Lowie, Helen Marot, Albert Sonnichsen. Louis B. Boudin came on and Walter Lippmann went off in May 1915. The *New Review* started as a weekly, then became a monthly, a biweekly, and finally a monthly again.
20. *New Review,* July 1913, pp. 657–61; September 1913, pp. 772–80; December 1913, pp. 964–70.
21. Ibid., May 1, 1915, p. 3, and December 1915, p. 339, for Boudin on Hillquit; September 15, 1915, p. 233, for Fraina on Hillquit.
22. Ibid., January 1915, pp. 7–20; May 15, 1915, p. 26; January 15, 1916, p. 36 (italics in original).

CHAPTER 4: INFLUENCES AND INFLUENCERS

1. The Dutch Social Democratic party had only about 600 members in 1916 (*American Labor Year Book,* 1916, p. 195). The Dutch Social Democratic Labor party had about 25,000 members (ibid., 1917–1918, p. 257).
2. Paul Frölich, *Rosa Luxemburg* (London: Gollancz, 1940), p. 202. Also *New Review,* November 1914, p. 663. Pannekoek's residence in Bremen was noted beside his name in the *International Socialist Review,* October 1914. For the Bremen Left Wing, see Ossip K. Flechtheim, *Die KPD in der Weimarer Republik* (Offenbach: Bollwerk-Verlag, 1948), pp. 12–13.
3. He was so called in the *International Socialist Review,* May 1915, p. 645. For Gorter's group, see Arthur Rosenberg, *A History of Bolshevism* (London: Oxford, 1934), pp. 59 and 129.

NOTES: CHAPTER 4

4. Borkenau (see Key), p. 66.
5. *International Socialist Review,* October 1914, pp. 198–204.
6. Anton Pannekoek, "The Downfall of the International," *New Review,* November 1914, pp. 621–30. This article was evidently first published in the Swiss Social Democratic paper, *Berner Tagwacht,* October 20–22, 1914, and constitutes one of the first calls of its kind (Lenin, *The Imperialist War,* p. 424).
7. Fine (p. 326) estimates that between 25,000 to 30,000 of the 80,000 members in 1915 belonged to the foreign-language federations.
8. Pronounced, in Lettish, Fritzish Rozinsh. He used the Anglicized form Rosin (*Strahdneeks,* October 5, 1915, p. 3), but in some places the spelling "Rozin" is used.
9. For Rosin's life, see *Latvju enciklopedija* (Stockholm, 1950–51), p. 2193. I am indebted to Miss Marta Aspers and Mr. Paul Ramans for help in research on this section.
10. He is listed as responsible editor, *Strahdneeks,* October 5, 1915, p. 3.
11. From a short sketch of the American Lettish Socialist movement by Martins Ogulis, *Strahdneeks,* September 9, 1915.
12. Letter of James Oneal, *The American Socialist,* December 23, 1916.
13. Letter signed by S. Bergin, John D. Williams, and John A. Perry, *New York Call,* January 21, 1917.
14. *Strahdneeks,* July 15, 1915; *New York Call,* June 27, 1915, p. 4.
15. See *Strahdneeks,* July 15, 1915, for the text of the resolutions.
16. *New York Call,* June 25, 1916, p. 5.
17. See *Strahdneeks,* July 15, 1915, for the report of the convention. There were 115 English-speaking, 98 Finnish, and 17 Jewish delegates at the convention (*New York Call,* June 27, 1915, p. 4).
18. See *Strahdneeks,* October 28 and 30, 1915, for the text, which was originally in English. Unfortunately, the 18 names were not given in full.
19. *Strahdneeks,* July 6, 1916. Also see James Oneal's letter, *New York Call,* February 4, 1917, for some Right Wing comments on the convention.
20. *New York Call,* December 11, 1916, p. 4.
21. See New York *World,* October 14, 1916, interview with Walling; October 16, 1916, letter from Walling.
22. *New York Call,* February 4, 1917.
23. See *Strahdneeks,* December 7, 1916, for a full report of this meeting.
24. Strangely enough, though he was secretary of the Massachusetts party in this period, James Oneal does not even mention the Socialist Propaganda League in his *American Communism* (Rand Book Store, 1927). Nor is it mentioned in the first Communist *History of the American Working Class* by Anthony Bimba (International, 1927). William Z. Foster (*From Bryan to Stalin,* International, 1937, p. 290), mentioned it as the first forerunner of the American Communist party and correctly placed it in Boston, 1915. But fifteen years later,

the same William Z. Foster, *History of the Communist Party of the United States* (see Key), p. 158, incorrectly stated that the Socialist Propaganda League "had been launched in Boston in November 1916, with S. J. Rutgers (who later returned to his homeland, Holland) as its leader." Foster was obviously misled the second time by Rutgers' article in the *International Socialist Review*. Citing Foster's first reference of 1937, however, Ira Kipnis (*The American Socialist Movement, 1897–1912*, p. 420), says that many revolutionary Socialists united in 1915 "as a party caucus under the name Socialist Propaganda League." Kipnis was apparently misled by Foster into believing that the original formation of the League had a wider significance than it deserved. Daniel Bell (in *Socialism and American Life*, p. 320; see Key), mentions the Socialist Propaganda League more generally. David A. Shannon (*The Socialist Party of America*), does not mention it at all. Julius Falk ("The Origins of the Communist Movement in the United States," *The New International*, Fall 1955, p. 158), comes closer to the truth, with some factually incorrect details. He mistakenly dates the Socialist Propaganda League as "early in 1915," instead of late 1915. He mistakenly attributes its organization to Rosin and Rutgers, though the latter did not get into the picture until a year after its original organization. Rosin was editor of the Lettish Socialist organ, *Strahdneeks,* and not "secretary of a Lettish socialist organization in Boston." Nor was Rutgers a "Bostonian." He lived in Brooklyn, New York, and merely cooperated with the Boston group.

25. *International Socialist Review*, December 1916, pp. 365–66.
26. Ibid., February 1917, pp. 483–85.
27. Unfortunately, I have not been able to locate a copy, but it is mentioned in the letter by J. Kreitz, secretary of the more moderate Lettish Branch No. 2, in the *Socialist Party Bulletin* (Chicago), March 1917, p. 16.
28. *Strahdneeks,* December 9, 1916, published the full text of Rutgers' article.
29. *International Socialist Review*, February 1917, p. 460–62, republished it.
30. Corey, F.B.I. Interrogation (see note 20, Chapter 5).
31. William English Walling, *Russia's Message* (Doubleday, Page, 1908), pp. 365–66, 369–70.
32. *New Review*, November 15, 1915, p. 321.
33. Corey, F.B.I. Interrogation, p. 89.
34. I am indebted to Max Eastman for permitting me to read a portion of the manuscript of his forthcoming autobiography, which says that the *Masses* group never heard of Lenin until November 1917.
35. Lenin, *The Imperialist War*, p. 309.
36. Lenin's *Letters* (see Key), p. 343, also 348.
37. Ibid., pp. 390–91.

38. Lenin, *The Imperialist War*, pp. 374–76, and note 196 on p. 439
39. Gitlow, *I Confess*, p. 23; Bell, p. 319.
40. *Lenin's Letters*, p. 391.
41. See Isabel de Palencia, *Alexandra Kollontay* (Longmans, Green, 1947), for a superficial biography which mentions only Mme. Kollontay's first trip to the United States (p. 72).
42. For mention of her first tour, see *The American Socialist*, October 23, 1915, which noted that she had just arrived; *New Yorker Volkszeitung*, November 8, 1915, p. 6, for a report of her activities; and *New York Call*, January 16 and February 13–14, 1916, for some details about her lectures and departure. Nevertheless, there is another, conflicting version of her first trip to the United States from no less a source than Ludwig Lore. According to an interview with Lore in the *New York Call*, March 19, 1918, p. 13, she came here in January 1915, not at the end of the year, but left after five months when she found out that her son had been conscripted in Russia. "She left secretly for Russia, organized a band of Socialists in the town where her son was in barracks; kidnapped him and spirited him out of Russia and to the United States, arriving in the spring of 1916." This unlikely story, which conflicts, at least in point of time, with contemporaneous references and reports of her trip, not the least in Lore's own paper, *New Yorker Volkszeitung*, November 8, 1915, may have some interest as an example of the romantic aura that clung to her at the time.
43. See *Lenin's Letters*, pp. 379, 380–81, 383–84, 390–91, 398, for Lenin's correspondence with Mme. Kollontay; Lenin, *Collected Works* (International, 1942), Vol. XIX, p. 30, for the speech in Berne.
44. "The Third International," *The American Socialist*, October 23, 1915; "Do Internationalists Want a Split?" *International Socialist Review*, January 1916; "The Attitude of the Russian Socialists," *New Review*, March 1916.
45. *New York Call*, interview with Lore, March 19, 1918, p. 13.
46. *American Labor Who's Who* (see Key), has a short biography (pp. 140–41).
47. *New Review*, December 15, 1915, p. 369.
48. *New York Call*, February 6, 1915, p. 8.
49. See Lenin, *Collected Works*, Vol. XXI, Book II, pp. 270–71, for a biographical note on Bukharin. Bukharin's first article in the *Novy Mir* appeared November 7, 1916. His election as editorial secretary was announced in the issue of January 12, 1917, p. 6.
50. *New York Call*, January 16, 1917.
51. *New York Times*, January 15, 1917. A representative of the Hebrew Sheltering and Immigrant Aid Society met Trotsky and his family at the pier and took them away. Deutscher (see Key), p. 184, discusses the Kiev newspaper for which Trotsky wrote.
52. *New York Call*, January 15, 1917. The interview continued: "I am a

disciple of Karl Marx, the great German Socialist. I am a man of peace, and my life has been devoted to an effort to bring concord among nations." The paper ran another full-length interview with Trotsky the following day.

53. *New York Call,* November 13, 1917, p. 4, interview with Alexander Menshoy. Forty years later, the poet W. H. Auden liked to call visitors' attention to the fact that he was living in the same house, but fortunately not in the cellar.
54. *New York Call,* January 21, 1918, p. 3, published the text of a Department of Justice report on Trotsky's activities in New York. The report was prefaced with the comment: "Every fact contained in it could have been gathered in 24 hours by any cub reporter," which would indicate its probable reliability.
55. See New York *Tribune,* May 23, 1918, for letter by Lore.
56. *New York Call,* February 6, 1917, p. 2.
57. *International Socialist Review,* January 1917, p. 441.
58. Ibid., July 1917, pp. 37–38.
59. See George E. Roewer's letter, *New York Call,* February 10, 1916, p. 6, for Nuorteva's background.
60. See Jesse D. Clarkson, "'Big Jim' Larkin: A Footnote to Nationalism," in *Nationalism and Internationalism* (Columbia University Press, 1950) for a short sketch of Larkin's background. Professor Clarkson says little of Larkin's American period, for which Larkin's own testimony in his trial of 1920, *People of the State of New York against James Larkin* (Hall of Records, 31 Chambers Street, New York City, room 703) is indispensable.
61. *American Labor Who's Who,* p. 300.
62. See *New York Call,* March 20, 1917, p. 4, for advertisement.

Chapter 5: The Left at War

1. Ludwig Lore, "Leon Trotsky," in *One Year of Revolution,* a 32-page brochure "celebrating the First Anniversary of the founding of the Russian Soviet Republic" (Brooklyn, N.Y.: Socialist Publication Society, 1918), pp. 7–8.
2. Sen Katayama, *The Revolutionary Age,* July 26, 1919.
3. Lenin's *Letters* (see Key), p. 410.
4. Leon Trotsky, *My Life* (Scribner, 1930), pp. 273–74.
5. Lenin's *Letters,* p. 411.
6. *Novy Mir,* February 21, 1917.
7. *International Press Correspondence,* January 6, 1927, p. 39.
8. *New York Call,* March 5, 1917, and *Novy Mir,* March 6, 1917. Also see Fraina's letter in the *New York Call,* March 18, 1917. The majority resolution merely pledged "a vigorous and independent campaign against war and militarism on distinct working-class lines" and, if war should come, "to hasten the return of peace, minimize

NOTES: CHAPTER 5

the evils which war inflicts upon the workers, preserve the working-class movement . . . against any suspension or curtailment of their right to organize and strike. . . ." The Right Wing point of view was carefully worded to stay within the law.

9. Louis Waldman, *Labor Lawyer* (Dutton, 1944), p. 68.
10. Lenin, *Collected Works,* Vol. XIX, p. 404.
11. Deutscher (see Key), p. 241.
12. Trotsky, op. cit., p. 278.
13. I have been told by Max Shachtman, a long-time former leader of the American Trotskyist movement and one of Trotsky's translators, that he often tried to draw out Trotsky about his experiences in the United States and always found that Trotsky regarded them as quite unimportant. G. A. Ziv, Trotsky, *Kharakteristika po Lichnym Vospominaniam* (New York, 1921), has a quite uninformative chapter on Trotsky's American period. Trotsky's latest biographer, Isaac Deutscher, skims over it lightly (pp. 241–46).
14. Lenin, *Collected Works,* Vol. XX, p. 19.
15. See *New York Call,* March 26, 1917, for the advertisement, and March 27, 1917 for the story.
16. James Bunyan and H. H. Fisher, *The Bolshevik Revolution, 1917–1918* (Stanford University Press, 1934), pp. 106, 120. Chudnovsky, originally a Menshevik, joined the Bolsheviks in 1917 and died in 1918.
17. See *The Communist International,* No. 3, July 1, 1919, pp. 351–52, for a commemorative article on Volodarsky (Moisei Markovich Goldstein). He came to the United States in 1913 and also joined the Bolsheviks in 1917. Also see Bunyan and Fisher, op. cit., p. 733.
18. See *New Review,* May 1916, for the announcement. The last issue was dated June 1916. The last editorial board, as of May 1916, was composed of Louis B. Boudin, Louis C. Fraina, Felix Grendon, Martha Gruening, Isaac Hourwich, and Moses Oppenheimer.
19. Almost four decades later, the author was able to get in touch with John D. Williams. In a letter, dated August 21, 1954, he explained the reason for his presence at the Brooklyn meeting, which he vividly remembered. He also recalled that it took place at the home of Ludwig Lore. According to Corey (F.B.I. Interrogation), Williams was editor of *The Internationalist*.
20. The rest of the information in this paragraph is taken from an interrogation of Lewis Corey by two agents of the Federal Bureau of Investigation at Yellow Springs, Ohio, in 1949–50 (the exact date is missing from the 150-page stenographic transcript). I am indebted to Mrs. Esther Corey for permitting me to consult the copy in her possession. It is referred to in these notes as Corey, F.B.I. Interrogation. *The New International,* Vol. I, No. 2, lists A. S. Edwards as secretary of the Socialist Propaganda League, with headquarters in Boston, Louis C. Fraina as editor, and a press committee composed

of A. S. Edwards, S. J. Rutgers, S. Freiman, and J. C. Rovitch. I have not been able to locate a copy of Vol. I, No. 1, which was dated April 22, 1917. I am indebted to Granville Hicks for six of the eleven copies of *The New International.* Vol. I, No. 11, is dated April, 1918.

21. *The New International,* May 5, 1917, p. 3 (italics in original).
22. *Masses,* August 1917, p. 5.
23. Paul Fröhlich, *Rosa Luxemburg,* pp. 197–202.
24. See *Die Neue Zeit* (Berlin), November 22 and December 6, 1912, for Pannekoek's first articles; December 13, 1912, for Kautsky's reply; and January 10, 1913, for Pannekoek's final answer. Also see the historical reference in Rutgers' article, "The Left Wing: Mass Action," *International Socialist Review,* October 1916, p. 237.
25. *Proceedings,* National Convention of the Socialist Party, 1912 (Chicago: Socialist Party, 1912), p. 248.
26. Austin Lewis, "Syndicalism and Mass Action," *New Review,* June 1913, p. 578. Also see the answer to Lewis by Gustave Eckstein, "What is Mass Action?," ibid., August 1913, pp. 680–88. For Lewis' background, see *The American Labor Who's Who,* p. 137.
27. Editorial, signed M. E. M. (Mary E. Marcy), *International Socialist Review,* December 1916, pp. 367–69.
28. See Wolfe, *Three Who Made a Revolution,* p. 592, note, for some incisive remarks on antimilitarism in the prewar Socialist movement.
29. See S. J. Rutgers, "The Left Wing: Mass Action," *International Socialist Review,* October 1916, pp. 235–237 for a full exposition of "mass action." Also see Herman Gorter, "Mass Action the Answer," ibid., September 1916. Gorter was one of the fathers of the concept, but Pannekoek and Rutgers were much more active in presenting it for American consumption. Gorter devoted a chapter to "mass action" in his book, *Imperialismus, der Weltkrieg und die Sozial-Demokratie* (Amsterdam, 1915; original edition in Dutch, 1914), the same work in which he was one of the first to call for a Third International.
30. *The New International,* "Industrial Unionism and Mass Action," June 2, 1917, p. 3 (italics in original).
31. Louis C. Fraina, *Revolutionary Socialism* (The Communist Press, 1918), pp. 195–96 and 202–203. His indebtedness to Rutgers was gratefully acknowledged in the preface: "I wish to express the deep appreciation I feel to my good Comrade, S. J. Rutgers, my colleague for one year on *The New International,* who read the manuscript of this book, making many an acute criticism and suggestion. A member of the revolutionary Social Democratic Party in Holland, Comrade Rutgers' sojourn of two years in this country and his activity in the Socialist Propaganda League were a source of inspiration and ideas to the comrades associated with him" (p. iii).

After the Bolshevik revolution, Fraina gave the phrase a Russian derivation befitting the new dominant influence. He found a passage in one of Trotsky's writings, translated as "The Proletariat and the Revolution," in *Our Revolution,* the volume edited by Olgin, published in 1918 (pp. 41–42), and proclaimed it the "final and complete form of 'mass action,'" though Trotsky never uses the phrase as such (*The Revolutionary Age,* March 15, 1919, p. 3). Russian writers like Trotsky and Lenin frequently used the term "masses," of course, but never in the transcendental sense that "mass action" had for the Dutch.

32. Interview with L. E. Katterfeld, September 7, 1956.
33. See *New York Call,* April 8, 9, 12, 13, 1917; Fine, pp. 307–16; and Morris Hillquit, *Loose Leaves from a Busy Life* (Macmillan, 1934), pp. 165–66, for the subcommittee of three. My interpretation of Boudin's role is quite different from that of Shannon who believes that Boudin held a "middle-ground position" (p. 96).
34. Bell (see Key), p. 311.
35. *New York Call,* January 3, 1919.
36. New York *Tribune,* March 9, 1917.
37. Evans Clark, *New York Call,* April 10, 1918.
38. In his mayoralty campaign in New York City in 1917, Hillquit demanded "peace" in his acceptance speech (*Loose Leaves from a Busy Life,* p. 183). But after the election, William Hard of the *New Republic* asked him whether he favored withdrawing from the war and he answered in the negative (*New Republic,* November 24, 1917, and *New York Call,* December 15, 1917).
39. Fine (see Key), p. 322.
40. *New York Call,* December 19, 1917. (The paper's name was changed to *The Evening Call* from December 3, 1917, to August 12, 1918, but it is more convenient to use the original name throughout.)
41. *The New International,* June 16, 1917, p. 3.
42. *The Class Struggle,* May–June 1918, p. 338.
43. *New York Call,* August 4, 1917.
44. *The Workers' World* (Kansas City, Mo.), July 18, 1919, when the seven went to jail.
45. *The New International,* October 1, 1917.
46. Shannon (see Key), pp. 112–13.
47. Ibid., pp. 114–16.
48. *New York Call,* July 2, 1917.

Chapter 6: The Reflected Glory

1. *The Worker,* November 4, 1922; *The Workers Monthly,* October 1925, p. 531, and September 1926, p. 483.
2. Karl Marx and Frederick Engels, *The Russian Menace to Europe,* selected and edited by Paul W. Blackstock and Bert F. Hoselitz (Free Press, 1952), pp. 217, 228, 235.
3. Lenin, *The Imperialist War,* p. 357.

4. Lenin, *Collected Works,* Vol. XX, Book I, pp. 85–87.
5. Leonard Schapiro, *The Origin of the Communist Autocracy* (Harvard, 1955), pp. 32–34. In 1924, Stalin admitted that he was one of those who differed with Lenin for about two weeks in April 1917 (J. V. Stalin, *Collected Works,* Moscow: Foreign Languages Publishing House, 1952, Vol. VI, p. 348).
6. See *New York Call,* August 17, 1917, p. 6, and *American Labor Who's Who* (see Key), pp. 230–31, for biographical data.
7. *New York Call,* April 29, 1917.
8. Ibid., May 20, 1917.
9. Ibid., May 5, 1917.
10. Charles Louis [Louis C. Fraina], "The Seizure of Power," *The New International,* May 5, 1917, p. 1 (italics in original).
11. Ibid., p. 30.
12. *The New International,* "Lenin on the Russian Revolution," July 21, 1917; "Lenin on the Russian Land Problem," November 1, 1917.
13. Ibid., Anton Pannekoek, "Russia, Germany, America," July 21, 1917; "The Clash After the War," June 16, 1917.
14. I have followed the Gregorian calendar. According to the Julian calendar, which prevailed in Russia until 1918, the revolutions of 1917 took place in February and October respectively.
15. *The New International,* November 1, 1917.
16. *The Class Struggle,* November–December 1917, p. 85.
17. Ibid., January–February 1918, pp. 29–67.
18. *The Communist,* October 25, 1919, p. 3.
19. Boudin was ousted from the editorial board in the issue of September–October 1918. In the issue of February 1919, Eugene V. Debs replaced him. In the issue of November 1919, Jack Carney replaced Debs.
20. O. Piatnitsky, *Communist International* (London), December 1, 1933, p. 835.
21. V. I. Lenin, *Selected Works,* Vol. VII, p. 294.
22. Ibid., Vol. VIII, p. 33.
23. Ibid., Vol. VII, p. 291.
24. Ibid., Vol. VIII, p. 345.
25. N. Lenin and Leon Trotsky, *The Proletarian Revolution in Russia,* edited by Louis C. Fraina (The Communist Press, 1918), p. xix. (See note 31, Chapter 6.)
26. Bell (see Key), p. 320: "The left of 1918 was completely unlike the left of 1912." Also Falk, op. cit., p. 156: ". . . the American Communist movement began from virtually nothing. It was not the continuation of the Left Wing of 1912, and was fundamentally different from it."
27. J. C. Rovitch, "Confusion and Compromise," *The New International,* June 16, 1917, p. 2.
28. "The Bolshevik Policy," *The New International,* February 1918, p. 7.

29. The first name, Friends of the Russian Revolution, was used at the first public meeting on December 4, 1917 with Alexander Trachtenberg, George R. Kirkpatrick, Art Young, and Hutchins Hapgood (see *New York Call*, December 4, 1917, p. 2, for advertisement and list of full committee; December 5, 1917, pp. 1–2, for report of the meeting). The second name, Friends of New Russia, was used at the outdoor demonstration on December 21, 1917, with the speakers listed as Joseph D. Cannon, Frank Harris, Juliet Stuart Poyntz, and Ludwig Lore (see *New York Call*, December 21, 1917, p. 7, for advertisement with a smaller and somewhat different committee, though most of the names are similar).

30. The five Russian organizations were the Russian Socialist federation, the New York group of Social Revolutionists, the Russian branch of the Socialist party, the New York branch of the Russian Bolsheviki, and the *Novy Mir* (*New York Call*, February 2, 1918).

31. *The Proletarian Revolution in Russia*, op. cit., pp. 78, 81, 83, 84, 401–402. A section of this book appeared as a separate pamphlet, entitled *The Soviets at Work* (Rand School of Social Science, 1918). This pamphlet, actually the text of an address by Lenin to the Supreme Soviet, played an exceptional role in winning sympathy for the Bolsheviks among Left Wing Socialists. In his forthcoming autobiography, Max Eastman tells how this pamphlet revived his revolutionary fervor and made him a Communist sympathizer. Whittaker Chambers went through the same experience six years later (*Witness*, Random House, 1952, p. 194). I have chosen to quote from the original translation, but a more adequate one may be found in Lenin's *Selected Works*, Vol. VII, pp. 313–50. Trotsky's book, *The Bolsheviki and World Peace* (Boni and Liveright, 1918) appeared a few months before *The Proletarian Revolution in Russia* but it was mainly a blown-up translation of an old pamphlet by Trotsky, originally entitled *The War and the International*, published in 1914. Trachtenberg tells the story of the race by American publishers to get out something by Trotsky (*New York Call*, February 9, 1918). This unauthorized translation took a pamphlet of 60 pages and converted it into a book of 239 pages.

32. *New York Call*, March 1, 1918. See March 12 and 20, 1918, for other meetings.

33. Many of these messages, including the full text of the second, may be found in *Revolutionary Radicalism* (see Key), Vol. I, pp. 634–636. But parts of both are also reported in the *New York Call*, February 28, 1918.

34. *The New International*, April 1918, p. 2, reported two meetings held on February 28 and March 12, 1918. *New York Call*, March 1, 1918, reported that a delegation had been sent to Washington but failed to get the War Department's approval.

35. Michael Gold, "How I Came to Communism," *New Masses*, September 1932.

416 THE ROOTS OF AMERICAN COMMUNISM

36. See *Revolutionary Radicalism*, Vol. I, p. 631, and *New York Call*, February 27, 1918, p. 5, for Nuorteva's appointment as Finnish representative; and *New York Call*, March 1, 1918, p. 5, for Sirola's American activity.
37. See *New York Call*, June 10, 1918, p. 4, for advertisement.
38. The New York *World*, February 24, 1919, called Nuorteva the chief pro-Bolshevik propagandist. See *New York Call*, March 9, 1919, p. 8, for Nuorteva's comment.
39. *National Office Review*, February 1918. This first proclamation on Russia was adopted February 4, 1918. A typewritten copy is included in the Socialist Party Collection at Duke University Library.
40. *Special Official Bulletin*, September 17, 1918 (typewritten copy at Duke University Library). This conference was held August 10–12, 1918.
41. See *Jewish Daily Forward*, May 17, 1918, and *New York Call*, May 30, 1918, p. 6, for translation.
42. Morris Hillquit, "Labor and the War," *The Liberator*, July 1918, p. 21.
43. Quoted in Shannon (see Key), p. 119.
44. Quoted in Bell, p. 319.
45. *The Liberator*, May 1919.
46. Harrison George, *The Red Dawn* (Chicago: I.W.W. Publishing Bureau, 1918). Most of this pamphlet was written in early December 1917 (p. 22), making it the first of its kind. It was published in February 1918, and the I.W.W. sold thousands of copies until the anti-Soviet faction won control in 1920. See Art Shields, *Daily Worker*, August 10, 1937, p. 9, for details about the pamphlet.
47. *Bill Haywood's Book*, p. 308.
48. Cannon to Draper, April 21, 1954.
49. Harold Lord Varney, "Left Wing or I.W.W.—The Way to Unity," *The Revolutionary Age*, April 19, 1919, p. 8. Floyd Dell called *Revolt* "the best example so far produced in America of a significant new kind of fiction—the Novel of Proletarian Revolt" (*The Liberator*, July 1919, p. 49). The father of the "proletarian novel" soon became the father of confessions by ex-radicals. Varney wrote a series of articles for the New York *World* in 1920, "exposing" the I.W.W., which set a pattern. In the nineteen-thirties, he became the editor of *The Awakener*, a magazine of the extreme Right.
50. Lenin's *Letters* (see Key), pp. 391, 411.
51. Arthur Ransome, *Russia in 1919* (Huebsch, 1919), pp. 120–21.
52. *The Weekly People*, May 11, 1918.
53. *The American Labor Year Book, 1919–1920*, pp. 420–21.
54. Lenin, *The Imperialist War*, p. 149.
55. *New York Call*, December 24 and 26, 1917.
56. Ibid.; see letter signed by sixteen names, December 27, 1917, p. 6, and Fraina's letter, January 5, 1918, p. 7.

NOTES: CHAPTERS 6 AND 7

57. Ibid., December 26, 1917, p. 6.
58. Ibid., Bela Low, September 14, 1918, p. 7.
59. Ibid., Joseph Shaplen, letter, December 6, 1918, p. 8. Also see article by Bela Low, January 12, 1919, and report of Shaplen's talk in Brooklyn, January 13, 1919.
60. Melech Epstein, *Jewish Labor in U.S.A., 1914–1952* (Trade Union Sponsoring Committee, 1953), p. 64.
61. *The Red Dawn*, p. 25.
62. *The American Labor Year Book, 1919–1920*, pp. 420–21: "This process of organization, and the result—the Soviets, corresponds to the industrial union program long ago formulated by the Socialist Labor Party, with such differences, of course, as naturally result from the differences between the two countries (Russia and the United States of America)."

CHAPTER 7: ROADS TO MOSCOW

1. James Oneal, *Socialist Party Bulletin* (Chicago), May 1917, p. 7.
2. The first pamphlets were published by the Socialist Publication Society, which also published the magazine *The Class Struggle*. Of its first ten pamphlets, two were by Price—*The Old Order in Europe and the New Order in Russia* and *The Soviet, the Terror, and Intervention*—and one by Ransome—*Open Letter to America*. Pamphlets by Williams—*The Bolsheviks and the Soviets* and *Soviet Russia*—were published by The Rand School of Social Science and Charles H. Kerr & Co. respectively. Williams also mentions Madeleine Z. Doty of *Harper's* and Louis Edgar Brown of the *Chicago Daily News* (*The Bolsheviks and the Soviets*, p. 19).
3. Williams was introduced as "an authorized messenger to the American people from Lenin and the Soviet Government" in *The Liberator*, December 1918, p. 24, note. His contribution has been overshadowed by Reed's, but he was not far behind as a sympathetic interpreter of the Bolshevik regime.
4. *The Autobiography of Lincoln Steffens*, p. 799.
5. Ibid., p. 799.
6. *The Letters of Lincoln Steffens* (Harcourt, Brace, 1938), Vol. II, p. 539.
7. *The Autobiography of Lincoln Steffens*, p. 817.
8. *New Masses*, June 1931, p. 5.
9. Hicks (see Key), pp. 223–24, touches on Reed's support of Wilson, but Reed's innermost thoughts seem to be contained in a letter, dated October 13, 1916, evidently sent to Socialist party headquarters (in the Duke University Library Collection).
10. Hicks, p. 259. No one can write about John Reed without making this book the chief source, though I have not always followed it in interpretation, or, farther on, for material.
11. Reed's plans were divulged to Lenin by Alexander Gumberg, a former manager of the New York *Novy Mir*, who acted as go-between for

the Bolshevik officials and the American representatives in Moscow. Gumberg's version is given by George F. Kennan in *Russia Leaves the War* (Princeton, 1956, pp. 405–10). Gumberg claimed that Reed had proposed the publication of an official American Russian-language newspaper in Petrograd and had negotiated with various Soviet officials concerning future Soviet-American commercial relations. Hicks says that Reed had considered a proposal to edit an official American propaganda newspaper in Russia (p. 296). Eastman says that Reed concocted a "scheme by which American capital was going to be piped over to Petrograd in floods, and employed all unbeknownst to itself, by some ingenious system of social ducts and by-passages, in building up a great newspaper and explaining everything to everybody and making the world safe for proletarian revolution" (*Heroes I Have Known*, Simon & Schuster, 1952, pp. 214–15). Ironically, after exposing Reed's capitalistic inclinations in order to quash the consular appointment, Gumberg came back to the United States and became personal adviser to a real American capitalist.

12. Hicks, p. 342.
13. Joseph North, *Robert Minor* (International, 1956) is the official Communist biography. It is almost a *reductio ad absurdum* of Communist hagiology. For most of his Communist career, Minor was a slavish follower, first of Lovestone, then of Browder, both of whom he betrayed. Neither Lovestone nor Browder are ever mentioned in this book. North's book does not always agree on details with previous articles on Minor in the Communist press: Philip Sterling, *Daily Worker*, September 11, 12, and 15, 1933; Orrick Johns, *New Masses*, August 28, 1934, pp. 16–18. There is other biographical material of unequal quality in Benjamin Gitlow, *The Whole of Their Lives*, pp. 70–82, and Joseph Freeman, *An American Testament*, pp. 303–308. Of much greater interest is an early autobiographical sketch by Minor himself, "How I Became a Rebel," *The Labor Herald*, July 1922, pp. 25–26. North and Sterling say that Minor joined the Socialist party in 1907; Minor said that the date was about 1908. North says that Minor worked for the New York *World* in 1914–1915. It was *The Evening World*, a separate paper, though the publishers were the same. In order to make him one of the founders of the Communist party, which he was not, Johns took the liberty of claiming that Minor "had been a member since the Party was formed in 1919." Subsequently, an article in the *Daily Worker* by Beth McHenry said that he joined the Communist party in 1920 (May 23, 1938, p. 5). There was an obituary of Minor's father, Judge Robert B. Minor, who died at the age of 84, in the *Daily Worker*, June 22, 1935, p. 1. Another son, Houston, was a San Antonio deputy sheriff.
14. Robert Minor, *Sunday Worker*, January 8, 1939. Minor's pro-Mooney pamphlet was entitled *Shall Mooney Hang?* (1918).

NOTES: CHAPTER 7

15. New York *World*, February 4, 1919.
16. Robert Minor, "I Change My Mind A Little," *The Liberator*, October 1920, pp. 5–11.
17. Max Eastman, "A Statesman of the New Order," *The Liberator*, September 1918, pp. 11–12.
18. Floyd Dell, *The Liberator*, May 1919, p. 45.
19. Joseph Freeman, *An American Testament*, (Farrar & Rinehart, 1936), p. 103.
20. Irwin Granich (Michael Gold), "Max Eastman—A Portrait," *New York Call*, February 9, 1918. From the same article: "How can I hope to embody in poor words the personal essence of the man, so humane and charming, so melodious yet deep as the dark river of life itself?"
21. Michael Gold, *The Modern Quarterly*, Vol. 3, No. 3, 1926, p. 161. Dell began to develop a social interpretation of literature in a number of book reviews in *The Liberator* in 1919. He set forth his main ideas at length in a long essay entitled "Literature and the Machine Age" (*The Liberator*, October 1923–October 1924), later republished in book form as *Intellectual Vagabondage* (Doran, 1926).
22. *The Liberator*, September 1918, p. 10.
23. Ibid., December 1919, pp. 23–25.
24. Ibid., June 1921, pp. 5–7 (italics in original).
25. Ibid., April 1918.
26. Ibid., December 1918, p. 45.
27. Ibid., June 1921, p. 7.
28. Floyd Dell, *Homecoming* (Farrar & Rinehart, 1933), pp. 346–47.
29. Irwin Granich (Michael Gold), "Towards Proletarian Art," *The Liberator*, February 1921, p. 20.
30. Max Eastman, *Colors of Life* (Knopf, 1918).
31. Bertrand Russell, "Democracy and Revolution," *The Liberator*, May and June 1920. The quotation is from May 1920, p. 14.
32. Bertrand Russell, "Soviet Russia—1920," *The Nation*, July 31, 1920, pp. 121–26, and August 7, 1920, pp. 152–54.
33. *The Liberator*, September 1920, pp. 5–10, 27–29.
34. Max Eastman, *Since Lenin Died* (London: Labour Publishing Co., 1925), p. 129; for his own version of his Russian trip, Max Eastman, *Reflections on the Failure of Socialism* (Devin-Adair, 1955), pp. 11–15.
35. *An American Testament*, p. 383.
36. Michael Gold, *New Masses*, June 1930, p. 5.
37. *An American Testament*, p. 571. Freeman also wrote: "The unbounded admiration for Trotsky was not confined to Mike Gold; it marked all the extreme radicals of this country, who followed Russian events at a distance in both space and time" (p. 384).

Chapter 8: The Revolutionary Age

1. *The New International*, June 16, 1917, p. 4.
2. Corey, outline for "One Rebel's Years." In his F.B.I. Interrogation, he said that he was called to Boston in May or June 1918.
3. The first issue of *The Revolutionary Age* was dated November 16, 1918, but it was not until the fourth issue, dated November 27, 1918, that it claimed to be the official organ of the Boston local.
4. Reprinted in *The Revolutionary Age*, January 4, 1919, p. 4.
5. *Latvju enciklopedija, 1950–1951*, op. cit., p. 2193.
6. *Revolutionary Radicalism* (see Key), Vol. I, p. 261.
7. Schlüter died in January 1919, and Lore replaced him as editor of the *New Yorker Volkszeitung* (*New York Call*, January 31, 1919).
8. *The Revolutionary Age*, November 20, 1918, p. 1.
9. The articles were called, "The Background of the German Revolution" and the book, *The Social Revolution in Germany*. (*The Revolutionary Age*, 1919). His other books were *Revolutionary Socialism* (1918) and *The Proletarian Revolution in Russia*, which he edited (1918).
10. *The Revolutionary Age*, November 16, 1918, p. 1.
11. This is from the original translation in *The Revolutionary Age*, December 28, 1918, pp. 4–5. There is a slightly different translation in Lenin, *Collected Works* (International, 1945), Vol. XXIII, pp. 192–204. This "Letter" and a second one in 1919 were two of the earliest Communist pamphlets to be widely circulated.
12. *The Revolutionary Age*, December 18, 1918, p. 3.
13. Ibid., January 18, 1919, p. 8 (italics in original).
14. See *American Labor Year Book, 1917–1918*, p. 340, for the party and federation figures for 1917; Germer's Report, *New York Call*, September 2, 1919, for the middle of 1919.
15. Table of monthly membership figures for the foreign-language federations in the Duke University Library Collection from October 1917 to March 1919 (photographic copy in possession of the author).
16. *New York Call*, January 7, 1919, p. 7.
17. *The Class Struggle*, February 1919, pp. 114–115.
18. Caro Lloyd, *Henry Demarest Lloyd* (Putnam, 1912), Vol. I, p. 44.
19. From Isaac E. Ferguson's testimony in the court record of *The People of the State of New York against Isaac E. Ferguson and Charles E. Ruthenberg*, pp. 757–60, 777, 819–20.
20. *The Revolutionary Age*, March 1, 1919, p. 8.
21. Ibid., February 8, 1919, p. 8.
22. Hicks (see Key), p. 343.
23. *The New York Communist*, April 19, 1919, p. 2.
24. An interview in the *New York Call*, October 18, 1918, p. 3, men-

tions Gitlow's attendance at law school. The rest of this paragraph is based on his autobiography, *I Confess*, pp. 3–21.
25. Interview with Bertram D. Wolfe, June 16, 1956.
26. See *American Labor Who's Who* (see Key), p. 245, and *Daily Worker*, June 20, 1932, p. 3, for Weinstone's background. It was a point of honor for Communist leaders to claim involvement in the revolutionary movement at the earliest possible age. In Weinstone's case, the first source gives his membership in the Socialist Party at the age of 18, the second at 16. The same confusion arises in Lovestone's background. In the Hearings before a Special Committee on Un-American Activities, House of Representatives, 76th Congress, 1st Session, he testified that he became a political organizer in 1912, which would mean at the age of 14 (*Investigation of Un-American Propaganda Activities in the United States*, 1939, Vol. XI, p. 7097). In his testimony in the trial of Harry M. Winitsky in New York in 1920, Lovestone said that he joined the Socialist party at the end of 1916 or early in 1917 (p. 376 of court record). Lovestone's background was most fully given by himself at the trial in 1923 arising from the Bridgman raid (*People vs. Ruthenberg* [see Key], pp. 133–34 of the court record). *The Intercollegiate Socialist* (organ of the Intercollegiate Socialist Society), October–November 1916, p. 31, lists Jacob Liebstein (Jay Lovestone) as secretary of the C.C.N.Y. chapter, and, October–November 1917, as president (p. 22), with William Winestein (Weinstone) as secretary (p. 31). Evidently the names were changed in 1919.
27. *The Revolutionary Age*, May 24, 1919, p. 7.
28. See *New York Call*, March 7, 1919, p. 8, for his debate with Joseph Shaplen.
29. See ibid., March 1, 1919, p. 9, for Trachtenberg's letter, and March 2, 1919, p. 9, for Cohen's reply. Also see the contemptuous reference to Trachtenberg in *The New York Communist*, April 19, 1919.
30. See Moissaye J. Olgin, *The Soul of the Russian Revolution* (Holt, 1917), p. viii, for the commendation in Professor Simkovitch's introduction; and p. 376, for the characterization of the Mensheviks and Bolsheviks.
31. Leon Trotsky, *Our Revolution* (Holt, 1918), p. iv of Olgin's preface, and Olgin's biographical notes, pp. 3–22. This volume contains four of Trotsky's contributions to the New York *Novy Mir*.
32. In a review of the book, Trachtenberg remarked that Olgin was "not in agreement with the policies of the present government in Russia" (*New York Call*, March 30, 1918).
33. M. J. Olgin, *Trotskyism: Counter-Revolution in Disguise* (Workers Library Publishers, 1935).
34. The statement of this group, headed by David P. Berenberg, was published in the *New York Call*, March 23, 1919.

35. *The New York Communist,* April 26, 1919, p. 5.
36. See *New York Call,* January 26, 1919, p. 3, for a report of a lecture by Nearing; and April 28, 1919, p. 1, for the prediction.
37. Scott Nearing, *Violence or Solidarity? or Will Guns Settle It?* (People's Print, 1919); *The New York Communist,* June 7, 1919, p. 7.
38. *The Revolutionary Age,* November 30, 1918, p. 1.
39. See *New York Call,* January 19, 1919, p. 8, for Algernon Lee's letter explaining his vote in favor of the Victory Arch; and May 29, 1919, p. 2, for article by Evans Clark, research director for the Socialist alderman, for an authoritative version of the two votes.
40. The chief source for the account of the break in New York is "The Growth of the Left Wing" by Maximilian Cohen in *The Revolutionary Age,* March 8, 1919, p. 7. A less detailed version was given in the New York *Tribune,* January 6, 1919, p. 5, which Algernon Lee called "fairly accurate" (*New York Call,* January 8, 1919, p. 8). Foster's *History* (see Key) confuses the date of the founding of the Left Wing Section on February 15 with this meeting held earlier (p. 162).
41. The author found a complete set of the Minutes of the Left Wing Section in the musty old files of the Lusk committee deposited in the New York State Library, Manuscript Division, in Albany, New York (photographic copies in possession of the author). The Minutes for February 2, 1919 show that a City Committee was in existence and Cohen was functioning as Executive Secretary at that time. Cohen's article in *The Revolutionary Age,* March 8, 1919, has created confusion by appearing to start the organization of the Left Wing Section on February 15. The first county organizers were Carl Brodsky (New York County), Edward Lindgren (Kings), Benjamin Gitlow (Bronx), and Aarons (Queens). For a copy of the membership blanks, see *Revolutionary Radicalism* (see Key), Vol. I, p. 681.
42. Cohen, op. cit., gives the date as February 15, 1919, but a note in *The Revolutionary Age,* March 22, 1919, p. 4, has February 16, which is also given by Gitlow (*I Confess,* p. 25).
43. Benjamin Gitlow, Nicholas I. Hourwich, Fanny Horowitz, Jay Lovestone, James Larkin, Harry Hiltzik, Edward I. Lindgren, Milton Goodman, John Reed, Joseph Brodsky, Dr. Julius Hammer, Jeannette D. Pearl, Carl Brodsky, Mrs. L. Rovitch, and Bertram D. Wolfe (City Committee); Gitlow, Hourwich, George Lehman, Larkin, L. Himmelfarb, George C. Vaughn, Benjamin Coser, Lindgren, and Cohen (Executive Committee).
44. Minutes of the Left Wing Section, March 22 and April 6, 1919.
45. *The New York Communist,* April 19, 1919, p. 5.
46. *Revolutionary Radicalism* (see Key), Vol. I, p. 682.
47. The two versions were published in *The Revolutionary Age,* February 8, 1919, pp. 4–6, and March 22, 1919, pp. 4–5.

CHAPTER 9: THE REAL SPLIT

1. J. Fineberg, *The Communist International*, 1929, Nos. 9–10 (Tenth Anniversary Issue), pp. 443–44.
2. New York *World*, February 4, 1919, p. 2.
3. B. Reinstein, *The Communist International*, op. cit., pp. 428–35.
4. Arthur Ransome, *Russia in 1919* (B. W. Huebsch, 1919), p. 35.
5. Gazette of the Temporary Workers' and Peasants' Government, No. 31. For full text, see *Recognition of Russia* (see Key), Part 2, p. 207.
6. See *The Revolutionary Age*, March 1, 1919, p. 1, for the original text.
7. *The Revolutionary Age*, March 29, 1919, p. 6, mentions the merger of the Socialist Propaganda League and the Left Wing Section in New York in an editorial note relating to a pamphlet by S. J. Rutgers. Nevertheless, a meeting under the auspices of the Socialist Propaganda League was announced in the *New York Call*, April 4, 1919, p. 8. No further sign of life of the League was found.
8. Fineberg, op. cit., p. 444.
9. Reinstein, op. cit., p. 432.
10. Reinstein's role seems so embarrassing that Foster's *History* (see Key) goes to the trouble of demoting him to an "unofficial representative" (p. 159, note). The official records of the First Congress list him with the official delegates, and Reinstein himself told the story of his unauthorized "official" representation.
11. Fineberg, op. cit., p. 444.
12. Eberlein, *The Communist International*, op. cit., p. 437.
13. Eberlein, op. cit. The best account of the entire episode is in Branko Lazitch, *Lénine et la IIIe Internationale* (Switzerland: Ed. de la Baçonniere, 1951), pp. 96–113.
14. *Der I. Kongress der Kommunistischen Internationale: Protokoll der Verhandlungen* (Verlag der Kommunistischen Internationale, 1921), p. 35.
15. *The Revolutionary Age*, March 1, 1919, p. 1.
16. Ibid., May 10, 1919, p. 7.
17. *New York Call*, March 23, 1919. The other signatories were F. G. Biedenkapp, Evans Clark, Walter M. Cook, Jacob Lawn, Flore M. Line, Moses Oppenheimer, Albert Pauly, and Henry Sipos.
18. *The Revolutionary Age*, March 29, 1919, p. 3.
19. Minutes of the Left Wing Section, April 23, 1919.
20. *New York Call*, April 15, 1919, p. 6.
21. Minutes of the Left Wing Section, April 20, 1919.
22. *The New York Communist*, April 19, 1919, p. 8.
23. *New York Call*, letters by Moses Oppenheimer, April 21, 1919, p. 5; Israel Amter, April 25, 1919; and nine signatories, April 28, 1919.
24. Maximilian Cohen, *The New York Communist*, May 24, 1919, p. 6.
25. See *New York Call*, September 7, 1919, p. 7, for the official figures.

Slightly different figures may be found in the Report of Louis C. Fraina to the Communist International, *Manifesto and Program* (Chicago: Communist Party of America, 1919), pp. 33–34.

26. *New York Call,* May 21, 1919, p. 8.
27. *The New York Communist,* May 24, 1919, p. 7.
28. Each side gave out different figures for the expulsions. The Left Wing claimed that nearly 40,000 were expelled or suspended. The official figure was about 27,000 (circular letter by Adolph Germer, June 21, 1919, in possession of the author). The Michigan party was credited with 6115 members in March 1919 and only 3131 in May 1919 (Report of Adolph Germer to the N.E.C., August 27, 1919). This monthly fluctuation, common to all units of the party, largely accounts for the different estimates. The seven suspended foreign-language federations claimed a total membership of over 30,000, but I have chosen to use the more conservative official estimate in order to make it consistent with the other official figures.
29. See *National Bulletin,* June 15, 1919, for the complete Minutes of this meeting of the National Executive Committee, May 24–29, 1919.
30. Report of Adolph Germer to the National Executive Committee, August 27, 1919.
31. See *The Proletarian* (Detroit), June–September 1919, for a series of articles on "Revolutionary Political Action," the fullest exposition of the Michigan program.
32. See *Russian Propaganda:* Hearing Before a Subcommittee of the Committee on Foreign Relations, U.S. Senate, 66th Congress, 2nd Session (Government Printing Office, 1920), for Martens' testimony.
33. See Hearings of the Joint Legislative Committee Investigating Seditious Activities, New York State, 1919 (Lusk Committee), Stenographic Minutes, testimony by Martens, p. 1138, for the reference (unpublished, in the New York State Library, Albany, New York). Parts of this testimony were used in the report, *Revolutionary Radicalism* (see Key), Vol. I, pp. 627–57.
34. Nicholas I. Hourwich, "Problems of the Soviet Representative," *The Revolutionary Age,* April 19, 1919, p. 6 (italics in original).
35. Minutes of the Left Wing Section, April 20, 1919.

CHAPTER 10: THE GREAT SCHISM

1. *The Revolutionary Age,* April 26, 1919, p. 1.
2. *The Communist* (Vol. 1, No. 5), August 23, 1919, p. 11. This is the first publication with this name, put out by the Michigan–foreign-language-federations group. Vol. 1, No. 1, was dated July 19, 1919. (See note 21, Chapter 13, for fuller explanation.)
3. Hourwich, *The Revolutionary Age,* April 5, 1919, p. 4.
4. Foster's *History* (see Key) always has the embarrassing problem of excluding names that later became *persona non grata* and including

names that remained *persona grata*. In this case, he mentions Alexander Bittelman, W. W. Weinstone, and Charles Krumbein as if they were delegates to the conference, and omits most of the real delegates (p. 164). The delegation from New York was made up of Larkin, Wolfe, Reed, Cohen, Lindgren, MacAlpine, Hourwich, Gitlow, Paul, Zucker, Carl Brodsky, and Waton; with three alternates, Lovestone, Hiltzik, and Fanny Horowitz (Minutes of the Left Wing Section, May 25, 1919). Both Bittelman and Weinstone were New Yorkers, but they were not elected delegates. There is a list of 79 names of conference delegates in the Larkin Trial, pp. 81–82.

5. See *The Revolutionary Age*, July 5, 1919, for the official record of the First National Conference of the Left Wing, June 21–24, 1919; and July 19, 1919, for "All Power to the Left Wing!" by Louis C. Fraina, pp. 7–8, and I. E. Ferguson's letter, p. 14.

6. Lewis Corey, "One Rebel's Years" (outline).

7. See *The Revolutionary Age*, July 5, 1919, p. 6, or *Revolutionary Radicalism*, Vol. 1, pp. 716–38, for the text.

8. Fraina and Ferguson, *The Revolutionary Age*, July 19, 1919, pp. 7 and 14.

9. *The Communist* (National Organization Committee), July 19, 1919, p. 3.

10. *The Revolutionary Age*, July 19, 1919, p. 8.

11. This connection between the date of the Communist organization and the struggle for control between the English-speaking elements and the foreign-language federations was keenly analyzed by Alexander Bittelman in "A Memorandum on the present situation in the Communist movement of America, adopted by the Communist Unity Committee for submission to the Executive Committee of the Third Communist International," *Communist Unity*, Vol. 1, No. 2, February 1, 1921, p. 3. In the thirties, Bittelman became the more or less official historian of the American Communist movement and wrote a pamphlet, *Milestones in the History of the Communist Party*, which is of little value. For the very early period, however, the Memorandum is candid and revealing. There is also a historical sketch written by Bittelman, apparently as a synopsis for lectures, at the end of 1923 or the beginning of 1924 and published in *Investigation of Communist Propaganda*, 1930 (see Key, Bittelman). These two early historical efforts by Bittelman show a keen mind permitted to become hopelessly partisan and pedantic.

12. The full committee was made up of Dennis E. Batt, D. Elbaum, Oakley C. Johnson, John Keracher, S. Kopnagel, J. V. Stilson, and Alexander Stoklitsky (*The Communist*, July 19, 1919, p. 2). For the Call, see *Novy Mir*, July 7, 1919.

13. The first issue is dated July 19, 1919.

14. *The Revolutionary Age*, August 2, 1919.

15. Gitlow, *I Confess*, pp. 37–38.

16. *The Revolutionary Age,* August 23, 1919.
17. An inside view of how the Russian leaders played with the English-speaking groups and ultimately chose between them is given by Bittelman (see Key), pp. 441–42.
18. See *The Revolutionary Age,* August 23, 1919, for the text of the Call.

CHAPTER 11: THE SIBLING RIVALRY

1. There are as many versions of this incident as there are sources. I have mainly followed Shannon (see Key), pp. 143–45, based partially on a personal interview with Germer; a letter from Germer to the Members of the Socialist Party in Virginia, dated September 29, 1919 (Duke University Library Collection); Minutes of the Left Wing Caucus, August 29, 1919; and Gitlow, *I Confess,* pp. 44–47. There are other versions in Hicks (see Key), pp. 359–60; Max Eastman, *The Liberator,* October 1919, pp. 7–8; *New York Call,* August 31, 1919; and Harry Laidler, *Socialist Review,* December 1919, p. 106. The main dispute is over who called the police. Germer told Shannon the story about Wagenknecht's indiscretion to the *Chicago Tribune* reporter. However, Gitlow, Eastman, and Hicks assume that Germer called the police. It would be impossible to make all these versions consistent, but they agree on the main point: the Left Wing was thrown out by the police after a scuffle between Reed and Germer.
2. Herman Michelson, *New York Call,* September 1–2, 1919; Laidler, op. cit., pp. 106–107; Oneal, op. cit., pp. 61–64. Different sources give different figures for the second wave of walkouts from the Socialist convention.
3. *Historical Review of the Split in the Socialist Party and the Organization of the Communist Labor Party and the Communist Party* (Brooklyn Branch of the Communist Labor Party, signed by A. Pauly, organizer, mimeographed, 3 pp., September 1919), p. 2 (in possession of the author). The official roster of delegates numbered 82 (*The Ohio Socialist,* September 10, 1919). But 92 delegates from 22 states were claimed in an *Official Report of the Chicago Convention,* published by the Communist Labor Party (a 2-p. printed circular). The *Historical Review* claimed regularly elected delegates from 23 states without giving any number.
4. *The Ohio Socialist,* September 17, 1919, pp. 2–3, published the official proceedings of the Communist Labor party convention.
5. Most of this incident is based on Max Eastman, "The Chicago Conventions," *The Liberator,* October 1919, pp. 18–19, and Gitlow, op. cit., pp. 52–53. The first version of Boudin's last words is from Eastman, the second from Shannon, p. 148.
6. Gitlow, op. cit., p. 53, and *New York Call,* September 6, 1919, p. 2.
7. *The Communist,* October 25, 1919, p. 3. This is the second series

NOTES: CHAPTER 11

of the same name, published by the Communist party of America. Vol. 1, No. 1, of this series was dated September 27, 1919. (See note 21, Chapter 13.)

8. Katterfeld moved from the state of Washington to Kansas in 1917.
9. This paragraph is based on Max Eastman, *The Liberator,* October 1919, p. 14; I. E. Ferguson, "The Communist Party Convention," *The Communist,* September 27, 1919, pp. 4–5; *New York Call,* September 2 and 3, 1919; New York *World,* September 2, 1919; and Jacob Spolansky's testimony at the St. Joseph, Michigan, trial in 1923, *People vs. Ruthenberg* (see Key), p. 21. As usual, some of the details vary. Eastman has Batt arrested by Detective Sergeant Egan, *The Call* by Detective Sergeant Lawrence McDonough. *The Call* also reported that the protesting Communist lawyer, L. M. Montgomery, was beaten unconscious, but Eastman merely says that a lawyer was arrested besides Batt. For one of the police photographs of the convention in session, see *Revolutionary Radicalism* (see Key), Vol. I, opposite p. 750, which also gives twenty-two names identifying individuals in the picture. For the exact number of delegates, *The Communist,* September 27, 1919, p. 11.
10. *The Communist,* September 27, 1919, pp. 10–12, for the exchange of proposals.
11. I. E. Ferguson's article in *The Communist,* September 27, 1919, is the basic source for the factional struggle at the Communist party's convention. An interesting inside view of the foreign-language federations' control and tactics was once given by Alexander Bittelman of the Jewish federation (p. 441; see Key): "Leadership of federation caucus knew that it must have the services and support of an English-speaking group in order to form and lead the party. Two English-speaking groups to choose from. The Michigan group or the group of *The Revolutionary Age.* Each of the two groups presents its program to the federation caucus. . . . After long struggle, federation caucus accepts program of the group of *Revolutionary Age.*"
12. *New York Call,* September 2, 1919.
13. Ibid., September 6, 1919.
14. The Central Executive Committee was composed of Ruthenberg, Fraina, Ferguson (Illinois), Schwartz (Lettish federation), Karosses (Lithuanian federation), Charles Dirba (Minnesota), Harry M. Wicks (Oregon), Oscar Tywerousky (Russian federation), Petras (Hungarian federation), Maximilian Cohen (New York), D. Elbaum (Polish federation), Alexander Bittelman (Jewish federation), John J. Ballam (Massachusetts) and Jay Lovestone (New York). The smaller Executive Council was made up of the first seven. Ruthenberg, Hourwich, Stoklitsky, and Ferguson were also elected International Delegates.

One of the odd things in Foster's *History* (see Key) is the lack of interest, judging by the shortage of space, in the two founding conventions, which are described in a little over a page, and their programs, which get two pages. The extreme compression at this point, after 170 pages for the pre-Communist period, avoids the problem of telling what happened at the conventions or mentioning those delegates who had become *persona non grata*. One might imagine that the names of the first Central Executive Committee would be of some interest, at least in a footnote, but then such forbidden figures as Fraina and Lovestone would have to be mentioned and Foster himself would have stood out by reason of his absence.

15. Gitlow, op. cit., pp. 55–56.
16. *The Communist*, October 4, 1919, p. 6.
17. Ibid., October 18, 1919, p. 2.
18. This section is largely based on the parties' programs, which may most conveniently be found in *Revolutionary Radicalism*, Vol. I, pp. 776–98, for the Communist party, and Vol. I, pp. 809–17, for the Communist Labor party. The Communist party's Manifesto, Program, and Constitution was originally published in *The Communist*, September 27, 1919, and reprinted in a pamphlet, *Manifesto and Program* (Chicago: Communist Party of America, 1919). The Communist Labor party's Platform, Program, and other documents were originally published in the 2-page circular, *Official Report of the Chicago Convention*. The versions in *The American Labor Year Book, 1919–1920*, pp. 414–19, are only excerpts.
19. These figures varied, sometimes in the same issue of a single paper. The 58,000–10,000 figures were handed down because they appear in the pamphlet, *Manifesto and Program* (pp. 37–38). They also appeared in *The Communist*, September 27, 1919, pp. 11–12, but the same issue gives the Communist party "more than 60,000" (p. 2). Two months later, the Communist party reduced the figure to "approximately 50,000" and specifically stated that it was based on "convention credentials" (ibid., November 29, 1919, p. 6). By the end of 1919, it called itself "an organization of Fifty Thousand Workers" (ibid., December 27, 1919, p. 7). Two years later, Ruthenberg said that there were ten or fifteen thousand members in the Communist Labor party and forty or fifty thousand in the Communist party (David Damon [Ruthenberg], *The Communist* [U.C.P.], July 1921, p. 26). Ruthenberg and Bedacht later asserted that the two parties had 50,000 to 60,000 members (Damon and Marshall [Ruthenberg and Bedacht], "Problems of Communist Organization in the U.S.," *The Communist*, July 1922, p. 23).
20. *Historical Review of the Split in the Socialist Party and the Organization of the Communist Labor Party and the Communist Party*, p. 2. *The Official Report of the Chicago Convention* (p. 2) claims more

than 30,000 members for the Communist Labor party, without offering any figures for the Communist party.
21. *The Communist*, November 29, 1919, p. 7. New Jewish and German federations were organized after the convention.
22. *The Communist*, September 27, 1919, p. 12.
23. "The Convention of Revolutionists" by Y.F. [I. E. Ferguson], *The Communist* (U.C.P.), June 12, 1920, p. 3.
24. See *The Communist* (C.P.) August 1, 1920, p. 6, for the two sets of figures.
25. Gitlow, op. cit., p. 57.
26. Ibid.
27. *The Communist* (pro-Ruthenberg faction), May 8, 1920, p. 3.
28. *The Communist* (C.P. of A.), September 27, 1919, p. 9.
29. *The New York Communist*, June 14, 1919, p. 2.
30. Melech Epstein, *Jewish Labor in U.S.A. 1914–1952* (New York: Trade Union Sponsoring Committee, 1953), pp. 106–107.
31. *The New York Communist*, June 14, 1919, p. 6. Epstein has misplaced the split in 1920 (op. cit., p. 107).
32. *The Communist* (C.P. of A.), October 25, 1919, p. 7. This is further proof from contemporary sources that Epstein's version of the formation of the Jewish Communist federation cannot be correct in its date.
33. See the table on p. 189.
34. Ella Reeve Bloor, *We Are Many*, pp. 160–62; Al Richmond, *Native Daughter: The Story of Anita Whitney* (San Francisco: Anita Whitney 75th Anniversary Committee, 1942); for Rose Pastor Stokes, see *Daily Worker*, June 20, 1939, p. 7, and *New Masses*, June 1933, pp. 23–24; for Juliet Stuart Poyntz, *American Labor Who's Who* (see Key), p. 188.
35. This paragraph is mainly based on Ruthenberg's own testimony at the St. Joseph trial, p. 117 of the court record; *A Communist Trial* (New York: National Defense Committee, 1922), extracts from the testimony of C. E. Ruthenberg in the New York trial in 1921; an early newspaper article about him in the *Cleveland Press*, October 18, 1912; and the *Daily Worker*, July 9, 1927, March 2, 1928, and February 28, 1931. The older official Communist version of his life was given by Jay Lovestone, introduction to *Speeches and Writings of Charles E. Ruthenberg* (International, 1928) and *Ruthenberg, Communist Fighter and Leader* (International, 1928); the newer one by Elizabeth Gurley Flynn, *Debs, Haywood, Ruthenberg* (Workers Library Publishers, 1939).
36. *Cleveland Press*, October 18, 1912.
37. *New York Call*, July 30, 1912, p. 4.
38. C. E. Ruthenberg, *Are We Growing Toward Socialism?* (Local Cleveland, Socialist party, 1917), pp. 38 and 48.

39. *The Liberator*, June 1919, p. 9.
40. See *The Ohio Socialist*, May 8, 1919, for the most gory report.
41. Virtually the same words were used by Lovestone in his pamphlet on Ruthenberg (op. cit., p. 1) and a quarter of a century later by Foster in his *History* (p. 264). When Lovestone used them, he considered himself Ruthenberg's heir; when Foster used them, Ruthenberg was the least dangerous to Foster's prestige of all the possible founders in terms of the party's subsequent history.

Chapter 12: The Underground

1. *The Liberator*, February 1923, p. 13.
2. *The Revolutionary Age*, February 15, 1919, p. 2.
3. *The Communist*, September 27, 1919, p. 2.
4. Ibid., October 4, 1919, p. 1.
5. Ibid., October 11, 1919, p. 5.
6. Ibid., October 18, 1919, p. 2.
7. Ibid., November 29, 1919, p. 3 (italics in original).
8. *The Workers Monthly*, September 1926, p. 484.
9. For confirmation, see Bittelman (see Key), p. 441.
10. *The Communist*, October 4, 1919, p. 3.
11. Ibid., September 27, 1919, p. 3.
12. Frederick Lewis Allen, *Only Yesterday* (Harper, 1931), p. 46.
13. "Report upon the Illegal Practices of the United States Department of Justice," *To the American People* (Workers Defense Union, 1920), p. 3.
14. Clayton R. Lusk was chairman of the Joint Legislative Committee Investigating Seditious Activities. The committee's report, *Revolutionary Radicalism* (see Key), is a valuable repository of early documents, though much of the material must be handled critically.
15. Gitlow tells about his experiences in prison in *I Confess*, Chapter III.
16. Emma Goldman relates her experiences on the *Buford* in *Living My Life* (Knopf, 1931), Vol. II, pp. 711–26.
17. Robert K. Murray, *Red Scare* (University of Minnesota Press, 1955), pp. 210–38, describes the national and state government campaigns.
18. See *The Communist*, February 15, 1920, p. 4, and April 5, 1920, p. 7.
19. "Rules for Underground Party Work," signed by Central Executive Committee, Communist Party of America, *The Communist International*, Nos. 16–17 (1921), pp. 120–21.
20. See *The Communist*, August 1, 1920, p. 6, for the following two sets of figures.
21. Gitlow, op. cit., p. 66.
22. *People vs. Ruthenberg* (see Key), p. 178.

Chapter 13: The Second Split

1. Bittelman (see Key), p. 443.
2. For Ruthenberg's side of the story, see his statement, *The Communist* (C.P.), May 1, 1920, pp. 5, 8, and "What Kind of Party?" in *The Communist* (pro-Ruthenberg), May 8, 1920, p. 3. For the anti-Ruthenberg side, see "Statement to the Membership," *The Communist* (C.P.), May 1, 1920, pp. 6–7. (See note 21, Chapter 13.)
3. *The Communist* (C.P.), November 8, 1919, p. 12, and November 22, 1919, p. 3.
4. Bittelman, *Communist Unity*, February 1, 1921, pp. 3–4; *The Communist* (C.P.), February 15, 1920, p. 4.
5. See *Communist Labor* (C.L.P.), May 15, 1920, pp. 5–6, for the exchange of correspondence.
6. *Communist Labor* (C.L.P.), May 15, 1920; "Statement to the Membership," op. cit., p. 6, and "What Kind of Party?", op. cit., pp. 4 and 8.
7. "What Kind of Party?", op. cit., p. 4.
8. "Statement to the Membership," op. cit., p. 6 (capitalization in original).
9. Bittelman says that Ruthenberg finally agreed "to frankly state our position on armed insurrection" (p. 442). But it is clear that Ruthenberg never changed his mind on the main issue ("What Kind of Party?", op. cit., p. 4).
10. *The Communist* (C.P.), May 1, 1920, p. 8.
11. *Communist Labor*, May 15, 1920, p. 7; *The Communist* (U.C.P.), July 3, 1920, p. 4. According to another version in *Communist Labor*, May 1, 1920, the vote against Ruthenberg was 5 to 4, with the minority of four, all the district organizers except one, and the representatives of the German, Ukrainian, South Slavic, Esthonian, and Polish federations breaking away.
12. Damon [Ruthenberg], "Make the Party a 'Party of Action'," *The Communist* (pro-Ruthenberg), April 25, 1920, p. 4.
13. *The Communist* (C.P.), May 1, 1920, pp. 2, 8 (capitalization in original).
14. "What Kind of Party?", op. cit., p. 8.
15. *The Communist* (C.P.), May 1, 1920, p. 8.
16. *The Communist* (pro-Ruthenberg), May 8, 1920, p. 2.
17. *Communist Labor*, May 15, 1920, p. 7.
18. The date of the Unity Convention is given as May 26–31, 1920, in an American report to the Communist International (*Berichte zum Zweiten Kongress der Kommunist. Internationale* [Hamburg: Verlag der Kommunistischen Internationale, 1921], p. 367). Foster's *History* (see Key) gives the date as May 15, 1920, which seems to be incorrect.
    The Communist (U.C.P.), June 12, 1920, p. 3, mentions the Com-

intern's representative. The opposition Communist party protested that this "representative" had no such mandate (*The Communist* [C.P.], November 15, 1920, pp. 4–5. According to Katterfeld, a Russian member of the Comintern happened to be passing through the United States on his way to another country and incidentally attended this convention (interview, September 8, 1956).

19. For this and the following references, see "The Convention of Revolutionists" by Y.F. [I. E. Ferguson] in *The Communist* (U.C.P.), June 12, 1920, pp. 3–5 and 7; also the Constitution (pp. 6–7) and Program (pp. 8–16).

20. Foster's *History* incorrectly states that Ruthenberg was elected executive secretary of the U.C.P. (p. 177). The official report clearly states that "Meyer" was appointed to this position (*The Communist* [U.C.P.], June 12, 1920, p. 2).

21. To avoid confusion, the different publications called *The Communist* have been accompanied by the initials of the party. By 1920 there were four: (1) Published by the National Organization Committee, Vol. 1, No. 1, dated July 19, 1919; (2) Published by the Communist party of America, Vol. 1, No. 1, dated September 27, 1919; (3) The same as the foregoing but representative only of the pro-Ruthenberg "minority," three issues only, dated April 25, May 8, and May 22, 1920; (4) Published by the United Communist party, Vol. 1, No. 1, dated June 12, 1920. The Communist and United Communist organs were published from the summer of 1920 to the summer of 1921 with the same names. In 1922, there were further splits and more series of *The Communist* which are identified in note 4, Chapter 21.

William A. Nolan in his *Communism versus the Negro* (Regnery, 1951, p. 214) incorrectly assumes that there were only three different publications bearing the identical title of *The Communist*. The listings under this title in the *Bibliography on the Communist Problem in the United States* (The Fund for the Republic, 1955, p. 459) are also inadequate.

22. Bittelman, p. 443.

23. The Communist party claimed that it had 12,740 members before the split and 8350 afterward. The difference was 4390, but it also claimed that only 3490, or about 28 per cent, had gone over to the United Communist party (*The Communist* [C.P.] August 1, 1920, p. 6). Ruthenberg claimed that 6119, or about 60 per cent of the C.P.'s membership, followed him into the U.C.P. Added to 4525 for the C.L.P., this gave the U.C.P. a total of 10,644 (*Berichte zum Zweiten Kongress*, op. cit., p. 355). If Ruthenberg was right, only about 4000 were left in the C.P. Subsequently, however, statements were permitted certifying an average membership for the period July–October 1920 of 7552 for the C.P. and 4561 for the U.C.P. (*The Communist* [C.P.], December 15, 1920, p. 8). The U.C.P. protested that the

C.P.'s figures were inflated and itself rated both of them equal in size (ibid., January 5, 1921, p. 5). Ruthenberg later admitted that he had inflated the C.L.P. figure by over 400 per cent. When the U.C.P. went out of existence in 1921, he admitted that "there were less than a thousand of the original ten or fifteen thousand members of the Communist Labor Party who came into the United Communist Party" (*The Communist*, Vol. 1, No. 1, of the Communist party of America series, dated July [1921], p. 26) though he had previously claimed 4525 for the C.L.P.

Gitlow's estimate seems to have changed with the passing of time. In his first book, *I Confess* (1939), he wrote: "A few months after the Chicago conventions both parties together had only from eight to ten thousand members. In fact, so badly was the movement disorganized that it was impossible to check up on its membership in order to determine its actual number" (p. 65). In his second book, *The Whole of Their Lives* (1948), he wrote: "The 16,000 Communist party members who remained in the two communist parties, after the raids, voluntarily undertook the perils of Communist party membership" (p. 63). It seems to this writer that Gitlow was more nearly right the first time.

24. *The Communist* (C.P.), August 1, 1920, p. 5.
25. *The Communist* (U.C.P.), June 12, 1920, p. 7.
26. *Revolutionary Radicalism* (see Key), Vol. II, pp. 1900–901.
27. *The Communist* (U.C.P.), Vol. 1, No. 7 (1920), p. 1 (capitalization in original). The last dated number of this series is Vol. 1, No. 5, August 15, 1920. The issues from No. 6 on are not dated. Previously the paper had been issued every two weeks. Vol. 1, No. 7, was probably issued early in September 1920.
28. See *The Communist* (C.P.), August 1, 1920, for the text of the program and constitution adopted at the second convention of the Communist party of America.

CHAPTER 14: SPIES, VICTIMS, AND COURIERS

1. *To the American People*, op. cit., p. 3.
2. *New York Times*, January 3, 1920, p. 2.
3. C. E. Ruthenberg, "The Story Nosovitsky Didn't Tell," *Daily Worker*, December 19, 1925.
4. Corey, F.B.I. Interrogation, p. 44.
5. New York *American*, September 20, 27, October 4, 11, 18, 25, November 1, 8, 15, 1925. Ruthenberg's article in the *Daily Worker*, December 19, 1925, was written in answer to Nosovitsky's series.
6. This particular detail was confirmed thirty years later. Nosovitsky said that Fraina went as "Ralph Snyder" (New York *American*, October 25, 1925), and Lewis Corey also recalled that he had used

the name of "Snyder" (F.B.I. Interrogation, p. 46). Nosovitsky said that Fraina used a British passport. Corey implied that it was Canadian.

7. *Stenographic Record of the "Trial" of Louis C. Fraina* (Issued by the Central Executive Committee of the Communist Party of America, 1920).
8. Ibid., p. 22.
9. New York *American*, November 8, 1925.
10. *The Communist* (C.P.), April 5, 1920, p. 3.
11. New York *American*, November 8 and 15, 1925.
12. *The Communist* (C.P.), May 1, 1920, p. 4.
13. Fraina gave the date as February 10–17, 1920, in *The Communist* (C.P.), May 1, 1920, p. 4. However, the opening of the conference was dated February 3, 1920, in a previous issue (April 5, 1920, p. 3).
14. Corey, F.B.I. Interrogation, p. 47.
15. Murphy (see Key), pp. 87–89.
16. *The Communist* (C.P.), April 5, 1920, p. 3.
17. *The Communist* (C.P.), May 1, 1920, p. 5.
18. *The Communist* (U.C.P.), June 12, 1920, p. 2, and *The Communist* (C.P.), April 5, 1920, p. 1.
19. *The Communist* (C.P.), July 3, 1920, p. 8.
20. New York *American*, September 20, 27, 1925.
21. See *New York Times*, September 3, 1953, for Borodin's obituary.
22. Clare Sheridan, *Russian Portraits* (London: Jonathan Cape, 1921), p. 86.
23. I am indebted to Carl Sandburg for giving me the information about this incident. The foregoing three paragraphs are based on a letter, dated February 25, 1956; an informal memorandum; and a conversation with Mr. Sandburg, April 23, 1956, in New York City.
24. Manavendra Nath Roy published many installments of his memoirs in *The Radical Humanist*, a Calcutta weekly, in 1953 and 1954. The Borodin story was contained in the issues of August 9, 16, and 30, 1953. D. H. Dubrowsky's testimony is in *Investigation of Un-American Propaganda Activities in the United States:* Hearings before a Special Committee on Un-American Activities, 1939, Vol. 8, pp. 5157–59. Jacob Spolansky's *The Communist Trail in America* (Macmillan 1951), pp. 172–75, adds some personal details to Dubrowsky's story. Corey, F.B.I. Interrogation, p. 91, contains Fraina's version.
25. This story was related to Max Eastman, in a letter dated August 17, 1956, by a famous Irish statesman who was personally involved in the entire incident. The author of the letter gave Mr. Eastman authorization to permit me to tell the story in this book, but requested that his name should not be used. Confirmation of the main details may be found in the Dáil Debates (1948), Vol. 110, col. 172, and Vol. 113,

NOTES: CHAPTERS 14 AND 15

col. 1526. The Irish Government Information Bureau also issued a statement on April 1, 1950, informing the public that the loan had been repaid and the jewels returned.

26. A German version first appeared in the *New Yorker Volkszeitung*, January 4, 1920. The English version appeared in the *New York Times*, January 25, 1920; *The Communist*, March 1, 1920, p. 4; *Revolutionary Radicalism* (see Key), Vol. I, pp. 468–74.
27. *Current History*, February 1920, pp. 303–304. A different translation was published in *Investigation of Communist Propaganda*, 1930, Part III, Vol. 2, pp. 78–79. There are significant differences in the two versions. Instead of ordering the American Communists to organize the party in Moscow, the second version states: "Upon the formation of the Communist Party, measures should be taken to have a representative at Moscow."
28. New York *World*, March 29, 1920. The full text was later published in *The Communist* (U.C.P.), August 15, 1920, pp. 5 and 11, entitled "The Communist International to the American Movement." It is also in *Revolutionary Radicalism*, Vol. II, pp. 1902–907, in a different translation.
29. The New York *World*, March 29, 1920, devoted only a single sentence to this agreement. The full text was later published in *The Communist* (U.C.P.), July 17, 1920, p. 5, and reprinted in *Revolutionary Radicalism*, Vol. II, pp. 1908–909.
30. The full text was published in *Solidarity*, August 14, 1920; and reprinted in Gambs, *The Decline of the I.W.W.*, op. cit., pp. 207–22, as well as *Revolutionary Radicalism*, Vol. II, pp. 1933–46.

CHAPTER 15: THE CRISIS OF COMMUNISM

1. *The Liberator*, October 1921, p. 6.
2. See Lenin, *Selected Works*, Vol. X, p. 27, for Lenin's statement at the First Congress; *Manifest, Richtlinien, Beschlüsse des Ersten Kongresses—Aufrufe und offene Schreiben des Exekutivkomitees bis zum Zweiten Kongress* (Hamburg: Verlag der Kommunistischen Internationale, 1920, p. 91), for the Comintern's May Day proclamation; Lenin, *Collected Works* [in Russian] (Moscow, 1932, Vol. XXIV, p. 381), for Lenin's speech in July 1919.
3. Emma Goldman, *My Disillusionment in Russia* (Doubleday, Page & Co., 1923), pp. 15 and 48.
4. V. I. Lenin, *"Left-Wing" Communism: An Infantile Disorder* (International, rev. ed., 1934), pp. 50–54.
5. Lenin, *Selected Works*, Vol. IX, p. 338.
6. Ibid., Vol. X, p. 332.
7. Hicks (see Key), pp. 366–71.
8. Ibid., pp. 372–74.
9. Based on Corey, "One Rebel's Years" (outline). Murphy's story

(see Key) is in much greater but somewhat different detail (pp. 99–105).
10. *The Communist* (U.C.P.), No. 11 (1920), p. 8.
11. Corey, F.B.I. Interrogation, p. 50.
12. *The Communist* (U.C.P.), No. 11, p. 8.
13. Corey, "One Rebel's Years" (outline).
14. *The Worker*, July 29, 1922, p. 5.
15. *The Communist* (C.P.), November 15, 1920, p. 2. The official *Protokoll* of the Second Congress lists seven American delegates. The other three were Chabrow and Jurgis of the Independent Young People's Socialist League, and Gildei, unidentified, with a voice but not a vote (p. 780).
16. John Reed, *The Communist* (U.C.P.), No. 10 (1920), p. 3.
17. Hicks, p. 391.
18. Lazitch, op. cit., p. 144. (But Lazitch, p. 142, is mistaken about the American delegates to the Second Congress.)
19. Hicks, p. 391.
20. *Der Zweite Kongress der Kommunistischen Internationale: Protokoll der Verhandlungen* (Verlag der Kommunistischen Internationale, 1921), p. 523.
21. Ibid., p. 629.
22. Ibid., pp. 482–501.
23. See *The Communist* (C.P.), April 1921, pp. 5–8 and 14, for Fraina's full explanation.
24. *Der Zweite Kongress der Kommunistischen Internationale* (Vienna: Verlag der Arbeiter Buchhandlung, 1920), p. 98. This is the condensed version, not to be confused with the fuller Protokoll published the following year. Oddly, the earlier "condensed" version has important material not included in the larger one.
25. *Der Zweite Kongress* (*Protokoll*), p. 647.
26. John Reed, *The Communist* (U.C.P.), No. 10 (1920), p. 3.
27. Murphy, pp. 164–65, also p. 124.
28. *Der Zweite Kongress* (condensed version), pp. 19, 20, 27, 28.
29. *The Theses and Statutes of the Communist International*, as adopted at the Second World Congress (issued by the Central Executive Committee of the Communist Party of America, from the original published by the Communist International in Moscow, 1921), pp. 25–30.
30. *Izvestia*, December 17, 1918 (translated in *Soviet Documents on Foreign Policy*, ed. by Jane Degras, Oxford, 1951, Vol. 1, pp. 127–128).
31. *The Communist* (C.P.), August 1, 1920, p. 8.
32. *Manifesto and Program, Constitution, Report to the Communist International* (Chicago: Communist Party of America, 1919), p. 19.
33. *The Party Organization* (Chicago: Workers Communist Party of America, 1925), p. 27.

NOTES: CHAPTERS 15 AND 16   437

34. *The Theses and Statutes of the Communist International*, op. cit., p. 8.
35. James P. Cannon, *The Fifth Year of the Russian Revolution* (Workers Party of America, 1923), p. 21.
36. *Investigation of Communist Propaganda*, 1930, Part I, Vol. 4, p. 384.

CHAPTER 16: TO THE MASSES!

1. *Der Zweite Kongress (Protokoll)*, pp. 607–608.
2. *The Unity Proceedings* (Statement of the C.E.C. of the Communist Party on Unity and International Relations, 4 pp., n.d., probably November 1920), p. 1.
3. *The Communist* (C.P.), November 1, 1920, p. 8.
4. Ibid., November 15, 1920, pp. 2, 5.
5. Ibid., September 15, 1920, p. 2. Other figures were 7552 claimed by the C.P. and 4561 by the U.C.P., in *Unity Proceedings* to December 15, 1920 (U.C.P., 4 pp., n.d., probably end of December, 1920), p. 1.
6. *The Communist* (U.C.P.), No. 13 (January 1921), p. 1.
7. Bittelman (Raphael) was the leader of this committee which published at least four numbers of a bulletin, *Communist Unity*. He criticized the sectarianism of the C.P. but supported the foreign federations against the criticism of the U.C.P.
8. *The Communist* (U.C.P.), No. 15 (March 1921), p. 5.
9. His original name was Carl Jansen, but he changed the spelling to Johnson. Later he was usually known by his party name, Scott, and it is easier to follow him by it.
10. *The Communist* (U.C.P.), No. 16 (April 1921), p. 3.
11. The differences in detail were revealed in the *Official Bulletin No. 1* (probably June 1921), published by the Communist Party of America, pp. 1–2.
12. The Joint Unity Convention was reported in Vol. 1, No. 1 of *The Communist* (series published by the Communist Party of America, dated July 1921); see p. 3 for this passage. Professor Jacob W. Hartmann, a philologist by profession and a prolific translator, who was then editing the magazine *Soviet Russia*, served as "impartial chairman" at this convention.
13. Ibid., p. 26.
14. Ibid., p. 2.
15. *Official Bulletin No. 2* (issued by the Central Executive Committee of the Communist Party of America, undated, probably August 1921), pp. 4–7.
16. Ibid., p. 6.
17. See J. Carr [L. E. Katterfeld], *The Communist International*, December 1921, p. 390 for the figures at the end of 1921.
18. See *The Communist* (C.P. of A.), July [1921], pp. 19–23, for the full text of the Constitution of the Communist Party of America.
19. Clara Zetkin, *Protokoll des III Kongresses der Kommunistischen In-*

ternationale (Verlag des Kommunistischen Internationale, 1921), p. 287; Ruth Fischer, *Stalin and German Communism* (Harvard University Press, 1948), pp. 174–75.
20. *Protokoll des III Kongresses,* p. 90.
21. Leon Trotsky, *The First Five Years of the Communist International* (Pioneer Publishers, 1953), Vol. II, p. 38.
22. *Protokoll des III Kongresses,* p. 509 (English translation in Lenin's *Selected Works,* Vol. X, pp. 279–88).
23. See *The Communist,* August 1921, for English translation.
24. *Protokoll des III Kongresses,* pp. 571–73.
25. Ibid., pp. 823–27, 850–58.
26. The meeting with Lenin was described at length by Max Bedacht in an interview, June 1, 1954, and in two letters, dated July 30, 1954, and January 20, 1955. Bedacht also wrote about the meeting in the *Daily Worker,* January 2, 1932. Minor's version appeared in the *Daily Worker,* June 19, 1928. and January 6, 1934. All of these sources agree substantially but details vary. Minor says six Americans were present. Bedacht recalls only four.
27. The first edition of this pamphlet was published by the Communist Labor party, in late 1919 or early 1920. It was reprinted by the Contemporary Publishing Association, New York, in 1920.
28. Interview with Katterfeld, September 8, 1956.
29. Lenin, *Selected Works,* Vol. XII, pp. 190–282.
30. Katterfeld was expelled early in 1929 because he refused to submit to party control a magazine devoted to the subject of evolution, which he had founded in 1927.

CHAPTER 17: THE REVOLUTION DEVOURS ITS CHILDREN

1. Hicks (see Key).
2. Hicks to Draper, letter dated February 17, 1954: "I still regard with extreme skepticism the stories about Reed's disillusionment."
3. Hicks, p. 395.
4. *Modern Monthly,* October 1936, p. 18, and December 1936, pp. 14–21. These articles were later reprinted as a chapter on John Reed in Eastman's *Heroes I Have Known,* pp. 201–37, with some additional material.
5. Benjamin Gitlow, *The Whole of Their Lives* (Scribner, 1948), pp. 33–36.
6. Emma Goldman, *My Further Disillusionment in Russia* (Doubleday, Page, 1924), p. 26.
7. Emma Goldman, *Living My Life* (Knopf, 1931), Vol. II, p. 851.
8. Emma Goldman, *My Disillusionment in Russia* (Doubleday, Page, 1923), p. 16.
9. Hicks to Draper, February 17, 1954. Hicks alluded to this bizarre

story without mentioning Irwin's name or the gist of the allegation in his letter to the *Modern Monthly,* May 1937, p. 16.
10. Hicks to Draper, February 17, 1954. Also Hicks's letter, *Modern Monthly,* May 1937, p. 16.
11. Angelica Balabanoff, "John Reed's Last Days," *Modern Monthly,* January 1937, pp. 3-6, contains the fullest account. Mme. Balabanoff's autobiography, *My Life as a Rebel* (Harper, 1938), leaves out some of the details.
12. Angelica Balabanoff (Rome) to Theodore Draper, April 4, 1954. This is similar to what Mme. Balabanoff told Max Eastman in 1936, though in much greater detail (*Modern Monthly,* December 1936, p. 20).
13. This letter from Lewis Corey to Granville Hicks, dated December 30, 1935, was made available to me by Mrs. Esther Corey.
14. Corey, "One Rebel's Years" (outline).
15. Corey, F.B.I. Interrogation, p. 52.
16. Quoted by Hicks in the *Modern Monthly,* May 1937, p. 16, from the letter mentioned in note 13.
17. Hicks to Draper, February 17, 1954.
18. Introductory biographical and critical essay by John Stuart in *The Education of John Reed* (International, 1955), especially pp. 37-38.
19. John Reed, "The World Congress of the Communist International," *The Communist* (U.C.P.), No. 10 (1920), pp. 1-3.
20. "Last Days with John Reed," a letter from Louise Bryant, *The Liberator,* February 1921, p. 11. There is no hint of Reed's disillusionment in this letter.
21. J. Stalin, *Collected Works,* Vol. VI, p. 339.
22. A long note was devoted to Fraina by James Oneal in *American Communism* (1927, pp. 97-98). It took revenge on Fraina for his share in splitting the Socialist party by solemnly repeating Nuorteva's charges and inexplicably omitting all mention of the investigation and exoneration in Moscow. Oneal implied that the mystery of Fraina was "reminiscent of the old days of Czarist Russia when the revolutionary occasionally turned out to be a spy of the Czar."

Gitlow's first book, *I Confess* (1939, pp. 323-24) was comparatively restrained on the subject of Fraina. He makes Nosovitsky into "a very good personal friend of Fraina" and mentions the New York "trial" while passing over all the other efforts made to check on the charges, all in Fraina's favor. His reference to the accusation of embezzlement "a few months later for example," shows that he was very hazy about the whole period in which these events took place. But Gitlow permitted himself much greater liberties in his second book, *The Whole of Their Lives* (1948, pp. 10-16). After repeating Nuorteva's old charges, he does his best to give them credence without taking responsibility for them by assuming that Nosovitsky had a mysterious hold over Fraina. The difference between Gitlow's two books is amusingly illustrated by the following example: in 1939, Gitlow wrote that Fraina dropped out of the Communist movement a "few months" after the New York "trial." In 1948, he wrote that Fraina "won the confidence of Zinoviev" and "became one of Zinoviev's powerful and dreaded inner circle that dominated Comintern affairs." He does not bother to explain, for the benefit of his earlier readers, how and why Fraina should have dropped out of the movement in the very months when he was becoming such a powerful and dreaded figure in the Comintern. It should be remembered that Gitlow himself spent 1920–22 in jail and could hardly have had firsthand knowledge of Fraina's movements in this period.

23. *The Communist* (U.C.P.), No. 11 (probably November 1920), p. 8.
24. *Attorney General A. Mitchell Palmer on Charges Made Against Department of Justice by Louis F. Post and Others:* Hearings before the Committee on Rules, House of Representatives, 66th Congress, 2nd Session (Washington, D.C.: Government Printing Office, 1920), pp. 51–54. Many years later, the author put the same question of Fraina's alleged connection with the Department of Justice to Jacob Spolansky, who of all people was in a position to know in the early twenties. Spolansky scoffed at the very suggestion and ruled it out as a possibility.
25. *The Radical Humanist,* January 17, 1954, p. 30.
26. In the F.B.I. Interrogation, the figures given are: $25,000 to Murphy, $20,000 to Scott, and $10,000 remaining in Fraina's possession (pp. 80–86). In a typewritten memorandum by Lewis Corey, the total figure is given as $55,000, with $20,000 to Murphy and $10,000 to Scott mentioned. In the outline for "One Rebel's Years," the only figure given is $50,000 for the total.
27. *The Communist* (United Toilers), February 1922, p. 11.
28. Corey, F.B.I. Interrogation, p. 113.
29. Ibid., p. 83. In an interview on September 8, 1956, L. E. Katterfeld recalled that he had been asked in Moscow, toward the end of 1922, about Fraina's debt to the Comintern, and that a sum of about $5000 was mentioned. Katterfeld knew nothing about the matter.
30. Gitlow, *The Whole of Their Lives,* p. 15, mentions $386,000.
31. Cannon to Draper, June 15, 1954 (reprinted in the *Fourth International,* Spring 1955, pp. 58–59).
32. Gitlow, op. cit., p. 16. Gitlow also says that Fraina "spent many years in Mexico."
33. *New Republic,* April 17, 1929, p. 247. Other articles appeared in the issues of January 26, 1927; August 10, 1927; and May 2, 1928.
34. George Soule of the editorial staff of the *New Republic* asked Professor Wesley C. Mitchell to comment on the second article. Professor Mitchell replied that he had but "minor criticisms to make." Professor Frank H. Knight, then of the College of Commerce of

the University of Iowa, wrote to Lewis Corey after the second article to tell him how much he liked it, asking who he was, expressing the desire to look up other of his writings and assuring him that he intended to watch for more in the future (correspondence in the possession of Mrs. Esther Corey).

35. The review by David Ramsey in the *Daily Worker*, November 9, 1934, made some minor criticisms. It declared: "The volume under review represents a serious and, to a large extent, successful effort to give a factual and documental verification of the Marxian analysis of the decline of capitalism in terms of the American scene." A large order was placed by the party's literature department, subsequently cancelled, and the Workers Bookshop on 13th Street in New York City gave it a full window display for a few days.

36. Alexander Bittelman and V. J. Jerome, *Leninism, the Only Marxism Today* (Workers Library, 1934). This is a reprint of two articles in *The Communist*, October 1934, pp. 1033–56, and November 1934, pp. 1125–56.

37. *The Crisis of the Middle Class* was reviewed in friendly fashion by David Ramsey in the *New Masses*, December 17, 1935. The book was given away with subscriptions for a time (see advertisement on back cover, December 10, 1935).

38. *New Masses*, April 7, 1936. Corey was listed as "chairman of the editorial committee" which prepared the issue.

39. Cannon to Draper, June 15, 1954 (reprinted in the *Fourth International*, Spring 1955, p. 59).

40. "One Rebel's Years" (outline). In Corey's F.B.I. Interrogation he said: "The first big jolt, the final jolt that finally made me see that even this general faith and hope that Soviet Communism would still move in the right direction had to be abandoned—were the purges of 1936, 1937." But other material in the Corey papers indicates that he did not call himself an anti-Communist until 1939.

41. *The Nation*, February 17, 24, and March 2, 1940. Also see the comments on his viewpoint in the issue of March 9, 1940, by Norman Thomas, Earl Browder, Bertram D. Wolfe, Algernon Lee, and Max Shachtman.

42. Corey and Murray Gross, a trade-union official, took the initiative in November 1940 to form the Union for Democratic Action, of which Murray Gross became the secretary and Freda Kirchwey the treasurer. The first Provisional Committee was composed of Jack Altman, Robert Bendiner, John S. Childs, Lewis Corey, George S. Counts, Kenneth G. Crawford, Franz Daniels, Eduard Heimann, Alfred Baker Lewis, Reinhold Niebuhr, Nora Piore, A. Phillip Randolph, and Mark Starr. Its program was contained in the pamphlet *A Program for Americans* (1941). In 1946, the U.D.A. called a meeting to expand by taking in New Dealers ousted by the Truman administration; the result was the transformation of the U.D.A. into

Americans for Democratic Action—another example of the peculiar seminal influence which Corey exerted on organizations in which he never stayed long enough to enjoy any power.
43. *Daily Worker,* June 12, 1941, p. 6.
44. One of his former students voluntarily sent him a statement that a representative of the Ohio Communist party had come to a meeting of the Young Communist League at Antioch with instructions to "get rid of Corey." The extreme Rightist leaflet was reported in the Antioch student paper, *The Record,* December 6, 1946.
45. The author asked the Immigration and Naturalization Service of the Department of Justice for permission to consult the record of the hearings, but was informed, in a letter dated May 3, 1954, signed by Assistant Commissioner Carl B. Hyat, that the Service's records were confidential and the request was therefore refused. According to an article by William V. Shannon in the *New York Post,* October 20, 1953, Gitlow testified that he "had no reason to know" that Corey had become an anti-Communist. The author communicated with Mr. Corey's lawyer, Jack Wasserman, of Washington, D.C., who was present at the hearing, in an attempt to verify this account, and received the reply quoted in the text September 17, 1954. Subsequently, Mr. Wasserman tried to obtain the minutes of the hearing in a letter to the Immigration and Naturalization Service, dated March 19, 1956. This request was also refused. Finally, the author wrote Mr. Gitlow a letter, dated August 3, 1956, in an effort to obtain an explanation of this and other points for the purposes of this book. Mr. Gitlow did not reply.

In the Corey papers are two letters that were never sent. One was written in 1947 to E. P. Dutton & Co., publishers of an enlarged edition of James Oneal's *American Communism,* with additional material by G. A. Werner. The other, written in 1948, was addressed to Max Eastman, who contributed the introduction to Benjamin Gitlow's *The Whole of Their Lives.* Both protest bitterly against what Corey considered the books' malicious misrepresentations. They were never sent, evidently because Corey decided that he could never catch up with the "dastardly distortions" spread against him. At the time of his death, however, he had made up his mind to write an autobiography. One of the major human and political documents of our time was lost. There is a short appreciation, "Lewis Corey, 1894–1953," in the *Antioch Review,* December 1953, pp. 538–40.

For those interested in Lewis Corey's intellectual development, the following incomplete bibliography may be helpful: "The New Capitalism," in *American Labor Dynamics* (1928); *The House of Morgan* (1930); *The Decline of American Capitalism* (1934); *The Crisis of the Middle Class* (1935); articles in *The Marxist Quarterly* (1937); "Marxism Reconsidered," *The Nation,* February 17, 24, and March 2, 1940; "A Liberal Looks at Life," in *Frontiers of Democracy,* May

15, 1941; *The Unfinished Task* (1942); *Meat and Man* (1950); "A Plea for Liberal Socialism," in *The New Leader*, July 15, 1950. At his death, he was engaged on a new biography of Frances Wright, which was partially completed; and he left outlines for two more books: his autobiography, entitled "One Rebel's Years: A Contribution to the Autobiography of a Generation," and a 7000-word outline of his last political faith, "Towards an Understanding of America."

Chapter 18: New Forces

1. *People vs. Ruthenberg*, pp. 133–34 (see Key and note 7, Chapter 22); interview with Lovestone, June 21, 1954.
2. *American Labor Who's Who* (see Key), p. 245.
3. Max Bedacht, interview, June 1, 1954 and letter, Bedacht to Draper, December 13, 1954; Philip Sterling, *Daily Worker*, October 13, 1933, p. 5.
4. James P. Cannon, "The I.W.W.," *Fourth International*, Summer 1955, pp. 75–86, a nostalgic article commemorating the fiftieth anniversary of the founding convention of the I.W.W. in 1905. It contains a sympathetic appreciation of Vincent St. John.
5. Based on interview, September 23, 1955; and James P. Cannon, "The Debs Centennial," *Fourth International*, Winter 1956.
6. *The Workers' World*, September 26, 1919, p. 1.
7. The direct line to the *Daily Worker* runs through *The Toiler*, First there was the *Ohio Socialist*, organ of the Socialist party of Ohio. It became an official organ of the Communist Labor party and changed its name to *The Toiler*, in the issue of November 26, 1919. *The Toiler* was transferred from Cleveland to New York in October 1921 and changed its name to *The Worker* in February 1922. The change from a weekly to a daily came in January 1924.
8. This paragraph is based on a letter from Cannon to Draper, April 21, 1954.
9. Vol. 1, No. 1, of *The Workers' World*, published by the reinvigorated Workers' Educational League, was dated April 4, 1919. E. R. Browder was listed as managing editor in the issue of June 20, 1919, and James P. Cannon from the issue of July 18, 1919, to the end, November 28, 1919. I am indebted to Mr. Browder for a complete file of this rare publication.
10. The foregoing account of Earl Browder's family, professional, and political background is based mainly on a letter to the author, dated February 29, 1956. It was written by Mr. Browder in response to a series of questions by the author pointing out the misstatements and contradictions abounding in the official Communist biographical sources from the time of Browder's leadership. The chief of these sources is M. J. Olgin, *That Man Browder* (Workers Library Publishers, 1936), reprinted from a series of articles in the *Daily Worker*,

444   THE ROOTS OF AMERICAN COMMUNISM

October 1936. Two others are Joseph North, "Earl Browder; A Profile," *New Masses*, April 30, 1935, pp. 13–15; and Alexander Taylor, "Browder," *New Masses*, August 11, 1936, pp. 38–39.

11. Based on letter, Cannon to Draper, August 4, 1954 (reprinted in the *Fourth International*, Fall 1955, pp. 127–31). A letter to the author from Earl Browder dated January 24, 1956, stated that Cannon's version was "relatively accurate." Browder pointed out, however, that he came to New York on his own and that Cannon was mistaken in writing that he had made a motion to bring Browder to New York. This subject also figured in an interview with Browder, October 22, 1954.

12. Foster told the story of his life in his autobiographies, *From Bryan to Stalin* (1937) and *Pages from a Worker's Life* (1939). Also see official Communist sources: Elizabeth Gurley Flynn, *Labor's Own: William Z. Foster* (New Century, 1949) and Joseph North, *William Z. Foster: An Appreciation* (International, 1955); and Arnold Petersen, *W. Z. Foster: Renegade or Spy?* (New York Labor News Co., 1932) for a hostile version of his early years.

13. See *Syndicalism* by Earl C. Ford and Wm. Z. Foster (Chicago, 1912), for Foster's point of view after his return from Europe.

14. *The Communist* (C.P.), September 27, 1919, p. 2.

15. *Investigation of Strike in Steel Industries:* Hearings before the Committee on Education and Labor, U.S. Senate, 66th Congress, 1st Session (Washington, D.C.: Government Printing Office, 1919):

SENATOR WALSH: What was your attitude toward this country during the war? . . .

FOSTER: My attitude toward the war was that it must be won at all costs.

WALSH: Some reference was made by Mr. Fitzpatrick about your purchasing bonds or your subscribing to some campaign fund. Do you mind telling the committee what you did personally in that direction?

FOSTER: Well, I did the same as everybody else.

WALSH: What was that?

FOSTER: I bought my share, what I figured I was able to afford, and in our union we did our best to help make the loans a success.

WALSH: Did you make speeches?

FOSTER: Yes, sir.

WALSH: How many?

FOSTER: Oh, dozens of them.

WALSH: . . . I would like to have you, for the sake of the record, tell us how many speeches you made, what time you devoted, and what money you expended for bonds, for the Red Cross or for any other purposes.

NOTES: CHAPTER 18

FOSTER: Well, I think I bought either $450 or $500 worth of bonds during the war. I cannot say exactly.

WALSH: You made speeches for the sale of bonds?

FOSTER: We carried on a regular campaign in our organization in the stockyards.

WALSH: And your attitude was the same as the attitude of all the other members of your organization?

FOSTER: Absolutely. (Pp. 398–399.)

CHAIRMAN: And you say now to the Committee that your views have so changed that you are in harmony with the views of Mr. Gompers?

FOSTER: Yes, sir, I don't know that it is 100 per cent, but in the main they are. (P. 423.)

16. Ibid., pp. 76 and 111–12.
17. *From Bryan to Stalin*, pp. 126–31. This repudiation and recantation is written so disingenuously that it is hard to take it seriously. Foster refers to "the stories current about my selling war bonds being without foundation," as if his own testimony was not the source of the stories (p. 131).
18. Gambs, op. cit., pp. 77–78.
19. *Report of the International Council of Red Trade and Industrial Unions*, July 15, 1920–July 1, 1921 (Moscow: Press Bureau of the First International Congress of Red Trade and Industrial Unions, 1921), pp. 12, 87, and 106.
20. Ibid., p. 23.
21. Information from Earl Browder.
22. William F. Dunne, *The Struggle Against Opportunism in the Labor Movement—For a Socialist United States* (New York Communications Committee, n.d., p. v). The biographical preface in this pamphlet, written after Dunne was expelled from the Communist party in 1946, differs in some respects from the information given by Dunne himself to Joseph Freeman in the previous decade (*An American Testament*, pp. 292–93). I have followed Dunne's pamphlet, except that he there chose to make himself a charter member and founder of the Communist party instead of the Communist Labor party, probably because he did not think his readers would be familiar with the circumstances surrounding the formation of the first two Communist parties. Two letters from Vincent R. Dunne, dated January 24 and February 14, 1956, enabled me to confirm that *American Labor Who's Who*, p. 64, incorrectly gives his birthplace as Canada. Vernon H. Jensen, *Heritage of Conflict* (Cornell University Press, 1950, pp. 435, 439, 447) refers to Dunne's role in the Butte strike.
23. See Charles Rumford Walker, *American City* (Farrar and Rinehart, 1937, pp. 192–199), and John Wickland, *Minneapolis Sunday Tribune*, December 4, 1949, p. 12, for Vincent R. Dunne's background.

24. *Resolutions and Decisions of the First International Congress of Revolutionary Trade and Industrial Unions* (Chicago: The American Labor Union Educational Society, 1921), pp. 33, 50, 73, and 77.
25. Ibid., p. 31.
26. George Williams, *The First Congress of the Red Trades Union International at Moscow, 1921* (Chicago: Industrial Workers of the World, 1922), pp. 32–33.
27. A syndicalist International Workingmen's Association was formed at an international conference in Berlin, December 25, 1922–January 3, 1923 (*American Labor Year Book, 1923–1924*, pp. 287–88).
28. See Gambs, op. cit., p. 89, where, however, the estimate is based on Communist as well as I.W.W. sources. Foster's *History* (see Key) cites these figures from Gambs without mentioning that he got them partially from the Communists themselves (p. 183).
29. Deutscher (see Key), pp. 221–22.
30. Foster, *From Bryan to Stalin*, pp. 157–58.
31. Wm. Z. Foster, *The Russian Revolution* (Trade Union Educational League, 1922), p. 28. This booklet is a collection of Foster's articles.
32. Browder, "A Political Autobiography" (in manuscript), p. 169.
33. Foster, *From Bryan to Stalin*, p. 163; *History of the Communist Party of the United States*, p. 185. Browder says that Foster declared his intention to join the party when he returned from Europe (op. cit.). Cannon states that Foster told him, after his return, that the party could have his application for membership whenever it wanted. Cannon informed the other leaders and Foster's admission followed (interview, April 24, 1956). Gitlow says that Foster joined the Communist movement in Moscow (*I Confess*, p. 174).
34. Foster's *History*, p. 185, mentions only five names in his group: Jack Johnstone, Jay Fox, Joseph Manley, David Coutts, and Sam Hammersmark. Cannon, close associate of those days as he was, says that he never encountered Fox, a veteran of the Haymarket period, or Coutts, in the Communist party (letter to Draper, August 4, 1954), though Fox wrote a pamphlet, *Amalgamation*, for the Trade Union Educational League. Johnstone joined the Communist party independently, before Foster, in 1920 (Browder, letter to the author, February 7, 1956). Hammersmark, a veteran of the I.W.W., also apparently joined the party, before Foster, in 1919 (*Daily Worker*, September 23, 1937, p. 3). If this information is correct, most of the five names mentioned by Foster came into the party without him or not at all.
35. Ruthenberg wrote about his visit to Debs in 1920 in the *Daily Worker*, November 8, 1926, p. 6; for the Communists' reaction to Debs's telegram on behalf of the Russian Social Revolutionaries, see *The Worker*, August 12 and 19, 1922, September 2, October 14 and 21, 1922. Theodore Debs's letter was published in *The Worker*, August 26, 1922;

the reply to Debs's statement on Sovietism came in an editorial in *The Worker,* December 9, 1922.

36. Ginger's book, the best available biography of Debs, falls short on this score; it gives indications of both sides of Debs's attitude toward communism but fails to mention Ruthenberg's visit in 1920 or Theodore Debs's letter in 1922; the full extent of the gap between Debs and the Communists is somewhat blurred, and Debs's more sympathetic references to the Communists receive undue emphasis. On the Communist side, the worst offender is *Gene Debs* by Herbert M. Morais and William Cahn (International, 1948). It is so one-sided that an innocent reader might find it hard to understand why Debs did not become a Communist. Foster's *History* says that Debs "was an important forerunner of the Communist Party, despite the fact that, old and sick when the Party was formed, he did not grasp its significance and never joined it" (p. 124). This illustrates the patronizing attitude toward Debs adopted in Communist writings; Debs is usually portrayed as well-meaning but not very bright. It would be much closer to the truth to say that Debs did not join the Communist party because, in some respects, he did grasp its significance. On the Socialist side, McAlister Coleman, *Eugene V. Debs: A Man Unafraid* (New York: Greenberg, 1930), stresses Debs's differences with the Russian and American Communists. Arthur M. Schlesinger, Jr., in his introduction to the *Writings and Speeches of Eugene V. Debs* (Hermitage Press, 1948, pp. xii–xiii), gives a fair summary of Debs's sympathies. Bell (see Key) has a short but extremely illuminating analysis of Debs's character (pp. 299–302).

CHAPTER 19: THE LEGAL PARTY

1. *"Left-Wing" Communism,* pp. 66–69 (italics in original). Zinoviev admitted that the idea for the united front derived from Lenin's advice to the British Communists in *"Left-Wing" Communism* (*Die Taktik der Kommunistischen Internationale gegen die Offensive des Kapitals:* Bericht über die Konferenz der Erweiterten Exekutive der Kommunistischen Internationale, Moskau, vom 24. Februar bis 4. März 1922, Verlag der Kommunistischen Internationale, 1922, pp. 36–37).

2. "Overwhelmed by opportunism, the Second International has died," Lenin wrote on November 1, 1914. The context shows that he meant it to be taken literally, because the Social Democratic parties were warring on each other (*Collected Works,* Vol. XVIII, p. 89).

3. Bukharin: "One must admit that in the course of the recent years, let us say up to the middle of 1926, membership in the foreign Communist Parties was almost continually dwindling" (*Report of the XV Congress of the Communist Party of the Soviet Union,* published by the Communist Party of Great Britain, London, 1928, p. 257). In

1929, official Comintern figures compared the respective Communist and Socialist parties as follows:

	Communists	Socialists
Germany	124,729	867,671
Czechoslovakia	150,000	194,960
France	52,376	99,106
Britain	9,000	3,338,256 (Labour Party)
Austria	6,250	683,786
Belgium	500	597,971 (Labor Party)

(B. Vassiliyev, "The Forces of the Comintern and its Allies," *International Press Correspondence*, March 29, 1929, p. 334.)

For the decline of the European Communist movement in the early twenties, the official Comintern figures are:

	1921	1924
Germany	360,000	121,394
Czechoslovakia	360,000	138,966
France	131,000	68,187
Sweden	14,000	7,011
Great Britain	10,000	4,000

(Ibid., April 5, 1929, p. 362.)

4. Zinoviev, *Bericht über den IV Kongress der Kommunistischen Internationale* (Verlag der Kommunistischen Internationale, 1923), p. 12.
5. *Resolution and Theses of the Fourth Congress of the Communist International* (London: Communist Party of Great Britain, 1923), pp. 30–31.
6. *Die Taktik der Kommunistischen Internationale gegen die Offensive des Kapitals*, op. cit., p. 35.
7. Writing in 1929, when the Comintern policy turned "Left," Manuilski declared that "the application of the united front tactics worked out by the Third and Fourth Congresses of the C.I. applied to the period of the decline of the revolutionary wave of 1918–1919. Today the forms must be determined by the rise of the international working class movement. That is the fundamental difference in the situation." (*The Communist International*, London ed., June 28, 1929, p. 666.)
8. Zinoviev, *Protokoll der Konferenz der Erweiterten Exekutive der Kommunistischen Internationale, 12–23 Juni 1923* (Verlag Carl Hoym, 1923), pp. 9–10.
9. *The Communist* (U.C.P.), No. 10, 1920, pp. 5–6. Also see Oneal, *American Communism*, pp. 64–66, 99–100; *The American Labor Year Book, 1921–1922*, pp. 392–93.
10. *The American Labor Year Book, 1921–1922*, p. 407. Whereas Epstein says (p. 110), that a "majority of the membership" left the Jewish federation, this source suggests that the minority in the con-

NOTES: CHAPTER 19   449

vention probably represented a majority of the federation's membership.
11. *The Workers' Council,* October 15, 1921, pp. 120–21.
12. J. Carr [Katterfeld], *Internationale Presse Korrespondenz,* November 9, 1922, p. 1537; James Ballister [Minor], *The Communist* (Workers party), February–March 1922, p. 14.
13. *The Toiler* (Cleveland), August 6, 1921, p. 1. Harrison was later replaced by Elmer Harrison (ibid., November 19, 1921, p. 13).
14. Lovestone's Report, *Recognition of Russia* (see Key), p. 255.
15. *Official Bulletin of the Communist Party of America,* No. 2, p. 2.
16. Bittelman (see Key), pp. 446–47.
17. James Ballister [Minor], *The Communist* (Workers party), February–March 1922, pp. 8–11.
18. Foster's *History* (see Key), p. 194.
19. *People vs. Ruthenberg* (see Key), p. 187 (punctuation is not in original).
20. "Riley" was a Lithuanian member of the Central Executive Committee. The "Riley Company shipments" probably refers to money obtained in Moscow for the Lithuanian Communist paper or the Lithuanian federation. "Car arrived" probably refers to the arrival in Moscow of Carr [Katterfeld] as the American representative to the Comintern. Benjamin Gitlow testified that the Comintern donated $35,000 when the *Daily Worker* was started in 1924 (*Investigation of Un-American Propaganda Activities in the United States,* 1939, Vol. VII, p. 4557).
21. See *The Communist* (Workers party), February–March 1922, p. 24, for the full text.
22. Bittelman, p. 446.
23. Melech Epstein seems to be mistaken on this point. He says that the Communists agreed to disband their underground party (op. cit., pp. 112–13). Both J. B. Salutsky and J. P. Cannon, the latter having served as chairman of the Workers' Council–Communist party negotiating committee, denied that any such pledge was made. Cannon points out correctly that the Communist press of this period "contained articles explaining how we conceived the functioning of both a legal and an illegal party and the relations between them" (Cannon to Draper, April 21, 1954). The Workers' Council was fully forewarned that the new legal party was going to be controlled by the illegal Communist party.
24. Epstein, op. cit., p. 113.
25. *Minutes of the Convention of the Workers Party of America* (mimeographed by the Publicity Department, Workers Party, 7 pp., 1921), session of December 23, 1921, p. 1. Foster's *History* (p. 190) gives the total number incorrectly as 150. Max Eastman's figures in *The Liberator,* February 1922, p. 1, are also incorrect. In addition to the

94 official delegates, there were 14 or more fraternal representatives (the exact number is missing because the list in the Minutes fails to give the number for the "I.W.W. Committee for the Red Trade Union International").

26. See *The Toiler*, January 7, 1922 for Cannon's speech, the Program and Constitution of the Workers party. The latter can also be found in *Investigation of Un-American Propaganda Activities in the United States*, 1940, appendix, Part 1, pp. 233–45, a valuable collection of Communist documents.
27. Interview with J. B. Salutsky (Hardman), February 15, 1954.
28. The first Central Executive Committee of the Workers party was made up of Alexander Trachtenberg, New York; Ludwig Lore, New York; James P. Cannon, Kansas; J. Louis Engdahl, Illinois; J. B. Salutsky, New York; Henry Askeli, Illinois; Mrs. Marguerite Prevey, Ohio; Elmer T. Allison, Ohio; A. Bittelman, New York; J. Wilenkin, New York; Arne Swabeck, Illinois; Caleb Harrison, Illinois; Robert Minor, New York; Jay Lovestone, New York; Meyer Loonin, Michigan; J. Anderson, New York; and W. W. Weinstone, New York. Seven alternates were also elected: Charles Baker, Ohio; Earl Browder, Kansas; William Kruse, Illinois; Jack Carney, Illinois; Harold Ware, New York; Edgar Owens, Illinois; and Thomas O'Flaherty, New York (Minutes of session of December 26, 1921, p. 2).
29. *The Toiler*, January 21, 1922. Foster's *History* incorrectly states that Ruthenberg was chosen secretary, but that since he was in jail, Caleb Harrison, appointed assistant secretary, was named acting secretary (p. 191). There is no evidence for this in any of the existing records.
30. *The Toiler*, January 14, 1922, p. 8. Also *Investigation of Un-American Propaganda Activities in the United States*, appendix, Part 1, pp. 238–39.
31. A. Raphael [Bittelman], *The Communist* (C.P. of A.), October 1921, p. 4.
32. See Harry Gannes, *Daily Worker*, April 22, 1935, p. 3, for the most detailed, official account; *The Communist International*, No. 5 (probably September), 1919, p. 77; *Revolutionary Radicalism* (see Key), Vol. I, p. 769; Arthur G. McDowell, "The Socialist Youth Movement," *American Socialist Quarterly*, III (Summer 1934), p. 44. The first National Executive Committee of the Young Workers League consisted of Oliver Carlson, G. Schulenberg, Harry Gannes, John Marks, Herbert Zam, Jacobs, and Martin Abern, with Abern as secretary (*The Worker*, May 27 and June 17, 1922).
33. Among them, Jack Stachel, John Williamson, Sam Darcy, Harry Gannes, Harry Haywood, John Steuben, Pat Toohey, Carl Winters, Gil Green, and Phil Frankfeld.

Chapter 20: The Manipulated Revolution

1. Roger B. Nelson [Lovestone], "Have We Retreated?", *The Communist* (C.P. of A.), October 21, 1921, p. 12.
2. *Thesen und Resolutionen des III. Weltkongresses der Kommunistischen Internationale* (Hamburg: Verlag der Kommunistischen Internationale, 1921), p. 48.
3. A. Raphael [A. Bittelman], "The Task of the Hour," *The Communist* (C.P. of A.), October 1921, p. 3.
4. James A. Marshall [Max Bedacht], "The Socialist Party and Revolution," *The Communist* (C.P. of A.), November 1921, p. 32.
5. A. Raphael [A. Bittelman], op. cit., p. 6 (italics in original).
6. *The Worker*, April 22, 1922, p. 2.

Chapter 21: The Two-Way Split

1. A. Raphael [A. Bittelman], *The Communist* (C.P. of A.), October 1921, p. 3.
2. J. P. Collins [J. P. Cannon], ibid., p. 21.
3. J. Carr [L. E. Katterfeld], *The Communist International,* December 1921, p. 390, put the figure at 12,000 to 13,000 in a report to the Comintern. Raphael [Bittelman], op. cit., gave the membership figure as only 10,000. The latter figure was generally accepted, but should be considered the maximum estimate for official purposes.
4. See *The Communist* (United Toilers), February 1922, pp. 1–3, for the background of the split and report of the "emergency convention," held January 7–11, 1922.

   Two more series of *The Communist* appeared in 1922 as a result of this split, one representing the old organization, the other the new one. Three numbers of the latter were available to the author, dated February, March, and June, 1922. There were probably six to eight numbers published. In order to differentiate the two series, they have been designated by placing in parentheses the so-called legal parties with which they were identified, the old one the Workers party, the new one the United Toilers. These two series of *The Communist* in 1922 bring the total number to six—and that was not the end. A seventh series began publication in 1927. To add to the confusion, it should be noted that the Workers party issued its own organ, *The Toiler,* and the United Toilers its own organ, *Workers' Challenge.* Thus the two Communist organizations in 1922 published underground organs bearing the same name and "open" organs with different names. (See note 21, Chapter 13.)
5. *The Communist* (United Toilers), March 1922, p. 14.
6. *The Communist* (Workers party), July 1922, p. 2.
7. Ibid., p. 5.

8. J. Ballister [Robert Minor], "The Blight of Purity," *The Communist* (Workers party), July 1922, p. 9.
9. *Workers' Challenge* (New York), March 25, 1922 (Vol. 1, No. 1), pp. 3–4.
10. *The Communist* (United Toilers), June 1922, p. 8.
11. *Recognition of Russia* (see Key), p. 260.
12. The entire issue of *The Communist* (United Toilers), June 1922, was devoted to the documents from Moscow, "John Moore's" [Ballam] report and the repudiation of the Ballam-Katterfeld-Rákosi "declaration."
13. See R. M. Whitney, *Reds in America* (The Beckwith Press, 1924), facing p. 36, for reproductions of both cablegrams, which lacked punctuation in the original. These documents and others mentioned or cited in this chapter and the next have their origin in the Bridgman raid in August 1922. The documents were produced in court at the trial, *People vs. Ruthenberg* (see Key), in St. Joseph, Michigan, in April 1923. Many of them were reproduced in the court record, not easily available for general consultation. They were also made available to R. M. Whitney, director of the Washington Bureau of the American Defense Society, a radical-hunting organization of the period, who used them in a series of articles appearing in the Boston *Transcript* in 1923. An enlarged version of the same material was put out as a book, *Reds in America*. This volume is full of unbalanced, irresponsible, and distorted statements and innuendoes. Nevertheless, the documents made available from the Bridgman raid and the St. Joseph trial, especially in the first six appendixes, were accurately reproduced. Some of the documents were also reproduced in *Recognition of Russia*. For the sake of convenience, these two sources have been cited wherever possible.
14. Both Ruthenberg and Lovestone freely translated code names at the trial (*People vs. Ruthenberg*, especially pp. 135–36 of Lovestone's testimony).
15. *The Communist* (Workers party), January 1922, pp. 11–12.
16. Bertram D. Wolfe, *Three Who Made a Revolution*, pp. 367–68, 523–527; N. Popov, *Outline History of the Communist Party of the Soviet Union* (International, 1934), Vol. I, pp. 198–202, 234–36; *History of the Communist Party of the Soviet Union* (International, 1939), pp. 132–35.
17. *The Worker*, May 20, 1922.
18. Damon [Ruthenberg] and Marshall [Bedacht], "Problems of Communist Organization in the U.S.," *The Communist* (Workers party), July 1922, pp. 23–24. The passage on "armed insurrection" reads: "There is an element in the Party which holds that the Party can only come into the open when it can advocate as part of its program 'the principle of mass action and armed *insurrection.*' This view is a hang-

over from that 'leftist nonsense' which felt it necessary to preach 'armed insurrection' to the workers when there was a street car strike or some other struggle of the workers over wages and working conditions. There is no magic in the words 'armed insurrection' which makes it necessary to a program in order that it can be a communist program. The test of a communist program is whether it advocates mass action, the Soviet State and the proletarian dictatorship, and includes affiliation with the C.I. To make a test of the possibility of an open CP the advocacy of 'armed insurrection' by the program is to say that there can be no open CP until the time of revolution, a condition which is given the lie by the greater number of existing open Communist Parties all over the world" (p. 24).

19. Gitlow tells the story the following way: "The name 'Goose Caucus' originated in the course of a stormy debate, when William Dunne, exasperated by Jakira's unceasing and persistent stuttering, interjected, 'Jakira, you make me sick; you cackle like a goose,' and Amter, springing to the defense of his fellow-factionalist, retorted, 'But the geese saved Rome and we shall yet save the Party,' while Lovestone, counterattacking with ridicule, shouted back, 'All right, then; from now on you're the Goose Caucus!' " (*I Confess*, p. 133).

20. J. Ford [Israel Amter], and A. Dubner [Abraham Jakira], "Theses on the Relations of No. 1 and No. 2," *The Communist* (Workers party), July 1922, pp. 12–13.

21. "Theses on Relations of the C.P. to an L.P.P.," by the Central Executive Committee of the C.P. of A., ibid., pp. 1–3. Also see the commentary, "The Blight of Purity," by J. Ballister [Robert Minor], ibid., pp. 8–10.

22. Damon and Marshall [Ruthenberg and Bedacht], op. cit., p. 23.

23. Gitlow says that the Goose caucus was the largest (*I Confess*, p. 133). Cannon wrote: "It is my impression that the forces were quite evenly divided, with the Goose Caucus having a slight advantage." (Cannon to Draper, May 5, 1954).

Chapter 22: The Raid

1. *Recognition of Russia* (see Key), p. 261.
2. Ruth Fischer, op. cit., p. 202. According to the catalogue of the New York Public Library, Valetski's real name was Max Horwitz.
3. *I Confess*, pp. 135–36.
4. Bedacht to Draper, December 9, 1954.
5. These minutes are part of a collection extending from the end of May to the end of December 1922 (in possession of the author).
6. "A View of Our Party Condition," extract from Report of the Representative of the Communist International to the Presidium of the C.I. (*The Communist*, August–September 1922, pp. 10–14).

7. The story of Francis A. Morrow and the Bridgman raid is based on the following sources:

   People vs Ruthenberg (see Key). The original trial in St. Joseph, Michigan, was held in 1923, the appeal to the Supreme Court of Michigan in 1924, and the appeal to the Supreme Court of the United States in 1925. A large portion of the original testimony was reproduced in the transcript of record of 1925 available to the author. This record has been used as the main source whenever possible.

   New York Times, April 8, 1923, an unsigned article on the case, based on the testimony at the Foster trial and information from government agents.

   Jacob Spolansky, *The Communist Trail in America*, pp. 23–30. The author is also indebted to Mr. Spolansky for an unpublished chapter originally written for this book dealing with "K-97," and for two personal interviews.

   Benjamin Gitlow, *I Confess*, pp. 137–46.

   William Z. Foster, *Pages from a Worker's Life*, pp. 232–34.

8. *The Communist* (Workers party), July 1922, p. 23; August–September 1922, pp. 6–7.
9. *The Communist* (Workers party), August–September 1922, p. 11.
10. Interview with Bertram D. Wolfe, June 16, 1956.
11. According to Lovestone, this vote took place on the motion to accept his report (interview, November 15, 1954). Gitlow says that it took place on "a minor question of a point of order" (*I Confess*, p. 141).
12. *The Communist* (Workers party), August–September 1922, pp. 2, 5.

Chapter 23: The Transformation

1. Gérard Walter, *Histoire du Parti Communiste Français* (Paris: Somogy, 1948, pp. 77–123) for a running account of the crisis in the French party. Borkenau (p. 228; see Key) says the membership of the French Communist party was reduced from 150,000 to 50,000. Ruth Fischer (*Stalin and German Communism*, pp. 180–86) gives a rather confused version of the struggle in the German Communist party and fails to mention her own struggle against the united front. See *Protokoll des Vierten Kongresses der Kommunistischen Internationale* (Hamburg, 1923, pp. 81–82) for Ruth Fischer's speech against the whole new line, as well as much first-hand material in the speeches of the French, Italian, Spanish, and other delegates.
2. *Protokoll des Vierten Kongresses der Kommunistischen Internationale*, p. 33.
3. Borkenau, p. 229.
4. *The Worker*, June 24, 1922.
5. Gitlow, *I Confess*, p. 157. *The Toiler*, November 26, 1921, p. 5, said

NOTES: CHAPTER 23

that the Communists received 3000–4000 votes in the New York municipal election of 1921.

6. *The Worker*, April 29, 1922, p. 5.
7. Ibid., August 5 and 12, 1922.
8. Harry Rogoff, *An East Side Epic: The Life and Work of Meyer London* (Vanguard Press, 1930), pp. 298–303. Bedacht (Marshall) discussed the Communist policy of withdrawing in favor of London at the Fourth Congress (*Protokoll des Vierten Kongresses*, pp. 181–82).
9. *The Worker*, November 4, 1922, p. 5.
10. Alexander Bittelman, "In Retrospect," *The Workers Monthly*, December 24, 1924, p. 86.
11. Quoted by Ruthenberg, *The Liberator*, February 1923, p. 13.
12. *The Worker*, June 24, 1922.
13. *The Communist* (Workers party), August–September 1922, p. 11.
14. "A Political Letter to the Party" from the Special Representative Sent to America by the C.I., *The Communist*, Vol. 1, No. 12, 1922 [undated, probably December]. This document is dated October 7, 1922, and is signed by "Michelson," Valetski's post-Bridgman pseudonym.
15. *For a Labor Party*, A Statement by the Workers Party (Workers Party of America, October 15, 1922), pp. 12, 14, 47. The first edition of this pamphlet was unsigned. An enlarged edition published in 1923 was signed by John Pepper [Joseph Pogany].
16. Bittelman, *The Workers Monthly*, December 1924, p. 87.
17. James P. Cannon, *The History of American Trotskyism* (Pioneer, 1944), pp. 16–17.
18. One paragraph in the C.E.C. minutes of May 29, 1922 reads: "Motion to approve of action of resident members when they approved decision of Jewish Bureau to send Raphael [Bittelman] to get some funds for *Freiheit* through Jewish ZB of RKP and other sources. Carried." (In the author's possession.)
19. Cannon to Draper, May 10, 1954 (published in the *Fourth International*, Winter 1955, pp. 15–18).
20. *Protokoll des Vierten Kongresses der Kommunistischen Internationale*, pp. 50–51, 144, 181–84.
21. *Thesen und Resolutionen des IV. Weltkongresses der Kommunistischen Internationale* (Hamburg, 1923), p. 24. The paragraph ended by recommending the issue of unemployment as the best means of weakening Gompers' influence; and it still persisted in believing that the "special task" of the American Communists was winning over of the "best elements of the I.W.W."
22. Cannon to Draper, May 10, 1954 (published in the *Fourth International*, Winter 1955, p. 17). Commenting on this story, Bedacht wrote to the author (December 1, 1954): "It seems to me that Cannon's memory is influenced by later developments, especially his own. The interview with Trotsky was one of the interviews we tried

to get and did get with leading members of the Russian and other Parties. None of these interviews was in itself decisive." Claude McKay tends to confirm Cannon: "I think Trotsky was the first of the big Russians to be convinced that there should be a legal Communist party in America, then Rakovsky and finally Zinoviev, a little reluctantly. Bukharin was for the illegal group. He said: 'Remember what Jack London has told us about the terror and secret organization in America in his *Iron Heel*.' That was so rare that I had to smile. While Cannon was informing the Russians about actual conditions in America, Bukharin was visualizing the America of Jack London's *Iron Heel*" (*A Long Way from Home,* Furman, 1937, pp. 178–79). Max Eastman does not recall the exact circumstances of the interview with Trotsky.

23. The Memorandum is entitled *Die Amerikanische Frage* (in possession of the author). I am indebted to Mr. Bedacht for his copy of the Memorandum. German was the language most commonly used in the Comintern.

24. Bedacht to Draper, December 1, 1954.

25. Cannon to Draper, May 10, 1954, for the material in the foregoing three paragraphs.

26. "To the Communist Party from the Executive Committee of the Communist International," *The Communist*, Vol. 1, No. 13, 1923 [probably January 1923]. The full text was reprinted in *Recognition of Russia* (see Key), pp. 282–84.

27. "A Statement of the Problem in America and The First Step Towards Its Solution," submitted by Max Eastman to Lenin and Trotsky in Moscow, 1923 (10-page typewritten copy in possession of Mr. Eastman).

28. *Protokoll des Vierten Kongresses,* pp. 692–97 for Huiswoud (Billings) and pp. 697–701 for McKay (Mackay). Rose Pastor Stokes, "The Communist International and The Negro," *The Worker*, March 10, 1923, contains an English text of the "Theses on the Negro Question." Mrs. Stokes (Sasha) served as reporter for the Negro Commission. A more official German version of the Theses may be found in *Thesen und Resolutionen des IV. Weltkongresses,* pp. 52–54. Claude McKay gave his impressions of the Fourth Congress and his Russian visit in his autobiography, *A Long Way From Home.* Wilson Record, *The Negro and the Communist Party* (University of North Carolina Press, 1951, p. 54), fails to do justice to the decisions of the Fourth Congress. William A. Nolan, *Communism versus the Negro* (Regnery, 1951, p. 26), falls even farther from the mark with a flat statement: "The events of 1922 scarcely touch the problems of this book."

29. *Minutes of the C.E.C. Meeting of September 29, 1922* contains Valetski's report (as "Michelson") of the Opposition's convention. Attached to these Minutes are seven demands and Valetski's answer.

This collection also contains the Minutes of the Committee for Unification of September 30, 1922, and a report of the same committee of October 5, 1922 (in possession of the author). Foster's *History* (p. 194; see Key) makes the mistake of dating the liquidation of the United Toilers at the Bridgman Convention in August. The decision was actually made over a month later.
30. Cannon, *The History of American Trotskyism*, pp. 18–19.
31. Cannon to Draper, May 21, 1954.
32. The new C.E.C. consisted of Amter (New York); Bittelman (New York); Browder (Chicago); Cannon (Kansas City); Dunne (New York); Marion L. Emerson (New York); Engdahl (New York); Jakira (New York); Katterfeld (New York); Kruse (Jersey City); Lindgren (New York); Lore (New York); Lovestone (New York); Theodore Maki (Brooklyn); Minor (New York); Michel Nastasiewsky (New York); Olgin (New York); Pepper (San Francisco); Ruthenberg (Cleveland); Stokes (New York); Trachtenberg (New York); Wagenknecht (Cleveland); Weinstone (New York); Wicks (New York). (*The Worker*, January 6, 1923, p. 1.)

The Executive Council was composed of Bittelman, Cannon, Dunne, Emerson, Engdahl, Lindgren, Lore, Maki, Olgin, Ruthenberg, and Wicks. (Ibid., January 20, 1923, p. 2.)
33. *The Second Year of the Workers Party of America* (Chicago: Literature Department, Workers Party of America, 1924), pp. 73–86.
34. *The Worker*, January 27, 1923, p. 2.
35. *The Communist*, Vol. 1, No. 12, 1922, pp. 1–2.
36. *The Worker*, April 28, 1923, p. 6.
37. See *The 4th National Convention* (Chicago: Daily Worker Publishing Co., 1925), pp. 27–29, for these figures. There are slightly different figures in *The Second Year of the Workers Party of America*, pp. 29–30, but I have chosen to use the former source because the figures there are more complete in every respect. Ruthenberg once gave the figure of 8319 for March–June 1922 (*The Worker*, December 9, 1922, p. 1).
38. Jay Lovestone, *Daily Worker*, May 24, 1927, explained the effect of the "dual-stamp" system. Referring to the sudden drop in the membership figures, *The Communist International between the Fifth and Sixth Congresses, 1924–1928* (London: Communist Party of Great Britain, 1928, p. 351) remarked: "This figure shows how inaccurate the previous statistics of the Workers' Party had been, as it is not to be conceived that the Party actually lost 5,000 members in the process of its reorganization."
39. See *The Fourth National Convention*, p. 30, for the membership by districts. When the "dual-stamp" system was abolished in 1925, the New York percentage rose from one-quarter to one-third.
40. *The Communist*, Vol. 1, No. 12, 1922, p. 3.
41. *The Worker*, January 6, 1923, p. 2.

42. *The Second Year*, p. 31.
43. *The Worker*, May 26, 1923, p. 5.
44. See *The Second Year*, p. 31, for the industrial registration of one-third of the party membership. A much fuller registration was reported in *The Fourth National Convention*, pp. 40–41, but it refers to a later period. The difficulty of determining the "non-proletarian" percentage in 1923 arises from the vagueness of the available figures. Of the 6862 registered, 2806, or almost one-third, were classified as "Miscellaneous (including laborers and housewives)." Presumably most of the "non-proletarian" members were covered by this classification.
45. See *American Labor Year Book, 1923–1924*, p. 125, for the 1923 membership; also Shannon (see Key), pp. 163–64.
46. Scott Nearing, "What Can the Radical Do?", reported by Ruth Stout from a Rand School lecture, *New York Call*, February 4, 1923.
47. *The Worker*, February 24, 1923, pp. 1–2.

Acknowledgments

The Roots of American Communism is the first volume of a history of the American Communist movement which I intend to bring up to 1945. My work was started in 1952 on a part-time basis with the encouragement and generosity of Max Ascoli. Since June 1955, I have devoted my full time to the work as part of the project sponsored by the Fund for the Republic on the Study of Communist Influence in American Life, directed by Professor Clinton Rossiter. I am deeply indebted to Max Ascoli and to the Fund for the Republic for support which enabled me to work in complete freedom and independence.

In the Introduction as well as in the Notes I have referred to the information and material obtained from personal sources. These interviews and letters generally covered a larger period than this volume and, therefore, only a portion of this material has been used. I have spent many hours with Earl Browder, before and after my association with the Fund for the Republic's project. A long correspondence was carried on with James P. Cannon, supplemented by two personal meetings. Three interviews were held with Jay Lovestone. I had two interviews and exchanged several letters with Max Bedacht. Bertram D. Wolfe gave me the benefit of his personal experience on three occasions.

All these men devoted their time and knowledge without conditions or stipulations. Though personal sources of information account for only a small portion of this volume, these participants in some of the events contributed intimate insights and different points of view that could not be obtained in any other way. It was obviously impossible to write anything that could please all of them, and none of them could be sure that I would write anything that would please even one. I have tried to base this work on documentary sources as much as possible; I do not think that it would have been materially different without personal sources of information.

Mrs. Esther Corey permitted me to consult the papers of the late Lewis Corey and always lent her assistance with warmth and sympathy. Carl Sandburg and Max Eastman contributed valuable details. Granville Hicks sent me a box of old Communist papers which included some that I could not locate anywhere else. Philip J. Jaffe made available to me the unrivaled collection of Communist material in his extraordinary library.

I owe a special debt of gratitude to those who gave me that most ungrateful form of helpfulness—criticism. Clinton Rossiter performed a heroic service in behalf of greater clarity and accuracy. I came again and again to Joseph Freeman for unfailing inspiration and rich critical judgement. Bertram D. Wolfe enabled me to profit from his vast knowledge of the subject of Communism in all its ramifications. Earl Browder and James P. Cannon read and criticized earlier versions of the manuscript. I was lucky to get the expert advice of my colleagues on the Fund for the Republic's project, Dr. David A. Shannon and Daniel Bell, both of whom had made special studies of the American Socialist and radical movements. Murray J. Rossant and Philip J. Jaffe labored long and hard over the entire manuscript and contributed a wealth of detailed criticisms. I have benefitted greatly from Marshall Best's editorial counsel.

This is not the kind of book the slightest responsibility for which can be shared with anyone else. It would have had many more defects and shortcomings if so many different people had not come to my assistance without any assurance that their advice would be heeded. It should not cause surprise, therefore, to find some of them expressing very different opinions than my own on any aspect of

ACKNOWLEDGMENTS

this book. All these relationships, most of them new to me, have been entirely happy because they were completely free—on both sides.

And I am particularly grateful to Frances Alexander for her devoted technical assistance, made possible by the grant from the Fund for the Republic.

I cannot resist a final thought: at a time when much is said and written about the unhealthy political pressures exerted on American scholars, this book was made possible at different stages by Max Ascoli and the Fund for the Republic in the great tradition of American intellectual liberty. No one could have respected that tradition more ably and scrupulously than the director of the Fund's project, Clinton Rossiter.

Index

Aarons, Queens organizer, Left Wing, 422 *n.* 41
Abern, Martin, member, National Executive Committee, Young Workers League, and secretary of League, 450 *n.* 32
Adjustment Commission, 365; *see* Disarmament Commission
African Blood Brotherhood, 387
Agent provocateur, 226–27, 229; *see also* Agents
Agents, Department of Justice, at Foster trial, 372; at Fraina trial, 230–32; *see* Morrow, Francis A.; Nosovitsky, Jacob; Peterson, Ferdinand; Shanahan, Edward; Spolansky, Jacob
Agrarian revolt, 37; in Oklahoma, 34
Allen, Frederick Lewis, 202
Allison, Elmer T., on first Central Executive Committee, Workers party, 450 *n.* 28
Amalgamated Clothing Workers, 20, 340
Amalgamated Meat Cutters and Butcher Workmen, A.F. of L., 301
American Agency, American Communists to be united by, 270; Browder approved for Profintern work by, 310; Comintern appoints, 269; in United States, 270
American Bolshevik Bureau of Information, 107–108, 415 *n.* 30
American Bureau, outgrowth of Amsterdam conference, 234
American Commission (1922), 356; appointed by Comintern, 356
American Commission (Fourth Comintern Congress), 382–85
American Communists, *see* Communist party
American Defense Society, and Nosovitsky, 236
American Federation of Labor, 16, 29, 31, 42, 88, 135–36, 224; Browder and, 308; in Chicago, 198, 312; Comintern letter on, 243–44; Communists oppose, 186; Communists working inside, 304; Debs on, 326; formation of, 12–13; Foster and, 312–14, 320; in Left Wing manifesto, 168; membership, 20, 198; Profintern policy, 316–18; Reed on, 283; and Second Comintern Congress, 256–57; and strikes, 199; and Third Comintern Congress, 279; United Communist party on, 220
American Freedom Foundation, in American Labor Alliance, 337
Americanization, 159; Communist party attack on, 187–88; in Left Wing manifesto, 168; and Left Wing split, 172–73; and Russian domination, 395; in Ruthenberg split, 218; and Workers' Council, 333–34
American Labor Alliance, 336; Com-

American Labor Alliance (*continued*) intern reaction, 337; merger with Workers' Council proposed, 337; organizations included, 337
American Labor Union, 16
American Railway Union, 15
American Testament, An, 129
American Trade Union Delegation, 316
Amsterdam Bureau, *see* Amsterdam conference
Amsterdam conference, 227, 251–52; American Bureau of, 234; Central European Bureau, 234; International Sub-Bureau, 234; mandate revoked by Moscow; 235; Pan-American Provisional Bureau, 234–235; political action opposed, 234; program, 233–34; representation at, 233; spies at, 233; trade-union policy of, 234
Amsterdam International, *see* International Federation of Trade Unions
Amter, Israel, 39, 128, 296; on Central Executive Committee, Workers party, 457 *n.* 32; in Goose caucus, 360–61; pseud., "J. Ford," 360; Valetski on, 365
Amtorg, *see* Produce Exchange Corporation
Anarchism, 13, 21, 22, 45, 122, 129; *see also* Anarcho-syndicalism, Syndicalism
Anarchist Squad, Chicago police, at Communist founding convention, 182
Anarcho-syndicalism, and communism, 322; philosophy of I.W.W., 17; *see also* Anarchism, Syndicalism
Anderson, J., on first Central Executive Committee, Workers party, 450 *n.* 28
Anderson, Sherwood, 41
Andrew, *see* Hourwich, Nicholas
Andreychine, George, 96
Anti-alien drive, *see* Deportations
Antioch College, 300–301
Appeal to Reason, 38, 41, 42, 305, 308; Lenin on, 75
Ashkenudzie, George, in Left Opposition, 335; in Left Opposition appeal to Comintern, 339–40; pseud. "Henry," 357; suspended, 339
Ashleigh, Charles, 96
Ashworth, Francis, *see* Morrow, Francis A.
Askeli, Henry, on first Central Executive Committee, Workers party, 450 *n.* 28
Associated Toiler Clubs, in American Labor Alliance, 337

Baker, Charles, arrest, 95; on Communist Labor party labor committee, 181; Workers party Central Executive Committee alternate, 450 *n.* 28
Baku Congress, and Reed, 284–85, 287–90
Bakunin, Michael, 13
Bakuninist influence, 22
Balabanoff, Angelica, accounts of Reed, 285, 287–88, 290–92
Baldwin, *see* Tywerousky, Oscar
Ballam, John J., on Communist party Central Executive Committee, 184, 427 *n.* 14; concedes to federations, 175; in Left Opposition, 335; in Left Opposition appeal to Comintern, 339–40; in Moscow, 356–57, 363; pseud., "Moore," 356; suspended, 338; tours United States, 358; in United Toilers, 355; yields to Comintern, 357–58
Barbusse, Henri, 127
Baruch, Bernard M., 115
Basle congress, 52
Batt, Dennis E., 160, 165, 167; at Communist founding convention, 182, 184; editor, *The Communist,* 173; National Organization Committee secretary, 173, 425 *n.* 12; and Profintern, 316; signs joint convention call, 175
Beard, Charles A., 40
Bebel, August, 52
Bedacht, Max, 190, 207, 337–38, 343, 388; background, 305; at Bridgman convention, 373; in Central Execu-

tive Committee majority, 335; on Communist Labor party National Executive Committee, 180-81; leadership emerges, 304; and Lenin, 281; a Liquidator, 360, 362; in Moscow, 356; pseud., "James A. Marshall," 205; sentenced, 204; at Third Comintern Congress, 275; and Valetski, 364-65

Bell, Daniel, 94, 399, 447 *n*. 36

Bellamy, Edward, 14, 16

Benson, Allen L., 56; leaves Socialist party, 93; Socialist presidential candidate, 70

Berenberg, David P., 154, 156

Berger, Victor L., 30, 33, 46, 56, 58, 93, 95, 156, 347; "American Bernstein," 27; arrest, 94; member of Congress, 27, 42

Berkman, Alexander, 111, 122, 404 *n*. 32; deported, 203

Berle, Adolph A., 298

Bernstein, Eduard, 27; on war, 52

Berzin, J. A., 54

Bilan, Alexander, on Communist Labor party National Executive Committee, 181; in Moscow, 252

Billings, *see* Huiswood, Otto

Billings, Warren K., 123

Bittelman, Alexander, 343, 348, 399; approach to workers, 349; background, 305; on Communist party Central Executive Committee, 184, 427 *n*. 14; forms Communist Unity Committee, 269, 437 *n*. 7; editor, *Der Kampf*, 192; expelled temporarily, 269; Fraina refuted by, 299; at Fraina trial, 230-32; on language federations, 425 *n*. 11, 426 *n*. 17, 427 *n*. 11; leadership emerges, 304; in Moscow for *Freiheit*, 382, 455 *n*. 18; pseud., "A. Raphael," 205; on Workers party Central Executive Committee, 450 *n*. 28, 457 *n*. 32, on Executive Council, 457 *n*. 32

Block and Co., 339, 357

Bloor, Ella Reeve, 39, 47; in Communist Labor party, 193; in Profintern, 316

Bohemian Socialist federation, leaves Socialist party, 332

Bohn, Frank, on board of *New Review*, 404 *n*. 35, 406 *n*. 19

Bohn, William, on board of *New Review*, 404 *n*. 35, 406 *n*. 19

Boland, Harry, and the Russian jewels, 240

Bolshevik revolution, 97-100, 159, 228; and Ruthenberg split, 218; Zinoviev and, 259; *see* Revolution, Russian Revolution

Bolshevik section, Russian Social Democratic Workers party, 83

Bolsheviks, 74, 101-102, 106, 111, 119-120, 136, 143-44, 154, 171, 195, 201; aims, 107-108; attitude to United States, 265-66; concept of the party, 261-63; and European revolution, 248-49; improvisation, 250; influence, 265-66, on Letts, 34, on Reed, 283; on legality, 360; major personalities, 258-59; and revolution, 352; and revolutionary defeatism, 53; splitting tendency, 164, 166; typed, 364; and underground, 207; on violence, 214; and Western communism, 232; win Left Wing support, 415 *n*. 31

Bolshevism, in America, 135; Debs on, 325; in Left Wing manifesto, 168; Third Comintern Congress interpretation, 276

Bookkeepers, Stenographers and Accountants union, 308; Browder local president, 308

Borkenau, Franz, 377

Borodin, Michael, at Amsterdam conference, 233; background, 236; courier to United States, 236-41; real name Michael Gruzenberg, 236; Roy converted by, 239; and the Russian jewels, 238-41; and Carl Sandburg, 237-38

Boston police strike, 197

Boudin, Louis B., 30, 48, 63-64, 76, 79-80, 85-87, 92, 95, 120, 139-40, 155, 414 *n*. 19; anti-war, 59-60; background, 57-58; on board of *New Review*, 406 *n*. 19, 411 *n*. 18;

Boudin, Louis B. (*continued*)
at Communist Labor party convention, 179–80; correspondence, 405 *n*. 10; questions Russian revolution, 100; in St. Louis Convention minority, 93, 413 *n*. 33; theoretician, 57-60

Bourderon, A., 73

Boycott of elections, 200–201, 225; Lenin on, 280; United Communist party on, 221

Brandler, Heinrich, 356

Bridgman convention, 364–65; arrangements, 369–70; Comintern domination, 373–74; decisions, 373–375; and electoral activity, 378; Goose faction majority, 373; representation, 373; raid, 371–72; trade unionists, 373; underground route to, 368

Bridgman defendants, *see* Bridgman convention

Bridgman raid, *see* Bridgman convention, Raids

Bridgman unity conference, 219, 306

Briehl, Fred, 139

British Labour party, 197; Lenin on, 257; and united-front tactic, 327–328, 379

British Socialist Party, 151

Brodsky, Carl, 141–42; at National Left Wing conference, 167, 424–25 *n*. 4; on New York Left Wing City Committee, 422 *n*. 43; New York Left Wing organizer, 422 *n*. 41

Brodsky, Joseph, 141–42; on New York Left Wing City Committee, 422 *n*. 43

Brookings Institution, 298

Brooklyn Left Wing meeting, 80–82

Brooks, *see* Valetski, H.

Browder, Earl Russell, 7, 36, 39, 322–324, 343; alternate, Central Executive Committee, Workers party, 450 *n*. 28; arrest, 95, 309, 372; background, 307–308, 443–44 *n*. 10, 444 *n*. 11; on Central Executive Committee, Workers party, 457 *n*. 32; in cooperatives, 309; editor, *The Workers' World*, 309, 443 *n*. 9; and Foster, 310–11; in jail, 309; leaves Socialist party, 47, 308; pseud., "Joseph Dixon," 316; and Russian revolution, 309; in Socialist party, 308–309; and Syndicalist League, 308

Browder, Ralph W., 309; arrest, 95

Browder, William, 307

Browder, William E., 309; arrest, 95

Bross, William, 138

Bryant, Louise, accounts of John Reed, 285–87

Bryan, William Jennings, 37, 305, 311

Buford, deportations, 203–204

Bukharin, Nikolai, 280, 356; on American Commission, 382, 384–85; biographical material, 409 *n*. 49; on E.C.C.I., 259; in Left Wing, 80–85; and Lozovsky, 319; quarrel with Trotsky, 81; and Reed, 289; at Reed's funeral, 284; on Western communism, 235, 447–48 *n*. 3; in United States, 76–77

Bull Moose movement, 41

Bullitt Mission, 115

Bureau of Immigration, 207

Bureau of Investigation: agent K-97, 366–72; Chicago office, 368–69; at Communist founding convention, 182; and Fraina, 296; General Intelligence Division, 367

Bureau of International Revolutionary Propaganda, 120

Burns, William J., 368, 371

Butte, Montana: Central Labor Council, 316; *Daily Bulletin*, 316; "Soviet," 139; strike, 139

Cahan, Abraham, 59, 110

Cannon, James P., 322, 324, 388; background, 305–306; and Browder, 308–10; on Central Executive Committee, Workers party, 450 *n*. 28, 457 *n*. 32; chairman, Workers' Council-Communist party negotiating committee, 449 *n*. 23; editor, *The Toiler*, 306; editor, *The Workers' World*, 309, 443; on Executive Council, Workers party, 457 *n*. 32; at Fourth Comintern Congress, 383–85; and Fraina, 296, 300; leaves I.W.W., 110; Liquidators send to Moscow, 381; gratitude to Moscow, 394; at National Left Wing Conference, 166–67; in new leadership, 304; in New York, 306; pseud., "Cook," 384; in Socialist party, 111; on Soviet Russia, 265; and Trotsky, 384; and underground Letts, 388–389; at Workers party convention, 341–42

Capitalism and Agriculture in the United States of America, 280–81

Carlson, Oliver, 343; member, National Executive Committee, Young Workers League, 450 *n.* 32

Carney, Jack, 78–79; at Communist Labor party convention, 179; on Communist Labor party National Executive Committee, 181; Workers party Central Executive Committee alternate, 450 *n.* 28

Carr, *see* Katterfeld, Ludwig E.

Carver, Thomas Nixon, 298

C.E.C. majority, 1921 faction, 335

Central Committee, Communist party, 8; Russian, 384

Central European Bureau, outgrowth of Amsterdam conference, 234

Centralization, Comintern policy, 235

Chafee, Zechariah, Jr., 202

Chabrow, delegate to Second Comintern Congress, 436 *n.* 15

Chaliapin, Feodor, 255

Cheidze, Nicholas S., 99

Cheyney, Ralph, arrest, 95

Chicago: District committee, and Ruthenberg group, 214; Executive Council and Ruthenberg group, 214; Federation of Labor, 198, 312; Left Wing, 138

Chicherin, Georgi Vassilievich, 148–149

Christian socialism, 14; and Socialist party, 15

Chudnovsky, Grigorii Isakovich, 80, 86

C.I., *see* Comintern

Clark, Evans, in Russian Soviet Government Bureau, 162

The Class Struggle, 87, 95, 100; divided on Communist split, 181

Coal strike, 197

Codes, Communist, American-underground, 367; cables, 452 *n.* 13; international, 339, 357–58, 449 *n.* 20

Coeur d'Alene strike, 21

Cohen, Dr. Maximilian, 141–42, 145, 157; on Communist party Central Executive Committee, 427 *n.* 14; forms Communist Unity Committee, 269; concedes to federations, 175; temporarily expelled, 269; at National Left Wing conference, 424–25 *n.* 4; on New York Left Wing Executive Committee, 422 *n.* 43; New York Left Wing secretary, 422 *n.* 41

Coldwell, Joseph M., leads walk-out, Socialist convention, 178

College of the City of New York (C.C.N.Y.), 141

Colonialism, and the Negro question, 387

Colonization, Debs and, 15

Comintern (C.I., Communist International), 8, 149, 153, 252, 256, 306

and American communism: American Agency, 269; American Labor Alliance rejected, 337; American representatives, 269–71, 363–64, 371, 431–32 *n.* 18; American rivalry for support of, 251; American unity planned by, 244, 267–70; arbiter of American disputes, 258; attitude to United States of, 265–66; backs C.E.C. majority, 335; cracks down on American parties, 268; on Communist party conventions, 186; federations limited by, 244; Geese vs. Liquidators problem settled by, 381–85; instructions for 1922 convention of, 358; on Labor party, 379; Left Opposition opposed, 340; Left Wing affiliation, 174; for legal, mass party, 303; letter on parliamentarianism, 241, on revolutionary tactics, 242, on unity, 243–45; Negro

Comintern (*continued*)
Commission, 387; proposed composition of American party, 242; role in United States of, 338–39; supported by both parties, 187; supported for nationalist reasons, 191; on underground convention, 338–40; on United States Congress, 243; and Workers Council, 333; on Workers party, 390
and Amsterdam Bureau, 235; centralization, 377
Congresses: First, 148–54; Second, 253–64; Third, 269–77; Fourth, 382–87; *see also* First Comintern Congress, etc.
concept of Communist party by, 263–64; control of parties through representatives of, 262; discipline, 263; factionalism in, and Fraina, 252–53, 294–96; "General Staff" concept, 264; identification with Soviet regime, 259, 262; supports I.W.W., 242, 435 *n.* 30, writes to I.W.W., 245; influence, 394–95; intervention in Communist parties, 261–64; monolithic character, 262; Profintern relations, 315, 317–19; Red International of Labor Unions, 269–70; and John Reed, 290–92; and Reed's funeral, 284; Russian control, 256; statutes, 263; subsidization, 261–62, 340; symbolism, 255; twenty-one points of admission, 262; united-front policy, 330, 375–76; and world revolution, 248; Zinoviev's policies, 260–64

Commissariat for Foreign Affairs, 149–50

Committee for Third International, attacked by Communists, 332; in Socialist party, 332–33

Communism, 34, 115–17, 311–23; American, 303, and Labor party, 381; choice between art and, 128; Debs on, 325; effect of underground on, 208–209; and Fourth Comintern Congress, 383; and immediate demands, 348–50; independent, 395; nature of, 352; as science, 124–25; and syndicalism, 318; and united front, 329

Communist, The, explanation of publications, 432 *n.* 21, 451, Ch. 21, *n.* 4

Communist, The (1919), A.F. of L. attacked by, 199; official organ of Communist party, 185; replaces *Revolutionary Age,* 185

Communist, The, organ of National Organization Committee, 1919, 173

Communist, The (Ruthenberg group) April–May 1920, 215

Communist, The (United Communist party) 1920–21, 222

Communist, The, organ of (new) Communist party, 1922, 354

Communist, The, organ of united party, 1921, 304

Communist International, *see* Comintern

Communist Labor, see Voice of Labor

Communist Labor party, 251, 304–305, 354; Comintern letter to, 244; decline of, 207; delegates to founding convention, 426 *n.* 3; on dictatorship of proletariat, 187; differences with Communist party, 179, 185–88; on electoral action, 185; endorses I.W.W., 186; and federations, 179–80; founding convention, 178–79, 426 *n.* 4; headquarters, 181; internal divisions, 180; Labor party opposed, 199–200
membership, 188–89, 428 *n.* 19, *n.* 20; geographical distribution, 188–189; national composition, 190
Negro policy, 192; officers, 180–81; Ohio delegation split, 195; organizational structure, 186–87; outside labor movement, 198–99; program, 185–88, 428 *n.* 18; raids, 202–203; trade-union policy, 186; underground, 205; United Communist party, 221
unity, first attempts, 183–84; proposed with Communist party, 211–212; with Ruthenberg group, 219–221

INDEX

Communist Manifesto, 26, 180
Communist movement:
  American, 10, 70; character of, 393; childhood, 393; international implications, 396; and Left Wing National conference, 166; weakness, 393; *see also* Communism
  Chinese, 10
  Russian, 10
Communist party, 97, 129, 227, 251, 318, 324–26
  background: differences in Left Wing, 169–73, 175; foreign-language federations, 173, 182–84; founding convention called, 169–171, 173, 427 *n.* 9; future leadership, 167–68; intellectuals, 127; middle class in, 30; Populist influence, 39
  Central Executive Committee, 357, 427 *n.* 14; Bridgman convention election of, 374; Comintern Representative to, 364–65; Department of Justice representative, 372; divides on legality, 335; Goose caucus majority, 374; on insurrection, 213; on Labor party, 379; Michigan group acted on, 211; policy for legal party, 341–42; in Ruthenberg split, 214; on strikes, 199; on underground convention, 338; Woodstock convention, 272; Young Communist League on, 374
  and the Comintern: American Agency, 269; application-card references, 263; attitude to Russian revolution, 265–66, to Soviet Russia, 265; instructions for 1922 convention, 357; intervention in Communist parties, 270; letters to American party, 241–45; merger of legal and illegal parties demanded, 386; relationships between, 261–66; rival Pan-American Bureaus, 235; role of Comintern representative, 364–65, 371–74; Second Congress, 254, delegates, 275; Third Congress, 277–78, delegates, 275, changed attitude of, 278
  factionalism: advance guard of working class theory, 349; factions, 335, 362; 1921 issues, 354–55; Left Opposition split, 353–54; new factions, Geese and Liquidators, 360–362; struggle over underground convention, 337–39; Workers' Council, the Right opposition, 333–334, 337, merges, 340–41
  foundations: character of new party, 185–88; convention, 181–85; differences with Communist Labor party, 185–88; English-speaking groups in, 185–86; factions in, 182–184; headquarters, 185; Michigan group, 182–85, Michigan-federation split, 184; negotiations with Communist Labor party, 183; organizational structure, 186–87, Executive Council and National Organization Committee, 428 *n.* 18; program, 185–88; Russian influence, 182
  labor policies: opposes Labor party, 199–200; outside labor movement, 198–99; on strikes, 199; Trade Union Educational League, 321–22, and Foster's leadership, 321–22; trade union policy, 273–74; unionism opposed, 224
  legality: Bridgman unity convention and, 364, 369–72; Comintern instructions on, 357, 386; Communist party becomes Workers party, 389–390; electoral policy changes, 378–379; Geese-Liquidator struggle ended, 360–62, 381–85; merger of legal and illegal organizations Comintern decision, 386; third national convention, 390; Workers party organized, 358
  membership: in 1919, 188, 428 *n.* 19; leadership, 196; national composition, 190–91; Negroes, 192; Slavic preponderance, 191; women, 193; in 1920, 222–23, 432–33 *n.* 23; preponderantly foreign, 223; in 1921, 272, 351, 451, Ch. 21, *n.* 3; in 1922, 360–62; in 1923, 391–93
  Ruthenberg group: Communist Labor party unity proposals, 211–12; membership, 222–23; policy issues

Communist party (*continued*)
  on elections, 224–25, insurrection, 223, unionism, 224; split into second Communist party, 214; unity with Communist Labor party, 219
  underground: agent K-97 in, 366–372; Communist party goes underground, 205; code used, 367; convention, 364, 369–72; effect of raids, 207; federations in, 206; functioning, 205; membership, 206; New York first, 203; pseudonyms in, 205; raids, 202; rules, 205–206; structure, 205
  unity at Woodstock: convention, 270–74; finances, 272–73; federations, 273; membership, 272; negotiations with United Communist party, 268–69; organizers, 273; parliamentarianism, 274; political-action policy, 273–74; publications, 273; on revolution, violence and insurrection, 274, 354–55; structure, 273; trade-union policy, 273–74; underground and illegality, 274
  See also: Communist Labor party, Left Opposition, Workers party
Communist party (Left Opposition, 1922), 362; federations predominate, 354; Left Opposition forms, 353–54; Workers party program attacked by, 354–55; *see also* Left Opposition
Communist party (Ruthenberg group), 214–21
Communist programs, 428 *n.* 18
Communist Propaganda League, 150; organized, 138
Communist sources, analyzed, 5, 9
Communists, basic questions about, 4; decision-making by, 8; formative influences, 16
Communist Program, The, 280
Communist revolution, 250; *see also* Bolshevik revolution, Russian revolutions
Communist Unity, 437 *n.* 7
Communist Unity Committee, 269, 437 *n.* 7

Congress of Oriental Nations, *see* Baku Congress
Congress, United States, Comintern on, 243
Connolly, in Socialist Propaganda League, 69
Cook County Labor party, 197
Cooperative League of America, 309; Browder on board, 309
Corey, Lewis, *see* Fraina, Louis C.
Coser, Benjamin, on New York Left Wing Executive Committee, 422 *n.* 43
Couriers, Russian, 162, 241–43
Criminal anarchy, laws against, 202
Criminal syndicalism, laws against, 202
Cripple Creek strike, 21
Crisis of the Middle Class, The, 299
Cosgrove, Pascal B., pseud., "Crosby," 316; in United Toilers, 355
Crosby, *see* Cosgrove, Pascal B.
Crown jewels, *see* Jewels, Russian
Cunard line, and government agents, 228
Current History, publication of Comintern letters to American party, 242

Daily People, The, 62
Daily Worker, The, 301; Comintern proposal for, 340; predecessors, 443 *n.* 7
Damon, David, *see* Ruthenberg
Darcy, Sam, party leadership from Young Communist League, 450 *n.* 33
Daughters of the American Revolution, 372
Davidson, *see* Reinstein, Boris
Davidson, Jo, 115, 403 *n.* 32
Day, *see* Morrow, Francis A.
Debs, Eugene Victor, 15, 48, 59, 93, 156; American Federation of Labor opposed by, 19; arrest, 95; Canton speech, 95; and Communist Labor party, 178; and Communist party, 324–26; 446–47 *n.* 35, *n.* 36; and dictatorship of proletariat, 324–25;

interpretations of, 447 n. 36; leaves I.W.W., 16; and Lenin, 75, 280; Populist and Democrat, 38; in prison, 324; reforms opposed, 24; on Russian revolution, 110, 325–26; on Russian Social Revolutionaries, 324–25; and Soviet government, 325; on violence, 22; vote in 1912, 41, 70; World War I opposed by, 56

Debs, Theodore, 324
Decentralization, Amsterdam Bureau potential, 235
"Declaration of Intellectual Independence," 127
Decline of American Capitalism, The, 299
DeLeon, Daniel, 14, 27, 29–30, 49, 62, 111, 123, 141, 149; immediate demands opposed by, 23; I.W.W. ousts, 16, 18; and Lassalleans, 19; and Marx, 15; for revolutionary unions, 18; on violence, 22
DeLeonism, in Left Wing manifesto, 168
Dell, Floyd, 49, 124, 127–28, 404 n. 32; on board of *New Review*, 404 n. 35, 406 n. 19; praises *Revolt*, 419 n. 49; social interpretation of literature, 419 n. 21
Department of International Propaganda, 149
Department of Justice, Agent K-97, 366–72; agents, 226; and Mexico, 236; Jacob Nosovitsky, 227–28, 232–33; Ferdinand Peterson, 229–230; raid of Bridgman convention, 369–71; on Trotsky, 412 n. 54; *see also* Bureau of Investigation; Burns, William, J.; Shanahan, Edward; Spolansky, Jacob
Deportations, 202–203
Detroit Central Labor Council, 316
Detroit convention of Socialist party, 332
DeValera, Eamon, and Russian jewels, 240–41
Diamonds, *see* Russian jewels
Dimitroff, George, 319
Dirba, Charles, on Communist party Central Executive Committee, 184, 427 n. 14; on Communist party Executive Council, 427 n. 14; in Left Opposition, 335; in Left Opposition appeal to Comintern, 339–40; pseud., "Dobin," 356; suspended, 339
"Direct action," 22
Disarmament Commission, 365, 373; *see* Adjustment Commission
Dixon, Joseph, *see* Browder, Earl
Dobin, *see* Dirba, Charles
Dodge, Mabel, 43, 118, 403 n. 32
Dogmatism, 7, 27; in Communist theory, 250; Lenin's, 352
Dolsen, James H., leads Socialist convention walk-out, 178
Dreiser, Theodore, 62
Dual unionism, 19–20, 43; Communist policy on, 186, 273–74; and Profintern, 317–18, 320; at Third Comintern Congress, 278–79, 317; United Communist party on, 220
Dubner, A., *see* Jakira, Abraham
DuBois, W.E.B., 49; on board of *New Review*, 404 n. 35, 406 n. 19
Dubrowsky, D. H., and the Russian jewels, 239–40
Dunne, Grant, 317
Dunne, Miles, 317
Dunne, Vincent R., 317
Dunne, William F., 308, 324; background, 316, 445 n. 22; on Central Executive Committee and Executive Council, Workers party, 457 n. 32; in Communist Labor party, 317; gubernatorial candidate, 378; in Montana labor movement, 316; in Socialist party, 317
Durant, Kenneth, in Russian Soviet Government Bureau, 162; heads TASS, 162
Dutch Left Wing (Dutch Social Democratic party), 65; at Amsterdam conference, 233; influence in United States, 66; members in United States, 66; syndicalist influence, 151
Dutch influence on Left Wing, 64–66, 72–73

INDEX

Eastman, Max, 56–57, 73, 88, 118–19; autobiography, 408 *n.* 34; background, 126; and communism, 127–128; Communist sympathizer, 415 *n.* 31; disillusionment, 129–30, 155; eulogy by Joseph Freeman, 126–27; eulogy by Michael Gold, 127, 419 *n.* 20; at Fourth Comintern Congress, 383–84, 386–87; in Left Wing, 126; *Masses,* 48–49; *New Review,* 49, 404 *n.* 35; and John Reed, 284–86, 288, 290, 292, 418 *n.* 11; and Russian jewels, 434–35 *n.* 25; in Socialist party, 47; and Trotsky, 383–84; on the undergrounds, 247; on violence and sabotage, 47

Eberlein, Hugo, 151–53

E.C.C.I., *see* Executive Committee of the Communist International

Economic Interpretation of the Constitution of the United States, An, 40

Edwards, A. S., 69; on press committee, Socialist Propaganda League, 412 *n.* 20

Elbaum, D., on Communist party Central Executive Committee, 427 *n.* 14; on Communist party National Organization Committee, 425 *n.* 12

Emerson, Marion L., on Central Executive Committee and Executive Council, Workers party, 457 *n.* 32

Emigration to Russia, 114, 137, 191, 392

Emmett, Robert, 305

Emmons, *see* Knight, Joseph

Encyclopedia of the Social Sciences, 298

Engdahl, J. Louis, 335; arrest, 94; and Debs, 324–25; at Socialist convention, 178; in Socialist Left Wing, 330–31; on Third International, 332; Workers' Council secretary, 333; on Workers party Central Executive Committee, 450 *n.* 28, 457 *n.* 32, and Executive Council, 457 *n.* 32

Engels, Frederick, 24, 29, 88, 180, 401; on Americanization, 32; and Knights of Labor, 26; on Labor party, 26, 30; and Russian revolution, 98; on United States, 25–26; visits United States, 25; on war, 50–51

English-speaking groups, 161; at Bridgman convention, 371, 373; at Communist founding convention, 182–84; Communist potential in, 159; effect of raids on, 207

and federations, alliance, 184, needed by, 166, opposed to, 172–73, 425 *n.* 11, 426 *n.* 17, 427 *n.* 11, support for, 175

long-run leadership provided, 192; mass influence favored, 173; minority in Communist party, 190–91; proportion of Workers party, 392; in Ruthenberg group, 212–13; split opposed, 167; struggle in Communist party, 210–12; underground, 206; undifferentiated, 160; *see also* Communist party: membership

Epstein, Melech, in Jewish federation, 332; on founding of Jewish Communist federation, 429 *n.* 31, *n.* 32; and Workers' Council–Communist party negotiations, 448–49 *n.* 10, 449 *n.* 23

Espionage Act, 1917, 94

Esthonian Socialist federation, in Communist party, 188; membership, 189; in underground, 206

European Communists, *see* Western Communists

European revolution, 98; Lenin on, 104; and Second Comintern Congress, 328; and Third Comintern Congress, 275–77, 328; *see also* Western revolution

Evolutionary Socialism, 27

Executive Committee of the Communist International (E.C.C.I.): clears Fraina, 253, 293; power and function, 261–64; and Reed's membership, 257, 284–86, 288–91; Valetski at Bridgman conference for 219; Zinoviev chairman of, 259

INDEX

FF-22, see Peterson, Ferdinand
Farmer-Labor party, see Labor party
Farmers, and Labor party, 380
F.B.I., see Bureau of Investigation
Federations, see Foreign-language federations
Federated Press, 320
Ferguson, Isaac E., 138–39; at Communist founding convention, 183–184; on Communist party Central Executive Committee and Executive Council, 427 n. 14; concedes to federations, 174–75; on federations vs. English-speaking groups, 427 n. 11; indicted, 203; international delegate, 427 n. 14; joint convention call signed by, 175; on Left Wing National Council, 168; Left Wing national secretary, 168; at National Left Wing conference, 167; sentenced, 204
Ferrer, Francisco, 62
Fine, Nathan, 94, 400
Fineberg, J., 148
Finnish foreign-language federation, 78, 109; affiliates with Socialist party, 32; in American Labor Alliance, 337; predominately Right Wing, 192; withdraws from Socialist party, 332; in Workers party, 342, 392
First Comintern Congress, see First Congress of Third International
First Congress of Red International of Labor Unions (Profintern), 310, 316–18; planned, 269; and Third Comintern Congress, 317
First Congress of the Third International (Comintern), 148–50, 153–154; contrasted with Second Congress, 254; Lenin's policy, 248; Western representation, 232; see also Comintern
First International (International Workingmen's Association), 11; American section, 11; split, 12
Fish, Hamilton, Jr., 117
Fitzgerald, C. W., 69
Fitzpatrick, John, 197–98, 312–13

Flynn, Elizabeth Gurley, in I.W.W., 43
"Force and violence," see Violence
Ford, J., see Amter, Israel
Ford, James W., 299
"Foreign agents," 263, 265
Foreign Commissariat (U.S.S.R.), and the Russian jewels, 238, 240
Foreign-language federations, in American Labor Alliance, 336–37; Comintern would limit, 244; Comintern defied by, 245; and Communist Labor party, 180
  and Communist party, 169; dominate party, 212–18; faction in, 210; at founding convention, 182–85; majority, 190–91; in (new) Communist party, 354; form National Organization Committee for, 173–174
  on Communist Unity Committee, 437 n. 7; dues question, 213; effect of raids, 207; English-speaking leadership, 160; against English-speaking groups, 172–73, 210–14, 425 n. 11, 427 n. 11; fundamentalism, 345–46; growth, 137–38; hostility to Ruthenberg, 196, to Ruthenberg group, 213–14, 431 n. 11; joint convention call issued, 175; in Left Opposition, 335; in Left Wing, 146, 153, 155–57, 190; in Left Wing National Council, 174–175, national conference, 306; on legality, 336; Michigan alliance, 165, 169, 171, split, 184; non-voters in, 200; orthodoxy of, 170; on political action, 200; political composition, 192; prepare split, 165–66; Russian leadership, 159; in Socialist party, 32, 66–67, 407 n. 7; suspended by Socialist party, 158; and Third Comintern Congress, 279; underground membership, 206, 207; unity, with Communist Labor party, 212, with United Communist party, 269; at Woodstock convention, 271–273; in Workers party, 392–93
Forest House, 369

Forward, Jewish Daily, 59, 99, 110, 112, 341

Foster, William Z., 36, 39, 60, 299, 322–24, 326, 334, 342–43; in American Federation of Labor, 312–14; approach to workers, 350; arrest, 372; background, 311–12, 444 *n.* 12; at Bridgman convention, 370, 373; and Browder, 308, 310–11; joins Communist party, 321–22, 446 *n.* 33; "E. Z. Foster," 313; and Gompers, 313, 351; *History*, 6, 400, 424–25 *n.* 4, 427–28 *n.* 14; International Trade Union Educational League, 312; in Moscow, 316, 320–321; opportunism, 351; packinghouse campaign, 312; and Red International of Labor Unions, 314–16, 319; on Ruthenberg, 430 *n.* 41; sectarianism, 351; in Socialist party, 311; in steel strike, 198–99, 313; syndicalist, 311, 314, 320, 322, 350; in Syndicalist League of North America, 312; testimony on steel strike and war, 313, 444–45 *n.* 15; in Trade Union Educational League, 314, 446 *n.* 34; trips to Europe, 311, 316–17; on war, 313, 445 *n.* 17

Foster group, 330

Fourth Congress of the Comintern, 329, 382–87; effect on American Communism, 383; Geese-Liquidators problem at, 382–85; on illegality, 385, 389; on immigrants vs. natives, 386; instructions to American Communists, 385–86; on Labor party, 386; on the Negro question, 387, 456 *n.* 28; trade-union policy, 455 *n.* 21; "united front" defined by, 329

Fraenkel, Osmond K., 47

Fraina, Louis C., 72–73, 76, 80, 84–88, 105, 112, 120, 133, 142, 145, 156–57, 174, 278

early radicalism: background, 61–62; in I.W.W., 43, 62; at Lawrence strike, 43; and *New Review*, 49, 63, 86, 404 *n.* 35, 411 *n.* 18; in Socialist Labor party, 43, 62, leaves, 62; in Socialist party, 62; for Third International, 64, 66

in new Left Wing, 80; arrest, 95; to Boston, 131; Communist founding convention, 182–84; concedes to federations, 175; director, American Bolshevik Bureau of Information, 107–109; editor, *Revolutionary Age*, 132, 168; on Left Wing split, 172; Left Wing manifesto, author of, 168; on mass action, 89–91; at National Left Wing conference, 167, on National Council, 167; on *New International*, 411–12 *n.* 20; on Russian revolution, 99–100; Rutgers, debt to, 412–13 *n.* 20; on World War I, 410 *n.* 8

in Communist party: at Amsterdam conference, 233–35; break with Comintern, 295–96, 300; and Comintern funds, 294, 296, 300, 440 *n.* 26, *n.* 29; in Germany, 252; and Lenin, 281; in Moscow, 252; and Nosovitsky, 227–28; and John Reed, 288–91; at Second Congress of Comintern, 253–58, 267, 283, 293, 295; pseud. "Ralph Snyder," 229, 433–34 *n.* 6; trip to Russia, 227, 251; to United States, 270

in Mexico, 294, 296–97

positions held in party: on American Agency, 269, 294, 310, 363; on Central Executive Committee and Executive Council, Communist party, 184, 427 *n.* 14; editor, *The Communist*, 184–85; International secretary, 184, 227, 251; Moscow representative of Communist party, 211; Moscow representative to Mexico, 294

repudiation by American Communist party, 295; and the Russian jewels, 240; and Ruthenberg, 196 *trials:* 293, 439–40 *n.* 22, 440 *n.* 24; in Moscow, 252–54, cleared, 253; in New York, 230–32, cleared, 232; and Nosovitsky, 230–32; and Peterson, 229–32; called "provocateur," 229–30

INDEX

in underground, 227; vanishes, 282, 293
anti-communism: 300, 441 *n.* 40; autobiography, 406 *n.* 16, *n.* 17, 408 *n.* 30, 420 *n.* 2; bibliography, 442–443 *n.* 45; Communist attacks, 299, 301–302, 442 *n.* 44; death, 302; deportation ordered, 301; economic writings, 298–300, 440–41 *n.* 34; Foster-Ford campaign, 299; Gitlow testimony against, 301, 442 *n.* 45; as Lewis Corey, 298–302; and Lovestone, 300; Marxism reconsidered, 300; name wiped out, 60; pseud. "Joseph Charles Skala," 297; and Trotskyists, 299–300; in Union for Democratic Action, 301, 441–442 *n.* 42; and World War II, 300–301
Frankfeld, Phil, party leadership from Young Communist League, 450 *n.* 33
Frankfurter, Felix, 202
Fraser, Alexander, president, *New Review* publishing company, 404 *n.* 35
Freiheit, Jewish Daily, Comintern proposal for, 340; established, 341; subsidization, 382
Freeman, Joseph, 126–27, 129–30, 403 *n.* 32
"Free silver," 37, 39
French Communist party, 376, 454 *n.* 1
Friends of the Russian Revolution (*also* Friends of the New Russia), 106, 415 *n.* 29
Friends of Soviet Russia, in American Labor Alliance, 337
From Bryan to Stalin, 39
Fundamentalists, 345; foreign-born, 345; *see also* Orthodoxy

Gallacher, William, 257
Gannes, Harry, party leadership from Young Communist League, 450 *n.* 33; on Young Workers League National Executive Committee, 450 *n.* 32
Gaylord, Winfield R., leaves Socialist party, 93

"Geese" (Goose caucus): at Bridgman convention, 373–74; and legality, 389; one-vote majority, 373, 454 *n.* 11; in Moscow, 381–85; origin of name, 360, 453 *n.* 19; party majority, 361–62, 453 *n.* 23; theses, 360–61
General Staff of the World Revolution, *see* Comintern
George, Harrison, 96, 110, 113
George, Henry, supported by Daniel DeLeon, 14
Gerber, Julius, 140, 144–45, 156; at Socialist convention, 177
German-American Socialist Labor party, 32; *see* Socialist Labor party
German Socialist federation, 74, 76; attitude toward Communists doubtful, 192; in underground, 206
German immigrants, 11, 25–26, 31–33
German Communist party, and insurrection, 275; and Secretariat for Western Europe, 234; and united front, 378, 454 *n.* 1
German revolution, failure, 275–77; subsidization, 262
German Social Democracy, 33; collapse, 104; conflict in, 88–89
German-Soviet Pact, 300
Germer, Adolph, 92, 174, 424 *n.* 28, *n.* 30; arrest, 94; at Socialist convention, 177, 426 *n.* 1.
Ghent, William J., leaves Socialist party, 93
Gibbs, in Socialist Propaganda League, 69
Gildei, delegate to Second Comintern Congress, 436 *n.* 15
Giovannitti, Arturo, on board of *New Review,* 404 *n.* 35, 406 *n.* 19
Gitlow, Benjamin, 37, 139–40, 190, 304, 308, 327, 343; background, 140; Bronx organizer, Left Wing, 422 *n.* 41; business manager, *The Voice of Labor,* 175; at Communist Labor party convention, 178–80; on Communist Labor party labor committee, 181; cited on Communist party membership, 432–33 *n.*

Gitlow, Benjamin (*continued*)
23; federations opposed by, 175–176, 306; in Goose caucus, 361; and Haywood, 186; indicted, 203; in Left Wing, 141, 145; on Left Wing National Council, 168; at National Left Wing conference, 167, 424–25 *n.* 4; in "new minority," 175; on New York Left Wing City Committee and Executive Committee, 422 *n.* 43; pseuds., "Tom Paine," "John Pierce," 205; on John Reed, 285–86, 290; sentenced, 204; at Socialist convention, 176–77; testimony against Fraina, 301–302, 442 *n.* 45; on Valetski, 363–64; versions of Fraina trials, 439–40 *n.* 22

Glassberg, Benjamin, 154; editor, *The Workers' Council*, 333; at Socialist convention, 178; in Socialist Left Wing, 331

Gold, Michael, 116, 127–29, 404 *n.* 32; on Eastman, 419 *n.* 20; as Irwin Granich, 419 *n.* 20; Red Guard recruit, 109

Goldman, Emma, 111; deported, 203; and Lenin, 248; and Reed, 286–87; and Zinoviev, 248

Gompers, Samuel, 12, 19–20, 42, 135, 347; and Foster, 313, 347; and Socialists, 29

Goodman, Milton, on New York Left Wing City Committee, 422 *n.* 43

Goose caucus, *see* Geese

Gormley, Jim, *see* John Reed

Gorter, Herman, 65, 66, 73; on mass action, 412 *n.* 29

Green, Gil, party leadership from Young Communist League, 450 *n.* 33

Greenback movement, 36

Grendon, Felix, on board of *New Review*, 404 *n.* 35, 406 *n.* 19, 411 *n.* 18

Group of Social Revolutionaries, 83

Gruber, J., Comintern delegate from Austria, 152–53; pseud., "Steinhart,"

Gruening, Martha, on board of *New Review*, 411 *n.* 18

Gruzenberg-Borodin, 368; *see* Borodin

Guesde, Jules, 52

Hammer, Dr. Julius, on New York Left Wing City Committee, 422 *n.* 43

Hankins, Martha, 307

Hardman, J. B. S., *see* Salutsky, J. B.

Hardy, George, 96

Harriman, Job, 45, 46

Harrison, Caleb, 336, 360; on first Central Executive Committee, Workers party, 450 *n.* 28; secretary, Workers party, 342, 450 *n.* 29

Harvard Socialist Club, 117

Hayes, Max, 42

Haymarket Square, 21

Haywood, Harry, party leadership from Young Communist League, 450 *n.* 33

Haywood, William D. (Big Bill), 16, pathy for, 47–49, 70, 92; Los Angeles *Times* dynamiting, 45; Paterson strike, 43; repudiation by Communists, 279; sentenced, 96; and Socialist party fight on violence, 45–46, Haywood recall from National Executive Committee, 46; at Third Comintern Congress, 278–79; trip to U.S.S.R., 278; on violence, 22

Heimin, 78

Heller, Abram A., in Russian Soviet Government Bureau, 162

Henderson, Arthur, 327

Henry, *see* Ashkenudzie, George

"Henry, Curtis Dow Company," 357

Herron, George D., 56; leaves Socialist party, 93

Hervé, Gustave, 52

Heywood, Harry, party leadership from Young Communist League, 450 *n.* 33

Hicks, Granville, 400; on John Reed, 284, 288–90, 291–92, 400, 418 *n.* 11, 438–39 *n.* 9

Hillquit, Morris, 33, 45–46, 58–59, 63, 84, 140–41, 157–58, 178, 330; and Russian revolution, 110; in

Russian Soviet Government Bureau, 162; at St. Louis convention, 92–93; on Third International, 331–32; on war, 56, 93–95, 413 *n.* 38

Hiltzik, Harry, alternate at National Left Wing conference, 424–25 *n.* 4; on New York Left Wing City Committee, 422 *n.* 43

Himmelfarb, L., on New York Left Wing Executive Committee, 422 *n.* 43

History of the Communist Party of the United States, 6, 60, 400

Homestead steel strike, 21

Horowitz, Fanny, alternate at National Left Wing conference, 424–425 *n.* 4; on New York Left Wing City Committee, 422 *n.* 43

Hourwich, Isaac A., 163; on board of *New Review,* 404 *n.* 35, 406 *n.* 19, 411 *n.* 18

Hourwich, Nicholas I., 107, 132, 163; at Communist founding convention, 184; Moscow representative, 211, 427 *n.* 14; at National Left Wing conference, 167, 424–25 *n.* 4; on New York Left Wing City Committee and Executive Committee, 422 *n.* 43; pseud., "Andrew," 214; quarrel with Ruthenberg, 211, 431 *n.* 2; remains in Russia, 280; and Russian Soviet Government Bureau, 163; at Second Comintern Congress, 268; for split, 165–66; at Third Comintern Congress, 275, 279–80; leaves United States, 191

House of Morgan, The, 298

Hughan, Jessie Wallace, 58

Hughes, Charles Evans, and Nosovitsky, 236

Huiswoud, Otto, at Fourth Comintern Congress, 387; pseud., "Billings," 387

Hungarian foreign-language federation: Comintern representative to, 364; in Communist party, 188; membership, 189; potential Communists, 159; Ruthenberg group attacks, 212; suspended by Socialist party, 158; in underground, 206

Hungarian Workers federation, in American Labor Alliance, 337

Hunter, Robert, leaves Socialist party, 93

Hyndman, H. M., 52

Illegality, 45, 205, 208, 330; American party ends, 388–90; and Bolshevism, 207; changing Comintern attitude on, 244; factions on, 335–36; and Fourth Comintern Congress, 382, 386; a principle, 345; at Third Comintern Congress, 277–78; and Woodstock convention, 274; and Workers Council, 334

Illinois Socialist party, controlled by Left Wing, 159

Immediate demands, 23–24, 27, 30, 346–47; difference between Socialist and Communist, 349; *see also* Reforms

Immigrants, in American socialism, 31–35; Comintern decision on, 386; *see also* German, Irish, etc.

Independent Young People's Socialist League, 343; affiliates with Third International, 343; delegates to Second Comintern Congress, 436 *n.* 15

Industrial Socialist League, 336–37; in American Labor Alliance, 337

Industrial unionism, 14–15, 18–19, 69, 113; Reed on, 290; United Communist party on, 220

Industrial Workers of the World (I.W.W.), 64, 88, 135–36, 140, 324, 416 *n.* 46; Browder and, 308; Cannon and, 306; in Chicago, 19

and Comintern, 150; approved by, 242; hostile to, 316; letter from, 245; and Profintern, 315–18; and Second Comintern Congress, 255–257; and Soviet Russia, 315; and Third Comintern Congress, 278–279; and Third International, 315, split on International, 318, 446 *n.* 28

and Communist Labor party: at

I.W.W. (*continued*)
convention, 178–79; endorsed by, 186; C.L.P. vs. C.P. on, 224 composition, 22; decline, 105, 393; in Detroit, 19; dual unionism, 19; first convention, 19; formation, 16; Foster and, 312, 314; General Executive Board, 315; heyday, 42–43; on immediate demands, 24; immigrants in, 32; influence, 323; Left Wing in, 17; and Left Wing, 28; in Left Wing manifesto, 168; and political action, 200; raids, 204; Reed on, 283, 302; and Russian revolution, 110–13; syndicalist, 18; union policy opposed by Communist party, 274; United Communist party on, 220; on violence, 22, 34; war prosecution, 96

Informers, *see* Agents

Ingerman, Dr. Anna, 112

Insurrection, Comintern letter on, 243; Communists advocate, 223–24; issue in Communist party split, 213–214, 431 *n.* 9; Lenin's policy, 259; Liquidators on, 360; and Woodstock convention, 274; and Workers party, 342; Workers party on, 452–453 *n.* 18; *see also* Violence

Intellectuals, 282, 299, 363; Communist, 41; and the *Masses*, 49; in Progressive movement, 40; protest Haywood recall, 47; and Russian revolution, 125–29; self-taught, 63; in strikes, 43

Intelligence Branch, United States Army, 368

Intercollegiate Socialist Society, 42, 141

International Conference of Socialist Organizations and Groups, 82–83

International Federation of Trade Unions, 315

International Ladies Garment Workers Union, 193

International Socialist Bureau, 52

International Socialist Review, 48, 57, 60, 66, 68, 71–73, 76, 78, 89; mass action, 412 *n.* 24, *n.* 29

International Soviet Republic, 248

International Sub-Bureau: created at Amsterdam conference, 234; subsidiaries: American Bureau, 234; Central European Bureau, 234; Pan-American Provisional Bureau, 234

International Trade Union Educational League, 312

International Workingmen's Association (First International), 11; *see also* Syndicalists

Internationalism, 264; vs. Americanization, 187–88; and Russian nationalism, 264

Internationalist, The, 71–72, 86; name changed to *The New International*, 86

Irish American Labor League, in American Labor Alliance, 337

Irish Free State, and the Russian jewels, 240–41, 434–35 *n.* 25

Irish immigrants, 21

Irish Nationalist movement, 78–79

Irish Transport and General Workers Union, 79

Irish Worker, The, 79

"Iron law of wages," 11

Irwin, Will, 287

Italian foreign-language federation, attitude toward Communists doubtful, 192

I.W.W., *see* Industrial Workers of the World

Izvestia, 262, 268

Jacobs, member, National Executive Committee, Young Workers League, 450 *n.* 32

Jakira, Abram, in Goose caucus, 360–61; pseud., "A. Dubner," 360; Valetski on, 365; on Workers party Central Executive Committee, 374, 457 *n.* 32

Jansen (Johnson), Carl, *see* Scott, Charles E.

Jerome, V. J., refutes Fraina, 299

Jewels, Russian, and Borodin's mission, 238–41, 434 *n.* 24; and Irish government, 434–35 *n.* 25

Jewish Bureau of the Russian Communist party, 382

INDEX

Jewish Communist federation, 305; organized, 192, 429 n. 31, n. 32; publication, 192; Ruthenberg group attacks, 212; in underground, 206; in Workers party, 342

Jewish Daily Forward, see Forward

Jewish foreign-language federation: and Communist party, 173, 189; Left Wing in, 192; leaves Socialist party, 332–33, 448–49 n. 10; Right Wing predominates, 192; split in, 192

Joffe, A. A., 262

Johnson, Oakley C., on National Organization Committee, Communist party, 425 n. 12

Joint Unity Convention, *see* Woodstock convention

Jungle, The, 41

Jurgis, delegate to Second Comintern Congress, 436 n. 15

K-97, *see* Morrow, Francis A.

Kamenev, Leon, at Third Comintern Congress, 277

Kampf, Der, 192

Kansas City Socialist party, controlled by Left Wing, 159

Kapital, Das, 16

Kapp Putsch, 252

Karklin, C., 89

Karosses, on Central Executive Committee and Executive Council, Communist party, 427 n. 14

Katayama, Sen, 80, 82, 85, 132, 356; on American Agency, 269, 294, 310, 363; in Japan, 78; pseud., "Yavki," 269; sent to United States, 270; in United States, 77–78

Katterfeld, Ludwig E.: on Communist Labor party National Executive Committee, 181; on Communist party Central Executive Committee, 374; expelled, 281, 438 n. 30; at Fourth Comintern Congress, 381–382, 385; in Goose caucus, 361; leadership weakens, 304; in Left Wing, 92, 158; and Lenin, 280–81; pseud., "Carr," 382; sentenced, 204; at Socialist convention, 177; in Socialist party, 92; temporary Socialist party secretary, 174; on Workers party Central Executive Committee, 457 n. 32

Kautsky, Karl, 27, 58, 89; on war, 52

Kenneday, Paul: on board of *New Review,* 404 n. 35, 406 n. 19

Keracher, John, 160, 165; on National Organization Committee, Communist party, 425 n. 12

Kerensky, Alexander, 99

Kerr, Charles H., and Co., 48, 75–76

Kienthal conference, 55

Knight, Joseph, pseud., "Emmons," 316

Knights of Labor, 13–14, 19, 26, 36, 305, 323

Kollontay, Alexandra, 60, 80, 82, 85–86; background, 74; biographical material, 409 n. 41, n. 42, n. 43; Lenin's representative, 74–76; second trip to United States, 76; in United States, 74–76

Kopnagel, S., on National Organization Committee, Communist party, 425 n. 12

Kremlin, 252, 279

Krumbein, Charles, 424–25 n. 4; at Bridgman convention, 370; sentenced, 204

Kruse, William F.: arrest, 94; at Socialist convention, 178; in Socialist Left Wing, 330; and Third International, 331–32; on Workers party Central Executive Committee, alternate, 450 n. 28, member, 457 n. 32

Kuusinen, Ottomar V., 356; chairs American Commission, 382

"L.P.P." (Legal Political Party, 1922), 358–59

Labor party, 135–36, 208; at Bridgman convention, 380; Communist definition of, 380–81; Communist interest in, 379–80; Communist opposition to, 185, 199–200, 223; Communist support for, 380–81; in Cook County, 197; becomes Farmer-Labor party, 201; Fourth Com-

Labor party (*continued*)
  intern Congress on, 383, 385–86; in Left Wing manifesto, 168; Lenin on, 253, 280; movement in United States, 197, 379; national convention called, 198; and united-front policy, 379; Valetski favors, 380
Lang, *see* Pogany, Joseph
Langley, *see* Lovestone
Lansing, *see* Swabeck, Arne
Lapland, 229–30, 332
Larkin, James Joseph: biographical material, 410 *n.* 60; on federations, 175; indicted, 203; on Left Wing National Council, 168; at National Left Wing conference, 167, 424–25 *n.* 4; in "new minority," 175; on New York Left Wing City and Executive Committees, 422 *n.* 43; sentenced, 204; in United States, 78–79
Lassalle, Ferdinand, 11
Latvian Communist party, 148
Lawrence strikes: 1912, 43, 62; 1919, 139, 197
Lazzari, Costantino, 73
Leadville strike, 21
League of Nations, 240
Lee, Algernon, 69, 92, 94, 142
Left Opposition, 1921–1922; appeals to Comintern, 339–40, 355–358; Comintern supported by, 388; becomes (new) Communist party, 354; convention, 388, 456 *n.* 29; emergency convention, 353; as a faction, 335; failure, 351; foreign-language composition of split, 353; legal party established, 355; rival (illegal) party planned, 340; reunification, 389; 1922 split, 353; suspensions, 339, 353; suspensions upheld, 340; United Toilers of America, 355; Valetski's influence, 388, 456–57 *n.* 29
Left Wing (historic): continuity with Communist party, 186–87; defeat of Haywood, in Socialist party, 46; dualism, 20; evaluated, 346, 348; identified with proletariat, revolution, 27–30; immediate demands opposed by, 23–24, 34; immigrant character, 34; for industrial unionism, 19–20; and I.W.W., 18, 28; isolation, 30; Labor party opposed, 380; and middle class, 30; publications, 48–49; rival groups in, 17; roots of, 17; and 1912 strikes, 43; on violence, 22
Left Wing (new), 50, 76, 88, 118, 131, 136–37, 139, 306, 311, 314, 317; alignments in changed by war, 52; Americanization, 168; Bolsheviks supported by, 415 *n.* 31; in Boston, 131, 144; Brooklyn meeting of, 80; in Chicago, 138, 144; Chicago convention called by, 169; Communist Propaganda League part of, 138; contrast with historic Left Wing, 414 *n.* 26; dual organization formed by, 155; Dutch influence on, 64–66, 72–73; expulsion of, from Socialist party, 157–58; growth of, 137; Jewish influence in, 142; language groups in, 153, 160; Lettish influence, 68–71, 89, 132; in Massachusetts, 68–72; in Michigan, 210–11; national conference called, 157, 164; National Council of, 175; National Organization Committee of, 173–74; new minority in, 175; in New York, 83–84, 139–41, 144–145, 153–57; on orthodoxy vs. opportunism, 169–70; on parliamentarianism, 241; potential of in Socialist party, 156, 159–60; primaries contested by, 200; publications of, 160; Russian influence on, 81, 106, 132, 138, 160; effects of Russian revolution on, 101–104; and Russian Soviet Government Bureau, 162; at St. Louis convention, 92–93; at Socialist emergency convention, 176–77, 426 *n.* 1, removed from, 177, walkouts, 178; Socialist party, fight for control of, 164–65; National Executive Committee, 174; split in, 167, 276; and Socialist Propaganda League, 69–75; states controlled by, 159–60; strength of, 166; Trotsky-Bukharin difference

INDEX

on tactics of, 81; on war position of Socialist party, 94–96; women in, 193

Left Wing manifesto, grounds for indictment, 203

Left-Wing Communism: An Infantile Disorder, 248, 251, 327, 352

Left Wing in the labor movement, Comintern on, 386

Left Wing Section of the Greater New York Locals of the Socialist Party, *see* New York Left Wing

Left Wing socialism, and communism, 322

Left Wing, Socialist party, 330–33, *see* Socialist party

Left Wing trade unionists, Foster and, 322

Legal, mass party: American Labor Alliance formed as, 336; Bridgman decision for, 374; Comintern decision for, 274, 303, 385–86; Fourth Comintern Congress and, 385–86; Lenin on, 279–80; separate conventions of American Labor Alliance and Workers' Council planned, 337; and Third Comintern Congress, 275–77; Workers' Council for, 334

Lehman, George, on New York Left Wing Executive Committee, 422 *n.* 43

Lenin, V. I. (Vladimir Ilyich Ulianov), 10, 15, 49, 52, 58, 73, 81–82, 84–85, 99, 111, 116, 119–20, 123–124, 127, 141–42, 147, 152, 159, 171, 187, 191, 196, 237–38; on American Left Wing, 72–76; and American policy at Third Comintern Congress, 279–81; Americans meet with, 279–81, 438 *n.* 26; on American revolution, 248; on British Labour party, 379; and Communist founding convention, 181; and Debs, 324–25; dogmatism, 352; on economic development of Russia, 248, 250; at Fourth Comintern Congress, 384, 386; and Fraina, 253, 255, 293; and Haywood, 278; on Labor party, 253, 280; letter to American workers, 133–34; and Liquidators, 384; New Economic Policy for Russia, 249; opportunism of, 248–49, 251; personal influence, 100, 102, 259–60, 265, 279–281; program, 107–109; and Reed, 252, 255–56, 283, 285; on reform, 249, 346; on revolutionary defeatism, 53; on Russian revolution, 98, 104; on Second International, 53, 328, 447 *n.* 2; on Social Democrats, 327–29; struggle for succession to, 395; at Third Comintern Congress, 275–77; and Third International, 148; on trade unions, 255; unitedfront policy, 327–29, originator of, 447 *n.* 1; and Western revolution, 104, 247–48, 266; on World War I, 53; writings translated, 104, 107; and Zinoviev, 258–60

Letter to American Workingmen, A, 133; brought to United States, 238; published in *Revolutionary Age* and *Liberator,* 238

Letters to Americans, 1848–1895, Marx and Engels, 401 *n.* 11

Letters of Lenin, The, 400

Lettish branch No. 1, Socialist party, 83

Lettish Communists, 269; *see* Lettish foreign-language federation

Lettish foreign-language federation (Lettish Left Wing, Lettish Social-Democratic Workers party): in Communist party, 188; at Fourth Comintern Congress, 383; in Massachusetts Socialist party, 68–71, 89, 132; membership, 189; potential Communists in, 159; and Russian Left Wing, 67; in Socialist party, 67; suspended by Socialist party, 158; in underground, 206

Lettish influence, 67–71

Lettish Left Wing, *see* Lettish foreign-language federation

Lettish Social-Democratic Labor party, in Russian Social-Democratic Labor party, 73–74

Lettish Social-Democratic Workers party, *see* Lettish foreign-language federation

INDEX

Lettish (Socialist) immigrants, Left Wing character of, 33

Lettish Workers Society of Boston, 68, 70

Lewis, Austin, 89

Lewis, John L., 393

Lewis, Sinclair, 41

Liberator, The, 128, 155, 195

Liebknecht, Karl, Letts greet, 68; war denounced by, 52

Liquidators, 360; at Bridgman convention, 373–74; defeated, 361; in Moscow, 381–85; Russian origin of name, 360; trade-union sympathizers, 362; and Trotsky, 383–84, 455–456 *n.* 22

Lindgren, Edward I., 139; on Communist Labor party National Executive Committee, 181; in Goose caucus, 261; Kings organizer, Left Wing, 422 *n.* 41; at National Left Wing conference, 424–25 *n.* 4; on New York Left Wing City and Executive Committees, 422 *n.* 43; pseud., "Flynn," 267; at Second Comintern Congress, 267–68; on Workers party Central Executive Committee and Executive Council, 457 *n.* 32

"Line," Communist, 301, 377, 395; change in, 250; changes to "Left" again, 448 *n.* 7; of Third Comintern Congress, 275

Lippmann, Walter, 48–49, 117; on board of *New Review,* 404 *n.* 35, 406 *n.* 19

Lithuanian branch, Socialist party, Manhattan, 83; Brooklyn, 83

Lithuanian foreign-language federation, 173; in Communist party, 188; membership, 190; potential Communists, 159; suspended by Socialist party, 158; in underground, 206

Litvinov, Maxim, and the Russian jewels, 240

Living My Life, 286

Livingston, Arthur, 49; on board of *New Review,* 404 *n.* 35, 406 *n.* 19

Lloyd, Caro, 41

Lloyd, Henry Demarest, 41, 138

Lloyd, William Bross, 41, 138; chairman, National Left Wing conference, 166

Lochner, Louis P., 154

London Daily News, 115

London, Jack, 41, 56, 62

London, Meyer, 59, 94–95; Fourth Comintern Congress discussion of, 383, 455 *n.* 8; Workers party candidate withdraws in favor of, 378–79, 383

Looking Backward, 14, 16

Loonin, Meyer, on first Central Executive Committee, Workers party, 450 *n.* 28

Lore, Ludwig, 120; background, 76; in "Center," 154; *Class Struggle* editor, 87, 100; and Communist Labor party, 180–81; speaks for friends of New Russia, 415 *n.* 29; in Left Wing, 80–82, 139, 143; *Revolutionary Age* editor, 132; and Trotsky, 77, 79, 85; on Workers party Central Executive Committee, 450 *n.* 28, 457 *n.* 32, Executive Council, 457 *n.* 32

Los Angeles *Times* dynamiting, 45

Lovestone, Jay, 7, 140, 192, 308, 332, 339, 343, 388; background, 141, 421 *n.* 26; at Bridgman convention, 373–74; at Communist founding convention, 183; on Communist party Central Executive Committee, 184, 304, 427 *n.* 14; on C.E.C. majority, 335; editor, *The Communist,* 304; and Fraina, 300; at Fraina trial, 230–32; as Jacob Liebstein, 205; a Liquidator, 362; alternate at National Left Wing conference, 424–25 *n.* 4; national secretary, 3–4; on New York Left Wing City Committee, 422 *n.* 43; pseuds., "Langley," "Nelson," "Wheat," 205; cited on Ruthenberg, 430 *n.* 41; goes with Ruthenberg in 1920 split, 214; and Valetski, 364–65; on Workers party Central Executive Committee, 450 *n.* 28, 457 *n.* 32

Low, Bela, 112

Lowie, Robert H., 49, 56; on board of

INDEX

New Review, 404 *n.* 35, 406 *n.* 19
Lozovsky, A., 319, 321; on American Commission, 382; as Solomon Abramovich Dridzo, 319; background, 319; and power struggle in U.S.S.R., 319
Lusk committee, 146; raids, 203, 227; report, 430 *n.* 14
Luxemburg, Rosa, 52, 73, 89, 152, 363; on war, 52–53

MacAlpine, Eadmonn, 78–79, 132, 146; opposes federations, 175; at National Left Wing conference, 424–25 *n.* 4; in new minority, 175
MacDonald, Ramsay, 52
Majority, Comintern attitude toward, 356–57
Maki, Theodore, on Central Executive Committee and Executive Council, Workers party, 457 *n.* 32
Manchester Guardian, 115
Manuilsky, Dmitri Z., 376; on tactics, 448 *n.* 7
Marks, John, member, National Executive Committee, Young Workers League, 450 *n.* 32
Marot, Helen, on board of *New Review,* 404 *n.* 35, 406 *n.* 19
Marsh, Henry W., and Nosovitsky, 236
Marshall, James A., *see* Bedacht, Max
Martens, Ludwig C. A. K., 107; background, 161; and Fraina, 227–30, 239, 243; and Russian Soviet Government Bureau, 161–63
Martov, Julius, 52, 54
Marx, Karl, 11, 13, 24, 29, 37, 88, 110, 136, 147, 180–81; and DeLeon, 15, 27; on immediate demands, 25; and Lenin, 249; on Russian revolution, 97; on United States, 25
Marxian Educational Society, in American Labor Alliance, 337
Marxian Socialists, in U.S., 11
Marxists, 16; evaluation of Russian revolution, 266
Marxism: and American conditions, 26; and Bernstein revisionism, 27; Fraina on, 300; orthodox, 24; Russian, 191
"Mass action," 66, 72, 88, 95, 412 *n.* 26, *n.* 29, 412–13 *n.* 30; Communist attitude, 187, 198; defined, 89–90; election boycott as example, 201; in Left Wing manifesto, 168; in Socialist party, 89
Massachusetts Socialist party: center of Left Wing, 68–70; control by Left Wing, 159; emigration from, 114; *Revolutionary Age* published by, 131
Masses, 72, 86, 88, 118–19, 126–27, 284; initiated, 48
Masses: contempt for, 350; Third Comintern Congress slogan, To the, 276–77
Mass organization, approved by Comintern, 244
Mass party, *see* legal mass party
Mauretania, 228
McKay, Claude: as Mackay, 403 *n.* 32; at Fourth Comintern Congress, 387
McNamara, J. B., 45
McNamara, J. J., 45
Means, Gardiner C., 298
Meat and Man, 301
Mehring, Franz, 73
Mensheviks, 99, 128, 136, 143, 159, 354, 383; and Bolshevik split, 164; on legality, 360; on violence, 214
Mexican Communist party, and Nosovitsky, 236
Mexico, Fraina mission to, 294
Meyer, *see* Wagenknecht
Michael, Joseph, secretary, *New Review* publishing company, 404 *n.* 35
Michelson, *see* Valetski, H.
Michigan group, 210–11; leaves Communist party, 211; named Proletarian party, 212; *see also* Michigan Socialist party
Michigan Socialist party: charter revoked, 158; at Communist founding convention, 182–84; and Communist party, 169, 173; differs from Left Wing, 160; emergency state

Michigan Socialist party (*continued*) convention, 165; foreign-language federation alliance, 165, 169, 171, broken, 184; national convention called, 166; program, 160–61; split prepared by, 165–68; for Third International, 165

Middle class, 28, 30

Ministerialism, 90

Minneapolis Trades and Labor Council, 316

Minnesota Left Wing conference, 173

Minnesota Socialist party, controlled by Left Wing, 159

Minor, Robert, 121, 324, 338, 361, 403 *n*. 32; anarchist, 122; background, 121; biographical material, 418 *n*. 13, 419 *n*. 16; cartoonist, 122; on Central Executive Committee, Workers party, 450 *n*. 28, 457 *n*. 32, in C.E.C. majority, 335; conversion to communism, 124–26; in Goose caucus, 361; in I.W.W., 121; and Lenin, 280; and Mooney-Billings case, 123; pseud., "Ballister," 278; joins Socialist party, 122; at Third Comintern Congress, 275, 277–79; and Valetski, 364–65; on violence, 355

Modern Corporation and Private Property, The, 298

Molly Maguires, 21

Montana Federation of Labor, 316

Montana State Legislature, 316

Mooney, Tom, 123

Moore, *see* Ballam, John J.

Morrow, Francis A.: breaks underground code, 367; Camden section organizer, 366; in Communist party, 366; Department of Justice agent K-97, 366; pseuds., "Ashworth," 371, "Comrade Day," 366; in Socialist party, 366; sources, 454 *n*. 7; testimony, 372; at underground convention, 367–72

Moscow, 8, 247–48, 258, 323, 338–39, 356; abolishes Amsterdam Bureau, 235; Comintern leadership from, 377; domination, 394–95; factionalism in, 381; on Labor party, 379; instructions from, 239, 371; representation to, 211; symbolism of, 255; usefulness of, 394–95; *see also* Comintern

Moscow Congress, *see* Third International, First Congress

Most, Johann, 13

Moyer, Charles H., arrested, 21

Municipal Ownership Leagues, opposed by Communist party, 185

Murphy, John T., 252, 294; influenced by Lenin, 259–60

Mussolini, Benito, 116

Myers, Gustavus, leaves Socialist party, 93

My Further Disillusionment with Russia, 286–87

N-100, *see* Nosovitsky

Nastasiewsky, Michel, on Central Executive Committee, Workers party, 457 *n*. 32

Nation, The, 128, 300–301

National Conference of the Left Wing, 157, 425 *n*. 5; call for, 164; capture of Socialist party planned, 167; and Communist party, 169; delegates, 166–67, 424–25 *n*. 4; manifesto, 168; meeting, 166–69; National Council, 167–68; split on tactics, 166, in organization, 167–170

National Council of the Left Wing: and Communist founding convention, 182–83; and Communist party, 169; elected, 167–68; and federations, 174–75; joint convention call issued, 175; the new minority, 175; Socialist party National Executive Committee meeting held, 174

National Defense Committee, in American Labor Alliance, 337

National emergency convention of Socialist party, called, 158

National Labor Union, 25

National Organization Committee, 173–74; joint convention call of, 175

INDEX

National Steel Committee, 312–13

Naye Welt (New World), 331

Nearing, Scott, 132, 143–44; on American radicalism, 394; in "Center," 154; dismissal, 132; fears Moscow domination, 394

Negro Commission, at Fourth Comintern Congress, 387

Negro question, at Fourth Comintern Congress, 387; theses on, 387, 456 n. 28

Negro World Congress, planned, 387

Negroes, in Communist parties, 192; policy on, 192

Nelson, Roger B., *see* Lovestone

Neue Zeit, Die, 58

New Economic Policy, 249

"New Freedom," 41

New International, The, 86–88, 90, 99–100, 106, 131; on mass action, 412 n. 30; *see Internationalist*

New Masses, 299

New Republic, 298

New Review, 58, 60, 63, 66, 68, 72–73, 89; banned by Right Wing, 48; board of, 48; ends, 86; established, 49

New York Call, 59, 68, 77, 98–99, 112, 122, 153, 157; Fraina and, 410 n. 8; Friends of Russian Revolution in, 415 n. 29; Hillquit on war, 413 n. 38; Nuorteva in, 410 n. 59; Socialist Propaganda League in, 423 n. 7; St. Louis convention division in, 413 n. 33; Trotsky in, 409–10 n. 52

New York *American*, 297

New York Communist, 146, 156

New York Communist party, first underground, 203

New York District, Communist party, electoral question, 378

New York Left Wing, 139–42, 150; the break, 422 n. 40; committee membership, 422 n. 43; minutes, 422 n. 41; organized, 144–45; program, 146–47; publication, 146

New York Section of the Russian Bolshevik, 107

New York Socialist party, "Center," 142–44; Left Wing, 139–42; struggle in, 144–45

New York State Assembly, Socialists expelled, 202

New York Times, 77, 297; Comintern letter published, 241; on government agents, 226; on Trotsky, 409 n. 51

New York World, publishes Comintern letters, 243–44

New Yorker Volkszeitung, 76–77, 409 n. 42

Nicholas II, Czar, 148; abdication of, 85

Niles, Alfred S., 202

"No. 1" (Communist party, 1922), 358–59, 365

"No. 2" (Workers party, 1922), 358–359, 365

Non-Partisan League, opposed by Communist party, 185

Norris, Frank, 40, 62

Nosovitsky, Jacob: at Amsterdam conference, 233; background, 228; and Fraina, 227–36, 293; Fraina leaves, 235–36; at Fraina trial, 230–32; as government agent N-100, 228; Martens' courier, 227; in Mexico, 236; newspaper articles, 297; pseud., "Dr. James Anderson," 233

Novick, Paul, in Jewish federation, 332

Novy Mir, 82–83, 85, 132, 162–63; in American Bolshevik Bureau, 415 n. 30; and Bukharin, 77, 409 n. 49; and Trotsky, 77

Nuorteva, Santeri, 79; in Finland, 78; attacks Fraina, 229–32, 293; at Fraina trial, 230–32; and Peterson, 229; represents Finland, 109; in Russian Soviet Government Bureau, 162; in Russian Soviet Recognition League, 107; and Sandburg, 237; on Socialist party National Executive Committee, 78; in United States, 78

Ochrana, 207

Octopus, The, 40

O'Flaherty, Thomas, alternate, Central Executive Committee, Workers party, 450 n. 28

O'Hare, Kate Richards, 157

Ohio Socialist, The, Left Wing organ, 160

Ohio Socialist party, controlled by Left Wing, 159

Old Guard Socialists, 180

Olgin, Moissaye J., 143; editor, Jewish Daily *Freiheit,* 341; in Jewish federation, 332; in Socialist Left Wing, 331; leaves Socialist party, 332; in Workers' Council, 332, 340; on Workers party Central Executive Committee and Executive Council, 457 n. 32

Oneal, James, 110, 407 n. 12, n. 19, n. 24; attack on Fraina, 439-40 n. 22, 442 n. 45; secretary of Massachusetts Socialist party, 68, 70

One Big Union of Canada, 316

Oppenheimer, Moses, on board of *New Review,* 411 n. 18; treasurer, *New Review* publishing company, 404 n. 35

Opportunism: Lenin's, 248-49; vs. orthodoxy, 169-70, 395; in Ruthenberg-group split, 216-17

Orthodoxy: vs. opportunism, 169-70, 395; in Ruthenberg-group split, 216-217

Outlook, The, 115

Owens, Edgar, alternate, Central Executive Committee, Workers party, 450 n. 28

Pacifism, 141, 144, 202

Packing-house workers organizing committee, 312-13

Paine, Tom, *see* Gitlow

Palmer, A. Mitchell, raids, 204, 206-207, 211-12, 241, 334, 343; retired, 303

Paul, delegate to National Left Wing Conference, 424-25 n. 4

Pierce, John, *see* Gitlow

Pan-American Provisional Bureau: outgrowth of Amsterdam conference, 234; split by Ruthenberg split, 234-35

Pan-American Sub-Bureau, split from Pan-American Provisional Bureau, 235

Panken, Judge Jacob, at Socialist convention, 178

Pannekoek, Anton, 64-66, 72-73, 86, 89, 100; on mass action, 412 n. 24, n. 29

Parliamentarism, 45, 90; Comintern letter on, 241; Fraina on, 295; in Left Wing manifesto, 168; Lenin on, 248; and Woodstock convention, 295

Paterson textile strike, 43, 118

Pearl, Jeannette D., on New York Left Wing City Committee, 422 n. 43

Penney, Owen W., 290

People's Council of America, 112; opposed by Comunist party, 185

Pepper, John, *see* Pogany, Joseph

Petersen, Arnold, 111, 113

Peterson, Ferdinand: accuses Fraina as agent, 229, 293; at Fraina trial, 230-32; government agent FF-22, 229

Petras, on Central Executive Committee, Communist party, 427 n. 14

Petrograd Soviet, Zinoviev president, 259

Pettibone, George, arrested, 21

Plekhanov, George, 52

Pogany, Joseph: at Bridgman convention, 372; Comintern representative, 364; on Labor party, 381; pseuds., "Lang," 364, "John Pepper," 381; on Workers party, Central Executive Committee, 457 n. 32

Polish foreign-language federation: in Communist party, 188; membership, 190; potential Communists, 159; suspended by Socialist party, 158; in underground, 206

Political action vs. economic action, 16, 17, 45, 90, 304; Amsterdam conference on, 234; Communist attitude on, 186, 200; Lenin on, 251; United Communist party on, 220-

221; United Communist party vs. Communist party on, 224–25; and united-front line, 378–81
Political Bureau, Communist party, 8
"Political Communists," 319
Pollitt, Harry, 319
Populism, 36; anti-capitalism, 37; anti-socialism, 38; influence on Communists, 39, 305, 308, 323
Portland "Soviet," 139
Pound, Dean Roscoe, 202
Poyntz, Juliet Stuart: in Communist party, 193; Friends of New Russia speaker, 415 *n.* 29; in International Ladies Garment Workers Union, 193; in Left Wing, 193
Pravda, 86
Preparedness, 58, 76
Present Economic Revolution in the United States, The, 298
Presidium: American, 373; highest Comintern body, 338
Prevey, Mrs. Marguerite, on first Central Executive Committee, Workers party, 450 *n.* 28
Price, P. Philips, 115
Produce Exchange Corporation, receives Russian jewels, 240
Profintern: American delegation, 269–270, 310, 314–21; on American Federation of Labor, 317–18; and Comintern, 315, 317–19; first conference, 315; functioning, 318–19; independence an issue, 317; I.W.W. rebuffed, 317–18; planned, 8; provisional council, 315; Reinstein represents, 364; Russian control, 315; subsidization, 315
Progressivism, 36; anti-capitalist, 40; influence on Communists, 41; and intellectuals, 40–41; and literary renaissance, 41; middle-class character of, 37; and muckraking, 40
Proletarian party, 211
Proletarian Revolution in Russia, The, 107
Proletarian University, 210
Proletariat, 27–31, 38, 115, 333, 343; proportion in Workers party, 393

dictatorship of, 147, 154, 320, 361; Communist Labor party and, 185, 187; Communist party and, 187, 345; issue in 1922 split, 354; in Left Wing manifesto, 168; in Profintern, 315, 317; United Communist party on, 220; Workers party on, 342, 389, 452–53 *n.* 18
Prosecutions, government, 202; effect on Communists, 208; influence on tactics, 213–14, 355
Pseudonyms, underground, 205
"Purges," 300
"Putschism," 275

Radek, Karl, 54, 363; on American Commission, 382, 385; on E.C.C.I., 259; and Reed, 257, 283, 285–89, 291; at Second Comintern Congress, 256–57; at Third Comintern Congress, 277; and Western communism, 235
Raids, government, anti-Communist, 203; attack on in Twelve Lawyers' Report, 203; on Bridgman convention, 369–71; Chicago, 204; at Communist founding convention, 182; effect on Communists, 205; 1919–1920 epidemic of, 202; on I.W.W., 96; of Lusk Committee, 203; Palmer, 204, 206–207, 211–212, 241, 334, 343; on Socialist party, 94
Railroad brotherhoods, 20
Railway Carmen's Union, A.F. of L., 312
Raivaaja, 78
Rákosi, Mátyás, 356–57
Rand School of Social Science, 99, 141, 330
Ransome, Arthur, 115, 149, 404 *n.* 32
Raphael, A., *see* Bittleman
Red Dawn, The, 110
Red Guard, American, 108–109
Red International of Labor Unions, *see* Profintern
Reed, John, 40–41, 111, 115, 118–119, 126, 132, 134–37, 145–46, 149–150, 157–74, 278, 282, 305; American Federation of Labor opposed

Reed, John (*continued*)
by, 256–58; background, 117; at Baku Congress, 284–88, 287–89; at Communist Labor party convention, 178–80; death, 284; differences with Comintern, 283; disillusionment, accounts of, 284–92, 438 *n.* 2; on E.C.C.I., 257–58; accounts of E.C.C.I. resignation, 284–86, 288–291; editor, *Voice of Labor*, 175; and Fraina, 257, 293–94; government agent, called, 287, 438–39 *n.* 9; and Haywood, 186; indictments of, 204; international delegate, 181, 251; and I.W.W., 43; and *Masses*, 118–19, 404 *n.* 32; in Moscow, 252; at National Left Wing conference, 167, 424–25 *n.* 4; in new minority, National Council, 175, 306; on New York Left Wing City Committee, 422 *n.* 43; pseud., "Jim Gormley," 251; and Radek, 257; report to United Communist party, 257; in Russia as correspondent, 119; and Russian revolution, 110–11, 115; at Second Comintern Congress, 254–58, 283, 287; at Socialist convention, 176–77; on Socialist Labor party, 111; in Socialist party, 120; sources, 417 *n.* 9, *n.* 10, 417–18 *n.* 11; and second Communist split, 215; and Stalin-Trotsky split, 292–93; and war, 118; last writings of, 290–91

Reform, 27; in Cleveland campaign, 194; Communist Labor party and, 185; Communist party and, 185; issue in Jewish federation, 192; Lenin on, 249; New York Left Wing on, 146–47, 154; in program of Socialist party, 44, and Ohio Left Wing, 44; and revolution, 347

Reformers, 345; Americanization, 346

Reinstein, Boris, 111, 148; on American Commission, 356; at First Comintern Congress, 149–50, 153, 423 *n.* 10; Profintern representative, 364; pseud., "Davidson," 364; in Socialist Labor party, 149; in United States, 149, 364

Retail Clerks Union of New York, 140

Revisionism, 24, 27

Revolt, 111

Revolution, 16, 27–28; American, dismissed, 277; and Communist party, 345; Foster's theory, 320; an illusion, 249; manipulated, 352; nearness of, 153, 266; and strikes, 198–199; Trostky on, 275; underground road to, 207; and united front, 329; Workers' Council and, 333–34; world, 246, 250–51, 260, 266, 275, 333–34; *see also* European revolution, Russian Revolution

Revolutionary Age, The, 131–33, 145, 154, 160, 203; European orientation, 133; Left Wing official organ, 168; origin, 420 *n.* 3; replaced by *The Communist*, 185; Socialist party organ, 174; on Socialist Propaganda League, 423 *n.* 7

Revolutionary defeatism, 53

Revolutionary Socialism, 91

Revolutionary Socialist party: organized, 13; unites with anarchists, 13

Richardson, R. E., on labor committee, Communist Labor party, 181

Right Opposition, 1921, *see* Workers' Council

Right Wing, 28, 175, 341, 347; alignments changed by war, 52; Comintern attacks, 154; Finnish federation in, 192; immediate demands supported, 23; Jewish federation in, 192; Liquidators attacked as, 383; majority in Massachusetts, 68; in New York, 140, 142, 155–57; primaries contested, 200; revisionism, 27; at Socialist convention, 175, 177; split blamed on, 165; in 1921 split, 332

Roland-Holst, Henriette, 54, 65, 86; on International Sub-Bureau Executive Committee, 234

Rolland, Romain, 127, 403 *n.* 32

Roosevelt, Franklin D., 39

Roosevelt, Theodore, 1912 vote for, 41

INDEX

Rosin, Fr., background, 67–68; editor, *Strahdneeks*, 68, 407–408 n. 24; in Lettish federation, 68; Lettish name Fricis Rozins, 67; return to Europe, 132; in Russian Bureau, Latvian Communist party, 148

Rosmer, Alfred, 252–53

Rovitch, Mrs. L., 108; on New York Left Wing City Committee, 422 n. 43

Roy, M. N., on Borodin, 238–40; becomes Communist, 239; to Moscow, 239

Rozins, Fricis, see Rosin, Fr.

Rudniansky, A., 253

Russell, Bertrand, 130, 430 n. 32; trip to Russia, 128

Russell, Charles Edward, 40, 56, 59, 76, 95; leaves Socialist party, 93

Russian branch, Socialist party, 83; in American Bolshevik Bureau, 415 n. 30

Russian Communist party, 8, 129, 319–20; factions in, 381

Russian influence, 72–77, 81–82, 91, 392; at Communist founding convention, 182–85; in Communist party, 190–91; on Slavic nationality groups, 264; at Third Comintern Congress, 277; wins in first split, 175; see also Foreign-language federations

Russian leadership, 426 n. 17; in foreign-language federations, 159; in Left Wing split, 172–73

Russian Left Wing, 67, 98, 368

Russian-Michigan alliance, see Foreign-language federations, Michigan Socialist party

Russian revolution (1905), 77–78; American parallels, 359–60

Russian revolution (March 1917), 90

Russian revolution (November 1917), 67, 72–73, 116, 124–25, 129, 137–141, 144, 146–47, 168, 191, 193, 201, 236, 299, 302, 326, 331, 352; control, 112–13; influence, 101–104; 264–65; 306, 309, 323, 330, 333, 394; need for Western revolution, 246–48, 265–66; and Third Comintern Congress, 275–76; world support for, 110; Workers' Council, 333–34; see Bolshevik revolution, European revolution

Russian Right Wing, 98

Russian Social-Democratic Labor party, 74

Russian Social Democratic party, 360

Russian Social Democratic Workers party, 83

Russian Social Revolutionaries, defended by Debs, 324–26

Russian foreign-language federation, 77, 107, 176, 305, 392; in American Bolshevik Bureau, 415 n. 30; changed position, 386, 392; and Communist founding convention, 181; in Communist party, 188; domination, 159; growth, 138; and Left Wing split, 172–73; membership, 190; and Martens' Bureau, 243; Nosovitsky hired, 228; orthodoxy, 170–71; potential Communists, 159; and Russian Soviet Government Bureau, 162–63; second split caused, 215; suspended by Socialist party, 158; in underground, 206

Russian Soviet Government Bureau, 161–62, 227–28; autonomy, 243; and Fraina case, 227–32; Martens' Bureau, 161; Nosovitsky employed by, 227–28; and Peterson, 229

Russian Soviet Recognition League, 109

Russian trade unions, dominate Profintern, 315

Russia's Message, 73

Rutgers, S. J., 60, 78, 100, 407–408 n. 24; in American Bolshevik Bureau, 107; American Left Wing theorist, 66; at Amsterdam conference, 232–34; Comintern representative to West, 232; on Executive Committee of International Sub-Bureau, 234; at First Comintern Congress, 151, 232; Fraina on influence of, 412 n. 31; *Internationalist*, 72; in Left Wing, 80, 139; on mass action, 89–90, 412 n. 24, n. 29; and *New*

Rutgers, S. J. (*continued*)
International, 86; and Socialist Propaganda League, 70–72, 107–108

Ruthenberg, Charles Emil, 36, 97, 156–57, 174, 190–92, 207, 308, 322, 343, 388, 392; on Americanization, 218; arrests of, 95, 371; background, 194, 429 *n*. 35, 430 *n*. 41; at Bridgman convention, 371, 373; campaigns for mayor, 194–95; on Central Executive Committee and Executive Council, Communist party, 184, 427 *n*. 14; at Communist founding convention, 183–84, 195; and Communist Labor party, 179; and Debs, 324; editor, *The Communist*, 222; foreign-language groups oppose, 195, 211–15; alleged founder of Communist party, 196; and Fraina, 196, 296; and Hourwich, 211, 431 *n*. 2; indictment of, 203; on insurrection, 213–14, 431 *n*. 11; international delegate, 427 *n*. 14; in jail, 223, 304; in Left Wing, 194; and Lenin, 196; a Liquidator, 360–62; on National Council, 167, 195; at National Left Wing conference, 166–67, 195; national secretary, Communist party, 184, 196; and Nosovitsky, 227–28; pseud., "David Damon," 205; on reform, 44; release from prison, 360–61; sentenced for anti-war activities, 195; at St. Louis convention, 92, 194–95; at Socialist convention, 177; in Socialist party, 194; split of group analyzed, 216–218, 431 *n*. 11; in United Communist party, 222; at unity conference, 219–21; and Valetski, 365; on violence, 47; on Workers party Central Executive Committee and Executive Council, 457 *n*. 32, secretary, 360

Ruthenberg group: in Communist party, 212–14; division in split, 431 *n*. 11; federations attacked by, 212; on insurrection, 213–14, 431 *n*. 9; split with Communist party, 214; United Communist party result of merger, 222; unites with Communist Labor party, 219–21; unity campaign of, 212

Sabotage, in Socialist party constitution, 46

Sacco-Vanzetti case, 43

Safarov, George Ivanovich, chairman of Comintern Negro Commission in 1922, 387

Saltzman, Rubin, in Jewish federation, 332

Salutsky, J. B., as Hardman, 331; in Jewish federation, 332; leaves Socialist party, 332; at Socialist convention, 178; in Socialist Left Wing, 331; in Workers' Council, 332, 340; and Workers' Council-Communist party negotiations, 449 *n*. 23; at Workers party convention, 342; on Workers party first Central Executive Committee, 450 *n*. 28

Sandburg, Carl, 41, 237–38, 403 *n*. 32; and Borodin, 237–38

Schlüter, Hermann, 132

Schulenberg, G., member, National Executive Committee, Young Workers League, 450 *n*. 32

Schwartz, on Central Executive Committee and Executive Council, Communist party, 427 *n*. 14

Scotland Yard, and Nosovitsky, 228, 232–33

Scott, Charles E., 269–70, 294, 310, 363; real name, Jansen, Carl, 269, 437 *n*. 9

Seattle Central Labor Council, 316

Seattle general strike, 139, 197

Second Congress of the Comintern, 260, 262, 278, 310; American unity asked, 254; Borodin and Roy attend, 239; character, 255; concept of the party, 261–64; delegates, 254, 436 *n*. 15, *n*. 18; and Fraina, 253, 293, 295; and Reed, 254–55, 283–84, 287–91; Russian control, 258; Russian predominance, 254; trade-union policy dispute, 255–57, 436 *n*. 24; twenty-one points of admission to Comintern, 262; and united front, 328

Second convention of the Communist party, 262, 295; program and constitution, 433 *n.* 28
Second International, 64, 66, 149, 156, 158, 165, 171; Communist criticism of, 264; International Socialist Bureau of, 52; Lenin considers dead, 447 *n.* 2; membership compared with Communist parties in 1920s, 447–48 *n.* 3; and war, 51
Secretariat, Communist party, 8
Secretariat for Western Europe, 234
Sedition, laws against, 202
Senate, U.S., Comintern on, 243
Shame of the Cities, The, 40
Shanahan, Edward, Department of Justice agent, at Bridgman convention, 369–71
Shannon, David A., 16, 33, 401
Shaplen, Joseph, 112
Shaw, George Bernard, 62
Sheridan, Clare, on Borodin, 237
Shoe Workers Union, 316
Shop Stewards' movement, 256
Skala, Joseph Charles, *see* Fraina, Louis C.
Simkhovitch, V. G., 143
Simons, A. M., leaves Socialist party, 93
Simpson, Herman, on board of *New Review,* 404 *n.* 35, 406 *n.* 19
Since Lenin Died, 129
Sinclair, Upton, 41, 62, 403 *n.* 32; leaves Socialist party, 93
Single tax, 14, 36
Sirola, Yrjo, 109, 148
Slavic federations, 386–87
Slavic preponderance, 191, 392; *see also* Foreign-language federations, Russian influence
Snowden, Philip, 327
Social Democratic parties, Western: comeback, 328; Communist criticism, 276; and International Federation of Trade Unions, 315; split questioned, 276
Social Democratic party, organized by Debs, 15
Social Democratic party of Holland, 151

Social Democratic party of North America, 12
Socialism and War, 59, 73, 75–76
Socialism, 23, 27, 34–35, 88, 122, 135–36, 142, 146–47, 309, 323; Bellamy's, 14; Christian, 14; Debs converted to, 15; and Fraina, 300; modern American, 12; and populism, 38; and Profintern program, 317; and Progressivism, 41; war crisis and, 64
Socialist Labor party of North America, 12, 14–15, 39, 64, 69, 82, 111, 148–49; Comintern invites, 150–51; Comintern mentions split, 242; decline, 105, 393; Hillquit rebels against, 15; immigrants in, 31–32; in Left Wing manifesto, 168; Reed misleads, 111; and Soviets, 417 *n.* 62; split, 13; trade-union policy, 18–19
Socialist party, 64, 69, 81, 89, 135, 137, 140–41, 143–44, 302, 305–306, 308, 311, 324, 354
prewar: Center in, 24; composition, social, 15; convention, first, 23; formation of, 15; Haywood expelled from, 46; on immediate demands, 23; immigrants in, 33; on Labor party, 30; Left Wing, historic, in, 17, 33, 94–95; office-holders of, 42; Populists in, 38; publications of, 42; Right Wing domination, 33; and revisionism, 27; on trade unions, 18; vote, 1912, 41–42; 1916, 70
World War I and Communist split: Agent K-97 in, 366; candidates elected, 201; Center in, 142–43; convention (emergency), called, 158, held, 176–78, 426 *n.* 1; convention (St. Louis), 92–93; decline in membership, 105, 189, 330, 393–94; expulsions from, 157–58, 424 *n.* 28, *n.* 29, *n.* 30; language federations and, 83, 158, 332; Left Wing, new, in, 164–65, 167–69, 171, 174–75; Left Wing, 1920–21, 330–31, 333; Michigan charter revoked by, 158; National Executive Committee of, 45–46, 78, 110, 156–58, 171, 174;

Socialist party (*continued*)
and New York State Assembly, 202; raids on, 94–95, 202; Russian revolution supported by, 110, 331; and Ruthenberg group, 217; St. Louis resolution on war, 93; split of prowar group from, 93; and Third International, 331–32; United Communist party and, 220; united-front approach to, 378, 383; and war, 55–57

Socialist Party of Canada, 160

Socialist Party of Great Britain, 151, 160

Socialist Propaganda League, 80, 83, 86, 89, 96, 107, 407–408 *n*. 24, 411 *n*. 20; activities, 70–71; debt to Rutgers, 412 *n*. 31; end of, 423 *n*. 7; formed, 69; leadership, 69; and Lenin, 75; manifesto, 69, 74; mentioned by Comintern, 242; merger, 423 *n*. 7; and Nuorteva, 78; and Red Guard, 107–108

Socialist Publication Society, pamphlets about Soviet Russia, 417 *n*. 2

Socialist Trade and Labor Alliance, 19

"Social patriots," 154

Sonnichsen, Albert, on board of *New Review*, 404 *n*. 35, 406 *n*. 19

Soul of the Russian Revolution, The, 143

South Slavic foreign-language federation: in Communist party, 188; membership, 190; potential Communists, 159; suspended by Socialist party, 158; in underground, 206

Souvarine, Boris, 356

"Soviet Ark," The, 203

Soviet Russian Trade Delegation, financing, 238

Soviets, 72, 98, 113, 146, 218, 220, 242, 361; Butte, 139; Comintern letter on, 243; Debs on, 325; platform for American, 243; Portland, 139; translated, 88; and Workers party, 342

Soviet Union: Communist attitude toward, 263–66; contrasted with United States, 265–66; Debs on, 325; I.W.W. on, 315

Soviet World, 139

Spargo, John, 56; in prowar minority, 93; leaves Socialist party, 93

Spartacus group, 136, 151–52

Spies, *see* Agents

Splits: and Fourth Comintern Congress, 384; from I.W.W., 318; of Left Opposition, 1922, 340, 353–54; in new Left Wing, 1919, 173–75; of Ruthenberg group, 217; in Socialist party, 1919, 158, 306; in 1921, 330–333

Spolansky, Jacob: background, 368–369; and Borodin, 239; Bridgman convention raided by, 370–72; in Bureau of Investigation, 368; at Communist founding convention, 182; in Intelligence branch, U.S. Army, 368

Stachel, Jack, party leadership from Young Communist League, 450 *n*. 33

Stalin, Joseph, 98, 129; and Lozovsky, 319; and Reed, 292–93; and Zinoviev, 260

Steel strike, 197, 313

Steffens, Lincoln, 40, 117–19, 124, 126; conversion, 116; visits Russia, 115

Steinhart, *see* Gruber, J.

Steinmetz, Charles, 56

Steuben, John, party leadership from Young Communist League, 450 *n*. 33

Steunenberg, Frank, 21

Stilson, J. V., National Organization Committee treasurer, 173, 425 *n*. 12

St. John, Vincent, 18

St. Louis anti-war resolution, 93–94

Stokes, J. G. Phelps, 193

Stokes, Rose Pastor, 48; arrest, 95; at Communist founding convention, 182; in Communist party, 193; at Fourth Comintern Congress, 456 *n*. 28; pseud., "Sasha," 456 *n*. 28; on Workers party Central Executive Committee, 456 *n*. 32

Stoklitsky, Alexander: at Communist founding convention, 184; international delegate, 427 *n*. 14; National Organization Committee organizer,

175, 425 n. 12; at Second Comintern Congress, 254, 267; leaves United States, 191
Strahdneeks (The Worker), 68, 407–408 n. 24, n. 28
Strasser, Adolph, 12, 22
Strikes: Boston, 187; Brooklyn Rapid Transit, 223; Butte, 139; coal, 197; Coeur d'Alene, 21; Comintern on, 244; Communists in, 43; Cripple Creek, 21; Homestead, 21; insurrection the goal of, 223–24; Lawrence, 1912, 43, 62; Lawrence, 1919, 139, 197; Leadville, 21; packing house, 312–13; Paterson, 43, 118; Pullman, 15, 21; railroad, 21; Seattle general, 139, 197; steel, 197–198, 313; Telluride, 21
Stuart, John, 287
Student movement, 141
Stuttgart congress, 52
Subsidization: by Comintern, 261–62; of Communist press, 340, 382; Germany, 262; Mexico, 294; of Profintern, 315
"Sullivan": at Fourth Comintern Congress, 383; in Left Opposition, 388; and Trotskyists, 388–89
Swabeck, Arne: at Fourth Comintern Congress, 384; pseud., "Lansing," 384; on Workers party first Central Executive Committee, 450 n. 28
Syndicalism, 16, 34, 64, 88, 146; and Browder, 309; and communism, 318; differences with Communists, 186; and Foster, 311–12; in Left Wing manifesto, 168; and Profintern, 315–18
Syndicalist League of North America, and Browder, 308; and Cannon, 308; and Foster, 308, 312
Syndicalists, 16; European, in Profintern, 318; International Workingmen's Association formed, 444 n. 27
Swift, in Socialist Propaganda League, 69

Taft, William Howard, 1912 vote for, 41

Tailism, 171
Tanner, Jack, 256
TASS, 162
Telluride strike, 21
Ten Days That Shook The World, 110; in Stalin-Trotsky split, 292–93
Theoretical System of Karl Marx, The, 57
Theoreticians, 57–60, 63, 305–306
"Theses on Tactics," 277
Third Congress of the Comintern, 305, 306, 337; American delegation to, 275; and German counterrevolution, 275; legal, mass party asked, 275, planned, 269; and Western revolution, 275–77, 328, 347
Third International (Communist International, C.I., Comintern): called for, 64, 66, 68–69, 75, 83; Committee for, 332; and Communist Labor party, 180; first Congress, 148, 150, 156; formation of, 148; Fraina representative to, 227; I.W.W. on, 315; Left Wing supports, 170–71; and Michigan group, 165; and political action, 200; and Socialist party admission, 331–32; and Socialist party split, 1921, 331–332; at Zimmerwald, 55; *see also* Comintern
Toiler, The (Cleveland), supports Communist Labor party, 181
Toiler, The (Kansas City), 308
Toiler, The, organ of Workers party, 451, Ch. 21, n. 4
Toiler, The, organ of United Communist party, 306
Toohey, Pat, party leadership from Young Communist League, 450 n. 33
Trachtenberg, Alexander L., 98–99, 109, 142–43; in Friends of the Russian Revolution, 415 n. 29; at Socialist convention, 178; in Socialist Left Wing, 330; on Workers party Central Executive Committee, 450 n. 28, 457 n. 32
"Trade-union Communists," 319, 322
Trade Union Educational League (T.U.E.L.), 314; Debs on, 325;

T.U.E.L. (*continued*)
formed by Foster, 314; at Fourth Comintern Congress, 384; members, 446 *n.* 34; Profintern accepts, 321; relation to Communist party, 321–322

Trade unionism: Amsterdam conference opposes, 234; at Bridgman convention, 373–74; Browder on, 308–10; Cannon and, 306–307; Communists and, 350; Communist policy on, 186, 198–200, 208; conflict with political socialism, 12; divorce from politics, 303; early radical opinion on, 12; Foster and, 250, 312–15; at Fourth Comintern Congress, 383, 386, 455 *n.* 21; Fraina on, 295; and Labor party, 380; Lenin on, 248, 251; Michigan group on, 160; "pure and simple," 12, 22; and Profintern, 315–19; Reed on, 283, 290; at Second Comintern Congress, 255–57; and united front, 383; *see also* Red International of Trade Unions, Trade Union Educational League

Transmission apparatus, 343

Trotsky, Leon, 53–54, 66, 73, 99–100, 120, 129, 142–43, 147, 159, 356, 386; admiration of American Communists for continues, 419 *n.* 37; and Communist founding convention, 181, 187; and Debs, 324; at Fourth Comintern Congress, 275–277; and Fraina, 300; influence, 265; inspiration, 102–103; in Left Wing, 80–85; compared to Lenin, 259; aids Liquidators, 383–84, 455–56 *n.* 22; and Lozovsky, 319; in New York, 77, 79, 409 *n.* 51, 409–10 *n.* 52, 410 *n.* 54, 410 *n.* 1; on New York, 411 *n.* 13; and Reed, 252, 292–93; at Third Comintern Congress, 275–77; writings translated, 104, 107; and Zinoviev, 260

Trotskyists, 299–300, 317; and underground Letts, 388–89

Truth, Left Wing organ, 160; supports Communist Labor party, 181

Truth Seeker, The, 62

Tucker, Irwin St. John, arrest of, 94
Twelve Lawyers' Report, 203, 226
Twenty-one points, admission to Comintern based on, 262–63
Tywerousky, Oscar: on Communist party Central Executive Committee, 427 *n.* 14; pseud., "Baldwin," 275; at Third Comintern Congress, 275, 279

Ukrainian branch, Socialist party, 83
Ukrainian foreign-language federation: in Communist party, 188; membership, 190; potential Communists, 159; suspended by Socialist party, 158; in underground, 206
Ukrainian Workers Club, in American Labor Alliance, 337
Underground, the, 195, 304, 330; agents in, 226; Bridgman convention decision on, 374; Comintern on underground convention, 338; in Communist theory, 208; contrasted with Comintern letter, 241–242; control of Workers party by, 358–59; convention an issue in split, 353; effect on membership, 208–209; ended, 388–90; factionalism in, 247; factions on, 335–36; foreign preponderance in, 207; function, 205; importance for American communism, 246–47; Lettish hold-out in, 388–89; Liquidators and, 360–61; membership of, 206; New York the first, 203; permanent nature of, 361; press, 247; Socialist Left Wing attitude on, 331; Third Comintern Congress on, 278; underground convention demanded, 337–338; and Woodstock convention, 274; Workers' Council opposed to, 334, 340

Underground convention, *see* Bridgman convention

Unfinished Task, The, 300

Union for Democratic Action, 301, 441–42 *n.* 42

United Communist party, 354; autonomy of federations opposed, 225;

Browder and, 310; Cannon and, 306; Central Executive Committee of, 222, 300; Comintern intervention, 270; election-boycott favored, 224–25; foreign preponderance in membership, 223; formation of, 218–22; insurrection advocated, 224; I.W.W. supported, 224; membership, 222–23, 432–33 *n*. 23; officers, 222, 432 *n*. 20; and Pan-American Bureau, 235; publications, 222, 272; Reed's report to, 257; representative on American Agency, 269; at Second Comintern Congress, 267; and Third Comintern Congress, 277; unity asked by Comintern, 254; unity negotiations, 270–72; Woodstock unity convention and, 270–72; Zinoviev attacks, 256

United Toilers of America, 355, 362; Comintern decision challenged, 452 *n*. 12; at Fourth Comintern Congress, 383; Left Opposition's legal party, 355–56; and legality, 389

United front: American reaction, 377–379; derivation from Lenin, 447 *n*. 1; electoral activities in, 378; and Fourth Comintern Congress, 329; implications of, 327–30; "Left" line replaces, 448 *n*. 7; objections to, 376; and Workers party, 343

Unity: at Bridgman convention, 431 *n*. 18; Comintern asks, 244, 254, 388–89; Comintern representatives and, 431–32 *n*. 18; Communist Labor party proposals, 211–12; of Communist Labor party with Ruthenberg group, 219–21; and Fourth Comintern Congress, 384, 386; and Woodstock convention, 270–74, 303

Utopianism, 15

Valetski (Walecki), H., on American Commission, 382; at Bridgman convention, 371–74; at Central Executive Committee meeting, 364–65; Comintern representative, 363; convention dominated by, 373; on Labor party, 380; and Left Opposition, 388, 456–57 *n*. 29; pseuds., "Brooks," 364, "Michelson," 455 *n*. 14; real name Max Horwitz, 453 *n*. 2; report to Comintern, 365

Varney, Harold Lord, 111, 416 *n*. 49

Vaughn, George C., on New York Left Wing Executive Committee, 422 *n*. 43

Villa, Pancho, 118

Violence or Solidarity? or Will Guns Settle It?, 144

Vlag, Piet, 48

Voice of Labor, The, 175; supports Communist Labor party, 181

Volodarsky, V.: biographical material, 411 *n*. 17; in United States, 80, 86

Violence: Bridgman conference on, 219–20; Communists on, 345, 349; issue in Communist party, 213–14; in labor movement, 21–22; and Left Wing, 47; in Socialist movement, 34; in Socialist party constitution, 46; in strikes, 223–24; and Woodstock convention, 274

Vorbote, 86

Wagenknecht, Alfred, 158, 222, 304; arrest of, 95; chairman, Communist Labor party convention, 178, 180; Communist Labor party executive secretary, 181; in Goose caucus, 361; at National Left Wing conference, 166; pseud., "Meyer," 222; at Socialist convention, 177; Socialist party temporary secretary, 174; United Communist party executive secretary, 222; on Workers party Central Executive Committee, 457 *n*. 32

Waldman, Louis, 84, 110

Walecki, *see* Valetski, H.

Walling, William English, 48–49, 56–57, 70, 72; on board of *New Review*, 404 *n*. 32, 406 *n*. 19, 407 *n*. 21; leaves Socialist party, 93

Walsh, Frank P., 202

War: and Marxism, 50; and Second International, 51; Socialist emergency convention on, 92–94; So-

cialist Propaganda League on, 71
Warbasse, James P., 47
Ware, Harold, alternate, Central Executive Committee, Workers party, 450 *n.* 28
Waton, Harry, delegate to National Left Wing Conference, 424–25 *n.* 4
Wealth Against Commonwealth, 41
Weaver, James B., 36
Weinstein, Gregory, 132, 138; editor, *Novy Mir,* 138; at Fraina trial, 230–232; in Russian Information Bureau, 162
Weinstone, William W., 140–41, 378; background, 421 *n.* 26, 424–25 *n.* 4; on Central Executive Committee, Communist party, 304; on Central Executive Committee, Workers party, 450 *n.* 28, 457 *n.* 32; New York organizer, 304; as Winestein, 421 *n.* 26
Wells, Hulet, 316
Western communism, 351
Western Communist parties: comparison with Socialist parties, 447–448 *n.* 3; membership dropping, 447–48 *n.* 3; and Third Comintern Congress, 276–77; Zinoviev's influence, 260; *see also* Amsterdam conference
Western Communists: influence of Lenin, 259; Russian leadership, 266; and united front, 329, 375–77
Western Federation of Miners, 20; leaves American Federation of Labor, 16
Western Labor Union, 16
West-European Secretariat of the Comintern, replaces Amsterdam Bureau, 235
Western revolution, 266; abandoned, 248; Russian need for, 265–66; and Third Comintern Congress, 347; *see also* Western revolution
Wheat, *see* Lovestone
Whitney, Charlotte Anita, in Communist Labor party, 193
Wicks, Harry M.: at Communist founding convention, 184; on Communist party Central Executive Committee and Executive Council, 184, 427 *n.* 14; on Workers party Central Executive Committee and Executive Council, 457 *n.* 32
Wilenkin, J., on first Central Executive Committee, Workers party, 450 *n.* 28
Williams, Albert Rhys, 115, 149; importance as interpreter of the Bolshevik regime, 417 *n.* 3
Williams, George, 316; opposes Comintern, 317–18
Williams, John D., 69, 80, 86, 407 *n.* 13; at Brooklyn Left Wing meeting, 411 *n.* 19
Williams, Tyrell, 202
Williamson, John, party leadership from Young Communist League, 450 *n.* 33
Willard, Colonel, 229
Wilson, J. Stitt, leaves Socialist party, 93
Winitsky, Harry M., 142; indicted, 203; sentenced, 204
Winters, Carl, party leadership from Young Communist League, 450 *n.* 33
Why I Am A Socialist, 41
Wilson, Woodrow, 41, 58, 70, 107, 118; 1912 vote for, 41
Wolfe, Bertram D., 140, 300, 308, 404 *n.* 1; background, 141; at Bridgman convention, 372–73; concedes to federations, 175; in Left Wing, 145; unites with Liquidators, 373; at National Left Wing conference, 167, 424–25 *n.* 4; on National Council, 168; on New York Left Wing City Committee, 422 *n.* 43; pseud., "Albright," 372
Women in Communist parties, 193
Woodstock unity convention, 270–74, 304, 437 *n.* 12; *see also* Comintern, Communist party, Communist Labor party
Workers' Challenge, 355, 451, Ch. 21, *n.* 4
Workers' League, 378
Workers (Communist) party, 263, 390

INDEX

"Workers' control," 317
Workers' Council: and Americanization, 333; and Comintern, 333; and Communist party, 334, 337; joins Communist party, 340–41; divisions in, 340; illegality opposed, 334–35; merger with American Labor Alliance proposed, 337; negotiations on illegality, 449; organization of, 333; and Russian revolution, 333; at Workers party convention, 341–42
Workers' Council, The, 333
Workers' Educational League, 308, 443 n. 9
Workers International Industrial Union, 150, 186
Workers party of America: American Labor Alliance in, 341; and Bridgman convention, 368; as cause of split, 353, 356, 362, 381; Central Executive Committee of, 342, 389, 450 n. 28, 457 n. 32; Comintern accepted by, 390; Communist party merged into, 390; constitution of, 342; on dictatorship of proletariat, 452–53 n. 8; in elections, 378–79; electoral campaign of, 379; Executive Council of, 389; factions on electoral policy, 378; federations in, 342; first convention, 341–42, 449–50 n. 25, n. 26; formation of, 341; on insurrection, 452–53 n. 18; on Labor party, 379
Membership of, 391, 457 n. 37, n. 38, n. 39; in Chicago, 392–93; contrast with other radical groups, 393–94; foreign-language proportion in, 392–93; geographical distribution of, 391; immigrants in, 393; national composition of, 392; occupational status of, 393; urban character, 391–92
nature of, 341–42; Negroes in, 387; officers of, 342; organization of, 358–59; program of, changed, 389; relation to Communist party, 358–359; relation to Moscow, 394–96; Salutsky opposed to, 342; second convention of, 389; trade-union policy of, 342; underground control of, 341; and united front, 342, 377; Workers' Council in, 341; youth organization of, 343–44
Workers' World, The, 309, 443 n. 9; Left Wing organ, 160; supports Communist Labor party, 181
World Congress, *see* Fourth Congress of the Comintern
Working Men's party of the United States, 12
Wortis, Rose, 142; in Communist party, 193
Wulfskeel, Mr. and Mrs. Karl, 369–70
Wynkoop, D. I., on International Sub-Bureau Executive Committee, 234

"X" (Trade Union Educational League), 358–59

Yochichago, of I.W.W., 315
Young Communist League: at Fourth Comintern Congress, 384; organization of, 344; party leadership supplied by, 344, 450 n. 33; relation to Communist party, 344
Young People's Socialist League, 330; split, 343
Young Workers League: National Executive Committee members, 450 n. 32; organization of, 344

Zam, Herbert, member, National Executive Committee, Young Workers League, 450 n. 32
Zimmerwald; conference, 54, 69; manifesto, 73; movement, 75, 83
Zimmerwald Left, 55
Zinoviev, Gregory, 54, 73, 129, 153, 340; on American unity, 268; Americans attacked by, 256; Comintern letters to America signed by, 244; and Comintern policies, 261, 264; at Fourth Comintern Congress, 382, 384–85; importance in Comintern, 258–60; on intervention in Communist parties, 261–62; Lenin credited with originating united front by, 447 n. 1; and Lozovsky, 319; and Profintern, 315; and Reed,

Zinoviev, Gregory (*continued*)
283, 285–89, 291–92; at Second Comintern Congress, 256–58; at Third Comintern Congress, 277; and united front, 329, 377; and Western communism, 235; on world revolution, 260

Zola, Emile, 62

Zucker, Morris, delegate to National Left Wing Conference, 424–25 *n.* 4